P9-DEP-661

WORLD IN CONFLICT 1914-45

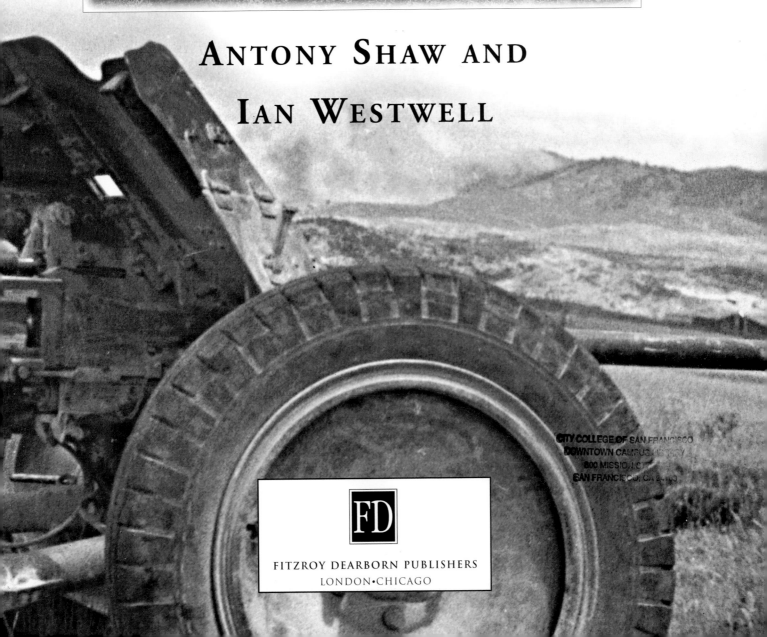

WORLD IN CONFLICT 1914-45

ANTONY SHAW AND

IAN WESTWELL

FD

FITZROY DEARBORN PUBLISHERS
LONDON·CHICAGO

© Brown Partworks Ltd, 2000

All rights reserved, including the right of
reproduction in whole or in part in any form

For information, write to

Fitzroy Dearborn Publishers
310 Regent Street
London W1R 5AJ
UK

or

Fitzroy Dearborn Publishers
919 North Michigan Avenue
Chicago, Illinois 60611
USA

British Library Cataloguing in Publication Data.
A catalogue record for this book is available
from the British Library

A Cataloging-in-Publication record for this book
is available from the Library of Congress

ISBN 1-57958-212-5

Cover designed by Philip Lewis

This edition first published by
Fitzroy Dearborn Publishers 2000

Printed in Great Britain by
Butler & Tanner Ltd

PAGE 1: *Groundcrew of the US Eighth
Air Force carry out routine maintenance
on a B-17 Flying Fortress, while the
squadron's artist adds to the bomber's
impressive tally of sortie symbols for
operations over Nazi Germany.*

PAGES 2–3: *Nationalist rebels and
Italian troops man a German anti-tank
gun during the Spanish Civil War.*

THESE PAGES: *Battlecruisers of the
British Home Fleet pictured shortly
before the outbreak of World War I.*

Editors: Peter Darman, Antony Shaw,
and Ian Westwell
Art Editor: Duncan Brown
Production: Matt Weyland
Cartographer: William Le Bihan
Indexer: Kay Ollerenshaw

CONTENTS

FOREWORD	6
WORLD WAR I: INTRODUCTION	8
1914	12
1915	50
1916	84
1917	122
1918	158
INTERWAR YEARS	188
WORLD WAR II: INTRODUCTION	210
1939	214
1940	220
1941	242
1942	276
1943	306
1944	336
1945	368
AFTERMATH	390
APPENDICES AND BIBLIOGRAPHY	394
INDEX	410
ACKNOWLEDGMENTS	416

FOREWORD

The twentieth century remains the most violent era in human history. Despite being a period of unprecedented progress in all realms of human endeavor, events showed that men were still prey to the most base emotional response – that of violence against other humans. In the first 50 years of the century the world was rent by conflicts that were more ferocious and often more widespread than any experienced before. To many, even down to the present, the defining moments of this 50 years of struggle remain the two world wars fought between 1914–18 and 1939–45. Their legacy was, in rough total, around 60 million dead, many more injured, and countless others traumatized by their experiences. The stark numbers remain in many ways incomprehensible and reveal nothing of the individual suffering of both the dead and those who survived.

While undoubtedly terrifying and terrible, the two world wars bookended two decades that, though less analyzed and mythologized, were similarly murderous. There was little peace between 1918 and 1939 – civil wars, localized territorial disputes, and colonial campaigns continued to add to the half-century's death toll. In retrospect, it seems ironic that World War I, that first great bloodletting, was dubbed "The War to End All Wars" by English novelist H.G. Wells in 1914.

Those who supported his view believed that the horrors of world war were likely to be so unspeakable that no such similar event – at least involving the world powers – would occur again. There were fine and decent motives behind many of the pronouncements of those who promulgated the slogan and sought to use negotiation to resolve issues during the two decades after World War I, but they, without the luxury of our hindsight, were sadly misguided. Others who had also lived through World War I and were to achieve political prominence in the interwar era drew entirely different conclusions. In reality, World War I decided one set of political issues regarding the hegemony of Europe but in its concluding peace treaties it created a fragile political framework that would lead to the even more lethal World War II.

What were the causes of these various wars, both national and international, in the first half of the century? Put simply, they revolved around power and influence. They were chiefly fought for status and recognition; the competitive desire of one country or people within one country to be acknowledged and, in their own minds, respected by their peers. To achieve these ends, countries, individuals, and political groups were willing to embark on campaigns of violence in which the voice of reason or that of the dissenting individual were rendered silent beneath the clamor of the manipulated masses for action.

The political message of all the leaders of states or political factions that fought wars in the first five decades of the twentieth century was that they were going to war for "just" and "legitimate" reasons – to right an economic, political, or morale injustice of some sort. More often than not these seemingly fine and usually populist sentiments were nothing more than a convenient veil to cover baser motives and used as a patriotic call to drag a sometimes less-than-willing populace into shedding blood for an often dubious cause.

WORLD WAR I

World War I's origins dated back to the fourth quarter of the nineteenth century when Europe's – and the world's – leading powers embarked on a dangerous game of political brinkmanship. This chiefly involved Austria-Hungary, Britain, France, Germany, and Russia. Their rivalries, motivated by rampant nationalism, centered around economic expansion, the scramble for colonies, and the pursuit of military prestige. Part of this race for power and recognition was Germany's Kaiser Wilhelm II, a militarist who dubbed himself Germany's "First Soldier" but who was also indecisive and easily swayed. He came to power in 1888.

Colonialism, the domination of an area and its people by another state, was fueled by nationalism, the belief than one race is superior to another.

European colonists thought that they were somehow superior, and that they had the right to take the territory of peoples they considered inferior.

VALUABLE COLONIES

To Europe's leading powers, as well as the United States and Japan, colonies had two benefits. Behind the mask of bringing civilization to their indigenous peoples, they knew that colonies guaranteed their industries raw materials and potential markets, and gave their governments prestige among their peers. Colonies were costly to run and were usually exploited by private ventures, but European governments became fixated with keeping up with their rivals, whatever the cost.

Colonial expansion got into its stride in the second half of the nineteenth century. In 1870 some 70 percent of

the globe was controlled by the European powers; by 1914 the figure was 85 percent. In this period colonial interest centered on Africa, which had previously escaped major colonization.

Many early African colonizers had succumbed to rampant diseases; however, advances in medical science conquered or alleviated killers like yellow fever. Technology in the form of modern weapons allowed relatively small numbers of Europeans to crush any local opposition.

By the latter part of the nineteenth century it was clear that new colonies were becoming increasingly difficult to find. The leading powers were coming into conflict – if not outright

▼ *Germany's Kaiser Wilhelm II (center, left) attends one of the German Army's annual training exercises.*

innovation in military technologies. Weapons were becoming increasingly powerful, more deadly, and available in huge numbers thanks to standardization and mass production.

The naval arms race typified the desire for military parity, if not outright superiority. In the late 1890s Britain, the greatest colonial power, maintained the world's largest navy. However, it was being increasingly challenged by France and Russia.

The British increased their warship production with the intention of

◄ *British troops move forward against the Boer farmers of southern Africa, who were backed by Germany.*

▼ *An armaments factory capable of mass producing the destructive weapons that would come to dominate World War I.*

war – with each other as each attempted to grab areas ripe for colonization. In 1898 Britain and France came close to war when a French expedition marched into Fashoda, a town in British-controlled Sudan. In 1911 Germany sent a gunboat to Agadir, Morocco, which had recently been taken over by the French, to challenge France's right to the country.

Powers were also sometimes willing to intervene indirectly in regions controlled by their rivals. For example, the Boer farmers of gold-rich southern Africa went to war with Britain in 1899 to keep their independence, and received support from Germany during the protracted fighting.

The great European powers also embarked on an arms race that ran in tandem with the scramble for colonies. They needed to protect their far-flung colonies, secure their trade with them, and maintain a balance of military power with their neighbors in Europe. None of the powers was willing to see another gain an unassailable military advantage. The arms race coincided with rapid industrialization and

creating a navy that could take on the combined Russian and French fleets. This, however, was a costly strategy, particularly once Britain became involved in a naval arms race with Germany shortly thereafter. The British answer was to build better warships, a process that reached its apotheosis with the launching of HMS *Dreadnought*, a battleship incorporating several new technologies that was far superior to any vessel afloat, in 1906. Britain's rivals, seeing the

◄ *The British* Dreadnought *marked a new era in warship design and helped to fuel the ongoing arms race between the world's great powers.*

9

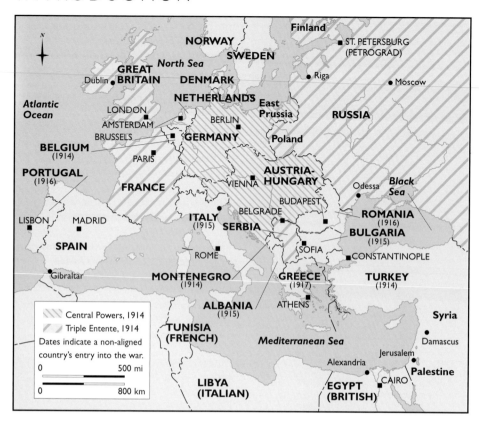

▲ *The geopolitical map of Europe on the eve of World War I, showing the members of the rival power blocs.*

those areas it controlled in the Balkans, where its power was being challenged by ardent nationalists in Serbia. France was politically unstable, industrially weak, and full of resentment at its defeat during the Franco-Prussian War (1870–71).

Before the outbreak of World War I Europe's powers had entered into a series of often-shifting alliances with each other, depending on which country was seemingly threatening the balance of power. From the 1890s attention focussed on Germany, whose Kaiser Wilhelm II embarked on a strategy that he intended would make Germany the leading European power. This became increasingly central to Wilhelm's foreign policy as Germany could not embark on any expansion of its overseas possessions as there were few countries left to colonize.

ALLIES AND RIVALS

Germany became allied with Austria-Hungary, the two known as the Central Powers. Arrayed against them were Britain, France, and Russia – the Triple Entente. These networks of alliances, both informal and formal, effectively guaranteed that an attack on one alliance member was considered an attack on all. Kaiser Wilhelm had ambitions to expand German territory into Russian-dominated Eastern Europe, a move that would precipitate war with France, Russia's ally and Germany's old rival in Western Europe. If Germany was to expand into Eastern Europe, it would need a reason to go to war.

All the European powers were aware of the network of alliances, and most developed war plans based on the

sudden vulnerability of their costly fleets, began to build their own dreadnought-type battleships.

Colonial, economic, and military rivalries impacted on the balance of power that regulated the relationships between Europe's leading nations. In the past, if one nation gained an advantage of some type, its chief rival or rivals would act to negate the advantage in some way. The European – and world – balance of power depended on no single nation or nations gaining an unassailable lead.

By the beginning of the twentieth century it was clear that Britain and Germany had clear water between themselves and their rivals. Germany was military superior on land, had a dynamic industrial base, and was intent on extending its power in Europe. Britain was the largest colonial power, had the most powerful navy, and a strong, if declining, industrial base.

In contrast, Russia remained a virtually feudal agricultural society and its armed forces suffered a humiliating defeat during the Russo-Japanese War (1904–05). Austria-Hungary was riven by ethnic tensions, particularly in

▼ *Japanese field artillery in action during the Russo-Japanese War, which was a disaster for the Russian armed forces.*

premise that once a war broke out between any two rival alliance members, the others would react immediately. Thus it became necessary to develop plans for the rapid mobilization of armies and their swift movement, usually by rail, to the front.

This need was most acutely felt in Germany, which faced a possible war on two fronts against Triple Entente members France and Russia. Rapid mobilization followed by a pre-emptive strike against France, which was likely to mobilize faster than Russia, became the key element of Germany's war strategy. This also involved an attack through Belgium, whose coal fields would be a valuable addition to Germany's heavy industries. However, Belgium's neutrality was guaranteed by Britain – and all the other major European powers, including Germany.

The flashpoint between the two alliances was the Balkans, a region rent with ethnic divisions and nationalistic aspirations, all overlain with the ambitions of two rival alliance members – Austria-Hungary and Russia, who were both eager to take advantage of Turkey's waning influence in the region. Serbia, whose security was guaranteed by Russia, was an ambitious Balkan power, aiming to curb Austro-Hungarian expansion in the region and establish a "Greater Serbia."

COUNTDOWN TO WAR

The security of Austria-Hungary, the weaker of the Central Powers, was guaranteed by Germany. Indeed, Kaiser Wilhelm II had told his planners to prepare for war in late 1912 to early 1913, when a local conflict in the Balkans saw Serbia gain territory from Turkey and threaten Austro-Hungarian possessions in the northern Adriatic. Austria-Hungary, backed by Germany, stated that it would go to war if Serbia did not give up its gains along the Adriatic. Such a move would have prompted a Russian response, thereby drawing in France. Serbia did back down due to diplomacy. However, the possible route for a local conflict to spark a Europe-wide war, which some were actively seeking, was revealed.

Germany did not have to wait for long to take advantage of a similar political incident. On June 28, 1914, the heir to the Austro-Hungarian throne, Archduke Ferdinand, was assassinated by a Serbian nationalist while touring Sarajevo, the capital of Bosnia, an Austro-Hungarian province.

In 1914 most countries, their civilians and politicians alike, believed that they were going to war for the right reasons. War enthusiasm was rife, but it was destined to die, along with scores of thousands of troops, in the face of machine guns, artillery, and trenches during the first year of war.

▼ *German troops on maneuvers in the years before the outbreak of World War I.*

1914

To many people in Europe the outbreak of war in August 1914 was welcome and seen as an opportunity to right many perceived wrongs, irrespective of either their political or economic validity. The politicians and generals who plunged Europe into this industrial-based war believed it would not last beyond a few months. By December, however, hopes of a swift and decisive victory were dashed against a backdrop of huge casualties, general stalemate, and a widening conflict.

JUNE 28

POLITICS, *BOSNIA*

Archduke Franz Ferdinand, heir to the throne of the Austro-Hungarian Empire, and his wife are assassinated in Sarajevo, the capital of Bosnia, which is a province of the empire. A radical Bosnian-Serb, Gavrilo Princip, is arrested along with other conspirators. Princip is a member of a Serbian nationalist organization, the Black Hand, which is dedicated to the creation of a Serbia-dominated Balkans. Austria-Hungary suspects the direct involvement of Serbia in the plot.

◀ *Austria-Hungary's Archduke Franz Ferdinand is greeted by a Bosnian official shortly before his assassination, June 28.*

JULY 23

POLITICS, *AUSTRIA-HUNGARY*

Austria-Hungary delivers an ultimatum to Serbia after several meetings with Germany's Kaiser Wilhelm II and his advisers, who back Austria-Hungary's actions. The demands of the ultimatum would, if agreed, destroy Serbia as an independent state. Austria-Hungary demands a reply within 48 hours.

JULY 25

POLITICS, *SERBIA*

The Serbians, while mobilizing their armed forces, agree to meet all but one of the 10 demands outlined in the Austro-Hungarian ultimatum. The Austro-Hungarians find this unacceptable and Emperor Franz Joseph orders the mobilization of his forces to begin on the following day. Russia's Czar Nicholas II and his minister of war, Grand Duke Nicholas, agree to partly mobilize their forces to protect Serbia from any Austro-Hungarian invasion. Germany, along with Italy one of Austria-Hungary's allies in the Triple

◄ Germany's Kaiser Wilhelm II. His willingness to back Austro-Hungarian military action against Serbia effectively guaranteed the outbreak of World War I.

▶ Austro-Hungarians in Vienna celebrate the opening of hostilities with Serbia.

Alliance, threatens to begin mobilizing its forces if Britain and France, Russia's allies, do not succeed in curbing Russia's war preparations.

JULY 28

POLITICS, *AUSTRIA-HUNGARY*
Austria-Hungary declares war on Serbia at noon.

POLITICS, *BRITAIN*
The government orders its warships to their various war bases. The main force, the Home Fleet, begins to assemble at its anchorages in Scapa Flow in the Orkneys off the northeast coast of Scotland from where it can dominate the North Sea and block the German fleet's access to the world's oceans.

STRATEGY & TACTICS

WAR PLANS IN THE EAST

The war strategies of both the Austro-Hungarians and Russians were very much shaped to fall in line with Germany's war strategy. Austria-Hungary had two plans. First, there was the strategy known as Plan B to fight in the Balkans, with Serbia as the enemy. Second, there was Plan R to fight on two fronts against Serbia and its ally, Russia.

In the later, more likely, scenario it was planned that the Austro-Hungarian armies would fight in support of their German counterparts, which would be based in East Prussia. The Austro-Hungarian armies were under orders to launch an attack into Russian-controlled Poland in the south to divert Russian troops from East Prussia. Other Austro-Hungarian forces were earmarked to attack Serbia.

Russia also had two war plans. First, if Germany attacked Russia, the Russian armies would fight a defensive war. If, however, Germany chose to attack France first, Russian troops would march into East Prussia as quickly as possible.

Serbia's strategy was defined by the comparatively small size of its armed forces. Its commanders could realistically only fight a defensive war, hoping to delay any attacker for long enough until events on other fronts would force the enemy to pull some of its troops out of Serbia.

JULY 29

POLITICS, *BULGARIA*
The Balkan state declares its neutrality.

POLITICS, *GERMANY*
The navy is ordered to mobilize. This includes the main force, the High Seas Fleet, which begins to assemble along the Jade River. Russia is also informed that its recent partial mobilization will trigger a wider war.

POLITICS, *RUSSIA*
Czar Nicholas II puts his signature to a partial mobilization order, which comes into force on August 4.

BALKANS, *SERBIA*
In the first engagement of what will become World War I, Austro-Hungarian warships on the Danube River bombard Belgrade, the Serbian capital. Serbian artillery replies.

JULY 30

POLITICS, *NETHERLANDS*
The Dutch government declares its neutrality in the war.

JULY 31

POLITICS, *GERMANY*
General Helmuth von Moltke, chief of the General Staff, informs his Austro-Hungarian counterpart, General Franz Conrad von Hötzendorf, that Germany will mobilize its forces. Russia is told that it must cease all war preparations by noon on August 1, and the

French government is requested to explain its political position on any conflict between Germany and Russia.

▼ Franz Conrad von Hötzendorf, the Austro-Hungarian chief-of-staff, was an advocate of pre-emptive wars to curb Italian and Serbian expansionism.

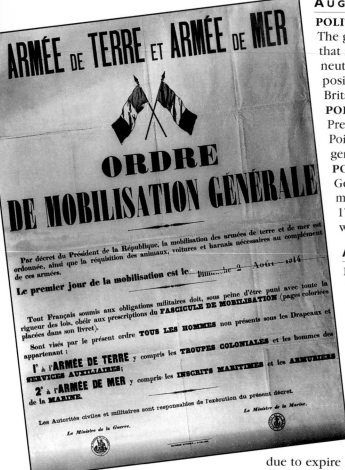

AUGUST 1

POLITICS, *BELGIUM*
The government proclaims that it will maintain its armed neutrality in any conflict, a position guaranteed by Britain and France.

POLITICS, *FRANCE*
President Raymond Poincaré agrees to issue a general mobilization order.

POLITICS, *GERMANY*
Germany begins to mobilize against Russia at 1700 hours and declares war at 1910 hours.

AUGUST 2

POLITICS, *GERMANY*
While German troops occupy neutral Luxembourg, an ultimatum is delivered to Belgium at 1900 hours demanding that German forces be allowed to move through Belgian territory unhindered to pre-empt a French attack on Germany. The ultimatum is due to expire in 12 hours. There are reports of border clashes between French and German troops.

POLITICS, *TURKEY*
War Minister Enver Pasha, an aggressive nationalist eager to restore Turkey's fortunes as a major regional power, arranges a secret military alliance with Germany as a means of protecting his country from possible Russian attack.

▲ The general mobilization order issued by the French Army and naval authorities on the eve of World War I.

▼ German troops head westward at the opening of their great offensive against Belgium and France, August 1914. They appear confident of a swift victory.

AUGUST 3

POLITICS, *BELGIUM*
The Belgian government rejects the German ultimatum demanding that its forces have free passage through Belgian territory and also receives confirmation that Britain and France will provide armed support to combat any German attack.

POLITICS, *BRITAIN*
A general mobilization order is signed.

POLITICS, *GERMANY*
Germany declares war against France.

POLITICS, *ITALY*
Much to the annoyance of its partners in the Triple Alliance – Germany and Austria-Hungary – Italy declares its neutrality. The Italian government argues that Austria-Hungary's attack on Serbia is an act of war not covered in the essentially defensive provisions of the Triple Alliance treaty.

POLITICS, *ROMANIA*
Despite ailing King Karol's wish to join Germany and Austria-Hungary, his government opts for a position of

◄ *Enver Pasha, an ardent expansionist, was made the Turkish Army's deputy commander-in-chief on August 3.*

► *The mobilization order published by the British government in the name of King George V.*

BY THE KING.

A PROCLAMATION

For Calling out Men of the Royal Naval Reserve and Royal Fleet Reserve, and Officers and Men of the Royal Naval Volunteer Reserve.

GEORGE R.I.

[body of proclamation in small print]

Given at Our Court at Buckingham Palace, this Third day of August, in the year of our Lord one thousand nine hundred and fourteen, and in the Fifth year of Our Reign.

GOD SAVE THE KING.

armed neutrality. However, a secret government agreement with Russia made in early October agrees that Romania will gain territory if Russia's armed forces are successful in their war against both Germany and Austria-Hungary. Evidence of Romania's true interests becomes clear on October 23, when it closes its borders to German supplies bound for Turkey.

POLITICS, *TURKEY*
Turkey declares its armed neutrality and mobilizes its forces.

▼ *The German light cruiser* Breslau, *a gift for Turkey along with the* Goeben.

AUGUST 4

POLITICS, *BRITAIN*
The government declares war at 2300 hours as the Germans reject the British ultimatum requesting that their troops leave Belgian soil.

POLITICS, *GERMANY*
The government declares war on Belgium and its armies invade in force across a narrow front. Leading the main attack are the First Army commanded by General Alexander von Kluck and General Karl von Bülow's Second Army.

STRATEGY & TACTICS

BRITAIN'S COMMITMENT

Uniquely, Britain was the only major European power that did not have some form of conscription at the outbreak of World War I. Its regular army, although much smaller than its European counterparts, was an all-volunteer force. Man for man, however, it was probably the best. Its regular infantry regiments were highly trained, skilled in most aspects of warfare, and renowned for the volume and accuracy of their rifle fire.

One British regular soldier described the impact of accurate rifle fire on a company of Germans at Mons in August 1914: "[They] were simply blasted away to heaven by a volley at 700 yards [680 m], and in their insane formation every bullet was almost sure to find two billets."

The army that Britain sent to France in 1914 was known as the British Expeditionary Force and consisted at the outset of around 100,000 men. It was a generally well-balanced force, but was later found to be lacking trench-busting medium and heavy artillery. It was also short of machine guns – just 120 in total in August 1914. In stark comparison, the German Army, although considerably larger, had 10,500.

At the outset of the war Britain's greatest contribution was its powerful navy of over 500 vessels. In the key area of dreadnought battleships and battlecruisers the British naval forces enjoyed a 28:18 superiority over Germany's High Seas Fleet.

POLITICS, *UNITED STATES*
The government declares its neutrality.

SEA WAR, *MEDITERRANEAN*
Two German warships, the battlecruiser *Goeben* and the light cruiser *Breslau*, under the command of Vice Admiral Wilhelm von Souchon, open

▲ *British recruits gather in central London at the outbreak of war. Like thousands of young men across Europe, many saw the conflict as a great adventure.*

▼ *British troops, part of the force earmarked to protect the neutrality of Belgium, entrain for the Western Front.*

fire on Bône and Philippeville, two ports in French Algeria, for 10 minutes. After the attack Souchon heads for Turkey. As he sails east across the Mediterranean, his small squadron runs into two British battlecruisers, the *Indefatigable* and *Indomitable*, sailing west.

The British commander, Vice Admiral Sir A. Berkeley-Milne, refrains from opening fire as the British government's ultimatum demanding that German forces inside Belgium should withdraw or face war does not expire until midnight. Souchon also avoids action and continues on to Turkey.

AUGUST 5

POLITICS, *AUSTRIA-HUNGARY*
Austria-Hungary declares war on Russia at 1200 hours.

POLITICS, *MONTENEGRO*
The government of this Balkan state, which has close links with Serbia, declares war on Austria-Hungary.

WESTERN FRONT, *BELGIUM*
German troops launch a night attack on Liège but fail to capture any of the outer ring of 12 powerful forts protecting the city, which is the key border defense in eastern Belgium and a railroad center. It also blocks the route of the German First and Second Armies as they attempt to head for the French border before swinging south toward Paris as part of the Schlieffen Plan, the German war strategy.

AUGUST 6

POLITICS, *SERBIA*
The government declares war on Germany.

WESTERN FRONT, *BELGIUM*
General Erich Ludendorff of the German Second Army wins great fame in his homeland by leading troops through part of Liège's defensive ring of forts to establish a lodgment that threatens the city's Belgian garrison. However, he is cut off until the 10th.

SEA WAR, *EAST AFRICA*
The *Königsberg*, a German light cruiser, attacks and sinks the British light cruiser *Pegasus* off the port of Mombasa. The German warship sailed from Dar-es-Salaam on 31 July; its role

▼ *A column of German infantry moves through the shell-blasted remains of a Belgian village in early August.*

is to interdict British commerce in the Indian Ocean. The British move to deal with the threat posed by this German raider and the *Königsberg* is forced to seek shelter in the Rufiji River, German East Africa, on October 30.

AUGUST 6–7

SEA WAR, *MEDITERRANEAN*
German Vice Admiral Wilhelm von Souchon, pursued by Vice Admiral Sir A. Berkeley-Milne's two British battle-cruisers, continues to lead his two

STRATEGY & TACTICS

THE SCHLIEFFEN PLAN

In 1893 France and Russia signed a military alliance that greatly alarmed Germany's chief of the General Staff, Count Alfred von Schlieffen. Schlieffen was acutely aware of the dangers of Germany fighting a major war on two fronts and saw France as the most immediate threat in any conflict involving the three countries. He then developed a plan (see below) to knock France out of any war in a matter of weeks before Russia could mobilize its vast armies.

Schlieffen realized that France's border defenses with Germany were far too strong to be taken quickly, and that rapid movement through Switzerland's mountainous terrain was impossible. He therefore opted to violate Belgian and Dutch neutrality by sending a massive force, some 90 percent of the total German Army, through these countries and then swing southward to head for Paris. Only five percent of the army would defend Alsace-Lorraine, where Schlieffen, correctly, expected – and wanted – the French forces to attack. The region's strong border fortifications backed by a resolute defense would tie up a large part of the French Army.

The remaining five percent of the army would hold East Prussia. It was expected that these forces would block the Russians

until German forces, fresh from their rapid victory over France, could be rushed east to defeat Russia in turn. Central to the plan were rapid mobilization and the speedy movement of troops by rail.

Schlieffen retired in 1906 and his successor, General Helmuth von Moltke, made modifications to the original plan. Moltke saw that Russia could mobilize more quickly than Schlieffen believed and therefore earmarked 15 percent of the German Army to defend East Prussia. Moltke did not want to give up any of Alsace-Lorraine to France, no matter how temporarily, and therefore increased the forces there to 25 percent. He was also concerned to protect German industry in the adjacent Rhineland. Thus only 60 percent of the German Army was available for the decisive sweep into northern France through Belgium.

Finally, Moltke decided not to attack through the neutral Netherlands, believing that Britain might not go to war to save Belgium if Dutch neutrality was honored. Consequently, the planned attack had to take place on a much narrower front than that envisaged by Schlieffen. It also forced the Germans to contemplate neutralizing the massive defenses of Liège, Belgium, which stood directly in their path.

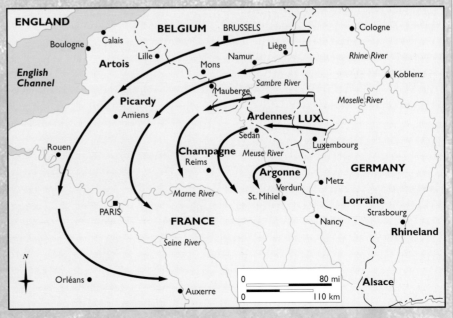

warships, the *Goeben* and *Breslau*, through the Mediterranean. Southwest of Greece he maneuvers to avoid a squadron of British cruisers led by Rear Admiral E. C. Troubridge, which has been sent to block his route to Constantinople, the Turkish capital.

STRATEGY & TACTICS

FRANCE'S PLAN XVII

France's greatest humiliation following its defeat at the hands of Germany in the Franco-Prussian War (1870–71) was the loss of Alsace-Lorraine on its eastern frontier. France expected to go to war with Germany again at some time in the future and its military leaders developed a war strategy to win back the lost provinces.

Between 1911 and 1914 General Joseph Joffre, the French commander-in-chief, devised Plan XVII. It called for the various French armies to assemble along the key frontier from Switzerland to Belgium, and launch an immediate, devastating attack in strength into Alsace-Lorraine. Joffre did recognize that the Germans might violate Belgium's neutrality in any attack on France, but believed that they could not advance past the Meuse River in northeast France without becoming dangerously overextended. The French also had an informal arrangement with the British that guaranteed that their army would plug any gap on the Franco-Belgian border.

Plan XVII had two key weaknesses. First, Joffre underestimated the quality of the German Army and the speed with which it could mobilize and move. In the event of war this would allow the Germans to have a possibly greater initial front-line strength than the French and permit a movement through Belgium that would not leave them particularly overstretched.

The second weakness of Joffre's war plans was that the French adhered to the doctrine of constant attack. They believed that a resolute attack could fight through any defense. All that was needed was the will power of the ordinary French soldier to carry out what was termed *offense à l'outrance* ("offense at the utmost"). Consequently, French training concentrated on attack and neglected defense. For their part the Germans did train to both attack and defend aggressively – and their infantry units were equipped with a greater proportion of machine guns. As the French learned in 1914, resolute attacks in the face of defensive machine-gun fire could lead to very heavy casualties.

AUGUST 7

WESTERN FRONT, *FRANCE*
The advance guard of the 100,000-strong British Expeditionary Force reaches France. The arrival of this army is completed over the following few weeks and the force takes up a position in the southeast corner of Belgium, around the town of Mons. Field Marshal Sir John French is named as its commander.

AUGUST 8

POLITICS, *BRITAIN*
Field Marshal Sir Herbert Kitchener, the recently appointed secretary of war, calls for 100,000 volunteers to join the British Army. He later poses for a recruitment poster, which depicts him pointing an accusing figure at the viewer and stating "Your Country Needs You." The message first appears on September 5; 175,000 volunteer over the next week.

▼ *French troops with a guard dog keep watch for German troops during their attack into Lorraine, August 1914.*

▶ *Serbian Marshal Radomir Putnik, although severely outnumbered, defeated an Austro-Hungarian invasion in 1914.*

WESTERN FRONT, *FRANCE*
In accordance with a prewar strategic blueprint for war against Germany known as Plan XVII, France's Army of Alsace under General Paul Pau advances against the German-held city of Mulhouse in Alsace, heralding a series of battles along the French and Belgian borders.

AUGUST 10

POLITICS, *FRANCE*
The government declares war on Austria-Hungary.

WESTERN FRONT, *BELGIUM*
The first of Liège's 12 forts falls to the Germans following a pounding by 17-in (42-cm) howitzers brought up by Second Army commander General Karl von Bülow.

SEA WAR, *MEDITERRANEAN*
The German warships *Goeben* and *Breslau* pass through the Dardanelles seaway and their British pursuers call

off the chase. The German ships, along with their crews, become part of Turkey's naval forces operating in the Black Sea. The "gift" of the two warships acts as an encouragement to the Turks to join the war, particularly as two Turkish battleships under construction in British shipyards had been commandeered by the British at the outbreak of the war.

AUGUST 12

POLITICS, *BRITAIN*
The government declares war on Austria-Hungary.

AUGUST 12–21

BALKANS, *SERBIA*
Advancing across the border into Serbia from the north and northwest, some 200,000 Austro-Hungarian troops led by General Oskar Potiorek invade. Although outnumbered, the Serbians forces under Marshal Radomir Putnik put up stout resistance during the Battle of the Jadar River, forcing the invaders to begin withdrawing by August 16.

AUGUST 14

HOME FRONT, *BRITAIN*
Novelist H.G. Wells calls the conflict "The War to End All Wars."

AUGUST 14–22

WESTERN FRONT, *FRANCE*
Southeast of Metz two French armies, the First under General Auguste Dubail and the Second commanded by General Noël de Castelnau, initiate the first of a series of engagements that become known as the "Battle of the Frontiers" by attacking into Lorraine.
  Two German armies make a slow but coordinated withdrawal to give time for reinforcements to arrive. The German counterattack on the 20th forces the French back. A defensive action by General Ferdinand Foch's XX Corps on high ground outside Nancy prevents a major defeat.

AUGUST 15

POLITICS, *JAPAN*
The Japanese demand that the Germans evacuate their colony based at the port of Tsingtao in China.

AUGUST 16

POLITICS, *GERMANY*
Austrian-born Adolf Hitler volunteers to fight with the German Army. He will serve throughout the conflict on the

AUGUST 17-19

General Max von Prittwitz's thinly-spread Eighth Army. However, the Russian armies are widely separated, chiefly by the Masurian Lakes, and are lacking in most types of equipment. Prittwitz's troops, although overstretched and outnumbered, act as a delaying force.

On the 17th German forces inflict a defeat on Rennenkampf's advance guard at Stallupönen, causing 3000 casualties and pushing the Russians back to the East Prussian frontier. The German commander at Stallupönen, General Hermann von François, then falls back to Gumbinnen.

AUGUST 18

WESTERN FRONT, *BELGIUM*
King Albert orders the Belgian Army, some 75,000 men, to retreat to the port of Antwerp, which has a garrison of 60,000 men. The move is completed by the 20th and the Germans deploy some 60,000 men to keep Leopold bottled up in the fortified city as the bulk of their forces push toward the Franco-Belgian border.

▲ *Russian troops in a Polish town prepare to march to the front. Although the army had a strength of over four million, it lacked ammunition and equipment.*

Western Front as a messenger, suffer wounds, and receive various medals for valor.

WESTERN FRONT, *BELGIUM*
After days of intense bombardment from the massive German 17-in (42-cm) howitzers, which leave the defenders' forts in ruins, the garrison of Liège surrenders. With the Belgian fortress neutralized, the German First Army commanded by General Alexander von Kluck and the Second Army led by General Karl von Bülow push westward across the Meuse River. The Belgian Army begins to withdraw, destroying bridges as it retreats.

AUGUST 17-19

EASTERN FRONT, *EAST PRUSSIA*
Two Russian forces, the First Army under General Pavel Rennenkampf and General Alexander Samsonov's Second Army, invade East Prussia from the east and southeast, where they are met by

▶ *A German 17-in (42-cm) howitzer is readied for action. It could lob a large shell accurately to a range of 10,000 yards (9140 m) with a flight time of around 60 seconds.*

▶ *German troops subject Belgian citizens to a thorough search. German policy in occupied countries was to use physical force and intimidation to pre-empt any civilian resistance.*

AUGUST 19

WESTERN FRONT, *BELGIUM*
German troops shoot 150 civilians at Aerschot, one of many – often unconfirmed – reports of atrocities committed against non-combatants. It is known that the Germans openly avow the policy of *Schrecklichkeit* ("frightfulness") to cow and intimidate the local population in occupied areas.

AUGUST 20

WESTERN FRONT, *BELGIUM*
German forces occupy Brussels, the Belgian capital.

EASTERN FRONT, *EAST PRUSSIA*
At Gumbinnen, the Germans, who fear encirclement, confront the slowly advancing Russian forces of Rennenkampf. General Hermann von François, who acts decisively, unlike the dithering Prittwitz, drives Rennenkampf back some five miles (8 km) – but other German attacks are unsuccessful. Prittwitz is relieved of his command and is replaced by the elderly General Paul von Hindenburg, who is recalled from retirement. Hindenburg's chief-of-staff is confirmed as the dynamic General

▼ *Belgian civilians look on as a German supply column prepares to move out from Brussels, the recently captured capital.*

Erich Ludendorff, fresh from his role in capturing the crucial Belgian frontier fortress of Liège.

AFRICA, *CAMEROONS*
Some 400 British troops invade German Cameroons from Nigeria.

AIR WAR, *GERMANY*
The German high command is asked to authorize long-range Zeppelin airship bombing attacks on London, key British ports, and a number of major naval bases.

AUGUST 20–25

WESTERN FRONT, *BELGIUM*
The "Battle of the Frontiers" switches to the wooded Ardennes region to the north of Metz. Two French

armies advancing at all possible speed into Belgium run into two German armies rushing through Luxembourg and southeast Belgium on the 22nd. Three days of bitter, confused fighting follow, with the outnumbered French blunting the German attacks and then launching their own counterattacks.

French losses are severe. Their Third Army (General Pierre Ruffey) is virtually destroyed and General Fernand de Langle de Cary's Fourth Army badly mauled. The French, pursued by the Germans, fall back to positions between the Meuse and Marne Rivers, with their right wing resting on the fortifications of Verdun.

▲ *A French three-inch (75-mm) field gun in action. A lightweight design, it could be moved around the battlefield with ease and thus offer immediate support in both defense and attack. It could also fire up to 20 rounds a minute.*

▼ *German infantry await the order to advance on the Eastern Front.*

AUGUST 22

EASTERN FRONT, *EAST PRUSSIA*
Ludendorff quickly takes charge of the German forces confronting Rennenkampf and Samsonov. He orders the wholesale realignment of the outnumbered German troops facing the Russians, directing the bulk of his units against Samsonov's Second Army in the south of the province by both road and rail. A

▲ *German troops advance during the fighting in the French Argonne sector of the Western Front.*

single cavalry division is directed to delay Rennenkampf in the north. The Germans plan to defeat Samsonov before his forces can link up with Rennenkampf. Unbeknown to Ludendorff and Hindenburg, Lieutenant Colonel Max Hoffmann, Prittwitz's chief of operations, has already begun such a maneuver.

AUGUST 22–23

WESTERN FRONT, *BELGIUM*

North of the Ardennes three German armies are continuing to sweep through western Belgium and are beginning to advance to the south and southwest for France. In the third engagement of the "Battle of the Frontiers" the French commander-in-chief, General Joseph Joffre, orders General Charles Lanrezac's Fifth Army into position between the Sambre and Meuse Rivers to block the unexpected switch in the main axis of the German attack into France.

Again, the French fight stubbornly to halt the German advance, but suffer unacceptably high casualties. Lanrezac seeks and is granted permission by Joffre to withdraw. As this battle is taking place, German troops are using their heavy howitzers to smash the Belgian garrison of Namur. The fortress is finally captured on the 25th.

KEY PERSONALITIES

FIELD MARSHAL PAUL VON HINDENBURG

Hindenburg (1847–1934) actually retired from the German Army in 1911, but was recalled to command the Eighth Army in East Prussia, with General Erich Ludendorff as his subordinate, in August 1914. Together, the two men scored notable victories over the Russians at the Battle of Tannenberg and the Masurian Lakes the same year. Hindenburg was promoted to command all German and Austro-Hungarian troops on the Eastern Front and made a field marshal later the same year.

In 1915 Hindenburg won significant victories in Poland, but was later highly critical of the transfer of some of his forces to the Western Front to take part in the Battle of Verdun in 1916. On August 29 Hindenburg replaced Erich von Falkenhayn as chief of the General Staff. Due to the weakness of Kaiser Wilhelm II and the German parliament, Hindenburg and Ludendorff effectively took over as military dictators.

Among his key decisions during this period was to announce unrestricted submarine warfare (January 1917), and he oversaw the talks at the Treaty of Brest-Litovsk with Russia in the following December. His final role as chief of the General Staff was to back Ludendorff's series of offensives on the Western Front between March and June 1918, which were finally unsuccessful.

In the final days of the war Hindenburg was forced to sue for peace and, although he retired from public life in 1919, he returned to serve two terms as German president. He was made chancellor by Adolf Hitler on January 30, 1933, but was little more than a figurehead until his death on August 2, 1934.

Hindenburg (left) and Ludendorff (right) discuss war strategy with Kaiser Wilhelm II.

AUGUST 23

KEY PERSONALITIES

FIELD MARSHAL SIR JOHN FRENCH

Field Marshal Sir John French (1852–1925) commanded the British Expeditionary Force from August 1914 until replaced by General Sir Douglas Haig in September 1915. French had won fame as a cavalry commander during the Second Anglo-Boer War (1899–1902) and risen in seniority.

In 1914 French faced several immediate problems, not least the sweeping early successes of the German Army, which dislocated any Anglo-French war plans, and the need to preserve the British Expeditionary Force. Although he had great charisma and was undoubtedly brave, he was not an easy man to get along with. French quarreled with General Charles Lanrezac, whose French Fifth Army he claimed was offering insufficient support to his own forces. French also got on badly with Lord Kitchener, who was the British secretary of state for war, and relied too heavily on General Henry Wilson, his headstrong deputy chief of the General Staff.

In March 1915, after the Battle of Neuve-Chapelle, French severely criticized the British government (with some justification) for its alleged inability to provide him with sufficient artillery shells, and then dismissed General Sir Horace Smith-Dorrien for failure at the Second Battle of Ypres in April. The crunch came in September, when French failed to commit his reserve corps during the Battle of Loos. Although French had powerful political allies in Britain, he was nevertheless dismissed.

▲ Crowds in Paris turn out to watch the departure of heavy cavalry for the front at the height of the August fighting.

AUGUST 23

POLITICS, *JAPAN*
The government declares war on Germany and two days later opens hostilities with Austria-Hungary. The Japanese refuse to become involved in the war in Europe and concentrate their efforts against the German colony-port of Tsingtao in China.

WESTERN FRONT, *BELGIUM*
At Mons, in the final encounter of the "Battle of the Frontiers," the British Expeditionary Force meets General Alexander von Kluck's German First Army. Although heavily outnumbered the British repulse the first German attack, inflicting severe casualties with accurate and

▶ A lone German sentry stands guard over the remains of one of Namur's shell-blasted forts, August 25.

▲ *German infantrymen move through a French wood. Hot weather and heavy equipment soon tired the troops.*

◄ *A British cavalry unit falls back after briefly slowing the pace of the German attack at the Battle of Mons.*

high-volume rifle fire. Subsequent German attacks force the British back just three miles (5 km). Because of the withdrawal of Lanrezac's French Fifth Army a little to the east, the British are forced to conduct an orderly retreat.

Mons marks the end of the "Battle of the Frontiers." To Helmuth von Moltke, the German chief-of-staff, this sprawling series of battles seems to herald a great victory. French casualties are high (some 300,000 men), and both they and the British are in seemingly disorganized retreat.

On this basis he modifies the Schlieffen Plan further. He orders his forces in northeastern France to continue their wide sweep aimed toward Paris but sends the reinforcements earmarked for them elsewhere – Lorraine – for a new attack. Two corps from the German right wing are also sent to the Eastern Front, where the Russian mobilization has been more rapid than expected. Other German units from the key right wing are to lay siege to Antwerp, where much of the Belgian Army is holding out, and to besiege the French-held fortress-city of Mauberge.

Moltke's evaluation of the strategic situation is false, partly due to his poor communications with his army commanders. In contrast, the French commander-in-chief, General Joseph Joffre, recognizes that, although his

▶ *A German field forge and smithy on the Eastern Front.*

casualties are heavy, the morale of his forces remains high. Joffre, by now aware of the location of the German armies, prepares a counterattack in northeast France. His forces in contact with the Germans are ordered to continue their orderly withdrawal, while armies around Verdun are to remain in position to act as an anchor for the offensive. Two new armies, the Sixth commanded by General Michel Maunoury, and General Ferdinand Foch's Ninth Army, are created.

Joffre plans to place the Sixth Army to the west of the far right wing of the German forces marching through northeastern France, and the Ninth is moved to bolster the line confronting the German forces advancing a little way to the northeast of Paris. However, the plan is thwarted for the moment by the speed of the German advance, which continues to force the French and British southward.

AUGUST 23–24

EASTERN FRONT, *GALICIA*
While the Germans are preparing to take on the Russians in East Prussia, their Austro-Hungarian allies launch an

▼ *The German victory at Tannenberg cost the Russians 125,000 casualties and 500 guns – against 15,000 German losses.*

offensive from around Lemberg in their province of Galicia into Russian-controlled Poland. The plan, masterminded by the Austro-Hungarian chief-of-staff, General Franz Conrad von Hötzendorf, involves the movement of three armies on a 200-mile (320-km) front. Their objective is to crush the four armies of General Nikolai Ivanov's Russian Southwest Army Group,

which are based southwest of the extensive and barrier-like Pripet Marshes. The main Austro-Hungarian advance begins well, with their First Army pushing back the Russian Fourth Army at the Battle of Krasnik.

AUGUST 24

EASTERN FRONT, *EAST PRUSSIA*
German troops successfully delay

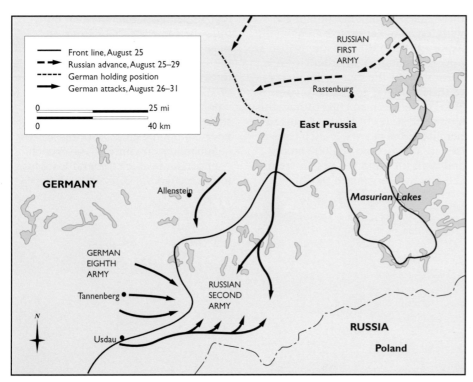

Front line, August 25
Russian advance, August 25–29
German holding position
German attacks, August 26–31

0 — 25 mi
0 — 40 km

RUSSIAN FIRST ARMY

Rastenburg

East Prussia

GERMANY

Allenstein

Masurian Lakes

GERMAN EIGHTH ARMY

Tannenberg

RUSSIAN SECOND ARMY

Usdau

RUSSIA

Poland

Samsonov's advance in southern East Prussia in a day-long battle at Orlau-Frankenau, thereby allowing other German units to concentrate at nearby Tannenberg for their forthcoming battle against Samsonov. The Russian high command remains unaware that its uncoded radio traffic is being intercepted by the Germans, who have detailed knowledge of the Russian strength, dispositions, and plans.

AUGUST 25–27

WESTERN FRONT, *FRANCE*
The British Expeditionary Force continues to retreat southward across northeast France, fighting almost continuous rearguard actions against General Alexander von Kluck's First Army. At Le Cateau the British II Corps, some 40,000 men, fights for its life as the Germans attempt to surround it. The German attacks are beaten off but at terrible cost to the corps, which suffers 7800 casualties.

AUGUST 26

AFRICA, *TOGOLAND*
An Anglo-French expedition operating inside the German colony of Togoland in West Africa wins a decisive victory at Kamina, which effectively destroys the German presence.

AUGUST 26–31

EASTERN FRONT, *EAST PRUSSIA*
The Germans strike at Samsonov's Second Army outside Tannenberg from the north and south, and also in the center. By nightfall on the 29th Samsonov has been surrounded and he is believed to have committed suicide. Attempts by Rennenkampf in the north to come to the aid of Samsonov's beleaguered forces come to nothing. Tannenberg is a major German victory. Russian losses are enormous, their invasion of East Prussia is decisively rebuffed, and France and Britain's faith in their ally on the Eastern Front is severely shaken by the crushing defeat.

AUGUST 26–SEPTEMBER 1

EASTERN FRONT, *GALICIA*
The Austro-Hungarian broad-front offensive against the four armies of General Nikolai Ivanov's Russian Southwest Army Group in Poland continues with mixed results. At the Battle of Zamosc-Komarów the Austro-Hungarian Fourth Army pushes back the Russians. However, two Russian armies, the Third and Eighth, strike against the Austro-Hungarian Third Army at the Battle of Gnila Lipa, forcing it back to Lemberg, the base for the Austro-Hungarian attack.

▼ *Lines of Russian prisoners, some of the more than 90,000 captured by the Germans during the Battle of Tannenberg in East Prussia, queue for field rations in early September.*

KEY PERSONALITIES

MARSHAL JOSEPH JOFFRE

Marshal Joseph Joffre (1852–1931) was the commander-in-chief of the French Army between 1911 and December 1916, when he was replaced by General Robert Nivelle and took no further part in the war. Joffre (above, left) was a methodical officer and can claim credit for holding the Germans in 1914, chiefly through the rapid transfer of forces from his right flank to the threatened left flank along the Marne River.

Renowned for his calm manner, he was also held in great affection by the French troops and was known as "Papa Joffre." His stock reached its zenith during the fluid campaign of 1914, but he was less suited to the demands of static trench warfare, despite his background as a military engineer.

Joffre failed to adapt to the realities of trench warfare and was blamed by some for choosing the wrong places to launch attacks, chiefly at Loos in September 1914 and the Somme in 1916. Both were costly British failures, which soured his relationship with his main ally.

Also in 1916 he was blamed for the parlous state of Verdun's defenses when it was attacked by the Germans, although he displayed considerable skills in the early stage of the battle. Nevertheless, the credit went to General Henri-Philippe Pétain and Nivelle, Joffre's successor.

AUGUST 27

POLITICS, *TURKEY*

German General Liman von Sanders is made commander of the Turkish First Army.

AUGUST 28

SEA WAR, *NORTH SEA*

British cruisers launch a foray into German waters as part of a plan to lure elements of the German High Seas Fleet into an unequal fight, and also prevent German warships from attacking convoys transporting follow-on units of the British Expeditionary Force across the English Channel to France. The engagement, known as the Battle of Heligoland Bight, begins at 0700 hours. British light cruisers and destroyers under Commodore Tyrwhitt catch the Germans by surprise and enjoy success against German torpedo-boats.

However, the Germans recover from their surprise and their more powerful warships get up steam and sail out from their anchorage in the Jade River to attack the

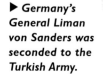

▶ *Germany's General Liman von Sanders was seconded to the Turkish Army.*

British. The German warships threaten to inflict severe losses, but the sudden arrival of reinforcements, chiefly five battlecruisers under Admiral Sir David Beatty, cover the withdrawal of the initial British force. No British ships are sunk during the battle, while four German vessels are sent to the bottom. The battle is seen as a clear-cut success by the British, but

▲ *French cavalry on the move during the build-up to the decisive Battle of the Marne, late August 1914.*

their euphoria serves to mask severe shortcomings, particularly in the planning and conduct of complex multi-force naval operations. However, the British raid has a profound impact on the morale of the German high command. Kaiser Wilhelm II warns his

naval commanders that the High Seas Fleet, already outnumbered by the British navy, cannot afford such losses. Plans to use the High Seas Fleet in large-scale offensive operations in the North Sea are shelved.

AUGUST 29–SEPTEMBER 2

WESTERN FRONT, *FRANCE*

General Joseph Joffre, the French commander-in-chief, orders the French Fifth Army to launch a flank attack against the German First Army around Guise to take some of the pressure of the withdrawing British Expeditionary Force to the west. The attack makes little progress, but the Fifth Army's I Corps under General Louis Franchet d'Esperey temporarily stops the advance of the German Second Army under General Karl von Bülow in a supporting attack.

Bülow now calls on the commander of the German First Army, Alexander von Kluck, to come to his aid. Kluck is under orders to advance to the west of Paris but any support for Bülow would take his forces to the east of the capital. However, Kluck believes the British are effectively defeated and that there are no sizeable enemy forces menacing his exposed right flank. (He is unaware of the newly-created

French Sixth Army assembling a little to the north of Paris.) Kluck cannot reach Moltke, the chief of the German General Staff, for clarification, so moves to support Bülow on his own initiative. By September 2 his army is stretched out from the Marne River at Château-Thierry to the Oise River.

▲ *A horse-drawn German field artillery battery on the move.*

▼ *The advance of the German Army through Belgium and northern France, August–September 1914. The bold sweeping movement was finally halted at the Battle of the Marne.*

▼ *German troops maintain the pace of their drive through northern France.*

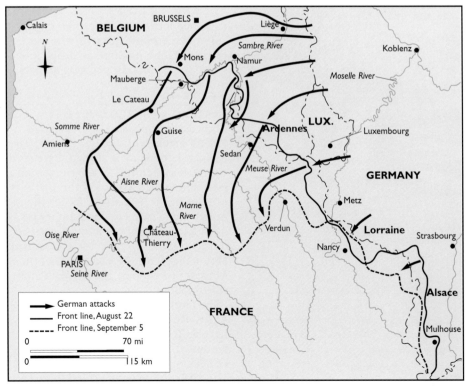

DECISIVE WEAPONS

THE FRENCH "75"

The three-inch (75-mm) Field Gun Model 1897 was a revolutionary design. The key to its success was axial recoil, which made firing more accurate and faster. To fire the weapon, the loader simply opened the breech and threw in the round, then closed the breech with a swift flick of the wrist.

Once the gun was fired, the recoil did not roll the carriage backward as in older designs. The 75's carriage remained perfectly still, but the gun barrel itself flew backward in its holding cradle to a distance of some four feet (1.2 m) and then slid back to its original position due to the hydraulic recoil system. As the barrel returned, the loader could simply flick open the breech, which automatically ejected the spent cartridge, and then throw in another round.

The military benefits of this firing system were obvious. The crew did not have to jump clear when the gun was fired as they would have had to do if the carriage moved. Consequently, they were in position to reload quickly. Second, the gun remained in position and therefore did not need relaying on its target after each round was fired. The "75" was capable of delivering six or so rounds a minute with accuracy up to ranges of 7500 yards (6900 m). However, in extreme circumstances up to 20 rounds a minute could be fired.

A French 75-mm field gun captured at the moment of the barrel's maximum recoil. The crew is poised to reload the weapon immediately.

▲ *Austro-Hungarian prisoners of war are marched into captivity by the Russians after their defeat in Poland.*

Thanks to air reconnaissance General Joseph Joffre, the French commander-in-chief, is aware of Kluck's change of direction and has set his plans for a massive counteroffensive along the line of the Marne River by French and British forces accordingly.

AUGUST 30

AIR WAR, *FRANCE*
Paris becomes the first capital city to suffer aerial bombardment when a German Taube monoplane drops four small bombs and propaganda leaflets.

SEPTEMBER 3–11

EASTERN FRONT, *GALICIA*
The Austro-Hungarian offensive into Poland meets with further disaster. The Russian Fifth Army is able to drive a wedge between the Austro-Hungarian First and Fourth Armies at the Battle of Rava Ruska. The attack forces the Austro-Hungarians to abandon their main base at Lemberg and retreat 100 miles (160 km) back to the Carpathian Mountains. With the exception of the fortress of Przemysl, the Russians now control all of Galicia.

The faith of the Germans in their Austro-Hungarian ally, whose forces have suffered 350,000 men killed, wounded, or taken prisoner in the Galician campaign, is severely shaken. The Austro-Hungarian armed forces are

clearly not able to fight a modern industrial war. It also becomes clear that the Russians are preparing further attacks and that the Austro-Hungarians can only survive with extensive German military assistance.

SEPTEMBER 4

WESTERN FRONT, *FRANCE*
General Joseph Joffre orders a major attack against the overextended German armies holding the line south of the Marne River to the east of Paris. It begins the next day.

SEPTEMBER 5

WESTERN FRONT, *FRANCE*
The French and British launch their counterattack against the German forces along the Marne River between Paris and Verdun. The key to the plan is for the French Sixth Army to strike at the exposed western flank of General Alexander von Kluck's First Army to the east of Paris, around Château-Thierry, with the British Expeditionary Force advancing into the gap between Kluck's force and General Karl von Bülow's Second Army. This offensive, known as the Battle of the Marne, has six main phases.

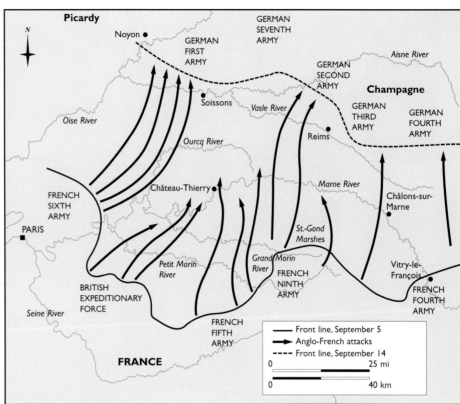

▼ *French General Joseph Galliéni commanded the Sixth Army during the opening phase of the Battle of the Marne.*

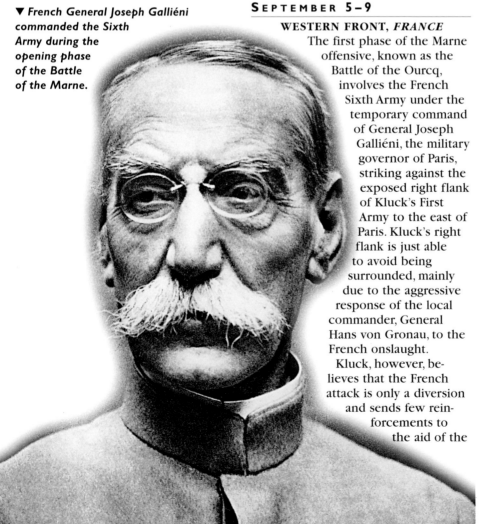

SEPTEMBER 5-9

WESTERN FRONT, *FRANCE*

The first phase of the Marne offensive, known as the Battle of the Ourcq, involves the French Sixth Army under the temporary command of General Joseph Galliéni, the military governor of Paris, striking against the exposed right flank of Kluck's First Army to the east of Paris. Kluck's right flank is just able to avoid being surrounded, mainly due to the aggressive response of the local commander, General Hans von Gronau, to the French onslaught.

Kluck, however, believes that the French attack is only a diversion and sends few reinforcements to the aid of the

▲ *The successful French and British attack along the Marne exploited the gap between two German armies.*

hard-pressed Gronau. The remainder of the First Army continues to push to the south, chasing the British Expeditionary Force until Kluck realizes on the 7th that the French attack is crucial.

The German commander immediately pulls his army back over the Marne River and heads westward to confront the French Sixth Army, now back under the command of General Michel Maunoury. The Germans launch powerful attacks that come close to breaking Maunoury, but the tide is stemmed by Galliéni, who rushes some of the much-needed reinforcements from Paris to the front in taxicabs.

SEPTEMBER 6-10

WESTERN FRONT, *FRANCE*

While the Battle of the Ourcq is raging, the British Expeditionary Force to the southeast moves slowly into the widening gap that has opened up between Kluck's First Army and von Bülow's Second Army. The French Fifth Army, now commanded by General Louis Franchet d'Esperey, also exploits the gap and then swings eastward to launch its greater strength against the right flank of the German Second

31

Army in what becomes known as the Battle of the Two Morins. After hard fighting von Bülow withdraws his right flank some six miles (9 km) and realigns it to face westward, thus further opening the gap between himself and Kluck's First Army. The British, meanwhile, are pushing northward, crossing the Marne River on September 9, and thereby drawing ever closer to the rear of Kluck's First Army.

As the Battle of the Two Morins rages, the French Ninth Army under General Ferdinand Foch attacks the left flank of von Bülow's Second Army. At the same time elements of the German Third Army run into Foch's right wing.

Foch's forces meet great resistance and fall back, pursued by the Germans. Despite repeated assaults, the Germans are unable to achieve a decisive break-through of Foch's front and the French hold. Foch telegraphs his situation to Joffre, his superior: "My center is falling back. My right retreats. Situation excellent. I attack!" This engagement, the Battle of St.-Gond, ends on the 8th.

To the east of Foch, the fifth engagement of the Marne offensive, the Battle of Vitry-le-François, is taking place between General Langle de Cary's French Fourth Army and Duke Albrecht of Württemburg's German

Fourth Army, which is supported by elements of the German Third Army. The French attack on the 6th but are quickly counterattacked. For three days the Germans batter unsuccessfully against the front of the French.

The final component of Joffre's Marne offensive is the attack of the French Third Army led by a new commander, General Maurice Sarrail. Sarrail attacks the Crown Prince's German Fifth Army from around Revigny in the Argonne Forest to

A French priest looks on as a column of soldiers advances to the front during the opening stages of the successful Marne counterattack.

the north of Verdun. The French attack on the 6th begins just as the Germans open their own. There is fierce fighting and, although the Germans almost break through to Sarrail's rear, the French hold firm.

Although not strictly part of the Marne offensive, there is also fighting between the

◄ *British officers look on as a French field gun, with its ammunition caisson close by, is readied for action.*

the chief of the German General Staff, sends a subordinate, Lieutenant Colonel Richard Hentsch, to von Bülow's embattled Second Army to assess the situation. Hentsch arrives on the 8th to find von Bülow under great pressure from the French Fifth Army, which is threatening to turn his right flank, and planning to withdraw. Hentsch is also made aware that the British Expeditionary Force is advancing on the rear of von Kluck's First Army.

French First and Second Armies and the German Six and Seventh Armies in Alsace-Lorraine to the southeast of Verdun. The Germans lead the way with powerful attacks, which begin on the 4th, but the French just manage to stem the tide. The Germans call off their onslaught on the 10th.

SEPTEMBER 7–17

BALKANS, *SERBIA*
Austro-Hungarian troops under General Oskar Potiorek launch a second invasion of Serbia. They establish a number of positions across the Drina River, which are repeatedly attacked by the Serbians under Marshal Radomir Putnik. After 10 days of intense combat Putnik pulls his exhausted troops, who are short of supplies, back to positions around Belgrade, the Serbian capital, thus ending the Battle of the Drina River.

SEPTEMBER 8

WESTERN FRONT, *FRANCE*
While the Battle of the Marne is raging, General Helmuth von Moltke,

▲ *French troops escort German prisoners to the rear – some of the 29,000 captured during the fighting along the Marne.*

▼ *British troops come under accurate German artillery fire during the Battle of the Marne.*

SEPTEMBER 9

WESTERN FRONT, *FRANCE*
Lieutenant Colonel Hentsch concurs with von Bülow that the German Second Army should withdraw and later orders von Kluck's First Army to fall back from the east of Paris. These movements are confirmed by von Moltke, who also orders his armies to undertake a general withdrawal to a line stretching from Noyon on the Oise River to Verdun. The move is completed in five days.

The German withdrawal ends the Battle of the Marne. Although the Germans are far from crushed, they have suffered a decisive strategic defeat of profound consequence. The original Schlieffen Plan had called for a single sweeping victory over France in the first few weeks of the war. The Battle of the Marne makes this an

impossibility. Von Moltke's watered-down Schlieffen Plan has been unsuccessful and its failure brings about the nightmare scenario that it is meant to avoid – Germany facing a war on two fronts.

WESTERN FRONT, BELGIUM

King Albert launches an attack against the German forces outside Antwerp. The Belgian sortie so worries Kaiser Wilhelm II that he orders the immediate capture of the port. Over the next few weeks German reinforcements and large-caliber

▶ General Erich von Falkenhayn was made chief of the German General Staff on September 14.

howitzers threaten to overwhelm the garrison, despite the arrival of some British naval infantry.

SEPTEMBER 9–14

EASTERN FRONT, EAST PRUSSIA

Swift to capitalize on their recent victory against the Russian Army outside Tannenberg, the Germans strike against Rennenkampf's First Army at the Masurian Lakes. The Germans again attempt to surround the

▲ Cooks of a small field kitchen prepare food for German troops in East Prussia on the Eastern Front.

▼ British infantry take cover by a French roadside during the series of battles that became known as the "Race to the Sea."

Russians, but Rennenkampf launches a limited but successful counterattack, which allows his battered forces to escape. Nevertheless, the action at the Masurian Lakes is a major German success. In addition to losing 150 artillery pieces and 50 percent of their transport, the Russians have 125,000 men killed, wounded, or captured. The German casualties total 40,000 men.

SEPTEMBER 14

POLITICS, *GERMANY*
General Helmuth von Moltke pays the price for the failure of the Schlieffen Plan and strategic defeat in the Battle of the Marne. He is sacked and replaced as chief of the General Staff by General Erich von Falkenhayn.

SEPTEMBER 15–18

WESTERN FRONT, *FRANCE*
Planning to exploit his success at the Battle of the Marne, Joffre orders the French and British armies to attack the withdrawing German armies in what becomes known as the Battle of the Aisne. The main effort is by the British against the Chemin des Dames Ridge between Soissons and Craonne in the direction of Laon. The attack meets stubborn resistance. Joffre calls off the British and French offensive.

▲ *A German transport column moves into Galicia, a province of Austria-Hungary, during the successful attempt to prevent a Russian attack into Silesia, one of Germany's key industrial areas.*

Both sides now attempt to outflank each other – the Germans by attacking the French and British left flank, while they in turn strike against the opposing German right flank. What follows is a succession of similar turning actions that gradually take the rival forces ever closer to the North Sea as the year draws to a close. These indecisive encounters become known as the "Race to the Sea."

SEPTEMBER 17

POLITICS, *AUSTRALIA*
Prime Minister Andrew Fisher states that Australia will support Britain "to the last man and the last shilling" during an election campaign speech.

SEPTEMBER 17–27

EASTERN FRONT, *GALICIA*
Having roundly defeated the Russian forces menacing East Prussia, Generals Paul von Hindenburg and Erich Ludendorff rush troops by rail to support the badly-mauled Austro-Hungarians in Galicia.

They believe, correctly, that the Russians are preparing to strike into Silesia, one of Germany's key mining and industrial centers. The rail transfer is speedy, allowing the creation of the new German Ninth Army under Hindenburg's personal command in the vicinity of Cracow.

SEPTEMBER 22

SEA WAR, *NORTH SEA*

In a severe blow to British morale, the German submarine *U-9* sinks three British cruisers, the *Aboukir*, *Hogue*, and *Cressy*, in rapid succession off the Dutch coast. The loss of life totals over 1400 men.

SEA WAR, *INDIAN OCEAN*

A German light cruiser, the *Emden* under Captain Karl von Müller,

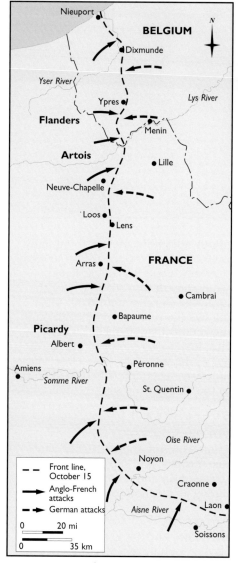

The "Race to the Sea" map.

Front line, October 15
Anglo-French attacks
German attacks

0   20 mi
0   35 km

bombards British oil facilities at Madras, India. The *Emden*, which has been in action since August 22, continues to operate in the Indian and Pacific Oceans until it is sunk by the Australian cruiser *Sydney* off the Cocos Islands on November 9.

AIR WAR, *GERMANY*

The British launch their first air raid on Germany. Four Royal Navy Air Service Tabloids drop bombs on Zeppelin airship facilities at Cologne and Düsseldorf.

◀ *The "Race to the Sea" across northern France and Flanders took place between September and October. Neither side gained any advantage.*

▼ *British infantry move north in the attempt to attack the open right flank of the German forces on the Western Front.*

SEPTEMBER 22–24

WESTERN FRONT, *FRANCE*

German attacks against the fortress-city of Verdun are repulsed, but the French are forced to withdraw from the St. Mihiel salient, which the Germans will hold until 1918.

SEPTEMBER 22–26

WESTERN FRONT, *FRANCE*

The Battle of Picardy involves flank attacks by the French and Germans. The fighting is hotly contested and losses on both sides are severe. Neither gains an advantage and the offensives, part of the

"Race to the Sea," succeed only in extending the front northward across the Somme River in the direction of the French towns of Péronne and Albert.

SEPTEMBER 27–OCTOBER 10

WESTERN FRONT, *FRANCE*
The "Race to the Sea" continues with the Battle of Artois. It opens with Falkenhayn directing his commanders, who have received substantial reinforcements, to attack around the French and British left flank. However,

◀ *French cavalry and infantry officers study the progress of the fighting during the engagement along the Aisne River during September.*

▶ *Belgian troops oversee the destruction of a rail bridge to slow the German advance through their country.*

▼ *German infantry, in open order to reduce casualties from enemy fire, await the order to advance.*

Joffre is equal to the threat and rushes troops from the far right of his line and elsewhere in France to block the German attacks. Again, there is no decision beyond stretching the front line farther north to the Lys River in the area of the Franco-Belgian border. Over the following days the British Expeditionary Force moves into Belgium to prepare for the climax of the "Race to the Sea."

SEPTEMBER 28–NOVEMBER 1

EASTERN FRONT, *GALICIA*
Although Hindenburg's 19 German divisions are outnumbered by 60 Russian divisions, his Ninth Army strikes against the Russians west of the Vistula, reaching the river to the south of Warsaw, the Polish capital, on October 9. The German offensive runs out of steam three days later in the face of stiffer Russian resistance.

▲ *Australian infantry at Melbourne embark on the transports that will take them to the Western Front.*

◀ *Austro-Hungarian troops, supported by heavy machine guns, advance against the Russians in Galicia during October.*

Hindenburg, who has disrupted the Russian plans for their offensive into Silesia, now executes a careful, coordinated withdrawal, which begins on October 17. His units lay waste to the countryside as they retreat. Austro-Hungarian armies to the south of Hindenburg also make some progress against the Russians before being forced to withdraw.

▶ *German prisoners trudge to the rear watched over by their British escorts. As 1914 drew to a close, exhaustion, heavy losses, and bad weather ended the fighting on the Western Front.*

On November 1 Hindenburg is promoted to commander-in-chief of the Eastern Front, but is told he can expect to receive no reinforcements because of German commitments on the Western Front. Nevertheless, he plans a pre-emptive strike against the Russians in the area of Lódz.

OCTOBER 6

WESTERN FRONT, *BELGIUM*
The Belgian defenders of the port of Antwerp are close to being totally cut off. It is agreed that what remains of the Belgian field army should be evacuated. The evacuation is completed by the 8th and those troops who escape are landed between Zeebrugge and Ostend. Antwerp surrenders on the 10th.

OCTOBER 11

MIDDLE EAST, *TURKEY*
The commander of the Turkish Third Army reports that ethnic Armenians are deserting and that arms are being supplied to the Armenians by Russia.

OCTOBER 13

HOME FRONT, *BRITAIN*
The first Canadian troops in Europe land at Plymouth.

OCTOBER 16

HOME FRONT, *NEW ZEALAND*
The New Zealand Expeditionary Force sails for Europe from Wellington, after the arrival of a stronger naval escort.

OCTOBER 17

HOME FRONT, *AUSTRALIA*
Around 20,000 troops embark to fight on the Western Front in France.

OCTOBER 18–28

WESTERN FRONT, *FRANCE/BELGIUM*
Field Marshal Sir John French orders the British Expeditionary Force to advance toward Menin, Belgium, and Lille, France, on the 18th in the opening stage of the Battle of the Yser. However, this move is pre-empted by

▼ *The Belgian countryside was flooded to slow the German advance on the Channel ports used by the British.*

the Germans, who had begun a slow advance a few days earlier aiming to capture the Channel ports used by the British. Falkenhayn has rushed massive reinforcements to the sector.

The British, with the aid of the French, are able to hold the German attack but at great cost. However, to the north, Belgian forces with limited French support struggle to contain the enemy advance. Eventually, King Albert of Belgium orders the opening of canal and sea-defense sluice gates. This

OCTOBER 20

desperate act floods a key area in the path of the German advance along the low-lying Belgian coast and brings it to a standstill.

On the 19th the newly-arrived British I Corps under General Sir Douglas Haig counterattacks the Germans from its positions around the Belgian city of Ypres. Haig's move effectively ends the German offensive and the British launch their own counterstroke.

This, however, fails due to the heavy rains that have turned the low-lying fields of Flanders into a morass and the stubborn German defense of the low-lying hills that circle around the north, east, and south of Ypres. French and British losses are heavy in what is the preliminary round of what becomes known as the First Battle of Ypres. The fighting around Ypres continues into late November.

OCTOBER 20

SEA WAR, *NORTH SEA*
The British *Glitra* becomes the first merchant ship to be sunk by a submarine. It is intercepted, boarded, and scuttled by the German *U-17* a few miles off the Norwegian coast.

OCTOBER 23

MIDDLE EAST, *MESOPOTAMIA*
British Indian Army forces land in Turkish-controlled Mesopotamia from their base on the island of Bahrain in the Persian Gulf, where they have been defending the British protectorate's oil installations. The limited British attacks are sufficient to evict the Turkish garrisons in southern Mesopotamia. The region's main port, Basra, located

close to the confluence of the Tigris and Euphrates Rivers, falls to the British on November 23.

OCTOBER 29

POLITICS, *TURKEY*
The government declares war. The decision to go to war is announced by the Turkish fleet bombarding the Russian Black Sea ports of Odessa, Sevastopol, and Theodosia. The fleet is commanded by German Vice Admiral Wilhelm von Souchon and includes the former German *Goeben* and *Breslau*.

Turkey's siding with the Central Powers closes the Dardanelles, the vital seaway linking the Mediterranean to the Black Sea. Crucially, the closure of this major route by Turkey prevents France and Britain sending military equipment to Russia and also cuts off the return trade in foodstuffs from the Russian Ukraine.

▼ *British forces, part of an artillery battery, move through the deserted streets of a Belgian village during the First Battle of Ypres.*

▲ *Soldiers of the British Indian Army occupy a roadside embankment during the fighting around Ypres in late October.*

◀ *Turkish troops drill outside the walls of Constantinople, their capital.*

OCTOBER 29–NOVEMBER 24

WESTERN FRONT, *BELGIUM*

General Erich von Falkenhayn, the chief of the General Staff, has steadily been building up the strength of the German Fourth and Sixth Armies around British-held Ypres to break through to the ports of Calais and Boulogne. Locally, the Germans enjoy an advantage of six-to-one and are superior in medium and heavy artillery. The offensive opens well and, despite French and British reserves being rushed to the sector, German units come close to breaking through southeast of Ypres on the 31st. Desperate fighting by the French and British stems the tide.

In early November the Germans renew their attempts to break through. Some progress is made and they take Dixmunde, to the north of Ypres, from the Belgians on the 11th. However, the British, who are bearing the brunt of the onslaught, finally halt the major German attacks on the same day.

Despite several German pushes over the following days, the worst of the fighting is over. The first snows fall on

▶ *A German six-inch (15-cm) howitzer goes into action during the opening phase of the main attack against Ypres in October. This stalemated battle ended with both sides digging trench systems.*

the 12th, heralding an end to the campaigning season. This, the First Battle of Ypres, is a success for the French and British, but it has been won at high cost. Half of the British Expeditionary Force are casualties. All sides now begin digging in earnest the trenches that will soon stretch from the North Sea to the Swiss border.

NOVEMBER 1

SEA WAR, *PACIFIC*

A powerful squadron of German warships commanded by Admiral Maximilian von Spee inflicts a major defeat on Vice Admiral Sir Christopher Cradock's British squadron off Coronel, Chile.

Spee, whose warships have been taking on coal from German colliers in Chilean waters, leads his two heavy cruisers, the *Gneisenau* and *Scharnhorst*, and three light cruisers, the *Dresden*, *Leipzig*, and *Nürnberg*, into battle in the late afternoon and in heavy seas.

November 2

Cradock's force, which has been hurriedly assembled to deal with Spee, consists of two old heavy cruisers, the *Good Hope* and *Monmouth*, the light cruiser *Glasgow*, and an armed former ocean liner, the *Otranto*. A fifth vessel, the aging battleship *Canopus*, has been left behind in the Falklands, a British coaling station in the South Atlantic, because it could not keep up with the rest of Cradock's squadron.

Spee's two heavy cruisers use the longer range of their main guns to smash Cradock's cruisers and frustrate the maneuvers of the British, who try to get to close range to use their smaller guns. Both the *Good Hope* and *Monmouth* go down with all hands, including Cradock, in the early evening. The *Glasgow* and *Otranto* escape under cover of darkness. The British are fearful that Spee's squadron will move into the Atlantic to disrupt their commerce and quickly send a squadron of warships under Vice Admiral Sir F. D. Sturdee to intercept Spee's warships.

▶ *A German mine has destroyed the bow of this British vessel. German surface vessels and submarines laid scores of mines in British waters during the campaign to starve Britain into surrender.*

▼ *Admiral Maximilian von Spee, the victor of the Battle of Coronel (far left).*

AIR WAR, *GERMANY*
Grand Admiral Alfred von Tirpitz, commander-in-chief of the Imperial Germany Navy, demands mass firebomb raids on London.

November 2

POLITICS, *SERBIA/RUSSIA*
Both countries declare war on Turkey. The Russian I Caucasian Corps invades

▶ *The German heavy cruiser* Gneisenau *was one of Admiral Maximilian von Spee's warships at the Battle of Coronel.*

▶ *Damage caused by the German naval bombardment of British ports.*

Turkish-governed Armenia at five points, but is repulsed by a Turkish counterattack on the 11th.

NOVEMBER 3

SEA WAR, *NORTH SEA*

German warships begin to bombard and lay mines off a number of towns along Britain's east coast. The raids reach their peak on December 16, when German heavy cruisers led by Admiral Franz von Hipper attack the ports of Whitby and Hartlepool and cause over 700 casualties.

Although the brief raids have little military impact, the death toll of civilians and damage to property sends shockwaves through the British establishment. Of more military value are German mine-laying operations in British inshore waters.

NOVEMBER 3–4

AFRICA, *GERMAN EAST AFRICA*

A British amphibious assault directed against Tanga, a German-held port, is decisively defeated by General Paul von Lettow-Vorbeck.

▶ *German-officered local troops – known as askaris – drill in East Africa.*

Lettow-Vorbeck's force consists of a few German companies and local troops – askaris. Tanga marks the beginning of a four-year-long guerrilla war by Lettow-Vorbeck, which will see him operate at will throughout East Africa, tying down increasingly large British and Commonwealth forces with little aid from Germany. His campaign is a model of guerrilla warfare.

NOVEMBER 5–30

BALKANS, *SERBIA*

In the face of a renewed Austro-Hungarian offensive directed toward Belgrade and desperately short of ammunition, Marshal Radomir Putnik's Serbian troops holding positions outside the capital city withdraw slowly and in good order. However, Austro-Hungarian troops cannot be prevented from occupying Belgrade on December 2.

NOVEMBER 7

POLITICS, *TURKEY*

The government declares war on Belgium.

NOVEMBER 8

ESPIONAGE, *BRITAIN*

The naval high command forms the decoding unit known as Room 40, which becomes the hub of Britain's intelligence-gathering operations.

NOVEMBER 10

FAR EAST AND PACIFIC, *JAPAN*

After a siege that began in late August, the Japanese secure the formal surrender of the German base at Tsingtao, China.

NOVEMBER 11–25

EASTERN FRONT, *GALICIA*

The German Ninth Army, which has been commanded by General August von Mackensen since Hindenburg's recent promotion, is launched against the Russians. Mackensen's main aim is to drive a wedge between the Russian First and Second Armies and defeat each in turn. General Pavel Rennenkampf's First Army is overwhelmed by Mackensen and the Russian Second Army is virtually surrounded near Lódz.

However, an unusually swift Russian counterattack turns the tables on the Germans, and one of Mackensen's spearhead units, General Reinhard von Scheffer-Boyadel's XXV Reserve Corps, is surrounded. However, Scheffer-Boyadel displays exemplary powers of leadership, breaking out of the Russian encirclement and taking 16,000 Russian prisoners and more than 60

▶ *Japanese siege artillery bombards the German colony of Tsingtao in China prior to an infantry assault on the defenses.*

▼ *Serbian forces launch an attack against the larger Austro-Hungarian forces that are menacing their capital Belgrade in late November.*

artillery pieces with him in a running fight that lasts nine days in atrocious winter weather.

Although the Russians have rebuffed the German offensive directed against Lódz, the strategic initiative remains with Hindenburg, who, although still outnumbered, has thwarted the Russian plan to invade the German industrial heartland of Silesia. German casualties in the battle total 35,000 men killed or wounded; Russian casualties are at least three times as many.

DECEMBER 1

MIDDLE EAST, *CAUCASUS*
Renewed fighting sees the Russians capture Sarai and Batumi.

▶ *Survivors from the German heavy cruiser* **Gneisenau** *make for the British battleship* **Inflexible** *following the Battle of the Falklands.*

▼ *Russian soldiers captured by the Germans during the fighting around Lódz await the arrival of transportation to take them to their prison camps.*

him. Spee had intended to destroy the British coaling and communication facilities at Port Stanley in the Falkland Islands, but unknown to him a British squadron commanded by Vice Admiral Sir F. D. Sturdee, which arrived two days earlier, is waiting for him.

On sighting the British, Spee orders his warships to withdraw. However, Sturdee's two dreadnought battleships, the *Inflexible* and *Invincible*, give chase supported by a number of armored cruisers commanded by Rear Admiral Stoddart. As the two dreadnoughts emerge from Port Stanley harbor, the aging battleship *Canopus*, which escaped the British defeat at Coronel, opens fire on Spee's ships from the harbor, where the vessel has been beached to create a steady gun platform.

Spee's position is hopeless: the British warships are faster and carry heavier armaments. The *Scharnhorst*,

▼ *Damage caused to the British cruiser Kent by a German shell during the Battle of the Falklands.*

DECEMBER 3–9

BALKANS, *SERBIA*

Serbian forces under Marshal Radomir Putnik, now supplied with ammunition by France, launch a major attack on the Austro-Hungarian forces inside Serbia. The Battle of Kolubra is a major Serbian victory. The Austro-Hungarian armies collapse under the Serbian assaults and are thrown out of Serbia.

The Austro-Hungarian commander, General Oskar Potiorek, is sacked for this humiliating defeat and replaced by Archduke Eugene. Austro-Hungarian casualties in the campaign, which began in September, are enormous – roughly 50 percent, some 230,000 men. The Serbian casualty list in the campaign totals 170,000 men out of 400,000 engaged.

DECEMBER 4

MIDDLE EAST, *MESOPOTAMIA*

At the First Battle of Qurna, an initial British landing party is blocked by Turkish forces, but the town is captured on the 9th.

DECEMBER 8

SEA WAR, *ATLANTIC*

German Admiral Maximilian von Spee, fresh from his victory at Coronel, Chile, in early November is surprised by a British squadron sent to intercept

December 14

Spee's flagship, is the first of the two German armored cruisers to be sunk and is followed by the other, the *Gneisenau*. Two of Spee's other three vessels are also sunk. The light cruisers *Nürnberg* and *Leipzig* are sent to the bottom by the armored cruisers *Kent* and *Cornwall* respectively.

Spee's last warship, the light cruiser *Dresden*, escapes from the Falklands. However, the *Dresden* is cornered three months later in Chilean territorial waters by the *Glasgow* and

▶ *Turkish artillery in action during Enver Pasha's large offensive into the Russian-occupied areas of Armenia.*

Kent. Unable to evade its British pursuers, the last of Spee's squadron is scuttled by its crew.

December 14

WESTERN FRONT, FRANCE/BELGIUM
Despite the worsening weather and the growing strength of the German

defenses, the French and British undertake a general offensive along the Western Front, from the North Sea to Verdun. They believe, correctly, that they outnumber the Germans, who have rushed large numbers of men to the Eastern Front. However, they underestimate the strength of the German trench system or the excellent qualities of the German soldiers.

Most of the attacks end by December 24 and little progress is made. Only in Champagne, where the French have made moderate gains at the expense of huge casualties, does the fighting go

◀ *British artillerymen prime shells and prepare to fire a light field gun from behind rudimentary defenses in the Ypres sector.*

▼ *The German cruiser* Dresden *settles on the seabed after being scuttled by its crew off Chile.*

been killed, wounded, or taken prisoner, while the equivalent figures for Austria-Hungary are up to one million and for Russia some 1.8 million.

In the Balkans the Austro-Hungarians have suffered 225,000 men killed, wounded, or taken prisoner, while Serbia acknowledges casualties totaling around 170,000 men.

DECEMBER 18

POLITICS, *BRITAIN*
To secure their strategic position in the Mediterranean and Middle East, the British declare a protectorate over Egypt and begin to move troops to defend the Suez Canal, the strategic waterway that connects the British with the oil-producing regions around the Persian Gulf and their key colonial possession, India.

MIDDLE EAST, *ARMENIA*
Despite the onset of winter, Enver Pasha prepares to launch a complex offensive against the Russian forces in Armenia and the Caucasus. This begins on the 21st and has forced three Russian divisions to retreat by the end of the year.

DECEMBER 29

MIDDLE EAST, *CAUCASUS*
The Russian commander General Vorontsov thwarts the Turkish advance toward Kars in the Caucasus at the Battle of Sarikamish, but the fighting continues. Neither side is able to gain a victory.

on over the winter months. The First Battle of Champagne continues into 1915, but elsewhere the fighting dies down as both sides come to recognize that their belief in a swift victory is totally misplaced.

World War I is just six months old and the casualty lists are unparalleled in the history of warfare. On the Western Front alone the French, British, and Belgians have suffered more than one million casualties, of which the vast majority are French. The Germans have had around 675,000 troops killed, wounded, or missing in action.

Equally, losses on the Eastern Front are unprecedented. Some 275,000 Germans have

KEY MOMENTS

CHRISTMAS TRUCE

By Christmas 1914 the soldiers on the Western Front were exhausted and shocked by the scale of the losses they had suffered since August. At dawn on the 25th the British holding trenches around the Belgian city of Ypres heard carols ringing out from the opposing German positions and then spied Christmas trees being placed along the front of the German trenches. Slowly, lines of German soldiers climbed out of their trenches and advanced to the halfway point of no-man's land, where they called on the British to join them. The two sides met in the middle of the shell-blasted wasteland, exchanged gifts, talked, and played games of football.

Such events were common all along the line where British and German troops sat in opposition to each other and the fraternization continued for up to a week in some places until the military authorities ordered it to be stamped out. There were, however, no such truces in the sectors where French and German forces opposed each other.

British and German soldiers fraternize in the middle of no-man's land around Ypres in Belgium during the 1914 Christmas truce.

1915

In 1915 the war became much more global – Italy sided with Britain and France and the Bulgarians threw in their lot with the Central Powers. Both sides were confronted by strategic dilemmas over where they could best exploit their military might to advantage. Equally, the list of casualties was growing ever longer as the stalemate of the trench fighting intensified. Neutral powers, particularly the United States, were also feeling the war's impact.

JANUARY 1–3

MIDDLE EAST, *CAUCASUS*
The Battle of Sarikamish, which began in late December 1914, continues. Some 100,000 Russian troops are opposing a Turkish advance toward the city of Kars. The Turkish attack is badly managed by Enver Pasha, whose 95,000-strong army is suffering severely from the bitter cold. A sudden Russian counterattack forces the Turks to retreat to Erzerum. Some 30,000 Turks are killed in the battle and around only 19,000 of those who escape to Erzerum are fit for further service. Enver Pasha renounces his command. The Russian commander, General Vorontsov, shows little drive in pursuing the Turks and is replaced by General Nikolai Yudenich.

JANUARY 11

POLITICS, *BRITAIN*
An offer of Turkish territory in return for Greek military support of Serbia is rejected by the Greek government. It is made by the British foreign secretary, Sir Edward Grey. Similar offers are rebuffed over the following weeks, chiefly because the Greeks demand Anglo-French forces to protect their sovereignty.

JANUARY 13

POLITICS, *AUSTRIA-HUNGARY*
Foreign Minister Count Leopold von Berchtold resigns and is replaced by Hungarian Baron Burian.
POLITICS, *BRITAIN*
A council of war decides upon a naval attack against Turkey with the aim of opening the Dardanelles seaway to the

◀ *Turkish cavalrymen operating against the Russians in the Caucasus pictured at their field camp.*

▼ *German destroyers move cautiously while rescuing survivors from the Blücher, a battlecruiser sunk at the Dogger Bank.*

◀ Djemel Pasha (left), the commander of the Turkish forces involved in the attack on the British-controlled Suez Canal.

any German incursion into the North Sea. The interception of German radio traffic means that the British are informed of Hipper's raid.

On the 24th Beatty and Hipper meet at the Dogger Bank shoals roughly in the center of the North Sea. Hipper, surprised by the British, orders a withdrawal but is soon caught by Beatty's faster and better-armed warships. The first of Hipper's ships to suffer from British fire is the *Blücher*, which sinks shortly after midday. However, Beatty's flagship, the *Lion*, suffers extensive damage from one of *Derfflinger*'s shells and falls out of the battle line. Helped by the confusion caused by Beatty's need to transfer his flag to the *Princess Royal*, Hipper is able to make his escape.

▼ Admiral Franz von Hipper led the German battlecruiser squadron at the Battle of the Dogger Bank. He was able to outrun a larger British force.

flow of supplies between Russia and France and Britain. The British seek French approval, which is given on the 26th. First Lord of the Admiralty Sir Winston Churchill is the chief advocate of the operation.

JANUARY 14

MIDDLE EAST, *PALESTINE*

Some 25,000 Turkish troops backed by more than 50 artillery pieces begin an advance from Beersheba in Palestine against the British troops defending the Suez Canal in Egypt. Their commander is Djemal Pasha, the Turkish minister of marine.

JANUARY 19–20

AIR WAR, *BRITAIN*

The Germans launch their first Zeppelin airship raid. Two Zeppelins, the *L3* and *L4*, bomb eastern England, causing 20 casualties among civilians.

JANUARY 24

SEA WAR, *NORTH SEA*

A clash between elements of the British Home Fleet and Germany's High Seas Fleet is partly brought about by public disquiet at the seeming ease with which German warships are bombarding ports on the east coast of England. On the 23rd Admiral Franz von Hipper's German battlecruiser squadron of four ships (*Blücher, Derfflinger, Moltke,* and *Seydlitz*) with destroyer, light cruiser, and airship cover sails to attack ports and the British fishing fleet. However, the British have already moved a force of warships under Admiral Sir David Beatty from distant Scapa Flow in the Orkneys to Rosyth in southern Scotland, from where it can more easily intercept

▲ *The engine room of a German U-boat. These submarines bore the brunt of efforts to strangle the flow of supplies to Germany's enemies.*

▼ *General August von Mackensen (left) was one of Germany's most successful commanders on the Eastern Front.*

The Battle of the Dogger Bank curtails German naval raids on Britain, but also highlights certain weaknesses in British naval procedures. The gunnery of Beatty's warships has been extremely poor – just 73 hits out of 958 shells fired. Equally, the orders between the various British vessels has been slow and ambiguous. Neither shortcoming is properly addressed.

On the plus side Hipper has been forced to withdraw after losing one vessel. Although the British do not know it, he has also suffered damage to the *Seydlitz*; a severe fire in one of its turrets has killed 159 sailors. The Germans study the causes of the fire and introduce new safety regulations.

JANUARY 29

POLITICS, *BRITAIN*
Government minister David Lloyd George suggests to the British War Council that Anglo-French forces be sent to Salonika, Greece, to encourage various Balkan states to declare war on Austria-Hungary. However, the Greeks reject the offer.

JANUARY 30

SEA WAR, *ENGLISH CHANNEL*
Two British ships are torpedoed without warning by the German submarine *U-20*, marking an escalation in the naval war. Previously, submarines have stopped suspect vessels and allowed their crews to abandon their ships before sending them to the bottom.

JANUARY 31

POLITICS, *AUSTRIA-HUNGARY*
As relations between erstwhile Triple Alliance allies Austria-Hungary and Italy deteriorate, the Austro-Hungarians

complete the transfer of 30 battalions to protect their long and mountainous border with the Italians.

POLITICS, *SOUTH AFRICA*
The authorities introduce adult male conscription.

EASTERN FRONT, *RUSSIA*
The German Ninth Army under General August von Mackensen attacks toward Warsaw. The advance, known as the Battle of Bolimov, is opened by 600

DECISIVE WEAPONS

GAS WARFARE

Gas was first used in 1915, initially by Germany and then Britain and France. Some of the early gas attacks were launched from cylinders sited in forward trenches and required a favorable prevailing wind for the clouds to drift toward the enemy. This method of discharge was unsatisfactory, so gas shells were developed. Germany used gas shells to little affect on the Eastern Front in January 1915, but France developed the most practical device. This consisted of a shell largely filled with gas and only a small explosive device to crack the casing and allow the gas to escape.

There were also a number of different gas types used. The first was xylyl bromide, a type of tear gas. This was followed by chlorine. However, lethal gas types were soon developed, chiefly phosgene and mustard gas. The latter was the most feared: not only did it attack the body through the lungs, it also burned the skin and damaged the bloodstream, and could cause permanent blindness. It was also a persistent agent and would usually lie on the ground for three days or so after an attack.

The British Livens gas projector was a simple steel tube sunk into the ground. A gas shell and propellant were placed in the tube and fired by electric charge.

▲ *German artillerymen prepare to fire a Krupp-manufactured six-inch (15-cm) howitzer in Galicia. The howitzer, however, has yet to be elevated.*

artillery pieces bombarding the Russian positions with 18,000 poison gas shells – the first time poison gas has been used in the war. However, the intense cold and adverse winds minimize the impact of the poison gas to such an extent that the Russians hardly notice its use and fail to notify their allies. Russian counterattacks on February 6 recapture ground lost to the Ninth Army at a cost of 40,000 casualties. German losses total 20,000.

Bolimov is, in fact, a diversionary attack designed to mislead the Russians as to the true nature of the forthcoming German and Austro-Hungarian offensive. Directed by Field Marshal Paul von Hindenburg, the forthcoming offensive, scheduled to begin on February 7, has been planned as a massive pincer attack. In the north two German armies, the Eighth and Tenth, are poised to strike eastward into Russia from around the Masurian Lakes in East Prussia.

▲ *Russian troops receive supplies of ammunition. Although numerically strong, the Russian Army was short of many basic military necessities.*

▼ *German troops move forward rapidly during their attempted breakthrough to the besieged fortress of Przemysl.*

From their positions along the Carpathian Mountains to the south, three other armies are poised to strike northward into the Austro-Hungarian province of Galicia, much of which was captured by the Russians in 1914. The Austro-Hungarian and German army commanded by German General Alexander von Linsingen is under orders to drive toward the fortress of Lemberg, which was lost to the Russians on September 3, 1914.

This attack is supported by General Karl von Pflanzer-Baltin's Austro-Hungarian Seventh Army. General Svetozan Borojevic von Bojna's Austro-Hungarian Third Army is tasked with breaking through the Russian forces outside Przemysl, whose Austro-Hungarian garrison has been besieged on and off since September 1914.

FEBRUARY 1

POLITICS, *GERMANY*
The government agrees to permit an unrestricted submarine campaign – ships, even those of neutral countries, can now be sunk without warning.

HOME FRONT, *GERMANY*
The authorities introduce bread and flour rationing in the capital, Berlin.

FEBRUARY 3

MIDDLE EAST, *EGYPT*
Turkish forces attempt to cross the Suez Canal, but the attack is repulsed by British-officered Indian troops. The Turks fall back to Beersheba, Palestine, after suffering close to 2000 casualties.

▲ The sweeping successes enjoyed by German and Austro-Hungarian armies on the Eastern Front in 1915.

▼ British-officered Indian troops occupy shallow trenches during their defense of the Suez Canal against the Turks.

FEBRUARY 4

POLITICS, *GERMANY*
The authorities announce that submarines will blockade Britain from the 18th. All vessels, whether sailing under combatant flags or not, are deemed legitimate targets.

FEBRUARY 7–22

EASTERN FRONT, *EAST PRUSSIA*
Field Marshal Paul von Hindenburg begins his pincer offensive against the Russians by sending his German Eighth and Tenth Armies against the Russian Tenth Army. The Eighth Army attacks first in the face of a blizzard. It nevertheless strikes hard against the left flank of the Russian Tenth Army. On the 8th, General Hermann von Eichhorn's German Tenth Army attacks the Russian Tenth Army's right.

The Russians fight back hard but are forced back into the Augustow Forest, where only the heroic action of the Russian XX Corps prevents a complete disaster. The corps is

▲ German troops continue their advance into northern Russia following the Second Battle of the Masurian Lakes.

forced to surrender on the 21st, but its action has allowed the Russian Tenth Army's other three corps to escape encirclement. Nevertheless, the Russian front line has been pushed back some 70 miles (112 km). The Germans capture some 90,000 Russians during this action, which is known as the Second Battle of the Masurian Lakes.

After their defeat at the Masurian Lakes, the Russians hastily form the Twelfth Army under General Wenzel von Plehve, who launches a counter-attack against the German right flank with some success on the 22nd.

FEBRUARY 12

POLITICS, *GERMANY*
Kaiser Wilhelm II issues an order regarding the prosecution of the air war against Britain. The list of key

▲ German cavalrymen escort Russian prisoners to the rear – some of the 60,000 taken at the fall of the town of Czernowitz in Galicia.

targets includes fuel stores, dockyard facilities, and military bases – but it specifically excludes raids on urban residential areas and royal palaces.

FEBRUARY 14

POLITICS, *TURKEY*
The three-man Committee of Union and Progress agrees to launch a genocidal war against the Armenians, who occupy the country's northern border with Russia and are suspected of having close links with the Russians.

FEBRUARY 17

EASTERN FRONT, *GALICIA*
General Karl von Pflanzer-Baltin's Austro-Hungarian Seventh Army captures the Russian-held town of Czernowitz as part of the joint German and Austro-Hungarian drive into Galicia from their positions along the line of the Carpathian Mountains. However, progress elsewhere is limited due to the awful weather, Austro-Hungarian incompetence, and Russian resistance. General Alexander von Linsingen's army fails to reach Lemberg and

General Svetozan Borojevic von Bojna's Austro-Hungarian Third Army fails to make any significant progress in the attempt to relieve the besieged garrison of Przemysl.

FEBRUARY 19

SEA WAR, *MEDITERRANEAN*
Several French and British warships commanded by Vice Admiral Sackville Carden bombard Turkish forts protecting the Dardanelles seaway between the Mediterranean and Black Sea. Operations against the forts intensify over the following weeks.

FEBRUARY 20

MIDDLE EAST, *EGYPT*
Australian and New Zealand troops training in Egypt are earmarked to take part in operations against the Turkish-controlled Dardanelles.

FEBRUARY 22

AFRICA, *SOUTHWEST AFRICA*
General Louis Botha, the prime minister of the Union of South Africa, leads a reconnaissance into German Southwest Africa. Over the following weeks

▲ *Russian troops march through a town in the Austro-Hungarian province of Galicia in an attempt to block advancing enemy forces.*

▼ *Austro-Hungarian troops man the firestep of a trench in Galicia.*

an invasion force of some 43,000 South Africans is massed at four points. German troops total 9000. The invasion begins on March 7.

FEBRUARY 24

HOME FRONT, *AUSTRIA-HUNGARY*
The government takes over the direct distribution of both grain and flour supplies.

MARCH 1

POLITICS, *BRITAIN*
The government, with French backing, announces that it "would prevent commodities of any kind entering or leaving Germany," thus marking the

beginning of a naval-led economic blockade. There are protests from, among others, the United States.

AIR WAR, *FRANCE*
The first ever specialized fighter unit is established by Commandant Baron de Tricornet. Its pilots fly Parasol two-seater aircraft.

MARCH 6

POLITICS, *AUSTRIA-HUNGARY*
The Austro-Hungarian chief-of-staff, General Conrad von Hötzendorf, informs General Erich von Falkenhayn, the chief of the German General Staff, that war with Italy is inevitable.

MARCH 10

POLITICS, *BRITAIN*
Secretary of War Lord Kitchener tells General Sir Ian Hamilton that he will command the ground forces earmarked for the attack on the Gallipoli Peninsula in Turkey. The first landings are scheduled for April.

AIR WAR, *WESTERN FRONT*
The British Royal Flying Corps develops five innovations to support the Neuve-Chapelle offensive: a "clock system" whereby observers can plot the fall of an artillery shot on a celluloid disk; the coordination of bombing attacks with the ground offensive;

▼ *South African mounted troops prepare to advance into German Southwest Africa. Some South Africans opposed supporting the British and launched a short but unsuccessful rebellion.*

▲ *Camouflaged British howitzers begin the 35-minute bombardment that heralded the opening of the attack at Neuve-Chapelle on March 10.*

patrols to identify counterattacking German troops; photo-mosaic mapping of the German trench system; and protective patrols over British troops moving up to the battlefield.

MARCH 10-13

WESTERN FRONT, *FRANCE*

Field Marshal Sir John French's British Expeditionary Force launches a limited offensive at Neuve-Chapelle in Artois, northeastern France. Following a short bombardment by some 350 artillery pieces, four British and Indian divisions attack along a 4000-yard (3660-m) front. Early progress is comparatively good – Neuve-Chapelle falls, as do several lines of German trenches. However, ammunition shortages and rapid German counterattacks blunt the advance. The British dig in on the captured ground and beat off subsequent German attacks. British casualties total 11,500 men by the end of the offensive on the 13th. The British conclude that artillery fire is the key to success in trench warfare.

▼ *British troops man a fairly basic front-line trench. As the war progressed, they would be dug deeper and strengthened. Men would be protected by dug-outs and their trenches fronted by barbed wire.*

◄ *A Russian 11-inch (280-mm) howitzer outside the Austro-Hungarian fortress of Przemysl, which fell on March 22.*

▲ *A French six-inch (155-mm) gun is readied for action. An obsolete design, it was in service due to artillery shortages.*

MARCH 18

AFRICA,
SOUTHWEST AFRICA
General Louis Botha leads 21,000 troops in the main invasion of German Southwest Africa.

SEA WAR, MEDITERRANEAN
The final Anglo-French attempt to force a way through the Dardanelles by naval power alone fails. Three warships from the fleet commanded by Rear Admiral John de Robeck are sunk by Turkish mines and three badly damaged. De Robeck orders his surviving warships to withdraw from the Dardanelles.

▶ *Rear Admiral John de Robeck failed to break through the Dardanelles with naval power.*

Unbeknown to de Robeck, the Turks are in fact on the point of collapse – they are short of ammunition and many of their batteries are inoperable. However, the British and French begin to push ahead with their planning for an overland attack aimed at Constantinople via the Gallipoli Peninsula. French and British troops are already gathering for the landings. However, problems with loading men and equipment push back the operation to late April. The Turks, who are aware of the invasion, begin to strengthen

their defenses. German General Liman von Sanders is placed in charge of the 60,000 Turkish troops in the area.

MARCH 22

EASTERN FRONT, GALICIA
The 110,000-strong Austro-Hungarian garrison of Przemysl surrenders to the Russians following the recent unsuccessful attempts to relieve it by the Austro-Hungarian Third Army. It has been under almost constant bombardment since early February.

MARCH 27

HOME FRONT, BRITAIN
The press begin a campaign criticizing the shortage of artillery shells following the publication of Field Marshal Sir John French's letter concerning the same issue in *The Times* newspaper. French's superiors are outraged.

APRIL 5

WESTERN FRONT, FRANCE
The French launch their First and Third Armies in an attack against the German-held St. Mihiel salient in the Meuse–Argonne region. Progress is limited due to a combination of poor

weather, thick mud, and the extensive German defenses. The attack peters out within a few weeks, but small-scale skirmishing continues over the following months.

APRIL 8

POLITICS, *TURKEY*
Turkish troops begin to crush any support for the Russians in Armenia and Armenian desires for independence. A systematic campaign of great brutality follows: men are murdered, while women and children are deported to other Turkish provinces.

▲ *Turkish cavalrymen advance through an Armenian village. The Armenians, a Christian minority in a Muslim country, were ruthlessly persecuted by the Turks.*

By September some estimates suggest that one million Armenians have been killed outright or died through neglect or starvation. A further 200,000 Armenians have been forced to convert to Islam from Christianity. The surviving Armenians revolt against the Turks.

APRIL 12

MIDDLE EAST, *MESOPOTAMIA*
A Turkish advance on the British base at Basra is defeated at Shaiba. Although outnumbered two-to-one by 12,000 Turks, the British troops inflict some 3200 casualties.

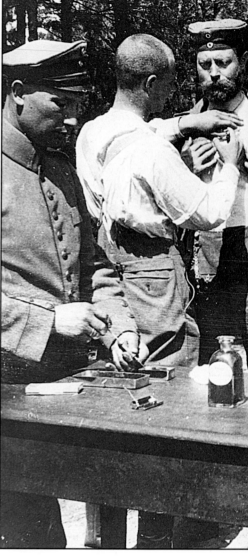

▲ German troops are vaccinated against cholera on the Eastern Front.

◄ Germany's commitment to the Eastern Front grew in 1915 due to the increasing military weakness of Austria-Hungary and a belief that Russia could be knocked out of the war quickly.

STRATEGY & TACTICS

EAST VERSUS WEST

Both Germany's military planners and their enemies faced a strategic dilemma in 1915: where was the war to be won? On the Western Front the Germans held French and Belgian territory and had no immediate need to attack. They could extend their defense lines, launch counterattacks, and give up unimportant ground if necessary. Matters were different on the Eastern Front, where the fighting was more fluid and more suitable to the sweeping flanking attacks the Germans favored. Germany had already won several spectacular victories on the Eastern Front, but also had to lend extensive support to the less competent Austro-Hungarian Army.

If Russia was comprehensively defeated then the German forces on the Eastern Front could be sent west to deliver a knock-out blow against the British and French. Hindenburg and Ludendorff favored an all-out onslaught to smash Russia, while Falkenhayn believed that the war could only be won on the Western Front and that victories against Russia would have only a limited overall impact. Hindenburg and Ludendorff, backed by Kaiser Wilhelm II, won the argument.

The British faced a similar dilemma. Some, mainly politicians, believed that the Western Front was a slogging match that offered little more than a growing casualty bill for negligible gain. They argued that action on other fronts, in the Middle East and the Balkans, might achieve more by knocking out of the war one or both of the two weaker Central Powers – Turkey and Austria-Hungary. Their opponents, chiefly senior military figures, argued that victory could only be achieved by defeating Germany on the Western Front. In 1915, at least, the politicians had their way.

APRIL 13

POLITICS, *GERMANY*

Kaiser Wilhelm II accedes to the demands of his military planners that German military efforts must focus on the Eastern Front, particularly in the light of recent Austro-Hungarian offensive shortcomings. Eight divisions are to be transferred by rail from the Western Front to the south of Cracow and a new German Eleventh Army under General August von Mackensen is formed on the 16th. General Erich von Falkenhayn travels east to take overall command of the forthcoming attack, although he believes that victory can only be truly won on the Western Front.

The offensive involves Field Marshal Paul von Hindenburg's forces north of Warsaw launching limited attacks to occupy the Russian forces opposite them. The key attack will, however, take place to the south and be led by Mackensen's Eleventh Army. Mackensen's army will launch a broad-front offensive directed toward the towns of Gorlice and Tarnow. Austro-Hungarian troops will also take part in the attack.

APRIL 14

▶ *Dutch aviation engineer Anthony Fokker developed a device allowing machine guns to fire through propellers.*

APRIL 14

POLITICS, *GREECE*

The government rejects an offer of Turkish territory if it joins the war against the Central Powers.

APRIL 17

SEA WAR, *MEDITERRANEAN*

The British *E17* becomes the first submarine to break through the Turkish defenses (forts, mines, and nets) guarding the Dardanelles in 1915. Others will follow in the wake of the *E17* and score many successes against German and Turkish shipping operating in the Black Sea.

APRIL 19

TECHNOLOGY, *GERMANY*

Aviation engineers working for Dutch-born Anthony Fokker develop the mechanical interrupter gear, which allows machine-gun bullets to be fired through the blades of a rotating aircraft propeller. This greatly facilitates the development of dedicated single-seater fighters.

APRIL 20

MIDDLE EAST, *ARMENIA*

Some 1300 armed Armenian rebels and 30,000 non-combatants are besieged in the city of Van by Turkish forces. They successfully hold out until the siege is broken by Russian forces on May 19.

APRIL 22

WESTERN FRONT, *BELGIUM*

The Second Battle of Ypres begins with the first use of poison chlorine gas on the Western Front. The Germans have amassed 4000 gas cylinders,

▶ *The Second Battle of Ypres, fought in April and May, saw the Germans reduce the size of the British-held salient around the Belgian town.*

▼ *A British submarine, the E11, is cheered home after a successful sortie against enemy shipping in the Black Sea.*

Map of Belgium showing: Langemarck, Passchendaele, Pilckem, St. Julien, BELGIUM, Frenzenberg, Bellewaarde, Ypres, Wytschaete

Front, April 22
Front, May 24

0 — 3 mi
0 — 4 km

N

▲ German troops in a reserve trench on the Western Front wear an early form of gas-mask consisting of a gauze pad tied around the mouth and nose.

▶ German machine-gunners begin to move their Maxims into the front line.

which they use to open an attack by their Fourth Army. Having no protection against the gas, several units holding the northern flank of the salient panic and run away, opening a gap in the front line some five miles (8 km) wide. A second gas attack takes place the next day.

APRIL 23

MEDITERRANEAN, *SKYROS*
British poet Rupert Brooke dies of blood poisoning on a hospital ship lying off the Greek island.

APRIL 24

WESTERN FRONT, *BELGIUM*
The Germans use gas in their offensive against the Ypres salient. Their attack concentrates on St. Julien, which is held by the 1st Canadian Division. The Canadians improvise gas protection by

KEY PERSONALITIES

MUSTAFA KEMAL

Later known as Ataturk and regarded as the founding father of modern Turkey, Mustafa Kemal (1881–1938) remains a national hero to many modern Turks. A professional soldier, he served in the Turco-Italian War (1911–12) and the Balkan Wars (1912–13). He rose to public prominence for his role in defeating the Anglo-French landing at Gallipoli in 1915, where his energy and drive prevented the invaders from capitalizing on their surprise attack.

After Gallipoli Kemal served in the Caucasus and Syria, where his radical proposal for the abandonment of many provinces of the Turkish Empire in the Middle East offended his superiors. He was sent on indefinite sick leave (December 1917), but was recalled to active service in the late summer of 1918, just in time to witness Turkey's defeat.

After World War I Kemal became head of an alternative government to that in Constantinople and fought to prevent the dismemberment of Turkey. In 1922 he advanced on the capital from his base around Ankara, securing the withdrawal of the occupying World War I victors.

He was proclaimed president of the new secular Republic of Turkey in October 1923 and established a new capital at Ankara. He also instituted wide-ranging reforms to modernize the country. Held in great popular esteem, he was given the name Ataturk, meaning "Father of Turks," in 1934.

▲ *A British field hospital in Belgium during the fighting around Ypres. Medical orderlies attend the lightly wounded.*

▼ *German troops enjoy a break before the opening of the attack toward the towns of Gorlice and Tarnow, both of which capitulated in early May.*

using handkerchiefs soaked in water or urine, and prevent a major German breakthrough.

APRIL 25

MIDDLE EAST, *TURKEY*
The Anglo-French invasion of the Gallipoli Peninsula begins. The plan calls for three initial landings, totaling 30,000 men. The first involves British troops landing at Cape Helles on the very tip of the peninsula. The second involves the Australian and New Zealand Army Corps (ANZAC) forces coming ashore to the north of Cape Helles at Ari Burna. The third is designed as a diversionary attack and involves French troops landing at Kumkale on the opposite side of the Dardanelles.

Naval gunfire is used to support each attack and there is a demonstration by warships against Bulair, some 50 miles (80 km) north of Cape Helles to distract the attention of the local commander, German General Liman von Sanders.

The landings on the peninsula do not go smoothly. At Cape Helles the British 29th Division comes ashore at five beaches in the face of intense fire from the local Turkish defenders. Despite heavy casualties, elements of the division almost reach their chief objective – the commanding heights

of Achi Baba and the town of Krithia – on the 28th. However, confusion reigns and some of the troops stop to make tea. The Turks rush troops forward and occupy both positions, from where they can shoot down on the British landing beaches.

The ANZACs at Ari Burna are also tasked with capturing high ground – the ridge of Chunuk Bair. The area is relatively lightly defended and the ANZACs come very close to capturing it. However, the prompt action of a Turkish officer, Mustafa Kemal, who rushes reserves to the sector just in time, prevents the ANZACs from taking their primary objective.

APRIL 26

POLITICS, *ITALY*

The government agrees to become involved in the war against its former ally Austria-Hungary and has been promised substantial territorial gains in the event of victory. The Austro-Hungarians rapidly move reinforcements to their border with Italy from the Eastern Front and Serbia to strengthen their defenses.

APRIL 28

MIDDLE EAST, *TURKEY*

The British launch an attack to capture the Turkish positions around the town of Krithia on the Gallipoli Peninsula. They advance just two miles

▲ *A Turkish shell explodes close to one of the piers used by the British to land troops and supplies at Cape Helles on the tip of the Gallipoli Peninsula.*

▼ *The Anglo-French landings at Gallipoli were a costly failure.*

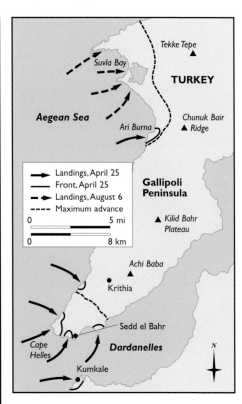

(3 km) at the cost of 3000 casualties. The Turks, who are rushing reinforcements to the peninsula, launch a succession of counterattacks.

MAY 1

EASTERN FRONT, *GALICIA*

The German attack toward Gorlice and Tarnow begins, heralded by a four-hour barrage from more than 600 artillery pieces, which fire both conventional and gas shells. German and Austro-Hungarian forces advance along a 28-mile (45-km) front, smashing the Russian Third Army. Gorlice falls on the following day and Tarnow on the 6th. The German forces capitalize on their early gains and continue their advance deep into Galicia over the following weeks.

SEA WAR, *ATLANTIC*

The *U-30* sinks the first US merchant ship, the *Gulflight*, without warning.

MAY 6

WESTERN FRONT, *BELGIUM*

The commander of the British Second Army at Ypres, General Sir Horace Smith-Dorrien, is removed from his post after suggesting that a tactical withdraw would reduce pressure on the salient. His superior, Field Marshal Sir John French, disagrees strongly and continues to order counterattacks,

The Cunard Liner LUSITANIA

▲ *The British liner* Lusitania, *bound for England from New York, was sunk by a German submarine without warning off the coast of Ireland. Its loss hardened US public feeling against Germany.*

none of which recaptures any significant territory. Smith-Dorrien's replacement is General Herbert Plumer.

MIDDLE EAST, *TURKEY*
The British at Gallipoli again attempt to capture the town of Krithia from the Turks. The advance stalls quickly, gaining only 600 yards (550 m) at a cost of 6500 casualties. The British commander, General Sir Ian Hamilton, receives more reinforcements.

MAY 7

SEA WAR, *ATLANTIC*
The *Lusitania* is sunk without warning by the German submarine *U-20*. Among the dead are 124 US citizens.

MAY 8

WESTERN FRONT, *BELGIUM*
In the Second Battle of Ypres the Germans capture Frenzenberg Ridge and hold it despite facing counterattacks.

MAY 9

WESTERN FRONT, *FRANCE*
General Sir Douglas Haig, commander of the British First Army, attacks on either side of Neuve-Chapelle. His aim is to secure Aubers Ridge, which lies some 3000 yards (2740 m) from the town. The British are supporting a major French offensive in Artois. The opening barrage is poorly coordinated and does little to undermine the German defenses. There are also concerns over the quality and quantity of the shells provided for the artillery. The attack, which makes little progress, grinds to a halt the next day. British casualties amount to 11,600 men.

While the British batter away at Aubers Ridge, the French open the Second Battle of Artois. Led by the corps of General Henri-Philippe Pétain, the French advance some four miles (6 km) in 90 minutes to reach the key Vimy Ridge, a vital piece of high ground. Mounting losses convince Pétain that further frontal attacks on the ridge would be too costly, however. The fighting continues and centers on the town of Souchez.

MAY 11

MIDDLE EAST, *MESOPOTAMIA*
The commander of the much-enlarged British forces in Mesopotamia, General Sir John Nixon, outlines a major offensive devised to advance on and capture Baghdad. He is unaware that the Turks are also building up their strength in the region.

MAY 12

AFRICA, *SOUTHWEST AFRICA*
South African troops led by General Louis Botha occupy Windhoek, the capital of German Southwest Africa. In a meeting with the German governor on the 20th, Botha demands unconditional surrender.

▼ *A lone soldier looks out across no-man's land during the Festubert battle.*

MAY 13

POLITICS, *BRITAIN*
The government agrees to intern all enemy aliens who are of military age.

MAY 15

WESTERN FRONT, *FRANCE*
The commander of the British Expeditionary Force, Field Marshal Sir John French, remains under severe pressure to support the major French

▲ *German wounded and prisoners take shelter in a shell crater with their British captors at Aubers Ridge.*

offensive in Artois and orders his First Army under General Sir Douglas Haig to attack Festubert. The British attack under cover of darkness for the first time and the onslaught is preceded by a 60-hour bombardment of the German trench line. There are early

MAY 19

gains by the British, but a mixture of rain, mist, and a stiffening of German resistance prevent any exploitation. The British shortage of artillery shells becomes increasingly acute.

MAY 19

MIDDLE EAST, *TURKEY*

The Australians and New Zealanders at Gallipoli, some 17,000 men, defeat a major counterattack by 40,000 Turks, inflicting over 3000 casualties.

MAY 23

POLITICS, *ITALY*

The government announces that Italy is at war with Austria-Hungary – but not Germany. The subsequent fighting is concentrated in two mountainous areas in northern Italy – the Trentino and along the Isonzo River. The major effort is directed across the Isonzo toward the Austro-Hungarian port of Trieste, but the Italians are also hoping to initiate an advance to help hard-pressed Serbia.

MAY 24

WESTERN FRONT, *BELGIUM*

A German attack at Ypres directed against the British-held Bellewaarde Ridge enjoys early success, but many of the initial gains are lost to British counterattacks. The fighting ends on the 25th and marks the last act of the Second Battle of Ypres. The British have had 58,000 casualties since the opening of the offensive, the Germans 35,000, and the French around 10,000. The Ypres salient has been reduced to a depth of just three miles (5 km).

▲ *Australian infantrymen await the order to attack the Turks at Gallipoli.*

▼ *Winston Churchill, (center, with cane) pictured after his dismissal from Britain's government over the Gallipoli fiasco.*

MAY 25

POLITICS, *BRITAIN*
A coalition government is formed, drawing together 12 Liberals and eight Tories in the cabinet. Liberal firebrand David Lloyd George is made minister for munitions.

MAY 26

POLITICS, *BRITAIN*
First Lord of the Admiralty Sir Winston Churchill is dismissed from his post by Prime Minister Herbert Asquith after the failure of the naval attack on the Dardanelles. In November Churchill is dropped from the government altogether because of the failure of the land operation on the Gallipoli Peninsula. He goes to fight on the Western Front.

SEA WAR, *ADRIATIC*
Italy introduces a naval blockade of Austria-Hungary.

MAY 27

WESTERN FRONT, *FRANCE*
The British attack at Festubert ends. The British commander-in-chief, Field Marshal Sir John French, contacts the government stating that there can be no further attacks until his stock of artillery shells is replenished. The British have won territory a mile in depth across a 3000-yard (2700-m)

▲ *French troops, captured during the fighting around the Ypres salient in Belgium during the spring of 1915.*

front but at a high price – some 16,000 casualties. German losses total 5000 men.

AIR WAR, *GERMANY*
French Voisin bombers carry out their first major long-range raid, dropping bombs on poison-gas producing facilities at Ludwigshafen.

MAY 31

MIDDLE EAST, *MESOPOTAMIA*
Under orders from General Sir John Nixon, General Sir Charles Townshend defeats a Turkish force at Qurna. Townshend is in command of a division-size force supported by a flotilla of gunboats and is under orders to test the feasibility of an advance on Baghdad. A second amphibious assault captures Amara on June 3. Townshend, however, is stricken with illness.

JUNE 1

POLITICS, *GERMANY*
The government makes an official apology to the United States for the sinking of the tanker *Gulflight* by one of its submarines off the Scilly Isles on May 1.

JUNE 2

POLITICS, *GERMANY*
Kaiser Wilhelm II backs plans to launch a limited encirclement of the Russian forces in the salient around Warsaw, despite opposition from Hindenburg and Ludendorff. The plan calls for General Max von Gallwitz's new German Twelfth Army to strike south toward Warsaw, while the German and Austro-Hungarian forces in the south engaged in exploiting

▶ *British General Sir Charles Townshend, who was ordered to advance on Baghdad despite a lack of resources.*

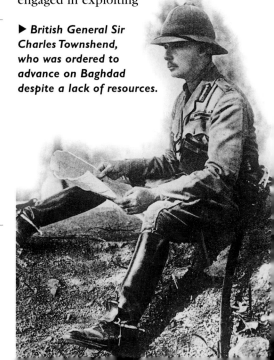

JUNE 3

lack of progress lead to the sending of further reinforcements. However, doubts about the operation grow.

JUNE 6–7

AIR WAR, *BRITAIN*
German Zeppelin airships launch a major raid against east coast ports and London. Zeppelin *L9* strikes the port of Hull, where 64 casualties result from a 20-minute attack. The key mission is against London. Three Zeppelins complete their attack but their fortunes are mixed. *LZ38* returns

◀ *British women at work in an armaments factory, a growing part of the country's war effort.*

▼ *German troops enter Przemysl.*

the recent Gorlice–Tarnow break-through should advance north.

HOME FRONT, *BRITAIN*
The British government passes the Munitions of War Act, which leads to the mass employment of women workers – 46,000 rush to enhance the country's war production in the first week after the act becomes law.

JUNE 3

EASTERN FRONT, *GALICIA*
Capitalizing on their breakthrough at Gorlice–Tarnow the previous month, the Germans and Austro-Hungarians recapture the fortress of Przemysl.

JUNE 4

MIDDLE EAST, *TURKEY*
The British at Gallipoli attempt to capture the Turkish-held town of Krithia for the third time. Some 30,000 men attack but gain only a few hundred yards at a cost of 6500 casualties. Mounting losses and the

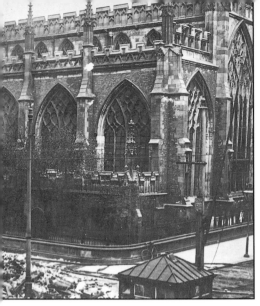

to its base near Brussels, but is destroyed by bombs dropped from British naval aircraft; elsewhere Flight Sub-Lieutenant R. Warneford chases Zeppelin *LZ34* from Ostend to Ghent in Belgium and, despite heavy protective fire, destroys it by dropping bombs on it from above; and the *LZ39* returns home safely.

JUNE 16

WESTERN FRONT, *FRANCE*
The Second Battle of Artois carries on with the French launching a major 20-division attack against the Germans, who have received large reinforcements. The offensive is aimed at Vimy Ridge, but only one French division gains a brief foothold on the commanding heights.

JUNE 18

WESTERN FRONT, *FRANCE*
Although fighting will continue until the end of the month, the Second Battle of Artois grinds to a halt. The French claim to have recaptured some

◀ *French gunners stand ready to open fire during the Second Battle of Artois.*

▼ *Austro-Hungarian troops man trenches high above the Isonzo River.*

25 square miles (65 sq km) of German-occupied French territory. Losses on both sides are high.

JUNE 22

EASTERN FRONT, *GALICIA*
The Austro-Hungarian Second Army recaptures the fortress of Lemberg, which has been occupied by the Russians since September 1914. This victory is a result of the recent Gorlice–Tarnow breakthrough engineered by General August von Mackensen, who is promoted to the rank of field marshal the same day.

JUNE 23–JULY 7

WESTERN FRONT, *ITALY*
The Italians open the First Battle of the Isonzo, marking the beginning of a series of 11 engagements in northeast Italy along the border with Austria-Hungary that will continue until 1918. The offensive plans to capture the Austro-Hungarian port of Trieste, two-thirds of whose inhabitants are Italians. However, the Italians have to overcome considerable physical obstacles, chiefly the Isonzo River itself, which meanders along the border and is backed by precipitous mountains.

The 200,000 Italians, who initially outnumber the Austro-Hungarians by approximately two-to-one in men and artillery pieces, make some progress in the opening phase of the battle but their main offensive, which begins on

June 24

the 30th, ends in failure. Italian forces attack on a 20-mile (32-km) front, but gain only a single foothold on the east bank of the Isonzo.

A renewal of the attack on July 5 achieves little. The Italian armies, the Second under General Pietro Frugoni and the Duke of Aosta's Third, spearhead the onslaught. Despite a superiority of six-to-one, they advance little more than a mile. Casualties are heavy – the Italians lose 5000 men, some 4000 alone in the battle for Gorizia; Austro-Hungarian losses total 10,000.

June 24

POLITICS, *FRANCE*
Meeting at Chantilly, the French commander-in-chief, General Joseph Joffre, and the British Expeditionary Force's Field Marshal Sir John French agree that the Western Front is the decisive theater of war and plan to launch a major offensive in late summer. Both need time to gather reinforcements.

HOME FRONT, *UNITED STATES*
Some 70,000 attend the National German–American meeting at New York's Madison Square Garden.

▼ *The bodies of Italian dead are examined by a party of Austro-Hungarians at the end of the First Battle of the Isonzo.*

▲ *A column of Italian infantry, known as Bersagliari, moves through a village on the way to the First Battle of the Isonzo.*

July 2

HOME FRONT, *UNITED STATES*
A bomb planted by a German student from Cornell University destroys a reception room in the Senate. The perpetrator, who later commits suicide in prison on the 6th, also shoots and wounds the pro-British banker William Pierpoint Morgan.

July 9

AFRICA, *SOUTHWEST AFRICA*
The remaining German forces in German Southwest Africa surrender to the South Africans.

HOME FRONT, *BRITAIN*
Secretary of War Lord Kitchener makes a speech at London's Guildhall calling for greater recruitment to the country's armed forces. By the end of the month, two million men have answered his call to arms. Many are enthusiastic volunteers, who form units based on their home towns.

July 11

POLITICS, *UNITED STATES*
Secretary of State Robert Lansing privately writes: "Germany must not be allowed to win this war, or to break even."

SEA WAR, *AFRICA*
The German raider *Königsberg*, holed up in the Rufiji River, is badly damaged after 90 minutes of shelling by two British monitors, whose fire is directed by a spotter plane. The *Königsberg* is scuttled by its crew, but its valuable main guns are salvaged by the Germans and used in land operations in East Africa.

July 13

EAST FRONT, *POLAND*
General Max von Gallwitz's German

Twelfth Army, a force of some 120,000 men, launches its offensive directed toward Warsaw by attacking on a 25-mile (40-km) front. The army has advanced some five miles (8 km) by the 17th. Russian morale is reported to be falling and German troops enter Warsaw on August 5. The salient around the Russian held-city is collapsing rapidly under the attacks from the north and south.

JULY 17

POLITICS, *BRITAIN*
Women march demanding to make a fuller contribution to the war effort.

POLITICS, *BULGARIA*
Although declaring its continued neutrality, Bulgaria signs a secret treaty with Germany and Austria-Hungary. As part of the deal Bulgaria receives some 600 square miles (1550 sq km) of frontier territory from Turkey.

▲ *The shattered German surface raider Königsberg lies scuttled on the bed of the Rufiji River in East Africa. After sustaining damage from British warships, its captain ordered his vessel to be disabled. However, its armaments were saved for use on land.*

▼ *A lone German soldier keeps watch over a party of Russian prisoners captured around Warsaw.*

JULY 18–AUGUST 3

WESTERN FRONT, *ITALY*

The Italians and Austro-Hungarians clash in the Second Battle of the Isonzo. The commander-in-chief of the Italian Army, General Luigi Cadorna, has sent more artillery to the front in the hope of achieving the decisive breakthrough to Trieste. For their part the outnumbered Austro-Hungarians have reinforced their positions with just two divisions – but it is enough.

The battle begins with a shorter, more accurate barrage by the Italians, and their Second and Third Armies make some initial progress, taking 4000 Austro-Hungarian prisoners by the 22nd. However, a lack of shells and heavy artillery combine to slow the advance, which breaks down in front of the still intact Austro-Hungarian trench systems protected by barbed wire. The few gains that the Italians make are recaptured by the Austro-Hungarians. The battle ends on the 3rd.

JULY 24

MIDDLE EAST, *MESOPOTAMIA*

British Major General George Gorringe, who has been ordered to advance up the Euphrates River in support of General Sir Charles Townshend's push along the adjacent Tigris River in the direction of Baghdad, defeats the Turkish at Nasiriya, 100 miles (160 km) from Basra.

▼ *Austro-Hungarian artillery fires at Italian positions during the fighting along the Isonzo River.*

▲ *General Luigi Cadorna, chief of the Italian General Staff, 1914–17.*

AUGUST 1

POLITICS, *GERMANY*

Germany's war planners agree on the need to defeat Serbia as soon as possible, preferably with the aid of Bulgaria. Defeat of Serbia will free their forces to redouble their efforts on the Eastern Front.

AIR WAR, *FRANCE*

German pilot Max Immelmann scores his first air victory, in part due to his

aircraft, a Fokker EI fitted with an interrupter device that allows machine-gun rounds to be fired through its propeller blades. It begins a period of German air dominance over the Western Front, which becomes known as the "Fokker Scourge."

AUGUST 4

ESPIONAGE, *BELGIUM*

The Germans arrest British-born nurse Edith Cavell, who is implicated in

◄ A Fokker E1 monoplane fighter. It easily outperformed its rivals and helped establish German air superiority in 1915.

aiding more than 200 prisoners-of-war to escape. Cavell is convicted by a German court martial, which convenes on October 7, and is executed five days later. Her last words are: "Patriotism is not enough. I must have no hatred or bitterness toward anyone."

AUGUST 6

MIDDLE EAST, TURKEY
In an attempt to break the deadlock at Gallipoli, the British launch an amphibious assault on Suvla Bay on the north of the peninsula adjacent to the original landing beach at Ari Burna. The plan is to outflank the Turkish defenders to the south, who have confined the British to the tip of the peninsula. The landings are to be made in conjunction with an

▼ British naval ratings escort the coffin carrying the remains of executed nurse Edith Cavell on its arrival in England.

AUGUST 12

Australian and New Zealand attack against the high ground known as Chunuk Bair.

Although the ANZACs attack with great determination, their few gains are won at a high cost. They briefly capture the summit of Chunuk Bair on the 8th, but a Turkish counterattack led by Mustafa Kemal evicts them two days later. The landings at Suvla are unopposed, but the local commander, Sir Frederick Stopford, fails to take advantage of the situation, allowing Turkish reinforcements to gain the high ground overlooking Suvla Bay.

AUGUST 12

TECHNOLOGY, *BRITAIN*
British inventors begin work on what will become the world's first tracked

▲ *British forces led by General Sir Charles Townshend begin their advance toward Turkish-held Kut-el-Amara.*

▼ *A party of Turkish prisoners captured during a British attack on the town of Krithia on the Gallipoli Peninsula.*

armored vehicle. Nicknamed "Little Willie," it makes its debut on September 8. Suggestions by Winston Churchill on December 24 that the secret weapon should be described as a water tank is accepted and the term "tank" enters the common language.

AUGUST 17

MIDDLE EAST, *TURKEY*
The commander of the Gallipoli operation, General Sir Ian Hamilton, asks the British secretary of war, Lord Kitchener, for a further 95,000 reinforcements. There is growing political dismay at the lack of progress and the growing list of casualties at Gallipoli.

AUGUST 19

SEA WAR, *IRISH SEA*
Submarine *U-24* sinks the liner *Arabic*; among the 44 killed are three US citizens. US war protests mount.

AUGUST 20

POLITICS, *ITALY*
Declares war on Turkey.

AUGUST 21

POLITICS, *RUSSIA*
Czar Nicholas II takes personal command of the Russian armed forces, sacking his commander-in-chief, Grand Duke Nicholas, despite the latter's steadying influence during the recent and ongoing German and Austro-Hungarian encircling offensive against the salient around Warsaw. The grand duke is sent to command the forces fighting in the Caucasus, while the czar makes General Mikhail Alekseyev his chief-of-staff.

AUGUST 25

EASTERN FRONT, *RUSSIA*
Driving into the rear of the Warsaw salient from the south, General Alexander von Linsingen's forces take Brest-Litovsk from the Russians.

AUGUST 26

POLITICS, *GERMANY*
The authorities announce that merchant ships will not be attacked

without warning and also order their U-boats not to sink liners without warning four days later.

AUGUST 27

MIDDLE EAST, *MESOPOTAMIA*
British General Sir Charles Townshend, recently returned from sick leave in India, is ordered to advance on Kut-el-Amara, a major Turkish base on the Tigris River, some 300 miles (480 km) to the north of the main British base of Basra. Townshend believes his force of some 11,000 troops is inadequate.

▲ *An early British attempt to test the ability of tracked vehicles to cross small obstacles. The vehicle is a Killen Strait Tractor fitted with a wire-cutter.*

▼ *Australian troops advance at the run with fixed bayonets against the Turkish trenches at Gallipoli.*

AUGUST 28

DECISIVE WEAPONS

THE STOKES MORTAR

In October 1914 British troops on the Western Front complained bitterly of a German trench device that could lob a shell to a range of 600 yards (550 m) to which they could not reply. In response the British simply made copies of a captured German *Minenwerfer* ("mine-thrower"), but also asked their arms manufacturers to come up with similar devices.

By mid-1915 the government had been inundated with potential designs, but most were far from practical. Like the *Minenwerfer* many of these were no more than mini-howitzers – large, costly, and often of little use in the confines of a trench system. However, one individual, engineer Wilfred Stokes, had a practical, if revolutionary, design. His weapon consisted of a short barrel, which fitted to a bedplate, and a bipod, which could be slid up or down the barrel to give the correct firing elevation. In trials the mortar was remarkably accurate. Stokes then designed a shell that exploded on impact, rather than by a preset fuse.

Stokes's device was simple, cheap, easily manhandled, and could be brought into use rapidly. It also proved its worth in 1918, when the stalemate of trench warfare ended. The Germans had to abandon their heavy trench mortars, while each Stokes mortar and its ammunition could be brought forward by a few men.

Two examples of the successful mortar created by Wilfred Stokes. Their portability and high rate of fire became the basis for all subsequent designs.

▲ *German six-inch (15-cm) howitzers are moved to a new firing position somewhere on the Western Front.*

His offensive, which begins on September 12, is severely hampered by intense heat, a lack of river transport, and the need to detach one of his two infantry divisions to protect his tenuous lines of communication. However, he arrives outside Kut-el-Amara on September 16. The Turkish defender of Kut, Nur-ud-Din Pasha, commands 10,000 entrenched troops backed by nearly 40 artillery pieces.

AUGUST 28

POLITICS, *RUSSIA*
Rebuffing offers of peace from Germany, the government announces that peace cannot be agreed until all German soldiers have left Russia.

SEPTEMBER 6

POLITICS, *BULGARIA*
Bulgarian representative Colonel Gancev meets with General Erich von Falkenhayn, chief of the German General Staff, and Austria-Hungary's chief-of-staff, General Franz Conrad von Hötzendorf. They sign a military pact that binds them to crush Serbia. The Bulgarians issue a mobilization order on the 22nd.

SEPTEMBER 18

POLITICS, *GERMANY*
The government, bowing to mounting US protests about its unrestricted submarine campaign, decides to withdraw its U-boats from the southwest approaches to Britain and the English Channel. Many are transferred to the Mediterranean, where they begin a major campaign in early October.

EASTERN FRONT, *RUSSIA*
The Germans captures Vilna, marking the high point of the offensive against the salient around Warsaw that began in June. In the space of just a few months the Russians have been pushed out of Galicia and Poland, retreating some 300 miles (480 km). Although there is further fighting on the Eastern Front, little territory is lost or gained by both sides in the final months of the year. Heavy rains turn the roads into a morass and movement becomes all but impossible.

The Russians have taken a severe pounding but have escaped total encirclement, chiefly due to the efforts of the recently sacked Grand Duke Nicholas. However, their losses have been great and will total some two million men by the year's end. German and Austro-Hungarian casualties are suspected to be a little over one million men.

SEPTEMBER 24

MIDDLE EAST, *CAUCASUS*
Russia's Grand Duke Nicholas arrives in the region as overall commander but retains General Nikolai Yudenich as his main senior officer. They begin planning for a major offensive against the Turks in 1916.

SEPTEMBER 25

WESTERN FRONT, *FRANCE*

Following a three-day bombardment by 2500 artillery pieces, two French armies attack the Germans on a 15-mile (24-km) front, opening the Second Battle of Champagne, one of three major Anglo-French offensives to begin simultaneously on the Western Front. The aim is to give aid to Russia, which is under 'ferocious attack, and wear down the German forces.

Early gains are made – in the center the French advance some 3000 yards (2700 m) – and on the second day they break through to the German second line. The fighting continues into November, but becomes increasingly bogged down.

The second French attack, known as the Third Battle of Artois, also begins and they capture the town of

▲ *French guards move German prisoners to the rear at the height of the Second Battle of Champagne.*

Souchez. After five days of heavy fighting they briefly capture the commanding heights of Vimy Ridge – for the third time. However, subsequent gains are limited and bought at a high price as German resistance stiffens. The fighting continues into November, but the French are unable to capitalize on their early successes. French casualties are estimated at some 48,000 men; the Germans have losses totaling 30,000.

Also as part of the grand offensive, General Sir Douglas Haig's First Army launches an attack between Lens and the La Bassée Canal, opening the Battle of Loos. The British, short of artillery ammunition, use gas for the first time in the war. However, adverse winds

blow some of the gas back over the British lines and the terrain – strongly fortified villages and slag-heaps – makes progress difficult. The first-day advance totals 4000 yards (3660 m) and the assault troops capture part of the Hohenzollern Redoubt, Loos village, and Hill 70.

The German second line holds, however. French troops earmarked to support the British are slow to advance and their attack on the morning of the 26th is defeated. German counterattacks recapture the Hohenzollern Redoubt. The fighting continues into October.

SEPTEMBER 27

POLITICS, *GREECE*

The Greek government agrees to allow 150,000 Anglo-French troops to occupy Salonika, which will act as a base for operations in support of Serbia. The force will be commanded by two generals, France's Maurice Sarrail and Britain's Bryan Mahon.

SEPTEMBER 27–28

MIDDLE EAST, *MESOPOTAMIA*

British General Sir Charles Townshend launches his forces against the Turks defending Kut-el-Amara. The attack is successful, with the Turks suffering 5300 casualties, including 1300 men taken prisoner. However, the Turkish commander, Nur-ud-Din Pasha, makes a measured retreat to the next blocking position south of Baghdad, Ctesiphon. British losses reach 1230 men.

▼ *The build-up of forces in the Greek province of Salonika continues. Here, French troops wait to move out.*

SEPTEMBER 30

MIDDLE EAST, *TURKEY*

The British 10th Division is withdrawn from the stagnating battle for Gallipoli and sent to Salonika, Greece.

OCTOBER 2

POLITICS, *BULGARIA*

Bulgaria agrees to fight alongside Austria-Hungary and Germany in the forthcoming invasion of Serbia.

OCTOBER 6

WESTERN FRONT, *FRANCE*

The Second Battle of Champagne continues with a renewed French offensive against the German front line. French gains are limited. The fighting drags on into November but is stalemated. French losses to October 6 total 144,000 men; the Germans suffer 85,000 casualties.

BALKANS, *SERBIA*

Two German and Austro-Hungarian armies open the invasion of Serbia by attack across the northern border. The initial advance is followed by two Bulgarian armies striking from the east on the 14th – one moves on Nis; the other makes for Skopje. The joint operation is commanded by Field Marshal August von Mackensen. Outnumbered by nearly two-to-one, the Serbian Army escapes being surrounded but is forced to retreat to the southwest.

OCTOBER 8

MIDDLE EAST, *TURKEY*

To add to the problems faced by the troops occupying the trenches at

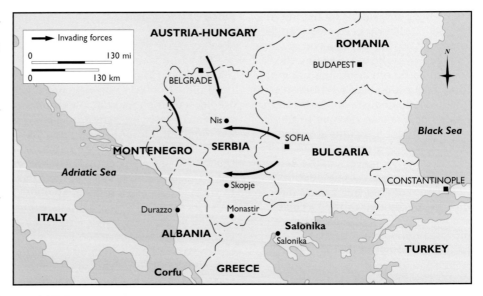

◀ *British wounded trudge through the streets of a shell-blasted town during the the Battle of Loos, October 13.*

Gallipoli, storms damage several piers used for the unloading of supplies and the evacuation of casualties.

OCTOBER 9

BALKANS, *SERBIA*

Austro-Hungarian troops occupy the capital Belgrade, while others attack Montenegro, Serbia's ally.

OCTOBER 11

POLITICS, *BRITAIN*

Secretary of War Lord Kitchener evaluates the risks of evacuating Gallipoli and states that "abandonment would be the most disastrous event in the history of the British Empire." The commander at Gallipoli, General Sir

Ian Hamilton, estimates he will lose some 50 percent of his troops in such an enterprise.

OCTOBER 13

AIR WAR, *BRITAIN*

In the heaviest Zeppelin raid of the year, five German airships strike against various targets. In London, bombs dropped by *L13, L14,* and *L15* cause about 150 casualties. Elsewhere, there are 49 other civilians either killed or wounded.

OCTOBER 13–14

WESTERN FRONT, *FRANCE*

The British 46th Division captures part of the German-held Hohenzollern Redoubt at the end of the Battle of Loos and successfully beats off German counterattacks. British casualties total 62,000 men, while the Germans have about 26,000 men killed, wounded, or captured. The commander of the British Expeditionary Force, Field Marshal Sir John French, is widely blamed for the poor handling of his reserves during the battle and calls to replace him grow ever more strident.

OCTOBER 14

POLITICS, *BALKANS*

Bulgaria and Serbia declare war against each other.

◀ *The twin-pronged attack on Serbia in 1915 involved troops from Bulgaria, Germany, and Austria-Hungary.*

▼ *A German cavalry detachment advances through Serbia.*

▲ *A German Zeppelin airship is framed by two searchlights while on a bombing raid on London.*

OCTOBER 15

POLITICS, *BRITAIN*

The government declares war on Bulgaria, which has invaded Serbia. Montenegro, a close ally of threatened Serbia, follows suit.

OCTOBER 16

POLITICS, *FRANCE*

The government declares war on Bulgaria.

MIDDLE EAST, *TURKEY*

The commander of the Gallipoli forces, General Sir Ian Hamilton, receives notice that he is to be replaced by General Sir Charles Monro, who takes charge on the 28th. His first request is for winter clothing.

OCTOBER 18–NOVEMBER 4

WESTERN FRONT, *ITALY*

The Italians again hammer away at the Austro-Hungarians defending the line of the Isonzo River as they continue their attacks toward Trieste. Despite having stockpiled over one million shells for the three-day barrage by 1200 artillery pieces that opens their attack on the outnumbered Austro-Hungarians, the Italians make little progress. What little ground they gain is swiftly retaken. Heavy rain and mud also slow the Italian offensive.

The attacks are called off on November 4. Losses are large. The Italians have 67,000 men killed, wounded, or taken prisoner; the Austro-Hungarians suffer 42,000 casualties.

OCTOBER 19

POLITICS, *ITALY/RUSSIA*

Both declare war on Bulgaria.

OCTOBER 24

BALKANS, *SERBIA*

Invading Bulgarian forces effectively prevent any link up between the Anglo-French forces advancing northward from Salonika and the embattled Serbian Army.

NOVEMBER 5

BALKANS, *SERBIA*
The Bulgarian First Army captures the city of Nis, a vital railroad junction. Its fall means that a rail line now stretches unhindered from Germany and Austria-Hungary to Turkey.

NOVEMBER 7

SEA WAR, *MEDITERRANEAN*
The Austrian submarine *U-38* shells and then torpedoes the liner *Ancona* bound for New York from Italy. Among the 208 dead are 25 US citizens. The Austrian response to the protests of the US government is considered inadequate.

NOVEMBER 10–DECEMBER 2

WESTERN FRONT, *ITALY*
The Italians and Austro-Hungarians fight the Fourth Battle of the Isonzo. The Italian offensive is heralded by an intense four-hour bombardment. Although attacking in force, the

▼ *Ctesiphon, the scene of the battle between Turkish and British forces.*

▲ *After months of unsuccessful attacks and increasing casualties, the British begin the evacuation of Gallipoli.*

Italians make only limited gains and resort to leveling one of their key objectives – the town of Gorizia – with artillery fire on the 18th.

The fighting dies down on December 2, with the Italians having made little further progress. Again, the list of casualties on both sides is high: an estimated 49,000 Italians and 30,000 Austro-Hungarians.

NOVEMBER 11

MIDDLE EAST, *MESOPOTAMIA*
The British continue their advance toward the Turkish-held positions around Ctesiphon. The Turkish commander, Nur-ud-Din Pasha, has received large reinforcements, which bring his strength up to 18,000 men supported by 45 artillery pieces. In contrast the British commander, General Sir Charles Townshend, has 10,000 infantry, 1000 cavalry, and 30 artillery pieces with which to attack.

NOVEMBER 20

POLITICS, *CANADA*
The government declares war on both Turkey and Bulgaria.

NOVEMBER 22

POLITICS, *UNITED STATES*
The administration rejects a German offer of $1000 for each US passenger killed following the torpedoing of the *Lusitania* on May 7.

MIDDLE EAST, *TURKEY*
Lord Kitchener, the British secretary of war, who has been on a fact-finding mission to Gallipoli since the 10th, advises evacuation. He sails home on the 24th. No firm decision is made until December 7, when the British government agrees to evacuate the positions at Suvla Bay and Ari Burna.

NOVEMBER 22–26

MIDDLE EAST, *MESOPOTAMIA*
The British attack the Turkish positions at Ctesiphon, which lies some 20 miles (32 km) south of their main objective, Baghdad. The initial advance successfully pierces the Turkish front, but the British commander, General Sir Charles Townshend, lacks the reserves to exploit this success and Turkish counterattacks stabilize the situation. As the Turks receive more reinforcements, Townshend orders a withdrawal back to Kut-el-Amara on the 25th. Turkish losses total 6200 men, while Townshend's smaller force takes 4600 casualties. The Turkish pursuit is limited and the exhausted British reach Kut-el-Amara on December 3.

NOVEMBER 23

BALKANS, *SERBIA*
The badly-mauled Serbian Army, some 200,000 men, begins a 100-mile

◄ *Specialist Italian mountain troops, known as Alpini, trek to their mountain-top positions.*

DECEMBER 7

MIDDLE EAST, *MESOPOTAMIA*
The Turks lay siege to the much-weakened British forces at Kut-el-Amara. The British reject a call to surrender on December 9 and are later informed that a relief force is being prepared to come to their rescue. Several attacks later in the month are defeated by the town's garrison and the Turks begin to entrench.

DECEMBER 8

MIDDLE EAST, *TURKEY*
The evacuation of the Suvla Bay and Ari Burna bridgeheads at Gallipoli begins. Despite much foreboding, they are carried out with great success due to meticulous work of the plan's creator, General William Birdwood. The Turks do not interfere with the evacuation and some 83,000 men, 186 artillery pieces, 1700 vehicles, and some 4500 transport animals are whisked away. The process is completed by the 20th. Troops remain in position at Cape Helles on the tip of the peninsula, however.

DECEMBER 12

SEA WAR, *ADRIATIC*
Allied warships begin the evacuation of Serbian forces from Albania. The operation will continue into 1916.

(160-km) retreat to the west and southwest, aiming to reach Albania. Four columns embark on a crossing of the mountains that separate the two countries. Short of food and warm clothing, thousands of Serbians die.

DECEMBER 3

POLITICS, *FRANCE*
General Joseph Joffre becomes commander-in-chief of all the French forces on the Western Front.

DECEMBER 6

POLITICS, *FRANCE*
British and French strategists reconvene at Chantilly and agree to plan a general offensive on the Western Front in 1916. They also agree to maintain their large – and growing – presence in Salonika.

▼ *A Serbian heavy artillery battery prepares to open fire on advancing Austro-Hungarian forces.*

DECEMBER 17

POLITICS, *BRITAIN*
Field Marshal Sir John French is dismissed as the commander of the British Expeditionary Force. His replacement is General Sir Douglas Haig.

DECEMBER 21

POLITICS, *GERMANY*
Twenty-two out of 44 Social Democrats in the Reichstag (German parliament) vote against further loans to finance the war.

DECEMBER 26

SEA WAR, *NORTH SEA*
The German commerce-raider *Möwe* leaves Bremen. It sinks 14 vessels before returning on March 4, 1916.

DECEMBER 27

MIDDLE EAST, *TURKEY*
The British government agrees to evacuate Cape Helles on the Gallipoli Peninsula. It begins the next day.

DECEMBER 28

POLITICS, *BRITAIN*
The government agrees to introduce adult male conscription.

DECEMBER 29

POLITICS, *WESTERN FRONT*
France's General Joseph Joffre and Britain's General Sir Douglas Haig meet. They discuss a 1916 attack along the Somme River sector on the Western Front.

1916

In a year of large and costly offensives, the Germans attempted to smash the French Army at Verdun. They failed, but it required the British and Russians to relieve some of the pressure. On the Somme the Germans survived, despite suffering as many losses as the British and French. The Russians almost forced the surrender of Austria-Hungary but had to divert forces to aid new ally Romania. The year also saw vain attempts to reach an acceptable peace.

JANUARY 1

MIDDLE EAST, *ARABIA*
In Turkish-controlled Arabia Hussein, Grand Sherif of Mecca, agrees to an alliance with Britain and later requests money to purchase rifles and food. The British government accepts his request and the rebellion begins in May.

AFRICA, *CAMEROONS*
British troops occupy Yaunde, the capital of this German West African colony. The campaign, supported by other colonial nations, had begun in August 1914. However, the German defenders are far from subdued by the fall of the capital and slowly retreat into the Spanish colony of Muni, some 125 miles (200 km) from Yaunde.

SEA WAR, *TECHNOLOGY*
The British introduce the depth-charge as part of their ongoing battle against enemy submarines. However, they will be in short supply until 1917.

JANUARY 2

SEA WAR, *BLACK SEA*
The British end their highly successful submarine campaign against Turkish shipping. Some 50 percent of Turkey's merchant ships have been sunk and the remainder are short of fuel.

JANUARY 4

POLITICS, *AUSTRIA-HUNGARY*
Chief of the General Staff Conrad von Hötzendorf confides to Prime Minister

▼ *British and local troops operating a 4.5-inch (115-mm) howitzer in the German colony of Cameroons in West Africa.*

▶ *Local porters carry equipment belonging to the small German army operating in East Africa commanded by General Paul von Lettow-Vorbeck. The Germans avoided pitched battles and carried out hit-and-run raids against isolated enemy garrisons and railroads.*

▼ *Turkish troops prepare to entrain for Baghdad, Mesopotamia, to increase the pressure on the British garrison besieged in Kut-el-Amara and the force sent to relieve it.*

by German General Paul von Lettow-Vorbeck, who wages a successful and protracted guerrilla war.

JANUARY 8

BALKANS, *MONTENEGRO*
Some 50,000 mainly Austro-Hungarian troops launch a major offensive, which is heralded by a 500-gun barrage and supported by air and naval attacks.

▼ *General Paul von Lettow-Vorbeck led the German and local troops operating against British, Belgian, and Portuguese colonies in East Africa.*

Count István Tisza that "There can be no question of destroying the Russian war machine; England cannot be defeated; peace must be made in not too long a space, or we shall be fatally weakened, if not destroyed."

MIDDLE EAST, *MESOPOTAMIA*
The British launch their first attempt to reach Kut-el-Amara, which has been besieged by the Turks since December 1915. The relief column, General Fenton Aylmer's 19,000-strong Tigris Corps, is opposed by more than 30,000 Turks. Aylmer's force clashes with the Turks at the Battle of Sheikh Saad on the 9th.

JANUARY 6

AFRICA, *EAST AFRICA*
South African General Jan Christiaan Smuts takes over operations in the region from British General Sir Horace Smith-Dorrien, who is ill with pneumonia. Smuts embarks on a campaign to capture the German colonies in East Africa. He is close to success by the end of the year but fails to destroy the small army commanded

▼ *Austro-Hungarian troops advance through Serbia in overwhelming strength. The country was quickly overrun.*

JANUARY 10

◀ Serbian troops forced to retreat in the face of Austro-Hungarian, German, and Bulgarian attacks await evacuation by sea from Durazzo in Albania.

▶ The British prototype tank, known as "Mother," is put through its paces. There was a growing belief in Britain that tanks could end the deadlock on the Western Front.

Austro-Hungarian progress is rapid and Montenegro is forced to capitulate to the invaders on the 17th.

MIDDLE EAST, *TURKEY*
The British evacuation of the Gallipoli Peninsula is completed when the last troops (17,000 men and around 40 artillery pieces) are taken off the beaches at Cape Helles. There are no casualties during the complex operation. However, the campaign has cost the British, Commonwealth, and French some 252,000 casualties and the Turks some 250,000 men.

JANUARY 10

MIDDLE EAST, *ARMENIA*
The Turkish Third Army is forced back to the city of Erzerum following the Battle of Köprüköy on the border between Russia and Turkey, which heralds a major offensive by Russian commander General Nikolai Yudenich.

JANUARY 12

BALKANS, *ALBANIA*
The evacuation of the Serbian Army from the port of Durazzo begins. The troops are heading for Corfu, which has been occupied by French marines, despite neutral Greece's protests.

JANUARY 15

POLITICS, *UNITED STATES*
Outrage is widespread when details of payments made to pro-German agents by Germany's military attaché

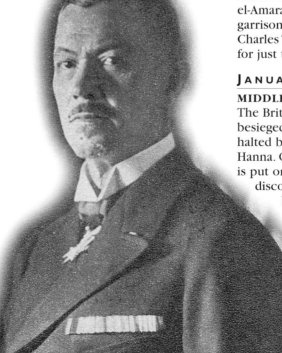

in Washington, Franz von Papen, are made public. Papen has already been recalled to Germany at the request of the US government.

JANUARY 16

MIDDLE EAST, *MESOPOTAMIA*
General Fenton Aylmer, leader of the British relief column making for Kut-el-Amara, is informed by the besieged garrison's commander, General Sir Charles Townshend, that he has rations for just two or three weeks.

JANUARY 21

MIDDLE EAST, *MESOPOTAMIA*
The British relief force heading for the besieged garrison of Kut-el-Amara is halted by the Turks at the Battle of Hanna. On the same day the garrison is put on half rations, although the discovery of an unknown store of barley alleviates matters somewhat. Over the following weeks the British rush

◀ Admiral Reinhard Scheer, commander-in-chief of the German High Seas Fleet from late January.

ZEPPELIN AIRSHIPS

The first Zeppelin airship raid against Britain took place on the night of January 19–20, 1915, and by 1918, 55 similar raids, most in 1915–16, had been made. In total, some 200 tons (203,000 kg) of bombs were dropped by airships and killed some 250 people. At first the British could do little to counter the high-altitude raids.

However, the advent of coordinated anti-aircraft defenses, chiefly bands of anti-aircraft guns with searchlights and high-altitude fighters, made the Zeppelins more vulnerable. They were increasingly replaced by long-range bombers, particularly the twin-engined Gotha, which made its first attack in April 1917. Zeppelins continued to be used elsewhere as bombers and also acted in the maritime reconnaissance role.

Zeppelins, named after Count Ferdinand von Zeppelin who produced aluminum-framed airships in the first decade of the twentieth century, were covered by an outer skin, which contained gas-filled bags that gave lift. By 1914 Germany had a fleet of 18 Zeppelins, operated by both the army and navy. Most could reach an altitude of 20,000 feet (6100 m) and had a speed of 80 mph (130 k/h).

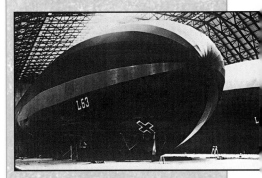

Two Zeppelins lie at anchor in one of the vast hangars built to protect them from the weather.

more troops to the theater and make plans to renew the relief operation, which recommences on March 7.

JANUARY 24

POLITICS, *GERMANY*
Admiral Reinhard Scheer is promoted to commander-in-chief of the German High Seas Fleet. Scheer, an advocate of offensive action against Britain's Home Fleet, later proposes luring the British navy into a decisive engagement in the North Sea, a strategy approved by Kaiser Wilhelm II the following month.

JANUARY 27

POLITICS, *GERMANY*
General Erich von Falkenhayn, the chief of the German General Staff, finalizes plans for an offensive against the French forces holding the fortress-city of Verdun in eastern France. Falkenhayn first proposed the attack in December 1915 and received the wholehearted backing of Kaiser Wilhelm II. Falkenhayn is planning to inflict massive casualties on the French at Verdun to sap their morale and will to fight on. The operation is scheduled to begin on February 12

and the Germans have positioned an extra 1220 artillery pieces around the city and delivered over 2.5 million shells to the front by the 1st.

JANUARY 29

AIR WAR, *FRANCE*
Paris suffers its second and last raid by Zeppelin airships, which produces 54 casualties. The French capital will not be attacked from the air again until January 1918.

TECHNOLOGY, *BRITAIN*
The first prototype tank, known as "Mother," starts a series of trials in great secret. These are successful and the commander of the British Expeditionary Force in France, General Haig, orders 40 on February 11. This figure is later increased to 100.

JANUARY 31

AIR WAR, *BRITAIN*
German airships launch their first attack on central and northwest England, key industrial areas. Seven Zeppelins are involved but the damage caused is small. One of the returning raiders, *L11*, goes down in the North Sea on February 2.

FEBRUARY 1

SEA WAR, *ENGLISH CHANNEL*
The British *Franz Fischer* becomes the first merchant ship to be sunk by air power, succumbing to an attack by Zeppelin bombs. It is one of only three ships to be sunk by the airships in the entire conflict.

FEBRUARY 7

AIR WAR, *WESTERN FRONT*
The British deploy their first single-seater fighter squadron.

FEBRUARY 9

BALKANS, *ALBANIA*

The evacuation of the remnants of the Serbian Army from various ports in Albania is completed.

FEBRUARY 11

POLITICS, *GERMANY*

Kaiser Wilhelm II permits German submarines to attack armed steamers, but forbids attacks on passenger liners. The order comes into force on the 29th. On the same day it is agreed to postpone the imminent offensive against the French at Verdun on the Western Front due to rain and snow. It is rescheduled for the 21st.

FEBRUARY 14

POLITICS, *BRITAIN/FRANCE*

Britain and France confirm that there can be no peace with Germany without the restoration and guarantee of Belgian neutrality. Their military planners agree to launch their Somme offensive on July 1.

FEBRUARY 16

MIDDLE EAST, *ARMENIA*

In a continuation of his winter offensive, Russian General Nikolai Yudenich captures the Turkish-held city of Erzerum and continues his advance.

FEBRUARY 21

WESTERN FRONT, *VERDUN*

The German offensive is heralded by a nine-hour barrage from 1240 artillery pieces, which fire both high-explosive and gas shells against an eight-mile (13-km) section of the French front line to the north of Verdun. This is followed by an advance by 6000

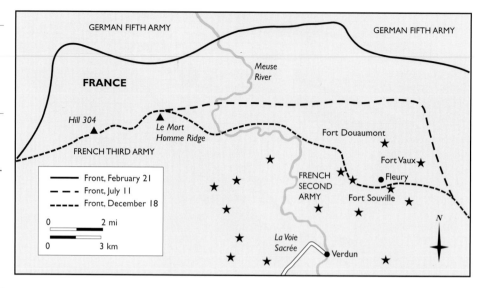

specialist German assault troops, some equipped with flame-throwers. These lead the way forward for the main force of some 140,000 men from Crown Prince William's Fifth Army. The French lose some ground in the face of these attacks.

▲ *Verdun, which lasted from February until November, was an attritional struggle and both the French and German forces suffered heavy casualties.*

▼ *German infantrymen advance in open order at the beginning of Verdun.*

FEBRUARY 22

POLITICS, *RUSSIA*

In an ill-judged move, the Russian high command appoints General Aleksey Kuropatkin as commander-in-chief of the North Front. The cautious Kuropatkin, aged 68, is a veteran of the Russo-Japanese War (1904–05). He will keep his post until July.

WESTERN FRONT, *VERDUN*

The French command agrees to create what becomes known as *La Voie Sacrée* ("The Sacred Way"). This is a narrow road stretching from Bar-Le-Duc to Verdun, and becomes the main

◀ *German artillerymen operating one of the 128 eight-inch (21-cm) howitzers deployed against Verdun.*

▲ French reinforcements are rushed to Verdun along the vital supply route known as La Voie Sacrée *("The Sacred Way").*

route for supplies and reinforcements entering Verdun. The road comes under frequent German artillery fire but damage is quickly repaired by teams of laborers earmarked for the vital task. Around Verdun itself German attacks, which gain some ground, are met by fierce French counterattacks.

FEBRUARY 23

POLITICS, *BRITAIN*
The government forms the Blockade Ministry under Lord Robert Cecil. Its role will be to coordinate efforts to cut off the flow of supplies by sea to Germany.

POLITICS, *PORTUGAL*
Acting on a British request, the government interns more than 70 German vessels and refuses German demands that they be released.

FEBRUARY 24

POLITICS, *RUSSIA*
The Russian high command decides to launch an offensive on the Eastern Front to relieve some of the pressure on the French, who are fighting for their lives at Verdun. The French

commander-in-chief, General Joseph Joffre, confirms the necessity of an immediate offensive on March 2.

WESTERN FRONT, *VERDUN*
The Germans cut through the second line of French defenses around Verdun and advance on the third, where one of the city's key positions, Fort Douaumont, lies.

FEBRUARY 25

WESTERN FRONT, *VERDUN*
One of the key French positions at Verdun, Fort Douaumont, just four miles (6 km) from the city, falls to German troops. Late in the day General Henri-Philippe Pétain takes charge of the French forces at Verdun.

Pétain re-invigorates the French troops and relies on defensive tactics rather than costly counterattacks, issuing the slogan *"Ils ne passeront pas"* ("They Shall Not Pass"). He also improves the flow of supplies to the front, brings better coordination to French artillery fire, and institutes a system whereby units suffering heavy casualties are withdrawn from the fighting to rest and recuperate. French morale does not break.

TECHNOLOGY, *FRANCE*
The French Army requests 400 tanks from manufacturer Schneider.

MARSHAL HENRI-PHILIPPE PÉTAIN

Pétain (1856–1951), who was commissioned in the late 1870s, saw no active service until World War I. However, in 1914 he was rapidly promoted, reaching the rank of general. His greatest moment came in 1916, when he was placed in charge of the French forces facing the Germans at Verdun.

Pétain, who excelled at defensive fighting, saw that the situation was critical but not irretrievable. He immediately set about improving the conditions for his troops: the flow of supplies and reinforcements to Verdun was increased; units were rotated into and out of the trenches on a more regular basis; and the strength of his artillery was increased. These reforms improved French morale and enabled them to hold the Germans and go over to the offensive.

In 1917 the French Army mutinied and Pétain, who had an excellent rapport with soldiers, was made commander-in-chief. He used harsh discipline against ringleaders but also introduced reforms, effectively ensuring that the army would fight on. In 1918 Pétain's defensive skills bore fruit during the defeat of the German spring offensive.

After World War I he was promoted to the rank of marshal. In 1940, after France had been invaded, Pétain was made prime minister and signed an armistice with Germany. Between 1940 and 1944 Pétain was head of the collaborationist Vichy regime in southern France, although it seems unlikely that he wielded much power due to the onset of senility. In 1945 he was convicted of treason and sentenced to death by the provisional government of Charles de Gaulle, who had also served at Verdun. This was later commuted to life imprisonment.

FEBRUARY 28

WESTERN FRONT, *VERDUN*
To add to the miseries of the French and German troops at Verdun, a sudden thaw turns the shell-blasted battlefield into a morass.

FEBRUARY 29

POLITICS, *GERMANY*
The German chancellor, Theobald von Bethmann Hollweg, suggests to Kaiser Wilhelm II that an unrestricted submarine campaign will precipitate US involvement in the war.

WESTERN FRONT, *ITALY*
Italian soldier Benito Mussolini is promoted to the rank of corporal for his good service record.

MARCH 2

POLITICS, *BRITAIN*
The government announces that all singled men aged 18–41 are liable for compulsory military service.

POLITICS, *GERMANY*
Germany's military planners inform several of their army commanders in occupied France and Belgium that they are to create a body of 50,000 forced laborers.

WESTERN FRONT, *VERDUN*
One of the French defenders of Fort Vaux, Captain Charles de Gaulle, is wounded and captured by the Germans. Along with Fort Douaumont, Vaux is one of the city's key defenses.

MARCH 4

POLITICS, *GERMANY*
Admiral Alfred von Tirpitz, secretary of state for the navy, fails to convince Kaiser Wilhelm II and his advisers that the need for unrestricted submarine warfare is overwhelming. Tirpitz feels that his position is undermined.

▼ **Le Mort Homme** *Ridge ("Dead Man" Ridge) at Verdun shows the results of prolonged artillery fire.*

MARCH 6

POLITICS, *BRITAIN*
The government forms the Women's National Land Service Corps to boost agricultural production and free male farm workers for military service.

WESTERN FRONT, *VERDUN*
The Germans open a new offensive to the northwest of the city. While the fighting around Fort Vaux continues, the Germans attempt to capture *Le Mort Homme* Ridge ("Dead Man" Ridge) and Hill 304.

MARCH 9

POLITICS, *GERMANY*
Declares war on Portugal, which is refusing to release interned German vessels. Austria-Hungary follows on the 15th.

▲ *French troops shelter in one of trenches dug on Verdun's* **Le Mort Homme** *Ridge ("Dead Man" Ridge).*

MARCH 11

WESTERN FRONT, *ITALY*
The Italians launch the Fifth Battle of the Isonzo. The attack against the Austro-Hungarians is in part designed to help relieve some of the pressure on the French at Verdun.

However, the Italian offensive is dogged by poor weather and their lack of artillery. Little ground is won

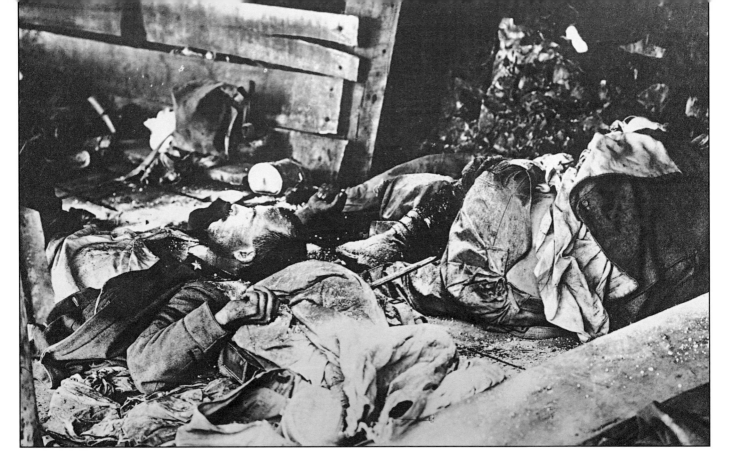

▲ *Italian troops killed in the fighting along the Isonzo River on the border between Austria-Hungary and Italy.*

or lost by either side in the battle and the fighting in the sector dies down at the end of the month.

MIDDLE EAST, *MESOPOTAMIA*
Following his botched handling of his forces during the Battle of Dujaila Redoubt on the 8th, General Fenton Aylmer is replaced as commander of the Tigris Corps, which is tasked with breaking the Turkish siege of Kut-el-Amara, by General George Gorringe. The British advance is delayed and does not recommence until April 5.

MARCH 12

POLITICS, *GERMANY*
Admiral Alfred von Tirpitz, head of the navy, resigns. He believes he has not been fully consulted over the role and deployment of the navy's increasingly important submarine fleet.

MARCH 15

POLITICS, *UNITED STATES*
President Woodrow Wilson orders General John Pershing to invade northern Mexico to track down rebel leader Pancho Villa. Villa's rebels have

▶ *Russian prisoners indicate the German victory at Lake Naroch. Some 120,000 were killed, wounded, or captured.*

executed 16 mining engineers, all US nationals, at Santa Isabel and attacked Columbus, New Mexico. Despite fighting a number of skirmishes, Pershing fails to capture Villa.

MARCH 18

EASTERN FRONT, *RUSSIA*
The Russians launch a major offensive designed to aid the French, who are

struggling to halt the major German offensive on Verdun. The Russian attack, which becomes known as the First Battle of Lake Naroch, involves a two-pronged advance into the Lake Naroch and Vilna areas. These are heralded by more than 1200 artillery pieces bombarding German positions for eight hours. The Russian Second Army then moves against the German

MARCH 19

Tenth Army. Some 350,000 Russian soldiers face just 75,000 German troops supported by 300 guns.

Despite their numerical superiority, the Russians make little progress – gaining just one mile (1.6 km) across a front of two miles (3.2 km) for the loss of 15,000 men. So heavy are their losses, the Russians resort to attacking under cover of darkness. However, subsequent Russian advances become bogged down in waterlogged terrain. The battle rages until mid-April.

AIR WAR, *WESTERN FRONT*
German fighter pilot Ernst Udet gains the first of his 62 confirmed victories in air combat.

MARCH 19

MIDDLE EAST, *EGYPT*
General Sir Archibald Murray replaces General Sir John Maxwell as commander of the British forces in Egypt.

MARCH 22

SEA WAR, *ATLANTIC*
U-68 becomes the first submarine to be sunk by depth-charge attack following an engagement with the British *Farnborough* off the coast of southwest Ireland. The *Farnborough* is a Q-ship, an armed vessel that is disguised to look like an ordinary merchant ship.

APRIL 4

EASTERN FRONT, *RUSSIA*
General Aleksey Brusilov, one of Russia most capable commanders, is placed in charge of the Southwest Front, which comprises four armies.

APRIL 5

SEA WAR, *ADRIATIC*
In the largest sea evacuation to date, warships complete the removal of Serbia forces from Albania – some 260,000 troops. Remarkably, there are no Serbian losses. However, 19 French, British, and Italian warships have been sunk in air and submarine attacks.

APRIL 6

MIDDLE EAST, *MESOPOTAMIA*
The British relief force making for Kut-el-Amara makes slow progress. At the First Battle of Sannaiyat, some 16 miles (24 km) east of Kut, the Turks are forced to retreat just 500 yards (450 m), but the British suffer heavy casualties and are little nearer to

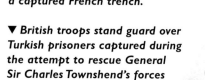

▲ *A lone German infantryman at Verdun keeps watch over Fort Vaux, one of the city's key defenses, from the remains of a captured French trench.*

▼ *British troops stand guard over Turkish prisoners captured during the attempt to rescue General Sir Charles Townshend's forces besieged by the Turks at Kut-el-Amara.*

their objective. A renewal of the fighting at Sannaiyat on the 9th sees the British lose their hard-won gains.

APRIL 9

WESTERN FRONT, *VERDUN*
The Germans launch a major offensive to the northwest of Verdun, against the high ground. Most of the attacks are repulsed by the French but the Germans capture front-line trenches on *Le Mort Homme* Ridge ("Dead Man" Ridge). General Henri-Philippe Pétain tells his troops: *"Courage, on les aura"* – "Courage, we'll get them."

APRIL 11

BALKANS, *CORFU*
The Serbian Army sets sail to join the ever-growing forces stationed in Salonika, Greece.

APRIL 14

EASTERN FRONT, *RUSSIA*
The Russian offensive around Lake Naroch ends. The battle, which began in mid-March, has resulted in an enormous Russian casualty list, some 122,000 men, but has produced few tangible results. The outnumbered Germans list 20,000 losses. Czar Nicholas II, who now formulates Russia's war strategy, meets with General Aleksey Brusilov, who agrees to launch a major summer offensive.

▼ *A German sentry moves a party of Russian machine-gunners captured at the Battle of Lake Naroch.*

▲ *Units of the Serbian Army arrive in Salonika, Greece, following their recent evacuation from Albania.*

APRIL 15

▲ *A British aircraft is readied to drop supplies to the garrison at Kut-el-Amara.*

Brusilov informs his four army commanders to prepare for a major attack by May 11. He tells them that they can expect no reinforcements.

APRIL 15

MIDDLE EAST, *MESOPOTAMIA*
British aircraft begin dropping food supplies to the besieged garrison of Kut-el-Amara. The garrison's commander, General Sir Charles Townshend, has stated that his stocks of food will be exhausted by the 29th.

The British column heading for Kut-el-Amara has been repulsed by the Turks the previous day.

APRIL 18

MIDDLE EAST, *ARMENIA*
Russia forces capture the Turkish Black Sea port of Trebizond, marking a key moment in their ongoing offensive.

APRIL 20

ESPIONAGE, *IRELAND*
Roger Casement, a supporter of Irish independence from Britain, lands from a German submarine with weapons

for the nationalists. He is captured on the 21st and later charged with high treason. He is convicted on June 29 and executed on July 3.

APRIL 21

POLITICS, *IRELAND*
Irish nationalists rebel against British rule. The rebellion, which becomes known as the Easter Rising, centers on Dublin, where the insurgents take

▼ *The aftermath of the fighting in Dublin, where British troops put down an uprising by Irish nationalists.*

▶ Members of the British garrison of Kut-el-Amara photographed after they have been released from Turkish captivity following an exchange of prisoners.

▼ Karl Liebknecht addresses a crowd of German workers in Berlin. Liebknecht formed the Spartacus League, which opposed the continuation of the war.

over and fortify several of the city's public buildings. The British declare martial law and their troops quickly recapture nationalist-held buildings.

The uprising ends on May 1. More than a dozen captured nationalists will be tried and later executed by the British. Seventy-nine receive prison terms. However, British fears that Irish troops fighting on the Western Front might be adversely affected by the rebellion prove unfounded.

APRIL 23

MIDDLE EAST, *MESOPOTAMIA*
With his food virtually exhausted and the advance of the relief force stalled, the commander of the British garrison at Kut-el-Amara, General Sir Charles Townshend, asks permission to begin surrender discussions with the Turks.

APRIL 25

SEA WAR, *NORTH SEA*
Four German battlecruisers shell the ports of Great Yarmouth and Lowestoft on the east coast of England for 20 minutes, causing around 20 mainly civilian casualties. At Great Yarmouth the German warships are forced to withdraw following the sudden arrival of British naval forces.

APRIL 29

MIDDLE EAST, *MESOPOTAMIA*
The British at Kut-el-Amara surrender. Some 13,000 are taken prisoner. Around 2500 sick and wounded are released by the Turks but the rest march into captivity. Some 4800 will die due to disease, illness, and neglect.

MAY 1

POLITICS, *GERMANY*
Radical politician Karl Liebknecht, along with Rosa Luxemburg a founder of the communist Spartacus League, is arrested during an antiwar protest by 10,000 Berlin workers.

ESPIONAGE, *HOLLAND*
Dutch-national Margaretha Zelle, who performs as an exotic dancer with the stage name of Mata Hari ("Eye of the Day"), is allegedly recruited as a spy by the Germans.

WESTERN FRONT, *VERDUN*
General Henri-Philippe Pétain is promoted to the command of France's Center Army Group. His replacement at Verdun is General Robert Nivelle, who is considered to be a more aggressive figure. Nivelle plans to launch major counterattacks against the Germans around Verdun.

◀ Mata Hari, the Dutch-born exotic dancer, was allegedly a spy for the Germans, although doubts have been expressed over the truth of the accusation.

MAY 2

MAY 2

BALKANS, *GREECE*
French forces, part of the large multi-national force building up in Salonika, advance to and occupy Florina close to the Serbian border and some 25 miles (40 km) from the enemy-occupied city of Monastir. Other troops are advancing with the French.

AIR WAR, *BRITAIN*
A raid by eight German Zeppelins against targets along the east coast causes 39 casualties. However, one of the raiders, *L20*, is wrecked by a fierce storm near Stavanger, Norway, as it is returning to its home base on the 3rd.

MAY 5

MIDDLE EAST, *ARABIA*
Backed by the British, Hussein, the Grand Sherif of Mecca, begins an uprising in the Turkish province. Hussein commands a force of 50,000 men, but has just 10,000 rifles. The Turkish presence in Arabia numbers 10,000. An early attack by his son Feisal on Medina is repulsed. However, the rebellion forces the Turks to withdraw some of their troops facing the British in Egypt to protect their communications.

▲ French colonial troops from what is now Vietnam prepare to advance deeper into Greece from their camp in Salonika.

▼ British vessels at anchor in the southern Italian port of Taranto. They are part of the Otranto barrage across the Adriatic.

MAY 9

POLITICS, *BRITAIN/FRANCE*
The British and French, with the agreement of Russia, sign the secret Sykes–Picot Agreement. It is named after its two chief negotiators, Britain's Sir Mark Sykes and France's Georges Picot. The convention agrees plans for the dismemberment of the Turkish Empire after an allied victory. Turkish-held territories across the Middle East are to be divided between and administered by the various allies. The agreement is made known to Italy in August, and it is agreed in 1917 that Italy will also receive Middle East lands.

MAY 13

MIDDLE EAST, *ARABIA*
In the first success of their rebellion against the Turks, Arabs fighting for

◄ Italian troops occupy a mountain-top post in the Trentino, where the Austro-Hungarians launched a major attack in mid-May.

▶ *An Austro-Hungarian trench mortar opens fire on the Italians in the Trentino.*

Hussein, Grand Sherif of Mecca, capture the holy city of Mecca. A further Turkish defeat follows on the 16th, when the city of Jeddah falls following naval and air attacks.

SEA WAR, *ADRIATIC*
The Austro-Hungarian submarine *U-6* becomes the only confirmed victim of the warships manning the Otranto barrage. The barrage comprises a semi-continuous line of small vessels stretching across the southern Adriatic. Its role is to deny German and Austro-Hungarian warships access into and egress out of the sea.

MAY 14

POLITICS, *CHINA*
The government agrees to supply France with 200,000 laborers to support its war effort.

MAY 15

WESTERN FRONT, *ITALY*
The Austro-Hungarians launch a major offensive in the Trentino region on the

north Italian border, which catches the Italians unprepared. The long-planned attack is opened on a 20-mile (32-km) front and, despite the mountainous terrain, the Austro-Hungarians make some progress, chiefly thanks to their specialist mountain troops. The Austro-Hungarian Eleventh and Third Armies, commanded by Archduke Eugene,

smash through the lines of General Roberto Brusati's Italian First Army in the next few days. On the 20th the Italian commander-in-chief, General Luigi Cadorna, orders the men of the First Army to fight to the death.

MAY 17

POLITICS, *UNITED STATES*
President Woodrow Wilson announces that the US may have to intervene in the war and should certainly have a role in any peace-making process.

MAY 20

POLITICS, *ITALY*
The Italian government, which is

▼ *Italian troops killed by Austro-Hungarian artillery fire in the Trentino.*

facing a crisis in the Trentino region due to an ongoing Austro-Hungarian offensive, asks the Russians to launch an immediate diversionary attack on the Eastern Front.

MAY 25

POLITICS, *BRITAIN*
The Military Service Act comes into force. All men between the ages of 18–41 are liable for military service and those previously rejected on whatever grounds are to be re-examined.

MAY 26

WESTERN FRONT, *ITALY*
The Austro-Hungarians maintain the momentum of their offensive in the Trentino by shifting the focus of their attacks toward the Asiago Plateau. Its

▲ *The British battlecruiser* Queen Mary *disappears in a cloud of smoke after being hit by shells from the German Derfflinger at Jutland.*

◄ *Admiral Sir John Jellicoe, commander of the British Home Fleet at Jutland.*

battlecruisers led by Admiral Sir David Beatty sets sail from Rosyth. The British plan to rendezvous at the Jutland Bank off the coast of Denmark. The German High Seas Fleet does not set sail until the 31st.

MAY 31

SEA WAR, *NORTH SEA*
The Battle of Jutland, fought between the British Home Fleet and the German High Seas Fleet, begins in the early afternoon, when rival light cruisers on picket duty spot each

capture will open the way into the lowlands of northern Italy. The Italians abandon the plateau on the 29th. However, the Austro-Hungarian offensive is slowing due to the problems of moving supporting artillery through the mountainous terrain.

MAY 27

POLITICS, *UNITED STATES*
President Woodrow Wilson suggests the creation of an international body with the authority to maintain peace and the freedom of the seas.

MAY 30

SEA WAR, *NORTH SEA*
Forewarned by the intelligence-gatherers of Room 40, the British Home Fleet puts to sea to intercept a major sortie by the German High Seas Fleet. The larger part of the Home Fleet, commanded by Admiral Sir John Jellicoe, sails from its bases at Scapa Flow and Invergordon. A strong force of

other and open fire. The main action opens shortly before 1600 hours when Admiral Sir David Beatty's battle-cruisers open fire on German Admiral Franz von Hipper's battlecruisers. Beatty attempts to sail south to cut Hipper off from his base in Germany. Hipper undertakes a withdrawal to the southeast, hoping to lure Beatty into an unequal struggle against the main part of the High Seas Fleet.

During this running fight Beatty is at a disadvantage as the low sun in the west highlights his own ships, while the German battlecruisers are partly hidden by haze and mist. In the ensuing action Beatty comes off worst: the *Indefatigable* is struck by salvoes from the *Von der Tann*, falls out of the line, and then disappears in a massive explosion. Twenty-five

minutes later, the *Derfflinger* lands a salvo on the *Queen Mary*, which is ripped apart by an internal explosion – only nine men survive of a crew of more than 1200.

Beatty's own flagship, the *Lion*, also suffers severe damage, and his battle-cruisers are perilously close to the battleships of the High Sea Fleet. He orders his depleted force to turn away from the German fleet and head north, where the British Home Fleet is in position. His withdrawal is covered by ships commanded by Rear Admiral Sir Horace Hood.

Meanwhile, Admiral Sir John Jellicoe has sent three battlecruisers to aid Beatty in his withdrawal. At 1735 these open fire on Hipper's ships, badly damaging the *Lützow* and hitting two light cruisers, the *Wiesbaden* and *Pillau*. Jellicoe, whose battle plans are made on poor and intermittent intelligence from his advance warships, now attempts a maneuver that will place his battleships in a position that will give them an enormous advantage over the main German fleet – in effect cutting the Germans off from their bases and allowing the British fleet to pound their warships to destruction.

The High Seas Fleet faces a line of British warships some nine miles (14 km) long, but continues the fight. One of the first ships to succumb is Hood's flagship, the *Invincible*, which is blown apart by the *Derfflinger* and *Lützow* at a

range of 10,500 yards (9500 m). The German fleet's commander, Admiral Reinhard Sheer, sensing the danger, opts to execute a turn away from the British, which will allow him to escape. However, Jellicoe is equal to this move and again attempts to block the German line of withdrawal.

To gain time for his main fleet, Sheer orders his light units, chiefly torpedo-boats and destroyers, and Hipper's battlecruisers – despite the odds – to attack. Sheer's attempt to escape under the cover of darkness is successful, but his fleet has several losses: the old bat-tleship *Pommern* is sunk by a torpedo; two light cruisers - the *Frauenlob* and *Rostock* – also sink; and the *Elbing* is sliced in half by the battleship *Posen* as it attempts to cross the bow of the larger ship. The battlecruiser *Lützow* has to be abandoned and is later sunk by a torpedo to prevent it from falling into British hands.

Nightfall effectively ends the Battle of Jutland and the German fleet is able to return through the minefields that

▼ *The British battlecruiser* Indefatigable *sinks after being hit by the German battlecruiser* Von der Tann *at Jutland. The British warship was blown apart.*

intelligence between ships and the poor design of some of the vessels, which led to several suffering devastating internal explosions after being hit by German shells.

◄ *Warships of the German High Seas Fleet head out into the North Sea to confront the British at Jutland.*

▼ *Russian troops advance through barbed wire under fire during the opening moves of General Aleksey Brusilov's offensive.*

protect the waters around its bases. However, one battleship, the *Ostfriesland*, is damaged by striking a mine on the morning of June 1.

In Germany, Jutland, or the Battle of the Skaggerak, is seen as a victory as three British battleships, three cruisers, and eight destroyers have

▼ *Damage inflicted on the German battlecruiser* Seydlitz *by the British during the Battle of Jutland.*

been sunk for the loss of a single battleship, as well as four cruisers and five destroyers.

However, the British fleet, although mauled, is still able to fight on and make sure that the High Seas Fleet remains bottled up in its home ports. The British handling of the battle is seen as poor, although they came close to inflicting a severe defeat on Sheer. Most concern is expressed over the badly-handled transfer of orders and

JUNE 1

MIDDLE EAST, *ARMENIA*

The Turks begin planning an attack against General Nikolai Yudenich's Russian forces. The operation is devised by Enver Pasha, the Turkish commander, and calls for a broad-front offensive. The Third Army under Vehip Pasha is ordered to advance along the coast of the Black Sea, while Ahmet Izzim Pasha's new Second Army makes for the Russian-held city of Bitlis. However, the Russian commander,

General Nikolay Yudenich, moves to counter the threat when the operation starts at the beginning of July.

JUNE 2

WESTERN FRONT, *BELGIUM*

A German attack against the Ypres salient, which becomes known as the Battle of Mount Sorrel, makes initial progress, but many of their gains are lost due to Canadian counterattacks.

SEA WAR, *NORTH SEA*

It is announced that the British Home Fleet is again ready for action despite its recent action at Jutland.

JUNE 3

BALKANS, *SALONIKA*

The British and French declare a state of siege in Salonika and remove all the region's Greek officials from their posts. They demand that the possibly pro-German Greek government is changed and its army mobilizes.

JUNE 4

EASTERN FRONT, *RUSSIA*

Russian forces led by General Aleksey Brusilov, the commander-in-chief of the Southwest Front, launch a major offensive against the Austro-Hungarian and German armies in former Russian Poland and Austria-Hungary itself. The starting date for the offensive had been planned for June 15 following

◀ *The territory regained by the Russians during the Brusilov Offensive, their most successful attack of the war.*

▲ *Serbian artillery in action during the fighting in Salonika, Greece. A spent shell case is being ejected from the gun.*

recent Austro-Hungarian successes against the Italians, whose high command has requested a Russian effort to draw Austro-Hungarian troops away from the fighting in Italy.

The Russian attack, which becomes known as the Brusilov Offensive, had been scheduled to coincide with the British onslaught along the Western Front's Somme River sector. Both the British and Russian attacks had been designed to relieve some of the pressure on the French at Verdun.

Brusilov plans to advance on a broad front of some 200 miles (320 km). His Third and Eighth Armies are ordered to strike against the Austro-Hungarian Fourth Army to the south of the Pripet Marshes. Farther south the Russian Seventh Army is directed against the Austro-Hungarian Seventh Army.

The operation is heralded by a bombardment from close to 2000 Russian artillery pieces and early progress is excellent, particularly in the north and south, where the Austro-Hungarians virtually collapse. Only in the center, where the Russians face German units, is the advance stalled. The battle continues into September.

JUNE 5

SEA WAR, *NORTH SEA*

The British cruiser *Hampshire* is sunk by a mine laid by the German

▲ *The remains of the aircraft of German ace Max Immelmann, who was shot down and killed over France on June 18.*

submarine *U-75* as it is making its way to Russia. Among the many dead is Secretary of War Lord Kitchener, who was to meet with Czar Nicholas II to discuss the flow of supplies between Russia and Britain. The incident is blamed on rough seas, poor mine-sweeping operations, and the ill-coordinated rescue operation.

JUNE 7

WESTERN FRONT, *VERDUN*
After weeks of bitter fighting and at high cost the Germans capture Fort Vaux from the French.

JUNE 8

WESTERN FRONT, *ITALY*
The Austro-Hungarians withdraw two divisions from their forces committed to the on-going Trentino offensive. They are rushed to the Eastern Front, where the Russian offensive led by General Aleksey Brusilov is making considerable territorial gains.

JUNE 10

POLITICS, *NEW ZEALAND*
The government passes a bill permitting compulsory military service.
POLITICS, *GERMANY*
The chief of the General Staff, General Erich von Falkenhayn, orders four German divisions in northern Russia and five from Verdun on the Western Front to move by rail to reinforce the defense against Brusilov's Offensive, which is close to totally defeating the

Austro-Hungarians. More will follow – 15 divisions will have been sent to the Eastern Front by mid-September.

JUNE 17

WESTERN FRONT, *ITALY*
The Austro-Hungarians call a stop to their Trentino offensive in the face of a mounting Italian counterattack, which began on the 16th. Backed by 800 artillery pieces, the Italians make steady but unspectacular gains. The campaign has cost the Italians 147,000 men, including 40,000 taken prisoner. The Austro-Hungarians, who pull back to more defensible positions over the next few days, admit to losses totaling 81,000, including 26,000 prisoners.
AIR WAR, *WESTERN FRONT*
Henri Navarre, France's first fighter ace, is shot down and badly wounded. He never takes to the air again. The following day German ace Max Immelmann is killed in air combat. He has 15 combat victories to his credit.

JUNE 23

WESTERN FRONT, *VERDUN*
There is intense German pressure against the French defenses around Verdun. The attacks concentrate on the French positions to the northeast of the city, where the Germans, advancing between Forts Douaumont and Vaux, move ever closer to Fleury and Fort Souville. Their capture would effectively seal the fate of Verdun.

▶ *Italian artillerymen attempt to place a three-inch (75-mm) gun on the summit of a mountain in the Trentino to help block the Austro-Hungarian offensive.*

JUNE 24

WESTERN FRONT, *SOMME*
The British begin their bombardment of the German trenches. Some 2000 British artillery pieces fire an estimated 1.7 million shells on the first day. However, as many as a third fail to explode, and many others are too light to inflict much damage on the German barbed wire or their strongly-constructed defenses. The barrage continues over the following week, further alerting the Germans to the impending offensive.

JUNE 27

POLITICS, *GREECE*
Under pressure from both Britain and France, the Greek government agrees to mobilize its armed forces.

JULY 1

WESTERN FRONT, *SOMME*
The British offensive begins at 0730 hours on an intensely hot day following the firing of 224,000 shells in an hour. Shortly before the advance begins, 10 huge underground mines are exploded beneath the German trenches, burying many of their occupants. Both the British commanders and the ordinary soldiers, most of whom are enthusiastic volunteers, believe that the first stage of the offensive, which becomes known as the Battle of Albert, will be an overwhelming success.

▼ *A British mine explodes underneath the German trenches near Beaumont Hamel at the beginning of the Somme attack.*

▲ *A German aerial photograph records the devastated remains of the French-held Fort Souville outside Verdun.*

The advance takes place along a front of some 25 miles (40 km). There are early gains to the east and southeast of the town of Albert: Montauban and Mametz, where the British Fourth Army led by General Henry Rawlinson attacks, and west of Péronne, where French colonial troops make some progress.

However, progress to the north of Albert is nothing short of disastrous. The attacking British infantry are confronted by uncut German barbed wire and intact defenses, particularly around Beaumont Hamel and Thiepval. Advancing at a walk and burdened

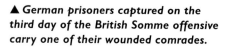

▲ *German prisoners captured on the third day of the British Somme offensive carry one of their wounded comrades.*

down with equipment, they meet a wall of machine-gun fire. By the end of the day British casualties total more than 57,000, of which 19,000 are killed. It is the greatest loss ever suffered by the British Army in a single day's combat. German losses are thought to be around 8000 men.

The British also find it difficult to rush reinforcements up to the exhausted troops holding what ground has been gained. There is poor communication between troops in advance positions and their head-quarters. German counterattacks are frequently successful. The British attempt to continue their offensive.

JULY 2

WESTERN FRONT, *VERDUN*
General Erich von Falkenhayn, chief of the German General Staff, orders the reduction of the German offensive at Verdun and the transfer of troops and artillery pieces to the Somme River, where the British have recently launched a major offensive. The fighting at Verdun, although less intense for the moment, continues.

SEA WAR, *ADRIATIC*
Austro-Hungarian agents in Taranto, southern Italy, use explosives to capsize the Italian battleship *Leonardo da Vinci*, killing 248.

JULY 4

POLITICS, *GERMANY*
Admiral Reinhard Scheer concludes his report to Kaiser Wilhelm II on the recent Battle of Jutland with the

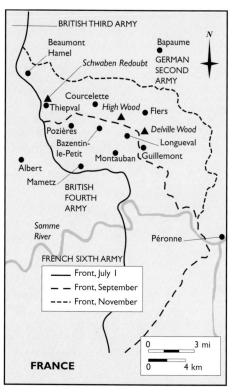

The map shows the Battle of the Somme area. Labels include:

BRITISH THIRD ARMY
Beaumont Hamel
Bapaume
Schwaben Redoubt
GERMAN SECOND ARMY
Courcelette
Thiepval
High Wood
Flers
Pozières
Delville Wood
Bazentin-le-Petit
Longueval
Albert
Montauban
Guillemont
Mametz
BRITISH FOURTH ARMY
Somme River
Péronne
FRENCH SIXTH ARMY

Front, July 1
Front, September
Front, November

0   3 mi
0   4 km

FRANCE

▲ *The Battle of the Somme, designed by the British to aid the French at Verdun and possibly knock Germany out of the war, produced huge casualties.*

◄ *The execution of Serbian guerrillas by Austro-Hungarians.*

statement that "A victorious end can only be achieved by using the submarines against British trade."

JULY 5

BALKANS, *SERBIA*

Serbian guerrilla units begin operating against the Austro-Hungarian occupation forces. Similar developments also take place in Montenegro.

JULY 7

POLITICS, *BRITAIN*

Liberal politician David Lloyd George becomes secretary of war following the recent death of Lord Kitchener.

JULY 10

EASTERN FRONT, *RUSSIA*

The Russian authorities announce that they have captured some 300,000 German and Austro-Hungarian prisoners since the opening of the Brusilov Offensive on May 4.

JULY 11

MIDDLE EAST, *MESOPOTAMIA*

General Sir Frederick Maude takes over the 95,000-strong Tigris Corps from General George Gorringe. Maude will be later promoted to command all of the British forces in the region (August 28). Before contemplating any renewal of the advance on Turkish-held Baghdad, he begins to build up his fleet of river steamers, which are vital for keeping his forces supplied in the field. He is anxious to avoid the logistical problems that dogged the first advance on the city.

JULY 14-20

WESTERN FRONT, *SOMME*

Four British divisions, preceded by a short barrage, achieve surprise,

▶ *David Lloyd George was made the British secretary of war in July after the death of Lord Kitchener.*

▲ *A British supply depot replenishes the ammunition stocks of an infantry unit on the Somme.*

▼ *The beginning of the Somme offensive – British infantrymen move forward slowly and methodically into a maelstrom of German machine-gun fire.*

taking 4000 German prisoners along with the villages of Longueval and Bazentin-le-Petit. On the following day the South African Brigade, just 3000 men, attacks and secures most of Delville Wood. The brigade is surrounded and is faced by three German divisions but manages to hold out until it is relieved on the 20th. The brigade has just 778 survivors. Delville Wood is abandoned but is later recaptured and held.

JULY 19

MIDDLE EAST, *EGYPT*
Turkish troops, some 15,000 men commanded by German General Kress von Kressenstein, launch their second attack against the British-held Suez Canal. They advance to within 10 miles (16 km) of Romani, a rail junction, and then establish defensive positions.

JULY 23

WESTERN FRONT, *SOMME*
The British attempt to restart their offensive in an attack that becomes known as the Battle of Pozières Ridge. Australian and New Zealand troops lead the advance toward Pozières to the northeast of Albert. The village is secured by the 25th, but the fighting then degenerates into stalemate.

JULY 25

MIDDLE EAST, *ARMENIA*
Russian General Nikolai Yudenich inflicts a major defeat on Vehip Pasha's Turkish Third Army at Erzincan, thereby blunting one of the two main attacks launched by Enver Pasha.

▲ *The first contingent of Russian troops to arrive in Salonika parades through the streets of a Greek town.*

▼ *British intelligence officers sift through the wreckage of a German Zeppelin airship shot down near London.*

Yudenich now turns his attention to Ahmet Izzim Pasha's Second Army, which is advancing on Bitlis.

JULY 29

POLITICS, *GERMANY*
Germany, Austria-Hungary, and Bulgaria agree to take direct military action against Romania.

AUGUST 1

WESTERN FRONT, *SOMME*
The British offensive is a month old and their casualties total 158,000 plus another 40,000 elsewhere on the Western Front. German losses on the Somme amount to 160,000 men.
BALKANS, *SALONIKA*
Some 5000 Russian troops arrive in Salonika, thereby contributing to the ever-growing presence in the province. Some 11,000 Italian troops arrive on the 11th.

AUGUST 2

AIR WAR, *BRITAIN*
Sixteen German airships attack London and southeast England. The results are poor due to bad weather

and technical problems. One of the raiders, *SL11*, is shot down by British pilot Lieutenant Leefe Robinson.

AUGUST 4

WESTERN FRONT, *ITALY*
The Italians launch the Sixth Battle of the Isonzo, but the key attack by the Duke of Aosta's Third Army does not begin until the 6th. The main assault opens at 1400 hours, after the Austro-Hungarian front line has been pounded by artillery for nine hours. The Italians gain some ground, chiefly Gorizia, which falls on the 8th.

MIDDLE EAST, *EGYPT*
The Turks commanded by German General Kress von Kressenstein attack the British-held rail junction at Romani, a little to the east of the Suez Canal. The surprise advance makes initial progress but is halted by New Zealand and other mounted forces. Turkish casualties are high in the battle – some 5000 men. The British losses total 1100.

AUGUST 5

MIDDLE EAST, *ARMENIA*
In the only noteworthy success of the Turkish offensive against General Nikolai Yudenich's Russian forces, Mustafa Kemal's corps captures Bitlis and then Mus on the following day. However, these gains will soon be lost.

AUGUST 8

POLITICS, *PORTUGAL*
The Portuguese government agrees to increase its military backing for the war against the Central Powers.

AUGUST 12

EASTERN FRONT, *RUSSIA*
General Aleksey Brusilov announces details of his continuing offensive. He claims to have captured 375,000 German and Austro-Hungarian prisoners as well as more than 400 artillery pieces, 1300 machine guns, and taken 15,000 square miles (38,850 sq km) of territory. Russian casualties total

▲ *Italian mountain troops move forward against the Austro-Hungarians during the fighting along the Isonzo River. The crew of a howitzer waits to advance once the infantry column has passed.*

▼ *Three wounded Turkish prisoners are escorted to the rear by British troops following fighting in the vicinity of the Suez Canal.*

550,000 men. Many of these troops were intensely loyal to Czar Nicholas II, but their replacements are less steadfast in their support for the Russian monarchy.

AUGUST 17

POLITICS, *ROMANIA*
The government agrees to join the war against the Central Powers with the aim of gaining territory.

WESTERN FRONT, *ITALY*
The Italians end the Sixth Battle of the Isonzo, their most successful attack

against the Austro-Hungarians to date. They have won territory and inflicted losses totaling 49,000. Italian casualties number 51,000.

BALKANS, *GREECE*
The Bulgarians launch a pre-emptive attack into the northern Greek region of Macedonia. There are early gains – the town of Florina falls on the 18th – and various enemy forces are pushed back to a line along the Sturma River.

AUGUST 18

SEA WAR, *NORTH SEA*
For one of the last times before its surrender in 1918 the German

▲ *Russian prisoners captured by the Germans during the Brusilov Offensive trudge into captivity.*

High Seas Fleet launches a major attack against Britain. The plan is to shell the port of Sunderland on the east coast of England and lure the British Home Fleet, which will sail from its bases to deal with the threat posed by the High Seas Fleet, into several groups of waiting submarines.

However, one German warship, the *Westfalen*, is torpedoed by a British submarine at the start of the sortie. The British commanders, thanks to their intelligence-gatherers in

▼ *German artillerymen on the Eastern Front lounge by their three-inch (77-mm) field gun awaiting orders. The gun's camouflaged ammunition caisson is nearly empty, suggesting that there has been recent action.*

Room 40, are aware of the attack, and Admiral Sir John Jellicoe has, in fact, already sailed to counter the threat.

AUGUST 19

SEA WAR, *NORTH SEA*
Two British cruisers, the *Nottingham* and *Falmouth*, part of the counter to the recently-launched sortie by the German High Seas Fleet, are sunk by German submarines. Their loss forces the British to break off their confrontation with the High Seas Fleet, which in turn heads for its home ports.

HOME FRONT, *GERMANY*
Coalminers in the Ruhr region go on strike to protest against inflation and shortages of food.

▲ *Serbian machine-gunners hold defensive positions outside the southern Serbian city of Monastir during their advance from Greece.*

◄ *A German submarine watches the Italian merchant ship that it has just intercepted burn. In 1916 such submarines sank 964 vessels of all types. Just 22 submarines were lost.*

▼ *Romanian troops advance into the southern Austro-Hungarian province of Transylvania, where there was a significant ethnic Romanian population. However, the territory captured by the Romanian forces was soon lost to swift counterattacks.*

AUGUST 20

SEA WAR, *MEDITERRANEAN*
The German submarine *U-35* commanded by Lothar von Arnauld de la Perière returns to its base at Cattaro in the Adriatic after a record-breaking 25-day cruise. It has sunk 54 ships, most Italian, in the Mediterranean. Many have been sent to the bottom by gunfire. Its captain will become the most successful submarine commander of all time.

AUGUST 27

POLITICS, *ROMANIA*
The government declares war on Austria-Hungary and mobilizes its armed forces, which immediately invade the Austro-Hungarian province of Transylvania, which has a large ethnic Romanian population. Germany and Turkey come to the aid of their ally and both declare war on Romania over the next few days.

STRATEGY & TACTICS

DEFENSE-IN-DEPTH

By late 1916 Germany's military planners were becoming seriously short of manpower on the Western Front due to recent losses, particularly at Verdun and on the Somme, and their commitments in several other war theaters. One of their solutions to this problem was to give up some territory on the Western Front and fall back to a more easily defensible – and shorter – front line. A shorter front would require few troops to defend it and free those not needed for service elsewhere.

Central to this revised strategy was a new defensive doctrine known as defense-in-depth, which called for a comparatively thinly-held front line, backed by lines of more extensive defenses stretching in depth to several miles. The aim was that the well-fortified but lightly-held front line would delay and break up any enemy attack, allowing time for fresh reserves to be rushed to the threatened sector. With fewer troops in the front line it was believed that the massive preliminary bombardments by the enemy would cause fewer casualties than in the past.

The plan was the brainchild of Marshal Paul von Hindenburg and the defenses were nicknamed after him, although their actual name was the Siegfried Line. Preliminary work on the Hindenburg Line began in late 1916. Its builders took advantage of any favorable high ground. The line, when completed in spring 1917, stretched from Arras, through St. Quentin to Soissons, and shortened the Western Front by some 25 miles (40 km). This contraction allowed around 14 divisions to be withdrawn from the front line.

The line itself consisted of a 600-yard (550-m) forward "outpost zone," which consisted of a series of positions held by a dozen or so men each. These were intended to break up or delay any enemy attack. The second line, the "battle zone," was 2500 yards (2300 m) in depth and contained two trench lines each dotted with prefabricated concrete machine-gun posts with interlocking zones of fire. This was the main line of defense and was held in greater strength. Troops were protected by deep underground bunkers. Both zones were masked by thick belts of barbed wire.

Behind the "battle zone" were one or two "rear zones" 6000 yards (5500 m) in depth in total, where reserves could be mustered for counterattacks if an enemy advance appeared successful.

AUGUST 28

POLITICS, *ITALY*
Declares war on Germany.

AUGUST 29

POLITICS, *GERMANY*
Marshal Paul von Hindenburg replaces General Erich von Falkenhayn as chief of the General Staff. Falkenhayn has been criticized for his offensive against the French at Verdun. It was to have inflicted massive casualties on the French and destroyed their will to fight on. Neither has happened and German casualties are as high as the French. Falkenhayn goes to the Eastern Front, where he takes charge of the Ninth Army. General Eric Ludendorff, Hindenburg's confident, is made his deputy. Both men believe a new strategy is needed on the Western Front – defense-in-depth.

AUGUST 31

POLITICS, *GERMANY*
The government's war minister receives a letter from Marshal Paul von Hindenburg demanding a doubling of

◄ *General Erich von Falkenhayn (center, with cane), the ex-chief of the German General Staff, with Ninth Army officers.*

▲ *German dead lie outside the shell-blasted remains of their machine-gun post near the Somme village of Guillemont.*

ammunition output by May 1917. Hindenburg also requests a three-fold increase in machine-gun and artillery production. He later meets leading industrialists to discuss his armaments needs and shortages of manpower. Hindenburg also presses for the immediate commencement of an unrestricted submarine campaign.

SEPTEMBER 1

POLITICS, *BULGARIA*
The government declares war on Romania.

SEPTEMBER 3

WESTERN FRONT, *SOMME*
Under mounting French pressure and needing to offer aid to Romania, which has recently joined the war, General Sir Douglas Haig agrees to yet another major renewal of the offensive, which has degenerated into a series of localized battles since its beginning.

◄ *While one man keeps watch out of a forward trench, other Bulgarian soldiers eat their rations.*

Supported by a French attack south of Albert, the main British effort is directed against the village of Guille-mont, which is captured by the 20th Division. However, attacks on German positions at High Wood and against the Schwaben Redoubt fail.

BALKANS, *ROMANIA*
German Field Marshal August von Mackensen, commanding a German–Bulgarian–Turkish force known as the Danube Army, invades southern Romania from Bulgaria.

BALKANS, *GREECE*
The troops in Salonika launch a counter-offensive against the Bulgarian forces operating in Macedonia, which they invaded in mid-August. They make early gains and push both Bulgarian and German forces back.

SEPTEMBER 5

WESTERN FRONT, *SOMME*
After two months of fighting, the British, with French support, secure all of the German second-line defenses. However, these were expected to fall in the opening phase of the battle.

111

September 8

WESTERN FRONT, *FRANCE*

Marshal Paul von Hindenburg and his deputy General Erich Ludendorff visit the Western Front, where the German forces are facing heavy fighting at Verdun and the Somme. Both realize that a new Western Front strategy needs to be implemented soon, particularly as German forces are being siphoned off to prosecute campaigns on the Eastern Front and in the Balkans. They finalize a new tactical doctrine, which becomes known as defense-in-depth.

September 13

WESTERN FRONT, *VERDUN*

France's president, Raymond Poincaré, visits the city and bestows on it the Legion of Honor. The French are planning to launch a major counterattack against the Germans.

September 14

WESTERN FRONT, *ITALY*

The Seventh Battle of the Isonzo opens at 0900 hours with the Italian Third Army attacking on a six-mile (10-km) front. The fighting will continue until the 17th. The Italians make some early gains, but bad weather and strong Austro-Hungarian resistance combine to thwart any major progress.

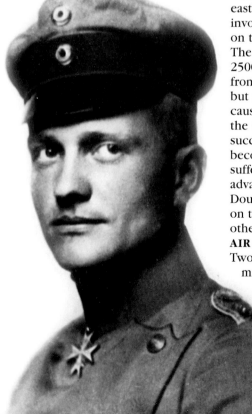

◀ Germany's Baron Manfred von Richthofen, the top-scoring fighter pilot of World War I with 80 victories to his credit.

▲ British troops and a Mark I tank pictured during a lull in the fighting around Flers–Courcelette on the Somme.

September 15

WESTERN FRONT, *SOMME*

The British again attempt to break the deadlock by launching what becomes known as the Battle of Flers–Courcelette, two villages to the northeast of Albert. Fourteen divisions are involved in the battle and tanks appear on the Western Front for the first time. The advance goes well, gaining some 2500 yards along a six-mile (10-km) front. Both villages are captured, but the slow-moving tanks, although causing some initial panic among the German defenders, are far from successful. Many are knocked out, become stuck in mud and ditches, or suffer mechanical failure during the advance. Nevertheless, General Sir Douglas Haig, the British commander on the Western Front, requests that another 1000 tanks be built on the 19th.

AIR WAR, *ADRIATIC*

Two Austro-Hungarian flying-boats make military history by becoming the first aircraft to sink a submarine. Their victim is the French boat *Foucault*.

September 16

WESTERN FRONT, *FRANCE*

Marshal Paul von Hindenburg announces the construction of a massive fortified position, which becomes known as the Hindenburg Line. The construction is to take place between five (8 km) and 30 miles (48 km) behind the existing front line. Work begins on the 23rd.

September 17

BALKANS, *GREECE*

French and Russian troops recapture the Macedonian town of Florina from the Bulgarians. The various contingents are planning to capture Monastir, some 20 miles (32 km) inside Serbia.

MIDDLE EAST, *EGYPT*

Capitalizing on their victory against the Turks at the Battle of Romani in early August, New Zealand and Australian mounted units successfully attack Mazar some 45 miles (72 km) east of Romani. The Turks are forced to retreat some 20 miles (32 km) to positions near El-Arish.

AIR WAR, *WESTERN FRONT*

German pilot Baron Manfred von Richthofen scores his first victory.

SEPTEMBER 16

BALKANS, *ROMANIA*

General Erich von Falkenhayn takes charge of the German Ninth Army. His immediate objective is to force the Romanians out of the Austro-Hungarian province of Transylvania and then secure several passes through the Transylvanian Alps. Their capture will allow his army to push into Romania itself.

SEPTEMBER 26

WESTERN FRONT, *SOMME*

A British attack spearheaded by 13 tanks succeeds in capturing the village of Thiepval. Fighting continues along much of the Somme front, with the British and French making some small gains at high cost over the following weeks. However, thick mud and strong German resistance make progress slow.

MIDDLE EAST, *ARMENIA*

The Turks abandon the recently occupied town of Mus, marking the end of their offensive against General Nikolai Yudenich's Russian forces. It has been a failure as the Russians still control most of Armenia. As the campaigning season ends, the Russians and Turks forces go into winter quarters.

OCTOBER 6

POLITICS, *FRANCE*

The government requisitions uncultivated land and livestock to improve agricultural output.

POLITICS, *GERMANY*

The authorities agree to resume attacks on merchant vessels, irrespective of their nationality, although it is specifically forbidden for submarine commanders to torpedo ships without warning them first.

OCTOBER 7

POLITICS, *UNITED STATES*

Democrat and serving president Woodrow Wilson is re-elected. He has campaigned on a ticket of maintaining US neutrality, despite increasing friction with Germany.

OCTOBER 8

POLITICS, *GERMANY*

The authorities agree to form an air force by uniting "all means of air

▲ *Female supporters campaign for US President Woodrow Wilson, who was re-elected in November.*

▼ *British stretcher-bearers carry a wounded man away from the fighting around Thiepval on the Somme.*

OCTOBER 9

▶ *French bystanders cover their ears as a 12-inch (30-cm) rail gun fires on German positions.*

combat and air defense with the army, in the field and in the home areas, into one unit."

SEA WAR, *ATLANTIC*
The German submarine *U-53* marks an escalation of the naval war by becoming the first boat to sink enemy vessels off the East Coast of the United States. Three British, one Dutch, and one Norwegian ships are its victims.

OCTOBER 9

WESTERN FRONT, *ITALY*
The Italians open the Eighth Battle of the Isonzo, with their Second and Third Armies striking the Austro-Hungarian Fifth Army. Again, the fighting is indecisive. The Italians gain just two miles (3 km) at a cost of 24,000 casualties. The battle ends on the 12th.

OCTOBER 10

POLITICS, *RUSSIA*
Czar Nicholas II orders that the highly successful offensive led by General Aleksey Brusilov is brought to a conclusion. However, the fighting drags on into mid-October.

BALKANS, *MACEDONIA*
German General Otto von Below is made the local army group commander and establishes his headquarters at Skopje. He is granted reinforcements from the Western and Eastern Fronts.

OCTOBER 16

MIDDLE EAST, *ARABIA*
Captain T.E. Lawrence, a member of the British Arab Bureau, arrives at Jeddah. His mission is to liaise between the leaders of the Arab revolt and the British establishment. He becomes the adviser to Prince Feisal, who is attempting to unite

▶ *Colonel T. E. Lawrence, the British liaison officer with the Arabs in Turkish Arabia.*

the various Arab tribes against the Turks. Lawrence, an advocate of the creation of an independent Arab state, will become known as "Lawrence of Arabia" because of his exploits.

OCTOBER 19

BALKANS, *ROMANIA*
The Danube Army commanded by German Field Marshal August von Mackensen, which has been

advancing steadily along the coast of southern Romania from Bulgaria since early September, gains a decisive breakthrough and advances on the key port of Constanza at the mouth of the Danube River on the Black Sea, which falls on the 22nd.

OCTOBER 24

WESTERN FRONT, *VERDUN*
The French launch their counterattack. Its aim is to capture territory to the northeast of Verdun. Advancing under cover of mist, the French recapture Fort Douaumont, taking 6000 prisoners. German attacks are defeated.

OCTOBER 21

POLITICS, *GERMANY*
The government agrees to establish the War Munitions Office to boost the country's output of much-needed ammunition, particularly for artillery. The body begins work on November 1.

▲ *The invasion of Romania was a chiefly German affair. The Romanian Army was no match for the invaders.*

▼ *French troops man a captured German machine gun amid the ruins of Verdun's Fort Douaumont.*

OCTOBER 28

AIR WAR, *WESTERN FRONT*
One of Germany's leading air aces, with 40 victories, and an outstanding tactician, Oswald Boelcke, is killed in a midair collision with a colleague.

NOVEMBER 1

WESTERN FRONT, *FRANCE*
The French commander-in-chief, General Joseph Joffre, outlines his plans for a combined Anglo-French offensive in 1917 to his British counterpart, General Sir Douglas Haig.

NOVEMBER 1–4

WESTERN FRONT, *ITALY*
The Ninth Battle of the Isonzo begins with attacks by the Italian Second and Third Armies against Austro-Hungarian positions east of the town of Gorizia. Bad weather and heavy casualties (28,000 men) force the Italian commander-in-chief, General Luigi Cadorna, to halt the attacks.

NOVEMBER 2

WESTERN FRONT, *VERDUN*
The Germans abandon what little remains of Fort Vaux, which is fully under French control by the 5th.

NOVEMBER 4

POLITICS, *ARABIA*
Despite several British and French protests, Hussein, Grand Sherif of Mecca, is crowned as king of the Arabs at Mecca.

▶ *German air ace Oswald Boelcke was killed in a midair collision on the Western Front in November.*

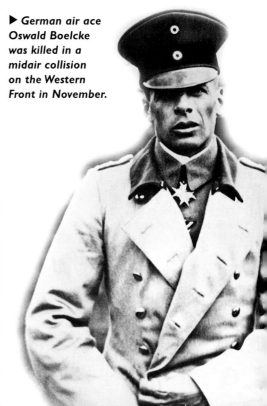

NOVEMBER 5

to the northeast of Albert. The British attack, heralded by the destruction of the German Hawthorn Redoubt by the detonation of an underground mine, is directed toward the village of Beaumont Hamel, which is captured. The fighting in the sector continues until the 18th.

NOVEMBER 15

POLITICS, *FRANCE*
The various allies confer at Chantilly, where General Joseph Joffre, the French commander-in-chief, chairs a meeting that discusses a joint offensive on the Western, Eastern, and Italian Fronts to begin in early

◀ *British troops negotiate the shell-cratered landscape along the Somme River at the close of their offensive during late 1916.*

▼ *Russian troops await the order to occupy Monastir in southern Serbia after its evacuation by Bulgarian forces.*

NOVEMBER 5

POLITICS, *FRANCE*
The government attempts to show its solidarity with occupied Serbia by sponsoring a national Serbian Soldiers' Flag Day.

POLITICS, *POLAND*
Germany and Austria-Hungary, conquerors of this former Russian territory, announce the creation of the "Kingdom of Poland," hoping to recruit Poles into their armed forces. Some Poles do join up, but many do not believe the German and Austro-Hungarian offer of independence goes far enough.

NOVEMBER 10

SEA WAR, *BALTIC*
Seven German destroyers are sunk in a Russian minefield.

NOVEMBER 12

POLITICS, *MEXICO*
A high-ranking German diplomat remarks to a Mexican official that "The imperial government would see with the greatest of pleasure the Mexican government's consent to a [submarine] base in its territory."

NOVEMBER 13

WESTERN FRONT, *SOMME*
The newly-created British Fifth Army commanded by General Sir Hubert Gough initiates the Battle of the Ancre

February 1917. It is believed that the Germans and Austro-Hungarians will be unable to counter such a widespread simultaneous offensive.

HOME FRONT, *GERMANY*
Germany's growing manpower shortage is highlighted when the 1918 conscription class, all under 19 years, is called up to fight. Medical reports note that many are undernourished, partly reflecting the growing success of the British naval blockade, which is preventing many supplies from overseas reaching Germany.

NOVEMBER 18

WESTERN FRONT, *SOMME*
The Battle of the Ancre ends, effectively concluding the British offensive on the Somme. British casualties are enormous; some 420,000 men. The French have lost 205,000 troops and the Germans some 500,000. At the end of their attacks the British have still not captured some of their first-day objectives. For example, they are still three miles (5 km) from Bapaume. Despite having gained little territory, the British have inflicted equally massive casualties on the Germans during the fighting and

contributed to their decision to withdraw to the Hindenburg Line.

WESTERN FRONT, *VERDUN*
General Robert Nivelle is given permission by General Joseph Joffre, the French commander-in-chief, to launch a final offensive. Nivelle has regained much of the territory to the northeast of Verdun lost to the Germans in the first months of the year and his stock with both the public and senior commanders is high. Part of his success is due to using a creeping barrage in which French troops advance behind a wall of artillery fire, which itself moves forward at a predetermined rate.

NOVEMBER 19

BALKANS, *SERBIA*
Serbian and French forces recapture the city of Monastir, which has been abandoned by its Bulgarian and German defenders who have fallen back a little way to the north.

NOVEMBER 21

POLITICS, *AUSTRIA-HUNGARY*
Emperor Franz Joseph dies at the age of 86. He is succeeded by his great nephew, 26-year-old Archduke Charles.

▲ *A German supply column negotiates a ford in Romania during the advance of the Ninth Army toward Bucharest.*

SEA WAR, *MEDITERRANEAN*
The British hospital ship *Britannic*, a companion-ship of the ill-fated *Titanic*, succumbs to a mine laid by a German submarine. The *Britannic* is not carrying wounded at the time and there are just 78 casualties among the crew of the former luxury passenger liner.

NOVEMBER 23

POLITICS, *GREECE*
The Greek provisional government in Salonika declares war on Germany and Bulgaria after much prompting by the French and British, who have substantial troops in the region.

BALKANS, *ROMANIA*
German Field Marshal August von Mackensen's Danube Army launches a second invasion of Romania to support his forces already attacking along the Black Sea coast. Units strike across the Danube River along a 30-mile (48-km) front. The plan is to link up with the German Ninth Army commanded by General Erich

von Falkenhayn, who is advancing through northwest Romania after negotiating the fortified passes of the Transylvanian Alps. Their objective is the Romanian capital, Bucharest. The two forces make contact on the 26th, by which stage they are less than 50 miles (80 km) from Bucharest. The struggle for the Romanian capital begins at the end of the month. The defeat of Romania will give the Central Powers access to its oil fields.

NOVEMBER 25

SEA WAR, *ATLANTIC*

The German submarine *U-52* sinks the French battleship *Suffren* as its sails off the coast of southern Portugal. There are no survivors.

NOVEMBER 28

AIR WAR, *BRITAIN*

Long-range German bombers launch the first daylight attack on London. A lone aircraft drops six small bombs on the center of the capital, wounding 10 civilians.

NOVEMBER 29

POLITICS, *BRITAIN*

Admiral Sir David Beatty is appointed to command the Home Fleet in place of Admiral Sir John Jellicoe, who is made First Sea Lord on December 4.

DECEMBER 1

POLITICS, *ROMANIA*

The government abandons the capital, Bucharest, and moves to Jassy.

DECEMBER 5

POLITICS, *BRITAIN*

Prime Minister Herbert Asquith resigns as head of the country's coalition government and is replaced by Liberal

▲ *German Field Marshal August von Mackensen celebrates the capture of Bucharest.*

David Lloyd George on the 7th. Lloyd George acts swiftly to reform and regularize Britain's war effort by establishing various powerful boards and committees.

POLITICS, *GERMANY*
The Auxiliary Service Law comes into effect. All males ages between 17 and 60 are compelled by the authorities to work in war-related industries.

DECEMBER 6

BALKANS, *ROMANIA*
German Field Marshal August von Mackensen, celebrating his 67th birthday, makes a triumphant entry into Bucharest mounted on his favorite white charger. There has been a three-day truce to allow the Romanians the opportunity to evacuate their capital. Romanian forces retreat into the northeast of their country in the direction of the border with Russia. They are pursued, although worsening weather slows the German advance.

▼ *A British gunboat on the Tigris River bombards Turkish positions at the opening of General Sir Frederick Maude's push to reach Baghdad, which began in mid-December.*

DECEMBER 11

BALKANS, *SALONIKA/SERBIA*
French General Maurice Sarrail, nominally the commander of all the forces operating in the theater is ordered to cease all offensive operations and place his forces in their winter quarters. Monastir remains under frequent artillery fire.

▲ *French troops march through the recently-captured city of Monastir in southern Serbia.*

DECEMBER 12

POLITICS, *FRANCE*
General Joseph Joffre is replaced as French commander-in-chief of the Armies of the North and Northeast by General Robert Nivelle, the hero of Verdun. On the same day General Ferdinand Foch is replaced as commander of the North Army Group by General Louis Franchet d'Esperey. Foch goes into semiretirement, but will soon return to active service.
POLITICS, *GERMANY*
The government sends a "peace note" to the various powers allied against it. It is rejected as being "empty and insincere" on the 30th.

DECEMBER 13

MIDDLE EAST, *MESOPOTAMIA*
The British commander, General Sir Frederick Maude, begins an offensive along the Tigris River. His force of 48,000 men is supported by more than 170 artillery pieces, 24 aircraft, and numerous armed river steamers. The Turks are able to muster 20,000 troops and 70 artillery pieces. However, heavy rains slow the British advance.

DECEMBER 15

DECEMBER 15

WESTERN FRONT, *VERDUN*

The French attack to the northeast of Verdun. Within a few days, the Germans have been forced away from key positions, including Forts Douaumont and Vaux. Although the fighting around Verdun will continue into 1917, this attack ends the main battle. Losses are enormous: 360,000 French troops and 336,000 Germans. The German plan to destroy the French Army at little cost has failed.

DECEMBER 19

POLITICS, *BRITAIN*

Prime Minister David Lloyd George makes his first speech. He rejects recent peace proposals, stating that "We shall put our trust rather in an unbroken army than in broken faith."

DECEMBER 21

MIDDLE EAST, *EGYPT*

Australian and New Zealand mounted units force the Turks to abandon their positions around El-Arish.

DECEMBER 26

POLITICS, *FRANCE*

General Joseph Joffre resigns as the French commander-in-chief but is

◀ Rasputin (1871–1916) became a close confident of the Russian royal family, but his influence over the appointment and dismissal of political and religious officials was greatly resented by many nobles. The monk was murdered in late December and his body dumped in a river in the Russian capital Petrograd, until 1914 known as St. Petersburg.

▲ German prisoners, some of the more than 17,000 captured at Verdun, are escorted to the rear by French troops.

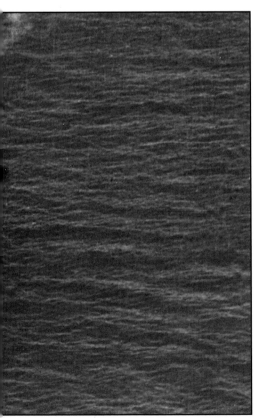

▼ *A victim of a German submarine sinks by the stern, one of 1157 vessels of all nations sunk during 1916.*

promoted to the rank of marshal. On the following day General Ferdinand Foch is made chief military adviser to the French government.

DECEMBER 29

WESTERN FRONT, *SOMME*
General Sir Douglas Haig completes his report on the prolonged battle. He claims that the British have fought half of the German Army, and have taken 38,000 prisoners and captured 125 artillery pieces of various calibers.

DECEMBER 31

POLITICS, *BRITAIN*
General Douglas Haig, the commander-in-chief of the British forces on the Western Front, is promoted to the rank of field marshal.

POLITICS, *RUSSIA*
Monk and mystic Rasputin, who many Russians believe has an untoward influence on the royal family, particularly the czarina, is murdered by a group of nobles.

SEA WAR, *ATLANTIC*
At the end of a successful month German submarines are credited with sinking 167 vessels. Of this total 70 belong to neutral countries. However, there are still calls for a greater effort.

KEY PERSONALITIES

FIELD MARSHAL SIR DOUGLAS HAIG

Douglas Haig (1861–1928) was the commander of the British forces on the Western Front between 1915 and 1918. In 1914 Haig was given command of I Corps, which he led during the Battles of Mons, the Marne, and First Ypres. Promoted to lead the First Army in December 1914, he played a prominent role in the Battle of Neuve-Chapelle. Haig is believed to have been involved in the dismissal of the increasingly unpopular Field Marshal Sir John French, the commander of the British Expeditionary Force, in December 1915.

Haig's period as commander-in-chief remains controversial. He was always looking for a decisive breakthrough on the Western Front. At the Battle of the Somme in 1916 and at Third Ypres in 1917 he persisted in attacking – at very great cost – even though chances of making a breakthrough were small. However, Haig proved adept in organizing, training, and supplying his forces, and was receptive to new ideas and technologies, such as the tank.

Haig's calmness during the German spring offensive of 1918 enabled the French and British to block the attack, and between August and November it was the British under Haig who won a string of victories against the Germans that effectively destroyed their army on the Western Front. Also, Haig was a prime-mover behind the creation of a joint Anglo-French command structure in 1918 – one led by the French.

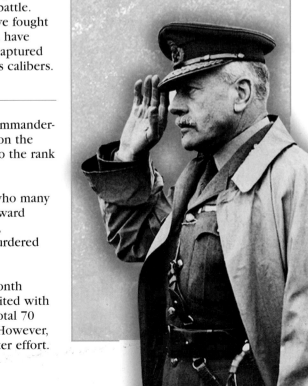

1917

▲ A column of Turkish cavalry moves out from a town in Palestine to confront the advancing British.

The year was dominated by the outbreak of the Russian Revolution, which would release Germans troops for service elsewhere, and the declaration of war on Germany by the United States. Italy came close to being knocked out of the war and the French Army mutinied, leaving Britain to bear the brunt of the campaign on the Western Front. German allies Austria-Hungary and Turkey were also in growing military and political decline.

JANUARY 8–9

MIDDLE EAST, *EGYPT*

The British forces massing in Egypt under the command of General Sir Archibald Murray begin to clear the Turks out of the Sinai Peninsula, prior to launching an invasion of Palestine. They win an important victory at the Battle of Magruntein, capturing some 1600 Turkish prisoners and a handful of artillery pieces. Murray's forces suffer a total of 487

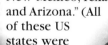

▶ A British-crewed howitzer in action during the fighting against the Turks in the Sinai Peninsula.

casualties. He now begins to plan an invasion of Palestine; his first targets will be the series of Turkish-held ridges stretching from Gaza on the Mediterranean coast to Beersheba in the interior, a distance of some 20 miles (32 km). Murray's ultimate objective is Jerusalem.

JANUARY 19

POLITICS, *MEXICO*

The German diplomatic representative receives a secret telegram penned by German Foreign Secretary Arthur Zimmermann. Its suggests forming a defensive alliance with Mexico if the United States declares war on Germany. The note concludes: "Mexico is to reconquer the lost territory in New Mexico, Texas, and Arizona." (All of these US states were

administered by Mexico, then a Spanish colony, in the past.) The message also suggests that Mexico should encourage Japan, which has plans to carve out an empire in the Pacific, to join the Central Powers. Unbeknown to the Germans, the British intercept and decode the sensitive message.

JANUARY 22

POLITICS, *UNITED STATES*
President Woodrow Wilson calls on all the combatant nations fighting in

▲ British-officered Indian troops armed with Lewis machine guns practise their anti-aircraft drill in the Sinai Peninsula.

◀ German submarines and destroyers are readied to attack enemy shipping.

World War I to agree to "peace without victory." The British and French reject the offer, finding some of the demands made by Germany unacceptable.

JANUARY 27

POLITICS, *UNITED STATES*
General John Pershing, who has been in charge of 4800 US troops attempting to capture rebel leader Pancho Villa in Mexico for some 10 months, is ordered to return to the United States.

JANUARY 31

POLITICS, *GERMANY*
After many months of often acrimonious debate the government agrees to launch an unrestricted submarine warfare campaign. This allows the 111

123

FEBRUARY 22–23

MIDDLE EAST, *MESOPOTAMIA*

General Sir Frederick Maude, the commander of the British forces pushing northward toward Baghdad, launches a major attack on the Turks at Kut-el-Amara. He conducts a feint drive against the Turkish right to cover his forces crossing the Tigris River, and then unleashes powerful attacks on both Turkish flanks. The Turkish commander, Kara Bekr Bey, orders his forces to retreat toward Baghdad following his defeat at what becomes known as the Second Battle of Kut. Kut-el-Amara is abandoned to the British on the 25th.

FEBRUARY 23

WESTERN FRONT, *FRANCE*

German forces begin their withdrawal to the newly-built defenses-in-depth of the Hindenburg Line, some 20 miles (32 km) behind the existing front and stretching from Arras to Soissons.

Between the old front line and their new positions the Germans destroy towns, villages, and lines of communications, cut down forests, and poison water supplies. The movement is secret and completed by April 5.

German U-boats currently available to sink any vessels at will. It is believed that such a campaign will starve Britain into surrender within as little as five months.

The German high command recognizes that the decision will have profound consequences on Germany's diplomatic relations with the United States, which is likely to declare war if its neutral vessels are sunk. However, it is thought that the United States will be unable to make any significant impact on the war in Europe for at least two years by which time the German planners believe that the Central Powers will have won the war.

A note concerning the submarine campaign is passed to the US Secretary of State Robert Lansing; it announces that all ships will be "stopped with every available weapon and without further notice."

FEBRUARY 3

POLITICS, *UNITED STATES*

The administration cuts its diplomatic ties with Germany following the latter's announcement that its navy will conduct unrestricted submarine warfare. President Woodrow Wilson announces: "This government has no alternative consistent with the dignity and honor of the United States." Other nations follow suit, including many in Latin American, and China. On the same day as Wilson's speech an American merchant ship, *Housatonic*, is sunk without warning.

▼ A section of the German Hindenburg Line with huge barbed-wire defenses.

◀ *Students and army deserters fire on police during the "February Revolution" in Petrograd, the Russian capital.*

MIDDLE EAST, *MESOPOTAMIA*
British forces under General Sir Frederick Maude, having brushed aside the Turkish Sixth Army under Halil Pasha and after three days of skirmishing along the Diyala River, enter Baghdad. Keen to prevent the Turks from regrouping, Maude sends some of his troops to scout along various rivers. However, the onset of intense summer heat will eventually bring a halt to operations until September.

MARCH 12

POLITICS, *RUSSIA*
Workers, left-wing politicians, agitators, and strike leaders meeting in the Russian capital form the Petrograd Soviet (Council of Workers' Deputies). One of its first acts is to issue "Order No. 1," which deprives Russian officers of their authority. Two days later the Duma (parliament) itself establishes a provisional government headed by Prince Lvov, although real power is wielded by Minister of War Alexander Kerensky. Neither body accepts the authority of the other, initially weakening the forces opposed to Czar

▼ *British troops march into Baghdad, Mesopotamia, on March 11 following its capture from the Turks.*

FEBRUARY 24

POLITICS, *BRITAIN*
The US ambassador to Britain, Walter Hines Page, is given a copy of the message written by German Foreign Secretary Arthur Zimmermann suggesting that Mexico should enter an alliance with Germany if the United States declares war on Germany. The ambassador passes the transcript of the so-called "Zimmermann Telegram" to the US State Department. Its contents cause an uproar when they are printed in newspapers on March 1.

MARCH 1

POLITICS, *AUSTRIA-HUNGARY*
Emperor Karl replaces General Franz Conrad von Hötzendorf as chief of the General Staff with General Arthur Arz von Straussenburg.

MARCH 8

POLITICS, *RUSSIA*
Riots, strikes, and mass demonstrations break out in Moscow. People are demonstrating against shortages of food and fuel, and the autocratic style of the government. The police use lethal force against the demonstrations, but the unrest continues over the following days. By the 10th an estimated 25,000 workers are on strike. Army units called in to deal with the growing unrest refuse to fire on the demonstrators. (The events become known as the "February Revolution" as the Russian calendar of the time was 11 days behind the Western one.)

MARCH 11

POLITICS, *RUSSIA*
Czar Nicholas II refuses to accede to calls for urgent political reforms from the president of the Duma (Russian parliament) and reacts by ordering the Duma to disband. However, it continues to sit in the increasingly lawless capital, Petrograd, whose garrison has rebeled the previous day. (The capital had been known as St. Petersburg until 1914, when it was give the less German-sounding name of Petrograd.)

KEY PERSONALITIES

VLADIMIR ILICH LENIN

Born in Simbirsk in 1870 with the name Vladimir Ilich Ulyanov, Lenin was the leader of the revolutionary Bolshevik Party, which played a dominant part in Russian politics in 1917 and won the subsequent Russian Civil War (1918–21).

Lenin studied law at university and developed his belief in revolutionary Marxism while in St. Petersburg during the 1890s. He was arrested in 1895 and sent into a three-year internal exile in Siberia. After his release he traveled to Western Europe, where he emerged as leader of the Bolshevik majority grouping within the Russian Social Democratic Workers' Party in 1903. Returning to Russia, he took part in the unsuccessful revolution of 1905 and then returned to Western Europe, basing himself in Switzerland from 1907.

In March 1917 he returned to Russia, which was in turmoil after the "February Revolution." The Bolsheviks emerged as the leading political force in Russia following the "November Revolution" the same year. Lenin led the Bolsheviks during the Russian Civil War, although Minister of War Leon Trotsky effectively commanded the ultimately victorious Red Army.

After the Civil War Lenin was primarily concerned with extending the Bolsheviks' control of Russia and developing the country's economy. However, he suffered from poor health and had a debilitating stroke in 1922. He died in 1924. Following a period of instability and infighting within the Russian leadership, Lenin's successor – Joseph Stalin – assumed power in 1927.

▲ *Russia's Czar Nicholas II abdicated as his war-weakened country descended into chaos in March.*

Nicholas II and his advisers. The chaos, which the army is both unwilling and unable to curtail, spreads throughout Russia. Pressure mounts on the czar to abdicate. One revolutionary in exile, Vladimir Lenin, the head of the radical Bolsheviks, misses the coup but is swiftly speeded back to Russia in a sealed train provided by the Germans.

MARCH 13

POLITICS, *UNITED STATES*
The US authorities announce President Woodrow Wilson's decision to arm all US merchant ships sailing in areas where German submarines are known to be active. His order is a counter to Germany launching an unrestricted submarine warfare campaign at the end of January.

MARCH 15

POLITICS, *RUSSIA*
Czar Nicholas II abdicates. Proposals to replace him with his son Aleksey are rejected by the czar, who favors his own brother, Grand Duke Mikhail.

MARCH 17

SEA WAR, *ENGLISH CHANNEL*
German destroyers launch one of their periodic sorties against enemy shipping plying the narrow seas between Britain and France. They are able to sink a pair of British destroyers and a single merchant ship in quick succession with no loss to themselves.

MARCH 18

SEA WAR, *ATLANTIC*
Three American vessels, the *City of Memphis*, *Vigilancia*, and *Illinois*, are sunk by German submarines; the incidents further anger the United States.

▼ *The US merchant ship* Illinois, *sunk on March 18, was a victim of Germany's unrestricted submarine campaign.*

MARCH 26

MIDDLE EAST, *PALESTINE*
British General Sir Archibald Murray begins his invasion of the Turkish province by attempting to break through the Gaza–Beersheba line with some 16,000 troops. The attack, led by units under the command of General Sir Charles Dobell, fails due to poor British planning, a lack of

▲ *A Turkish artillery battery fires on the British in Palestine, while a wounded man is carried away on a stretcher.*

communication between the infantry and cavalry units involved, acute water shortages, and Turkish resistance.

The Turks, who have a similar number of troops committed to what becomes known as the First Battle of Gaza, suffer some 2500 casualties in the fighting, while the British record losses of nearly 4000 men. Murray is, however, authorized to launch a second effort against the Turks.

APRIL 2

POLITICS, *UNITED STATES*
President Woodrow Wilson addresses Congress concerning the country's deteriorating relationship with Germany. Wilson states: "I advise that the Congress declares the recent course of the Imperial German government [the unrestricted submarine campaign and the Zimmermann correspondence] to be in fact nothing less than war against the government and

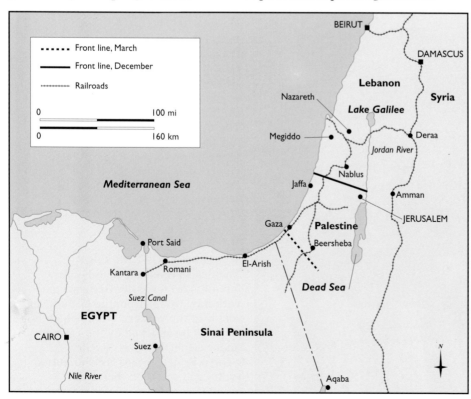

◀ *The 1917 campaign in Palestine. After a poor start the British were able to take Jerusalem from the Turks by December.*

▲ *President Woodrow Wilson addresses Congress on April 2, asking those present to support war against Germany.*

people of the United States ...[and] to exert all its power and employ all its resources to bring the government of the German Empire to terms and to end the war." Congress is asked to back what is a declaration of war.

APRIL 3

POLITICS, *RUSSIA*
Russian revolutionary Vladimir Ilich Lenin returns to Petrograd from exile. He intends to overthrow the Provisional Government and create a state headed by the Bolsheviks, but must first take control of various soviets (workers' councils). This is achieved by October.

▲ *German prisoners are marched to the rear as British troops move forward during the fighting at Arras.*

◀ *The crew of a British 12-in (30-cm) howitzer prepares to open fire at the beginning of the Battle of Arras.*

APRIL 6

POLITICS, *UNITED STATES*
President Woodrow Wilson's administration declares war on Germany. However, the US Army will have to be expanded before it can contribute to the war. The navy is more prepared. The United States does not become a full ally of the British, French, and Russians, preferring to be an "Associate Power." Wilson sees the war as a moral crusade and does not want to be associated with the motives of the other states arrayed against Germany.

APRIL 9

WESTERN FRONT, *FRANCE*
The British open the Battle of Arras, intending to force the Germans to withdraw troops from the Aisne River sector of the Western Front, which is about to be attacked by the French under General Robert Nivelle.

Three British armies are committed to the enterprise. In the center, around Arras, lies General Sir Edmund

Allenby's Third Army. It will lead the offensive. To the north, poised to strike at Vimy Ridge, is the First Army under General Sir Henry Horne containing the Canadian Corps led by General Sir Julian Byng. South of Allenby, General Sir Hugh Gough's Fifth Army is to strike at the Hindenburg Line around Bullecourt. Facing the onslaught are the troops of General Ludwig von Falkenhausen's German Sixth Army.

The British herald their attack with a five-day bombardment. They achieve considerable gains on the first day, particularly the Third Army's Canadian Corps, whose spirited assault captures Vimy Ridge, and its XVII Corps, which advances some four miles (6 km). However, Gough makes little progress.

The pilots of the British Royal Flying Corps suffer heavy losses due to the inferiority of their aircraft in comparison with the German Albatross D.III and the German tactic of diving on them from altitude. Some 33 percent of British pilots become casualties during April.

APRIL 11

WESTERN FRONT, *FRANCE*
The British continue the Battle of Arras

in the face of growing resistance from the reinforced German Sixth Army under General Ludwig von Falkenhausen. The British 37th Division captures the village of Monchy le Preux and elements of General Sir Hugh Gough's Fifth Army break into the Hindenburg Line at Bullecourt the next day. However, the battle is becoming a stalemate.

The British commander-in-chief, Field Marshal Sir Douglas Haig, opts to continue the Arras offensive into the middle of May, and the fighting centers on Bullecourt. Haig's decision is made in part to draw the German Army's

▼ *British troops investigate a German observation post disguised as a shell-blasted tree stump.*

▼ *Canadian troops commanded by General Sir Julian Byng consolidate their recently-won gains on Vimy Ridge.*

▲ The opening of the Nivelle Offensive –
French troops advance against the
German-held Chemin des Dames ridges.

▲ Paul René Fonck, France's top fighter
pilot, practises his marksmanship skills
at his home airfield.

attention away from the sectors of the
Western Front held by the French,
whose armies are in disarray following
widespread mutinies. At the close of
the offensive British casualties total
some 150,000 men killed, wounded, or
captured. German losses are 100,000.

APRIL 15

AIR WAR, *WESTERN FRONT*
Paul René Fonck joins one of France's
top fighter units, Groupe de Chasse
No. 12, better known as *Les Cigognes*
("The Storks"). He is destined to
become the country's top ace, scoring

75 victories by the end of the war,
although his unofficial score is 127.
On two occasions in 1918 – May 9
and September 26 – Fonck, an extra-
ordinarily lethal marksman, shoots
down six enemy planes in a day.

APRIL 16–20

WESTERN FRONT, *FRANCE*
General Robert Nivelle opens a major
offensive, which he has promised will
smash the German defenders on the
Western Front at little cost. However,
Nivelle's superiors are not convinced
of his plan and only agree to it after

▼ A German six-inch (15-cm) howitzer is
prepared to fire on the French at the
beginning of their Nivelle Offensive.

he has threatened to resign. The attack
involves offensives in Champagne and
along the Aisne River.

Committed to the enterprise are the
French Fifth Army under General
Olivier Mazel and General Charles
Mangin's Sixth Army. They are
supported by General Marie-Emile
Fayolle's First Army and the Tenth
Army commanded by General Denis
Duchêne. Nivelle has 102,000 men and
7000 artillery pieces. Opposing them
are two German armies: the First
under General Fritz von Below and
General Max von Boehn's Seventh.

The French advance takes place
along a front of some 40 miles (64 km)
between Soissons and Reims, with the
bulk of the troops committed to
capturing the Chemin des Dames, a
series of thickly-wooded ridges
running parallel to the front line.
Nivelle intends to use a creeping

artillery barrage to cover the main attacks. However, the Germans are fully aware of the onslaught, which becomes known as the Nivelle Offensive, as there has been little secrecy and the Germans have captured plans for the attack. Shortly before it begins, German aircraft destroy many French balloons used for artillery observation and strafe columns of French troops and tanks.

The German Seventh Army blocks the French advance into the Chemin des Dames, as does von Below's First Army to the east. French troops are met by heavy artillery fire and well-defended machine-gun positions. Their losses are heavy, some 118,000 men by the 20th.

By the 20th it is also clear that Nivelle is not going to achieve a decisive breakthrough. Despite capturing some 20,000 Germans, French territorial gains are limited, although a section of the Hindenburg Line on the Chemin des Dames falls by the end of the month. The fighting, which becomes increasingly bogged down, continues into May.

APRIL 17

WESTERN FRONT, *FRANCE*
A day after the opening of General Robert Nivelle's offensive, which has made little progress and produced severe casualties, the troops of the French 108th Regiment mutiny and abandon their trenches in the face of the enemy.

The mutiny spreads until some 68 of the French Army's 112 divisions are involved. Officers report a total of 250 cases of troops refusing to obey orders; some 35,000 men are

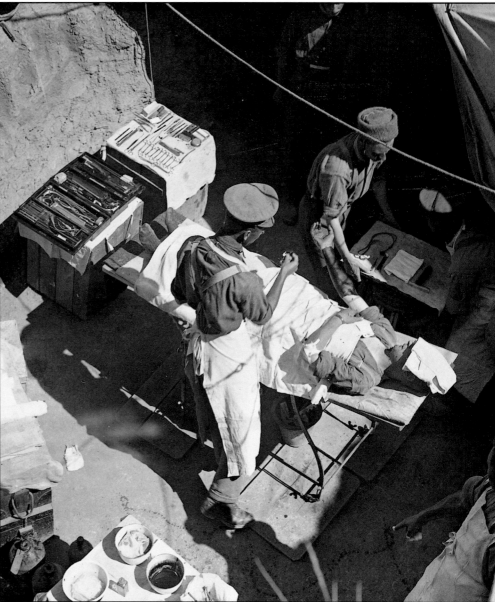

▲ *A wounded British soldier receives medical treatment in Palestine. A bullet has been removed from his arm.*

implicated in the mutiny. Many mutineers are willing to defend their positions, but refuse outright to advance against the enemy.

APRIL 17–19

MIDDLE EAST, *PALESTINE*
British General Sir Archibald Murray again attempts to invade the Turkish province by breaking through the enemy positions stretching between Gaza and Beersheba. As in the First Battle of Gaza fought in the previous March, the main effort is made by troops commanded by General Sir Charles Dobell. Dobell's frontal attack against well-entrenched Turkish forces

ends in high losses and no gains. British casualties reach a total of 6500 men, more than three times the recorded Turkish figure.

This action, the Second Battle of Gaza, has profound consequences on the British command structure in the region. First to pay the price of failure is Dobell, who is sacked by Murray. However, Murray's future is also in doubt as his recent failures at Gaza have angered the British government whose prime minister, David Lloyd George, has personally backed the attacks in Palestine.

APRIL 20–21

SEA WAR, *ENGLISH CHANNEL*
An attack by German destroyers on coastal shipping is foiled by two British destroyers, *Broke* and

Swiftsure, which sink two enemy destroyers. Their success halts German naval raids in the Channel until 1918.

APRIL 23

MIDDLE EAST, *MESOPOTAMIA*
Troops under British General Sir Frederick Maude, who captured Baghdad on March 11, continue their advance against the Turks by taking Samarra on the Tigris River. A Turkish counterattack is beaten off, but Maude is forced to end operations until September due to the intense heat.

AIR WAR, *ENGLISH CHANNEL*
Three British long-range Handley Page 0/100 bombers attack a flotilla of German torpedo-boats off Ostend, Belgium. Several boats are hit and damaged. However, subsequent losses in daylight operations force the bombers to abandon their daylight maritime patrol activities and concentrate on the strategic bombing of German targets under cover of darkness. One of their key roles will be to attack the airfields from which Germany's Gotha bombers operate.

MAY 5

TECHNOLOGY, *FRANCE*
The bulky and unmaneuverable Saint Chamond tank makes its first appearance in battle. It has a crew of nine, who operate four machine guns and a three-inch (75-mm) main gun.

MAY 7

AIR WAR, *WESTERN FRONT*
Captain Albert Ball, one of Britain's leading aces with more than 40 air victories to his credit, is shot down and killed.

▲ A French Saint Chamond tank in action. It was plagued by several design weaknesses, but 400 were built.

▼ An aerial view of the French Nivelle Offensive. It was France's only major attack on the Western Front in 1917.

MAY 7–8

SEA WAR, *ENGLISH CHANNEL*
British warships bombard Zeebrugge, Belgium, which is a major base for German destroyers and submarines. The attack does little damage, but other such operations follow.

MAY 9

WESTERN FRONT, *FRANCE*
General Robert Nivelle's attack along the Chemin des Dames is brought to a close. It has failed spectacularly. The French have been unable to break through the German defenses and have suffered enormous losses, some 187,000 men as opposed to around 163,000 German casualties. Ordinary French soldiers, who see little point in suffering such rates of attrition for no concrete advantage, are suffering from low morale, and some front-line units have mutinied.

MAY 9–23

BALKANS, *GREECE*
Serbian and French troops, some of

the 600,000 in the theater, launch an attack in Macedonia. Their aim is to break through the enemy and swing west across the Vardar River, while British troops attack around Lake Doiran. The offensive makes little progress and casualties total 14,000 men by the 23rd. There is growing disquiet over the competence of the commander, France's Maurice Sarrail.

▲ *A convoy of merchant ships and warships crosses the Atlantic. Losses to German submarines declined steadily once this system was introduced in May. Equally, German submarine losses began to soar as the escorts became effective.*

MAY 10

POLITICS, *BRITAIN*

Prime Minister David Lloyd George forces the British navy to institute the convoy system to protect merchant ships from enemy submarines. Recent losses to enemy submarines, which are rising alarmingly, are threatening to isolate Britain.

Henceforth, vessels will sail across the North Atlantic in large groups rather than singly and be protected by numerous warships. The system has an immediate impact – German submarine losses rise, while the rate of merchant ship sinkings declines equally dramatically.

MAY 12

POLITICS, *UNITED STATES*

General John Pershing is appointed the commander of the American Expeditionary Force, which is being formed to fight on the Western Front. It will take time to increase the strength of the US Army, but Pershing expects the number of American troops in France to reach one million by May 1918 and is planning for a force of three million if the war continues. Pershing also intends to make sure that his units will fight as a separate force and not be split into small units and placed under French or British command.

WESTERN FRONT, *ITALY*

The chief of the Italian General Staff, General Luigi Cadorna, finally initiates the delayed Tenth Battle of the Isonzo

GENERAL OF THE ARMIES JOHN PERSHING

Pershing (1860–1948) was commissioned as a junior officer in 1886 after graduating from West Point, and his early military experience was gained in several campaigns against Native Americans. After various peacetime appointments he saw overseas service in the Spanish–American War (1898–99), as a military observer in the Russo-Japanese War (1904–05), and in the Philippines. Between March 1916 and January 1917 Pershing led an unsuccessful punitive expedition into Mexico in pursuit of revolutionary Pancho Villa, whose forces had crossed the border and killed US citizens in Columbus, New Mexico.

When the United States entered World War I, Pershing was made commander of the American Expeditionary Force (AEF), which was earmarked for France, on May 12. He arrived in Europe on June 23 (below, center) and oversaw the massive build-up of US force in France, which began in earnest that summer and continued well into 1918. By May the AEF numbered more than 425,000 men. By the end of the war two million US troops had served overseas.

Pershing was successful in maintaining the AEF as an independent force with its own commanding officers and one able to carry out independent large-scale offensive operations. Pershing also oversaw the AEF's three main attacks on the Western Front in 1918: the Aisne–Marne (July–August), St. Mihiel (September), and Meuse–Argonne (September–November). He was made a six-star general and given the unique rank of general of the armies in 1919.

DECISIVE WEAPONS

THE GOTHA BOMBER

The German-built Gotha bomber, which began operating in early 1917, marked a new era in air warfare – for the first time heavier-than-air vessels could strike against an enemy at long range. This two-engined aircraft with a three-man crew was capable of speed of 80 mph (128 k/h), had a ceiling of 15,000 feet (4600 m), and could carry around 660 lb (300 kg) of bombs. Its defensive armament comprised two or three machine guns. Development work on the aircraft began in 1914 and the prototype took to the air in January 1915.

In April 1917 Gothas began attacking England from their bases in occupied Belgium. The Gothas' chief target became London in an operation known as *Türkenkreuz* ("Turkish Cross"). Their first attacks, which culminated in 14 Gothas bombing central London and killing 104 people with one direct hit on June 13, took place in daylight. Despite numerous British fighters being scrambled to meet the intruders, none was shot down. The lack of response caused public uproar.

However, the British strengthened their anti-aircraft defenses around the capital and the Gothas had to attack under cover of darkness. Between September 1917 and May 1918 the bombers flew 19 night missions against London. They killed some 830 people and wounded more than 1900. Sixty Gothas were lost during these attacks, although few fell to the British defenses. Most suffered from mechanical failures or crashes. The British conquered the Gotha threat by launching their own bomber offensive directed against the Gotha bases in Belgium.

Bombs in position under the fuselage and wing of a Gotha GV bomber prior to a mission against London.

in northeast Italy. The offensive had originally been timed to coincide with two attacks on the Western Front by the French and British in mid-April, but muddled planning and lack of organization have combined to delay the Italian effort.

The Tenth Battle of the Isonzo lasts for 17 days and the Italians fail to make any significant gains in the face of mountainous terrain and stubborn Austro-Hungarian resistance. The Italians record around 160,000 men killed, wounded, or taken prisoner by the close of their offensive, while the Austro-Hungarians report 75,000 casualties. Despite the lack of success on the Isonzo Front, Cadorna resolves to continue his efforts to break through to the Austro-Hungarian port of Trieste.

MAY 15

POLITICS, *FRANCE*
General Robert Nivelle, whose recent offensive on the Western Front has failed with massive casualties and provoked a widespread mutiny in the French Army, is sacked as commander-in-chief. He is replaced by General Henri-Philippe Pétain, the hero of Verdun. Pétain moves quickly to quell the mutiny.

Over the following months he tours the front listening to the grievances of the ordinary soldiers, agrees to improve their conditions, and arrests some of the ringleaders. The record of

disobedience peaks in July but is virtually over by the following month, although isolated incidents continue into early 1918. Some 50 men are tried and executed. Thanks to an efficient system of press censorship the Germans do not hear of the mutiny until it is virtually over and are unable to take advantage of the situation.

SEA WAR, *ADRIATIC*
Austro-Hungarian warships commanded by Captain Miklós Horthy, later the dictator of Hungary, attack several Italian vessels sailing off the Albanian coast. Fourteen are sunk before British, French, and Italian warships intervene, forcing Horthy to withdraw.

MAY 18

POLITICS, *UNITED STATES*
Congress passes the Selective Service Act, which allows for the registration and selective draft of men aged between 21 and 30.

MAY 23

AIR WAR, *BRITAIN*
Marking a new chapter in strategic bombing, 16 long-range German Gotha bombers attack London from their bases in Belgium. Darkness foils the attack on the capital, but the

▼ *A blindfolded volunteer draws out the assigned numbers of some of those Americans to fight on the Western Front.*

twin-engined aircraft drop their bombs to the east, killing some 100 Canadian troops at a military base.

JUNE 2

AIR WAR, *WESTERN FRONT*
Canadian fighter ace Billy Bishop carries out a singlehanded attack on a German airfield for which he will be awarded the Victoria Cross, Britain's highest award for valor. By the end of the conflict Bishop will be credited with 72 air victories.

▼ *A panorama of the German-held trenches captured by the British during the attack on Messines Ridge, Belgium.*

JUNE 4

POLITICS, *RUSSIA*
General Aleksey Brusilov is appointed commander-in-chief by the Provisional Government to replace General Mikhail Alekseev. However, it is clear that the Russian Army is disintegrating.

JUNE 7

WESTERN FRONT, *BELGIUM*
Field Marshal Sir Douglas Haig's British Expeditionary Force launches an attack against the German troops holding the high ground of Messines Ridge in southwest Belgium. Haig is planning to stage a major offensive

▲ *Canadian ace Billy Bishop pictured in front of his French-built Nieuport 17 fighter.*

between the North Sea and the Lys River in the hope of breaking through the German lines around Ypres to the north, but before he can contemplate such an attack the dominating ridge at Messines has to be captured.

The German defenses have been under constant artillery barrage from 2000 artillery pieces for 17 days, and shortly before the British infantry advance, a series of huge underground mines are exploded under the battered enemy positions.

June 12

The troops committed to the painstakingly-planned British attack are drawn from General Sir Herbert Plumer's Second Army and in a day's fighting they capture the ridge at a cost of 17,000 casualties. The German defenders suffer 25,000 casualties, of whom some 7500 are taken prisoner. The capture of the ridge paves the way for Haig's grand offensive, which is known as the Third Battle of Ypres, or Passchendaele. It begins in late July.

June 12

POLITICS, *GREECE*

King Constantine I, whose has pro-German sympathies (he is the brother-in-law of Germany's Kaiser Wilhelm II), is forced to abdicate. The new king is Constantine's second son, Alexander, who is more sympathetic to Britain and France. He appoints Eleuthérios Venizélos as his prime minister. They allow allied forces to move into Thessaly in northern Greece.

June 13

AIR WAR, *BRITAIN*

Fourteen German long-range Gotha bombers return to attack London in daylight, striking the center of the capital, killing 104 people, and wounding more than 400 without loss. Public outrage forces the government to improve its anti-aircraft defenses around the capital. This strengthening forces the Gothas to mount their attacks under cover of darkness.

June 24

WESTERN FRONT, *FRANCE*

US General John Pershing lands with the first contingents of the American Expeditionary Force. Other units will follow; some 180,000 men by the end of the year.

June 27

POLITICS, *GREECE*

The government enters the war against the Central Powers.

June 29

POLITICS, *BRITAIN*

The government replaces the commander of its forces in Egypt, General Sir Archibald Murray, with General Sir Edmund Allenby. Murray's failure to cut through the Turkish forces holding the Gaza–Beersheba

◄ *Civilians and military rescue workers survey the aftermath of a German bomber raid on central London.*

line on two previous occasions has brought about his downfall. His replacement, a cavalry officer with a reputation for clear-headed leadership and military flair, is ordered by the government to break through the enemy defenses and take "Jerusalem by Christmas."

▲ British General Sir Edmund Allenby was ordered to seize Jerusalem from the Turks by Christmas 1917.

attack. This, the Kerensky Offensive, begins well for the Russians. Their Eleventh and Seventh Armies make progress against German General Felix von Bothmer's Southern Army, and the Austro-Hungarian Second Army is also under intense pressure. In the south the Russian Eighth Army under General Lavr Kornilov attacks on the 7th and presses forward toward the oil fields at Drohobycz against the Austro-Hungarian Third Army.

However, there are growing signs that ordinary Russian soldiers are no longer willing to obey their officers. Many units have established their own

▲ The course of the war on the Eastern Front in 1917–18.

▼ A German howitzer bombards the retreating Russians during their disastrous Kerensky Offensive.

▲ US troops parade through central London, tangible evidence of the United States' commitment to the war.

JULY 1

EASTERN FRONT, *RUSSIA*
Despite growing political turmoil, the Russian commander-in-chief, General Aleksey Brusilov, launches a major offensive toward Lemberg at the behest of Minister of War Alexander Kerensky, who gives his name to the

soviets (workers' councils) and these are usurping the authority of the officers. The Kerensky Offensive begins to collapse as the Germans lay plans for a counteroffensive.

JULY 11

WESTERN FRONT, *BELGIUM*

The British begin a major air campaign over Ypres. Their intention is to sweep the Germans from the skies prior to the opening of a major offensive at the end of the month.

JULY 18

WESTERN FRONT, *BELGIUM*

The British begin the preliminary bombardment for their forthcoming attack in the Ypres salient. Some 1400 artillery pieces unleash high-explosive

▲ *Mata Hari, the convicted Dutch-born German spy, awaits execution at the hands of a French firing squad.*

and gas shells on the German trenches outside the city. The barrage will continue until the last day of the month, when the Third Battle of Ypres, also known as Passchendaele, begins with nine divisions leading the ground offensive.

However, the British barrage badly craters the low-lying ground, which has a high water table, and destroys the natural and manmade drainage systems.

▼ *German pilots prepare for a sortie over British-held Ypres in Belgium. The aircraft are Fokker DR.1 triplanes.*

JULY 19

POLITICS, *GERMANY*

Members of the Reichstag (parliament) pass a peace resolution, which effectively backs the plans for an end to the war proposed by US President Woodrow Wilson.

EASTERN FRONT, *RUSSIA*

German forces under the overall command of General Max Hoffmann launch their counteroffensive against the Russian forces involved in the recent Kerensky Offensive, which began on July 1. The Russian armies are riven by political unrest and begin to disintegrate. Many units simply refuse to advance or attack, and rates of desertion soar. The Germans quickly regain much of the territory lost during the initial Russian attacks, and rebuff a limited counterattack by the Russian Fourth Army and contingents of Romanians on the 22nd.

JULY 20

POLITICS, *BALKANS*

In a move that paves the way for the formation of what will become the state of Yugoslavia, the Serbian government-in-exile agrees the Pact of Corfu. It calls for Croats, Montenegrins, Serbs, and Slovenes to be united in a single state, which is to be headed by the Serbian royal family.

POLITICS, *RUSSIA*

Former Minister of War Alexander Kerensky is made head of the Provisional Government, although its status is not recognized by various left-wing revolutionary groups.

JULY 24

ESPIONAGE, *FRANCE*

Dutch-national Margaretha Zelle, who is better known by her stage name Mata Hari, stands trial on charges of spying for the Germans. She was arrested by French security personnel in Paris on February 13. Although the evidence is ambiguous, she is convicted and later executed.

JULY 26

AIR WAR, *WESTERN FRONT*

Faced with increasing numbers of more advanced enemy fighters, the Germans reorganize their own fighter forces by amalgamating various squadrons to form

▶ *British troops attempt to free a light field piece from the mud at Ypres.*

◀ *British troops examine a captured German heavy machine gun at Ypres. They are wearing body armor.*

to the northeast of Ypres toward Pilckem Ridge. Support is offered by the French First Army under General François Anthoine to the north and General Sir Herbert Plumer's Second Army to the south. The initial attacks are moderately successful, but strong German counterattacks limit British gains to around two miles (3 km).

AUGUST 2

POLITICS, *RUSSIA*
General Lavr Kornilov replaces General Aleksey Brusilov as the Russian commander-in-chief. Kornilov's chief problem is to restore discipline in the rapidly disintegrating Russian Army. However, he has little faith in the Provisional Government headed by Alexander Kerensky.

WESTERN FRONT, *BELGIUM*
The British offensive around Ypres, which began on July 31, is temporarily suspended due to unseasonal heavy rain. The heavily-cratered battlefield is turning into a sea of thick mud. It is hoped that the postponement will give time for the ground to dry out.

AUGUST 16–18

WESTERN FRONT, *BELGIUM*
The British offensive at Ypres, halted temporarily on the 2nd to allow the waterlogged ground to dry,

units consisting of 50 or so aircraft. One of the most famous, its aircraft painted in vivid colors, is nicknamed "Richthofen's Circus" after its commander, the charismatic ace Baron Manfred von Richthofen.

JULY 31

WESTERN FRONT, *BELGIUM*
Field Marshal Sir Douglas Haig launches what becomes known as the Third Battle of Ypres, or Passchendaele. His aims are ambitious: to smash through

General Sixt von Arnim's German Fourth Army, push several miles along the coast, and then swing northward to capture the ports of Ostend and Zeebrugge, from where German submarines and destroyers are operating. Once the ports have fallen, Haig intends to recommence his drive to evict the Germans from Belgium.

The main force committed to the operation consists of General Sir Hubert Gough's British Fifth Army, which is to attack

▲ *The battlefield of Third Ypres pictured with abandoned British tanks.*

recommences. The focus of the fighting is around the village of Langemarck, which is attacked by General Sir Hubert Gough's Fifth Army. Progress is slow due to the difficult conditions and the stubborn German defense. British progress is limited to a few hundred yards.

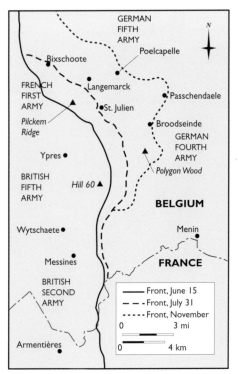

▲ *The Third Battle of Ypres was the major British offensive of 1917.*

AUGUST 17

POLITICS, *BRITAIN*
General Jan Christiaan Smuts makes a report to the government concerning means of improving the country's defenses against German air attack. Chief among his proposals is the creation of a single air force that is independent of either the British Army or navy. This will involve amalgamating the Royal Flying Corps and the Royal Naval Air Service. His report is accepted immediately. Air Marshal Sir Hugh Trenchard, a keen advocate of an independent air force and commander of the Royal Flying Corps, will be appointed its first commander.

AUGUST 18–SEPTEMBER 15

WESTERN FRONT, *ITALY*
The Italian commander-in-chief, General Luigi Cadorna, orders his forces to launch what becomes the Eleventh Battle of the Isonzo against the Austro-Hungarians. Two Italian armies are committed to the enterprise. The Second Army under General Luigi Capello, attacks to the north of the town of Gorizia, while the Duke of Aosta's Third Army attacks to the south

▶ *French fighter ace Georges Guynemer (second from right) pictured in front of his Morane-Saulnier Type L fighter.*

between Gorizia and Trieste. The Italian forces total some 52 divisions backed by 5000 artillery pieces.

General Svetozan Borojevic von Bojna's Austro-Hungarian Fifth Army swiftly halts the Duke of Aosta's advance, but the Italians make greater progress to the north. Here, the Italian Second Army takes the Bainsizza Plateau. Italian casualties are again very severe – around 166,000 men killed, wounded, or taken prisoner; the Austro-Hungarians admit to losses of 85,000. However, the Austro-Hungarian commanders believe that their troops are on the point of collapse and that they do not have the military resources to save the situation. They call on the German high command to send forces to stabilize the front.

SEPTEMBER 1

EASTERN FRONT, *RUSSIA*
Capitalizing on the growing unrest in Russia, the Germans launch an offensive directed against the port of Riga. Committed to this enterprise is the Eighth Army commanded by General Oskar von Hutier, who is opposed by the Russian Twelfth Army. Hutier uses new tactics – a brief preliminary bombardment followed by attacks by specialist stormtrooper assault infantry units, which push forward rapidly supported by mobile artillery and bypass enemy strongpoints.

Hutier's assault across the Dvina River is highly successful; the Russian Twelfth Army melts away. The Germans, whose casualties are

▲ *German troops rest in front of a church in the city of Riga, which they captured from the Russians in early September.*

minimal, take 9000 Russian prisoners. Many other Russian soldiers have simply deserted their posts.

SEPTEMBER 9–14

POLITICS, *RUSSIA*
General Lavr Kornilov launches a rebellion against the Bolsheviks, who dominate the Provisional Government in Petrograd, and are led by Vladimir Lenin and Leon Trotsky. However, Kornilov's attempted coup fails as his wavering forces are defeated by armed workers organized by the Bolsheviks.

SEPTEMBER 11

AIR WAR, *WESTERN FRONT*
Georges Guynemer is killed while operating over the Belgian city of Ypres. Guynemer, the top-scoring French ace of the war, gained his first victory in June 1915 and flew with the Third Squadron of the elite *Les Cigognes* ("The Storks") group.

SEPTEMBER 20

WESTERN FRONT, *BELGIUM*
The focus of the British offensive around Ypres switches to the south of

▼ *General Oskar von Hutier, one of the pioneers of Germany's successful stormtrooper tactics.*

STRATEGY & TACTICS

GERMAN STORMTROOPERS
By 1917 it was clear to some senior commanders on all sides that the established offensive doctrine of long preliminary bombardments followed by measured infantry attacks to capture all of an enemy's positions on a set step-by-step timetable was not working. Long artillery barrages warned the enemy, rarely destroyed his defenses or ability to fight back, and never produced massive casualties. Some tacticians began to consider new ways of fighting a battle based on surprise and rapid movement. Chief among these were two German officers on the Eastern Front, General Oskar von Hutier and Colonel George Bruchmüller.

They concluded that a sudden, unexpected artillery bombardment against key enemy positions using both gas and high-explosive shells would be more effective than a long barrage, particularly if the artillery pieces involved were brought into position shortly before the attack to avoid them being spotted.

They also argued that enemy positions surviving this initial rain of shells should be avoided to prevent the offensive from breaking down; far better that specially-trained assault units, their ranks filled with men known as stormtroopers, should infiltrate as quickly as possible into the enemy's rear areas, sowing confusion and disrupting communications as they went, rather than fighting against surviving strongpoints. Ideally, artillery, which in the past had failed to keep up with sudden breakthroughs, had to maintain pace with the infantry assault. Aircraft would support the advancing stormtroopers, shooting up enemy targets and pockets of resistance.

These ideas were not entirely unique. The British won a local victory at Messines Ridge on the Western Front in June 1917 using a brief bombardment. Equally, the French had used a similar tactic during the Nivelle Offensive in April. However, both Hutier and Bruchmüller saw that the surprise bombardment was clearly not enough: the specialist troops and mobile artillery were also essential.

The new German tactics were first tested on the Eastern Front in September 1917 and at Caporetto against the Italians in October. They were stunningly successful on both occasions. In the spring of 1918 the same tactics came very close to achieving a great German victory on the Western Front.

141

▲ *Turkish prisoners captured by the British at the Battle of Ramadi in Mesopotamia are led to the rear.*

the salient, where General Sir Herbert Plumer's Second Army is ordered to attack. The methodical Plumer decides to set limited objectives for a series of attacks that if successful will see his forces occupy the ridges to the south of Ypres. He opts to attack on a narrow front led by a creeping barrage.

Three battles follow: Menin Road (September 20–25), Polygon Wood (September 26), and Broodseinde (October 4). The British are aided by the drying out of the ground, a factor which has dogged progress since the opening of the Third Battle of Ypres in late July. Despite much heavy fighting, in which the Germans use mustard gas for the first time, Gough's limited, step-by-step attacks are successful. However, heavy rain again falls over the battlefield. The British commander-in-chief, Field Marshal Sir Douglas Haig, opts to continue.

SEPTEMBER 23

AIR WAR, *WESTERN FRONT*
German ace Werner Voss, who is credited with 48 victories in less than a year, is killed by British fighters led by James McCudden, who will win 57 victories before his death in 1918.

SEPTEMBER 27–28

MIDDLE EAST, *MESOPOTAMIA*
British and Commonwealth forces under the command of General Sir

Frederick Maude advance northward along the Euphrates River and confront the Turks at the Battle of Ramadi. The Turks are defeated and pursued by the British deep into central Mesopotamia. Maude's intention, once he has secured central Mesopotamia, is to drive northward along the Tigris River in the direction of Mosul, a vital oil-producing center.

OCTOBER 9–12

WESTERN FRONT, *BELGIUM*
The focus of the British offensive at Ypres switches back to the northeast of the town, but an attack led by Australian troops fails to make any significant progress. However, the battle continues, although it is clear that the British will not be able to achieve the decisive breakthrough that is planned. On the 12th they attack the village of Passchendaele without success. Although Field Marshal Sir Douglas Haig accepts that he cannot achieve his original ambitions of a decisive breakthrough, he nevertheless is determined to capture the high ground outside Ypres

before the onset of winter. He again makes the village of Passchendaele his main target.

OCTOBER 17

SEA WAR, *NORTH SEA*
A British convoy of 12 merchant ships, which is escorted by two destroyers, *Mary Rose* and *Strongbow*, is moving supplies from

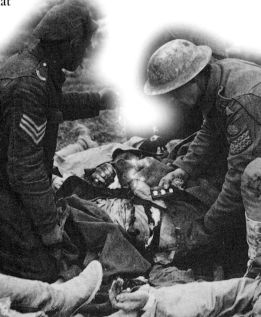

◄ Italian mechanized transport retreats during the disastrous Battle of Caporetto. The Germans provided specialist assault units to lead the highly-successful Austro-Hungarian offensive.

crash in enemy territory. This raid marks the end of major Zeppelin raids on Britain. Henceforth, they are used on naval-support duties in the North Sea or to carry out nuisance raids.

OCTOBER 24

WESTERN FRONT, *ITALY*

Austro-Hungarian artillery firing a mixture of high-explosive and gas shells open the Twelfth Battle of the Isonzo, also known as the Battle of Caporetto. In the previous month the Austro-Hungarians have been reinforced by several German divisions and specialist mountain units. Six of the German divisions and nine Austro-Hungarian have been formed into the

new Fourteenth Army, which is commanded by German General Otto von Below. Below's forces, assembled within Austro-Hungarian territory in the area of Tolmino, Caporetto, and Plezza along the Isonzo River, spearhead the offensive. The main target of the Fourteenth Army is General Luigi Capello's Italian Second Army, which has been slowly preparing defensive positions in readiness to meet the expected attack.

The main attack by the Fourteenth Army is backed by the advance of two further Austro-Hungarian armies. The Fifth, in the south opposing the Italian Third Army, is ordered to push along the north Italian Adriatic coast in the direction of Venice. The Third Army, to

▼ Italian dead, some of the 10,000 killed during the Battle of Caporetto. A further 275,000 were captured and around 20,000 wounded.

Scandinavia, but is surprised by the *Brummer* and *Bremse*, German light cruisers. Both destroyers and 75 percent of the convoy are sunk.

OCTOBER 19

AIR WAR, *BRITAIN*

German Zeppelin airships conduct what becomes a disastrous raid due to adverse weather and the British anti-aircraft defenses. Three of the 11 Zeppelins committed to the raid are smashed in a violent storm; one is destroyed by ground fire; a fifth drifts out to sea and is never seen again; while the other six fail to reach their targets and are either captured or

◄ British troops attempt to identify their own and German dead during the Third Battle of Ypres.

OCTOBER 26

the north of the Fourteenth Army is tasked with heading southwest into Italy, making for the line of the Piave River. It is hoped that elements of this force will deal with an Italian army known as the Carnic Force.

The opening barrage causes panic among many front-line Italian units, whose troops discover that their masks offer no protection against the enemy gas. Advancing through rain and mist, and bypassing points of resistance, the offensive makes rapid progress; by the 25th the attackers are exploiting a 15-mile (24-km) break-through in the Italian line, forcing the Italian commander-in-chief, General Luigi Cadorna, to consider with-drawing to the Tagliamento River.

However, Cadorna is unaware of the true extent of the breakthrough or the strength of the enemy forces he is facing, primarily due to poor commu-nications with his forward units. The order to withdraw to the next defen-sible barrier is finally issued on the 27th. The battered Italian armies are regrouping across the Tagliamento by the end of the month.

OCTOBER 26

POLITICS, *BRAZIL*
Brazil declares war on Germany, the only country in South America to do so. Brazilian merchant ships have been sunk by German submarines on a regular basis.

OCTOBER 26–NOVEMBER 10

WESTERN FRONT, *BELGIUM*
The British again attempt to capture the German-held village of Passchendaele outside Ypres. The Canadian Corps is committed to the

▼ *Disarmed Italian prisoners are hurried into captivity during the Battle of Caporetto, while German troops advance.*

attack, but the rate of advance is painfully slow due to the dreadful ground conditions and the extensive use of mustard gas by the enemy. The village finally falls on November 6, effectively ending the offensive that begun in late July.

The British commander-in-chief, Field Marshal Sir Douglas Haig, is widely criticized for prolonging the operation even though it rapidly became apparent that he could not achieve the breakthrough along the Belgian coast he desired.

OCTOBER 27

WESTERN FRONT, *ITALY*
During the on-going Battle of Caporetto a young German officer, Erwin Rommel, completes the capture of some 9000 Italian prisoners. For three days Rommel's 250 specialist mountain troops have fought to capture a critical position against heavy odds. For his bravery and leadership Rommel receives Germany's highest award, the Pour le Mérite.

OCTOBER 31

MIDDLE EAST, *PALESTINE*
The British and Commonwealth forces commanded by General Sir Edmund Allenby, some 88,000 men divided between seven infantry divisions and the horse- and camel-mounted Desert Mounted Corps, launch the Third Battle of Gaza.

Allenby has decided on a new plan to break through the Turkish-held Gaza–Beersheba line. Rather than

▲ *British troops move forward at dusk during the final stages of the Third Battle of Ypres.*

▼ *Australian and New Zealand troops of the Desert Mounted Corps advance at the opening of the Third Battle of Gaza.*

By any standards the Third Battle of Ypres has been an awful experience for the British. They have suffered some 310,000 men killed, wounded, or captured to advance a meager five miles (8 km), consuming all of their reserve forces on the Western Front in the process. The French have suffered some 85,000 casualties and the Germans list around 260,000.

▼ *British officers examine an abandoned Turkish field gun and ammunition limber during the Third Battle of Gaza.*

launch frontal attacks against the heavily-entrenched Turks around Gaza on the coast, he opts to use three of his divisions to launch a feint attack against the coastal town, while the bulk of his forces will drive inland against Beersheba to secure its vital water supply and turn the Turkish left flank. The key element is the rapid capture of Beersheba's water – without it Allenby's mounted forces will not progress far in the heat.

▶ *British Foreign Secretary Arthur Balfour (right), who backed the creation of a Jewish state in Palestine but one with the rights of local Arabs protected.*

▼ *Turks captured by the Australian Light Horse at Beersheba during the Third Battle of Gaza in Palestine.*

◄ *Turkish troops rise from their trenches to launch an attack on the British during the fighting in Palestine.*

Allenby is opposed by some 35,000 Turks, chiefly the Eighth Army and elements of the Seventh Army commanded by German General Kress von Kressenstein. Kressenstein also has a small number of German machine-gun, artillery, and technical detachments under his orders. However, his position is somewhat undermined by his long supply lines.

The attack on Beersheba, which will give an alternative name to the battle, lasts throughout the day, but culminates in a daring and successful charge by a brigade of Australian cavalry at dusk. Remarkably, the brigade charges through the Turkish defenses and machine-gun fire, taking Beersheba and its vital wells. The weak Turkish Seventh Army at Beersheba is forced

▲ *German assault troops and their artillery support pass through a recently-captured village in northeastern Italy during the Battle of Caporetto.*

◄ *Italian prisoners captured during the joint German and Austro-Hungarian crossing of the Tagliamento River during the climax of the Battle of Caporetto.*

into headlong retreat, leaving the Turkish left flank exposed to further British advances.

NOVEMBER 2

POLITICS, *BRITAIN*
Foreign Secretary Arthur Balfour writes to Lord Rothschild, the chairman of of the British Zionist Federation, expressing his support for the creation of a Jewish state in Palestine. This letter, known as the "Balfour Declaration," also expresses the need for safeguards to protect "the civil and religious rights of existing non-Jewish communities in Palestine."

WESTERN FRONT, *ITALY*
Capitalizing on the momentum of their advance, the German forces leading the Battle of Caporetto make a crossing of the Tagliamento River under cover of darkness, thereby breaking the recently-formed Italian defensive line.

The Italian commander-in-chief, General Luigi Cadorna, orders his forces to withdraw to the next feasible line of defense, the Piave

▲ German lancers, part of their country's limited manpower commitment to Turkey, patrol the Palestinian countryside.

▼ US troops prepare to disembark from their transport, which has just docked in a French port.

River. The retreat is completed by the 9th. Remarkably, despite their disorganization, casualties, and continuing enemy pressure, Italian resolve stiffens.

NOVEMBER 3

WESTERN FRONT, *FRANCE*
The first three soldiers of the ever-growing American Expeditionary Force are killed in action.

NOVEMBER 5

POLITICS, *ITALY*
The disastrous Italian defeat at Caporetto sparks a meeting at Rapallo of those nations opposing the Central Powers. Discussions broaden from providing military aid to Italy to include the establishment of a unified command structure. British Prime Minister David Lloyd George suggests creating what becomes known as the Supreme War Council. This will consist of the leaders (or their representatives) of Britain, France, Italy, and the United States.

NOVEMBER 6

MIDDLE EAST, *PALESTINE*
General Sir Edmund Allenby begins to

exploit his decisive breakthrough at Beersheba at the close of October; his main aim is to drive a wedge between the retreating Turkish Seventh Army and the Turkish Eighth Army, which is still holding defensive positions around Gaza on the coast. Leading the way is Allenby's Desert Mounted Corps, which is ordered to swing toward Gaza on the coast from its positions around Beersheba to the southeast. However, the Turkish Eighth Army is aware of Allenby's strategy and rapidly withdraws from Gaza along the coast. The Turkish Seventh Army inland retreats toward Jerusalem.

▲ *Turkish field artillery in action during the British advance through Palestine. The weapon is a German-built three-inch (75-mm) design.*

▼ *Dismounted Australian cavalrymen open fire on the Turks during the fighting in Palestine.*

Allenby, eager to maintain the momentum of his advance, orders his various units to pursue the Turks as closely as possible, despite his force's shortage of water.

NOVEMBER 6–7

POLITICS, *RUSSIA*

Bolshevik revolutionaries led by Vladimir Lenin and Leon Trotsky launch a successful attempt to overthrow the Provisional Government headed by Prime Minister Alexander Kerensky in Petrograd. The Bolsheviks will enter into negotiations with the Germans over an armistice.

NOVEMBER 12

WESTERN FRONT, *ITALY*

The Twelfth Battle of Isonzo, better known as the Battle of Caporetto, ends chiefly due to the Germans and Austro-Hungarians having overstretched their supplies. The offensive has been a disaster for the Italians.

Although the Italian commander-in-chief, General Luigi Cadorna, has been able to stabilize his front, his forces have taken a battering and have suffered around 30,000 men killed or wounded. Some 275,000 prisoners

◄ *Russian troops, probably deserters from the front, on the streets of an unidentified town reading propaganda leaflets printed by the Bolsheviks.*

▼ *British field artillery pieces are readied for action against the Turkish forces retreating through Palestine.*

have been captured by the German and Austro-Hungarian forces commanded by German General Otto von Below. In addition, 2500 artillery pieces and huge quantities of stores and other equipment have been lost. The Germans and Austro-Hungarian casualties total some 20,000 men, a remarkably low figure for such a major offensive.

In the space of a few weeks the Italians have been forced back from the Isonzo, where they have fought a series of fruitless battles since 1915, to a line running from just south of the city of Trent along the Piave River, which runs into the Gulf of Venice in the northern Adriatic Sea – leaving the Italians a new front line of some 60 miles (96 km).

◄ *German General Otto von Below of the Fourteenth Army, who led the attack against the Italians during the successful Battle of Caporetto.*

▲ *The German-led offensive in Italy known as the Battle of Caporetto was one of the most successful attacks of the entire war.*

The sweeping German and Austro-Hungarian success has two immediate and important consequences. The chief of the Italian General Staff, General Luigi Cadorna, is replaced by General Armando Diaz, and several French and British divisions under the command of General Sir Herbert Plumer are rushed to bolster the battered Italian units along the Piave.

Remarkably, the disaster of Caporetto transforms the Italian public's view of the war. Previously, the army has fought chiefly outside Italy, on Austro-Hungarian soil; Caporetto has been,

NOVEMBER 13-15

however, fought almost wholly in Italy. This fact and the scale of the Italian defeat are exploited by several Italian public figures, such as the ardent nationalist poet Gabriele D'Annunzio and soldier-turned-journalist Benito Mussolini. Both issued emotive calls for the invaders to be evicted from Italy. Many ordinary Italians responded to their call to arms.

NOVEMBER 13-15

MIDDLE EAST, *PALESTINE*
British General Sir Edmund Allenby continues his pursuit of the Turkish forces defeated at the recent Battle of Beersheba. The focus of his attack is the Turkish Eighth Army, which has recently abandoned its positions at Gaza and fallen back northward along the Mediterranean coast.

Allenby's troops are able to break through hastily-built Turkish defenses during the Battle of Junction Station – a source of much-needed water – and then turn eastward. However, Turkish reserves led by German General Eric von Falkenhayn slow Allenby's advance on Jerusalem.

NOVEMBER 17

AIR WAR, *AFRICA*
The German Zeppelin *L59*, which is on a 3500-mile (5600-km) supply mission to German East Africa in aid of

▲ *Turkish cavalrymen retreat through Palestine pursued by the British.*

▼ *Italian women dig trenches following the disaster at Caporetto.*

General Paul von Lettow-Vorbeck, is ordered to return to Europe while flying over the Sudan. It is believed, incorrectly, that Lettow-Vorbeck is about to surrender.

NOVEMBER 18

MIDDLE EAST, *MESOPOTAMIA*
The commander of the British and Commonwealth forces in the region, General Sir Frederick Maude, dies after contracting cholera from contaminated milk. He is buried just outside Baghdad. His replacement is named as General Sir William Marshall.

NOVEMBER 20

WESTERN FRONT, *FRANCE*
The British Third Army under General Sir Julian Byng opens the Battle of Cambrai. The main impetus of the

▲ *The funeral of British General Sir Frederick Maude at Baghdad.*

▼ *British tanks on their way to lead the attack at Cambrai.*

▲ British tanks move forward during the highly-successful opening phase of the Battle of Cambrai. In the left foreground is an abandoned German field gun. However, the offensive stalled as German resistance hardened.

tank-led attack falls on the section of the Hindenburg Line defended by General Georg von der Maritz's German Second Army. Byng's plan aims to cut through the German positions between the Canal de l'Escaut and the Canal du Nord. Cavalry are to move forward rapidly against Cambrai, while infantry units and tanks take Bourlon Ridge before advancing northeast to Valenciennes.

The battle begins with a short bombardment of the Hindenburg Line by 1000 artillery pieces, which have not been preregistered on their targets. The main attack is spearheaded by 476 tanks, marking the first use of such weapons en masse in the war. The tanks lead six of Byng's 19 divisions in an major advance along five miles (8 km) of the front.

The early attacks are spectacularly successful: the Hindenburg Line is pierced to depths of six–eight miles (9-12 km), except at Flesquières, where stubborn German defenders knock out a number of tanks and the poor coordination between the British infantry and tanks combine to foil the advance.

Despite the outstanding results in the first days of the battle, the British encounter increasing difficulties in maintaining the momentum of their offensive. Many tanks succumb to mechanical failure, become bogged down in ditches, or are smashed by German artillery at close range. The battle concentrates around Bourlon Ridge to the west of Cambrai. The fighting continues into December, with the Germans launching a series of successful counterattacks.

◀ General Sir Julian Byng, whose British Third Army led the attack at Cambrai.

▶ *A German light field gun opens fire on an enemy target during the fighting in East Africa.*

NOVEMBER 25

AFRICA, *GERMAN EAST AFRICA*
The outnumbered German General Paul von Lettow-Vorbeck, who is facing several large-scale enemy advances from neighboring colonies, is forced to order a total withdrawal into Portuguese East Africa in the face of overwhelming odds.

However, despite losing one-third of his army, which is surrounded and forced to surrender on the 27th, he continues to fight on, launching highly-successful guerrilla attacks until after the official end of the war in November 1918.

NOVEMBER 30

WESTERN FRONT, *FRANCE*
The German troops engaged against

▼ *German soldiers gather their equipment prior to launching a counterattack on the British at Cambrai.*

DECEMBER 3

British General Sir Julian Byng's British Third Army begin to launch counter-attacks to regain the ground lost on the opening day of the tank-led offensive. Crown Prince Rupprecht of Bavaria, the commander of the threatened sector, has rushed sizeable reinforcements to the aid of General Georg von der Maritz's Second Army, which has borne the brunt of the British onslaught so far.

The German attacks are highly effective chiefly due to three reasons: the use of a short bombardment, the employment of the new stormtrooper units, and the support offered to the advancing units by low-flying aircraft. The British, overextended and lacking immediate reserves, are forced to give up much of their hard-won gains over the following days.

On the same day as the opening of the German counterattack at Cambrai the US 42nd Rainbow Division, so named because it contains men from every state in the nation, arrives in France. The division's chief-of-staff and later commander is General Douglas MacArthur.

DECEMBER 3

POLITICS, *GERMANY/RUSSIA*
German and Russia delegates meet at Brest-Litovsk in former Russian Poland to discuss terms for a final peace (an armistice is already in operation) to the fighting on the Eastern Front. The Russians, led by Bolshevik Leon Trotsky, attempt to

stall negotiations. For their part the Germans want a swift conclusion so that they can transfer troops to bolster their forces battling on the Western Front.

WESTERN FRONT, *CAMBRAI*
Although Field Marshal Sir Douglas Haig, the British Expeditionary Force's commander, has rushed reinforcements to Cambrai to prevent the German counterattacks from breaking through the line held by General Sir Julian Byng's Third Army, he decides to withdraw his troops back to roughly the lines they occupied before the beginning of the battle on November 20.

Haig's order effectively ends the fighting by the 5th. Both the British and German forces have suffered roughly equal casualties – about 40,000 men – and the British have captured 11,000 troops to the 9000 taken by the Germans.

However, Cambrai highlights two important points. First, offensives do not have to be preceded by a prolonged artillery bombardment to be successful. Second, the mass use of tanks could achieve a major breakthrough, despite their mechanical unreliability and vulnerability to enemy fire. Both sides will take these lessons to heart in the offensive they are planning to launch during 1918.

DECEMBER 7

POLITICS, *UNITED STATES*
The government declares war on Austria-Hungary.

◄ *US General Douglas MacArthur, one of his country's most prominent generals in World War II, shown here commanding the 42nd Rainbow Division in 1918.*

▲ Turkish cavalrymen pictured in camp during the fighting against the British around Jerusalem.

▼ British tanks captured or abandoned at Cambrai are moved to the rear. Although Germany built its own tanks during the war, chiefly the A7V, it relied on the much more numerous British tanks that had been recovered from various battlefields. The larger A7V was found to have a poorer cross-country performance.

▲ British General Sir Edmund Allenby (foreground) makes his official entry into Jerusalem on December 11.

DECEMBER 9

POLITICS, *ROMANIA*
The authorities agree an armistice with the Central Powers, who have virtually total control of the country.
EASTERN FRONT, *RUSSIA*
Don cossacks revolt against the Bolsheviks, who are taking their land.
MIDDLE EAST, *PALESTINE*
The Turks abandon Jerusalem and British General Sir Edmund Allenby enters the city on the 11th.

DECEMBER 10

POLITICS, *FRANCE*
General Maurice Sarrail, commander of the vast multinational force operating in Greece, is sacked by French Prime Minister Georges Clemenceau, who appoints General Marie Guillaumat.

DECEMBER 30

FAR EAST AND PACIFIC, *JAPAN*
Taking advantage of Russia's instability, Japanese forces occupy the port of Vladivostok, much to the anger of Britain, France, and the United States, who doubt Japan's motives.

1918

This final year of the war the German high command gambled all on winning a clear victory on the Western Front before the arrival of US forces. They came close to victory but were halted. After this defeat Germany's allies gradually sought armistices, its own armed forces began to collapse, and its leaders had to seek an armistice themselves.

security, with disputes to be settled by an international body. The program, although not universally popular with America's allies, will subsequently be the basis on which Germany agrees to an armistice in November.

JANUARY 20

SEA WAR, *AEGEAN*
The former German warships *Breslau* and *Goeben*, which have been under Turkish control since 1914, make a final sortie into the Aegean Sea. Both run into an enemy minefield – the *Breslau* sinks and the *Goeben* is forced aground. Despite intense enemy air attacks, the *Goeben* survives and is towed to safety by the Turks.

JANUARY 1

POLITICS, *FINLAND*
The Bolshevik government recognizes the independence of this former Russian province, which had declared itself independent the previous month. However, tension mounts between Finland's political groups.

JANUARY 8

POLITICS, *UNITED STATES*
In a far-reaching speech to Congress, President Woodrow Wilson outlines his 14-Point Peace Program. It is designed to prevent destructive wars and at its heart are the principles of national self-determination and collective

▼ *British troops, part of the force led by General L.C. Dunsterville, advance through northern Mesopotamia on their way to Baku on the Caspian Sea.*

◄ *German troops and members of the Finnish "White Guard" militia parade in Helsinki, the country's capital.*

POLITICS, *FINLAND*

The country's Social Democrats, backed by their militia known as the "Red Guard," stage a coup and proclaim Finland a socialist workers' republic. The leader of the overthrown government, Pehr Svinhufvud, flees to Vaasa in eastern Finland, whose Russian garrison has been thrown out by General Karl von Mannerheim, the commander of the government's own militia, the "White Guard." Pro-German Svinhufvud calls on Germany for military aid against the "Red Guard."

FEBRUARY 1

POLITICS, *AUSTRIA-HUNGARY*

Austro-Hungarian sailors stage a mutiny at Cattaro, the navy's chief base on the Dalmatian coast.

FEBRUARY 18

POLITICS, *GERMANY/RUSSIA*

The German delegates who have been discussing the terms of a peace treaty with the Bolsheviks at Brest-Litovsk since the armistice agreement of December 1917, recommence hostilities, sending troops farther eastward into the Ukraine and toward Petrograd, the Russian capital. The Germans have become increasingly exasperated by the Bolsheviks'

▼ *Germans examine an armored car abandoned by the Bolsheviks during the renewed fighting on the Eastern Front.*

JANUARY 27

MIDDLE EAST, *MESOPOTAMIA*

A British force led by General L.C. Dunsterville is sent from Baghdad to take over the Russian oil fields at Baku on the Caspian Sea. With Russia in turmoil the Turks and Germans are also eager to grab the resources. "Dunsterforce" reaches Baku in August.

JANUARY 28

POLITICS, *ESTONIA*

The government of this former Russian province, which had declared its independence in November 1917, asks for German aid to deal with Russian Bolsheviks, who are attempting to regain power. The Germans occupy Revel on February 25 and succeed in expelling the Bolsheviks.

KEY MOMENTS

THE 14 POINTS

On January 8 US President Woodrow Wilson gave a speech that had profound consequences not only for World War I but also for the interwar map of Europe and for relations between states throughout the whole century. Wilson, who wished to distance himself from the secrecy that had governed relationships between powers before 1914, laid down principles that, he believed, should govern such relationships after 1918. His speech outlined key ideas that centered on openness in the relationships between countries and the right of self-determination. He hoped to reduce the suspicion between countries and prevent the rivalries that had sparked World War I. Among the 14 Points were:

1) Covenants of peace, openly arrived at, after which there shall be no private international understandings of any kind but diplomacy shall proceed always frankly and in the public view.

2) Absolute freedom of navigation, outside territorial waters, alike in peace and war, except as the seas may be closed by international action for the enforcement of international covenants.

3) The removal, so far as possible, of all economic barriers and the establishment of an equality of trade conditions among all the nations consenting to the peace and associating themselves for its maintenance.

4) Adequate guarantees given and taken that national armaments will be reduced to the lowest point consistent with domestic safety.

5) A free, open-minded, and absolutely impartial adjustment of all colonial claims, based upon a strict observance of the principle that in determining all such questions of sovereignty the interests of the populations must have equal weight with the equitable claims of the government whose title is to be determined.

14) A general association of nations must be formed under specific covenants for the purpose of affording mutual guarantees of political independence and territorial integrity to great and small states alike.

Points 6–13 were related to World War I, including the restoration of Belgian sovereignty, the return of French territory taken by Germany after the Franco-Prussian War (1870–71), and the self-determination of the various ethnic groups comprising what was the Austro-Hungarian Empire, certain parts of Russia, chiefly Poland, and Turkey.

FEBRUARY 24

▶ *German stormtroopers move forward at the opening of Operation Michael, the offensive begun on March 21.*

delaying tactics and are eager to impose an agreement to free their troops on the Eastern Front for service on the Western Front. The Bolsheviks do not have the forces or resources to block the renewed onslaught.

FEBRUARY 24

MIDDLE EAST, *ARMENIA*
Taking advantage of the collapse of the Russian Army in the wake of the 1917 Russian Revolution, Turkish forces reoccupy parts of Armenia they have lost to the Russians. However, they are most interested in securing the Russian oil-producing facilities at Baku on the Caspian Sea.

MARCH 3

POLITICS, *RUSSIA*
After weeks of prevarication the Bolshevik revolutionaries, who have a tenuous hold on the country, are forced to sign a stern peace treaty with the Germans at Brest-Litovsk. They are compelled to give up control of the Ukraine, Finland, the Baltic Provinces (Estonia, Latvia, and Lithuania), the Caucasus, Poland, and those areas of Russia controlled by the "White" Russians who are opposed to the Bolsheviks. German troops continue to occupy the Ukraine as its grain is vital to prevent wholesale starvation in Germany.

MARCH 21

WESTERN FRONT, *FRANCE*
General Erich Ludendorff has planned a knock-out blow on the Western Front. He recognizes that, with the imminent arrival of scores of thousands of US troops in France, Germany is likely to lose the war. However, Ludendorff plans to strike first. He transfers some 70 divisions of troops from the Eastern Front, where the turmoil following the Russian Revolution has effectively ended Russian involvement in the war. In

the short term, therefore, Germany has a clear numerical advantage over the British and French.

Ludendorff's plan is to exploit the differences between Britain's and France's strategies for facing any major German offensive. He believes the French will give priority to the defense of Paris, while the British are more concerned with defending the ports along the north French coast through which their supplies and troops flow. Ludendorff aims to attack at the juncture between the French and British forces in northeast France.

To this end he has three armies – the Seventeenth under General Otto von Below, the Second led by General Georg von der Marwitz, and General Oskar von Hutier's Eighteenth – prepare for the offensive. These are to advance along a 50-mile (80-km) front from Arras to St. Quentin and La Fère. This zone is defended by the British Third Army under General Sir Julian Byng and General Sir Hubert Gough's Fifth Army.

Ludendorff has 63 divisions, many led by elite stormtrooper units, earmarked for the attack, while the British can muster just 26. The offensive is code-named Operation Michael but is also known as the *Kaiserschlacht* ("Kaiser's Battle").

◀ *German officials greet the Russian Bolshevik delegates attending the peace negotiations at Brest-Litovsk.*

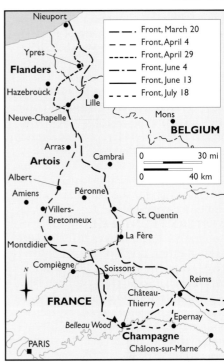

▲ British and French troops man hastily-prepared defenses during the opening phase of Operation Michael.

Operation Michael begins with a sudden five-hour bombardment on the British by 6000 artillery pieces. They fire both gas and high-explosive shells. Under cover of thick fog the Germans attack, with the specially-trained stormtrooper units leading the way. The surprise and shock of the onslaught overwhelms the thinly-spread British.

Gough's Fifth Army collapses in confusion, exposing the right flank of Byng's Third Army. However, Byng's forces, which are holding a narrower front than those of Gough, withdraw across the Somme River in good order. The attackers here, drawn from the German Seventeenth and Second Armies, make significantly less gains.

MARCH 23

WESTERN FRONT, *PARIS*
The Germans begin an intermittent bombardment of Paris with long-range eight-inch (21-cm) artillery pieces, which become known as the "Paris

Guns." There are seven of them and they can strike the French capital from ranges of 50 miles (80 km). The bombardment, which has little military value, continues until August 9. The "Paris Guns" fire a total of 367 shells, which kill 256 Parisians and wound 620. The guns are withdrawn in August as the German forces on the Western Front are forced to retreat.

MARCH 25

WESTERN FRONT, *FRANCE*
General Georg von der Marwitz's German Second Army breaks through the juncture of the British Third and Fifth Armies during the continuing Operation Michael. It appears to General Eric Ludendorff, the deputy chief of the German General Staff, that the British are on the point of collapse, so he issues new orders to

▼ One of the German "Paris Guns" undergoes test firing. They were designed by Krupp.

▲ The territory gained by the Germans during their series of offensives on the Western Front in the first half of 1918.

his commanders. He orders Marwitz to make for Amiens, while General Oskar von Hutier is directed to strike at Paris with his Eighteenth Army. General Otto von Below's Seventeenth Army is to continue to make for the ports along the coast of northern France.

The British commander-in-chief, Field Marshal Sir Douglas Haig, is rushing British troops to plug the gap in his line, but his French opposite number, Marshal Henri-Philippe Pétain is, as Ludendorff suspects, more concerned with protecting Paris, so sends few troops to aid the hard-pressed British.

MARCH 26

POLITICS, *FRANCE*
General Ferdinand Foch is made the coordinator of all the British, French, and American forces on the Western

Front following a meeting of the joint Supreme War Council. One of Foch's key supporters is Field Marshal Sir Douglas Haig, commander of the British Expeditionary Force.

Foch's chief concern is to stop the ongoing German offensive, Operation Michael, which has torn a hole in the British line in northern France. French reinforcements now flood into the threatened sector south of the Somme River, where they and British forces are placed under the command of France's General Marie Fayolle.

WESTERN FRONT, *FRANCE*
General Sir Julian Byng's British Third Army fighting north of the Somme River stops the German advance in part due to effective air support. The Germans attempt to relaunch their attack in this sector two days later, opening Operation Mars, which is aimed at Arras, but it fails. The defeat of Operation Mars signals the end of the German effort north of the Somme and the fighting now concentrates south of the river.

MARCH 27

WESTERN FRONT, *FRANCE*
German troops advancing south of the Somme River capture Montdidier. The town is some 40 miles (64 km) from their start point of March 21 and its fall leaves the German forces within striking distance of Amiens, their chief objective. However, the Germans are exhausted and are facing increasing

numbers of fresh British and French troops. The German attack is finally halted at the village of Villers-Bretonneux, some 10 miles (16 km) to the east of Amiens.

MARCH 29

AIR WAR, *WESTERN FRONT*
US pilot Edward Rickenbacker scores his first air victory. By the end of the war he will be acknowledged as his country's top ace with 26 kills.

▲ *US fighter ace Edward Rickenbacker, a renowned racing driver, was his country's top-scoring pilot of the war. Four of his 26 victories were against enemy balloons.*

APRIL 1

AIR WAR, *WESTERN FRONT*
The British Royal Air Force is created by the amalgamation of the Royal Flying Corps and the Royal Naval Air Service.

APRIL 3

POLITICS, *FINLAND*
Answering a call for military aid from the recently-ousted president, Pehr Svinhufvud, the German Baltic Division commanded by General Rüdiger von der Goltz arrives to aid the fight against the new pro-Bolshevik government and its militia, the "Red Guard."

APRIL 5

WESTERN FRONT, *FRANCE*
General Erich Ludendorff, the deputy chief of the German General Staff and instigator of Operation Michael, calls a halt to the offensive as it has become clear that he will not achieve a decisive victory along the Somme River. His forces have advanced some 40 miles (64 km) and inflicted around 240,000 casualties on the British and

◀ *German troops man an armored train during the fighting between rival political factions in Finland.*

French. German losses are equally severe, particularly among the stormtrooper units that spearheaded the onslaught. However, Ludendorff now switches his offensive to another sector of the Western Front.

APRIL 9–10

WESTERN FRONT,
FRANCE/BELGIUM
General Erich Ludendorff opens the second of a series of attacks on the

Western Front. Operation Georgette is directed at the British General Sir Herbert Plumer's Second Army and General Sir Henry Horne's British First Army, which are separated by the Lys River. Committed to the attack are General Sixt von Arnim's Fourth Army and General Ferdinand von Quast's Sixth Army. The offensive is to take place on a narrow front in the direction of the English Channel ports through which the British receive their supplies and reinforcements.

Following a three-day artillery bombardment, the attack begins on the morning of the 9th. The German Sixth Army advances from Neuve-Chapelle on a 12-mile (19-km) front against the left wing of Horne's First Army. Two divisions of Portuguese troops under Horne's command reel under the assault and are forced back some five miles (8 km).

The next day four divisions of General Sixt von Arnim's Fourth Army strike against elements of Plumer's Second Army, which is forced to retreat beyond Messines and Wytschaete.

APRIL 12

WESTERN FRONT,
FRANCE/BELGIUM
German forces attacking along the Lys River in the direction of the north

▼ *British troops take up position behind a railroad embankment during the fighting along the Lys River.*

MARSHAL FERDINAND FOCH

Ferdinand Foch (1851–1929) enlisted in the French Army in 1870 but did not see active service until 1914, when he played a significant role in the defeat of the German invasion of France. In the intervening 44 years he was a professor of strategy and tactics, and later commandant of the country's *Ecole de Guerre* ("School of War"). Both his lectures and writings emphasized the need for a general to gain psychological dominance over his opposite number and then to act offensively.

Despite a number of commands between 1914 and 1916, Foch was next tasked with a number of administrative roles, including that of Marshal Henri-Philippe Pétain's chief of staff in May 1917. Foch returned to action later the same year, when he coordinated the flow of Anglo-French reinforcements to Italy, which had suffered a catastrophic defeat at the Battle of Caporetto. He then joined the Supreme War Council, the body coordinating action against the Central Powers. During Germany's spring 1918 offensive on the Western Front the British suggested that Foch coordinate all the forces opposing the attack, a position that was later extended to other theaters. A thoughtful figure, renowned as an organizer and diplomat, he was able to overcome national self-interest to plan united action against the Germans.

French coast have created a break in the British line some 30 miles (48 km) wide and are closing in on one of their early objectives, the village of Hazebrouck, southwest of Ypres.

The British commander-in-chief, Field Marshal Sir Douglas Haig, issues an order prohibiting any further retreat: "With our backs to the wall and believing in the justice of our cause, each one must fight on to the end." The call to arms works and British resistance hardens.

▼ *French artillerymen go into action with a train-mounted naval gun during the fighting to halt the German offensive along the Lys River.*

APRIL 14

POLITICS, *FRANCE*
French General Ferdinand Foch is officially promoted to the position of commander-in-chief of all those forces of whatever nationality opposing Germany on the Western Front. In June this will be extended to include the Italian theater.

APRIL 17

WESTERN FRONT, *FRANCE/BELGIUM*
British and recently-arrived French troops fighting around Ypres

▲ *Open warfare breaks out on the Western Front for the first time since 1914 – German howitzers advance.*

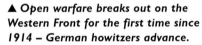

halt the German drive along the Lys River. Although there will be a series of attacks and counterattacks until the end of the month, the German attempt to reach the ports of northern France has failed. Both sides have lost around 100,000 troops in the fighting. However, General Erich Ludendorff, the deputy chief of the German General Staff, begins laying plans for a third offensive.

APRIL 21

AIR WAR, *WESTERN FRONT*
Baron Manfred von Richthofen, the leading ace of the war with 80 confirmed victories, is shot down and killed during a dogfight. He is buried with full military honors by the British. Richthofen's command is taken over by German ace (22 victories) Hermann Goering.

APRIL 23

WESTERN FRONT, *BELGIUM*
The British launch a surprise amphibious assault to curtail attacks by German submarines and destroyers operating in the English Channel from Ostend and Zeebrugge. The operation is masterminded by Vice Admiral Sir

▶ *The funeral service of German fighter ace Baron Manfred von Richthofen.*

Roger Keyes; his plan is to sink old warships across the canals that the enemy craft use to reach open water. In an operation that involves more than 70 vessels, the British concentrate their forces against Zeebrugge.

The attack on Zeebrugge begins with British naval infantry landing from the cruiser *Vindictive* on the harbor's sea-walls, and the destruction of an old submarine packed with explosives, the latter to isolate the German defenders of the sea-wall from the land.

As this action continues, three block-ships, *Thetis*, *Intrepid*, and *Iphigenia*, sail into Zeebrugge's inner harbor.

They are supposed to block the canal. *Thetis* grounds in the inner harbor, but *Intrepid* and *Iphigenia* reach their target only to be sunk in the incorrect position. The smaller attack on Ostend is even less successful – German raiders are still able to sail. A raid on Zeebrugge on May 9 also fails.

APRIL 25

AIR WAR, WESTERN FRONT Pilot Willy Coppens scores his first air victory, downing a German fighter. Belgium's leading ace of the war with 37 victories, he will become renowned for destroying observation balloons.

APRIL 28-29

POLITICS, *FINLAND* "White Guard" forces loyal to the former president, Pehr Svinhufvud, and commanded by General Karl von

▼ *The aftermath of the British raid on Zeebrugge, Belgium, a base for German submarines and destroyers.*

MAY 7

▶ *German stormtroopers cross a makeshift bridge during the drive against the French-held Chemin des Dames.*

Mannerheim win a decisive victory at Viborg over the "Red Guard" militia of the pro-Bolshevik government.

MAY 7

POLITICS, *ROMANIA*

Having been comprehensibly defeated in 1917 and forced to sign an armistice in December, Romania, which declared war on the Central Powers in August 1916, surrenders, signing the Treaty of Bucharest. Since the invasion the Romanian Army has suffered losses of some 400,000 troops and has had to retreat from some 80 percent of its territory.

However, the Romanian monarch, King Ferdinand, does not sign the document, which allows him to claim that his country never surrendered. This will permit Romania to claim full recompense for its efforts following the defeat of the Central Powers.

MAY 19

AIR WAR, *WESTERN FRONT*

Raoul Lufbery, one of the top-scoring US fighter pilots of the war with 17 victories, is killed during air combat. He had served with other American volunteers in the French *Escadrille Lafayette* (originally the *Escadrille Américaine* and credited with 38 air victories) before the United States' entry into the war. Lufbery was the commander of the famed 94th "Hat in the Ring" Aero Squadron at the time of his death. The squadron's nickname was derived from its emblem.

▼ *US troops supported by French-built Schneider tanks advance during the Battle of Cantigny, May 28.*

MAY 27

WESTERN FRONT, *FRANCE*

General Erich Ludendorff, the deputy chief of the German General Staff, opens his third offensive on the Western Front in 1918. It is a diversionary attack against the French forces holding the Chemin des Dames section of the Aisne River. Ludendorff's aim is to prevent the French from sending reinforcements to the aid of the British in northern France, where he is planning to attack again.

The offensive is led by General Max von Boehn's Seventh Army and the First Army under General Bruno von Mudra, a total of 44 divisions. The object of their advances, code-named Blücher and Yorck, is General Denis Duchêne's French Sixth Army, which consists of 12 divisions, including three British.

The German onslaught is heralded by a bombardment from 4600 artillery pieces, which is followed by an attack by seven divisions on a front of 10 miles (16 km). The Germans immediately capture the Chemin des Dames and advance on the Aisne River,

taking several intact bridges. By the end of the day the Germans have advanced some 10 miles (16 km).

Although the offensive is intended to be limited in scope, its early successes convince the German high command to press forward as Paris is just 80 miles (128 km) distant. However, the French are being sent reinforcements

by the commander of the American Expeditionary Force, General John Pershing. They are General Omar Bundy's 2nd Division and the 3rd Division under General J.T. Dickman. These will go into action on the 30th, by which stage the Germans are menacing the Marne River.

MAY 28

WESTERN FRONT, *FRANCE*

US forces undertake their first attack of the war on the second day of the German offensive along the Aisne River. However, the fighting centers on the village of Cantigny to the east of Montdidier on the Somme River sector to the north. Elements of the US 1st

▲ *Tangible proof of the United States' commitment to the Western Front – American troops march through the center of a French town.*

◄ *US and French troops rush ammunition supplies to the front during the fighting along the Aisne River at the height of the German offensives code-named Blücher and Yorck.*

Division under General Robert Lee Bullard are pitched against the German Eighteenth Army led by General Oskar von Hutier. Bullard's troops capture Cantigny, taking 200 prisoners, on the 28th and block a series of German counterattacks over the following days. American losses total some 1600 men, of whom 199 are killed.

JUNE 2–4

WESTERN FRONT, *FRANCE*

The US 3rd Division under General J.T. Dickman goes into action against the German troops threatening Château-Thierry on the Marne River. The division is able to prevent the German assault troops, who are part of the continuing operations code-named Blücher and Yorck, from crossing the Marne at Château-Thierry and then counterattacks with French support, forcing the Germans back across the Marne at Jaulgonne.

JUNE 4

WESTERN FRONT, *FRANCE*

General Erich Ludendorff calls off his twin offensives code-named Blücher and Yorck, which began on May 27. Although his assault units have advanced to a maximum depth of 20 miles (32 km) over a distance of 30 miles (48 km), they have run out of steam. He is also facing increasingly strong counterattacks from French and US forces.

German losses total some 125,000 men, a figure matched by those forces opposing the attacks. However, Ludendorff is already planning what will be his fourth offensive on the Western Front in 1918.

JUNE 6

WESTERN FRONT, *FRANCE*

As part of the ongoing counterattacks against the German forces holding their recently-won gains along the Marne River, the US 2nd Division under General Omar Bundy attacks at Belleau Wood, a little to the west of Château-Thierry. The division's US Marine Brigade and 3rd Infantry Brigade lead the way. Bundy's troops are facing the equivalent of four German divisions, yet the outnumbered US forces launch a succession

JUNE 9

▼ *The Austro-Hungarian battleship* Szent Istvan *keels over to starboard following a successful Italian attack.*

of attacks over the following weeks. After three weeks of fighting the wood is cleared. Bundy's casualties reach 1800 men killed and 7000 wounded.

JUNE 9

SEA WAR, *ADRIATIC*

An Austro-Hungarian attempt to break the enemy blockade of the Adriatic ends in failure with the dreadnought battleship *Szent Istvan* being sunk off the Dalmatian coast. It falls victim to Italian warships commanded by Commander Luigi Rizzo, who has already been credited with the sinking of the Austro-Hungarian battleship *Wien* in Trieste harbor during December 1917.

▼ *A badly-wounded French casualty is evacuated from a front-line trench during the German offensive along the Oise River.*

JUNE 9–13

WESTERN FRONT, *FRANCE*

Under orders from General Erich Ludendorff, the deputy chief of the German General Staff, General Oskar von Hutier's Eighteenth Army launches the fourth in a series of offensives. Ludendorff is aiming to unite two salients carved out in previous attacks in the Amiens and Aisne–Marne sectors.

Hutier is to attack westward along the Matz River, a tributary of the Oise River, in the direction of Noyon and Montdidier. However, the commander of the French Third Army, General Georges

▲ *A German eight-inch (21-cm) howitzer is readied for action during Operation Gneisenau, June 1918.*

Humbert, has been forewarned by deserters of the German attack and organized his defenses accordingly. He initiates an artillery bombardment on the enemy assault troops shortly before their onslaught.

However, this is unable to prevent the Germans gaining some five miles (8 km) on the first day of their attack, which is code-named Gneisenau. French resistance intensifies over the following days and the attempted link-up between Hutier's troops and the German Seventh Army under General Max von Boehn, which began an attack from Soissons on the 10th, fails.

Meanwhile, French General Charles Mangin has organized a counter-attacking force of three French and two US divisions. These strike the Eighteenth Army on the 12th, forcing Ludendorff to call off the operation the following day.

French and American casualties number some 35,000 men, while German losses are estimated to be considerably higher. Ludendorff, increasingly desperate to achieve a breakthrough, plans a fifth offensive elsewhere on the Western Front.

JUNE 13

WESTERN FRONT, *ITALY*
The Austro-Hungarians launch a diversionary attack against the Tonale Pass in northern Italy to mask their forthcoming offensive against the Italians along the Piave River.

JUNE 15–22

WESTERN FRONT, *ITALY*
The Austro-Hungarians, now fighting alone against Italy following the withdrawal of German forces to the Western Front, launch what becomes known as the Battle of the Piave River. Some 58 divisions are committed to a huge pincer attack across much of northern Italy. General Franz Conrad von Hötzendorf, who is operating in the Trentino region, is ordered to take

▶ *Italian troops holding the Piave River load an artillery piece protected by a sandbagged emplacement.*

Verona, while General Borojevic von Bojna is to fan out across the Piave River, making for the Adige River and the city of Padua.

However, the attacks are far from successful. In the north Hötzendorf's Tenth and Eleventh Armies are blocked on the second day of the advance and then vigorously counterattacked by the Italian Fourth and Sixth Armies, which contain several British and

▲ *French prisoners are escorted away from the fighting along the Aisne River during Operation Gneisenau.*

French units. The Austro-Hungarians are forced to retreat, having suffered 40,000 casualties.

To the east the Austro-Hungarians attack across the Piave on a wide front. Their Fifth and Sixth Armies gain three miles (4 km) on a 15-mile

(24-km) front before running up against the defenses of the Italian Third and Eighth Armies. The fighting in this sector continues over several days, with the Austro-Hungarians making some gains before a counter-attack on the 18th forces them back.

The Austro-Hungarian offensive begins to falter, partly due to the worsening weather and Italian air attacks, which weaken their lines of communication and undermines the flow of supplies. By the 22nd the Austro-Hungarians, who are in disarray, are forced back across the Piave. Their casualties, which include 24,000 prisoners, total 150,000 men. However, the chief of the Italian General Staff, General Armando Diaz, refrains from pursuing the defeated enemy and will spend until October building up his forces for a decisive offensive.

JUNE 23

POLITICS, *RUSSIA*
A joint Anglo-French force occupies the north Russian port of Murmansk to aid those forces – "White" Russians – opposed to the Bolshevik government. Similar occupations follow: Archangel and Vladivostok are both occupied in August, the latter by a contingent of US troops.

The two US regiments committed at Vladivostok are commanded by General William Graves. Unlike his allies in the north he is under strict orders not to interfere in internal Russian affairs. His roles are to prevent the Japanese, who have garrisoned Vladivostok since December 1919, from taking the port over permanently,

▲ *US troops keep watch over a section of the Trans-Siberian Railroad during their occupation of Vladivostok.*

▼ *General Max von Boehn, the commander of the German Seventh Army during 1918.*

and to aid in the repatriation of a 100,000-strong group of Austro-Hungarian prisoners later known as the Czech Legion.

US troops guard part of the Trans-Siberian Railroad to facilitate the possible evacuation of the Czech Legion, but they become involved in clashes with Bolshevik and anti-Bolshevik forces. American forces are destined to remain in the region until April 1920.

JULY 9

AIR WAR, *WESTERN FRONT*
One of Britain's top aces, James McCudden, is killed when his fighter crashes during a routine take-off.

JULY 11

POLITICS, *LITHUANIA*
German Prince Wilhelm of Urach accepts the crown and takes the name King Mindove II. The Germans have been occupying the former Russian province since 1915 and continue to exert influence through the Lithuanian Taryba, council of state.

JULY 15–17

WESTERN FRONT, *FRANCE*
German forces open their fifth offensive of 1918. The deputy chief of the General Staff, General Erich Ludendorff, is planning another diversionary attack, this time in Champagne, along the line of the Marne River, to draw his opponents' reserves away from northern France, where he still intends to cut through the British and seize ports along the English Channel. The attacks involves

▶ *Germans cross a bridge destroyed by the French during the fighting along the Aisne and Marne Rivers.*

three German armies: General Max von Boehn's Seventh Army, which is to strike across the Marne and then swing east toward Epernay, where it is intended to link up with General Bruno von Mudra's First Army advancing either side of Reims. To the east of Reims General Karl von Einem's Third Army is under orders to strike for Châlons-sur-Marne.

The French, through a combination of aerial reconnaissance and talkative German deserters, are aware of the offensive and pre-empt it with a bombardment of their own. The German Third Army makes little progress against General Henri Gouraud's First Army, being halted before noon on the 15th. Henceforth, the Germans concentrate their efforts to the west of Reims.

The German Seventh Army, with support from the Ninth Army under General Eben, attack on a 20-mile (32-km) front and cut through General Jean Degoutte's French Sixth Army to reach the Marne River between Château-Thierry and Epernay. However, attacks by the French Ninth Army under General M.A.H. de Mitry, supported by British

and US forces, prevent the Germans from exploiting their bridgeheads over the Marne. By the 17th Ludendorff accepts that his offensive has been stopped in its tracks.

Since the opening of his first offensive, Operation Michael, in March, his forces have suffered 500,000 virtually irreplaceable casualties. In contrast, US troops are arriving at a rate of 300,000 per month. Ludendorff, short of troops, plans a measured withdrawal from the salient he has created running south of

Soissons and Reims to shorten his line. However, the opposing commanders are intending to launch a counter-offensive before he can complete this withdrawal.

JULY 16–17

POLITICS, *RUSSIA*
Several members of the Russian royal family, including Czar Nicholas II and the czarina, are murdered by the Bolsheviks at Ekaterinburg, Siberia,

▼ *US troops open fire on a German sniper holed up in a ruined French village close to the Marne River.*

▲ *The room in the town of Ekaterinburg, Siberia, where the Russian royal family was murdered by the Bolsheviks.*

where they have lived in internal exile since late 1917.

JULY 18

WESTERN FRONT, *FRANCE*
Various French, British, and US forces launch a counterattack against the German forces in the salient they hold between Soissons and Reims in Champagne. The fighting becomes known as the Second Battle of the Marne. The attack is led by three French armies – the Tenth under General Charles Mangin; the Sixth under General Jean Degoutte; and General Henri Berthelot's Fifth. Support is offered by the French Ninth Army under General M.A.H. de Mitry.

The main attack involves the French Tenth Army and is spearheaded by the US 1st and 2nd Divisions, which take 8000 prisoners and 145 artillery pieces for the loss of 5000 casualties. Elsewhere, General Hunter Liggett's US I Corps fights alongside the French Sixth Army, which advances into the salient from the west along the Ourcq River. Three further US divisions from General Bullard's III Corps are attached to the French Ninth Army under General M.A.H. de Mitry, which is driving into the salient from the south close to Château-Thierry. The German defenders of the salient begin to collapse under these converging attacks and Ludendorff has to contemplate an urgent withdrawal.

JULY 20

WESTERN FRONT, *FRANCE*
General Erich Ludendorff, deputy chief of the German General Staff, calls off his proposed attack

against the British in northern France due to the deteriorating situation in the Second Battle of the Marne.

JULY 26

EASTERN FRONT, *RUSSIA*
A group of former Austro-Hungarian prisoners of war known as the Czech Legion occupy Ekaterinburg. They had been expecting to be repatriated but the plan has been blocked by the Bolsheviks. The troops of the Czech Legion respond by taking arms from Bolshevik units in order to force their way back to their homeland. They will, however, become embroiled in the Russian Civil War, fighting with anti-Bolshevik forces.

▲ Men of the Czech Legion, former prisoners of war fighting against the Bolsheviks, operate an armored train in Russia.

AIR WAR, *WESTERN FRONT*

Britain's top fighter pilot, Edward Mannock, is shot down and killed by German ground fire. He has been credited with 73 victories in air combat.

AUGUST 2–6

WESTERN FRONT, *FRANCE*

As part of the continuing Second Battle of the Marne the Germans are forced to abandon Soissons and over the next 24 hours fall back to the line of the Aisne and Vesle Rivers, effectively abandoning the salient they have recently captured between Soissons and Reims. The Second Battle of the Marne ends on the 6th. It has been a disaster for the German

▲ German prisoners captured by the French during the fighting of August 1918 await an escort to the rear.

forces, who have sustained losses totaling 168,000 men. Following a series of offensives since March, the Germans no longer have the resources to launch attacks. They have also suffered huge casualties among their best-trained troops – the stormtrooper units – and those who have survived are suffering from increasingly poor morale.

AUGUST 4

AIR WAR, *WESTERN FRONT*

America's second highest-scoring ace, Frank Luke, begins his short but distinguished career. He downs 14 observation balloons and four aircraft in a few weeks. However, he is forced down behind German lines in late September and, refusing to surrender, is shot.

AUGUST 6

POLITICS, *FRANCE*

In recognition for his outstanding performance in marshaling the various national forces under his overall command during the recent fighting along the Marne River, France's General Ferdinand Foch is promoted to the rank of marshal. Foch is contemplating a major Anglo-French offensive to the east of Amiens.

AUGUST 8–12

WESTERN FRONT, *FRANCE*

Field Marshal Sir Douglas Haig's British Expeditionary Force spearheads what becomes known as the Amiens

◀ Australian troops occupy a recently-captured German position during the Amiens Offensive.

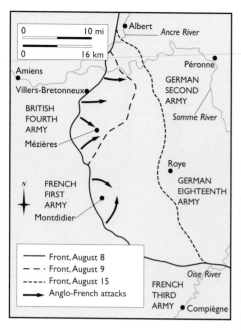

▲ The British-led offensive at Amiens heralded a series of attacks that smashed the German forces on the Western Front.

Offensive. The attack has been planned to clear parts of the railroad running from Amiens to Paris that have been held by the Germans since their Operation Michael in March.

The offensive is led by General Sir Henry Rawlinson's British Fourth Army, which stages a methodical

▲ Germans taken prisoner on the first day of the Amiens Offensive, a day termed the "Black Day of the German Army," march into captivity.

▼ US troops with French-built tanks move up to the front in the Meuse–Argonne sector of the Western Front.

advance along a 15-mile (24-km) front. The attack is preceded by a short bombardment and more than 400 tanks lead the way forward for the 11 British divisions earmarked for the first phase of the onslaught. Support is offered by the left wing of General Eugène Debeney's French First Army. The German defenses are manned by General Georg von der Maritz's Second Army and the Eighteenth Army under General Oskar von Hutier. The two generals have 14 divisions in the front line and nine in reserve. The Anglo-French attack is overwhelmingly successful with the Germans being forced back some 10 miles (16 km).

There are also more worrying signs for the future of the German Army: some front-line units have simply fled the fighting without putting up much resistance. Others, some 15,000, have quickly surrendered. When news of this reaches General Erich Ludendorff, the deputy chief of the General Staff, he calls August 8 the "Black Day of the German Army." Matters do not improve. The following day many more German troops are made prisoner.

On August 10 the focus of the Amiens Offensive shifts to the south of the German-held salient. Here, General Georges Humbert's French Third Army moves toward Montdidier, forcing the Germans to abandon the town and thus permitting the reopening of the Amiens to Paris railroad.

The first stage of the offensive is brought to a close in the face of increasing German resistance on the 12th. However, there is no disguising the scale of their defeat. German losses are 40,000 men killed or wounded and 33,000 taken prisoner. Anglo-French losses total some 46,000 troops.

AUGUST 21

WESTERN FRONT, *FRANCE*
General Sir Julian Byng's British Third Army opens the second phase of the Amiens Offensive, which began on August 8. Over the following days General Sir Henry Horne's British First Army and the French Tenth and Third Armies join in the attack. Ludendorff, who does not have the reserves to deal with these successive attacks, orders his forces to pull back from the salient to the east of Amiens and the Lys salient to the north. In effect, this is a general retreat.

AUGUST 30

WESTERN FRONT, *FRANCE*
The First Army of the General John Pershing's American Expeditionary Force moves into position around the German-held St. Mihiel salient to the south of Verdun along the Meuse River. Together with the French II Colonial Corps, the First Army will launch an attack on the position in mid-September.

▼ *The opening of the attack on St. Mihiel – three US infantrymen advance by one of their wounded colleagues.*

▲ *US gunners deploy German artillery pieces against their former owners during the attack on St. Mihiel.*

AUGUST 30–SEPTEMBER 2

WESTERN FRONT, *FRANCE*
The German withdrawal from the salient east of Amiens is threatened by repeated attacks by Anglo-French forces. Australian and New Zealand troops force their way across the Somme River, capturing Péronne and Mont St. Quentin. The subsequent capture of Quéant by the Canadian Corps on September 2 forces the Germans to consider withdrawing to the Hindenburg Line, from where they launched their spring offensive during the previous March.

SEPTEMBER 3–10

WESTERN FRONT, *FRANCE*
Closely pursued by Anglo-French forces, the German complete their withdrawal from Amiens and re-occupy the Hindenburg Line. The British are unable to continue their attacks due to a lack of reserves and the Amiens Offensive is brought to a close. The British and French have suffered some 42,000 casualties, but the Germans have sustained more than 100,000 losses, including 30,000 prisoners. General Erich Ludendorff, the chief of the German General Staff, becomes convinced that Germany can no longer win the war.

SEPTEMBER 8

WESTERN FRONT, *FRANCE*
General Erich Ludendorff, who is expecting a major US–French attack, begins to withdraw German forces from the St. Mihiel salient to the southeast of Verdun.

SEPTEMBER 12–16

WESTERN FRONT, *FRANCE*
The American Expeditionary Corps' First Army and the French II Colonial Corps launch an attack on the salient at St. Mihiel to the south of Verdun. It has been held continuously by the Germans since 1914. The advance is led by the First Army's I and IV Corps, which advance into the southern face of the salient, and V Corps, which

SEPTEMBER 14

moves against its west face. The French II Colonial Corps is positioned between the US forces.

The attack begins in thick fog and is supported by 600 aircraft commanded by US Colonel William Mitchell, a staunch advocate of the value of air power. The attackers are facing nine German divisions in the front line and a further five held in reserve. However, German resistance collapses on the first day with the US attacks from the south and west linking up at the village of Hattonchâtel. By the 16th the entire salient has been reduced.

The US troops capture some 15,000 German prisoners and 250 guns at a cost of 7000 casualties. Although General John Pershing, the commander of the American Expeditionary Force, could have continued the offensive, he has begun to transfer his forces away from St. Mihiel in preparation for the forthcoming offensive in the Meuse-Argonne sector of the Western Front.

SEPTEMBER 14

EASTERN FRONT, *RUSSIA*
Turkish forces occupy Baku, an important oil-producing center in the Caucasus, forcing a British force commanded by General L.C. Dunsterville to withdraw.

▼ *Oil-production platforms at Baku in Russia, which was targeted for capture by Britain, Germany, and Turkey.*

SEPTEMBER 15

BALKANS, *GREECE*
France's General Franchet d'Esperey, who has been in overall command in the theater since July, launches his large multinational force known as the "Allied Army of the Orient" against the Bulgarians.

The attack, which becomes known as the Battle of the Vardar River, is spearheaded by the Serbian First and Second Armies. The Bulgarian forces are split on the 25th and Skopje falls on the 29th. Bulgarian forces begin to collapse under the pressure.

▲ *Serbian troops advance against the disintegrating Bulgarians, who will be forced into headlong retreat.*

SEPTEMBER 19–21

MIDDLE EAST, *PALESTINE*
British General Sir Edmund Allenby opens what becomes known as the Battle of Megiddo against the Turkish forces in Palestine. The Turks have three armies, the Eighth, Seventh, and Fourth, commanded by German General Liman von Sanders. His 44,000 men are holding a long line stretching inland from just north of Jaffa on the Mediterranean coast to the valley of the Jordan River. However, they are demoralized and short of supplies, chiefly because Arab forces under British liaison officer T.E. Lawrence have been disrupting the Hejaz railroad along which their supplies flow. Allenby commands 69,000 troops.

Allenby has launched diversionary probes against the Turkish forces in the Jordan Valley, but actually intends to strike along the coast. To this end, real troop concentrations and supply dumps have been camouflaged in this sector, while nearer the valley dummy dumps and camps have been constructed.

Allenby intends his forces on the coast (some 35,000 men and 350 artillery pieces) to push through the Turkish defenders (8000 men and 130 artillery pieces) and then swing eastward, thereby cutting the northward line of retreat of the Turkish Seventh and Eighth Armies.

▶ *British cavalrymen, part of Sir Edmund Allenby's Desert Mounted Corps, pursue the Turks retreating through Palestine.*

The British offensive begins at 0430 hours, with Allenby's artillery opening fire along a 65-mile (104-km) front. This is followed by an attack along the Mediterranean coast, which quickly breaks through the overstretched Turkish line. This gap is exploited by Allenby's Desert Mounted Corps, which races northward in the direction of Megiddo and then swings eastward for the Jordan River. British aircraft bomb railroad lines and Turkish headquarters, effectively destroying their communications system. The Desert Mounted Corps covers 70 miles (112 km) in three days to secure its objectives.

Jerad Pasha's Turkish Seventh Army is virtually destroyed in the enveloping attack and Mustafa Kemal's Eighth Army attempts to escape eastward. Both are harried by British ground-attack aircraft. The retreat turns into a route and some 25,000 Turkish prisoners are captured. The Turkish Fourth Army, positioned around the Jordan Valley, stages a withdrawal northward in the direction of Damascus, but there is no hiding the scale of Allenby's victory. There is no longer any significant Turkish force available to oppose his advance northward toward Damascus and beyond.

SEPTEMBER 26–OCTOBER 3
WESTERN FRONT, *FRANCE*
The First Army of General John Pershing's American Expeditionary Force launches what becomes known as the Meuse–Argonne Offensive to the north of Verdun. It is one of several attacks planned by France's Marshal Ferdinand Foch to drive the Germans from the defenses of the Hindenburg Line and precipitate their surrender.

Pershing's First Army, some one million men split between three corps, is holding a front of some 17 miles (27 km) from Forges on the Meuse River into the Argonne Forest. To the left of the First Army is General H.J.E. Gouraud's French Fourth Army. The US forces are opposed by General Max von Gallwitz's Army Group, while the French are facing Crown Prince Frederick William's Army Group. The US and French deploy 37 divisions, while German forces

▼ *US infantrymen and French officers take a break during the fighting amid the remains of an Argonne wood.*

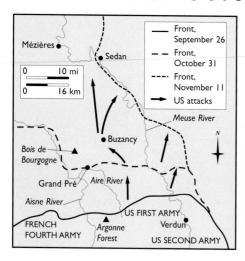

▲ The joint US and French offensive directed toward Sedan from north of Verdun along the Meuse River.

comprise 24 divisions. The Germans hold three strongly-fortified defensive lines in difficult terrain.

The attack begins at 0525 hours and the US forces make rapid gains, advancing some 10 miles (16 km) in the first five days of the offensive. French progress is somewhat less. The Germans rush reinforcements to the sector and slow the pace of the advance, although by the end of the first phase of the battle, on October 3, two of the three German defensive lines have been taken.

▼ Indian lancers and their British officers pose for the camera during a break in their pursuit of the Turks in Palestine.

SEPTEMBER 27–OCTOBER 4

WESTERN FRONT, *FRANCE*
Elements of Field Marshal Sir Douglas Haig's British Expeditionary Force and French units initiate part of French Marshal Ferdinand Foch's plan to crush the German forces on the Western Front. The aim is to attack toward Cambrai and St. Quentin with 41 divisions and break through the Hindenburg Line.

The offensive is led by the British First Army under General Sir Henry Horne and General Sir Julian Byng's Third Army, which break through the German positions, cross the Canal du Nord and advance to within three miles (5 km) of Cambrai on the first

▲ Canadian troops and German prisoners watch the continuing fighting around the Canal du Nord.

day. Elements of the Third Army finally occupy the town's western suburbs on the 30th.

On the 28th the Group of Armies of Flanders under Belgium's King Albert also joins in the general offensive, attacking from around Ypres against Crown Prince Rupprecht of Bavaria's Army Corps. Albert's British, French, and Belgian units quickly evict the Germans from the high ground around Ypres and begin advancing along the low-lying coast, although their progress is slowed by the waterlogged conditions.

On the 29th General Sir Henry Rawlinson's British Fourth Army joins in the attack, supported by General Eugene Debeney's French First Army and several US divisions. Under

▶ *Medical staff evacuate two wounded British soldiers by camel litter during the final push through Palestine.*

increasing pressure General Max von Boehn's Germany Army Group is forced to complete the abandonment of the Hindenburg Line on October 4. This precipitates the retreat of other German forces, which form a hasty defensive line along the Selle River, some 10 miles (16 km) from their original positions.

SEPTEMBER 30

POLITICS, *BULGARIA*
Following the collapse of its forces in the Balkans, the government agrees to an armistice, the first of the Central Powers to do so.

OCTOBER 1

MIDDLE EAST, *SYRIA*
Capitalizing on their recent overwhelming victory against the Turks at the Battle of Megiddo in September, forces commanded by British General Sir Edmund Allenby enter the capital Damascus, taking 20,000 Turkish prisoners. They are led by the Australian Third Light Horse.

  Their arrival has been preceded by Arab guerrilla forces. The Arabs, despite British worries, take charge of the running of Damascus. A day later Beirut is captured and Aleppo, some 200 miles (320 km) to the north, falls on the 25th.

OCTOBER 5

MIDDLE EAST, *LEBANON*
French naval forces occupy Beirut as a base for expanding their influence in the Middle East. It has been agreed that France will take over the former Turkish

province of Syria at the end of the war. However, this secret Anglo-French understanding will be disputed by the leaders of the Arab forces that have been waging a guerrilla war against the Turks.

OCTOBER 6

POLITICS, *GERMANY*
The German chancellor, Prince Max of Baden, contacts US President Woodrow

Wilson and requests an armistice based on Wilson's 14 Points outlined the previous January. However, it is made clear that there will be no negotiations until the removal of the country's military leadership.

OCTOBER 14

POLITICS, *TURKEY*
The Committee of Union and Progress, its members better known as the "Young Turks," resigns as the country's military situation worsens. The Young Turks are a nationalistic group dedicated to reviving Turkey's position as the region's leading power and have held effective power since 1908. A new government headed by Ahmed Izzet Pasha seeks an armistice.

OCTOBER 14–31

WESTERN FRONT, *FRANCE*
The second phase of the US and French Meuse–Argonne Offensive begins on the 14th, following a period of reorganization in which the US forces involved in the battle have been divided between two new armies: the First under General Hunter Liggett and

◀ *American artillerymen pound German positions with their six-inch (155-mm) howitzers, Meuse–Argonne.*

▲ *Italian troops take charge of an abandoned Austro-Hungarian position during the Battle of Vittorio Veneto.*

◄ *Growing evidence of the collapse of German morale on the Western Front – prisoners captured by the British.*

the fighting, which dies down at the end of the month, but Pershing"s troops have broken through the German third and final line of defense. The Meuse–Argonne Offensive is to be renewed at the beginning of November after a period of rest and reinforcement.

OCTOBER 17–31

WESTERN FRONT, *FRANCE*
British forces cut through the German defenders holding the line of the Selle River, taking 20,000 prisoners. By the end of the month they have pushed the Germans back behind the Scheldt River on a 20-mile (32-km) front. To maintain the pressure on the retreating Germans, the Group of Armies of Flanders under Belgium's King Albert also continues to attack from around Ypres.

OCTOBER 23

WESTERN FRONT, *ITALY*
The Italian commander-in-chief, General Armando Diaz, launches an offensive against the Austro-Hungarian forces in northern Italy from his line along the Piave River. His aim is to use

the Second commanded by General Robert Lee Bullard. General John Pershing has overall command of the two armies.

Liggett's First Army advances northward at a steady pace in the face of intense German resistance, while Bullard's Second Army moves to the northeast between the Meuse and Moselle Rivers. The Germans are forced to rush reinforcements from other threatened sectors of the Western Front to counter the French and Americans. All suffer heavy losses in

▲ *Turkish cavalrymen pull back in the face of the British drive from Baghdad toward Mosul.*

his Fourth Army to penetrate the center of the Austro-Hungarian line in the vicinity of Mount Grappa, while the Eighth Army, supported by the mainly Anglo-French Tenth and Twelfth Armies, is to make for the town of Vittorio Veneto.

The Italian forces committed to what becomes known as the Battle of Vittorio Veneto consist of 57 divisions, including three British and two French, backed by 7700 artillery pieces. The Austro-Hungarians, whose morale is already badly shaken, deploy 52 divisions and 6030 artillery pieces.

The Austro-Hungarians are able to block the advance from Mount Grappa by the Italian Fourth Army, but the key part of the battle is around Vittorio Veneto. Initially, the battle goes well

for the Austro-Hungarian Sixth Army, which blocks the advance of the Italian Eighth Army as it tries to cross the Piave River. However, the Twelfth Army, commanded by French General Jean Graziani, gains a foothold on the Austro-Hungarian side of the Piave, as does British General Earl of Cavan's Tenth Army. By October 28 both bridgeheads are secure and the Anglo-French forces are exploiting their successes.

MIDDLE EAST, *MESOPOTAMIA*
Taking advantage of what is seen as Turkey's imminent collapse, British forces under General A.S. Cobbe

advance from Baghdad with the intention of seizing the oil fields around Mosul to the north. They are opposed by General Ismael Hakki's Turkish Tigris Group. The Turks retreat slowly and make a stand at Sharqat. After a two-day battle on October 28–29, Hakki is forced to surrender his 11,300 troops and 51 artillery pieces. Cobbe continues his march on Mosul.

OCTOBER 26

POLITICS, *GERMANY*
General Erich Ludendorff is replaced as deputy chief of the General Staff by General Wilhelm Groener. Ludendorff

▼ *A lone British soldier stands watch over a batch of Austro-Hungarian prisoners taken at Vittorio Veneto.*

Fleet. Some 40,000 naval personnel are involved in the mutiny and they take over Kiel itself on November 4. Their actions spark risings across Germany, prompting the government to sue for peace before there is a revolution.

OCTOBER 30

POLITICS, *TURKEY*

The government agrees to an armistice following negotiations on the Greek island of Mudros. Under its terms hostilities end, Constantinople is to be controlled by the victorious powers, and all Turkish forces must withdraw from the Trans-Caucasus region.

WESTERN FRONT, *ITALY*

In the ongoing Battle of Vittorio Veneto, the British, French, and Italian drive against the Austro-Hungarians continues. They are able to capture Vittorio Veneto, effectively dividing the Austro-Hungarian forces in northern Italy. After a week of fighting the offensive has penetrated to a maximum depth of 15 miles (24 km) along a front of 35 miles (56 km).

It is clear that the Austro-Hungarian forces are disintegrating. Italian troops reach the line of the Tagliamento River on November 2, while in the Trentino British and French forces are heading rapidly for Trent. The fighting officially ends on November 3. The Austro-Hungarians have had some 300,000 troops taken prisoner, while Italian casualties total just 38,000 men.

has recently quarreled with his superior Field Marshal Paul von Hindenburg and has suggested that Germany seeks an armistice. It is clear that Groener shares Ludendorff's views.

OCTOBER 27

AIR WAR, *WESTERN FRONT*

Canadian pilot William Barker survives a crash-landing after inadvertently running into a flight of 60 German aircraft. Although totally outnumbered, he survives a one-sided battle lasting 40 minutes in which his Sopwith Snipe fighter is hit by enemy bullets some 300 times before being forced down. Barker has, however, downed three enemy aircraft during the encounter, taking his tally of air victories to 52.

OCTOBER 29

POLITICS, *GERMANY*

Sailors of the German High Seas Fleet mutiny at Kiel's naval base following suggestions by their newly-appointed commander, Admiral Franz von Hipper, that the navy should make one last "death ride" against the British Home

▲ *Wounded Italians receive front-line medical aid at the height of the Battle of Vittorio Veneto.*

▼ *US troops fight their way through the remains of a wood during their ongoing offensive in the Meuse–Argonne region. The fighting was intense and cost the American Expeditionary Force some 117,000 men killed or wounded.*

NOVEMBER 1

WESTERN FRONT, *FRANCE*

The third and final stage of the US-led Meuse–Argonne Offensive opens. The US First Army commanded by General Hunter Liggett resumes its northward

▲ *German troops are forced to pull back from the Western Front in the face of a series of large enemy offensives.*

advance and punches a way through the German defenses at Buzancy, thereby allowing the French Fourth Army to make a major crossing of the Aisne River.

German resistance is collapsing and the US forces move rapidly along the valley of the Meuse River in the direction of Sedan, which falls on the 6th. Although there is later progress in the offensive, it ends on the 11th with the signing of the armistice. The Meuse–Argonne

Offensive has been successful, but at a high cost – some 117,000 US troops have been posted as casualties since its opening on September 26.

MIDDLE EAST, *MESOPOTAMIA*
British cavalry units, part of General A.S. Cobbe's force advancing north-ward from Baghdad, arrive outside Mosul, center of the region's oil fields. Although an armistice has been agreed with Turkey, Cobbe is ordered to march into Mosul, which still has a Turkish garrison. The garrison's commander, Halil Pasha, finally agrees to abandon the town to the British during the middle of the month. The occupation of Mosul signals the end of the campaign.

SEA WAR, *ADRIATIC*
The flagship of the Austro-Hungarian fleet, the dreadnought battleship

Viribus Unitis, is sunk during an Italian attack.

NOVEMBER 2

POLITICS, *LITHUANIA*
The Lithuanian Taryba, council of state, repeals the German-sponsored appointment of Prince Wilhelm of Urach as monarch and announces the establishment of an independent republic. However, Bolshevik forces are preparing to take back this former Russian province.

NOVEMBER 3

POLITICS, *AUSTRIA-HUNGARY*
Following the recent catastrophic defeat at Vittorio Veneto, the authori-ties seek an armistice on the same day that an enemy naval expedition captures the port of Trieste in the north Adriatic.

The armistice is agreed the next day. It will fuel ethnic tensions between the many groups within the Austro-Hungarian Empire, which will break apart over the following months as its various provinces strive to gain their full independence.

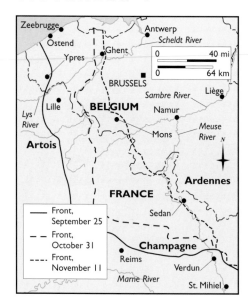

▲ Between September and the armistice on November 11 the German forces on the Western Front gradually collapsed. Although some troops put up fierce resistance, many – most war-weary – surrendered or headed for home.

NOVEMBER 7

POLITICS, *GERMANY*

A delegation headed by Matthias Erzberger meets with Marshal Ferdinand Foch to discuss terms for an armistice. Among Foch's demands are that German forces must immediately evacuate all occupied territory and Alsace-Lorraine; surrender substantial amounts of military supplies (including 5000 artillery pieces and 25,000 machine guns); evacuate German territory west of the Rhine River; allow three zones on the east bank of the Rhine to be occupied; surrender all of its submarines; and intern all other warships at ports indicated by the victors. The discussions, which last four days, take place in a rail carriage at Compiègne, northeast of Paris.

NOVEMBER 8

WESTERN FRONT, *FRANCE*

Forces under the command of Britain's Field Marshal Sir Douglas Haig complete the crossing of the Scheldt River in the face of crumbling German resistance and are close to occupying Ghent and Mons.

NOVEMBER 9

POLITICS, *GERMANY*

It is announced that Kaiser Wilhelm II has abdicated. He goes into exile in the Netherlands the next day. The victorious powers request halfheartedly that he be tried as a war criminal. A member of the chancellor's cabinet, Philipp Scheidemann, announces the creation of a republic. A new government and chancellor, Friedrich Ebert,

▼ Germany's Kaiser Wilhelm II (third from right) and his staff head for exile in the Netherlands after his abdication.

are appointed the next day. However, Germany is politically unstable, with various left- and rightwing political factions vying for control.

NOVEMBER 11

POLITICS, *EUROPE*

The armistice on the Western Front, negotiated over four days at Compiègne, comes into force at 1100 hours. It had been finalized just six hours earlier.

POLITICS, *AUSTRIA-HUNGARY*

Emperor Karl renounces his position as head of state, a move that prompts the creation of the separate Republics of Austria and Hungary the next day. These political upheavals spell the end of the multi-ethnic Austro-Hungarian Empire as its other various national groups will also clamor for autonomy.

POLITICS, *POLAND*

German troops are expelled from the former Russian province, whose independence has been recognized by Russia since March 1917. The commander-in-chief of the Polish forces who had fought for the Germans and Austro-Hungarians during World War I, Józef Piłsudski, becomes leader of independent Poland. His

▶ People take to the streets of Paris to celebrate the signing of the armistice.

most urgent task is to build up Poland's armed forces as large parts of the country are claimed by several of its neighbours, not least Russia.

Within days of coming to power he will be faced with an attack by Ukrainian forces, which invade, capture Lvov, and proclaim the establishment of the West Ukrainian Republic. It will take six months of fighting for Pilsudski to re-establish Polish authority over the region.

POLITICS, *TURKEY*
The recently-appointed government of Ahmed Isset Pasha falls.

NOVEMBER 12

SEA WAR, *MEDITERRANEAN*
Several allied vessels sail through the Turkish-controlled Dardanelles and anchor at Constantinople, the capital, the following day. Their presence reflects one of the clauses of the armistice agreed on the Greek island of Mudros on October 30.

NOVEMBER 13

POLITICS, *GERMANY*
Against a background of growing domestic political unrest, Bavaria's regent, Prince Otto, abdicates. Other monarchs of the states that make up Germany follow:

King Friedrich August III of Saxony on the same day and King Wilhelm II of Württemberg on the 30th.

NOVEMBER 14

POLITICS, *CZECHOSLOVAKIA*
Czechoslovakia, formerly part of the collapsing Austro-Hungarian Empire,

▲ *Marshal Jósef Pilsudski (seated) became independent Poland's first head of state.*

becomes an independent republic. The new state's first president is named as Tomás Masaryk.

NOVEMBER 15

POLITICS, *RUSSIA*
German troops leave the Ukraine, where they had been supporting the anti-Bolshevik "White" Russian General Pavel Skoropadski. However, Skoropadski is soon overthrown by Ukrainian socialists led by General Simon Petlyura. There is growing resistance to the Bolshevik revolutionaries, which is supported by Britain, France, and the United States.

NOVEMBER 16

POLITICS, *HUNGARY*
Count Mihály Károlyi becomes the first president of the newly-independent republic.

NOVEMBER 17

POLITICS, *GERMANY*
Under the terms of the recently-agreed armistice, German forces begin to leave those parts of France and Belgium that they still occupy.

EASTERN FRONT, *RUSSIA*
Turkish troops are forced to abandon the oil-producing center of Baku on the Caspian Sea following the arrival

NOVEMBER 18

◀ *General Karl von Mannerheim was able to defeat Finland's pro-Bolshevik forces with the help of the Germans.*

▶ *German troops head for their homes through the streets of Koblenz at the end of the war.*

Russia." He joins forces with the Czech Legion and enters eastern Russia to confront the Bolsheviks.

NOVEMBER 21

SEA WAR, *NORTH SEA*
British Admiral Sir David Beatty accepts the surrender of the German High Seas Fleet. His message is unambiguous: "The German flag will be hauled down at sunset and will not be hoisted again without permission." The fleet will later move to anchorages at Scapa Flow in the Orkneys off the coast of northern Scotland.

NOVEMBER 25

AFRICA, *NORTHERN RHODESIA*
General Paul von Lettow-Vorbeck finally surrenders at Abercorn, having belatedly been informed of the end of the war in Europe. His troops, who have waged an outstanding guerrilla war against vastly superior forces (some 130,000 men), consist at the end of 175 Europeans and 3000 askaris.

of a British naval force. They had taken Baku from the British during the previous September.

NOVEMBER 18

POLITICS, *RUSSIA*
A leader of anti-Bolshevik forces, Admiral Alexander Kolchak, a former commander of Russia's Black Sea Fleet, seizes control in Omsk, Siberia, and proclaims himself "Supreme Ruler of

NOVEMBER 26

POLITICS, *MONTENEGRO*
The assembly of the country, which has recently been liberated by the Serbians, announces that King Nicholas has been deposed and that it will unite with Serbia.

DECEMBER 1

POLITICS, *GERMANY*
British, French, and US forces move into

KEY MOMENTS

COUNTING THE COST

When World War I ended the scale of destruction and the loss of life was unparalleled in human history. Unlike previous wars, the fighting had been conducted, to a lesser or greater degree, almost constantly. From August 1914 until November 1918 rarely a day went by when there was no military activity.

Equally, the ferocity of the fighting, chiefly due to the nature of the predominantly trench-bound war and the destructive weapons employed by the warring nations, was previously unknown. It should be noted that all of the following figures for casualties are roughly-accurate estimates.

Out of the 65 million troops mobilized by all of the combatant nations, some eight million were killed and a further 21 million wounded. With regard to the Central Powers, the figures were: Germany, 11 million mobilized and 1.8 million dead; Austria-Hungary, 7.8 million and 922,000; Turkey, 2.8 million and 325,000; and Bulgaria, 1.2 million and 76,000.

The figures for those opposing the Central Powers were: France, 8.4 million mobilized and 1.36 million dead; the British Empire, 8.9 million and 908,000; Russia, 12 million and 1.7 million; Italy, 5.6 million and 462,000; the United States, 4.3 million and 50,000; Belgium, 267,000 and 14,000; Serbia, 707,000 and 45,000; Montenegro, 50,000 and 3000; Romania, 750,000 and 335,000; Greece, 230,000 and 5000; Portugal, 100,000 and 7000; and Japan, 800,000 and 300.

The loss of life in combat was mirrored in civilian casualties on an also unparalleled scale. Some 6.6 million died, chiefly in Russia and Turkey, which accounted for roughly two-thirds of the total. In the case of Turkey many of its 2.1 million civilian casualties were ethnic Armenians killed in Turkey by Turkish forces in their campaign of genocide against the Christian minority.

The fighting left both physical and mental scars on those who survived. Many ordinary soldiers suffered deep psychological trauma, what was termed "shell shock." Soldiers in 1914–18 had to face the threat of death or mutilation like warriors of earlier times. However, unlike their ancestors who might be in physical danger for a few hours at a time during a series of infrequent and usually brief battles, World War I soldiers faced a greater variety of dangers 24 hours a day for weeks — if not months — at a time.

the German Rhineland in accordance with the armistice agreement made on November 11.

POLITICS, *SERBIA*
The Serbian authorities, with the support of Montenegro and the former Austro-Hungarian provinces of Croatia and Slovenia, announce a political union. It will lead to the formation of the Federal Republic of Yugoslavia.

DECEMBER 9

POLITICS, *GERMANY*
Various parts of the German Rhineland are occupied: the British establish themselves at Cologne; the French at Mainz; and the Americans at Koblenz.

DECEMBER 12

POLITICS, *FINLAND*
General Karl von Mannerheim replaces

Pehr Svinhufvud as head of the provisional government. However, skirmishes between Mannerheim's forces and the pro-Bolshevik "Red Guard" continue.

DECEMBER 13

POLITICS, *UNITED STATES*
In a landmark event Woodrow Wilson arrives in France, becoming the first US President to travel outside the United States. He will also visit Britain and Italy, before playing a key role in the negotiations that will lead to the peace treaties that end World War I. He plans that the settlements should adhere to his 14-Point Peace Program.

DECEMBER 18

POLITICS, *FRANCE*
French troops occupy Odessa on the Black Sea, so that supplies can be sent to Ukrainians opposing the Bolshevik government, which is striving to consolidate its influence throughout Russia amid growing resistance.

◀ *Warships of the German High Seas Fleet at anchor in Scapa Flow as part of the armistice terms.*

INTERWAR YEARS

The treaties that ended World War I did not bring worldwide peace – various nations fought against each other or were torn apart by civil war. Also, the Treaty of Versailles left two dangerous legacies: a bitter, impoverished Germany and an Eastern Europe made up of small, politically-fragmented states. Interwar politicians, particularly nationalists and other rightwingers, began to exploit the situation created by Versailles. Their aggressiveness and opportunism, coupled with the political inertia of those who might have opposed them, led to World War II.

JANUARY 4, 1919

EASTERN FRONT, *LATVIA*
As part of the ongoing civil war in Russia, Bolshevik forces capture Riga in an attempt to reincorporate the former Russian province. They establish a government, but it is short-lived. With backing from Britain and France, German and Latvian troops evict the invaders. However, the Germans try to take over Riga until forced to return home by their backers on July 3.

JANUARY 18, 1919

POLITICS, *INTERNATIONAL*
Various victorious leaders assemble in Paris to discuss the terms on which peace should be agreed with the defeated Central Powers. Among

▼ *The World War I peacemakers gather – from left to right: Italy's Vittorio Orlando, Britain's David Lloyd George, France's Georges Clemenceau, and Woodrow Wilson of the United States.*

▲ British troops and local police pictured in Dublin at the height of the Anglo-Irish Civil War, 1919–21.

those present are President Woodrow Wilson of the United States, British Prime Minister Lloyd George, French Prime Minister Georges Clemenceau, and the prime minister of Italy, Vittorio Emanuele Orlando.

JANUARY 21, 1919

IRELAND, *CIVIL WAR*
Sinn Fein ("Ourselves Alone"), an Irish nationalist group, declares Ireland independent, sparking a rebellion against the British. There is fighting between Catholic nationalists and local Protestants, who favor maintaining links with Britain. The British deploy 100,000 troops and paramilitaries.

FEBRUARY 3, 1919

RUSSIA, *CIVIL WAR*
Revolutionary Bolshevik forces occupy Kiev as the first part of an advance that will see them evict the French troops occupying the Black Sea port of Odessa on December 18. The French have been supplying anti-Bolshevik "White" Russians.

▶ Members of a rightwing Freikorps unit on the streets of Berlin during the early days of the Weimar Republic.

FEBRUARY 11, 1919

POLITICS, *GERMANY*
Social Democrat Friedrich Ebert is elected the first president of the new republic. Ebert, a moderate socialist, will attempt to unite the various political factions within Germany from the seat of his government, the town of Weimar. Although his coalition is initially popular, it soon has to call on rightwing military bodies known as Freikorps to deal with pro-Russian

revolutionaries in Germany. However, the Freikorps dislike Ebert's regime only marginally less than they do the revolutionaries because of its contacts with Russia. In March 1920 one Freikorps unit stages a coup in Berlin. This rebellion, known as the "Kapp Putsch" after a rightwing politician, is defeated, but the violence continues.

MARCH 21, 1919

POLITICS, *HUNGARY*
President Mihály Károlyi resigns and a pro-Russian leader, Béla Kun, who has been in exile in Russia, is installed.

MARCH 28, 1919

POLITICS, *HUNGARY*
The pro-Russian regime of Béla Kun initiates a war with Czechoslovakia by invading Slovakia, which has a large Hungarian minority.

APRIL 10, 1919

POLITICS, *ROMANIA*
Romanian troops invade Hungary to forestall any Hungarian attempts to take over Transylvania, which has a large ethnic Hungarian population and has been occupied by Romania since the end of World War I.

APRIL 13, 1919

POLITICS, *INDIA*
Against a background of growing friction between Muslims and Hindus and the campaign of civil disobedience by supporters of former lawyer Mahatma Gandhi, British troops commanded by General Reginald Dyer commit a major

KEY MOMENTS

TREATY OF VERSAILLES

The treaty was signed at the Palace of Versailles, France, on June 28, 1919, and its provisions came into force on January 20 the following year. The victors of World War I, led by Britain, France, Italy, and the United States, had formulated the treaty's provisions at the Paris Peace Conference in early 1919. None of the defeated nations had any input into its contents.

The severity of the treaty came as a shock to the Germans present at Versailles. Germany had agreed an armistice in 1918 on the tacit understanding that any subsequent peace treaty would be based on US President Woodrow Wilson's 14-Point Peace Program. Although a number of the Versailles provisions reflected the spirit of Wilson's program, they also revealed the desire of some of the victors, chiefly Britain and France, to punish Germany for the war.

Germany lost some 10 percent of its prewar territory and population. This included surrendering Alsace and Lorraine to France, and having the Saarland placed under the supervision of the League of Nations until 1935. In the east, Germany was to give up West Prussia and Posen to Poland and a slice of territory that allowed Poland access to the Baltic. This, known as the "Polish Corridor," divided East Prussia from the rest of Germany. Danzig on the Baltic was made a free city. After a local vote part of Upper Silesia was also transferred to Polish control. Germany also lost its overseas possessions, which became territories administered by the victors.

Most galling of all to the German delegates was the demand that Germany accept a war guilt clause. Practically, this meant that Germany was burdened with huge reparations to pay for the damage suffered by the victors during World War I. The treaty also allowed the victors to take action if Germany defaulted on payments.

Germany's military power was curtailed. Its army was restricted to 100,000 men, the General Staff abolished, and the manufacture of aircraft, armored vehicles, gas, and submarines prohibited. All of Germany west of the Rhine and a zone 30 miles (48 km) east of it were to be demilitarized.

Many of the clauses of the treaty were modified during the interwar years, usually in Germany's favor, or were only halfheartedly imposed. Nevertheless, the "dictated" peace left many Germans resentful of their country's impoverishment, a situation that was exploited by rightwing politicians.

▲ *Germany's delegates attend Versailles, including General Hans von Seeckt (above, ll), World War I veteran and later the first commander of his country's much-reduced interwar army.*

atrocity at Amritsar in the Punjab. Dyer has been ordered to restore order following a riot in which several Europeans have been killed. His troops open fire on civilians, killing 379 and wounding 1208. Dyer avoids major official censure.

MAY 7, 1919

POLITICS, *INTERNATIONAL*
Various representatives gather at the Palace of Versailles, France, to finalize the peace treaty with Germany.

MAY 15, 1919

MIDDLE EAST, *TURKEY*
A Greek force lands at Smyrna on the coast of Asia Minor, as Turkey descends into civil strife and the victors of World War I squabble over what peace settlements to impose on the country. The Greeks, long-standing enemies of the Turks, commit various atrocities against civilians, prompting patriotic Turkish elements under Mustafa Kemal to form a new nationalist government. Kemal will establish his main base at Ankara in central Turkey.

JUNE 22, 1919

MIDDLE EAST, *TURKEY*
With formal backing from various allies, chiefly Britain, Greek forces in Turkish Asia Minor embark on a military campaign to crush the nationalists led by Mustafa Kemal. The Turks, who are riven by political infighting, do not offer any significant resistance to the Greeks at the outset.

JUNE 28, 1919

POLITICS, *INTERNATIONAL*
The Treaty of Versailles, created by the World War I victors and imposed on defeated Germany, is signed in

the Hall of Mirrors at the Palace of Versailles, France. The treaty's provisions shock the German delegation.

JULY 21, 1919

POLITICS, *GERMANY*
Many of the German High Seas Fleet's warships that surrendered and sailed into British waters in November 1918 are scuttled by their crews at Scapa Flow in the Orkneys.

AUGUST 1, 1919

POLITICS, *HUNGARY*
Pro-Russian President Béla Kun flees Budapest in the face of growing unrest and the approach of invading Romanians. His replacement is World War I hero Admiral Miklós Horthy.

SEPTEMBER 2, 1919

RUSSIA, *CIVIL WAR*
"White" Russians under General Anton Denikin drive into Bolshevik Russia, capturing Kiev. The "White" General Peter Wrangel's Caucasian Army has already captured Tsaritsin on June 17, but fails to meet up with Admiral Alexander Kolchak's Volunteer Army, which has been pushed back through the Urals. Wrangel retreats.

SEPTEMBER 10, 1919

POLITICS, *INTERNATIONAL*
The Austrians sign the Treaty of St. Germain at Versailles. Austria surrenders a large percentage of its German-speaking population as various territories are redistributed to Italy, Czechoslovakia, Yugoslavia, and Romania. Its army is reduced to 30,000 men and *Anschluss* ("Union") with Germany is forbidden.

SEPTEMBER 12, 1919

POLITICS, *ITALY*
Italian Nationalist Gabriele d'Annunzio takes control of the former Austro-Hungarian port of Fiume, which has a large Italian population but is also claimed by Yugoslavia. The Italian government disowns d'Annunzio and the rival claims are settled by the Treaty of Rapallo on November 12. Outraged by the perceived weakness of his own government, d'Annunzio declares war. However, his coup fails.

OCTOBER 24, 1919

RUSSIA, *CIVIL WAR*
"White" General Peter Krasnov's Don Army, advancing on Voronezh, is counterattacked by the Red Army and retreats. Exploiting the victory, the Red Army strikes westward, recapturing Kiev on December 17. The "Whites" retreat to the Black Sea.

OCTOBER 25, 1919

POLITICS, *GREECE*
King Alexander dies and is replaced by his father Constantine, who had been deposed in World War I.

DECEMBER 8, 1919

POLITICS, *POLAND*
The victors of World War I attempt to settle territorial disputes between Poland and Russia by demarcating a new border. This is known as the "Curzon Line" and follows the Bug River. However, it is unacceptable to the Polish government, which is intent on taking over former Polish territories to the east of the river – a move likely to provoke war.

FEBRUARY 7, 1920

RUSSIA, *CIVIL WAR*
Captured "White" Russian Admiral Alexander Kolchak is executed by the Bolsheviks. His execution marks the end of serious opposition to the Bolsheviks in Siberia. The Bolsheviks now turn to deal with the "Whites" in the Ukraine.

MARCH 27, 1920

RUSSIA, *CIVIL WAR*
The defeated "White" forces on the Black Sea escape surrender to the Red Army thanks to an evacuation carried out by British warships. This leaves just General Peter Wrangel's forces in the Crimea opposing the Bolsheviks. He launches an offensive northward in June but is forced to retreat back into the Crimea by early November.

APRIL 25, 1920

EASTERN FRONT, *POLAND*
Polish forces under General Jósef Pilsudski launch an ambitious pre-emptive strike into

◀ *Pro-Bolshevik troops, part of the Red Army commanded by Leon Trotsky, head off to battle "White" Russian forces.*

▶ *General Jósef Pilsudski, head of the Polish government and armed forces.*

the Russian-controlled Ukraine. Both Poland and Russia have claims to each other's territory. The complex Polish operation stalls in early May as the Russians plan a counterattack.

APRIL 23, 1920

POLITICS, *TURKEY*

A provisional nationalist government headed by World War I hero Mustafa Kemal is proclaimed in Ankara.

MAY 15, 1920

EASTERN FRONT, *RUSSIA*

Russian forces in the Ukraine under Marshal Mikhail Tukhachevski and General Semën Budënny counterattack General Jósef Pilsudski's Polish forces. Pilsudski's army is in danger of being surrounded and is pushed into head-long retreat. Warsaw, the Polish capital, is under threat by August.

JUNE 4, 1920

POLITICS, *INTERNATIONAL*

The Hungarians sign the Treaty of Trianon in France. It confirms that Hungary will lose two-thirds of its former territories. Among those benefiting from Trianon are Romania, Poland, Czechoslovakia, Austria, and the Kingdom of Serbs, Croats, and Slovenes (later Yugoslavia), which gains Croatia and Slavonia. Hungary's armed forces are restricted to just 35,000 men.

AUGUST 14, 1920

POLITICS, *CZECHOSLOVAKIA*

The government signs what becomes

▲ *Lenin addresses soldiers of the Red Army as they prepare to fight against the Poles. Leon Trotsky, their commander, stands on the right of the podium.*

▶ *"White" Russian forces pose with the bodies of dead Red Army troops.*

known as the Little Entente with Yugoslavia, chiefly to prevent Hungary taking back the lands given to both of the former at the Treaty of Trianon. A similar arrangement is reached with Romania on April 23, 1921.

AUGUST 16–25, 1920

EASTERN FRONT, *POLAND*

Polish forces launch a counterattack against the Russian armies arrayed around Warsaw. The attack smashes through the Russian center, forcing the two wings to retreat eastward and to the north. Russian casualties total 150,000 men; those of the Poles 50,000. The Poles pursue the mauled Russians eastward, and they are fighting on Russian soil by the middle of September.

AUGUST 20, 1920

POLITICS, *TURKEY*

Turkey accepts the Treaty of Sèvres, which effectively signals the end of the old Turkish Empire. The country gives up its provinces in the Middle East and North Africa, and grants independence to Armenia. It also has to surrender most of its European possessions and accept a Greek garrison in both Thrace and on the fringes of Asia

Minor. Italian troops occupy parts of the south coast of Asia Minor.

The Greek presence will spark the outbreak of a war that will rage until 1922. Turkish opposition to the occupiers is led by Mustafa Kemal, who does not accept the treaty.

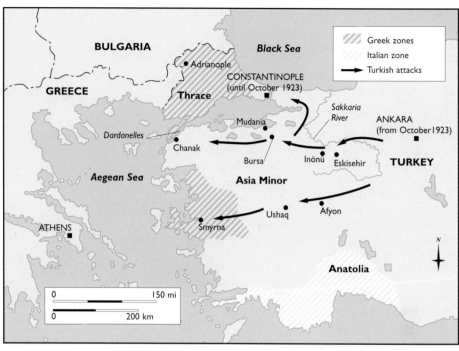

▲ *The course of the war between Greece and Turkey in Asia Minor, 1920–22. Both sides committed frequent atrocities.*

1920. The Poles have saved their country from occupation by Russia's Bolshevik regime, but a legacy of bitterness between the two Eastern European neighbors remains.

OCTOBER 14, 1920

POLITICS, FINLAND
The Finns finally win independence from Russia in the Treaty of Dorpat.

OCTOBER 12, 1920

POLITICS, RUSSIA
The authorities agree an armistice with the Poles, who have inflicted a number of defeats on them over the previous months. The armistice is ratified by the Treaty of Riga signed on March 18,

NOVEMBER 14, 1920

RUSSIA, CIVIL WAR
General Peter Wrangel's "White" forces are evacuated from the Crimea and transferred to Constantinople by British warships. This marks the end of effective opposition to the Bolsheviks.

MARCH 23, 1921

MIDDLE EAST, TURKEY
The Greeks renew their offensive deeper into Asia Minor, which had begun in January but was halted at the First Battle of Inönü. The Second Battle of Inönü on March 28–30 initially goes well for the Greeks, but the Turks finally defeat a succession of offensives.

JUNE 16–17, 1921

MIDDLE EAST, TURKEY
As part of their continuing attempts to secure territory in Asia Minor, the Greeks under King Constantine launch an offensive toward Afyon. Despite suffering high casualties in the intense fighting, the Turks are able to withdraw to the east. The Greek advance halts at the Sakkaria River due to exhaustion and supply shortages.

AUGUST 24–SEPTEMBER 6, 1921

MIDDLE EAST, TURKEY
The Battle of Sakkaria, part of the ongoing Greek–Turkish War, takes place. After several days of bitter fighting the Greeks under King Constantine are forced to retreat.

◄ *Red Army troops with one of the armored trains that allowed them to move across Russia to counter threats.*

193

November 12, 1921

The Turkish nationalists under Mustafa Kemal do not pursue closely. Kemal wishes to build up his military forces and strengthen his diplomatic relations with various foreign powers before launching an all-out offensive.

November 12, 1921

POLITICS, *INTERNATIONAL*
Several of the world's leading powers meet in Washington. They make several treaties designed to prevent any future war. The Four-Power Act is signed on December 13. It agrees that Britain, France, Japan, and the United States will be consulted over any problems arising in the Pacific between any two of the signatories to the act. An attached document states that they will respect each signatory's right to its colonial possessions and mandated territories in the region.

A further agreement, the Five-Power Naval Limitation Treaty, is signed by Britain, France, Italy, Japan, and the United States, on February 6, 1922. The signatories agree to scrap a large number of warships and set the relative strengths of the battleships in their fleets. They also are to cut back their shipbuilding programs for the next 10 years.

A final document, the Nine-Power Pact, agrees to respect China's territorial integrity. Aside from the five states already mentioned above, it is signed by Belgium, China, the Netherlands, and Portugal.

▲ A British warship at Constantinople. The Turkish capital was occupied from March 1920 until October 1923.

▼ British delegates at the Washington Conference, which attempted to limit the post-World War I naval race and reduce friction between the world's leading powers.

December 6, 1921

POLITICS, *IRELAND*
The British grant dominion status to southern Ireland, but six counties in the north with a Protestant majority keep their links with Britain. Many in southern Ireland, though agreeing the compromise, believe that the northern counties should be part of an Irish state and demand total independence.

August 18, 1922

MIDDLE EAST, *TURKEY*
Turkish nationalists under Mustafa Kemal launch a major offensive against the Greek forces occupying the coastal fringe of Asia Minor. The Greeks are

compelled to fall back. The Greek armies collapse, allowing the Turks to capture Smyrna on September 11. Its fall destroys the Greek presence in Asia Minor. Kemal next turns his attention toward Constantinople, which is occupied by foreign powers.

OCTOBER 3–11, 1922

POLITICS, *TURKEY*
Turkish nationalists led by Mustafa Kemal and the various foreign powers occupying Constantinople agree the Convention of Mudania. This promises to restore Thrace and the city of Adrianople to Turkey, and to make the Dardanelles neutral. Kemal takes the opportunity to announce the end of the Turkish sultanate, and the ruling sultan goes into exile on November 1.

▶ *French troops occupy the Rhineland following Germany's default in paying war reparations. They stayed until 1925.*

▼ *Italian fascist leader Benito Mussolini (second from right) and some of his supporters, known as "Blackshirts."*

OCTOBER 28, 1922

POLITICS, *ITALY*
Rightwing fascist leader Benito Mussolini leads his followers, the "Blackshirts," on what becomes known as the "March on Rome." Mussolini forces the government and king to give him dictatorial powers on November 28 and he initiates a reign of terror against leftwing opponents, which lasts from 1923 to 1925.

DECEMBER 30, 1922

POLITICS, *SOVIET UNION*
The Union of Soviet Socialist Republics comes into existence following the communist victory in the Russian Civil War. It initially comprises four soviet federated republics – the Russian, the Transcaucasian, the Ukrainian, and the Belorussian.

JANUARY 10, 1923

POLITICS, *UNITED STATES*
President Warren Harding withdraws the last detachments of US troops based in Europe.

JANUARY 11, 1923

POLITICS, *EUROPE*
French and Belgian troops march into the Ruhr, Germany's industrial heart. They are allowed to do so because of Germany's default on paying the war

JULY 24, 1923

reparations imposed by the Treaty of Versailles. The occupation forces remain until August 1925, by which time Germany has paid the outstanding reparations chiefly due to the US-sponsored Dawes Plan. This was able to reorganize Germany's parlous financial affairs in part due to large loans from the United States.

JULY 24, 1923

POLITICS, *TURKEY*
Following seven months of discussions the Treaty of Lausanne is agreed. It effectively repeals much of the Treaty of Sèvres, which was imposed on Turkey in 1919. Under the provisions agreed at Lausanne, Turkey regains much of Thrace from Greece and confirms that it will end all claims in the Middle East and elsewhere. The treaty is a triumph for Mustafa Kemal, the nationalist, who is proclaimed the first president of the new Turkish republic on October 29.

NOVEMBER 8–11, 1923

POLITICS, *GERMANY*
Extreme rightwingers of the National Socialist German Workers' Party (Nazis) under Adolf Hitler stage a coup

▼ Armed supports of the Adolf Hitler's National Socialist German Workers' Party in Munich during their coup attempt.

in Munich. They intend to overthrow the Bavarian government. However, the coup, known as the "Munich Putsch," ends in farce. Hitler is tried for treason and sentenced to five years in prison. However, he serves just nine months, spending the time writing a personal political testament, *Mein Kampf* ("My Struggle"). On his release Hitler continues his political career.

JANUARY 21, 1924

POLITICS, *CHINA*
Nationalist leader Sun Yat-sen chairs a conference of leading figures in the Kuomintang (National People's Party) at Canton. The discussions center on liberating the country from the various warlords who run its provinces as personal fiefdoms with no regard for central authority. To further their cause the Nationalists establish a military academy under the command of General Chiang Kai-shek.

POLITICS, *SOVIET UNION*
The death of leader Lenin sparks a political struggle as several former Bolshevik comrades vie for power. The turmoil continues until the second half of 1926 when Joseph Stalin emerges as the new leader.

NOVEMBER 26, 1924

POLITICS, *MONGOLIA*
Mongolian communists, who have

▲ Delegates at Locarno sign the various treaties designed to maintain security in Western Europe after World War I.

received support from the Soviet Union, announce the formation of the Mongolian People's Republic, which becomes a puppet of the Soviet Union.

APRIL 26, 1925

POLITICS, *GERMANY*
World War I hero Marshal Paul von Hindenburg is elected president.

JUNE 17, 1925

POLITICS, *INTERNATIONAL*
The League of Nations in Geneva, intent on controlling any arms race, attempts to limit the international arms trade. The Geneva Protocol prohibits the use of poison gas.

OCTOBER 5–16, 1925

POLITICS, *INTERNATIONAL*
Various nations meet under the aegis of the League of Nations. The discussions center on creating a framework that can help to provide a degree of security in Europe. Those present at the meeting, known as the Locarno Conference, agree several points. Belgium, Britain, France, and Germany are to mutually guarantee the frontiers between France and Germany and Belgium and Germany. Any disputes between Germany and Poland and Germany and Czechoslovakia are to go to arbitration, as well as any disputes

POLITICS, *INTERNATIONAL*
Britain, Japan, and the United States, their representatives meeting in Geneva, fail to agree a formula to establish the ratio of cruisers, destroyers, and submarines in their respective fleets.

AUGUST 1, 1927

POLITICS, *CHINA*
Communist elements within the Nationalist armed forces rebel in Nanchang. Although they are defeated, the rising marks the beginning of civil war. Other communist uprisings occur throughout the year, most notably in the province of Hunan where communist leader Mao Zhe-dong organizes a revolt of local peasants. However, Nationalists crush the communist-led resistance in Hunan.

SEPTEMBER 18, 1927

POLITICS, *GERMANY*
President Paul von Hindenburg rejects German responsibility for World War I, thereby denying a key part of the Treaty of Versailles.

NOVEMBER 22, 1927

POLITICS, *ITALY*
The government agrees the Second Treaty of Tirana with Albania. Under its provisions Albania becomes an Italian protectorate.

involving Germany and Belgium and Germany and France. Mutual assistance treaties are signed between France and Poland and also France and Czechoslovakia to prevent attack by Germany. However, France continues to build the Maginot Line defenses along its border with Germany.

MARCH 26, 1926

FAR EAST AND PACIFIC, *CHINA*
Chinese Nationalist forces under General Chiang Kai-shek capture the city of Nanking. This action is part of an ongoing offensive by the Nationalists, who are trying to unite the country and wrest power from the warlords who run the greater number of China's provinces.

APRIL 12, 1926

FAR EAST AND PACIFIC, *CHINA*
Chiang Kai-shek's Nationalist forces seize Shanghai in a move to prevent perceived subversion by both Chinese communists and leftwingers in the Kuomintang's national government. Following the action, which is denounced by the communists and leftwingers, Chiang establishes his own government in Nanking.

MAY 10, 1926

POLITICS, *UNITED STATES*
US Marines land in Nicaragua to stop a revolt. The United States will maintain a military commitment in the Central American country until 1933.

MAY 12–14, 1926

POLITICS, *POLAND*
The government is overthrown and a dictatorship headed by Marshal Jósef Pilsudski takes power.

NOVEMBER 27, 1926

POLITICS, *ITALY*
The government signs the Treaty of Tirana with Albania in which both agree to respect the territorial integrity of the other.

JANUARY 31, 1927

POLITICS, *INTERNATIONAL*
The Inter-Allied Military Control Commission, which had been created by the World War I victors to ensure Germany's compliance with the Treaty of Versailles' provisions, is dissolved. None of its members is willing to use troops to enforce Versailles, despite Germany's frequent flouting of its clauses. The League of Nations takes over its administration.

▶ *President Hindenburg rejected German responsibility for World War I.*

APRIL 12, 1928

APRIL 12, 1928

POLITICS, *CHINA*

Nationalist troops under Chiang Kai-shek launch an offensive against various warlords. The warlords are forced to accept Nationalist authority.

AUGUST 2, 1928

POLITICS, *ETHIOPIA*

The government signs the 20-Year Friendship Pact with Italy. Ethiopia gains trading rights in exchange for allowing Italian engineers to construct roads in Ethiopia.

FEBRUARY 6, 1929

POLITICS, *GERMANY*

The government accepts the Kellogg–Briand Pact, which has been under discussion since August 1928. Those signing renounce aggressive war. Also among the signatories are Britain, France, Italy, Japan, and the United States.

FEBRUARY 9, 1929

POLITICS, *SOVIET UNION*

Along with Estonia, Latvia, Poland, and Romania, Soviet delegates sign a pact rejecting aggressive war. It is named after the Soviet Union's chief negotiator, Maksim Litvinov.

OCTOBER 24, 1929

ECONOMICS, *INTERNATIONAL*

The US stock market crashes, heralding a period of worldwide economic failure, which becomes known as the "Great Depression." Among those badly hit is Germany, where inflation soars and unemployment rises to 25 percent of the work force by 1932. The insecurity prompts many Germans to support Adolf Hitler.

JULY 28, 1930

POLITICS, *CHINA*

Chinese communist forces capture Chang-sha in central China. The opposing Nationalists retake the city and initiate a series of "bandit suppression" campaigns. These are attempts to wipe out the communists.
By 1934 the campaigns are successful, forcing communists under Mao Zhe-dong to retreat to safe havens. The trek, which becomes known as the "Long March," covers some 6000 miles (9600 km) and ends in 1935.

APRIL 14, 1931

POLITICS, *SPAIN*

In a near-bloodless coup initiated by the country's pro-democratic bodies, King Alfonso XIII is deposed and Republican leader Alcalá Zamora is made head of the new government. He is named president on December 10. However, the country is far from stable.

◀ Chinese communists pictured on the "Long March," 1934–35.

SEPTEMBER 19, 1931

POLITICS, *CHINA*

The Japanese engineer an incident on the border between Manchuria, much of which they effectively control, and China. They claim that the Chinese Nationalists are planning to blow up key bridges along the railroad that links the Japanese bases at Port Arthur and Mukden. Chinese troops are forced to retreat from the area and the Japanese then continue their offensive. By February 1932 all of Manchuria is under their control.

FEBRUARY 18, 1932

POLITICS, *JAPAN*

The government announces the creation of the puppet state of Manchukuo, formerly Manchuria, which they have taken control of during the previous months. Former Chinese Emperor Pu-Yi is made nominal leader of state but is no more than a figurehead.

JUNE 16, 1932

POLITICS, *GERMANY*

Chancellor Franz von Papen ends the ban on the activities of members of the Nazi Party's SA (*Sturmabteilung* – "Storm Detachment"). Known as

▲ *Members of Hitler's "Brownshirts" attend the funeral of a comrade killed in political streetfighting with communists.*

"Brownshirts," they have been responsible in the past for considerable political violence. With the ban lifted, SA-inspired streetfighting rises.

JULY 25, 1932

POLITICS, *SOVIET UNION*
The authorities sign nonaggression pacts with Estonia, Latvia, Finland, and Poland. A similar agreement is reached with France the following November.

AUGUST 10, 1932

POLITICS, *SPAIN*
Republican President Alcalá Zamora, already facing growing calls for autonomy in some provinces, is faced by a rightwing revolt in Seville led by General José Sanjurjo. The revolt is quickly defeated, but the political violence continues.

NOVEMBER 8, 1932

POLITICS, *UNITED STATES*
Democratic contender Franklin Delano Roosevelt wins the presidential election in a landslide victory over incumbent Republican Herbert Hoover.

Roosevelt, who suffers from the debilitating impact of childhood polio, will prove to be one of his country's greatest leaders. He will serve as president for an unprecedented four terms, create policies designed to drag the United States out of the economic and social misery engendered by the worldwide Great Depression, and lead his country for most of its involvement in World War II.

NOVEMBER 17, 1932

POLITICS, GERMANY
The chancellor, Franz von Papen, resigns amid growing political unrest.

JANUARY 21– APRIL 22, 1933

POLITICS, *INTERNATIONAL*
Representatives of Britain, France, Italy, Japan, and the United States meet in London in an attempt to establish limits to their fleets. It is agreed to curb submarine tonnage and aircraft carriers. Britain, Japan,

▶ *US President Franklin D. Roosevelt was elected for the first of his four terms in office in 1932.*

and the United States sign an agreement to scrap certain types of warships by 1933. However, a clause allows any of the signatories to increase the tonnage of any particular type of vessel in their fleet if its national needs require it. The provisions of the London Naval Conference are to run until 1936.

JANUARY 30, 1933

POLITICS, *GERMANY*
Adolf Hitler, leader of the Nazi Party, becomes chancellor at the second time of asking following the resignation of Franz von Papen on November 17, 1932. Hitler refused the post the previous November as he was denied absolute power.

Hitler had already tried to gain power through another route by attempting to become president in November 1932. However, he was beaten by the incumbent, Paul von Hindenburg, polling just 36.9 percent of the vote on the second ballot.

FEBRUARY 27, 1933

POLITICS, *GERMANY*
The Reichstag (German parliament) building in Berlin is destroyed in a mysterious arson attack. A communist sympathizer is arrested and Chancellor Adolf Hitler uses the incident to warn

NOVEMBER 17, 1933

POLITICS, *UNITED STATES*
The administration recognizes the legitimacy of the Soviet Union.

JANUARY 26, 1934

POLITICS, *GERMANY*
The government signs a nonaggression agreement with Poland. Its central tenet is that each should accept the territorial rights of the other for the next 10 years.

FEBRUARY 8–9, 1934

POLITICS, *BALKANS*
Greece, Romania, Turkey, and Yugoslavia agree a pact in which each is pledged to consult the other signatories if its security is threatened. However, Bulgaria rejects the pact.

MARCH 17, 1934

POLITICS, *ITALY*
Officials from Italy, Hungary, and Austria meet in Rome and agree to establish closer economic ties and create a rightwing power bloc to

▲ The Reichstag (German parliament) after the mysterious and controversial arson attack in February 1933.

of a plot to take over the country. President Paul von Hindenburg outlaws communists and suspends various constitutional freedoms.

MARCH 5, 1933

POLITICS, *GERMANY*
Adolf Hitler's Nazi Party secures 43.9 percent of the popular vote in national elections, which have been marred by violence and intimidation by Nazi paramilitaries. On the 23rd the Reichstag passes a bill granting Hitler wide-ranging powers.

SEPTEMBER 15, 1933

POLITICS, *GREECE*
The administration signs a 10-year nonaggression pact with Turkey.

OCTOBER 14, 1933

POLITICS, *GERMANY*
The government resigns its seat in the League of Nations after disagreeing with plans to curb the expansion of armed forces and the growth of armaments production.

▶ A large poster exhorts ordinary Germans to vote for Nazi Party leader Adolf Hitler in 1933.

counter France's increasingly close ties with Czechoslovakia, Romania, and Yugoslavia. The latter three, known as the Little Entente powers, had already established various mutually-beneficial defensive agreements in 1920–21 to block German and Hungarian ambitions along the Danube River.

JUNE 30, 1934

POLITICS, *GERMANY*
More than 70 members of the Nazi Party are murdered in a purge ordered by Adolf Hitler, who believes they are a threat to his absolute authority. The action is known as "The Night of the Long Knives." Chief among those killed in the purge is Ernst Röhm, head of the Nazi Party's "Brownshirts."

JULY 25, 1934

POLITICS, *AUSTRIA*
Local Nazis assassinate Prime Minister Engelbert Dollfuss in an attempted coup. Although Chancellor Adolf Hitler denies all knowledge of the putsch, German troops are preparing to intervene. However, Hitler is forced to back down when both Italy and Yugoslavia mobilize their own forces.

AUGUST 2, 1934

POLITICS, *GERMANY*
President Paul von Hindenburg dies, allowing his chancellor, Adolf Hitler, to assume dictatorial powers by combining the posts of chancellor and president. The German people are permitted to vote on the matter – 90 percent are in favor. It also makes Hitler the supreme commander of all of the country's armed forces. Hitler receives the title of Führer ("leader") of the German Third Reich.

SEPTEMBER 18, 1934

POLITICS, *SOVIET UNION*
Joins the League of Nations.

OCTOBER 6, 1934

POLITICS, *SPAIN*
The government puts down leftwing revolts in the provinces of Asturias and Catalonia. There are reports that its troops have committed atrocities.

DECEMBER 5, 1934

EAST AFRICA, *ETHIOPIA*
Ethiopian and Italian forces clash over disputed territory on the border of Italian Somaliland. The League of Nations is unable to identify the instigator of the aggression.

▲ *The body of Prime Minister Engelbert Dollfuss lies in state following his assassination by Austrian Nazis.*

DECEMBER 19, 1934

POLITICS, *JAPAN*
The government rejects the Washington and London Naval Treaties, giving, as is required, two years' notice that it will no longer abide by the Washington Treaty and that it will not renew the London Treaty when it ends in 1936. The decision is sparked by Britain and the United States rejecting Japan's demands that it has parity with their fleets. Although Britain, France, Italy, Japan, and the United States will attend the Five-Power Naval Conference in December 1935, it also ends in failure when Japan's representatives walk out of the discussions.

MARCH 16, 1935

POLITICS, *GERMANY*
Hitler rejects the disarmament terms of the Treaty of Versailles, claiming that other nations are rearming. He embarks on a rearmaments program and reintroduces conscription.

MAY 2, 1935

POLITICS, *FRANCE*
Alarmed at Germany's announcement of a rearmaments program, the authorities agree an alliance with Russia. France begins rearming the next year.

MAY 16, 1935

POLITICS, *SOVIET UNION*
The authorities sign an alliance with Czechoslovakia to curb German expansionism into Eastern Europe.

JUNE 18, 1935

POLITICS, *GERMANY*
The government signs a naval agreement with Britain. Germany's fleet, excluding submarines, will have a tonnage no more that 35 percent of Britain's. The French authorities are outraged by the pact.

JULY 25, 1935

POLITICS, *SOVIET UNION*
Delegates attending the Third International agree to support those democracies arrayed against Europe's rightwing dictatorships, marking a major shift in the foreign policy of the Soviet Union.

KEY PERSONALITIES

GENERAL FRANCISCO FRANCO

Franco (1892–1975) was the dictator of Spain from the end of the Spanish Civil War (1936–39) until his death. Pro-monarchy and opposed to anti-Catholics, he was a careerist who entered the Toledo Infantry Academy in 1907 and whose abilities were recognized. By 1926 he was commanding the Spanish Foreign Legion, which defeated an Arab uprising in Spanish Morocco.

Franco fell out of favor following the overthrow of the monarchy and the election of a republican government in April 1931. He was sent to the Balearic Islands, returning in 1935 to suppress a leftwing revolt at the behest of the rightwing government of the time. However, Spain's volatile politics led to the election of a leftwing government and Franco was effectively exiled to the Canary Islands.

In 1936 Franco joined forces with other generals to launch a coup against the government, an act that sparked the civil war. Franco was made the rebels' chief of staff and by the end of the year he and his generals controlled roughly 50 percent of the country. At the end of the war Franco was the leader of the Nationalists and instigated a brutal campaign to crush all support for the former leftwing regime.

Although pro-Axis during World War II, Franco steadfastly refused to go to war in support of Germany and Italy, although Spanish workers were sent to Germany and a division of volunteers fought on the Eastern Front. As the war turned against the Axis, he became strictly neutral.

After 1945 Franco reorganized the Spanish government, concentrating even more power in his own hands, and made himself regent for the monarchy. His limited and short-lived political reforms in the 1950s did little to satisfy the aspirations of Spain's ethnic groups in the Basque country and in Catalonia. In his final years he ensured that the monarchy would continue after his death.

▲ Italian marines march in triumph through the streets of Addis Ababa, the Ethiopian capital, after its capitulation.

OCTOBER 3, 1935

EAST AFRICA, *ETHIOPIA*
Italian forces invade, although there has been no formal declaration of war. The military adventure is part of Italian dictator Benito Mussolini's plan to create an Italian empire in northern and eastern Africa. Four days later the League of Nations declares Italy the aggressor, and imposes sanctions the following month. The Italian offensive continues, despite fierce resistance from the Ethiopians.

NOVEMBER 12, 1935

POLITICS, *GERMANY*
The Saarland, which as part of the Treaty of Versailles settlement has been administered by the League of Nations, votes to return to direct German political control.

FEBRUARY 16, 1936

POLITICS, *SPAIN*
National elections lead to the formation of a new leftwing government headed by Manuel Azãna.

MARCH 7, 1936

POLITICS, *GERMANY*
Adolf Hitler renounces the Locarno Pact signed in 1925. It had been designed to guarantee territorial security in Europe, particularly in relation to Germany and its neighbors. Simultaneously, German forces reoccupy the Rhineland. Britain does not support the French government, which is ready to intervene, and the reoccupation goes unchallenged.

MAY 5, 1936

EAST AFRICA, *ETHIOPIA*
Invading Italian forces capture the capital, Addis Ababa, forcing Emperor Haile Selassie to flee his country. Four days later Italy formally annexes Ethiopia. Together with Eritrea and Italian Somaliland, it comprises Italian East Africa.

JUNE 18, 1936

SPAIN, *CIVIL WAR*
Twelve military garrisons on the Spanish mainland and five in Spanish Morocco rebel against Manuel Azãna's Republican government. General Francisco Franco, exiled in the Canary Islands, flies to Spanish Morocco and takes charge of the rebelling garrison

at Melilla. Meanwhile, anti-government troops, known as Nationalists, are flown from Spanish Morocco and establish bases at Algeciras and La Linea on the mainland. In northern Spain antigovernment forces are centered on Burgos.

AUGUST 15, 1936
SPAIN, *CIVIL WAR*
Nationalist rebels capture Badajoz from forces loyal to the Republican government.
They continue their advance toward Madrid, the capital, relieving the Nationalist troops under siege at Toledo on September 28. As the fighting intensifies, the Nationalists receive military aid from Germany and Italy; the Republicans are supplied by the

▶ *Italian guns are turned on their former owners during the Spanish Civil War.*

Soviet Union. Various foreign volunteers flock to both sides, but the bulk fight with the Republicans in units known as International Brigades.

AUGUST 26, 1936
POLITICS, *EGYPT*
The authorities enter into an agreement with Britain, which grants the country full independence. Britain is allowed to maintain a military presence along the Suez Canal and keep its naval base at Alexandria.

SEPTEMBER 4, 1936
POLITICS, *SPAIN*
The leftwing Popular Front government is formed under the leadership of Francisco Largo Cabellero in an attempt to unite the various political groups opposing the rebelling Nationalists, who appoint General Francisco Franco the chief of their rival Spanish state in October.

OCTOBER 27, 1936
POLITICS, *GERMANY*
Germany reaches an agreement with Italy. Italy agrees not to oppose the planned German take-over of Austria, while Germany pledges to recognize the legitimacy of Italy's conquest of Ethiopia. The arrangement marks the beginning of even closer ties between Nazi Germany and fascist Italy, the so-called Rome–Berlin Axis.

NOVEMBER 6, 1936
SPAIN, *CIVIL WAR*
Nationalist forces lay siege to Madrid but are unable to capture the capital. The fighting continues into 1937.

NOVEMBER 18, 1936
POLITICS, *SPAIN*
The authority of General Francisco Franco's Nationalist government is recognized by Germany and Italy.

NOVEMBER 25, 1936
POLITICS, *GERMANY*
The government signs what becomes known as the Anti-Comintern Pact with Japan. It is to reinforce the existing German–Italian power bloc, which opposes the French and Russian alliance.

MARCH 18, 1937
SPAIN, *CIVIL WAR*
Italian troops fighting for the Nationalist rebels are defeated at the Battle of Brihuega by forces loyal to the Republican government. The Nationalists call off their attempts to surround Madrid and push into northern Spain instead, capturing Bilbao in April.

MARCH 25, 1937
POLITICS, *ITALY*
The authorities sign an agreement with Yugoslavia, which guarantees the two countries' existing borders.

APRIL 25, 1937
SPAIN, *CIVIL WAR*
German aircraft, part of the Condor Legion which is fighting for the Nationalists, bomb the town of Guernica in the north. In what is considered an atrocity by many, some 1600 civilians are killed and nearly 900 wounded – one-third of the town's total population.

◄ *Japanese troops extricate their trucks from mud during their push into north-eastern China.*

MAY 17, 1937

POLITICS, *SPAIN*
The Popular Front coalition government of Francisco Largo Cabellero falls following political infighting between the various leftwing groups within the government. Juan Negrín is named the new leader.

JUNE 18, 1937

SPAIN, *CIVIL WAR*
Nationalist rebels capture the northern port of Bilbao from forces loyal to the Republican government. The Nationalist continue their attacks and by the end of the year will control all of northern Spain.

JULY 7, 1937

FAR EAST AND PACIFIC, *CHINA*
Japanese forces clash with Chinese units near the Marco Polo Bridge to the northeast of Beijing. The incident is engineered by the Japanese and heralds a full-scale invasion of China. The Chinese forces opposing the Japanese consist of some two million poorly-trained Nationalists under General Chiang Kai-shek and some 150,000 communist guerrillas. Relations between the Nationalist and communist forces are strained. The Japanese have a front-line strength of 300,000 men supported by 150,000 local troops. Some two million reserves are also available from Japan

itself. Japan's air force and navy are incomparably superior to those of the Chinese.

The initial Japanese attacks are overwhelmingly successful. Beijing falls on the 28th and Tientsin the following day. Despite increasing Chinese resistance and problems of resupply, the Japanese capture most of China north of the Yellow River by the end of the year. Chief among the Japanese victories, which are often

▼ *German forces occupy Austria, a gamble by Adolf Hitler that was unopposed by the international community.*

accompanied by atrocities against civilians, is the capture of Shanghai in early November.

OCTOBER 13, 1937

POLITICS, *GERMANY*
Adolf Hitler offers a guarantee that Belgium's borders will be respected with the key proviso that Belgium does not take any military action against Germany.

NOVEMBER 5, 1937

POLITICS, *GERMANY*
Adolf Hitler meets with his senior military commanders and foreign minister. The discussions, held in great secrecy, center on his plans for gaining *Lebensraum* ("living room") for the German people. He expects Austria, Czechoslovakia, Poland, and the Soviet Union to be seized by force between 1938 and 1943.

NOVEMBER 28, 1937

SPAIN, *CIVIL WAR*
Nationalist leader General Francisco Franco orders a naval blockade of Spain to prevent supplies from reaching the Republican government.

DECEMBER 11, 1937

POLITICS, *ITALY*
The government announces its withdrawal from the League of Nations.

DECEMBER 13, 1937

FAR EAST AND PACIFIC, *CHINA*
Japanese forces capture the city of

the country is now held by the Nationalists, who are preparing for a final offensive.

JULY 11, 1938

FAR EAST AND PACIFIC, *CHINA*
Fighting breaks out between the Soviet Union and Japan, which is occupying Manchuria and Korea, over a disputed border. Japanese attacks are beaten off by mid-August but tension remains.

In May the fighting flares up again. This time it occurs along a river, which the Japanese claim to be the true border between Manchuria and Soviet-occupied Mongolia. The Soviet response is to occupy the disputed territory lying between the river and Nomonhan, but Japanese attacks force the invaders back. However, a Soviet counteroffensive led by General Georgi Zhukov pushes the Japanese back and beats off several counter-attacks over the following months.

SEPTEMBER 15, 1938

POLITICS, *CHINA*
The fighting between Soviet and Japanese forces over a disputed border ends with a cease-fire.

POLITICS, *GERMANY*
Hitler demands that Czechoslovakia gives up its province of Sudetenland,

Nanking. Its fall is followed by several weeks of slaughter and looting by the Japanese. An estimated 42,000 civilians are killed. However, the horror of Nanking stiffens Chinese resolve against the Japanese, whose plans to take over China suffer a series of military setbacks.

MARCH 12, 1938

POLITICS, *GERMANY*
Hitler orders the take-over of Austria, where some six million Germans live. The operation is completed the next day. Italian dictator Benito Mussolini backs Hitler's political gamble of *Anschluss* ("Union") with Austria.

APRIL 15, 1938

SPAIN, *CIVIL WAR*
Nationalist forces reach the port of Vinaroz on the coast of Valencia in the east, effectively isolating Catalonia to the north from other Republican-held areas of the country.

JUNE 24, 1938

SPAIN, *CIVIL WAR*
Republican forces launch an offensive along the line of the Ebro River in an attempt to restore communications between isolated Catalonia and the other parts of the country held by their troops. The main attack is halted after just seven days, but the fighting continues into November, when the Republicans withdraw. More than half

▲ *The Soviet Union's General Georgi Zhukov (in peaked cap) holds a field briefing during the brief border war with the Japanese.*

▼ *The course of the Spanish Civil War, fought during 1936–39.*

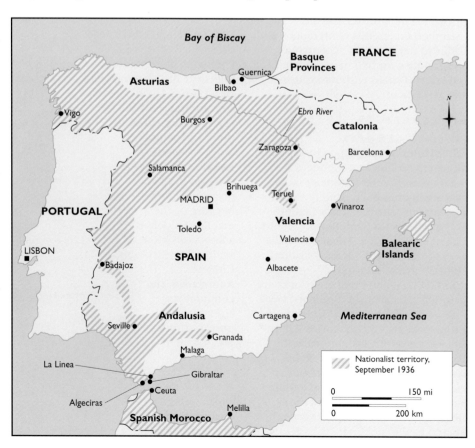

which contains some three million German-speakers. Hitler's propaganda machine has been demanding its return over the preceding two years. British Prime Minister Neville Chamberlain attends conferences with Hitler to negotiate an acceptable compromise on two occasions but returns to Britain without securing any agreement.

SEPTEMBER 29, 1938

POLITICS, *GERMANY*
Adolf Hitler, accompanied by Foreign Minister Joachim von Ribbentrop, meets with several European statesmen at Munich. Among those present are Italian dictator Benito Mussolini, his foreign minister, Count Ciano, British Prime Minister Neville Chamberlain and Edouard Daladier, France's prime minister.

Both Britain and France's leaders are painfully aware of their military weakness and believe that by acceding to Hitler's claims on Czechoslovakia they can secure a long-lasting peace in Europe. Hitler, who indicates this is his last territorial demand in Europe, is effectively given a free hand and the Sudetenland is incorporated into Germany. The Czech leaders are not invited to the meeting.

▲ *Bewildered Czech nationals look on as the German armed forces occupy the Sudetenland in 1938.*

OCTOBER 21, 1938

FAR EAST AND PACIFIC, *CHINA*
Following amphibious landings near British-controlled Hong Kong, Japanese forces capture Canton from the Chinese. The fall of the port is a temporary boost to Japanese morale, which has suffered in the previous months because of their inability to deliver a knockout blow against the Chinese Nationalists and communists attempting to prevent the take-over of their country.

▶ *Chamberlain and Hitler during the discussions over the Sudetenland.*

Nevertheless, the Japanese no longer hold out any hopes of conquering China quickly; they settle on a new strategy designed to wear down the Chinese. However, although the Japanese have captured China's major ports, the Chinese wage a guerrilla war and are still able to receive supplies from two directions. One is via a railroad that runs from Haiphong, a port in French-controlled Indochina, while the other is a road that begins in Burma, which is administered by the British. The latter, later known as the "Burma Road," will have an important role to play in World War II.

NOVEMBER 2, 1938

POLITICS, *HUNGARY*
Germany grants the country a large part of former Czech territory for the support it offered during the annexation of the Sudetenland.

NOVEMBER 9–10, 1938

POLITICS, *GERMANY*
Adolf Hitler's supporters launch attacks on Germany's Jewish community and their property, particularly synagogues. The events become known as *Kristallnacht* ("Crystal Night") because of the shards of window glass that litter the roads and sidewalks outside Jewish properties.

Kristallnacht marks an intensification in the persecution of

▲ *A synagogue burns following the Nazi attacks on Kristallnacht, which marked an escalation in anti-Jewish violence.*

Germany's Jews, who have already lost their legal rights as citizens. Since 1933 roughly half of Germany's 500,000-strong Jewish community has fled the country.

NOVEMBER 30, 1938

POLITICS, *ITALY*
Friction between Italy and France rises as the former demands that the latter surrenders Corsica and Tunisia.

DECEMBER 6, 1938

POLITICS, *FRANCE*
The government agrees a pact with Germany. It guarantees the integrity of their existing borders.

DECEMBER 23, 1938

SPAIN, *CIVIL WAR*
Nationalists forces launch an offensive to capture Catalonia, which has been effectively cut off from the rest of Republican-held Spain since April

1937. Republican morale begins to collapse in the face of the onslaught.

JANUARY 12, 1939

POLITICS, *UNITED STATES*
President Franklin D. Roosevelt requests Congress to approve a defense budget of $552 million, marking a significant rise in military spending.

JANUARY 26, 1939

SPAIN, *CIVIL WAR*
Barcelona, the Republican-held capital of Catalonia, is captured by the Nationalists.

▶ *Nationalist howitzers prepare to open fire on Republican positions in the battle for Catalonia, early 1939.*

FEBRUARY 27, 1939

POLITICS, *SPAIN*
The authority of the Nationalist regime of General Francisco Franco is recognized by Britain and France.

MARCH 5, 1939

POLITICS, *SPAIN*
The factions within the leftwing coalition government of Republican Juan Negrín disagree over the future of the war. Negrín is for fighting on despite the increasingly hopeless position; others favor an end to the war. Negrín is overthrown and replaced by Colonel Sigismundo Casado.

MARCH 10, 1939

POLITICS, *GERMANY*
Adolf Hitler begins the annexation of Bohemia and Moravia, both part of Czechoslovakia with sizeable German populations. The operation, which is in direct violation of the Munich Agreement, is completed by the 16th. Czechoslovakia ceases to exist, with only Slovakia remaining nominally independent. Hungary cooperates with Germany and gains Ruthenia.

MARCH 23, 1939

POLITICS, *GERMANY*
Adolf Hitler orders the annexation of Memel, Lithuania, and demands the return of the "Polish Corridor" and Danzig from Poland. His actions spark intense defensive negotiations between Britain and the Soviet Union over the following months.

MARCH 28, 1939

SPAIN, *CIVIL WAR*
Nationalist troops enter

▲ *Some of the German troops fighting for the Nationalists during the Spanish Civil War (right) march through Madrid, 1939.*

the capital, Madrid, thereby ending the fighting. Over the following weeks the various Republican forces surrender.

The civil war has cost the lives of some 300,000 Spaniards, perhaps a third killed in reprisals and atrocities by both Nationalists and Republicans. Nationalist leader General Francisco Franco sets out to eradicate those with strong Republican sympathies and an estimated 300,000 are killed in the subsequent purges.

MARCH 31, 1939

POLITICS, *BRITAIN*
The British government guarantees to aid Poland if the latter country is the victim of any external aggression. The arrangement is a last-ditch attempt to prevent Hitler from taking over the country, but Britain is ill-prepared to offer any immediate military aid to Poland. Similar pledges are later made to Greece and Romania. The French also give the same assurances.

APRIL 7, 1939

BALKANS, *ALBANIA*
Italian forces invade and quickly conquer the country. The attack is part of Mussolini's aim to create an Italian empire stretching along the Mediterranean coast.

APRIL 11, 1939

POLITICS, *HUNGARY*
The authorities withdraw from the League of Nations.

APRIL 13, 1939

POLITICS, *ROMANIA*
The country's independence is guaranteed by Britain and France. However, the value of the agreement is soon undermined when the Romanian government agrees closer economic ties with Germany.

APRIL 28, 1939

POLITICS, *GERMANY*
Adolf Hitler rejects Germany's 1934 nonaggression pact with Poland and the Anglo-German Naval Agreement signed in 1935.

MAY 3, 1939

POLITICS, *SOVIET UNION*
Maksim Litvinov, who is considered to be supportive of the Western democracies, is replaced as foreign minister by Vyacheslav Molotov. Although the Soviet Union continues to discuss alliances against Germany with Britain and France, Molotov does not trust their motives and the discussions stall without any formal or informal arrangements being made by any of the parties involved.

MAY 22, 1939

POLITICS, *ITALY*
The government agrees closer military ties with Germany. The strengthened alliance between the two becomes known as the "Pact of Steel."

MAY 23, 1939

POLITICS, *GERMANY*

Adolf Hitler orders his military high command to begin planning the invasion of Poland. Over the following months there are "border incidents" between Germany and Poland. These are usually instigated by German troops. They heighten tension between the two countries and one such event will be used to justify the German invasion in September.

AUGUST 22, 1939

POLITICS, *GERMANY*

Adolf Hitler gives his final approval for the invasion of Poland, and German forces move to their war stations along Poland's western border. The Germans plan to use a strategy of combining tanks, fast-moving troops, and aircraft to crush Polish resistance within a matter of a few weeks.

◄ *Adolf Hitler (far left), Hermann Goering, head of the Luftwaffe (sixth from right), and various military figures greet the Italian delegation during the "Pact of Steel" discussions, May 1939.*

▲ *Hitler's foreign minister, Joachim von Ribbentrop (center, standing), announces the signing of the nonaggression pact over Poland with the Soviet Union.*

AUGUST 23, 1939

POLITICS, *GERMANY*

Foreign Minister Joachim von Ribbentrop signs a nonaggression pact with the Soviet Union's foreign minister, Vyacheslav Molotov, in Moscow. The Soviet Union agrees not to oppose the German invasion of Poland and both countries agree to divide Poland between them. Eastern Europe is split between the two states' exclusive spheres of influence.

The Soviet leadership believes the agreement will give them time to reorganize their military forces, whose officer corps has been decimated by purges instigated by Joseph Stalin.

POLITICS, *JAPAN*

The government withdraws from the Anti-Comintern Pact with Germany and Italy following the former's recent surprise alliance with the Soviet Union concerning the immediate fate of Poland.

WORLD WAR II

World War I, "The War to End All Wars," was to create many of the conditions that would lead to the outbreak of an even more destructive conflict – World War II. At the end of World War I Germany was in dire straits: its population was near starvation and devoid of hope, and its army and navy were in disarray. The Treaty of Versailles of June 1919 added to Germany's woes as it removed its overseas possessions, implemented the occupation of part of the Rhineland to ensure Germany complied with provisions of the treaty, and imposed huge reparations for the damage inflicted on France and other countries during World War I.

The fact that Germany was almost bankrupt meant that it was extremely unlikely Germany would be able to pay, even less so when the world slump of 1921 arose. The next year German defaulted on reparations payments for the second year running. In retaliation, France, showing amazing shortsightedness, occupied the Ruhr, the center of German industry. This not only reduced the already slim chances of Germany paying any reparations, but also increased hostility between the two countries.

The stoppage of the Ruhr industries had a calamitous impact on the German currency, which plummeted in value. Overnight, savings were wiped out, leaving millions penniless and destitute, their careers, hopes, and finances totally destroyed.

ADOLF HITLER
In such an atmosphere people desperately searched for answers. They found them in the vitriolic oratory of an

▼ A Nuremberg rally. Each one was designed to increase support for both Hitler and Nazism.

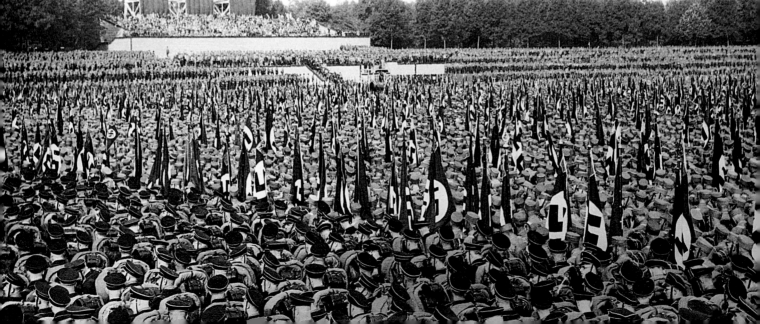

▶ German dictator Adolf Hitler, who was obsessed with the creation of German "living space" in Eastern Europe.

ex-soldier named Adolf Hitler, who belonged to the *Nationalsozialistische Deutsche Arbeiterpartei* (National Socialist German Workers' Party, or Nazi Party for short). The failure of Germany's Weimar government to cope with war debts and inflation made Hitler's claim that an alternative was needed seem sensible.

Notwithstanding his failure in the ludicrous 1923 Munich Beer Hall

▲ The 1936 Berlin Olympic Games, which provided Hitler with an opportunity to present Nazism on a world stage.

Putsch, the Nazi Party's membership continued to grow in the 1920s. The 1929 worldwide economic slump played into the Nazis' hands, for Hitler was able to blame the financial crisis on unpatriotic Jews and the conspiracies of communists – views that found receptive ears. In 1932 Hitler polled 36.9 percent of the vote, and after ingratiating himself with the World War I hero President Paul von Hindenburg, the latter invited the Nazi leader to become chancellor in 1933.

Once in power Hitler was able to establish a dictatorship. He created jobs by expelling Jews, by insisting that

women should stay at home and produce offspring, and by sending young men to labor camps (not to be confused with concentration camps). But there was a heavy price to be paid: the abolition of trade unions, and the persecution of Jews and communists. Hitler also renounced the Treaty of Versailles, began rearming, and reoccupied the Rhineland.

EXPANDING THE REICH
Having consolidated his position within Germany, Hitler now looked for *Lebensraum* ("living space") beyond its borders. His ambitions were helped by the peace treaties that followed World War I. For example, he wished to bring Czechoslovakia's Sudeten Germans back into the fold, while at the same time coveting Czechoslovakia's armaments industry.

As Austria and Czechoslovakia were absorbed into the Third Reich, the Western democracies dithered. Indeed, in both Britain and France there was a belief that the terms imposed on Germany by the Treaty of

▼ Benito Mussolini (left), the Italian dictator who came to power after the 1922 "March on Rome."

KEY MOMENTS

APPEASEMENT

Appeasement has, since the end of World War II, been equated with cowardice and is held in contempt by some. In the 1930s, however, appeasement as believed in by British Prime Minister Neville Chamberlain and French leaders such as Edouard Daladier encapsulated reasonable steps that might be taken to prevent Hitler taking the law into his own hands. It was also the manifestation of a very real desire to avoid another general European war and its many associated horrors.

Appeasement had its roots in the growing feeling in the early 1930s in Britain and France that the terms of the Treaty of Versailles had been harsh on Germany. Seen in this light, Adolf Hitler's demands for a rearmed Germany and the restoration of "German" territories appeared reasonable. Thus by agreeing to these essentially "just" demands, Chamberlain believed he could lay the foundations for a lasting peace.

Unfortunately, appeasement relied on the goodwill of both parties to be a success. Thus after the Munich talks in September 1938, Chamberlain and Daladier agreed to Hitler's demands for the incorporation into the Third Reich of German-speaking Czechoslovak Sudetenland. Chamberlain proclaimed the agreement heralded "peace with honor." For his part Hitler had expected a confrontation over the issue, and Britain and France's failure to stand up to him encouraged more brinkmanship. He occupied the rest of Czechoslovakia in March 1939, signaling the end of appeasement. This guaranteed that both Britain and France would fight to defend Poland.

Versailles had been harsh, and that by appeasing Hitler by assenting to his "just" demands, a basis for a lasting European peace could be laid.

But they were both mistaken. The belief that the Munich agreement of September 1938, whereby the Sudetenland was ceded to Germany, would lead to "peace in our time" was also wrong. This was confirmed in March 1939 when Germany occupied the rest of Czechoslovakia.

MUSSOLINI'S ITALY

World War II had, for all practical purposes, begun; the more so because Hitler had similarly belligerent allies in Europe and the Far East. In Italy, for example, Benito Mussolini fancied himself as a twentieth-century Caesar. His fascist regime had achieved some notable results in the country, such as the drainage and cultivation of marshes, the construction of factories and roads, the balancing of the budget, and, probably his greatest achievement, making the trains run on time. His regime built up the army, navy, and air force, and glorified war, while Mussolini himself talked of the Mediterranean as being *Mare Nostrum* ("Our Sea").

Mussolini realized that his armed forces required modern equipment, and so he picked his opponents carefully. His attack against Ethiopia (then Abyssinia) was regarded with disgust

by other European nations, as Italian warplanes dropped bombs and poison gas on spear-armed tribesmen. Nevertheless, the war confirmed the impotence of the League of Nations, which could not rally any of its members to take effective action.

THE AXIS ALLIANCE

In the Far East, Japan flexed its muscles. Having defeated Russia in 1904–05, it went on to annex Korea

▼ *Danzig, on the Baltic at the mouth of the Vistula River, was designated a "free city" by the League of Nations. Hitler demanded its return to Germany, along with the so-called "Polish Corridor."*

Poland now became the focus of Hitler's attention. Recreated after World War I, it had been given access to the sea via a corridor of land which reached the Baltic at Danzig. It had been formerly German territory, and Hitler was determined it would be again. Danzig was, in theory, a "free city" administered by the United Nations, but in reality the Nazis had gained control of the city in 1934 and did largely what they liked. Hitler ranted that it and the strip of land that divided Germany and East Prussia should be returned to the Reich.

Few people in the West knew or cared very much what the "Polish Corridor" was – some believed it to be an underground tunnel – but in March 1939 Britain and France took the fateful step of pledging themselves to the defense of Poland, which neither of them was in a military position to do. When German armies entered Poland on September 1, 1939, they had no choice but to declare war two days later. World War II had begun, little more than two decades after the end of the first great conflict.

and overrun the whole of Manchuria, which was renamed Manchukuo. When the League of Nations protested, Japan simply resigned its membership. In 1936 it signed the anticommunist Anti-Comintern Pact with Germany and Italy. Japan was now part of the Rome–Berlin–Tokyo Axis, which was seemingly further strengthened when Hitler and Joseph Stalin, the Soviet leader, signed a nonaggression pact on August 23, 1939, in which a secret clause divided up a conquered Poland between the two dictators (Stalin did not want German troops on the frontier of the Soviet Union itself).

▼ *The fruits of Nazi Germany's rearmament program – Hitler inspects a new warship at Kiel.*

1939

After months of diplomatic wrangling and "appeasement" bargaining, war erupted when Germany invaded Poland. Germany's Blitzkrieg offensive, which plunged Europe into conflict, heralded a new and dramatic style of modern warfare. Although there was no Allied advance into Germany in Western Europe, fighting flared up on the Eastern Front between the Soviet Union and neighboring Finland.

SEPTEMBER 1

EASTERN FRONT, *POLAND*

A German force of 53 divisions, supported by 1600 aircraft, crosses the German and Slovak borders into Poland in a pincer movement. Plan White, directed by General Walther von Brauchitsch, aims to totally paralyze Poland's 24 divisions by swift encirclement, thus cutting their lines of supply and communication. While Poland mobilizes its full strength, its forces in action, lacking both air and armored support, are largely placed on the country's borders. They are quickly overrun, and reinforcements often arrive too late to halt the German attacks.

SEPTEMBER 2

POLITICS, *ALLIES*

Ultimatums are delivered by Britain and France to Germany demanding its immediate withdrawal from Poland.

SEPTEMBER 3

POLITICS, *ALLIES*

Britain and France declare war on Nazi Germany after their ultimatums regarding the invasion of Poland expire. Australia and New Zealand also declare war. British Prime Minister Neville Chamberlain forms a war cabinet, which includes prominent antiappeasers First Lord of the Admiralty Winston Churchill and Secretary for the Dominions Anthony Eden.

▲ The German invasion of Poland began in September with air and ground attacks that quickly paralyzed the Polish forces.

◀ German troops tear down border posts as they advance into Poland.

▲ *French citizens cheer their soldiers after mobilization orders are issued in 1939.*

SEA WAR, *ATLANTIC*
The liner *Athenia* is sunk by the *U-30* after being mistaken for a British auxiliary cruiser, claiming 112 lives.

SEPTEMBER 4

AIR WAR, *GERMANY*
Britain's Royal Air Force (RAF) Bomber Command launches its first attacks against Nazi warships in the Heligoland Bight off northwest Germany, but the government will not authorize raids on targets within Germany.

SEPTEMBER 5

POLITICS, *SOUTH AFRICA*
Prime Minister Jan Christiaan Smuts declares war on Nazi Germany following the formation of a new cabinet after political disagreements over joining the conflict.
POLITICS, *UNITED STATES*
The authorities officially proclaim their neutrality.

SEPTEMBER 6

EASTERN FRONT, *POLAND*
The Polish government and high command leave Warsaw and order

▶ *German troops make a hasty river crossing during the invasion of Poland.*

their forces to withdraw to the line of the Narew, Vistula, and San Rivers. Nazi troops make a dramatic advance that reaches beyond Lódz. They also seize Cracow in the south.

SEPTEMBER 7

WESTERN FRONT, *GERMANY*
France begins minor skirmishes across the border with Germany near Saarbrücken.

SEA WAR, *ATLANTIC*
Britain's first convoys sail across the Atlantic. The system is already operating on Britain's east coast to protect merchant ships from U-boat attacks.

SEPTEMBER 8

EASTERN FRONT, *POLAND*
The German Tenth Army led by General Walter von Reichenau reaches the outskirts of Warsaw, the capital.

SEPTEMBER 9

▲ *Polish lancers head for the front.*

General Wilhelm List's Fourteenth Army reaches the San River around Przemysl, while General Heinz Guderian's tank corps reaches the Bug River to the east of Warsaw.

SEPTEMBER 9

EASTERN FRONT, *POLAND*
A Polish counterattack is launched by 10 divisions, which gather around Kutno under General Tadeuz Kutrzeba. The attack over the Bzura River against Germany's Eighth Army is the most effective Polish offensive of the campaign, but only achieves short-term success.

▼ *A grief-stricken Polish girl finds her sister has been killed during a German air attack on Warsaw.*

SEPTEMBER 10

POLITICS, *CANADA*
The government declares war on Germany.

WESTERN FRONT, *FRANCE*
Major elements of the British Expeditionary Force, led by General Lord Gort, begin to land in France. Some 160,000 men and 24,000 vehicles arrive throughout the course of September.

SEPTEMBER 13

POLITICS, *FRANCE*
Prime Minister Edouard Daladier forms a war cabinet and takes additional responsibility for foreign affairs.

SEPTEMBER 16–27

EASTERN FRONT, *POLAND*
Warsaw's defenders are encircled but refuse to surrender until the 27th. Elements of Germany's Fourteenth Army west of Lvov are still locked in battle, while other units advance to join General Heinz Guderian's units in action along the Bug River.

SEPTEMBER 17

SEA WAR, *ATLANTIC*
The British aircraft carrier *Courageous* is sunk by *U-29* during an antisubmarine patrol off southwest Ireland. The aircraft carrier *Ark Royal* has managed to escape a similar attack just three days beforehand. The naval authorities act quickly and withdraw Britain's aircraft carriers from such duties to preserve these valuable vessels for other maritime roles.

◀ *Polish forces surrendering to a German officer. Despite Poland's fighting spirit, its armies were decisively defeated by Germany's Blitzkrieg attack.*

formed and many fighters escape to join the Allies. Poland is split into two zones of occupation divided by the Bug River. Germany has lost 10,572 troops and the Soviet Union has 734 men killed in the campaign. Around 50,000 Poles are killed and 750,000 captured.

SEPTEMBER 21

POLITICS, *ROMANIA*
A local fascist group, the "Iron Guard," assassinates Romanian Prime Minister Armand Calinescu.

SEPTEMBER 27

POLITICS, *GERMANY*
Adolf Hitler's senior commanders are told of his plans for a western offensive at the earliest opportunity. This announcement is met with hostility by the military, who resent Hitler assuming direct control over strategic planning and also feel unprepared for this undertaking. His plan for invading the Low Countries, formulated as Plan Yellow on October 19, is constantly aborted due to bad weather. The plan is also modified and its objectives widened before the actual offensive in 1940.

▼ *The British aircraft carrier* **Courageous** *was sunk in September 1940 by a U-boat during an antisubmarine patrol. British aircraft carriers were quickly withdrawn from such duties.*

SEPTEMBER 17–30

EASTERN FRONT, *POLAND*
In accordance with a secret clause in their 1939 pact with Germany, the Red Army invades. Little resistance is encountered on Poland's eastern border as the Polish Army is fighting for its life to the west.

SEPTEMBER 18–30

POLITICS, *POLAND*
The Polish government and high command flee to Romania, only to be interned. A government-in-exile is

STRATEGY & TACTICS

BLITZKRIEG

Blitzkrieg ("lightning war") aimed to inflict a total defeat on an enemy through a single, powerful offensive. This was to be achieved by speed, firepower, and mobility. General Heinz Guderian's book *Achtung! Panzer!* (1933) articulated the strategy, which aimed to avoid the costly and indecisive trench warfare of 1914–18.

Germany exploited the developments in tanks, mobile artillery, and aircraft in its first Blitzkrieg, the attack on Poland. Blitzkrieg always avoided strong resistance in order to sustain the momentum of the assault, which concentrated on an enemy's rear areas to break his lines of supply and communication. Once this was achieved, less-mobile forces could annihilate isolated pockets of resistance.

Blitzkrieg not only required new technology; it also needed commanders with the tactical vision and flexibility to exploit opportunities and overcome obstacles in order to sustain an attack's momentum.

The Allies, having failed to appreciate the lessons of the Blitzkrieg strike on Poland, were equally stunned by the 1940 attacks against France and the Low Countries. Germany's formidable strategy, therefore, inflicted another major defeat.

A German Heinkel He 111 attacks Warsaw during the invasion of Poland. Aircraft were a vital component of the Blitzkrieg and acted as mobile artillery for the advancing land forces during an offensive.

SEPTEMBER 29

KEY PERSONALITIES

ADOLF HITLER

Adolf Hitler (1889–1945), the founder and leader of Nazi Germany, was born in Austria. His experiences as a failed artist in Vienna and decorated soldier in World War I helped shape his extremist political ambitions, which led to the Nazi Party's foundation.

He exploited Weimar Germany's political turbulence and social unrest to maneuver himself into power in 1933. Violence and intimidation secured his position as dictator. His Nazism fused nationalism with racism and created powerful expansionist ambitions. Hitler articulated the dream of creating an empire by destroying Germany's supposed racial and ideological enemies. His desire to realize his expansionist ambitions plunged Europe into diplomatic chaos and, ultimately, war.

Hitler's political skills centered upon his opportunistic character and mastery of propaganda. However, as Führer ("leader") Hitler also became Germany's military master. In this capacity Hitler's boldness and confidence were demonstrated in Germany's early Blitzkrieg successes.

By 1941 Hitler's skills were in decline, and his stubbornness and lack of strategic vision exacerbated the military problems. He became isolated from reality and refused to admit the war was lost.

Hitler survived an assassination attempt in 1944 but finally took his own life in 1945. Hitler's empire was finally crushed, but the destruction it wrought left the world re-molded by the bloodiest war in history.

▶ *Soviet forces in Finland dismantle antitank obstacles along the Mannerheim Line in the Karelian Isthmus.*

SEPTEMBER 29

POLITICS, *SOVIET UNION*
After occupying Poland, the Soviet Union concentrates on extending its control over the Baltic Sea region to safeguard against any German threat. During the next few weeks it gains bases and signs "mutual assistance" agreements with Lithuania, Latvia, and Estonia. Finland, however, will not agree to the Soviet Union's territorial demands and mobilizes its armed forces in October as political dialogue fails to resolve the crisis.

OCTOBER 14

SEA WAR, *NORTH SEA*
The British battleship *Royal Oak* is sunk, with 786 lives lost, after *U-47* passes through antisubmarine defenses at Scapa Flow in the Orkneys, where the Home Fleet is anchored. Defenses are improved at the base after this dramatic attack.

NOVEMBER 4

POLITICS, *UNITED STATES*
Changes to the Neutrality Act permit belligerent states to purchase arms from private suppliers on a "cash-and-carry" basis, whereby they have to pay for any weapons and then transport them using their own vessels. Given Britain's command of the Atlantic sea-lanes, this act is clearly intended to benefit the Allied nations.

NOVEMBER 26

POLITICS, *FINLAND*
Criticism of Finland in the Soviet press and a faked border incident further sours Soviet–Finnish relations. Joseph Stalin, the Soviet leader, subsequently withdraws from the nonaggression pact with Finland and breaks off relations. Finland, lacking allies or arms, fails to anticipate the attack, believing talks will avert a conflict.

NOVEMBER 30

EASTERN FRONT, *FINLAND*
A Soviet force of over 600,000 men, backed by air and naval power, attacks Finland in support of Otto Kuusinen's newly-proclaimed Finnish People's Government, which is sponsored by the Soviet Union. As aircraft bomb the capital, Helsinki, Field Marshal Karl von Mannerheim leads the nation's defense with a mainly reservist

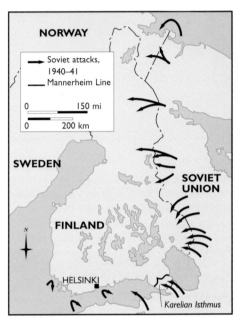

▲ *The Soviet invasion of Finland comprised land, air, and amphibious attacks.*

force, inferior in both numbers and arms. The main Soviet thrust through the Karelian Isthmus is obstructed by the Mannerheim Line, a 1914–18 system of fortifications that runs through rugged terrain and forest.

Other Soviet forces attack eastern and northern Finland, and also launch failed amphibious assaults on the southern coast. As the campaign progresses, highly-motivated Finnish troops exploit their familiarity with the terrain and use their ability to ski through snow-covered areas to launch hit-and-run raids on Red Army units bogged down by the weather.

DECEMBER 2

POLITICS, *FINLAND*
The League of Nations is asked by Finland to intervene in its conflict

with the Soviet Union. The League eventually agrees, but the Soviet Union opposes its involvement and is expelled from the organization on December 14.

DECEMBER 7

EASTERN FRONT, *FINLAND*
The Soviet 163rd Division approaches Suomussali village in eastern Finland. Halted by freezing conditions, its troops are targeted by the Finnish 9th Division, which severs its supply lines. The Soviet 44th Division, sent as a relief force, is blocked by Finnish attacks and both Red Army units attempt a breakout. By the end of the year these divisions have been forced to

▲ *Marshal Karl von Mannerheim led Finland's determined defense against the Soviet attack on his country.*

capitulate, after having 27,500 men killed by enemy action or the freezing temperatures. The Finns achieve similar successes in other engagements during the "Winter War."

DECEMBER 16

EASTERN FRONT, *FINLAND*
After advancing to the Mannerheim Line, the Soviet Seventh Army begins a major offensive. To compensate for their lack of armor and artillery, innovative sabotage techniques and improvised explosive devices ("Molotov Cocktails," named after the Soviet foreign minister) are used by Finnish ski-troops to destroy enemy tanks. The fighting will continue until February 11, 1940.

DECEMBER 13

SEA WAR, *ATLANTIC*
The British heavy cruiser *Exeter*, with light cruisers *Ajax* and *Achilles*, engage the German pocket battleship *Graf Spee* at the mouth of the Plate River, off Uruguay. The British vessels sustain severe damage as they maneuver to prevent *Graf Spee* delivering concentrated fire on a single vessel. *Graf Spee*, itself damaged, withdraws to neutral Uruguay for repairs. *Ajax* and *Achilles* are later joined by the heavy cruiser *Cumberland* to await *Graf Spee*'s emergence from Montevideo port. The *Graf Spee*, however, is scuttled by its crew on the 17th.

DECEMBER 23

POLITICS, *CANADA*
The first Canadian troops, some 7500 men, arrive in Britain.

▼ *Germany's pocket battleship* Graf Spee *is scuttled after being trapped by the Royal Navy in neutral Uruguay.*

1940

The German Army conquered much of Western Europe in 1940 in a series of spectacular Blitzkrieg victories. German armor and aircraft attacked and defeated a succession of Allied armies in Scandinavia, France, and the Low Countries. Germany's defeat in an aerial battle over Britain, however, saved that nation from any invasion. Britain's survival now depended on North American aid. Meanwhile, the war widened, with Italian offensives in Africa and the Balkans.

JANUARY 7–FEBRUARY 17

EASTERN FRONT, *FINLAND*
General Semyon Timoshenko assumes command of the Soviet invasion forces in the Karelian Isthmus and initiates a training program to improve service cooperation. After reorganizing and reequipping, his forces begin a determined attack on the Mannerheim Line on the 12th. The Finns complete a withdrawal to a secondary zone of defense on the line by February 17. Secret peace negotiations have already begun in late January.

JANUARY 10

WESTERN FRONT, *BELGIUM*
A lost German plane carrying two army officers lands at Mechelen.

▶ *Finnish officers discuss the battle against the Soviet invaders.*

Captured documents read by the Allies reveal an invasion plan for the 17th. For this reason, and because of poor weather, Adolf Hitler postpones the invasion until the spring.

JANUARY 14

POLITICS, *JAPAN*
Admiral Mitsumasa Yonai forms a new government in Japan after the resignation of Prime Minister Nobuyuki Abe's cabinet. Yonai's government, however, provokes opposition from the prowar military hierarchy.

FEBRUARY 5

POLITICS, *ALLIES*
The Allied Supreme War Council decides to intervene in Norway and Finland. This vague and indecisive policy relies on the cooperation of neutral Norway and Sweden. The main motivation is the Allied desire to deny Germany access to Swedish iron ore supplies, which pass through the ice-free port of Narvik in Norway.

FEBRUARY 16

SEA WAR, *NORTH SEA*
The British destroyer *Cossack* violates Norway's neutrality to rescue 299 British merchant seamen aboard the German transport *Altmark*. Germany accelerates its invasion preparations, believing that Britain is planning more military actions in Norway.

FEBRUARY 24

POLITICS, *GERMANY*
Plans for the invasion of Western Europe are revised. The main focus of

◄ *The British destroyer Cossack, which sailed into Norwegian waters to rescue 299 British sailors imprisoned on a German vessel.*

▼ *The British destroyer Glowworm sinks after ramming the German heavy cruiser Admiral Hipper.*

the offensive is changed to the Ardennes region after a suggestion by General Erich von Manstein. The bulk of the German Army's armored units are allocated to this radical plan.

MARCH 11

EASTERN FRONT, *FINLAND*
The Treaty of Moscow between Finland and the Soviet Union is agreed after the Red Army makes hard-won gains. Although Allied help to the nation is negligible, the Finnish Army has not capitulated. Finland retains its independence but has to surrender the Karelian Isthmus and Hangö – 10 percent of its territory. Campaign losses: 200,000 Soviet troops and 25,000 Finns.

MARCH 20

POLITICS, *FRANCE*
Prime Minister Edouard Daladier resigns after criticism of his failure to take the initiative to support Finland and thereby redirect the war away from France. Paul Reynaud succeeds Daladier on March 21.

◄ *Edouard Daladier, France's premier to March 1940.*

MARCH 28

POLITICS, *ALLIES*
Britain and France agree not to make any separate peace treaties. From April 5 they plan to mine Norwegian waters to force Nazi ships carrying Swedish iron ore into the open seas and expose them to naval attack. The minelaying is deferred to April 8. This is too late to prevent the Nazi invasion planned for the 9th.

APRIL 8

SEA WAR, *NORTH SEA*
The British destroyer *Glowworm* intercepts part of the German invasion fleet bound for Norway. It is sunk after ramming the heavy cruiser *Admiral Hipper*, but a British submarine then sinks the transport *Rio de Janiero*. However, Royal Navy vessels deployed in the North Sea have not received sufficient information about the German invading force and are unable to intercept it.

APRIL 9

WESTERN FRONT, *NORWAY/DENMARK*
A German invasion force, including surface ships, U-boats, and 1000 aircraft, attacks Denmark and Norway. Denmark is overrun immediately. The first ever airborne assault is made on Oslo and Stavanger airports in Norway, while ships land troops at six locations. Norway's six divisions have no tanks or effective artillery, while its coastal defenses and navy are generally inferior.

However, in Oslo Fiord, shore guns sink the German cruiser *Blücher*, claiming 1600 lives. This enables King Haakon to escape northward with his

APRIL 10–13

▶ *Germany's Blitzkrieg on Norway and Denmark began with combined airborne and amphibious landings.*

government. The British battlecruiser *Rodney* engages the battlecruisers *Scharnhorst* and *Gneisenau*, damaging the latter. The cruiser *Karlsruhe* is later sunk off Kristiansand by a British submarine.

APRIL 10–13

SEA WAR, *NORWAY*

Five British destroyers launch a surprise attack on 10 German destroyers and shore batteries to the west of Narvik. During short and confused engagements each side loses two destroyers, while eight German merchant vessels and an ammunition carrier are also sunk. The cruiser *Königsberg* becomes the first vessel to be sunk by dive-bombing during a British air attack on Bergen.

Subsequent air attacks on the *Gneisenau, Scharnhorst,* and *Admiral Hipper* by the British on the 12th fail. A British battleship and nine destroyers succeed in sinking eight German destroyers, plus a U-boat, by aerial attack in the Second Battle of Narvik on April 13.

APRIL 10–30

WESTERN FRONT, *NORWAY*

After securing their initial objectives, the Germans begin their conquest of Norway. Major General Carl Otto Ruge, Norway's new commander-in-chief, leads a stubborn defense around Lake Mjösa and the Glomma Valley.

APRIL 14–19

WESTERN FRONT, *NORWAY*

An Allied expeditionary force of over 10,000 British, French, and Polish

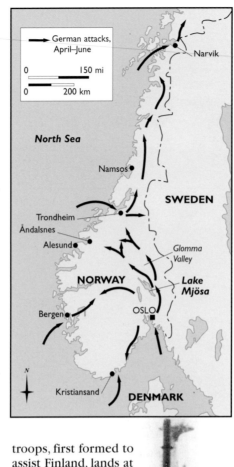

troops, first formed to assist Finland, lands at Namsos, Alesund, and Narvik. Its objective is to recapture Trondheim to secure a base in Norway, but its units

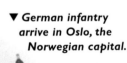

▼ *German infantry arrive in Oslo, the Norwegian capital.*

coordination with the Norwegian forces is poor, but the Germans in the area eventually withdraw at the end of April.

MAY 7-10

POLITICS, *BRITAIN*
Prime Minister Neville Chamberlain is severely criticized over the Norwegian

▲ Norwegian ski-troops were especially useful in disrupting German lines of communication.

▼ French mountain soldiers arriving in Norway to help repel the Nazi invasion. The Allies sent a force of British, French, and Polish troops to help the country.

▲ The German cruiser Königsberg *sinks after a British air attack.*

are ill-prepared for the campaign. There has been little liaison with the Norwegians. The various Allied units lack cohesion, training in arctic warfare, key supplies, air cover, and anti-aircraft weaponry.

APRIL 20-30

WESTERN FRONT, *NORWAY*
German troops defend Trondheim and wait for the arrival of more forces. German aircraft launch determined attacks against the Allies. British and French troops eventually evacuate Namsos and Åndalsnes on May 1-2.

APRIL 24

WESTERN FRONT, *NORWAY*
An Allied offensive on Narvik begins with a naval bombardment. Allied

◄ Eben Emael, the key Belgium fortress captured by German paratroopers.

and in Holland, to dislocate resistance. General Ritter von Leeb's Army Group C covers France's Maginot Line, the line of subterranean forts and other defensive positions running along its border with Germany.

In accordance with Allied planning, the left flank of the British and French line moves into Belgium. This decision facilitates Rundstedt's surprise Ardennes advance, which eventually divides the Allied armies in Belgium from those in France. The Allied armies advancing into Belgium up to the Dyle and Meuse Rivers above Namur, a position known as the Dyle Plan Line, are hampered by poor coordination with Dutch and Belgian forces.

campaign during a House of Commons debate. Chamberlain resigns after a significant fall in government support in a vote of confidence and the opposition Labour Party's refusal to serve under him in a coalition. Winston Churchill replaces him and forms a coalition government.

MAY 8
POLITICS, *SOVIET UNION*
General Semyon Timoshenko replaces Marshal Kliment Voroshilov as the Soviet commissar for defense.

MAY 10
WESTERN FRONT, *LUXEMBOURG/ HOLLAND/BELGIUM*
The Germany's Army Group A, under General Gerd von Rundstedt, and Group B, commanded by General Fedor von Bock, invade after preliminary air attacks. Successful airborne landings are made against Belgium's key frontier fortress of Eben Emael,

MAY 11–15
WESTERN FRONT, *HOLLAND/BELGIUM*
Dutch resistance to the German attack crumbles, despite opening the flood gates and mining the Rhine River to obstruct the enemy. German forces begin to approach the Allied Dyle Line, while Belgian defenders are driven back from the Albert Canal.

Queen Wilhelmina of the Netherlands escapes with the Dutch government to Britain on May 13. The city of Rotterdam is bombed before a cease-fire is declared on the 14th, and the Dutch Army capitulates the next day.

◄ British premier Neville Chamberlain, the appeasement advocate, who resigned after failing to save Finland and Norway.

▼ German troops crossing the Maas River during the invasion of Holland.

▲ *A six-inch (15-cm) howitzer in action with the French Second Army during the desperate fight to save France in 1940.*

◄ *Germany's offensive, which began on May 10, lured the Allies into the Low Countries, while a surprise attack went into France through the Ardennes.*

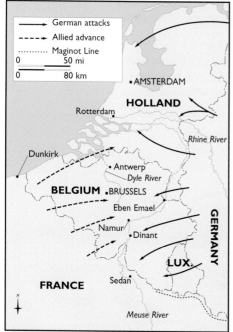

German attacks
Allied advance
Maginot Line

0   50 mi
0   80 km

AMSTERDAM
HOLLAND
Rotterdam
Rhine River
Dunkirk
Antwerp
Dyle River
BELGIUM BRUSSELS
Eben Emael
Namur
Dinant
GERMANY
LUX.
Sedan
FRANCE
Meuse River

MAY 12–14

WESTERN FRONT, *FRANCE*
German forces reach the Meuse River, the crossing of which is critical for the advance into France. Dive-bombers pound French positions and inflatable rafts are used to establish bridgeheads at Sedan and Dinant on the 13th. Despite Allied air attacks, German armor advances westward rapidly, opening a 50-mile (75-km) gap in the Allied line. This drives a wedge between the French Ninth

and Second Armies, which then mount a futile response.

MAY 15–20

WESTERN FRONT, *BELGIUM*
Germany's Sixth and Eighteenth Armies force the Allies to withdraw from the Dyle Plan Line to the Scheldt

KEY PERSONALITIES

PRIME MINISTER SIR WINSTON CHURCHILL

Winston Spencer Churchill (1874–1965), soldier, journalist, and statesman, had held ministerial offices but was relegated to the margins of political life in Britain during the 1930s for his anti-appeasement stance. He was propelled into power, however, as prime minister in 1940 as the Nazis appeared close to total victory.

Churchill reversed the fortunes of the nation by dismissing any sign of defeatism.

The bold but often impatient prime minister constantly urged his military commanders to take offensive action. Churchill forged a coalition of Allied nations, but it was the solid support he secured from the United States that was critical to Britain's survival.

A series of international conferences enabled Churchill and other Allied leaders to decide on the strategic direction of the war. Despite Churchill's anticommunist stance, he created a working alliance with the Soviet Union, although he correctly predicted that postwar Europe would be divided along political lines.

In domestic politics he secured the loyalty and cooperation of the House of Commons during the period of coalition government. Winston Churchill's mastery of propaganda, eccentricity, and powerful oratory helped galvanize the British people and secured their cooperation during the war years. Despite Churchill's popularity as Britain's war leader, he lost the 1945 election as many felt that a new premier was needed for the challenges of postwar Britain. Nevertheless, Churchill remains one of the twentieth century's most significant figures.

MAY 15

Line, west of Brussels, and the Dendre River. French forces have been forced to fall back from Holland, while the Belgians continue fighting between Antwerp and Brussels, finally retreating to the Escaut Canal and then to the Lys River, which is reached on the 20th.

MAY 15

AIR WAR, *GERMANY*
Britain launches its first strategic air attack on Germany with 99 aircraft hitting oil plants and railroad marshaling yards in the Ruhr region.

MAY 16–20

WESTERN FRONT, *FRANCE*
The French General Reserve and units south of the German forces are ordered to form the Sixth Army to bolster the vulnerable Allied lines, but this fails to halt the German advance. Brigadier General Charles de Gaulle's 4th Armored Division attempts to counterattack around Laon–Montcornet on May 17–19 but fails.

German tanks reach Cambrai on May 18, and finally the sea at Abbeville two days later. It now becomes critical for the Allies to cut the "corridor" made by the panzers or risk the isolation of their armies to the north from the forces in the south. The dismissal of General Maurice Gamelin, the Allied commander-in-chief, and the appointment of Maxime Weygand as his successor on the 19th further delays military decision-making, which reduces the potential for any action.

MAY 21–28

WESTERN FRONT, *FRANCE*
British tanks battle with the 7th Panzer Division at Arras until May 23. General Heinz Guderian moves toward Boulogne and Calais unaffected by the Allied "Weygand Plan," which attempts to split the tank spearhead from troops and supplies in the German "corridor." Boulogne and Calais capitulate after the naval evacuation of Allied troops.

Eager to preserve his panzers for taking Paris, Hitler halts General Gerd von Rundstedt's armor at Gravelines and allows the air force to attack the Allied "pocket" centering on

▲ *British troops surrender in Calais after trying to defend the port against attacking German armor and aircraft.*

▼ *General Maurice Gamelin, commander of the Allied armies in France, failed to halt the German Blitzkrieg.*

Dunkirk. British aircraft, however, resist the attacks, enabling the Allies to prepare for an evacuation.

MAY 25–28

WESTERN FRONT, *BELGIUM*
King Leopold of Belgium's forces are left surrounded as the Allies

Paris condemns King Leopold's surrender and assumes his powers.

MAY 26

WESTERN FRONT, *FRANCE/BELGIUM*

Operation Dynamo, the evacuation of Allied forces from the Dunkirk area, begins. A defensive perimeter established on the Aa, Scarpe, and Yser "canal line" covers the withdrawal, while an assorted rescue flotilla of pleasure boats, commercial craft, and naval vessels crosses and recrosses the English Channel.

MAY 31

POLITICS, *UNITED STATES*

President Franklin D. Roosevelt launches a "billion-dollar defense program" to bolster the armed forces.

JUNE 1–9

WESTERN FRONT, *NORWAY*

After Britain and France reveal to the Norwegians that they are to begin an evacuation, troops begin to withdraw

▼ *Plumes of smoke rise from Dunkirk's port area as troops sail back to Britain.*

withdraw to Dunkirk. Resistance seems futile and he decides to surrender on the 28th. Belgium has lost 7550 men killed. The surrender leaves the left flank of the Allied line increasingly vulnerable, and there is no hope of holding out in Belgium. The exiled Belgium government in

KEY MOMENTS

THE BATTLE OF FRANCE

Germany's sensational seizure of France and the Low Countries was the pinnacle of Blitzkrieg strategy and secured Adolf Hitler's mastery of Western Europe. The invasion that began on May 10 first struck the Low Countries, which had relied on their neutrality to save them, and were in no condition to resist the invaders.

As British and French forces rushed into Belgium in response to Germany's diversionary attack, the Nazis launched their main assault by advancing through the Ardennes forest. The Allies had dismissed this area as being unsuitable for any tank advances, which allowed the German units to move straight through against minimal opposition. This gateway into France enabled the fast-moving armored columns to advance into the Allied rear and disable communications. As the panzers raced westward to the sea, the Allied armies in the north were effectively isolated from potential reinforcements in the south. The Allies were unable to match Germany's effective exploitation of armor and aircraft or develop a credible strategy to counterattack the invaders.

As British, Belgian, and French forces completed the evacuation from Dunkirk, Germany launched the final phase of the offensive to complete the conquest. The Maginot Line, on which France's security had been entrusted, but had been completely bypassed by German forces, was eventually surrounded and penetrated.

As France's politicians floundered, the nation's high command attempted to regroup its faltering armies but resistance crumbled in the face of well-orchestrated German attacks that captured Paris on June 14. French and German officials signed an armistice agreement on June 22.

A French soldier surrenders to the German invaders.

▲ *Wounded troops return to Britain after being rescued from Dunkirk.*

on June 4. King Haakon and his government leave for Britain on the 7th, and 24,500 troops are evacuated. The king finally orders the Norwegians to stop fighting on June 9, after losing 1335 men in the campaign. Entire Allied losses include 5600 men, one carrier, two cruisers, nine destroyers plus other smaller craft, and 100 aircraft. German loses total 3692 men, 19 warships, and 242 aircraft.

JUNE 3–4

WESTERN FRONT, *FRANCE*
Operation Dynamo ends. The remarkable operation has rescued

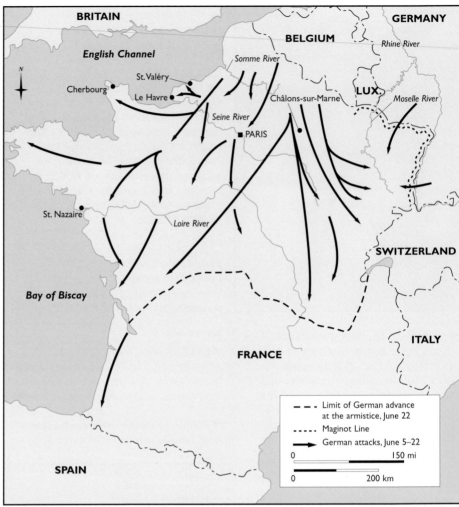

Limit of German advance
at the armistice, June 22

Maginot Line

German attacks, June 5–22

0 — 150 mi

0 — 200 km

▲ *Germany's conquest of France followed the Blitzkrieg principle. Armored thrusts bypassed the Maginot Line and other defensive positions. The Allied forces were then quickly isolated and defeated by air and ground attacks.*

338,226 men – two-thirds of them British – from the beaches of Dunkirk, although 243 vessels and 106 aircraft have been destroyed. General Lord Gort, the British Expeditionary Force's commander, leaves Lieutenant General Sir Harold Alexander in command after being evacuated on May 31. The Germans occupy Dunkirk on June 4 and capture 40,000 French troops.

JUNE 5–12

WESTERN FRONT, *FRANCE*
A German force of 119 divisions opens Operation Red, the conquest of France, with General Fedor von Bock's Army Group B attacking along the Somme River to reach the Seine River west of

◀ *German motorized units make rapid progress during the Battle of France.*

▶ *Triumphant German troops parade through Paris after conquering France.*

Paris by June 9. General Gerd von Rundstedt's Army Group A, moving toward the Moselle River in front of the Maginot Line, launches an offensive east of Paris. Rundstedt's tanks, reinforced by Army Group B panzers, overcome resistance from the French Fourth Army to break through at Châlons-sur-Marne on the 12th.

France's response, the Weygand Line, stretching along the Somme and Aisne Rivers, aims to protect Paris and the interior. Some of France's 65 divisions fight determined actions, but many units lack manpower and equipment. Air attacks and logistical problems also undermine General Maxime Weygand's vulnerable forces.

JUNE 8

SEA WAR, *NORTH SEA*
The German battlecruisers *Scharnhorst* and *Gneisenau* sink three empty vessels while hunting for convoys from Norway. They then sink the British carrier *Glorious* and two destroyers. These losses are blamed on the British failure to provide sufficient naval escorts for the Norway convoys.

JUNE 10

WESTERN FRONT, *FRANCE*
Some 11,000 British and other

French troops begin to evacuate from St. Valéry and Le Havre to Britain.

JUNE 10–11

POLITICS, *ITALY*
Italy declares war on France and Britain. Benito Mussolini, eager to capitalize on France's collapse, enters the war despite previous assertions that his nation will not have the capability to fight alongside Germany until 1942. Canada declares war on Italy on the 10th, as do Australia, New Zealand, and South Africa the following day.

JUNE 12–14

SEA WAR, *MEDITERRANEAN*
Britain launches a naval bombardment against the Italian base of Tobruk, Libya, on the 12th. The French Navy bombards the ports of

Genoa and Vado on the 14th. British air raids are also made on Turin and Genoa. Libyan and East African airfields are raided.

JUNE 13

POLITICS, *UNITED STATES*
President Franklin D. Roosevelt signs a $1.3 billion navy bill to improve the service. Shipments of arms also leave the country in response to Winston Churchill's request to Roosevelt for surplus weapons.

JUNE 13–25

WESTERN FRONT, *FRANCE*
Paris is declared an "open city" in order to save it from destruction and all French forces withdraw south of the capital, leaving the Maginot Line isolated. German troops enter Paris on June 14 as thousands flee the capital. Germany's Army Group C, deployed from the Maginot Line to the Swiss border, breaks through French

▼ *The German battlecruisers* Scharnhorst *(foreground) and* Gneisenau, *which attacked Allied ships evacuating troops from Norway in June 1940.*

◄ *French representatives sign articles of surrender in the railroad carriage in which Germany signed the 1918 documents.*

After Italy's armistice with France on the 24th, a cease-fire occurs on all fronts. French casualties since May 10 total more than 85,000 men, the British lose 3475 men, and German losses reach 27,074.

While Pétain's regime will collaborate with Nazi Germany, the French Army officer Brigadier General Charles de Gaulle begins broadcasting his opposition from London on the 18th with pledges to liberate the country.

JUNE 20

POLITICS, *UNITED STATES*
Democratic President Franklin D. Roosevelt appoints two anti-isolationist

defenses. German forces advance in all directions, crossing the Rhine and Loire Rivers. All of the coastal ports between Cherbourg and St. Nazaire are soon captured.

JUNE 15–25

WESTERN FRONT, *FRANCE*
The evacuation of the remaining Allied troops in northwest France begins. Operation Ariel extends this to the Biscay ports from the 16th. Some 214,000 troops are saved during the evacuation, although 3000 perish when the liner *Lancastria* is sunk on the 17th.

JUNE 16–24

POLITICS, *FRANCE*
Prime Minister Paul Reynaud fails to motivate his government to continue fighting and releases France from its agreement with Britain not to make any separate peace. France rejects a British idea to create a union between the countries.

Reynaud, after losing support, resigns and Marshal Henri-Philippe Pétain replaces him. Pétain requests Germany's armistice terms on the 17th, and the signing takes place at Compiègne, site of the World War I armistice agreement, on the 22nd. Under the terms Germany occupies two-thirds of France, including the Channel and Atlantic coastlines. The south, which becomes known as Vichy France, will have a nominal French administration and keep its colonies.

▶ *German troops enter Rouen during the offensive to conquer France.*

▲ Italian bombers on their way to strike Allied targets. Italy's poor performance in France, North Africa, and Greece contrasted sharply with propaganda about the nation's military prowess.

Republicans to his cabinet. Henry Stimson becomes secretary for war and Frank Knox is appointed secretary for the navy.

JUNE 20–21

WESTERN FRONT, *FRANCE*
Benito Mussolini launches attacks along the south coast. Offensives are also made along the Franco-Italian border. Italy also bombs the strategically-important island of Malta.

JUNE 26

POLITICS, *ROMANIA*
The government agrees to the Soviet occupation of Bessarabia and northern Bukovina, although Romanian troops attempt to halt the Red Army when it enters the country.

JUNE 30

WESTERN FRONT, *CHANNEL ISLANDS*
Germany invades the Channel Islands. This is the only British territory occupied during hostilities.

JULY 1

SEA WAR, *ATLANTIC*
The "Happy Time" begins for U-boat crews as their operational range is increased now that they have bases in French ports. This lasts until October. U-boat crews inflict serious losses on Allied convoys.

▶ A German officer speaks to a British police officer in the Channel Islands, the only part of Britain occupied in the war.

JULY 3-7

JULY 3-7

SEA WAR, *MEDITERRANEAN*

Britain, fearing that France's navy will be seized by Germany, sends two battleships, a battlecruiser, and a carrier (Force H) to neutralize French vessels at Oran and Mers-el-Kebir, Algeria. After negotiations fail, the British sink one battleship and damage two. In Britain, two French battleships, nine destroyers, and other craft are acquired with minimal force. French naval forces in Alexandria, Egypt, are disarmed on the 7th.

JULY 9-19

SEA WAR, *MEDITERRANEAN*

At the Battle of Punta Stilo, the British Mediterranean Fleet tries to separate the Italian Fleet from its base at Taranto in southern Italy. An Italian battleship and cruiser suffer damage, and Italian aircraft hit a British cruiser. On the 19th, the Australian light cruiser *Sydney* and four destroyers engage two Italian light cruisers. The Italians lose a cruiser and the *Sydney* is damaged.

JULY 10

AIR WAR, *BRITAIN*

The Battle of Britain begins. Hermann Goering, the Nazi air force chief, orders attacks on shipping and ports in the English Channel. The movement of Allied vessels in the Channel is soon restricted as a result of British naval and aircraft losses.

▲ *Barges being prepared for Operation Sealion, Germany's planned invasion of Britain that was to begin in the fall of 1940.*

▼ *British pilots rush to their Hurricanes during the Battle of Britain. The Nazis failed to destroy Britain's fighter capability in the aerial war over southern England.*

JULY 16-22

POLITICS, *GERMANY*

Adolf Hitler's Directive No. 16 reveals his military plan to invade Britain, code-named Operation Sealion. This requires control of the English Channel for transporting the invasion force and the destruction of Britain's fighter

▲ *Allied vessels under German air attack in the English Channel.*

▶ *Hermann Goering (right), the Nazi air chief, with Adolf Hitler (left).*

capability to ensure a safe crossing. The air force is made responsible for destroying the strength of the RAF and Royal Navy. Hitler's plans are further advanced after his final peace offer is rejected by the British on the 22nd.

JULY 18

POLITICS, *BRITAIN*
British Prime Minister Winston Churchill agrees to close the Burma Road to disrupt supplies to the Chinese in order to avoid a confrontation with the Japanese. The onset of the monsoon season means that the supply line would be disrupted anyway. The British will reopen the aid route in October.

JULY 21

POLITICS, *SOVIET UNION*
The authorities formally annex Lithuania, Latvia, and Estonia.

JULY 22

ESPIONAGE, *BRITAIN*
Britain establishes the Special Operations Executive (SOE) to secretly give support to resistance groups across Nazi-occupied Europe.

JULY 25

POLITICS, *UNITED STATES*
The United States introduces licensing to restrict the export of oil and metal products outside the Americas and to Britain. This measure is particularly directed toward Japan, which is heavily dependent upon imports of these

▼ *Peasants on the Burma Road, a key supply route to China during the war. Britain temporarily closed it to avoid a rift with the Japanese.*

resources. As a consequence, Japanese strategic planning devotes greater attention to the resources of the Dutch East Indies and Malaysia to relieve their raw material shortages.

AUGUST 1

POLITICS, *GERMANY*
Hitler issues Directive No. 17, which states that preparations for the invasion of England are to be complete by September 15, ready for an invasion between the 19th and 26th.

▲ *Air Chief Marshal Sir Hugh Dowding led the RAF's fighters to victory in the Battle of Britain.*

▼ *A German Heinkel bomber over the East End of London during the Luftwaffe's air offensive on Britain.*

AUGUST 2

SEA WAR, *MEDITERRANEAN*

A British naval force attacks the Italian naval base on the island of Sardinia.

AUGUST 3–19

AFRICA, *BRITISH SOMALILAND*

Italian forces, superior in manpower and artillery, attack the 1475-strong garrison in British Somaliland from neighboring Ethiopia.

AUGUST 5

POLITICS, *GERMANY*

General Franz Halder, the chief-of-staff, inspects the first plans for the invasion of the Soviet Union. He proposes a two-pronged offensive, principally

▲ *German pilots discuss their daring dog-fight tactics during the Battle of Britain.*

directed against Moscow, and a secondary attack on Kiev.

AUGUST 13–17

AIR WAR, *BRITAIN*

"Eagle Day" heralds a four-day German air offensive designed to destroy Britain's Fighter Command with raids on airfields and industrial targets. Hermann Goering, head of the Luftwaffe, postpones the early raids, however, and the later attacks are inconclusive.

AUGUST 15

AIR WAR, *BRITAIN*

Three German air fleets totaling 900 fighters and 1300 bombers launch massed daylight and night attacks on British airfields and ports to lure RAF fighters into combat. Air Chief Marshal Sir Hugh Dowding's 650 operational fighters, aided by effective radar defenses,

KEY MOMENTS

THE BATTLE OF BRITAIN

The Battle of Britain was Germany's attempt to achieve air superiority over the skies of southern England. With this achieved, it could then control the English Channel for the crossing of the invasion force, which was being prepared on the continent.

Germany's air force commander, Hermann Goering, assembled 2800 aircraft against Britain's 700 fighters. Widespread German attacks on ports, shipping, and airfields lured British fighters into action and inflicted heavy losses.

Britain's fate rested upon the bravery, determination, and skill of its fighter pilots. These men were drawn from the British Empire, North America, Czechoslovakia, Poland, and other Allied nations. The performance of the Hurricane and Spitfire fighters they flew also played a key role.

Crucially, a centralized command-and-control structure and radar network also enabled fighters to be effectively concentrated to meet enemy attacks. Germany's gravest strategical error was the decision, from September 7 onward, to concentrate on the bombing of British cities, despite eroding the capability of Fighter Command by widespread and incessant raids across southern England. This change in strategy enabled the RAF to concentrate its fighters and inflict heavier losses on the Luftwaffe. The RAF also benefitted from longer flying time as it operated over its own territory. In addition, crews who baled out were able to resume fighting, unlike their opponents who parachuted into captivity.

On October 31, after 114 days of aerial combat, Germany conceded defeat, having lost 1733 aircraft and 3893 men. The RAF, at a cost of 828 aircraft and 1007 men, had effectively saved Britain from invasion.

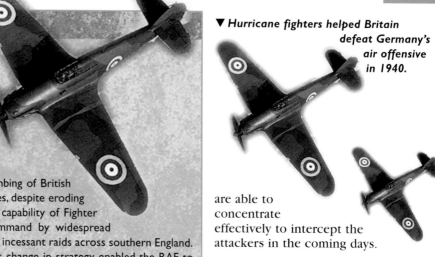

▼ *Hurricane fighters helped Britain defeat Germany's air offensive in 1940.*

are able to concentrate effectively to intercept the attackers in the coming days.

AUGUST 17

POLITICS, *GERMANY*
A total blockade of the British Isles is declared. Any Allied or neutral vessels found in British waters will be attacked on sight.

AUGUST 17–18

SEA WAR, *MEDITERRANEAN*
British naval vessels bombard Bardia and Fort Capuzzo, Libya, and shoot down 12 Italian bombers sent to attack them.

AUGUST 24–25

AIR WAR, *BRITAIN*
The Luftwaffe inflicts serious losses on the RAF during attacks on its main air bases in southeast England, straining the resources of Fighter Command to breaking point in a few days. London has also been bombed.

AUGUST 26–29

AIR WAR, *GERMANY*
The RAF launches a night raid with 81 aircraft on Berlin following a similar raid on London. Raids also take place against Düsseldorf, Essen, and other cities. The raids contribute toward a critical change in Germany's strategy, as aircraft are redirected to make retaliatory raids on London. This move relieves the pressure on Fighter Command's air bases.

SEPTEMBER 2

POLITICS, *BRITAIN*
Britain and the United States ratify a deal whereby 50 old destroyers, needed for convoy duties, are handed to

◄ *Police and rescue workers frantically clear debris after a German air raid on London. The Nazi bombing offensive quickly spread to other cities in Britain.*

bridgeheads on the south coast of England for an invasion force of nine divisions and 250 tanks.

SEPTEMBER 7–30

AIR WAR, *BRITAIN*

Full-scale bombing raids on London – the "Blitz" – begin with 500 bombers and 600 fighters. The RAF is initially surprised by the new German tactics, but adapts and concentrates its weakened forces against this threat. The bombing reaches its greatest intensity on the 15th, but the Luftwaffe is now

◄ *Civilians prepare to spend the night safe from the bombing by sheltering in one of London's underground stations.*

suffering heavy losses, especially during its daylight raids on English cities, which are largely abandoned by the 30th. Bomber Command raids in France and the Low Countries destroy a tenth of the Nazi invasion barges on the14th–15th.

SEPTEMBER 13–18

AFRICA, *EGYPT*

An Italian force of 250,000 men under Marshal Rodolfo Graziani advances from Libya into neighboring Egypt against the British Western Desert

▼ *Bomb damage to St. Paul's Cathedral. Nazi raids tore the City of London apart but failed to destroy public morale.*

Britain in exchange for bases in the Caribbean and Bermuda. Such exchanges will accustom the US public to aiding the Allied war effort.

SEPTEMBER 3

POLITICS, *GERMANY*

The Operation Sealion landings are postponed from September 15 to the 21st. Two airborne divisions will be used to establish three

▼ *Charles de Gaulle, the leader of the Free French forces based in Britain, opposed the puppet Vichy French regime.*

▶ *Italic forces invade Egypt from Libya. The offensive was later shattered by a British counterattack.*

Force of two divisions under General Sir Richard O'Connor. Graziani establishes fortified camps along a 50-mile (75-km) front, while the British remain 75 miles (120km) to the east. British plans to attack Graziani are delayed as units are redirected to Crete and Greece, where an Italian invasion is feared.

SEPTEMBER 15

POLITICS, *CANADA*
Men aged between 21 and 24 are to be conscripted.
POLITICS, *SOVIET UNION*
Men aged between 19 and 20 are to be conscripted.

SEPTEMBER 16-17

SEA WAR, *MEDITERRANEAN*
The British carrier *Illustrious* and battleship *Valiant* sink two Italian destroyers and two cargo ships at Benghazi, Libya.
HOME FRONT, *BRITAIN*
The Selective Service Bill permits the conscription of men aged between 21 and 35.

SEPTEMBER 17

POLITICS, *GERMANY*
Adolf Hitler decides to suspend Operation Sealion after Germany's failure to achieve aerial supremacy over southern England, while the General Staff inspects further plans for the invasion of the Soviet Union. General Friedrich von Paulus, deputy chief of the Army General Staff, suggests offensives toward Leningrad, Kiev, and Moscow, with the latter being the main thrust.

SEPTEMBER 20-22

SEA WAR, *ATLANTIC*
German U-boats launch their first successful "Wolf Pack" operation, sinking 12 ships. In this tactic some 15-20 U-boats are deployed across the approaches to Britain. When a U-boat finds a convoy, it tracks the vessels and awaits the gathering of the entire "Wolf Pack" for a combined attack.

◀ *Marshal Rodolfo Graziani, the commander of Italian forces in Libya, who was responsible for the attack against British, Indian, and Australian forces in Egypt.*

SEPTEMBER 21

POLITICS, *AUSTRALIA*
Prime Minister Robert Menzies wins another general election for the United Australia Party, although Labor remains the largest individual party.

SEPTEMBER 22

FAR EAST, *INDOCHINA*
Japanese forces enter the French colony after the powerless Vichy French authorities finally agree to the occupation. Some Vichy French resist the Japanese, who aim to prevent China obtaining supplies through the country.

SEPTEMBER 23-25

SEA WAR, *AFRICA*
A British and Free French expedition, code-named Menace, attempts to occupy Dakar, French West Africa, with naval forces, including the British aircraft carrier *Ark Royal*, and 7900 troops. The Free French commander Charles de Gaulle fails to reach any agreement with the Vichy authorities, whose warships open fire. The Vichy French lose a destroyer and two submarines. Prime Minister Winston

237

DECISIVE WEAPONS

RADAR

Radar uses synchronized radio transmitters and receivers that emit radio waves and process their reflections for display. This is especially useful for detecting aircraft. Although the United States and Germany had been working on this technology since the beginning of the century, it was Britain that first established a series of radar stations in 1938 in response to the threat of German bomber raids. The stations acted as a warning system to alert fighter aircraft to the presence of approaching bombers. This was critical in the Battle of Britain as the overstretched RAF was able to concentrate its fighter forces to repel enemy attacks. Axis aircraft could be detected over 70 miles (112km) from the stations in southeast England. Sector stations (as seen above) recorded the information from the various radar sites under their control and scrambled fighters to intercept the threat.

As the accuracy of ground-based radar increased, target range and direction information provided firing data for anti-aircraft guns. Eventually, guns received a stream of accurate information as radars "locked on" and automatically tracked the targets.

Aircraft radar, introduced in 1941, initially enabled nightfighters to locate targets and eventually aided bomber navigation. U-boats that surfaced in darkness for safety could also be detected by aircraft, which then illuminated the submarines with lights before attacking them. Ground-based radar also helped bomber crews hit targets by precisely tracking and relaying information to the aircraft. In the war at sea, radar was used to detect enemy aircraft and also directed gunfire, which could be effectively employed even in complete darkness with the new technology.

Churchill cancels Operation Menace after a Free French landing fails and British vessels suffer damage from Vichy French forces.

SEPTEMBER 24–25

AIR WAR, *MEDITERRANEAN*
Vichy France launches ineffective air raids on Gibraltar in retaliation for the British attack on Dakar.

SEPTEMBER 25

POLITICS, *NORWAY*
Nazi sympathizer Vidkun Quisling, who proclaimed himself Norway's leader following the German invasion, becomes head of the government. In reality Quisling remains a German puppet with limited authority.

SEPTEMBER 27

POLITICS, *AXIS*
Germany, Italy, and Japan agree a military, political, and economic alliance that pledges each country to fight any state that declares war on an Axis nation. The Tripartite Pact specifically aims to deter intervention by the United States in Europe or Asia.

▼ *Greek troops send letters home during the war against the Italian invasion. Italy's invasion, which was launched in October 1940, met fierce Greek resistance.*

OCTOBER 7

BALKANS, *ROMANIA*
German forces enter Romania on the pretext of helping to train the army of the fascist Iron Guard government. Germany's principal motive is to occupy the Ploesti oil fields.

OCTOBER 9

POLITICS, *BRITAIN*
Winston Churchill succeeds Neville Chamberlain, the former prime minister, as Conservative Party leader. Churchill was initially an unpopular figure in the party but his war leadership has gone a long way to reverse this.

OCTOBER 12

POLITICS, *GERMANY*
Hitler postpones Operation Sealion until spring 1941.

OCTOBER 15

POLITICS, *ITALY*
The Italian war council decides to invade Greece. Italy plans not to tell its Axis partner Germany about the operation, which is scheduled to commence at the end of October.

OCTOBER 16–19

POLITICS, *JAPAN*
The Dutch East Indies agrees to supply 40 percent of its oil production to

Japan for six months despite British attempts to obstruct this.

OCTOBER 18

POLITICS, *VICHY FRANCE*
The puppet Vichy regime introduces anti-Semitic laws.

OCTOBER 28

BALKANS, *GREECE*
Italy issues an ultimatum to Greece demanding the right to occupy the country for the war's duration. Before the ultimatum expires, eight divisions, led by General Sabasiano Visconti-Prasca, attack from Albania. Italy hopes for a rapid advance to rival Germany's conquests, but mountainous terrain and the absence of maps for commanders hamper the invasion. The winter weather limits air support and thousands die of cold. Greek forces, under General

▶ *Franklin D. Roosevelt was elected for a third term as US president in 1940. He prepared the nation for war and aided the Allies by expanding economic output.*

▲ *Greek troops carry brandy to the front. The ill-prepared Italian invaders lacked proper clothing and supplies to sustain their campaign during the freezing winter months in the mountains.*

Alexander Papagos, the commander-in-chief, mount stiff resistance.

OCTOBER 30–31

MEDITERRANEAN, *CRETE*
British forces occupy the Greek island.

NOVEMBER 5

POLITICS, *UNITED STATES*
President Franklin D. Roosevelt is elected for an unprecedented third term.
SEA WAR, *ATLANTIC*
The German pocket battleship *Admiral Scheer* attacks a British convoy of 37 ships escorted by the armed merchant cruiser *Jervis Bay*, which fights to save the convoy. The battleship rams and sinks *Jervis Bay*, but only five other vessels are lost. Eastbound convoys are suspended until the 17th while the Allies search for the *Admiral Scheer*.

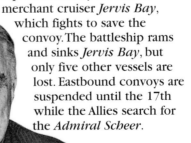

KEY PERSONALITIES

"IL DUCE" BENITO MUSSOLINI

Benito Mussolini, journalist, soldier, and politician, exploited the instability of inter-war Italy to become the dictator of a fascist state. After rising to power in 1922, he suppressed opposition and promised the nation that a new Roman Empire would arise. Mussolini presented himself as a tough alternative to previous liberal statesmen and a patriotic enemy of communism. Fascist propaganda hid his regime's economic instability, and the conquest of Ethiopia (1935–36) and Albania (1939) attempted to divert public attention away from domestic problems.

Mussolini established close relations with Adolf Hitler, but insisted that Italy would not be ready to enter into war until 1942. After the defeat of France in June 1940, however, he was keen to capitalize on Germany's conquests and declared war on the Allies. Military blunders in France, North Africa, and Greece left Italy dependent on German military assistance. Mussolini, physically and mentally weakened, faced growing public apathy and political threats as his country faltered.

In July 1943, Mussolini was overthrown by the Fascist Grand Council. The new regime agreed to an armistice with the Allies in September. Mussolini, now imprisoned, was then rescued by the Germans. Axis-controlled Italy remained under Berlin's direction but Hitler was benevolent toward Europe's first fascist leader. Italian partisans shot Mussolini in April 1945.

▲ *Marshal Pietro Badoglio, the Italian commander-in-chief, who resigned after the failure of the invasion of Greece.*

NOVEMBER 10

POLITICS, *ITALY*

General Ubaldo Soddu replaces General Sabasiano Visconti-Prasca as the Italian commander-in-chief in Albania.

NOVEMBER 11–12

SEA WAR, *MEDITERRANEAN*

At the Battle of Taranto British torpedo aircraft from the carrier *Illustrious* destroy three Italian battleships and damage two vessels during the raid on the Italian base. *Illustrious* loses only two aircraft. When the fleet leaves for Naples and Genoa, three British cruisers sink four vessels in the Strait of Otranto. This air attack on a fleet in harbor is closely studied by other navies, especially the Japanese.

NOVEMBER 14–22

BALKANS, *GREECE*

Greece launches a major counter-attack and 3400 British troops, plus air support, arrive from Alexandria, Egypt. When Greek forces finally enter Koritza they capture 2000 Italians and drive almost all the invaders back into Albania by December.

NOVEMBER 14

AIR WAR, *BRITAIN*

Germany sends 449 bombers to bomb the city of Coventry. The raid kills 500 civilians, leaves thousands homeless, and shocks the British public.

NOVEMBER 18

TECHNOLOGY, *BRITAIN*

British "Air-to-Surface-Vessel" radar

▲ *A German reconnaissance photograph of Coventry, the English city devastated by an air attack in November 1940.*

▶ *A Polish Jew in the Warsaw ghetto, which was created in November 1940.*

fitted to a Sunderland flying boat locates its first U-boat during a patrol in the Atlantic.

NOVEMBER 20

POLITICS, *HUNGARY*

Hungary joins the Axis powers. Since the Italian invasion of Greece, the Germans have been attempting to secure their food and oil supplies from the Balkans by pressing the countries of the region to join the Tripartite Pact.

NOVEMBER 23

POLITICS, *ROMANIA*

Prime Minister General Ion Antonescu leads Romania into the Axis alliance.

NOVEMBER 26

FINAL SOLUTION, *POLAND*

The Nazis begin creating a ghetto in Warsaw for the Jews, who will eventually be kept there in intolerable conditions.

DECEMBER 18

POLITICS, *GERMANY*
Adolf Hitler issues his plan for invading the Soviet Union, code-named Operation Barbarossa. His Directive No. 21 retains a three-pronged offensive but the weight of the invasion plan has now shifted northward to Leningrad and the Baltic area, where Army Groups North and Center are to annihilate the enemy forces, before attacking and occupying Moscow.

DECEMBER 29

POLITICS, *UNITED STATES*
In President Franklin D. Roosevelt's "fireside chat" broadcast, he describes how the United States must become the "arsenal of democracy" by giving maximum assistance to Britain in its fight against the Axis powers.

◀ *General Sir Archibald Wavell (right), the British commander-in-chief in North Africa who repelled Italy's attack on Egypt in December 1940.*

▼ *British, Indian, and Australian troops in Egypt halted the Italian offensive despite the numerical superiority of the invaders. This success was only reversed after the arrival of German forces.*

NOVEMBER 30

POLITICS, *JAPAN*
Japan officially recognizes the puppet government of President Wang Ching-wei in China.

DECEMBER 6

POLITICS, *ITALY*
Marshal Pietro Badoglio, Italy's commander-in-chief, resigns.

DECEMBER 9–11

AFRICA, *EGYPT*
General Sir Archibald Wavell, the commander-in-chief in the Middle East and North Africa, launches the first British offensive in the Western Desert. Major General Sir Richard O'Connor's Western Desert Force of 31,000 British and Commonwealth troops, supported by aircraft and long-range naval gunfire, is ordered to attack the fortified camps that have been established by the Italians in Egypt. Sidi Barrani is captured on the 10th and 34,000 Italians are taken prisoner as they retreat rapidly from Egypt. It is a famous victory in the face of overwhelming odds.

1941

The Allies continued fighting in North Africa, where they now faced General Erwin Rommel's Afrika Korps, and the war in the Balkans intensified with Germany conquering Yugoslavia and Greece. In the Mediterranean and Atlantic, the Allies fought a bitter campaign to defend their vital sea-lanes. The Axis powers' declarations of war on the Soviet Union and the United States proved a critical turning point. Germany undertook a bitter campaign on the Eastern Front, while Japan had to safeguard its conquests in the Pacific. The Axis powers had to face the might of the Soviet Union and the United States.

JANUARY 2
POLITICS, *UNITED STATES*
President Franklin D. Roosevelt announces a program to produce 200 freighters, called "Liberty" ships, to support the Allied Atlantic convoys.

JANUARY 3–15
AFRICA, *LIBYA*
General Sir Archibald Wavell's Middle East Force, renamed XIII Corps, with air and naval support, resumes its offensive into Cyrenaica. In Australia's first land action of the war, the Australian 6th Division leads the attack to capture Bardia, just across Libya's border with Egypt, on the 15th. Some 70,000 Italians, plus large amounts of equipment, are captured.

JANUARY 7–22
AFRICA, *LIBYA*
After the British 7th Armored Brigade encircles Tobruk, the Australian 6th Division leads

◄ Italian troops in Tobruk. Allied and Axis forces battled for control of the strategically-important port.

▶ Admiral Ernest King led the US Atlantic Fleet in 1941 and rose to become a key naval commander during the war.

the assault against the Italian defenders of the port, who eventually capitulate on the 22nd. Some 30,000 Italians, as well as port facilities, and vital supplies of fuel, food, and water, are seized. Major General Sir Richard O'Connor immediately sends forces farther west along the coast to capture the port of Benghazi.

JANUARY 19

AFRICA, *ERITREA*
British forces in the Sudan, led by General William Platt, begin attacking Italian forces, heralding the start of General Sir Archibald Wavell's campaign against Italian East Africa.

JANUARY 24

AFRICA, *LIBYA*
The British 4th Armored Brigade engages Italian tanks near Mechili. The Italian forces in Libya are now divided,

with units inland positioned around Mechili, and other forces on the coast around Derna. They do not support each other and both face encirclement.

JANUARY 29

AFRICA, *ITALIAN SOMALILAND*
British forces based in Kenya led by General Sir Alan Cunningham begin attacking the Italian colony's garrison in the next stage of their campaign against Italian East Africa.

POLITICS, *UNITED STATES*
A significant advance in Anglo-US cooperation begins with staff talks in Washington. A decision, code-named ABC1, is eventually made that places Germany's defeat as the principal Allied aim in the event of the US declaring war. These talks lead to a US mission in March to visit potential sites for military bases in Britain.

FEBRUARY 1

POLITICS, *UNITED STATES*
Major organizational changes to the US Navy lead to it being divided into three fleets: Atlantic, Asiatic, and Pacific. Admiral Ernest King is to lead the new Atlantic Fleet, and US naval forces will be strengthened in this vital war theater.

SEA WAR, *ATLANTIC*
The German heavy cruiser *Admiral Hipper*, operating from Brest in France, embarks on a series of highly-destructive raids on Atlantic convoys that last until April.

▼ A column of British tanks prepares for action against Axis forces in Libya.

SEA WAR, *ATLANTIC*
The German battlecruisers *Scharnhorst* and *Gneisenau* embark on commerce-destroying raids in the Atlantic. They succeed in dispersing

▼ *Prince George of Greece and Princess Bonaparte speak to Greek troops wounded while fighting the Italian invaders.*

numerous convoys and sink 22 ships before returning to the safety of French waters on March 22.

FEBRUARY 5–7

AFRICA, *LIBYA*
The Italians fail in their final attempt to escape encirclement at Beda Fomm, south of Benghazi, and surrender to the British 7th Armored Division. Meanwhile, the Australian 6th Division, advancing along the coastal roads, forces troops in Benghazi to surrender on the 7th.

This ends a two-month campaign in which the British have inflicted a complete defeat on a stronger enemy by executing a carefully-planned offensive using highly-trained troops backed by air and naval support.

FEBRUARY 14

POLITICS, *BULGARIA*
Bulgaria grants Germany access to its border with Greece. This move enables Germany to increase its power in the Balkans and provides a route for forces earmarked to invade Greece.

POLITICS, *SOVIET UNION*
General Georgi Zhukov is appointed chief of the General Staff and deputy commissar for defense. He has previously commanded the Red Army forces fighting against the Japanese in Mongolia in the summer of 1939.

AFRICA, *LIBYA*
In response to Adolf Hitler's offer to send an armored division to ensure that the Italians will not withdraw in Libya, the first detachments of General

▲ *Italian troops in action near Benghazi during the major British offensive into Cyrenaica, Libya.*

Erwin Rommel's Afrika Korps disembark at Tripoli.

FEBRUARY 19–23

POLITICS, *ALLIES*
A meeting of political and military leaders in Cairo, Egypt, decides to deploy forces to Greece. The Greek and British authorities subsequently agree to send 100,000 British troops to bolster the country's defenses.

FEBRUARY 25

AFRICA, *ITALIAN SOMALILAND*
British-led East and West African troops advance into Mogadishu, the capital. The defeated Italians begin evacuating the colony.

MARCH 1

POLITICS, *BULGARIA*
Bulgaria joins the Axis powers.
AFRICA, *LIBYA*
Free French forces from Chad seize the Italian air base and garrison at Kufra Oasis in the southeast after a 22-day siege.

▶ *General Erwin Rommel, the audacious commander of the German Afrika Korps, outlining his strategy for winning a battle against the British in North Africa.*

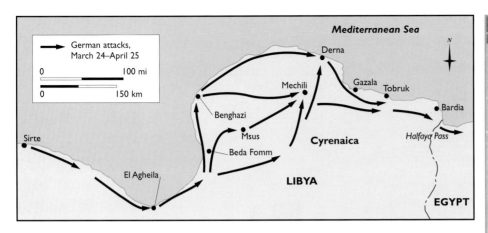

LEND-LEASE

Following the fall of France in June 1940, US President Franklin D. Roosevelt pursued a policy of supplying Britain with the military equipment it required to carry on the fight against Nazi Germany. As dependence on these imports increased, in December 1940 the British prime minister, Winston Churchill, proposed an arrangement whereby the Allied nations could obtain essential US goods and equipment but would repay the United States after the war.

In March 1941 Congress passed the Lend-Lease Act and gave Roosevelt wide-ranging powers to supply goods and services to "any country whose defense the president deems vital to the defense of the United States." Almost $13 billion had been allocated to the Lend-Lease arrangement by November 1941.

Although Britain now had the opportunity to increase the amount of US imports, its own war production had been increasing during this period. Food and oil from the United States, however, was still crucial to its survival.

Lend-Lease was terminated by President Harry S. Truman on August 24, 1945, although Britain was still under contract to receive large quantities of US goods for which it had to pay in dollars.

Britain was not the only beneficiary of the act. The British Commonwealth, the Soviet Union, and other Allied nations also became recipients of US aid in this manner to help their respective war efforts.

MARCH 4

WESTERN FRONT, *NORWAY*

A joint British and Norwegian commando raid and naval assault on the Lofoten Islands destroys fish-oil plants used in the production of explosives, captures 215 Germans, rescues 300 Norwegians, and sinks 10 ships.

MARCH 5

BALKANS, *GREECE*

The first contingent of British troops sails from Egypt. By April 2 some 58,000 troops will have been sent to help defend the country.

MARCH 9–25

BALKANS, *GREECE*

Italy launches a spring offensive between the Devoli and Vijosë Rivers in northwest Greece to counter the reverses it has suffered. Mussolini himself travels to Albania to supervise the deployment of

▲ *General Erwin Rommel's first offensive in the desert drove the British from Libya and threatened to seize Egypt.*

12 divisions for the attack. Greek intelligence and defensive preparations ensure that the poorly-planned Italian attacks from Albania are rebuffed.

MARCH 11

POLITICS, *UNITED STATES*

President Franklin D. Roosevelt signs the Lend-Lease Act that allows Britain to obtain supplies without having to immediately pay for them in cash. For the remainder of 1941, however, Britain is able to pay. The bill grants the president greater powers to supply military equipment to any nation he considers important to US security.

MARCH 24

AFRICA, *LIBYA*

General Erwin Rommel begins his first offensive in Libya by driving the British from El Agheila. He now begins a counteroffensive similar to the original attack by the British. While the 21st Panzer

US shipbuilding dramatically increased to provide vessels for the Atlantic convoys that sailed to Britain.

MARCH 25

Division races across the desert toward Tobruk, Italian forces take the longer coastal route.

MARCH 25

POLITICS, *YUGOSLAVIA*
Yugoslavia joins the Axis powers by signing the Tripartite Pact.

MARCH 27–30

POLITICS, *YUGOSLAVIA*
A coup by air force officers deposes Prince Paul's pro-Axis administration. King Peter II takes nominal charge of the country and General Dusan Simovic becomes head of government. The events alarm the Axis powers, chiefly Germany.

Adolf Hitler responds to the overthrow of Prince Paul by issuing Directive No. 25, the order for the invasion of Yugoslavia, which will commence alongside the attack on Greece, codenamed Operation Marita. Hitler approves of the army's proposals for the invasions, both of which are scheduled to begin on April 6.

MARCH 27

AFRICA, *ERITREA*
The Battle of Keren, in northeast Eritrea, ends with Italian forces being forced to retreat toward the capital Asmara. The Italians lose 3000 men compared to British fatalities of 536. Asmara falls five days later.

MARCH 28–29

SEA WAR, *AEGEAN*
The Italian fleet sails into the Aegean Sea to disrupt British convoys to Greece. A British force led by Admiral Henry Pridham-Wippell engages some Italian cruisers in a long-range bombardment. The Italians retire, fearing the presence of more enemy vessels.

▲ *British trucks carrying troops at the Battle of Keren during the campaign against the Italians in Eritrea.*

▼ *The Italian battleship* Vittorio Veneto *fires a salvo against the British in the Aegean Sea during the Battle of Cape Matapan. Torpedo-bombers hit the vessel during the action.*

KEY PERSONALITIES

FIELD MARSHAL ERWIN ROMMEL

Erwin Rommel (1891–1944) was a decorated World War I officer who commanded Hitler's bodyguard and was responsible for the Führer's personal safety during the Polish campaign. He then took command of the 7th Panzer Division for the 1940 invasion of France. His speedy advance across the Meuse River and drive to the English Channel earned him a reputation as a daring tank commander.

Following the failed Italian campaign in North Africa, he was sent there to lead the Afrika Korps in 1941. Rommel became a master of desert warfare tactics with his ability to exploit opportunities, employ unorthodox methods, and deploy his armored forces to maximum effect. After recapturing Tobruk in 1942, he pushed the Allies back to El Alamein in Egypt. The "Desert Fox" was promoted to field marshal, having led the Afrika Korps to a string of victories.

Rommel was forced to retreat into Tunisia after the British victory at El Alamein in November 1942 and the Allied Torch landings. He left North Africa in 1943. Rommel's next major appointment was in France, where he was tasked with establishing the anti-invasion program he had proposed to Hitler. He commanded Army Group B after the Allied landings in June 1944. Rommel was badly wounded during an air attack and returned to Germany. After being implicated in the failed July assassination attempt on Adolf Hitler, Rommel took poison to avoid a trial and the threatened reprisals against his family.

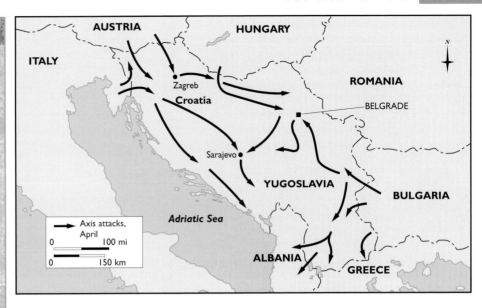

▲ *After Italy failed to seize Greece in 1940, the Germans conquered the Balkans with a successful campaign in 1941.*

Their fears are realized when the main British force, led by Admiral Sir Andrew Cunningham, sends two torpedo-bombers from the carrier *Formidable* to attack the Italian naval vessels. They damage the battleship *Vittorio Veneto* and cripple the cruiser *Pola*. Three British battleships then engage two cruisers sent to cover the *Pola*. The Battle of Cape Matapan claims five Italian ships sunk and 3000 men killed. The British lose just one aircraft in the action.

MARCH 30

POLITICS, *UNITED STATES*
The authorities confiscate 65 Axis ships, which are immediately taken into "protective custody."

APRIL 1–18

POLITICS, *IRAQ*
Nationalist politician Rashid Ali and army officers hostile to Britain depose Regent Faisal and form a pro-Axis

▼ *Prisoners-of-war captured during the invasion of Greece pass a variety of German armored vehicles.*

regime in Iraq. British troops begin arriving in Iraq on the 18th to safeguard access to key oil supplies.

APRIL 4

AFRICA, *LIBYA*
General Erwin Rommel's Axis troops are advancing across Libya in three groups. A predominantly Italian force on the coast takes Benghazi. Another group inland is advancing to Msus, while farther south a third force is also heading toward the same objective.

APRIL 6–15

BALKANS, *YUGOSLAVIA/GREECE*
Thirty-three German divisions, with Italian and Hungarian support, invade Yugoslavia from the north, east, and southeast. Aerial bombing centering on Belgrade dislocates the nation's military command and communication structure, and further undermines the ineffective mobilization of its 640,000-strong army. Major cities are quickly

▲ *German tanks crossing the desert during General Erwin Rommel's first offensive in the desert war.*

seized, including Zagreb, Belgrade, and Sarajevo, between the 10th and 15th.

In Greece, German forces attack the Greek Second Army on the fortified Metaxas Line along the country's northern border with Bulgaria. Air raids on Piraeus port destroy a British ammunition ship, which explodes and sinks 13 vessels. The Second Army, cut off after German forces reach the sea at Salonika on the 9th, soon surrenders. The British, after initially occupying positions between Mount Olympus and Salonika, are quickly forced back to a new defensive line just north of the mountain following the collapse of Greek forces on their left flank.

APRIL 6–9

AFRICA, *ETHIOPIA/ERITREA*

British General Sir Alan Cunningham, after an impressive advance of over 1000 miles (1600 km) from Kenya, captures Addis Ababa, Ethiopia's capital, and then continues to harass the retreating Italian forces. Allied

▲ *Italian troops were often unprepared for crossing freezing, mountainous terrain during the invasion of Greece.*

◄ *Following the conquest of Yugoslavia by Axis forces, Italian troops march into the province of Slovenia.*

forces in Eritrea then seize the port of Massawa on the 9th and capture 17 Axis merchant vessels and other assorted craft in the harbor.

APRIL 7

AFRICA, *LIBYA*

General Erwin Rommel captures Derna, along with British Generals Philip Neame and Sir Richard O'Connor, during his advance toward Tobruk.

APRIL 10

POLITICS, *YUGOSLAVIA*

The Ustachi political group in the province of Croatia declares the formation of an independent republic separate from Yugoslavia.

SEA WAR, *GREENLAND*

The United States begins occupying Greenland to prevent the Danish colony falling into German hands. Valuable weather-observation points for Britain are situated in Greenland.

APRIL 10–13

AFRICA, *LIBYA*

General Erwin Rommel begins the siege of Tobruk. The Allies, who repulse his first attacks, are determined to hold Tobruk as it is the only major port between Sfax in Tunisia and Alexandria in Egypt, a distance of 1000 miles (1600 km). It is therefore a strategic base for forces fighting in North Africa. Tobruk comes under constant air and ground attack, its caves providing the only real shelter, while the sea-lane to Egypt is to be its only lifeline.

APRIL 13

POLITICS, *SOVIET UNION/JAPAN*

A five-year nonaggression pact between the Soviet Union and Japan is signed, which enables the Red Army to move units from Siberia to bolster its forces preparing to meet any future German attack.

▼ *An Australian gun crew defending Tobruk. The besieged garrison and the ships supplying the defenders came under constant Axis attack.*

APRIL 17

POLITICS, *YUGOSLAVIA*

Yugoslavia signs an armistice with Germany. The country is now under military administration except for the Croatian puppet state. Immediately, guerrilla forces emerge to resist the Nazi occupation.

APRIL 18–21

BALKANS, *GREECE*

Greek positions are quickly collapsing as the German invaders advance. The British have fallen back from Mount Olympus to Thermopylae. A British evacuation appears inevitable as reinforcements from Egypt are canceled on the 18th. King George assumes temporary charge of the government after the premier, Alexander Koryzis, commits suicide. A British evacuation is finalized after General Alexander Papagos, the Greek commander-in-chief, realizing the situation is hopeless, recommends a withdrawal on the 21st. Greek forces fighting in Albania surrender on the 20th.

▼ *Yugoslavian soldiers surrender to the conquering Axis forces. Although the country was occupied, partisan forces carried on fighting to liberate the nation.*

APRIL 21–30

AIR WAR, *BRITAIN*
Two raids on the nights of the 21st–22nd and 29th–30th against Plymouth by 640 bombers claim 750 lives and leave 30,000 homeless.

APRIL 21–27

BALKANS, *GREECE*
British forces leave their lines around Thermopylae on the 24th after Greek forces in Thrace capitulate. The British evacuation operation now begins, and some 43,000 men are rescued by the Royal Navy from ports and beaches in eastern Greece, while under constant German air attack. Two destroyers and four transport ships are lost.

A German attack by paratroopers at Corinth on the 26th and an advance to Patras pose a threat to the British evacuation. German forces occupy Athens on the 27th, but the Greek government has already left for Crete. Campaign dead: Greek 15,700; Italian 13,755; German 1518; and British 900.

APRIL 25

POLITICS, *GERMANY*
Adolf Hitler issues Directive No. 28, ordering the airborne invasion of Crete, code-named Operation Mercury.

APRIL 30

AFRICA, *LIBYA*
The most intense Axis attack on Tobruk to date commences but meets determined resistance from

▲ *German parachutists engaged in street fighting with the Allies in Corinth during the invasion of Greece.*

▲ *Ethiopian fighters in action against Italian troops during the British campaign to destroy Mussolini's East African empire.*

the defenders. Four days later Axis forces secure a salient on the southwestern area of the defensive perimeter. Both sides then dig in for a lengthy campaign, with the garrison entirely dependent on supplies carried by the Royal Navy. German submarines, torpedo-boats, and medium and dive-bombers constantly

threaten the supply vessels, which are especially vulnerable when unloading.

MAY 1–17

MIDDLE EAST, *IRAQ*
Iraqi forces, totaling four divisions, commence attacks on British troops, which intensify in the following days. British forces are soon bolstered by reinforcements. Germany supports the Iraqis by launching air attacks.

MAY 3–19

AFRICA, *ETHIOPIA*
At the Battle of Amba Alagi in the mountains of northern Ethiopia, the Italians make their last major stand against the Allies in defense of their East African empire. The surrender of the Duke of Aosta and 7000 troops heralds an Allied victory in East Africa. Some 230,000 Italians have been killed or captured. The Allied victory safeguards the Suez Canal from any potential threat from East Africa and also secures control of the Red Sea for Allied shipping.

MAY 5

POLITICS, *ETHIOPIA*
Emperor Haile Selassie returns to Ethiopia after being exiled for five years by the Italians.

MAY 6–12

SEA WAR, *MEDITERRANEAN*
Operation Tiger, the first Gibraltar-to-Egypt convoy for many months, transports supplies intended for a British desert offensive. Two convoys also sail from Egypt to Gibraltar. The entire Mediterranean Fleet supports

▶ A British servicewoman shelters under a table in case an air raid occurs while she has a rest. Work carried on throughout the "Blitz" regardless of the dangers.

the convoy of five transports. They suffer attacks from Italian aircraft on the 8th. One transport, carrying 57 tanks, sinks after striking a mine. The convoy, however, delivers 238 tanks and 43 Hurricane fighters.

MAY 10

POLITICS, *BRITAIN*

Rudolf Hess, deputy leader of Germany, flies to Scotland on a strange mission to ask Britain to allow Germany a "free hand" in Europe in return for the Nazis leaving the British Empire intact. Hess flies to Scotland to see the Duke of Hamilton, whom he believes to be the leader of the antiwar party in Britain. Germany does not authorize his actions and the British imprison him. Martin Bormann, national party organizer, replaces Hess and becomes a key confidant of Adolf Hitler.

MAY 10–11

AIR WAR, *BRITAIN*

In the climax to the "Blitz," London is attacked by 507 bombers. This will be the last major German air raid for three years. The aerial bombing of Britain now affects Liverpool, Bristol, Belfast, and several other cities. Since September 1940, 39,678 people have been killed and 46,119 injured by Luftwaffe raids. Civil defense, fire, police, and medical organizations help the population to cope with the attacks. Infrastructure is quickly repaired and shelters provide some protection for people. The population in general remains resilient in the face of the onslaught, despite the dislocation and the strains caused by the bombing.

MAY 15–16

AFRICA, *EGYPT*

Operation Brevity, the first British operation against the Afrika Korps, attempts to throw the Axis forces back from the Egyptian frontier. Halfaya Pass and Sollum are recaptured in the operation.

MAY 20–22

MEDITERRANEAN, *CRETE*

A German force of 23,000 men, supported by 600 aircraft, attacks Crete. The German plan is to launch an airborne assault that can then be reinforced by a seaborne force. After preparatory air attacks, the Germans launch the first major airborne operation in history.

Paratroops come under attack while landing and meet determined resistance from the 42,000 British, New Zealand, Australian, and Greek troops stationed on the island. After an Allied battalion commander holding Máleme airfield mistakenly withdraws, the Germans gain a footing for

▼ German mountain troops en route to Crete, where many would die in the bitter battle to seize the island.

◀ Rudolf Hess, the Nazi who tried to make peace with the British.

▼ *The German battleship* Bismarck *fires a salvo at the British battleship* Hood. *The* Hood *was sunk during the fierce battle in the Denmark Straits.*

reinforcements to be landed. While the Germans are able to land some troops by glider and parachute, around 5000 men are lost on vessels sailing from Greece that are intercepted by British ships. The British Mediterranean Fleet in Cretan waters is subjected to massive German air attacks on the 22nd, forcing it to withdraw its ships off northern Crete.

MAY 23–27

SEA WAR, *ATLANTIC*

Two British cruisers, *Norfolk* and *Suffolk*, assisted by radar, find the German battleship *Bismarck* and cruiser *Prinz Eugen* in the Denmark Straits between Iceland and Greenland. However, the two Germans ships sink the battlecruiser *Hood* and damage the battleship *Prince of Wales*, which have been sent to engage them. *Bismarck*'s oil tanks, however, are hit and begin leaking. That night, a torpedo-bomber hits the ship but does little damage.

The German vessels make for Brest and the British lose radar contact

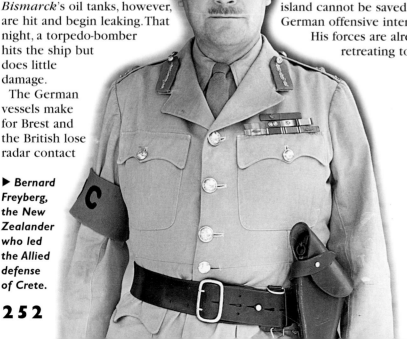

▶ *Bernard Freyberg, the New Zealander who led the Allied defense of Crete.*

for several hours. Aircraft from the carrier *Ark Royal* disable *Bismarck*'s steering with a torpedo on the 26th and other ships encircle her. Shelling from the battleships *Rodney* and *King George V* leave the *Bismarck* a shattered and burning wreck.

MAY 27

POLITICS, *UNITED STATES*

President Franklin D. Roosevelt declares that "an unlimited national emergency now exists." The government assumes wide-ranging powers over the economy and pledges to resist any act of aggression from Germany.

MAY 28–31

MEDITERRANEAN, *CRETE*

Major General Bernard Freyberg, the New Zealand commander responsible for defending Crete, decides the island cannot be saved as the German offensive intensifies. His forces are already retreating toward

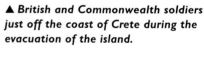

▲ *British and Commonwealth soldiers just off the coast of Crete during the evacuation of the island.*

Sfakia on the south coast. British losses are 1742 men, plus 2011 dead and wounded at sea, while Germany has 3985 men killed or missing. The Royal Navy's hazardous naval evacuation saves over 15,000 Allied troops but it loses nine ships in the process. Hitler suspends airborne operations on this scale in future after being informed of the devastating losses suffered by the paratroopers on Crete.

MAY 30

POLITICS, *IRAQ*

Iraq signs an armistice with Britain whereby the country agrees not to assist the Axis nations. It also agrees not to obstruct the stationing of British forces in Iraq. A pro-Allied government is subsequently installed.

MAY 31

AIR WAR, *EIRE*

The Luftwaffe mistakenly bombs the capital, Dublin, killing 28 people.

JUNE 8–21

MIDDLE EAST, *SYRIA*

An Allied force of 20,000 Free French, British, and Commonwealth troops, under General Sir Henry M. Wilson, invades Syria from Palestine and Iraq amid fears of increasing German influence in the country. They face 45,000 Vichy French troops under General Henri Dentz, plus naval forces that engage the Allies on the 9th.

In subsequent days the Allies encircle enemy units and use heavy artillery to overcome resistance. Vichy forces abandon the capital, Damascus, to the Allies on the 21st.

JUNE 13

FINAL SOLUTION, *VICHY FRANCE*

Over 12,000 Jews have been "interned" in concentration camps after being accused of disrupting relations between Vichy France and Germany. The Vichy authorities are increasingly persecuting Jews and passing legislation to deny them property rights.

JUNE 15–17

AFRICA, *LIBYA*

General Sir Archibald Wavell launches Operation Battleaxe to relieve Tobruk and break the German hold on

▶ *A soldier writes a defiant message outside a military post in Tobruk.*

▼ *A British truck pulls an antiaircraft gun across a dusty track in Syria during the Allied invasion of the country.*

Cyrenaica. An armored and infantry division crosses the Egyptian–Libyan border around Halfaya Pass, Fort Capuzzo, and Hafid Ridge. The new British tanks brought to strengthen the 7th Armored Division have suffered mechanical problems and their crews have had inadequate training. The understrength Allied divisions suffer heavily against the experienced German armor and antitank guns. Wavell halts Operation Battleaxe after losing 90 of his 190 tanks.

JUNE 17

POLITICS, *GERMANY*

Adolf Hitler decides to launch Operation Barbarossa, the invasion of the Soviet Union, on June 22. He has an extreme hatred of the Slav people and the communism that rules them. Hitler aims to enslave the "inferior" Slav peoples, exploit their resources, and occupy their lands as part of his *Lebensraum* ("living space") policy for the Aryan race.

▶ *An Italian mine-thrower crew in action during the desert campaign in Libya and Egypt against British and Commonwealth forces.*

JUNE 22

EASTERN FRONT, *SOVIET UNION*

Germany launches Operation Barbarossa, the invasion of the Soviet Union, with three million men divided into three army groups along a 2000-mile (3200-km) front. Hitler aims to achieve a speedy victory to destroy the Red Army before the summer ends and the Soviets can mobilize their immense resources. Army Group North, under Field Marshal Wilhelm Ritter von Leeb, strikes toward the Baltic and Leningrad. Army Group Center, under Field Marshal Fedor von Bock, aims to take Smolensk and then Moscow, and destroy communications. Army Group South, under General Gerd von Rundstedt, advances toward the Ukraine and the Caucasus.

Soviet forces are caught by surprise and lose a series of battles along the

▲ *Soviet soldiers surrendering to the invading German forces. Red Army units were often quickly encircled and destroyed by German tank formations.*

frontier. German air attacks quickly destroy 1800 Soviet aircraft on the ground. German forces make rapid progress in the north and center but meet stiffening resistance in the south.

JUNE 26–29

POLITICS, *FINLAND*

Finland declares war on the Soviet Union and launches an attack on the 29th. The Finns aim to recapture the territory lost to the Soviets during the Russo-Finnish War. When they finally achieve this objective, Adolf Hitler asks Marshal Karl von Mannerheim, the Finnish leader, to help Germany besiege Leningrad, but he refuses.

JUNE 26–30

EASTERN FRONT, *SOVIET UNION*

The fortress at Brest-Litovsk is taken after fierce resistance, while the important crossing of the Bug River by Army Group Center begins on the 26th. This group's initial objective is Minsk. The fast-moving panzers encircle Red Army units at Bialystok, Novogrudok, and Volkovysk, leaving them open to destruction by follow-on infantry forces. Unimaginative Soviet linear defensive tactics and weak divisions are proving vulnerable to rapid German panzer advances, especially on the flanks. In addition, Germany's total aerial superiority has led to heavy Red Army losses.

JUNE 27

POLITICS, *HUNGARY*
The government declares war on the Soviet Union.

JUNE 29

POLITICS, *SOVIET UNION*
Joseph Stalin assumes control of the federation's Defense Ministry and appoints a five-man council of defense.

▲ *A German tank drives among ruins during the invasion of the Soviet Union in the summer of 1941.*

◀ *Triumphant German troops aboard a Soviet train. Logistics were an essential element for both sides on the Eastern Front.*

JULY 1

POLITICS, *BRITAIN*
General Sir Claude Auchinleck replaces General Sir Archibald Wavell as the commander of British Middle East forces. Wavell's Middle East Command has achieved considerable success against numerically-superior Italian forces, despite supply shortages. However, subsequent commitments in Greece, Iraq, and Syria have overstretched his forces. Nevertheless, Prime Minister Winston Churchill wants a decisive offensive in the Western Desert and Wavell's failure to achieve this has led to his transfer.

JULY 1–11

EASTERN FRONT, *BELORUSSIA/UKRAINE*
The German advance continues. Army Group North crosses the Dvina River. Army Group Center moves across the Berezina River and efforts now center on bridging the Dniepr River in order to prevent the Soviets forming any defensive line that would obstruct the Moscow advance. Army Group South overcomes Soviet fortifications on the Stalin Line and moves forward on July 10. The panzer divisions are just 10 miles (16 km) from Kiev, the Soviet Union's third-largest city, by the 11th.

Such armored units, however, are unsuitable for urban fighting and risk suffering heavy losses, especially as Kiev is strongly defended. General Gerd von Rundstedt plans to lure the Soviet units into the open steppes with the threat of encirclement. Once exposed, they might be annihilated.

JULY 3

AFRICA, *ETHIOPIA*
Italian resistance ends in the south after 7000 men surrender.

◀ *Italian troops surrender during the campaign by Allied troops to liberate Ethiopia.*

KEY PERSONALITIES

JOSEPH STALIN

Joseph Stalin (1879–1953), the leader of the Soviet Union, had supported the 1917 Bolshevik Revolution and then proceeded to rise through the Communist Party's ranks. After the death of Lenin in 1924, he established a dictatorship by destroying all political opposition. The development of industry and agriculture was then achieved at enormous human cost, but it made Stalin's Soviet Union a formidable power.

As Europe moved closer to war in the 1930s, Stalin feared that a German attack on the Soviet Union was inevitable and delayed this with a nonaggression pact with Hitler in 1939. His occupation of half of Poland, Finland, and the Baltic states followed, but proper preparations for the impending German attack were not implemented. Stalin was stunned by Hitler's invasion in June 1941, and it was not until the fall that he properly mobilized the human and economic resources of the Soviet Union to mount an effective defense. Stalin controlled both civil and military affairs as Chairman of the People's Commissars. In both realms he displayed a grim determination to maximize the Soviet war effort and finally stood firm when Germany reached the gates of Moscow. He even exploited nationalist sentiments to maintain morale among Russians, appealing for a "holy war" to defend "Mother Russia."

At the great conferences held by the Allies, Stalin was a forceful negotiator who constantly demanded the establishment of a "Second Front" in Europe to relieve the Soviet Union and additional supplies for his war effort. As the war progressed, Stalin often bypassed the decisions of these meetings concerning the political profile of postwar Europe, and the Allies looked nervously on as Stalin maneuvered to create a series of communist "buffer states" around the Soviet Union.

JULY 4

POLITICS, *YUGOSLAVIA*
Joseph Broz, known as "Tito," emerges as the leader of the Yugoslavian resistance movement, although the government-in-exile does not support him. Tito, a communist, has popular support and proposes a Yugoslavian federation that overrides ethnic and national differences.

JULY 7

SEA WAR, *ICELAND*
US troops garrison the country to protect shipping from U-boat attacks.

JULY 10

POLITICS, *SOVIET UNION*
Joseph Stalin, in an attempt to halt the advancing Germans, appoints a number of "commander-in-chiefs of direction" in three command areas (fronts – groups of armies). These are Marshal Semën Budënny (South and Southwest Front), Marshal Semyon Timoshenko (Central West Front), and Marshal Kliment Voroshilov (Northwest Front).

▲ *Vichy French soldiers are marched into captivity after the surrender of Syria.*

JULY 12

POLITICS, *ALLIES*
Britain and the Soviet Union sign a Mutual Assistance Pact, which includes a declaration that neither will make a separate peace with the Axis powers.

AIR WAR, *SOVIET UNION*
Moscow suffers its first air raid. The bombing then intensifies with three large-scale attacks this month and 73 minor raids that last until the end of the year.

JULY 14

MIDDLE EAST, *SYRIA*
General Henri Dentz defies the Vichy French authorities and surrenders Syria to the Allies. British forces begin occupying the colony and pro-Allied administrations are formed in

◀ *Kliment Voroshilov, the Red Army commander of the Northwest Front.*

Syria and neighboring Lebanon. The Allies have sustained about 2500 casualties in the campaign, while the Vichy French forces have suffered some 3500 casualties defending their colonies in the region.

JULY 16

EASTERN FRONT, *SOVIET UNION*
Following the crossing of the Dniepr and Dvina Rivers, the encirclement of Smolensk by Germany's Army Group Center commences. The city falls after 300,000 Red Army troops and 3200 tanks are trapped in the vicinity of the city but, despite this, the surrounded Soviet forces are not finally defeated until August.

JULY 18

POLITICS, *CZECHOSLO-VAKIA*
Britain recognizes the Czech government-in-exile led by Edouard Benes. The Czechs also make a mutual assistance agreement with the Soviet Union and promise to form an army.

▶ *Edouard Benes, the leader of the Czech government-in-exile during the war.*

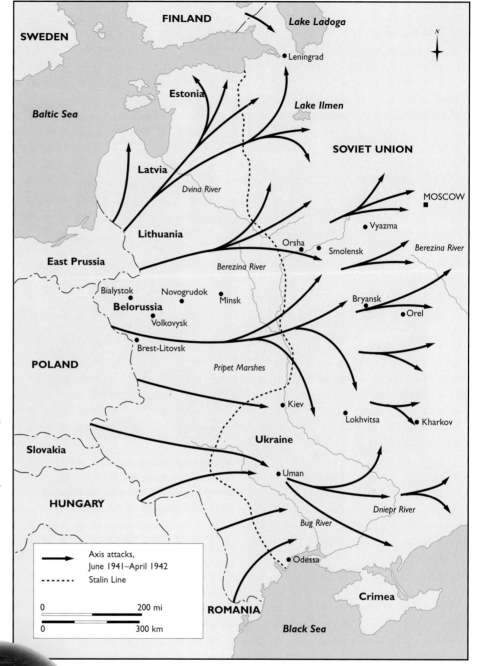

▲ *Germany's invasion of the Soviet Union was a huge operation stretching from the Baltic Sea to the Black Sea.*

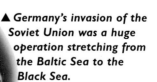

JULY 19-29

EASTERN FRONT, *SOVIET UNION*
General Heinz Guderian's 2nd Panzer Group, plus supporting infantry, leading the advance toward Moscow, receives orders to swing south and help tackle the Soviet Fifth Army, which is situated in the Pripet Marshes. This Soviet force vastly outnumbers the opposing German units and poses a serious threat to Field Marshal Walther von Reichenau's southern operations. Army Group Center's remaining panzer unit, the 3rd Panzer Group, is assigned to assist Army Group North take Leningrad. Guderian and other

257

▲ *Japanese industrial power relied on fuel and raw material imports. The nation's moves to war thus accelerated after vital imports of US oil ceased.*

◀ *Soviet fighters surrender during the German encirclement of Red Army forces in the Ukraine.*

commanders are hostile to this decision and attempt to persuade Adolf Hitler not to halt the Moscow advance, but to no avail.

JULY 21

SEA WAR, *MEDITERRANEAN*
Operation Substance, the British transportation of supplies from Gibraltar to Malta, begins. Besieged Malta, a naval base, occupies a key location across the short sea and air route between North Africa and Italy.

JULY 22

EASTERN FRONT, *BALTIC*
Germany's Army Group North halts west of Lake Ilmen, south of the city

of Leningrad. Troops and equipment along the entire front are suffering from the rigors of the advance and stronger Soviet resistance. During such rest periods the Soviets reinforce their lines, especially those in front of Moscow and Leningrad. The resources needed to take these two cities will be immense.

▶ *Reinhard Heydrich, the infamous head of the SS secret police and architect of the "Final Solution" to destroy the entire Jewish population of Europe.*

JULY 24

EASTERN FRONT, *UKRAINE*
Hitler orders Army Group South in the Ukraine to close the pocket around the concentration of Soviet forces based on Uman. They seal it 15 days later, isolating three Soviet armies from Red Army forces around Kiev. This leaves the Soviet South and South-west Fronts seriously weakened, and Odessa is now only accessible by sea. The Germans trap some 100,000 men and 317 tanks in the pocket.

JULY 26–29

POLITICS,
BRITAIN/UNITED STATES
Britain and the United States freeze Japanese assets in their countries. Japan retaliates likewise against both. Holland freezes Japanese assets in the Dutch East Indies on the 29th. As a consequence, much of Japan's foreign trade is lost.

JULY 31

POLITICS, *GERMANY*
Reinhard Heydrich, Germany's

security chief and head of the SS secret police, receives orders to begin creating a draft plan for the complete destruction of the Jews, which becomes known as the "Final Solution." Heydrich will become the infamous administrator of the state apparatus that persecutes and murders millions of people.

AFRICA, *LIBYA*
General Ludwig Cruewell takes command of the Afrika Korps and General Erwin Rommel takes charge of Panzer Group Africa (one infantry and two panzer divisions).

AUGUST 1

POLITICS, *UNITED STATES*
The United States bans the export of oil except to the British Empire and western hemisphere states. Japan, which is entirely dependent on oil imports, is severely affected by this and has to choose between changing its foreign policy or seizing oil by force.

AUGUST 5

POLITICS, *VICHY FRANCE*
Admiral Jean François Darlan assumes responsibility for Vichy-controlled North Africa.

EASTERN FRONT, *UKRAINE*
Romanian and German forces begin a 73-day siege of Odessa. The Soviet high command sends reinforcements to try to help form a line on the east bank of Dniepr River. Meanwhile,

troops delay the Germans on the west bank while industrial resources are destroyed or removed to beyond the Ural Mountains, where Soviet industry is being relocated.

AUGUST 6

POLITICS, *POLAND*
Lieutenant General Wladyslaw Anders is appointed to form a Polish army in the Soviet Union. Anders eventually forms an army but will lack the supplies to fight, while the Soviets will not permit the Poles to serve on the Eastern Front.

AUGUST 12

POLITICS, *GERMANY*
Adolf Hitler's Directive No. 34 outlines revisions to Operation Barbarossa, with the advance on Moscow being halted while the advance to Leningrad is resumed. The southern wheatlands and industries of the Ukraine have also become a higher priority than the Soviet capital.

AFRICA, *LIBYA*
Australian troops, at the request of their government, leave Tobruk; 6000 Poles relieve them.

AUGUST 14

POLITICS,
BRITAIN/UNITED STATES
A meeting between Winston Churchill and Franklin D. Roosevelt in Canada produces the Atlantic Charter. This

▶ *General Heinz Guderian, the talented armored warfare tactician, inspecting his men on the Eastern Front.*

AUGUST 18

asserts liberal policies that articulate their intentions not to acquire any territories or change national borders without the support of the populations concerned. People are also to be granted self-determination regarding how they are governed, and equal access is to be given to economic resources. The United States also secretly guarantees to defend any British possessions and to commence search-and-destroy patrols to support Atlantic convoys.

AUGUST 18

EASTERN FRONT, *UKRAINE*
Soviet forces in the Ukraine begin withdrawing across the strategically-important Dniepr River to form a defensive line farther north – the Bryansk front – leaving the Thirty-fifth Army in Kiev.

Hitler plans to trap and then destroy the bulk of the Red Army before it retreats across the Dniepr. To achieve this the Germans have to make wide encirclements to trap Soviet units. This move, however, creates large gaps through which Red Army troops can escape east.

▶ **British forces move into Iran to safeguard oil supplies inside the country.**

AUGUST 21

SEA WAR, *ARCTIC*
The first trial convoy to the Soviet Union from Britain transports vital supplies to the Russian port of Archangel. The Arctic convoy reaches its destination on the 31st.

AUGUST 23

EASTERN FRONT, *UKRAINE*
The German 2nd Panzer Group and 2nd Army Group strike southward aiming to link up with Army Group South to the east of Kiev.

AUGUST 25

MIDDLE EAST, *IRAN*
Soviet and British forces begin occupying Iran following fears that Germans are operating in the country. Allied forces seize vital oil installations and encounter little resistance.

AUGUST 30

EASTERN FRONT, *UKRAINE*
The Soviet Union launches a counter-attack with the Twenty-first Army

north of Kiev, but it fails and risks defeat by the 2nd Panzergruppe.

SEPTEMBER 1

EASTERN FRONT, *BALTIC*
German forces near Leningrad are now within artillery range of the city. Soon, the city's rail and road approaches are cut off and a bitter siege commences that lasts until early 1944. Leningrad is a key industrial center and is used by the Soviet Baltic Fleet, which potentially threatens vital Swedish iron ore shipments to Germany.

SEPTEMBER 3

FINAL SOLUTION, *POLAND*
Experiments using Zyclon-B gas chambers to slaughter Jews and others deemed "undesirable" by the Nazis are carried out in Auschwitz concentration camp, Poland. The experiments are a success, and will lead to the widespread use of the gas.

SEPTEMBER 4

SEA WAR, *ATLANTIC*
A U-boat mistakes the US destroyer *Greer* for a British vessel and attacks it. This is presented as an act of aggression and US warships are ordered to "shoot on sight" in waters integral to national defense.

SEPTEMBER 6

FINAL SOLUTION, *GERMANY*
Restrictions on Jews are reinforced with an order requiring them to wear a Star of David badge. Their freedom of movement is also restricted.

◀ **The British cruiser Sheffield sailing with an Arctic convoy of merchant ships taking vital supplies to the Soviet Union.**

OCTOBER 6–15

EASTERN FRONT, *UKRAINE*
Germany's Second Army and Second Panzer Army encircle three Soviet armies north and south of Bryansk on the 6th. Soviet forces begin evacuating 35,000 troops by sea from the besieged port of Odessa on the 15th.

OCTOBER 7–20

EASTERN FRONT, *SOVIET UNION*
After fierce fighting, six Soviet armies are encircled around Vyazma by the 14th. German forces elsewhere cover great distances, but the onset of heavy rains on the 8th severely limits mobility as the roads to Moscow become quagmires. Until the 20th, the Second Panzer Army also has to reduce the Bryansk pocket. The encirclements at Vyazma and Bryansk trap 673,000 troops and 1242 tanks, but also preoccupy the advancing forces, giving the Red Army time to establish new defensive positions.

OCTOBER 16

POLITICS, *JAPAN*
General Hideki Tojo, defense minister and

◄ *Japanese war leader General Hideki Tojo.*

SEPTEMBER 15

EASTERN FRONT, *UKRAINE*
Guderian's 2nd Panzer Group links up with Army Group South at Lokhvitsa, 100 miles (160 km) east of Kiev, trapping four Soviet armies. This seals the fate of the Soviet Southwest Front and its 500,000 men.

SEPTEMBER 17–19

EASTERN FRONT, *UKRAINE*
Soviet forces begin a fighting withdrawal from Kiev, having been delayed in abandoning the city by Joseph Stalin's insistence on holding it. This delay enables the Germans to cut off their escape routes. The Germans seize Kiev on the 19th, killing or capturing 665,000 men after 40 days of bloody combat. This seals the fate of the western Ukraine.

SEPTEMBER 24

SEA WAR, *MEDITERRANEAN*
The first U-boat enters the Mediterranean (half the entire U-boat force will be operating there later in the year). The Operation Halberd convoy leaves Gibraltar bound for Malta. During the six-day trip, Italian warships attempt to intercept the convoy, but an Italian submarine is sunk. The British bombard Pantellaria, an Italian island situated between Sicily and Tunisia.

SEPTEMBER 29

FINAL SOLUTION, *UKRAINE*
Nazi troops kill 33,771 Jews in Kiev.

SEPTEMBER 30

EASTERN FRONT, *UKRAINE*
The 1st Panzer Group begins the offensive against the southern Ukraine from the Dniepr and Samara Rivers, and immediately severs a vital Soviet rail line. The advance toward Rostov moves behind three Soviet armies. General Erich von Manstein's Eleventh Army then advances to trap 106,000 Soviet troops and 212 tanks between the two German forces on October 6 in a classic encirclement operation. One Soviet force, the weakened Twelfth Army, retreats northeastward.

EASTERN FRONT, *SOVIET UNION*
Operation Typhoon, the attack on Moscow, officially begins. Germany's Army Group Center's 73 divisions face 85 Soviet divisions plus 10–15 in reserve. General Heinz Guderian's Second Panzer Group thrusts toward Bryansk and Orel. Two days later, the 3rd and 4th Panzer Groups move to encircle Soviet forces around Vyazma.

leader of the militarist faction within Japan, replaces the more moderate Prince Fumimaro Konoye as prime minister. Konoye's attempts to satisfy the prowar military hierarchy and reach some form of settlement with the United States has failed. His

▲ *Female fighters march through Moscow. Thousands of Soviet women helped defend the city from attack.*

▼ *Soviet infantry in their winter clothing. German troops often lacked the kit needed for the freezing temperatures.*

successor exerts authoritarian control over the War and Home Affairs Ministries. This change signals the political ascendancy of the prowar faction in Japan and is a step closer to conflict with the United States and the Allies.

OCTOBER 19

EASTERN FRONT, *SOVIET UNION*
Joseph Stalin declares a state of siege

in Moscow. The Soviet Union is now in the process of mounting an enormous defensive operation. Reinforcements are arriving from northern and southern regions, and a formidable series of defensive lines are now being built by Moscow's citizens, who are also ready to fight in them. General Georgi Zhukov is to command the West Front responsible for defending Moscow.

Across the entire Eastern Front the Soviets are preparing strong defensive positions and mobilizing the entire population to support the war. Soviet resistance is fierce, and atrocities become commonplace on both sides. Agricultural and industrial resources are destroyed if they cannot be prevented from falling into German hands – a deliberate scorched earth policy.

OCTOBER 20–25

EASTERN FRONT, *SOVIET UNION*
Germany halts the original Typhoon offensive and sets more limited objectives, reflecting the deteriorating weather and strengthening Soviet

resistance. The Ukraine offensive has delayed the advance on Moscow. The Germans are now racing to beat the winter weather and the mobilization of Soviet men and equipment.

OCTOBER 24

EASTERN FRONT, *UKRAINE*
The German Sixteenth Army enters Kharkov, the Soviet Union's

fourth-largest city. Unlike the siege of Kiev, Joseph Stalin does not order a costly defense of the city. The Soviets' ill-equipped soldiers of the Southwest Front around Kharkov escape by making a gradual withdrawal.

OCTOBER 31

SEA WAR, *ATLANTIC*
The US destroyer *Reuben James*, part of an escort group accompanying a British convoy, is sunk by a U-boat, claiming 100 lives.

NOVEMBER 1

EASTERN FRONT, *UKRAINE*
Germany launches an offensive on Rostov, at the mouth of the Don River. The Soviet Ninth Army's deep and flexible defensive lines, together with the winter weather, obstruct the encirclement. A frontal assault from the coast on the 17th is then counterbalanced by the Soviet Thirty-seventh

▶ *A muddy German motorcyclist on the Eastern Front in the fall of 1941.*

◀ *The British aircraft carrier Ark Royal, which was hit by torpedoes and then sank after a fire broke out.*

Army's attack north of the city. The Germans capture Rostov on the 21st but the Soviets recapture it within eight days. General Gerd von Rundstedt then resigns after defying Hitler's orders concerning a tactical withdrawal from the city.

NOVEMBER 6

POLITICS, *UNITED STATES*
A loan of US $1 billion is made to the Soviet Union for Lend-Lease purchases.

NOVEMBER 13

SEA WAR, *MEDITERRANEAN*
Two U-boats attack the British carriers *Argus* and *Ark Royal* en route to Gibraltar after flying off fighters to Malta. *Ark Royal* is badly hit. The carrier sails to within

NOVEMBER 15

25 miles (40 km) of Gibraltar when a fire breaks out and the ship sinks along with 70 aircraft.

NOVEMBER 15

EASTERN FRONT, *SOVIET UNION*

The strength, mobility, morale, and logistical support of the German forces on the Eastern Front are severely affected by fierce winter weather. By the 27th, the panzer spearheads are only 20 miles (32 km) from Moscow, but the second phase of the advance is soon halted by Soviet counterattacks and freezing temperatures. Red Army troops, many newly equipped with the superb T-34 tank and Katyusha multiple rocket-launchers, are also properly clothed for winter operations. They are reinforced by partisan volunteers, whose hatred of the enemy is increased by Nazi atrocities against Soviet civilians.

NOVEMBER 18–26

AFRICA, *LIBYA*

The British Eighth Army in Egypt, under General Sir Alan Cunningham, launches Operation Crusader to relieve Tobruk by striking into Cyrenaica. British light tanks suffer serious losses (exacerbated by mechanical and tactical shortcomings) in various

▲ *Japanese Zero fighters take off from the carrier* Akagi *to escort bombers bound for Pearl Harbor US naval base.*

▼ *South African troops use a grenade to clear Germans from a building during Operation Crusader, the attempt to relieve Tobruk in North Africa.*

engagements with the Germans around Sidi Rezegh, southeast of Tobruk, from the 19th to the 23rd. On the 22nd, the Tobruk garrison attacks besieging Italian units in order to link up with the Eighth Army advancing to relieve it. General Erwin Rommel then strikes at the Allied flank but sustains heavy losses. He eventually retreats, relieving the pressure on Tobruk, although the fighting continues. On the 26th, General Neil Ritchie relieves Cunningham.

NOVEMBER 26

SEA WAR, *PACIFIC*

The Japanese First Air Fleet of six aircraft carriers, two battleships, three cruisers, nine destroyers, three submarines, and eight tankers leaves the Kurile Islands on a mission to destroy the US Pacific Fleet at Pearl Harbor, Hawaii. The carrier force,

under Admiral Chuichi Nagumo, sails 3400 miles (5440 km) and remains undetected by maintaining strict secrecy and radio silence. Japan's war aims are to destroy US naval power in the region, their only real threat, and then to seize territories in the Pacific and Far East. By establishing their "Greater East Asian Co-Prosperity Sphere," they can then obtain their economic resources and establish a defensive perimeter to repel attacks.

A series of diplomatic exchanges between Japanese and US officials has proved unsuccessful, and war appears inevitable. The United States mistakenly believes that Japan will launch its first offensive against the Philippines, Borneo, or the Malay Peninsula – Hawaii is not thought to be a likely target. Japan will thus take the US Pacific Fleet completely by surprise when its forces attack the naval base.

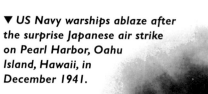

▼ *US Navy warships ablaze after the surprise Japanese air strike on Pearl Harbor, Oahu Island, Hawaii, in December 1941.*

NOVEMBER 27–28

AFRICA, *ETHIOPIA*
After an Allied attack on the city of Gondar, northwest Ethiopia, General Nasi, the local Italian commander, orders the surrender of 20,000 troops. Ethiopia's liberation by the Allies is complete.

NOVEMBER 30

SEA WAR, *ATLANTIC*
The first successful attack using Air-to-Surface-Vessel radar is made by a British bomber, which sinks *U-206* in the Bay of Biscay.

DECEMBER 6

POLITICS, *BRITAIN*
Britain declares war on Finland, Hungary, and Romania.

DECEMBER 7

AIR WAR, *PACIFIC*
A Japanese force of six carriers launches two

▲ President Franklin D. Roosevelt stands before the US Congress and asks for a declaration of war against Japan in 1941.

▲ Thousands of German troops perished as winter set in and Soviet resistance hardened on the Eastern Front at the end of 1941. Many more would die during Hitler's war in the Soviet Union.

▼ A German supply column smashed by the Soviets. Supply problems became critical with the onset of winter.

strikes on the US Pacific Fleet at Pearl Harbor on Oahu Island, Hawaii. Over 183 Japanese aircraft destroy six battleships and 188 aircraft, damage or sink 10 other vessels, and kill 2000 servicemen. The Japanese lose 29 aircraft. Five midget submarines are lost during a failed underwater attack. A planned third strike, intended to

destroy totally the harbor and oil reserves, is not launched for fear that the valuable Japanese aircraft carriers might be attacked by the remainder of the US Pacific Fleet. Japan then declares war on the United States and the British Commonwealth.

Despite information from Allied codebreaking operations, diplomatic

▶ *Australian troops in Tobruk take shelter in a cave during one of the frequent air attacks upon the besieged garrison.*

sources, and other warnings, the raid is a tactical surprise. The failure to take appropriate precautions at the base, exacerbated by failures in interservice cooperation, is severely criticized. Despite the attack's success, the US Pacific Fleet's aircraft carriers are at sea and thus survive, while the fleet itself is quickly repaired. In the United States there is outrage over the attack and popular support for declaring war.

DECEMBER 8

EASTERN FRONT, *SOVIET UNION*
Adolf Hitler reluctantly agrees to issue Directive No. 39, which suspends the advance on Moscow for the duration of the winter. Army Group Center begins withdrawing to less exposed positions farther west, much to Hitler's anger.

POLITICS, *ALLIES*
The United States, Britain, Australia, New Zealand, Holland, the Free French, several South American states, and Yugoslavia declare war on Japan in response to Pearl Harbor. China declares war on the Axis states.

December 8

▶ British and Commonwealth troops occupying defensive positions around the perimeter of the key port of Tobruk. The besieged garrison was finally relieved in December 1941 after the Axis forces under Rommel withdrew.

AFRICA, *LIBYA*

General Erwin Rommel finally decides to withdraw his greatly-weakened units from around Tobruk. He falls back to Gazala by the 11th and then withdraws toward El Agheila on the 16th. The naval operation to sustain Tobruk, finally ended on the 10th, has evacuated 34,000 troops, 7000 casualties, and 7000 prisoners. Around 34,000 tons (34,544 metric tonnes) of supplies have been brought in. Some 27 Allied vessels have been sunk.

▼ *Afrika Korps motorcyclists speed across the desert. Germany's forces attempted to drive the British and Commonwealth forces from Libya and then strike Egypt.*

▲ US troops in the Philippines prepare
to meet the Japanese invaders who
landed on the islands in December 1941.

◄ A Filipino family flees from their home
following a Japanese bombardment.
Thousands of civilians were affected
by the fighting in the islands.

PACIFIC, *PHILIPPINES*
Japanese air attacks destroy 100 US
aircraft at Clark Field, while a small
force lands on Luzon Island to build an
airfield. General Douglas MacArthur,
commanding the 130,000-strong US
and Filipino force in the Philippines,
had intended that US aircraft would
strike the invading Japanese force as his
troops are not capable of stopping any
landing. On the 10th, Luzon is invaded
and Guam Island quickly falls. The
Japanese forces also attack Wake Island
and capture it on the 24th – after two
invasion attempts.

▲ *Japanese troops wade ashore during the invasion of the Malayan Peninsula.*

FAR EAST, *HONG KONG*
The Japanese 38th Division attacks the 12,000-strong Hong Kong garrison. After the garrison refuses the Japanese surrender demand on the 13th, it faces an intense attack followed by amphibious assaults. Hong Kong finally surrenders on the 25th.

FAR EAST, *MALAYA/THAILAND*
A Japanese force of 100,000 troops (the 5th and 18th Divisions), under General Tomoyuki Yamashita, begins landing on the northeast coast of Malaya and in Thailand after initial air attacks. Japanese units quickly move southward down both sides of the Malayan Peninsula. British forces are mainly stationed in the south, having anticipated an attack nearer Singapore. Japanese aircraft soon destroy most of the British aircraft. British reluctance to move into neutral Thailand before a Japanese attack enables General Yamashita to complete his landings. British forces finally advance into Thailand on the 10th but cannot halt the Japanese invasion. Well-equipped and experienced Japanese troops continue pushing southward, many by bicycle.

DECEMBER 10

SEA WAR, *FAR EAST*
About 90 Japanese aircraft sink the British battleship *Prince of Wales* and the battlecruiser *Repulse* while they are attempting to intercept Japanese warships off Malaya. The attack claims 730 lives and leaves the Allies without a single battleship in the theater.

DECEMBER 11

POLITICS, *AXIS*
Germany and Italy declare war on the United States. The United States then declares war on the two Axis states. Romania declares war on the United

States on the 12th. Germany's declaration now confirms US participation in the European war.

DECEMBER 13

SEA WAR, *MEDITERRANEAN*
Three British and one Dutch destroyer sink the Italian fast cruisers *Alberico da Barbiano* and *Alberto di Giussano* off Sicily. The Italian warships are carrying fuel to North Africa, and the attack claims 900 lives. Off Messina, the British submarine *Urge* sinks two Italian transports and damages the battleship *Vittorio Veneto*, which is carrying supplies to Libya.

DECEMBER 14

SEA WAR, *ATLANTIC*
A British convoy of 32 ships, including the aircraft carrier *Audacity*, leaves Gibraltar for Britain. *Audacity* is the first British escort carrier introduced to provide Allied convoys with constant air cover by intercepting enemy bombers or U-boat "Wolf Packs" when they are beyond the operational range of land-based aircraft. During the voyage, the convoy suffers attacks from 12 U-boats, but destroys five of them. The convoy loses *Audacity*, a

▲ A British soldier is led into captivity by Japanese troops during the invasion of Malaya in December 1941.

▼ British troops prepare defenses in Hong Kong. Despite such measures, the colony was quickly overwhelmed.

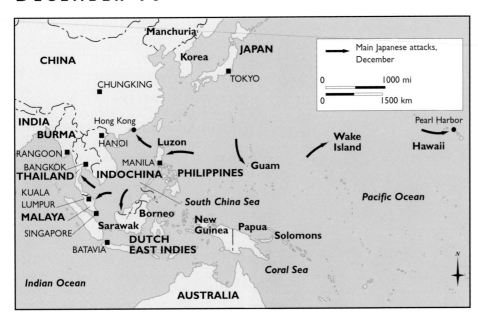

▲ *Japan launched a series of attacks across Southeast Asia in 1941 to seize strategic bases and economic resources.*

destroyer, and two merchant ships, before it reaches Britain on the 23rd.

DECEMBER 16

FAR EAST, *BORNEO*
The Japanese 19th Division makes three landings along the coast of Borneo. The British and Dutch forces defending the island set oil installations ablaze before retreating.

DECEMBER 17

POLITICS, *UNITED STATES*
Admiral Chester Nimitz replaces Admiral Husband Kimmel as commander of the Pacific Fleet following the attack on Pearl Harbor on December 7.

DECEMBER 18–19

SEA WAR, *MEDITERRANEAN*
The Royal Navy's Force K, operating from Malta, runs into a minefield off Tripoli. The cruiser *Neptune* and destroyer *Kandahar* are both sunk, while the remaining two cruisers are damaged. An Italian "human torpedo" attack upon the British Mediterranean Fleet in Alexandria, Egypt, sinks the battleships *Queen Elizabeth* and

Valiant. However, both vessels sink upright in shallow waters and are eventually repaired. Nevertheless, these losses severely reduce British naval power in the Mediterranean.

The "human torpedo," a midget submarine driven by two operators, is designed to enter defended harbors and clamp its warhead onto a ship's hull. The British soon develop their own version called "Chariot."

▲ *An Italian "human torpedo." These craft were used to great effect against British vessels in the Mediterranean.*

▶ *Allied convoys became increasingly vulnerable as naval forces were seriously overstretched and losses mounted.*

▼ *The British battleship* Queen Elizabeth *(front), which was sunk by an Italian "human torpedo" in Egypt.*

▲ *Adolf Hitler (center) discusses strategy with Field Marshal Walther von Brauchitsch (left) and General Franz Halder (right).*

DECEMBER 19

POLITICS, *GERMANY*

Adolf Hitler appoints himself as commander-in-chief of the army following Field Marshal Walter von Brauchitsch's resignation on the 7th. Brauchitsch resigned following a heart attack brought on by the strain of Soviet counterattacks. He was already under pressure to resign. His authority had been increasingly undermined by Hitler dominating strategic planning.

Hitler successfully keeps the Eastern Front armies in defensive positions during the winter. He develops an increasing skepticism toward the competence of his army commanders. Parallel to this is the expansion of the Waffen SS, seen by Hitler as being politically-reliable troops.

POLITICS, *UNITED STATES*

An amendment to the Selective Service Act requires all men aged 18–64 to register, and for men aged 20–44 to be liable for conscription.

DECEMBER 20–26

POLITICS, *UNITED STATES*

Admiral Ernest King becomes chief of naval operations.

PACIFIC, *PHILIPPINES*

Japanese forces invade Mindanao, the most southerly island, and Jolo. The islands offer Japan the chance to gain naval and air bases. The main invasion of Luzon commences on the 22nd. General Douglas MacArthur decides not to defend Manila, the capital, but declares it an open city in order to withdraw his forces westward to the Bataan Peninsula.

DECEMBER 22

POLITICS, *ALLIES*

US President Franklin D. Roosevelt and British Prime Minister Winston Churchill meet at the Arcadia Conference, Washington. Talks between the

▶ *African-American conscripts doing their war service with the US Army.*

▲ *Manila, the Philippines' capital, just after it was abandoned by the US and Filipino forces.*

respective political and military delegations reaffirm the "Germany First" strategic priority and establish the Combined Chiefs-of-Staff to direct Allied military action. They also agree to build up US forces in Britain in preparation for future military action against Nazi Germany and in order to continue the aerial bombing of Nazi-occupied Europe.

DECEMBER 26-28

SEA WAR, *NORTH SEA*
Britain launches Operation Archery, a commando attack against Lofoten Island, off Norway. The first force of 260 troops succeeds in destroying a fish-oil plant.

On December 27, a second landing by a further 600 troops successfully attacks fish-oil plants and radio facilities. The raids reinforce Hitler's fears that Britain is planning to invade the whole of Norway.

KEY PERSONALITIES

PRESIDENT FRANKLIN D. ROOSEVELT

Franklin D. Roosevelt, US president from 1933 to 1945, was the only person to be elected for three terms. He trained as a lawyer and subsequently pursued a political career in the Democratic Party, despite being stricken with polio. Roosevelt's peacetime administration, which began in 1932, generated popular support with its "New Deal" program to establish social and economic reconstruction during the Great Depression of the 1930s.

Once war broke out in 1939, he worked to overcome American "isolationism" and generate support for the Allied cause. Roosevelt was responsible for transforming the United States into the "arsenal of democracy" by expanding the economic capacity of the nation in order to sustain the Allies with war supplies and build up US military capability. A series of economic agreements were made with Allied states, while trade restrictions were imposed on Axis powers. Roosevelt also put the nation on a firm war-footing with military service legislation that provided the manpower for the expanding armed forces.

When the United States entered the war in 1941, Roosevelt ignored his critics and made the key decision to maintain the "Germany First" strategy rather than devoting greater effort to defeating Japan. He also took the crucial decision to demand the unconditional surrender of Japan and Germany. Roosevelt also rejected proposals by US commanders to invade Europe in 1942, and followed British plans to attack North Africa, Sicily, and Italy first.

Roosevelt adopted a conciliatory manner in inter-Allied relations, urging diplomacy between Britain and the Soviet Union to overcome the distrust that existed between these politically divergent states. This popular war leader died on April 12, 1945, three weeks before the end of the fighting in Europe.

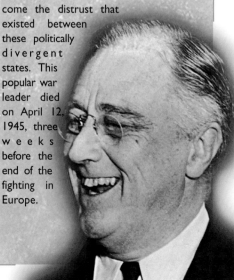

1942

J apan's territorial conquests appeared to signal its triumph over Europe's colonial powers in the Far East. The United States, however, was now on the offensive and won crucial strategic victories at sea over the Japanese. These had serious repercussions for Japan's ability to sustain both its domestic and overseas power. In North Africa and on the Eastern Front, Axis offensives, although initially successful, were halted and then defeated by a series of Allied counterattacks. Control of the sea-lanes continued to be a crucial factor in the war.

JANUARY 1

POLITICS, *ALLIES*

At the Arcadia Conference in Washington, 26 Allied countries sign the United Nations Declaration, pledging to follow the Atlantic Charter principles. These include an agreement to direct their "full resources" against the three Axis nations and not to make any separate peace agreements or treaties. This is a key development in the formation of the United Nations Organization.

JANUARY 2–9

PACIFIC, *PHILIPPINES*

US and Filipino forces under General Douglas MacArthur prepare defensive positions on the Bataan Peninsula and the island of Corregidor as Manila falls. MacArthur realizes that Japan has air and sea superiority. He also knows that no reinforcements will be sent. His troops begin a desperate resistance against Japanese attacks across the mountainous peninsula, which begin on the 9th. For several months the 80,000 troops will resist the Japanese, despite suffering from tropical diseases and being short of supplies.

JANUARY 3

POLITICS, *ALLIES*

Following the Arcadia Conference, British General Sir Archibald Wavell takes charge of the new American, British, Dutch, and Australian (ABDA) command. He is responsible for holding the southwest Pacific. Chinese Nationalist leader Chiang Kai-shek is made commander-in-chief of the Allied forces in his country.

JANUARY 5

EASTERN FRONT, *SOVIET UNION*

Joseph Stalin orders a general offensive against the German invaders, despite warnings from General Georgi Zhukov, the Western Front commander, that the Soviet Union lacks the resources for

◄ *A Japanese tank charges through a Philippines plantation as part of the relentless Japanese offensive to capture the islands from the Americans.*

▲ *Chiang Kai-shek took charge of Allied forces in China in January 1942.*

an attack on four fronts (Leningrad, Moscow, Ukraine, and Crimea). Zhukov advocates a concentrated attack against Army Group Center, which is threatening Moscow. However, the general offensive initially makes considerable inroads and captures trains, food, and munitions. German forces offer stiff resistance and are ordered to hold their positions. They set up defensive areas ("Hedgehogs") that frustrate the Red Army's attacks.

JANUARY 5–12

FAR EAST, *MALAYA*
Following the recent landing of Japanese troops on the northeast coast, British, Indian, and Australian forces are now retreating southward toward Singapore, unable to mount any meaningful defense against the Japanese. The British have underestimated the Japanese, who are well trained and equipped. Kuala Lumpur, the capital, falls to the Japanese on the 12th.

JANUARY 9–21

EASTERN FRONT, *SOVIET UNION*
The Battle of the Valdai Hills begins in the Moscow sector. During the 12-day battle Soviet troops make a 75-mile (120-km) penetration of the German lines that captures nine towns between Smolensk and Lake Ilmen.

JANUARY 10–11

FAR EAST, *DUTCH EAST INDIES*
A Japanese force, under General Tomoyuki Yamashita and Admiral Takahashi, begins attacking the Dutch East Indies to secure the oil assets of this island-chain. The Japanese Eastern Force lands on Celebes and Amboina before taking Bali, Timor, and east Java. The Central Force lands at Tarakan and

▶ *A Japanese tank crosses an improvised bridge during the invasion of Burma.*

▼ *Japanese troops occupy Kuala Lumpur, the capital of Malaya, following the hasty retreat of British forces from the city.*

aims to take Borneo. The Western Force moves from Indochina to attack Sumatra and Java. The remaining Allied troops under ABDA command in the region, including local forces of doubtful loyalty, attempt to resist the Japanese onslaught.

JANUARY 12

POLITICS, *YUGOSLAVIA*
General Dusan Simovic resigns as prime minister of the Yugoslavian government-in-exile. Professor Yovanovic replaces him.

AFRICA, *LIBYA*
General Erwin Rommel agrees to a plan proposed by his officers to counterattack the Allies. British naval strength in the Mediterranean has been eroded, which has enabled new German supplies to arrive. At the same time, Allied forces have suffered the departure of the 7th Armored Brigade plus two Australian divisions, which have been sent to the Far East.

JANUARY 12–31

FAR EAST, *BURMA*
The Japanese Fifteenth Army's two reinforced divisions, plus air support, move northwestward into Burma from neighboring Thailand. A small group under Burmese nationalist Aung Sang

supports Japan and encourages uprisings. British, Burmese, and Indian troops around the town of Moulmein unsuccessfully engage the invaders and withdraw. Already in the previous month the Japanese have taken a key

▼ Japanese offensives to conquer Burma drove the Allies back to the Indian and Chinese borders by May 1942.

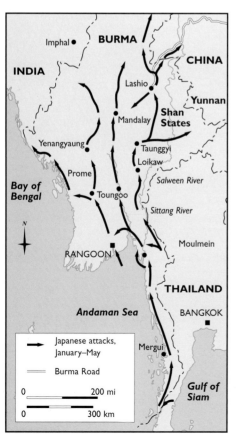

southern air base at Mergui, forming part of the air route between India and Malaya, which they have now blocked. Such airfields are then used for bombing missions. Burma has the only viable supply route to sustain the Chinese fight against Japan. The Allied possession of Burma also keeps India's northeast region secure from attack.

JANUARY 13

POLITICS, ALLIES
At a London meeting, the Allies agree to punish Axis leaders responsible for war crimes.

SEA WAR, ATLANTIC
Germany's U-boats launch attacks, code-named Operation Drum Roll, on shipping off the east coast of the United States. Approximately 20 ships are sunk in the first month of operations as a result of the US Navy's failure to take proper antisubmarine measures, despite British warnings. U-boats begin hunting in the Caribbean the following month.

JANUARY 16–19

POLITICS, GERMANY
Field Marshal Walther von Reichenau, commander of the German Army Group South on the Eastern Front, dies in a plane crash. Field Marshal Fedor von Bock replaces him on the 19th. Adolf Hitler removes Field Marshal Wilhelm von Leeb and replaces him

▶ Field Marshal Wilhelm von Leeb, one of the commanders whom Adolf Hitler blamed for failures on the Eastern Front.

▲ A female Soviet sniper in the Caucasus. Women made a valuable contribution to the Soviet war machine.

with General George von Küchler as Army Group North's commander. Since December, the Führer has removed over 30 senior officers, including two army group and two panzer group commanders, due to his impatience with their constant appeals to make withdrawals in the face of Soviet offensives.

POLITICS, *UNITED STATES*
Donald Nelson becomes head of the new centralized War Production Board.

JANUARY 17

AFRICA, *LIBYA*
The Axis garrison of Halfaya, besieged throughout the British Operation Crusader, finally falls and 5500 Germans and Italians are captured.

SEA WAR, *ARCTIC*
U-boats make their first attack on an Allied Arctic convoy. *U-454* sinks the destroyer *Matabele* and a merchant ship from convoy PQ-8.

JANUARY 18–27

EASTERN FRONT, *UKRAINE*
Soviet South and Southwest Front forces, under Marshal Semyon Timoshenko, make an attack aiming to cross the Donets River and then swing south toward the Sea of Azov to trap units of the German Sixth and Seventeenth Armies. The Donets River is crossed by the 24th, but the Soviet advance is halted by the 27th.

JANUARY 20

FINAL SOLUTION, *GERMANY*
At the Wannsee Conference, Berlin, deputy head of the SS Reinhard Heydrich reveals his plans for the "Final Solution" to the so-called "Jewish problem." Heydrich receives permission to begin deporting all Jews in German-controlled areas to Eastern Europe to face either forced labor or

▲ *Concentration camp prisoners receive rations from an SS officer in a carefully-staged propaganda photograph.*

extermination. The killing of Jews in Eastern Europe is already commonplace. Execution by shooting, however, is proving inefficient and a strain for the troops engaged. A more efficient way of killing using poison gas will soon become widespread.

SEA WAR, *PACIFIC*
In Japan's ongoing offensive against Allied possessions in the Far East, four carriers begin air strikes on Rabaul, New Britain (soon to become a major Japanese naval base), and two submarines shell Midway Island. US and Australian warships sink a Japanese submarine off Darwin. Japanese amphibious landings are made on Borneo, New Ireland, and the Solomons on the 23rd.

JANUARY 21–29

AFRICA, *LIBYA*
General Erwin Rommel begins his second desert offensive in North Africa, moving from El Aghelia to Agedabia on the 22nd. The British Eighth Army is caught unawares and the Germans capitalize on

KEY MOMENTS

WANNSEE CONFERENCE

The secret Wannsee Conference in Berlin officially launched the Nazi program to exterminate the Jewish people, who were regarded as the racial enemy of the "Aryan" Germans. The previous persecution and killing of Jews in Nazi-occupied Europe was transformed into a highly-efficient operation. European Jews were systematically herded into concentration camps in Eastern Europe, where they were worked like slaves. Millions died from maltreatment, exhaustion, disease, and starvation. In extermination camps, poison gas chambers were used to kill thousands of people. Many other people deemed "undesirable" by the Nazis, including gypsies, political opponents, and the mentally and physically disabled, also shared the same fate as the Jews.

Various efforts to save Jews were made. Some were hidden or smuggled to neutral states. Allied countries, however, were often too preoccupied with their struggle against Germany to provide any effective support, though they were aware of what was going on.

Jews who remained free were able to join resistance groups in Europe. The deportation of Jews from their ghettos in Poland for extermination led to various uprisings. In 1943, poorly-armed Warsaw Ghetto Jews resisted the Nazis for four months. The full horrors of the genocide were revealed when the first extermination camp was liberated in July 1944.

Over six million Jews were killed by the Nazis. Some of those responsible for the slaughter were tried at the Nuremberg War Crimes Trials. Thousands of others who served as guards during the "Final Solution" escaped justice, however.

The appalling sight of corpses from Buchenwald concentration camp, where many thousands died.

JANUARY 22

this by driving it back. Benghazi falls on the 29th.

JANUARY 22

EASTERN FRONT, *SOVIET UNION*
The besieged city of Leningrad evacuates 440,000 citizens over 50 days. Thousands are dying of starvation, typhus, and other diseases due to inadequate supplies reaching the city and the German shelling and bombing.

JANUARY 23–24

PACIFIC, *PHILIPPINES*
US and Filipino forces on Bataan begin withdrawing to a line running from Bagac in the east to Orion in the west.

SEA WAR, *FAR EAST*
At the Battle of Macassar Strait, four US destroyers, Dutch bombers, and a submarine attack a Japanese convoy off Borneo. Four Japanese transports are lost.

JANUARY 25

POLITICS, *THAILAND*
The government declares war on Britain and the United States.

▲ *Desert fighters from Germany's Afrika Korps make use of a captured truck during Rommel's second offensive against the British Eighth Army.*

▼ *T-34 tanks in Leningrad. Thousands of people were evacuated to escape the hardships of the besieged city.*

JANUARY 26

WESTERN FRONT, *BRITAIN*
The first US troop convoy of the war reaches Britain.

SEA WAR, *FAR EAST*
Several Japanese troopships off Malaya are struck by 68 British aircraft, of which 13 are lost. That night, the British increase their attacks. The destroyer *Thanet* and the Australian destroyer

Vampire are sunk while attacking the Japanese convoy.

JANUARY 29

POLITICS, *UNITED STATES*
Major General Millard Harmon succeeds General Carl Spaatz as United States Army Air Force chief-of-staff. Spaatz takes over the Air Force Combat Command.

JANUARY 30

FAR EAST, *SINGAPORE*
Retreating British and Commonwealth troops cross the Johore Strait, separating Singapore from the mainland, and partly destroy the connecting causeway. They abandon the rest of the Malayan Peninsula, where mobile Japanese units have constantly outwitted them. Singapore is designed to repel a naval attack. Its great guns have no suitable shells for bombarding land forces as the British believe that a land invasion through dense jungle is impossible, although the RAF has asked for more aircraft to meet a land attack from the north.

FEBRUARY 1

POLITICS, *NORWAY*
Nazi collaborator Vidkun Quisling becomes prime minister, although he will be controlled by Berlin.

SEA WAR, *ATLANTIC*
Germany adopts a new radio code for

▼ *Filipino troops prepare to fight alongside US forces in Bataan.*

▲ *Japanese troops cautiously scale a hill during their advance to Singapore. The British were shocked that the Japanese could move through dense jungle.*

U-boat communications in the Atlantic. Although the British are unable to crack the code until the end of the year, the detection of U-boats is made easier by photoreconnaissance and radio direction-finding technology.

SEA WAR, *PACIFIC*
The US Navy carriers *Enterprise* and *Yorktown*, together with the cruisers *Northampton* and *Salt Lake City*, attack the Marshall and Gilbert Islands.

FEBRUARY 4

AFRICA, *LIBYA*
Axis forces have overextended their lines of communication and a stalemate is developing in the desert. Allied forces are establishing a fortified line from

Gazala on the coast to Bir Hacheim farther inland. Both sides are building up their forces for a new offensive.

FAR EAST, *SINGAPORE*
Britain rejects Japanese demands for Singapore to surrender. Reinforcements are being sent to help defend the base, which is believed to be impregnable.

FEBRUARY 5

POLITICS, *UNITED STATES*
The US government declares war on Thailand.

FEBRUARY 8

▶ *Victorious Japanese soldiers celebrate their conquest of Singapore. The British had totally underestimated the military capability of the Japanese Army.*

FEBRUARY 8

POLITICS, *PHILIPPINES*
President Manuel Quezon proposes to the United States that his country should become independent, that both Japanese and US forces should withdraw, and Filipino units be disbanded. The United States rejects the proposal.

FEBRUARY 8–14

FAR EAST, *SINGAPORE*
Two Japanese divisions, supported by artillery and air bombardment, land on the northwest of the island, quickly followed by a third. Repairs to the Johore causeway enable tanks and 30,000 troops to advance, while in the air the Japanese achieve supremacy. Confused orders often result in the defenders making unnecessary withdrawals and much equipment is lost. Lieutenant General Arthur Percival, the Singapore commander, is forced to surrender on February 14 as the water supply for Singapore's residents and the 85,000-strong garrison is cut. Japan has fewer than 10,000 casualties in Malaya. British and Commonwealth forces have lost 138,000 men, and thousands more will die in captivity. The campaign is one of Britain's greatest defeats.

FEBRUARY 10

SEA WAR, *ATLANTIC*
Britain offers the United States 34 antisubmarine vessels with crews to battle the U-boats.

FEBRUARY 11–12

SEA WAR, *NORTH SEA*
The German battlecruisers *Gneisenau* and *Scharnhorst*, and the heavy cruiser *Prinz Eugen*, supported by destroyers and air cover, leave Brest and sail through the English Channel. RAF and Royal Navy strikes against the German ships are total failures, and 42 aircraft are downed. During the "Channel Dash" to the North Sea, both battlecruisers hit mines and need repairs. British operations to contain the threat of these

▼ *Lieutenant General Sir Arthur Percival's surrender of Singapore was a military disaster.*

commerce-raiders are easier while the vessels are in port. *Gneisenau* subsequently has to be rebuilt after being hit during an air raid against Kiel on February 26, but the project is never completed before the war's end.

FEBRUARY 13

POLITICS, *GERMANY*
Adolf Hitler finally abandons the invasion of Britain, Operation Sealion.

FEBRUARY 14

AIR WAR, *GERMANY*
Britain issues the "Area Bombing Directive," which outlines the strategic objectives of RAF Bomber Command. Bombing will now aim to destroy the psychological will of the German people as well as the country's war industry. Air raids will now aim to destroy residential areas to erode civilian morale.

FEBRUARY 18–23

FAR EAST, *BURMA*
Japanese forces are in constant pursuit of British forces. At the Battle of the Sittang River, the

British are withdrawing across a single bridge over the river when Japanese troops make a sudden crossing elsewhere. The British quickly blow up the bridge, losing much of their equipment with their forces only partially across; those left behind have to use boats. The Sittang River is the only major physical obstacle in the path of the Japanese forces moving toward Rangoon, the capital.

FEBRUARY 19

POLITICS, *UNITED STATES*
The virtually unknown General Dwight D. Eisenhower becomes head of the US Army General Staff War Plans Division. In this capacity he will advocate the intensification of Operation Bolero, the buildup of US forces in Britain, and press for the development of Operation Sledgehammer, a cross-Channel invasion of Europe from Britain.

◀ *General Dwight D. Eisenhower, who became a key figure in US strategic planning and commanded the North African landings in 1942.*

▼ *The German heavy cruiser Prinz Eugen, one of the commerce-raiders that evaded the British and sailed from France into the North Sea.*

KEY PERSONALITIES

AIR CHIEF MARSHAL SIR ARTHUR HARRIS

Arthur Harris (1892–1984) served as British Deputy Chief of Air Staff (1940–41) before taking charge of Bomber Command in 1942. He believed precision bombing was ineffective and favored area bombing against Germany, and he secured Prime Minister Winston Churchill's support to expand Bomber Command's size. Great bomber fleets therefore saturated districts with high explosives and incendiaries to destroy both industry and public morale.

The determination and inspiration shown by Harris encouraged his aircrews to undertake hazardous bombing missions. Raids increased in intensity, more night attacks were flown to avoid hazardous daylight missions, and photoreconnaissance improved bombing accuracy. Despite Harris's initiatives, though, there is still doubt over the success of his strategy.

The impact on Germany's civilians and economy have led some to question the morality of "Bomber" Harris's strategy. Harris himself, however, defended his strategy, claiming it saved many British lives by shortening the war.

A British Halifax bomber on a mission over Germany.

SEA WAR, *FAR EAST*
At the Battle of Lombok Strait, east of Bali, Dutch and US vessels fight several actions with the Japanese. A Dutch cruiser and a destroyer are sunk, while one Japanese destroyer is damaged.

AIR WAR, *AUSTRALIA*
Japanese carrier aircraft and land-based bombers attack Darwin, northern Australia. The raid sinks or damages 16 vessels, claims 172 lives, and causes widespread panic.

HOME FRONT, *UNITED STATES*
President Franklin D. Roosevelt signs Executive Order 9066 giving the secretary of war powers to exclude persons from military areas. This legislation is directed at the nation's Japanese-American population, which has faced growing public hostility since Pearl Harbor. The US Army subsequently removes 11,000 Japanese-Americans from the Pacific coast to camps in Arkansas and Texas

▲ *Scenes of devastation in Darwin after a Japanese air attack on the port. This attack on the Australian mainland shocked the population.*

for the war's duration (there are fears that they may aid a Japanese attack on the West Coast, which is regarded by many as a real possibility). Not a single Japanese-American, however, is convicted of spying for Tokyo during the war. Others go on to serve with distinction in the US armed forces, winning many awards for gallantry.

FEBRUARY 20

POLITICS, *VICHY FRANCE*
Political leaders of the Third Republic are tried by the Vichy Supreme Court, charged with being responsible for France's humiliating 1940 defeat. Former premiers Léon Blum, Paul Reynaud, and Edouard Daladier all defend their records with great skill. The trial, which quickly becomes a public joke, is never completed.

FEBRUARY 22

POLITICS, *BRITAIN*
Air Chief Marshal Sir Arthur Harris takes over Bomber Command.

FEBRUARY 23

POLITICS, *ALLIES*
Britain, Australia, the United States, and New Zealand ratify the Mutual Aid Agreement.

◀ The British Avro Lancaster bomber entered operational service in 1942.

FEBRUARY 24

SEA WAR, *PACIFIC*
The US aircraft carrier *Enterprise* leads a task force to attack the Japanese on Wake Island.

FEBRUARY 25

POLITICS, *ALLIES*
ABDA is disbanded and its commander, British General Sir Archibald Wavell, becomes commander-in-chief in India.

HOME FRONT, *UNITED STATES*
An air raid scare in Los Angeles results in a heavy antiaircraft barrage being fired.

FEBRUARY 27–29

SEA WAR, *FAR EAST*
Under the command of Dutch Rear Admiral Karel Doorman, five cruisers and nine destroyers from four Allied nations engage a Japanese force of four cruisers and 13 destroyers in the Java Sea. Following an inconclusive opening engagement, the Japanese inflict severe losses using their faster "Long Lance" torpedoes. Five Allied cruisers and five destroyers are sunk. Doorman is killed. Japan loses two transports, one cruiser is sunk, and six destroyers are damaged.

FEBRUARY 28

WESTERN FRONT, *FRANCE*
A British parachute assault destroys a German radar station at Bruneval near Le Havre. The force then escapes by sea with captured equipment.

MARCH 1–7

SEA WAR, *FAR EAST*
Two Japanese task forces, including four aircraft carriers, inflict serious losses on Allied shipping while sailing to Java in the Dutch East Indies. The Japanese surround the Allies and sink nine warships and 10 merchant vessels with close-range fire.

MARCH 2

POLITICS, *AUSTRALIA*
All Australian adult civilians become liable for war service.

MARCH 3

AIR WAR, *GERMANY*
The British Lancaster bomber undertakes its first operation by dropping mines in the Heligoland Bight in the North Sea.

MARCH 5

POLITICS, *BRITAIN*
General Sir Alan Brooke replaces Admiral Sir Dudley Pound as chairman of the Chiefs-of-Staff Committee responsible for the daily running of the war and future planning. Britain also extends conscription to men aged 41–45.

MARCH 5–7

FAR EAST, *BURMA*
Lieutenant General Sir Harold Alexander replaces Lieutenant General Thomas Hutton as British commander

◀ Chinese troops crossing the Sittang River during the campaign to save their vital supply road through Burma.

MARCH 9

in Burma. Two British divisions have been trying to resist Japanese advances toward Rangoon. Its port is the main point of entry for British supplies and troops. Alexander, however, evacuates Rangoon after realizing his dispersed forces cannot hold it. He himself narrowly escapes before the Japanese seize it on the 7th.

MARCH 9

POLITICS, *UNITED STATES*
Admiral Harold Stark replaces Vice Admiral Robert Ghormley as US naval commander in European waters. Admiral Ernest King assumes Stark's position as Chief of Naval Operations on the 26th.

FAR EAST, *DUTCH EAST INDIES*
Japan gains possession of its "Southern Resources Area" with the surrender of Allied

combatants in the Dutch East Indies. The capture of this resource-rich area and Malaya allows Japan to consider offensives against India and Australia.

MARCH 11

PACIFIC, *PHILIPPINES*
General Douglas MacArthur leaves his Far East command to become commander-in-chief of US forces in Australia. On leaving, he famously declares: "I shall return!"

FAR EAST, *BURMA*
US General Joseph Stilwell assumes command of the Chinese Fifth and Sixth Armies around the eastern Shan States and city of Mandalay. Their aim is to protect the Burma Road into China. The Allied ground forces are supported by one RAF squadron and up to 30 "Flying Tiger" aircraft flown by an all-volunteer force of US pilots. They face over 200 enemy aircraft.

MARCH 12

PACIFIC, *NEW CALEDONIA*
US Forces, including the first operational deployment of "Seabee" engineers, begin establishing a base in Noumea on New Caledonia in the southwest Pacific.

MARCH 13–30

FAR EAST, *BURMA*
Lieutenant General Sir Harold Alexander forms an Allied line below the central towns of Prome, Toungoo,

◄ *General Douglas MacArthur, the US commander in the Philippines, who directed the defense of the islands.*

and Loikaw near the Salween River and then eastward. Major General William Slim assumes command of the Burma Corps, the main elements of the British forces there on March 19. Japanese attacks begin on the 21st, directed at Chinese forces at Toungoo and the British at Prome.

MARCH 14

POLITICS, *AUSTRALIA*
Large numbers of US troops begin arriving in Australia.

MARCH 22–23

SEA WAR, *MEDITERRANEAN*
A superior Italian force engages a British convoy sailing from Alexandria to Malta. A relatively small escort of five light cruisers and 17 destroyers initially resists an attack led by the battleship *Littorio* at the Battle of Sirte. A storm, however, results in the loss of two Italian destroyers. The convoy subsequently faces air attacks and only 5000 of the original 25,000 tons (25,400 metric tonnes) of supplies arrive. British naval losses and commitments in the Mediterranean have reduced the number of ships available for convoy escorts.

MARCH 27

POLITICS, *BRITAIN*
Admiral Sir James Somerville assumes command of the Far East Fleet in Ceylon (modern Sri Lanka).

POLITICS, *AUSTRALIA*
Australian General Sir Thomas Blamey becomes commander-in-chief of the Australian forces and commander

◄ *Japanese troops pass a destroyed railroad bridge as they enter Burma from neighboring Thailand.*

main fleet, though, which is at sea. A British air attack against the Japanese force fails. Over several days, Japanese aircraft destroy the carrier *Hermes*, two heavy cruisers, an Australian destroyer, and several merchant ships.

APRIL 3-9

PACIFIC, *PHILIPPINES*
Japan launches its final offensive on Bataan, beginning with air and artillery bombardments. The US line is penetrated on the 4th. Major General Jonathan Wainright, commanding the US and Filipino forces, cannot mount an effective counterattack with his decimated units. Following the surrender on the 9th, some 78,000 US and Filipino troops are forced to make a 65-mile (104-km) march without sustenance, and are constantly beaten. Many die along the way. Wainright escapes with 2000 men to Corregidor Island off Bataan.

APRIL 10-23

FAR EAST, *BURMA*
Japan begins an offensive after reinforcements arrive. Lieutenant General

▲ *Japanese troops establish control in the Dutch East Indies following their conquest of the resource-rich islands.*

▼ *US troops captured by the Japanese following the capitulation of US and Filipino forces on Bataan, the Philippines.*

of Allied Land Forces in Australia, under the supreme command of US General Douglas MacArthur.

MARCH 28-29

AIR WAR, *GERMANY*
RAF bombers, including the new Lancaster, attack Lübeck on the Baltic coast. The raid on the historic, timber-built houses of the town signals a change in Bomber Command's strategy, which is now concentrating on the civilian population.

SEA WAR, *BAY OF BISCAY*
Britain's Combined Operations launches an operation to destroy the St. Nazaire dry-dock in France with a force of 611 men. The objective is to prevent the German battleship *Tirpitz* (currently in Norway) being able to use the only dock large enough to enable it to mount commerce-destroying operations in the Atlantic. An old destroyer, *Campbeltown*, is filled with explosives and destroys the lock gates after ramming them. A commando force attacks St. Nazaire's dock facilities, but 144 men die and over half are captured.

MARCH 29

POLITICS, *BRITAIN/INDIA*
Britain announces its proposals to grant India semi-independent status when the war ends.

APRIL 2-8

SEA WAR, *FAR EAST*
Japan's First Air Fleet attacks British air and sea bases in Trincomalee and Colombo, Ceylon. It fails to hit the

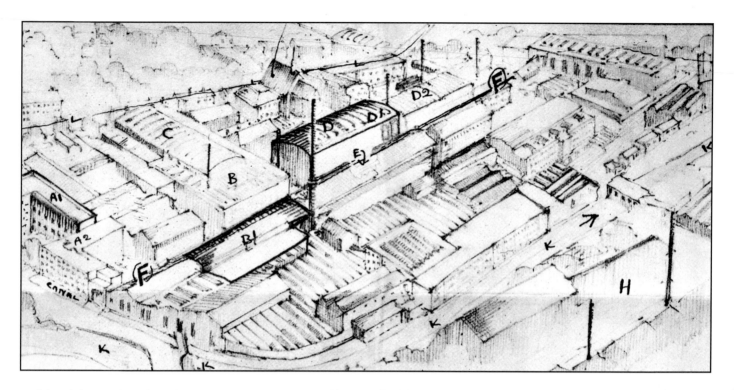

▲ A hand-drawn plan of the Augsburg diesel engine factory prepared for crew briefings before the raid to destroy it.

▶ James Doolittle, the pilot who led the first US air attack on Tokyo, presents awards to other airmen of the US Army Air Force.

William Slim fails to prevent the Japanese advancing on the oil fields at Yenangyaung in the south and sets large amounts of crude oil ablaze. The Chinese Sixty-fifth Army enters Burma to bolster the faltering defense against the Japanese. Around the central towns of Loikaw and Taunggyi, the Japanese 56th Division overwhelms the Chinese Sixth Army by the 23rd.

APRIL 17

AIR WAR, *GERMANY*
The RAF launch one of the war's most hazardous bomber raids, attacking a diesel engine factory in Augsburg. Seven of the 12 Lancaster bombers assigned to the daylight attack are lost and the other five sustain damage.

APRIL 18

POLITICS, *VICHY FRANCE*
Pierre Laval returns to head the government; Henri-Philippe Pétain continues as head of state. Laval is eager to enhance Franco-German relations and undermines the more hesitant approach advocated by Pétain.

AIR WAR, *JAPAN*
Lieutenant Colonel James Doolittle leads 16 B-25 bombers, launched from the aircraft carrier *Hornet,* on a daring mission to strike targets in Japan, including the capital Tokyo. The damage inflicted by the daylight raid is secondary to the impact on Japan's leaders, who are alarmed that US aircraft can strike at the heart of their homeland. This reinforces a decision to seek a decisive engagement to destroy US naval power in the Pacific.

APRIL 23

SEA WAR, *ATLANTIC*
The first "milch cow" submarine (*U-459*) delivers fuel and supplies to Germany's U-boats. This supply vessel doubles the operational range of the U-boats, which are no longer restricted by having to return to base for refueling.

APRIL 24

AIR WAR, *BRITAIN*
Germany bombs Exeter at the start of an air campaign against historic towns

and cities, following the British attack on Lübeck. Hitler has ordered raids against every English city featured in the famous Baedeker tourist books.

APRIL 29

FAR EAST, *BURMA*

The Japanese cut the Burma Road after seizing the town of Lashio, where the route ends. Chinese Nationalists are now almost wholly dependent on supply by air. The Japanese, being reinforced through the port at Rangoon, are advancing up the river valleys and plan to encircle the Allies in the Mandalay area. The Allies will then have to fight with their backs to the Irrawaddy River. The Burma Corps aims to fall back to India, whose defense is the main priority. Rapid Japanese advances, however, force the British to make a hurried (and potentially disastrous) retreat rather than an organized withdrawal.

APRIL 30

POLITICS, *SOVIET UNION*

Premier Joseph Stalin declares that the USSR has no territorial ambitions except to wrest its own lost lands from Nazi control.

▲ A U-boat in port. The "milch cow" supply submarines enabled U-boats to receive supplies at sea and thereby operate for long periods away from base.

▼ The German bombing of Bath damaged many fine buildings. This was one of the targets in the "Baedeker Raids" on historic English towns and cities.

MAY 1

FAR EAST, *BURMA*

The city of Mandalay falls to the Japanese. The Allies are now retreating, with the Chinese Sixth Army heading for the Chinese province of Yunnan. Units of the Fifth and Sixty-sixth Armies withdraw to Yunnan or northern Burma. General Joseph Stilwell leads a 100-strong group on a 400-mile (600-km) journey to Imphal, India. Heavy rain hampers the Allied retreat.

▲ *General Joseph Stilwell (right), the US commander of Chinese forces, leads his staff on a epic journey from Burma to India to escape the advancing Japanese troops.*

HOME FRONT, *SOVIET UNION*

A six-month evacuation commences, which is intended to move the besieged citizens of Leningrad to safety across Lake Ladoga. Around 448,700 people are taken out of the city.

MAY 2

SEA WAR, *PACIFIC*

Japan deploys a large carrier force to surprise the US Pacific Fleet in the Coral Sea as part of its plan to establish greater control of the Solomon Islands. A key aim is to seize Port Moresby on the southwest Pacific

▼ *The Japanese Navy's forces gather for the battle against the US Pacific Fleet in the Coral Sea.*

▲ *Major General Jonathan Wainright broadcasts the surrender of US and Filipino forces on Corregidor, the Philippines.*

island of Papua New Guinea, which would facilitate bomber attacks on Australia and help sever its communications with the United States. The Japanese have a Carrier Striking Force containing the carriers *Shokaku* and *Zuikaku* under Vice Admiral Takeo Takagi. They also have a Covering Group that includes the carrier *Shoho,* plus four heavy cruisers under Rear Admiral Aritomo Goto. There is also the Port Moresby Invasion Group and a support force. US codebreaking enables Admiral Chester Nimitz, the US Pacific Fleet commander, to prepare his forces. He deliberately withdraws from Tulagi in the Solomons before a Japanese attack in order to reinforce their belief that only one US carrier is operating in the area.

MAY 3

SEA WAR, *PACIFIC*
US Rear Admiral Frank Fletcher's Task Force 17, including the

▶ *British Royal Marines prepare to land on Madagascar in the Indian Ocean.*

carrier *Yorktown*, damages a Japanese destroyer, three minesweepers, and five aircraft off Tulagi during the Coral Sea engagement.

MAY 5–7

AFRICA, *MADAGASCAR*
Britain launches Operation Ironclad, the invasion of Vichy French Madagascar, with a battleship and two aircraft carriers carrying a landing force. The occupation is intended to deny Axis forces access to the island. An armed Vichy merchant cruiser and submarine are lost. A British

vessel is mined. The Diego Suarez naval base surrenders on the 7th.

MAY 5–10

PACIFIC, *PHILIPPINES*
US and Filipino forces on Corregidor finally surrender after a Japanese landing on the island. Some 12,495 US and Filipino troops (including Major Generals Jonathan Wainright and Edward King) are captured. The Philippines campaign has claimed 140,000 US and Filipino lives, plus 4000 Japanese dead.

◄ Canadian troops in Ontario. Thousands of men became liable for military service after full conscription was introduced.

US destroyer *Sims*, and the tanker *Neosho* (which is mistaken for a carrier) is scuttled. US forces successfully destroy the *Shoho* and 21 aircraft that attempt to engage the US carriers.

MAY 8

SEA WAR, *PACIFIC*

US aircraft damage the *Shokaku*, while *Zuikaku*'s aircraft losses are very serious in the Battle of the Coral Sea. Japanese aircraft hit the *Lexington*, which is later scuttled, and damage the *Yorktown*. This is the first ever battle fought exclusively with carrier aircraft. The US Navy loses a carrier but repairs to the *Yorktown* are speedy. Japan loses a smaller carrier while the other two Coral Sea carriers will be unfit for action in the approaching battle at Midway. Large numbers of Japanese aircraft and experienced pilots have also been lost. The abandonment of the Port Moresby landing is the first major blow to Japanese expansionism.

MAY 8–15

EASTERN FRONT, *CRIMEA*

The German Eleventh Army launches its attack against the Soviet Crimean Front. The Soviets resume their attempt to surround German units against the Sea of Azov in a battle around Kharkov. Germany's Eleventh Army captures the Crimean Kerch Peninsula on the 15th and continues to fight along the Donets River.

MAY 11

POLITICS, *CANADA*

Full conscription is introduced following a referendum on the issue, the only significant opposition being in Quebec province.

FAR EAST, *BURMA*

British and Commonwealth troops fight a last, bitter battle at Kalewa before the remaining forces in Burma finally enter the border region with

MAY 6–7

SEA WAR, *PACIFIC*

Although the opposing Japanese and US carrier groups are only 70 miles (112 km) apart, their reconnaissance flights fail to locate each other. Australian and US cruisers in Task Force 44, under British Rear Admiral Sir John Crace, are then sent to find the Port Moresby Invasion Group. Although poor weather prevents an attack, the unfolding battle leads the group to turn back to its Rabaul base on the 7th. Japanese aircraft sink the

▲ A German armored unit during Rommel's offensive against the British Eighth Army in Libya during 1942.

▼ US sailors abandon the Lexington during the Battle of the Coral Sea.

India and eventually reach Imphal. Japan now has control over some 80 percent of Burma.

SEA WAR, *MEDITERRANEAN*
A special German bomber force locates and sinks the British destroyers *Kipling*, *Lively*, and *Jackal* to the west of Alexandria, Egypt.

MAY 14

ESPIONAGE, *UNITED STATES*
US codebreakers deciphering Japanese radio messages obtain their first intelligence about the impending Japanese operation to destroy the US Pacific Fleet in the central Pacific Ocean by drawing into battle around Midway.

MAY 15

FAR EAST, *INDIA*
British and Commonwealth forces retreating from Burma begin to arrive in India. Some 13,463 British, Indian, and Burmese troops have been killed in the Burma campaign thus far.

The 95,000-strong Chinese force has been decimated, while Japan has suffered an estimated 5000–8000 casualties to date.

MAY 18

POLITICS, *BRITAIN*
Admiral Harwood assumes command of the British Mediterranean Fleet.

MAY 22

POLITICS, *MEXICO*
The Mexican government declares war on Germany, Italy, and Japan.

MAY 25

POLITICS, *AUSTRALIA*
Three people are arrested for conspiring to establish a fascist government to negotiate peace terms with Japan.

MAY 26–31

AFRICA, *LIBYA*
General Erwin Rommel attacks the Gazala Line in Libya. Italian armor strikes at Bir Hacheim, 40 miles (60 km) from the coast,

▲ *A view of the Germany city of Cologne after the British "1000 Bomber" raid.*

but is repulsed by Free French troops. Axis tanks try to outflank the Allied lines beyond Bir Hacheim. Although the British Eighth Army has 850 tanks (plus 150 in reserve), the Axis forces deploy their 630 tanks more effectively, and their antitank guns present a serious threat. British armor and aircraft engage Axis tanks at the Knightsbridge crossroads, behind the Gazala Line. Axis armor suffers serious fuel problems until the Italians penetrate the Gazala Line to bring up fresh supplies on the 31st.

MAY 27

HOME FRONT, *CZECHOSLOVAKIA*
British-trained Czech agents attack Reinhard Heydrich, the deputy chief of the SS, who has been appointed deputy governor of occupied Czechoslovakia. Heydrich is traveling in an open-top car without an escort when the agents strike.

MAY 30

AIR WAR, *GERMANY*
Britain launches its first "1000 Bomber" raid. The target is Cologne. Over 59,000 people are made homeless. The British lose 40 aircraft.

MAY 31

AIR WAR, *GERMANY*
British Mosquito bombers, constructed from wood, make the first of many raids over Germany.

◄ US dive-bombers in action against the Japanese during the decisive Battle of Midway.

the US base at Midway and then destroy the US Pacific Fleet commanded by Admiral Chester Nimitz. Japan deploys 165 vessels, including eight carriers, but they are too widely dispersed to provide mutual support. US code-breakers are able to warn the Pacific Fleet, which then converges to repel the Midway attack and is not diverted by a raid on the Aleutian Islands. The US Navy has a smaller force but has managed to gather three carriers.

The reconnaissance operation by Japan's 29 large cruiser submarines fails to establish the movements of the Pacific Fleet. Nagumo has no idea of US deployments when he first strikes Midway. Japan's I Carrier Striking Force

JUNE 1

AIR WAR, *GERMANY*
Britain launches a "1000 Bomber" raid against Essen and the Ruhr industrial area.

JUNE 4

SEA WAR, *PACIFIC*
The Battle of Midway begins. Japan's Admiral Chuichi Nagumo aims to seize

▼ A German woman collects water from a street tap. Water, gas, and electricity supplies were all disrupted by bombing.

▲ *The Japanese cruiser* Mogami *after sustaining an attack by US aircraft during the Battle of Midway.*

is decimated by US aircraft and three heavy carriers are lost. Japan's fourth carrier, *Hiryu*, then cripples the US carrier *Yorktown* before herself being fatally hit. Japan's attempt to destroy the enemy with its superior forces by luring it into a surface battle has failed. The loss of half of its carrier strength, plus 275 aircraft, puts Japan on the defensive in the Pacific.

JUNE 7

EASTERN FRONT, *UKRAINE*
The siege of Sebastopol intensifies with massive assaults by Germany's Eleventh Army. Sebastopol is under heavy shelling from German siege artillery, which includes the *Dora* gun, the world's largest mortar. The Soviet defenders continue to hold out, despite the intense bombardment.

JUNE 10

HOME FRONT, *CZECHOSLOVAKIA*
Reinhard Heydrich, the deputy governor of occupied Czechoslovakia and architect of the Nazi genocide program, dies after an attack by Czech agents on May 27. In retaliation, over 1000 Czechs accused of anti-Nazi activities are murdered, 3000 Czech Jews are deported for extermination,

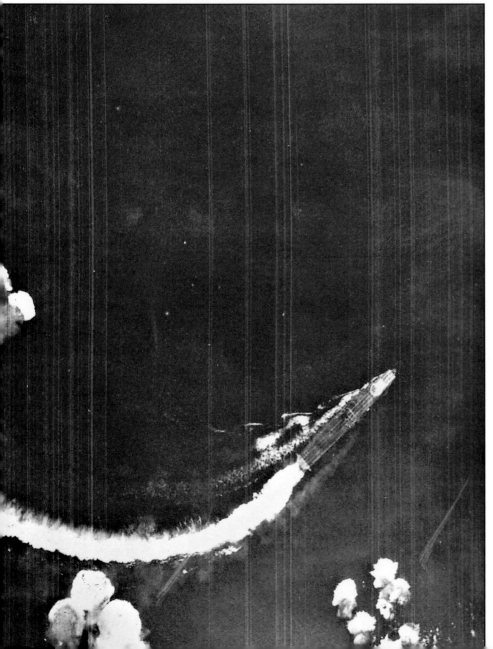

◄ *An aerial photograph of the Japanese carrier* Hiryu *during the Battle of Midway. The ship was set ablaze by a US air attack and subsequently scuttled.*

and 150 Berlin Jews are killed. The Czech village of Lidice is leveled. Its men are executed; its women and children are sent to concentration camps.

JUNE 10–13

AFRICA, *LIBYA*
Axis forces have created a fortified area ("the Cauldron") inside the Allied lines. Following the Free French withdrawal from Bir Hacheim on the 10th–11th, Axis armor advances east from the Cauldron to threaten the entire Eighth Army. British commander General Neil Ritchie orders a withdrawal on the 13th.

▼ *Soviet reinforcements being sent to Sebastopol. Despite fierce resistance, the port was captured by the Germans.*

JUNE 18

POLITICS, *ALLIES*
At the Second Washington Conference in the United States, British Prime Minister Winston Churchill and US President Franklin D. Roosevelt try to agree a strategy in Europe for 1942–43. Conditions appear unsuitable for a "Second Front" in France, so Churchill proposes a North African invasion. In July, Roosevelt accepts that Europe cannot yet be attacked and agrees to Churchill's North African option, later code-named Operation Torch. Cooperation in nuclear research is also agreed on.

▲ *British troops surrender to the Afrika Korps after the fall of Tobruk.*

AIR WAR, *GERMANY*
Britain launches a "1000 Bomber" raid on Bremen.

JUNE 21

AFRICA, *LIBYA*
Following the Allied withdrawal into Egypt, the Tobruk garrison suddenly falls following German land and air attacks. Some 30,000 men, rations, and fuel are seized. Newly-promoted Field Marshal Erwin Rommel continues chasing the retreating Allies, taking

Mersa Matruh on the 28th. General Sir Claude Auchinleck, British Middle East commander, takes personal charge of the Eighth Army and establishes a fortified line. This runs inland for 40 miles (64 km) from El Alamein on the coast to the impassable Quattara Depression. Rommel fails to penetrate the position, and the front stabilizes as his lines of supply in the Mediterranean are being strained by British air and sea attacks, assisted by intelligence from codebreaking.

JUNE 25

POLITICS, *UNITED STATES*
Major General Dwight D. Eisenhower assumes command of US forces in Europe.

JUNE 28

EASTERN FRONT, *UKRAINE*
Germany launches its summer offensive, with its Army Group South attacking east from Kursk toward Voronezh, which falls nine days later.

JULY 4–10

EASTERN FRONT, *CRIMEA*
The siege of Sebastopol ends with the Germans capturing 90,000 troops.
SEA WAR, *ARCTIC*
British Admiral of the Fleet Sir Dudley Pound gives a disastrous order for the PQ-17 convoy to disperse after air and U-boat attacks. The escorts therefore withdraw, leaving the convoy's isolated merchant ships vulnerable. PQ-17 loses 23 vessels out of 33 and enormous amounts of supplies during renewed German attacks.

JULY 13

EASTERN FRONT, *CAUCASUS*
Adolf Hitler orders simultaneous attacks on Stalingrad and the Caucasus, despite the strain this causes to his armies. Army Group B's advance toward Stalingrad is slowed after Hitler redeploys the Fourth Panzer Army to Army Group A's Caucasus drive. He believes Army Group A will not be able to cross the Don River without reinforcements. Field Marshal Fedor von Bock, leading Army Group B, is later dismissed for opposing this. The divergence of the two groups creates a gap through which Soviet forces are able to escape.

▲ *A British vessel from the PQ-17 Arctic convoy sinks after being torpedoed by a U-boat. The decision to scatter the convoy led to it suffering severe losses.*

JULY 21

POLITICS, *UNITED STATES*
Admiral William Leahy becomes the president's personal chief-of-staff. In this role he is closely involved in key military decisions.

JULY 23

EASTERN FRONT, *UKRAINE*
The city of Rostov is taken by

AUGUST 1

Germany's Army Group A, which then crosses the Don River and makes a broad advance into the Caucasus.

AUGUST 1

EASTERN FRONT, *UKRAINE*
Adolf Hitler moves the Fourth Panzer Army back to Stalingrad to accelerate the German advance. The Eleventh Army receives similar orders. This seriously strains the Caucasus advance.

AUGUST 7–21

PACIFIC, *SOLOMONS*
The US 1st Marine Division lands on Guadalcanal Island to overwhelm the 2200 Japanese garrison and capture the partly-built airfield that would enable bombers to strike Allied sealanes. Tulagi is also taken. US naval forces are subjected to air attacks and eventually withdraw. The Marines suffer supply shortages but are later relieved by air and sea. Japan sinks four cruisers on the 9th and starts landing forces by night to harass the Marines. US forces destroy the first major Japanese attacks on the Tenaru River on the 9th. Fighting now centers on the airstrip known as Henderson Field.

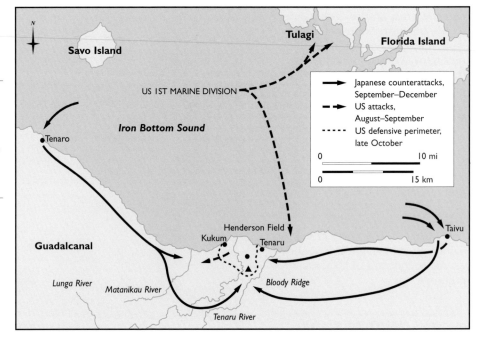

AUGUST 9

SEA WAR, *PACIFIC*
At the Battle of Savo Island, between Guadalcanal and Tulagi, the US Navy suffers one of its most serious defeats. A Japanese cruiser squadron, aiming to attack transports unloading off Guadalcanal, surprises five US and Australian cruisers. Superior night-fighting and gunnery skills enable the Japanese to sink four cruisers and damage the remaining one. The Japanese retire, fearing an air attack, while the US transports withdraw leaving the troops on Guadalcanal with serious supply problems.

AUGUST 10–15

SEA WAR, *MEDITERRANEAN*
Operation Pedestal, a 14-ship, Gibraltar-to-Malta

▼ *A German soldier leaps into action near Stalingrad.*

▲ *The fighting on Guadalcanal was among the most savage of the Pacific War, especially near Henderson Field.*

convoy, is devastated by enemy surface vessel, U-boat, and air attacks. Only four vessels reach Malta, but they enable the besieged island to survive.

AUGUST 12

POLITICS, *ALLIES*
Winston Churchill meets Joseph Stalin for the first time in talks that focus mainly on the decision to delay forming a "Second Front" in Europe.

AUGUST 13

POLITICS, *BRITAIN*
Lieutenant General Bernard Montgomery replaces General Neil Ritchie as Eighth Army commander. General Sir Harold Alexander replaces General Sir Claude Auchinleck as Middle East commander on the 18th.

AUGUST 17

AIR WAR, *FRANCE*
The first wholly US bomber raid over Europe strikes targets in France.

AUGUST 19

WESTERN FRONT, *FRANCE*
A force of 5000 Canadian, 1000 British, and 50 US troops attacks the port of Dieppe. It is a "reconnaissance in force" to gain experience and intelligence for landing a force on the continent. The assault is disastrous. Allied losses include almost 4000 men killed or captured.

▲ *American ground crew prepare an aircraft for action during US offensives against the Japanese on Guadalcanal.*

AUGUST 19–24

EASTERN FRONT, *SOVIET UNION*
Determined drives toward Stalingrad by Germany's Army Group B eventually reach the Volga River. Fierce resistance by the Soviet forces begins within a 30-mile (45-km) range of the city of Stalingrad.

AUGUST 22

POLITICS, *BRAZIL*
The government declares war on Germany and Italy.

AUGUST 22–25

SEA WAR, *PACIFIC*
In the Battle of the Eastern Solomons, Admiral Frank Fletcher's three-carrier task force engages a Japanese convoy bound for Guadalcanal, plus three other carriers operating in two separate groups. The Japanese light carrier *Ryujo*, a destroyer, plus 90 aircraft are lost. The US carrier *Enterprise* is damaged and 17 US aircraft downed.

AUGUST 23

AIR WAR, *SOVIET UNION*
A raid by 600 German bombers on Stalingrad claims thousands of lives.

AUGUST 30

AFRICA, *EGYPT*
Germany's tanks try to outflank the Allied line at El Alamein, but meet dense minefields and fierce resistance. The offense disintegrates under air attack and supply problems.

SEPTEMBER 2

FINAL SOLUTION, *POLAND*
The Nazis are "clearing" the Jewish Warsaw Ghetto. Over 50,000 Jews have been killed by poison gas or sent to concentration camps. The SS (*Schutzstaffel* – protection squad), a fanatical Nazi military and security organization, is chiefly responsible for Nazi persecution of the Jews and others deemed to be ideological or racial enemies of the Third Reich.

SEPTEMBER 9

POLITICS, *GERMANY*
Adolf Hitler dismisses Field Marshal Wilhelm List, commander of Army Group A laying siege to Stalingrad, for criticizing his Eastern Front strategy. General Paul von Kleist replaces him.

SEPTEMBER 12

SEA WAR, *ATLANTIC*
The liner *Laconia*, carrying 1800 Italian prisoners and Allied service

DECISIVE WEAPONS

CONVOYS

Convoys provided protective escorts for merchant vessels against enemy surface, submerged, or air attack. Allied convoys, often containing over 50 vessels, sailed in columns and weaved their way across the sea-lanes. In the Atlantic and Arctic, the atrocious weather reduced visibility, froze the crews, and created great waves that left vessels vulnerable to collision.

The main threat to Allied convoys were the U-boats, which inflicted critical losses on shipping. Antisubmarine measures gradually improved, however, with enhanced air and sea coordination, new tactics, and scientific innovations. Shipbuilding was also increased to replace lost vessels. The interception of German radio transmissions, centimetric radar, escort carriers, U-boat-detection technology (asdic and sonar), improved depth-charges, and launchers all helped protect convoys.

Germany's campaign to destroy Allied control of the Atlantic sea-lanes was especially critical as Britain came to rely upon North American aid. In the North Atlantic alone, some 2232 vessels were sunk, but the destruction of 785 U-boats secured Allied command of the sea-lanes.

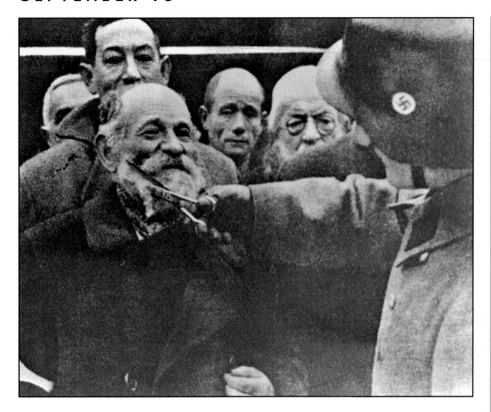

families, is sunk by *U-156*. A US bomber attacks *U-156* while it tries to aid the survivors. As a result, German navy chief Admiral Karl Doenitz instructs *U-156* to cancel the rescue. In future, no lifesaving attempts will be made by U-boats after an attack.

SEPTEMBER 13

PACIFIC, *SOLOMONS*
At the Battle of Bloody Ridge, 6000 Japanese try to seize Henderson Field, Guadalcanal, but are repulsed.

SEPTEMBER 15

SEA WAR, *PACIFIC*
Two Japanese submarines intercept a carrier force escorting troop transports to Guadalcanal. The US carrier *Wasp* and a destroyer are lost, but the troop transports arrive safely.

SEPTEMBER 24

POLITICS, *GERMANY*
General Franz Halder, chief of the General Staff, is replaced by General Kurt Zeitzler. Halder has made the mistake of criticizing Adolf Hitler's Eastern Front strategy, which demands that German troops should not retreat.

OCTOBER 18

POLITICS, *UNITED STATES*
Vice Admiral William Halsey replaces Vice Admiral Robert Ghormley as South Pacific Area commander.

▲ *A German soldier removes the beard of a Jewish man inside the Warsaw Ghetto. The abuse and terrorizing of Jews across Europe was Nazi policy.*

OCTOBER 22

AIR WAR, *ITALY*
Britain launches a series of raids on the industrial areas around Turin, Milan, and Genoa.

OCTOBER 23

AFRICA, *EGYPT*
The Battle of El Alamein begins. General Bernard Montgomery's carefully-prepared attack by 195,000 Allied troops against 104,000 Axis men begins with an enormous artillery bombardment and numerous decep-tion measures. Massive mine-clearance operations enable Allied armor forma-tions to push forward and leave the infantry to widen the gaps. Field Marshal Erwin Rommel is in Germany, but immediately returns after the temporary commander, General Georg Stumme, dies suddenly. First reports confirm that the Allies have made an excellent start, although Axis resis-tance is fierce.

OCTOBER 26

SEA WAR, *PACIFIC*
At the Battle of Santa Cruz, Japanese carriers approach Guadalcanal and fatally damage the US carrier *Hornet*

KEY PERSONALITIES

FIELD MARSHAL SIR BERNARD MONTGOMERY

Bernard Montgomery (1887–1976) began World War II leading a British division to France in 1939. After Dunkirk, he became a corps commander before Prime Minister Winston Churchill appointed him to lead the Eighth Army in the Western Desert.

Montgomery, exploiting the arrival of more men and supplies, halted Germany's drive into Egypt in 1942. Using careful planning and his ability to inspire confidence in his men, Montgomery inflicted the first British defeat on the German Army at El Alamein. This raised public morale and bolstered his reputation. After the landing of Allied armies in North Africa he helped secure the defeat of Axis forces in the desert.

After commanding the British Eighth Army in the 1943 invasions of Sicily and Italy, he was recalled to Britain in January 1944. Montgomery now had the task of helping prepare the enormous operation to invade northwest Europe. During the June 1944 D-Day landings he was commander of ground forces under US General Dwight D. Eisenhower's supreme command. From August, he became 21st Army Group commander. His relationship with US commanders was not always harmonious. He particularly disagreed with Eisenhower over the strategy for defeating Germany, favoring an all-out thrust rather than the more cautious "broad front" plan that was adopted. At the Battle of the Bulge in December 1944 Montgomery temporarily commanded two US armies, but then returned to 21st Army Group for the Rhine crossings to seal the defeat of Germany in 1945.

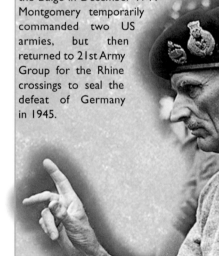

(leaving the US Pacific Fleet with one carrier). The Japanese cruiser *Yura* is sunk and the carrier *Shokaku* rendered ineffective by aircraft strikes.

NOVEMBER 2–24

AFRICA, *EGYPT/LIBYA*

Field Marshal Erwin Rommel, severely lacking supplies, decides to withdraw from El Alamein. He delays this for 48 hours, after Adolf Hitler's order to stand firm, but then continues following further Allied attacks. The Allies push him back to Tobruk, Benghazi, and then El Agheila by the 24th. Germany and Italy have lost 59,000 men killed, wounded, or captured. The Allies have suffered 13,000 killed, wounded, or missing. General Bernard Montgomery's victory saves the Suez Canal and raises Allied morale. Alamein is the first major defeat of German forces during the war.

NOVEMBER 5

AFRICA, *MADAGASCAR*

Vichy French forces in control of the island surrender.

NOVEMBER 8–11

AFRICA, *MOROCCO/ALGERIA*

Three Allied Task Forces, including five carriers, land 34,000 US troops near Casablanca, 39,000 US and British

▶ *Gurkhas of the British Eighth Army go on the attack during the Battle of El Alamein.*

▲ *A Japanese bomber in action against US warships during the Battle of Santa Cruz.*

troops near Oran (accompanied by a parachute assault), and 33,000 troops near Algiers. US General Dwight D. Eisenhower, the supreme commander, aims to seize Vichy French North Africa as a springboard for future operations to clear the whole of North Africa of Axis forces. Admiral Jean François Darlan, Vichy commissioner in Africa, causes

diplomatic turbulence by arranging a cease-fire and agreeing to support the Allies. The surprise invasion is a product of successful interservice planning, and Rommel is now fighting on two fronts.

NOVEMBER 11

WESTERN FRONT, *VICHY FRANCE*

German and Italian forces occupy Vichy France to prevent an Allied invasion from the former Vichy French territories in North Africa.

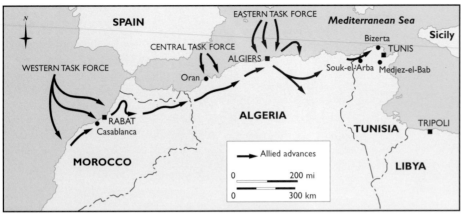

NOVEMBER 12–14

PACIFIC, *SOLOMONS*

A US cruiser-destroyer squadron inflicts serious losses on a Japanese naval force of 18 warships attempting to bombard Guadalcanal's Henderson Field, and also lands 11,000 troops.

NOVEMBER 17–28

AFRICA, *TUNISIA*

British paratroopers land at Souk-el-Arba and join a limited Allied advance toward Bizerta. Thousands of German reinforcements are arriving daily, and the Allies are not yet ready for a large offensive. By the 28th, they are within 20 miles (32 km) of Tunis but are halted by Axis counterattacks. Allied reinforcements from Algiers are slowed by rain and mud. A stalemate develops across much of Tunisia.

NOVEMBER 19

EASTERN FRONT, *UKRAINE*

General Georgi Zhukov launches a Soviet counteroffensive at Stalingrad with 10 armies, 900 tanks, and 1100 aircraft, to be carried out along a front of 260 miles (416 km). Soviet forces

▲ *The Allied landings in North Africa precipitated the surrender of the Vichy French forces stationed there.*

▶ *German troops trapped outside Stalingrad search the skies for the arrival of supplies being brought by aircraft.*

north and south of Stalingrad are to trap the Germans in a pincer movement. The attack is made during the frost, which assists tank mobility. It also coincides with the Allied North African landings, which divert Germany's attention. Allied supplies have equipped the Soviet forces for the advance. The German front buckles.

NOVEMBER 25

EASTERN FRONT, *UKRAINE*

The airlift to supply the German Sixth Army trapped around Stalingrad commences with 320 aircraft. The operation, which eventually requires 500 aircraft, lasts until February 1943.

NOVEMBER 27

SEA WAR, *MEDITERRANEAN*

Vichy French naval forces in Toulon are scuttled with the loss of 72

▼ *German troops in action during the desperate struggle against the Soviet forces outside Stalingrad.*

for postwar Britain that aim to provide a state pension and health care for everyone. This reflects aspirations for social justice to tackle society's problems.

DECEMBER 2

TECHNOLOGY, *UNITED STATES*
The first successful controlled nuclear "chain reaction" is made. It is a key step in making an atomic bomb. In this reaction, neutrons from the splitting of uranium atoms split other uranium atoms, releasing enormous energy rapidly in the form of a massive explosion.

DECEMBER 6–9

AFRICA, *TUNISIA*
Two German tank columns try to retake Medjez-el-Bab, 35 miles (40 km) southwest of Tunis. However, Allied armor and aircraft block one column as it advances, while artillery fire stops the second.

▼ *A German Junkers Ju 52 transport aircraft is refueled during the airlift that attempted to sustain the trapped Army inside the city of Stalingrad.*

DECEMBER 9

POLITICS, *UNITED STATES*
General Alexander Patch succeeds Lieutenant General Alexander Vandegrift as commander of operations on Guadalcanal. The 1st Marine Division is replaced by the US XIV Corps.

DECEMBER 10

PACIFIC, *SOLOMONS*
The Japanese are establishing a well-defended front some six miles (9 km) west of Henderson Field, Guadalcanal. Japan has a 20,000-strong force, however, while there are 58,000 US troops who are better equipped and supplied on the island. Japanese prospects are poor.

DECEMBER 11

SEA WAR, *FRANCE*
A British commando force of 10 men canoes up the Gironde River and disables six vessels in Bordeaux harbor with mines in a daring raid.

DECEMBER 19

EASTERN FRONT, *UKRAINE*
Field Marshal Erich von Manstein's attempt to relieve the German Sixth

vessels, including three battleships, before the Germans can seize them.

NOVEMBER 30

SEA WAR, *PACIFIC*
At the Battle of Tassafaronga, five US heavy cruisers and seven destroyers attack a Japanese convoy of eight destroyers bound for Guadalcanal. Japan loses one destroyer; the US four cruisers.

DECEMBER 1

POLITICS, *BRITAIN*
A report by Liberal economist Sir William Beveridge outlines proposals

DECEMBER 19

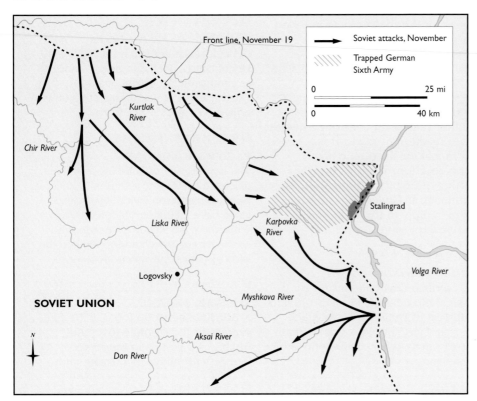

▲ *Dead Japanese troops lying in a river bed on Guadalcanal. Thousands of Japanese soldiers died on the island.*

▲ *The Red Army completely surrounded the German Sixth Army outside Stalingrad. A German counteroffensive failed to break the Soviet grip.*

▼ *Soviet troops battle their way forward in the ruins of Stalingrad as the Red Army tightens its grip on the city. The damaged buildings indicate the savage fighting.*

Army with an attack by Army Group Don (13 divisions formed from Army Group A in the north) advances to within 35 miles (56 km) of Stalingrad in the face of heavy resistance. Despite Manstein's pleas for General Friedrich von Paulus' Sixth Army to launch a break-out, Adolf Hitler orders him not to retreat, but fuel shortages limit any possible action anyway. The year ends with Soviet offensives pushing the German relief force westward. In Stalingrad, German troops are suffering severe hardships, chiefly due to the weather and supply shortages.

DECEMBER 24

POLITICS, *VICHY FRANCE*
Admiral Jean François Darlan, high commissioner in North Africa, is shot dead by a young Frenchman who accuses him of betraying the Vichy regime.

DECEMBER 30–31

SEA WAR, *ARCTIC*
At the Battle of the Barents Sea, the German pocket battleship *Lützow*, heavy cruiser *Admiral Hipper*, and six destroyers attempt to destroy the Allied Arctic convoy JW-51B. Although outnumbered, the British use superior tactics and exploit the German caution arising from orders not to sustain serious damage. Germany has one destroyer sunk, while the British also lose a destroyer and have one badly damaged. The battle outrages Adolf Hitler, who believes that the German

▲ *Henri-Philippe Pétain (left) with Admiral François Darlan, who ordered Vichy French forces in North Africa to surrender after the Allied invasion.*

fleet is tying down a huge amount of manpower and resources for very little result. Indeed, the Battle of the Barents Sea will lead to the end of significant sorties by major German surface vessels for the rest of the war.

1943

Allied successes in Papua New Guinea and the Solomon Islands, together with hard-won British and Chinese advances in Burma, forced the Japanese onto the defensive in the Pacific and Far East. Allied forces also triumphed in North Africa and went on to invade Italy, triggering the fall of Mussolini, while in the Soviet Union the clash of armor at Kursk resulted in a key German defeat.

JANUARY 1–3

EASTERN FRONT, *CAUCASUS*
Soviet troops launch offensives to encircle the German forces in the north of the region. Since August 1942 the Germans have been attempting to conquer the resource-rich area and reach the oil supplies of the Near and Middle East. The Soviet South Front moves toward Rostov and the Terek River, from where the Germans withdraw on the 3rd.

JANUARY 2

PACIFIC, *PAPUA NEW GUINEA*
US forces meet stubborn Japanese resistance after assaulting Buna on the east coast.

JANUARY 3

SEA WAR, *MEDITERRANEAN*
British Chariot "human torpedoes" damage the Italian cruiser *Ulpio* and a tanker in Palermo harbor, Sicily.

JANUARY 3–9

SEA WAR, *ATLANTIC*
U-boats destroy seven of nine tankers,

▼ *US Marine Corps pilots scramble to attack Japanese forces on Guadalcanal.*

JANUARY 9

POLITICS, *CHINA*

The Japanese puppet government declares war on both Britain and the United States.

JANUARY 10

EASTERN FRONT, *CAUCASUS*

Soviet attacks from the north, south, and east of Stalingrad split Germany's Sixth Army into pockets and isolate them from any sort of relief. Axis forces across southern Russia are under intense pressure.

JANUARY 10–31

PACIFIC, *GUADALCANAL*

A force of 50,000 US troops launches a westward offensive to destroy strong Japanese jungle positions. A disease-ridden and starving force of 15,000 Japanese troops mounts fierce resistance and fights a rearguard action at Tassafaronga Point. The Japanese have decided to evacuate Guadalcanal.

JANUARY 13

PACIFIC, *PAPUA NEW GUINEA*

The Japanese in New Guinea finally lose control of the Kokoda Trail – a major route across the Owen Stanley Range to Port Moresby, which they intended to use as an air base. Fighting between General Douglas MacArthur's Australian and US troops and the Japanese has been going on since March 1942.

carrying 100,000 tons (90,720 metric tonnes) of oil in the TM-1 convoy, which is sailing from the Caribbean to the Mediterranean.

▲ A German U-boat undergoes routine maintenance while on the lookout for Allied shipping in the Mediterranean.

▼ Admiral Karl Doenitz (third from left), replaced Erich Raeder as commander-in-chief of German naval forces.

JANUARY 5

AFRICA, *TUNISIA*

The US Fifth Army is formed under Lieutenant General Mark Clark. Allied forces form a line from Cape Serrat on the Mediterranean to Gafsa in the south. A stalemate arises in Tunisia until Field Marshal Erwin Rommel's offensive in February.

JANUARY 6

POLITICS, *GERMANY*

Admiral Erich Raeder resigns as commander-in-chief of naval forces following the blunders made at the Battle of the Barents Sea in December. Admiral Karl Doenitz replaces him.

JANUARY 6–9

SEA WAR, *PACIFIC*

At the Battle of Huon Gulf, the Allies gather aircraft from across the south-west Pacific to launch repeated attacks on Japanese convoys carrying troops to Papua New Guinea. Three transports and some 80 Japanese aircraft are lost. Allied casualties during the action are comparatively light.

JANUARY 14-23

JANUARY 14-23

POLITICS, *ALLIES*

British Prime Minister Winston Churchill and US President Franklin D. Roosevelt meet at Casablanca, Morocco. The conference highlights differences between them regarding the defeat of Hitler.

The British want to keep fighting in the Mediterranean before the main attack on Europe via the English Channel. They propose invasions of Sicily and Italy as a means of drawing German reserves away from France and the Low Countries, which will precipitate the fall of Mussolini; and establishing air bases in Italy, from where German armaments factories and Romanian oil-producing facilities can be bombed.

The Americans believe this will only dissipate resources for the cross-Channel invasion, and tie down forces in a sideshow. They believe the quickest way to defeat Hitler is an invasion of northern France. However, as a cross-Channel invasion is not possible in 1943, they grudgingly accept the invasion of Sicily (though no invasion of Italy is planned).

A further source of disagreement is Roosevelt's "unconditional surrender" call. Churchill wants to split the Axis by treating Italy differently, but is persuaded to go along with the US view after considering that a more lenient treatment of Italy will only antagonize Greece and Yugoslavia.

▼ *Prime Minister Churchill and President Roosevelt at the Casablanca Conference, where differences of strategy arose between Great Britain and the United States.*

JANUARY 15-22

AFRICA, *LIBYA*

The British Eighth Army attacks Field Marshal Erwin Rommel's forces at Buerat and pursues them to the Homs and Tarhuna area, approximately 100 miles (150 km) from Tripoli, the capital. British forces reach Homs on the 19th, and Rommel resumes his

▲ *Jewish fighters reinforce a strongpoint in the Warsaw Ghetto at the beginning of their uprising against the Germans.*

retreat toward Tunisia. Although Rommel has been ordered to defend Tripoli, he decides to save his troops and abandons the city on the 22nd to make a stand around Mareth.

JANUARY 16-17

EASTERN FRONT, *CAUCASUS*
The Soviet Fifty-sixth Army begins an attack to take the town of Krasnador. Southern Front forces are halted by German resistance between the northern Donets and Manych Rivers.

JANUARY 18

EASTERN FRONT, *POLAND*
Jewish fighters in the Warsaw Ghetto begin attacking German troops. Resistance was triggered by the resumption of deportations to extermination camps, which has been suspended since October 1942.

JANUARY 21

PACIFIC, *PAPUA NEW GUINEA*
After capturing Sanananda in New Guinea, the Allies prepare to advance northwestward to clear the Japanese from Salamua and Lae. Allied control of the sea and air around Papua New Guinea will force the Japanese finally to abandon the island.

JANUARY 29

PACIFIC, *PAPUA NEW GUINEA*
Allied troops force the Japanese to withdraw from Wau at the start of the Bulldog Track, the second route used by the Japanese for their offensive against Port Moresby.

JANUARY 30

AIR WAR, *GERMANY*
In the escalating Allied air offensive, British bombers make the first daylight bombing raid over Berlin.

KEY PERSONALITIES

GENERAL DOUGLAS MACARTHUR

Douglas MacArthur (1880–1964) was appointed commander of US troops in the Far East in July 1941. After the Japanese declared war in December, he directed the defense of the Philippines from the islands. He finally left for Australia in March 1942 to assume command of the whole of the Southwest Pacific theater.

MacArthur then led a campaign to free Papua New Guinea before commanding the Pacific "island-hopping" operations that finally reached the Philippines in October 1944. In April 1945, MacArthur became commander of the US Army in the Pacific and then Supreme Allied Commander for the occupation of Japan. In this role he accepted the Japanese surrender.

This flamboyant general always appeared to achieve his objectives yet maintain low casualty rates. His self-publicity has, however, led some historians to scrutinize the claims he made about his campaigns.

FEBRUARY 1-9

PACIFIC, *GUADALCANAL*
Japanese Navy warships evacuate 13,000 troops in night operations from the island. Their abandonment of Guadalcanal marks the first major land defeat of Japan. The Japanese have lost 10,000 men killed; the Americans some 1600.

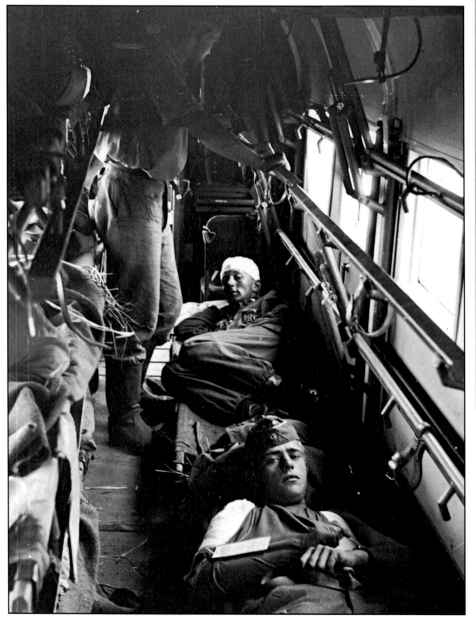

◄ *Some of the lucky ones: German casualties evacuated out of Stalingrad before the defeat of the Sixth Army.*

FEBRUARY 2

▶ *British Avro Lancaster heavy bombers were used against German U-boats in the Bay of Biscay.*

FEBRUARY 2

EASTERN FRONT, *CAUCASUS*

The siege of Stalingrad ends: Field Marshal Friedrich von Paulus and 93,000 German troops surrender. The Sixth Army has finally collapsed under the strain of supply shortages and constant attacks masterminded by Marshal Georgi Zhukov.

FEBRUARY 4

AIR WAR, *FRANCE*

British and US bombers launch Operation Gondola with a series of raids aimed at destroying U-boats in the Bay of Biscay. Bombers use immensely powerful searchlights to illuminate submarines during attacks.

▼ *Some of Orde Wingate's Chindits who operated behind Japanese lines in Burma in February 1943.*

FEBRUARY 8

EASTERN FRONT, *UKRAINE*

In their continuing offensive Soviet forces take the city of Kursk, which will be the site of a major battle.

FEBRUARY 9

SEA WAR, *MEDITERRANEAN*

An Axis convoy carrying reinforcements to Tunisia leaves Italy. Malta-based Allied aircraft sink 10 vessels between February 9 and March 22. Minefields and British submarines also destroy several of the ships.

FEBRUARY 12–14

EASTERN FRONT, *CAUCASUS*

The Soviets capture Krasnodar on the 12th and Rostov on the Don River two days later.

FEBRUARY 14–22

AFRICA, *TUNISIA*

Field Marshal Erwin Rommel launches an attack northwest from his fortified zone at Mareth to break through Allied forces between the Axis front and Bône on the coast. In the Battle of Kasserine Pass his forces strike the US II Corps and cause panic among the ranks.

US forces are 100 miles (160 km) from Gabès, a key part of Germany's Mareth Line because of its crossroads, port, and airfield. German troops exploit poor US command, land and air coordination, unit dispositions, and the inexperience of some troops. Attacks reach Thala until they lose momentum and Rommel orders a withdrawal. He loses 2000 men; the Americans 10,000.

FEBRUARY 15

EASTERN FRONT, *UKRAINE*

Kharkov and other cities are liberated as Soviet forces reoccupy territory held by the Germans. Stalin has begun to think of total victory in 1943.

FEBRUARY 16–21

HOME FRONT, *GERMANY*
Student demonstrations against Hitler's regime take place in Munich. Protests in other university cities in Germany and Austria then occur. Hans and Sophie Scholl, leaders of the anti-Nazi White Rose student group at the University of Munich, are beheaded on the 21st.

FEBRUARY 18

FAR EAST, *BURMA*
Brigadier Orde Wingate launches the first British Chindit mission. This 3000-strong, long-range penetration force aims to operate behind Japanese lines and disrupt communications. The Chindits are to be supplied by air. The six-week mission has limited military success but Prime Minister Winston Churchill is impressed by Wingate's unorthodox methods. As a result, further Chindit operations in Burma will be sanctioned.

▲ *An Allied merchant ship caught in heavy seas as a convoy makes its way across the Atlantic Ocean.*

FEBRUARY 18-27

EASTERN FRONT, *UKRAINE*
Field Marshal Erich von Manstein, commander of Army Group Don, launches a counteroffensive against the Red Army to crush the enemy thrust to the Dniepr River. Using four panzer corps, he isolates three Soviet armies, inflicting severe losses on the Red Army.

FEBRUARY 20-25

SEA WAR, *ATLANTIC*
During U-boat attacks, Allied convoy ON-166 loses 15 of its 49 ships. Only one German submarine is sunk.

FEBRUARY 21

PACIFIC, *SOLOMONS*
US forces land on Russell Island. This is their first move in the campaign to capture the island chain. The operation, code-named Cartwheel, eventually aims to seal off the key Japanese air and sea base at Rabaul in New Britain. The US Pacific commanders Admiral Chester Nimitz and General Douglas MacArthur have devised an "island-hopping" strategy whereby certain

◀ *Letters from home bring a smile to the faces of these two German soldiers of Army Group Don on the Eastern Front.*

◀ Italian troops in Tunisia lay a mine as Axis units try to halt the advance of the British Eighth Army.

▼ Twisting and turning in a desperate effort to escape, a Japanese destroyer is hit by bombs in the Bismarck Sea.

selected islands are retaken, while heavily-defended Japanese positions are bypassed. Allied aircraft and sea power will then isolate these strong-points, preventing them from being a threat. They will "wither on the vine."

FEBRUARY 23–24

SEA WAR, *ATLANTIC*
Seven tankers from the UC-1 Allied convoy are sunk by a U-boat group.

FEBRUARY 26–28

AFRICA, *TUNISIA*
Colonel General Jürgen von Arnim's Fifth Tank Army in northeast Tunisia finally launches a counterattack from

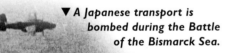

▼ A Japanese transport is bombed during the Battle of the Bismarck Sea.

the Mareth Line that should have been made during the previous series of attacks. It is unsuccessful.

FEBRUARY 28

POLITICS, *GERMANY*
General Heinz Guderian is appointed "Inspector-General of Armored Troops" and is given wide-ranging powers to strengthen Germany's tank arm.

WESTERN FRONT, *NORWAY*
Nine Norwegian paratroopers from Great Britain sabotage the Norsk Hydro power station where "heavy water" is made for atomic research.

MARCH 2–5

SEA WAR, *PACIFIC*
At the Battle of the Bismarck Sea eight Japanese transports and eight destroyers are attacked while sailing from Rabaul to Lae in New Guinea. US

◀ *German troops and armor await orders to advance against Kharkov in February 1943.*

nine, south of the Mareth Line. They attack across a broad front but fail to concentrate and are decisively thrown back. Field Marshal Rommel, whose morale and health are both deteriorating, leaves North Africa.

MARCH 6–20

SEA WAR, *ATLANTIC*
Two Atlantic convoys (HX-229 and SC-122) fight a running battle with 20 U-boats of a "Wolf Pack" in the Atlantic.

KEY PERSONALITIES

ADMIRAL CHESTER NIMITZ

Admiral Chester Nimitz (1885–1966) was appointed commander of the US Pacific Fleet just after the Pearl Harbor attack in December 1941. From April 1942, he was made commander of all naval, sea, and air forces in the Pacific Ocean Area.

Aided by US codebreaking efforts, he was able to anticipate and defeat Japanese plans at the Battles of the Coral Sea in May and Midway in June. These actions secured US naval superiority in the Pacific by inflicting decisive defeats on Japan's carrier capability. Nimitz then went on to lead a series of strikes against the Japanese Navy and supported the "island-hopping" operations to establish Allied control over the Pacific region. He was a strong advocate of this amphibious strategy, which pushed the Japanese back across the ocean to Japan. He was made a Fleet Admiral in 1944 and was present at the Japanese surrender in 1945. One of his strengths was being able to achieve his goals without antagonizing his colleagues.

▲ *Kharkov's battle-scarred Red Square following Manstein's brilliant capture of the city in March 1943.*

and Australian aircraft and torpedo-boats sink all the transports and four destroyers. The Allies lose six aircraft; the Japanese 25. This is the last Japanese attempt to reinforce their presence in New Guinea.

MARCH 5

AIR WAR, *GERMANY*
The British launch a four-month offensive against the Ruhr industrial area. A force of 367 bombers strikes the Krupp Works at Essen in the first attack; 14 aircraft are lost.

MARCH 6–9

AFRICA, *TUNISIA*
The Germans attempt to disrupt General Bernard Montgomery's preparations for a final offensive at Mede-

Although 21 ships are sunk, only one U-boat is lost. The Allies cannot afford such attrition.

MARCH 13

HOME FRONT, *GERMANY*
An unsuccessful assassination attempt is made on Adolf Hitler by army officers. They place a bomb in his aircraft but it fails to explode.

MARCH 14

EASTERN FRONT, *UKRAINE*
After his spearheads reached the Donets River, Manstein's forces have trapped and destroyed the Soviet Third Tank Army. In all, the Red Army has abandoned nearly 6,000 square miles (9,600 sq km) of newly-won ground in the face of Manstein's brilliant armored counteroffensive, which has stabilized the German front in southern Russia. Manstein has averted a total Axis collapse.

MARCH 15–31

EASTERN FRONT, *UKRAINE*

Germany's Army Group Don recaptures Kharkov, and Belgorod three days later. By the end of the month the Soviet Voronezh Front is back on the east bank of the northern Donets. The final phase of Manstein's offensive – a combined attack with Army Group Center's Second Panzer Army heading south from Orel toward Kursk – is halted by the spring thaw.

This victory encourages the German high command to launch Operation Citadel, an ambitious plan to destroy the Soviet Central and Voronezh Fronts in the Kursk salient to the north of Kharkov. Over 500,000 Red Army

▼ *Italian troops on the Mareth Line.*

troops occupy Kursk and a bulge of land stretching 100 miles (160 km) westward from the Soviet line.

MARCH 20–28

AFRICA, *TUNISIA*

Allied forces under General Bernard Montgomery launch a carefully-planned attack against the Mareth Line. The line's principal defenses along the banks of the Wadi Zigzaou are penetrated on the 21st–22nd but the 15th Panzer Division successfully counterattacks. Montgomery, however, develops an outflanking move into a major offensive, and by the 26th the Axis forces have retreated northward to the El Hamma Plain. The weakened German forces fall back to Wadi Akarit by the 28th, while many of their Italians allies surrender.

MARCH 26

SEA WAR, *PACIFIC*

At the Battle of the Kommandorsky Islands in the Bering Sea, two US cruisers and four destroyers engage four Japanese cruisers and five destroyers. The Japanese abandon the action just before they can exploit their numerical superiority. Both sides have a cruiser badly damaged.

MARCH 27

AFRICA, *TUNISIA*

General Sir Harold Alexander sends the US 34th Infantry Division to seize the Foundouk Pass but heavy artillery fire halts its advance.

MARCH 30

SEA WAR, *ARCTIC*

Britain suspends the Arctic convoys to the Soviet Union because it cannot provide enough escorts to guard against the increasing number of German warships in Norway.

APRIL 5–6

AFRICA, *TUNISIA*

The British Eighth Army attacks the Wadi Akarit Line, a defensive position situated across the route into Tunisia. The line cannot be outflanked. While

▲ *Trailing vapor, US B-17s Flying Fortresses bomb the German city of Dresden in daylight.*

the assault is successful, the British fail to exploit their breakthrough and Axis forces are able to regroup.

APRIL 7–10

AFRICA, *TUNISIA*

The British IX Corps, which includes the US 34th Infantry Division, attacks the Foundouk Pass but the Axis forces

▼ *Members of the Polish Commission look at evidence of the Katyn Forest massacre.*

hold the area until they can success-fully disengage the bulk of their units from the fighting.

APRIL 7–13

AIR WAR, *SOLOMONS*

Over 180 Japanese aircraft begin Operation I by attacking Allied ship-ping off Guadalcanal. On the 11th, the Japanese attack ships off New Guinea and raid Port Moresby airfield on the 12th, and British at Milne Bay the following day. They sink a destroyer, one corvette, one tanker, two cargo ships, and destroy some 20 aircraft. The massive aerial operation against shipping and airfields, however, does not achieve the scale of success that the Japanese anticipated.

APRIL 8

POLITICS, *JAPAN*

General Kawbe succeeds General Iida as commander of Japanese forces oper-ating in Burma.

APRIL 10–12

AFRICA, *TUNISIA*

British troops enter Sfax, one of the ports vital for reducing the long supply lines from Tripoli, and finally halt at Enfidaville, southeast of Tunis. Axis forces are now established in their final defensive line running from Cape Serrat on the Mediterranean to Enfidaville. Defeat for the Axis forces is inevitable. Allied sea and air control denies them any reinforcements. They are determined to fight on, however, in order to delay the Allied plan to invade Italy until the fall, when deteriorating weather is likely to disrupt any Allied landings.

APRIL 12

HOME FRONT, *POLAND*

The German authorities announce that they have found a mass grave in Katyn Forest. They claim that it contains the bodies of some 10,000 Polish officers executed by the Soviet secret police in 1939. The Soviets claim that this is deliberate German propaganda aimed at discrediting them. Subsequent investigations reveal the Soviets were indeed responsible for the massacre of 4500 officers at Katyn Forest.

APRIL 17

AIR WAR, *GERMANY*

The US 8th Army Air Force attacks Bremen's aircraft factories from its bases in eastern England. It is one of its largest raids to date. Sixteen of the 115 B-17 Flying Fortress bombers from the raid are lost.

▶ *A Jewish fighter surrenders in the Warsaw Ghetto as the SS fights its way through the city street by street.*

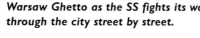

▲ *Admiral Minichi Koga, commander of the Japanese Combined Fleet.*

APRIL 18

AIR WAR, *TUNISIA*

An operation by 100 German transport aircraft to fly supplies to the Axis forces in North Africa suffers a devastating attack by US fighters. Over half the transport aircraft and 10 fighters are shot down.

APRIL 19–22

AFRICA, *TUNISIA*

General Bernard Montgomery, eager for his Eighth Army to seal victory in Tunisia, launches an offensive toward Enfidaville. The attack gains little ground and casualties are heavy.

APRIL 19

EASTERN FRONT, *POLAND*

The destruction of the Warsaw Ghetto begins with German SS troops making a large-scale attack. The Jewish fighters construct a network of hiding places and fight with small-arms or improvised weapons. Up to 310,000 Jews have already been deported from the ghetto, to be executed or imprisoned in labor camps.

APRIL 21

POLITICS, *JAPAN*

Admiral Minichi Koga succeeds Admiral Isoroku Yamamoto as commander-in-chief of the Combined Fleet. US codebreakers had learned that Yamamoto was visiting bases in the southwest Pacific and aircraft were deployed to intercept the fleet. The admiral was killed after his aircraft was destroyed by US fighters on the 18th.

APRIL 22

AFRICA, *TUNISIA*

The British First Army and US II Corps prepare to breach the series

▼ *Guns and vehicles of the British Royal Artillery Regiment on the road to Tunis during the last phase of the war in Africa.*

of interlocking strongpoints across the high ground above the approaches to Tunis. The First Army attacks between Medjez-el-Bab and Bou Arada while the US II Corps farther north strikes toward Mateur and Bizerta. The main thrust is made by the First Army's V Corps along a direct line toward Tunis from Medjez-el-Bab. To achieve this, they have to capture two major Axis positions on the high ground at Peter's Corner and Longstop Hill along the Medjerda River.

APRIL 26–30

AFRICA, *TUNISIA*

The First Army's V Corps captures Longstop Hill and reaches Djebel Bou Aoukaz. From April 28–30 the Germans counterattack and take Djebel Bou Aoukaz. Meanwhile, the US II Corps fights a bitter battle to capture Hill 609. The First Army's advance is being blocked by protracted engagements against strong Axis positions. To achieve a breakthrough across the Medjerda Valley, the Eighth Army sends two divisions and a brigade to bolster the offensive.

APRIL 28

SEA WAR, *ATLANTIC*

The Allied convoy ONS-5 begins a seven-day running battle against 51 U-boats. The convoy achieves considerable success despite the limited air

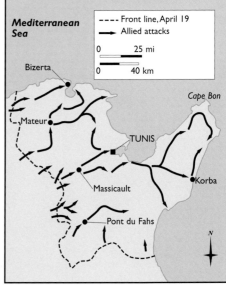

▲ *The final Allied victory in Tunisia brought an end to the North African campaign. Total Axis losses were 620,000 men, a third of them German. The Third Reich could not afford such wastage.*

support it receives. Seven U-boats are sunk and 17 damaged. The convoy loses 13 of its 42 ships.

APRIL 30

ESPIONAGE, *BRITAIN*

The British release a corpse, dressed as an officer and carrying false documents, into the Mediterranean Sea as part of a deception operation to divert German attention from Allied plans to invade Sicily. The corpse is recovered by the Germans, who find the false documents containing details of an Allied attack on Greece and Sardinia. As a result German reinforcements are sent to these areas.

MAY 3

POLITICS, *UNITED STATES*

General Frank Andrews, US commander in the European theater, is killed in an air crash. General Jacob Devers is named as his replacement.

MAY 5–7

AFRICA, *TUNISIA*

Reinforcements sent by the Eighth Army help the First Army recapture Djebel Bou Aoukaz and enable the British 7th Armored Division to advance into open "tank country." General Sir Harold Alexander can now exploit the numerical and material superiority of his armies against the

Axis forces defending Tunis. Massicault is reached on the 6th, and tanks enter Tunis on the 7th. The US III Corps reaches Bizerta the same day. The Axis forces in North Africa are facing imminent defeat, with no chance of escaping the Allies.

MAY 11–29

PACIFIC, *ALEUTIANS*

A US 12,000-man amphibious force attacks Attu Island, one of Japan's fortified positions in the northern Pacific. During the bitter offensive, only 29 of the 2500 Japanese survive. US forces sustain 561 fatalities and have 1136 men wounded.

▲ *Water gushes from the damaged Möhne dam following the successful raid by the British Royal Air Force.*

MAY 12–25

POLITICS, *ALLIES*

The Allied Trident Conference is held in Washington. Churchill and Roosevelt reinforce the "Germany First" strategy by agreeing to intensify bombing raids in Europe. A date is set for the cross-Channel invasion (May 1, 1944) and Britain urges that the Sicilian attack is extended to the Italian mainland. The British feel that the United States is committing increasing resources to the Pacific at the expense of European military operations.

MAY 13

AFRICA, *TUNISIA*

Axis forces officially surrender. Some 620,000 casualties and prisoners have been sustained by Germany and Italy. Allied campaign losses: French 20,000; British 19,000; and US 18,500.

MAY 16–17

AIR WAR, *GERMANY*

The dams on the Möhne and Eder Rivers are attacked by 19 British Lancaster aircraft, which are carrying

◀ *A happy Eisenhower (center) and General Montgomery after the Allied victory in Africa.*

317

MAY 23–29

AIR WAR, *GERMANY*
A massive British raid is made on Dortmund. Another offensive against Wuppertal on the 29th kills 2450 people. British bombers are intensifying their large-scale night attacks against industrial centers.

MAY 26

BALKANS, *YUGOSLAVIA*
An Axis force of 120,000 men attacks 16,000 communist partisans in Montenegro. A British military mission arrives on the 27th to meet partisan leader Joseph Tito, who confirms their intelligence reports that the rival Chetnik resistance group now supports the Axis forces. Since the fall of 1941, Tito has led a full-scale campaign in the province of Serbia but has since endured several major attacks from the Axis occupiers. Partisan forces have been preserved by withdrawing to the mountains and are now to be strengthened by large quantities of Allied aid.

JUNE 1–11

AIR WAR, *ITALY*
A round-the-clock naval and air bombardment of Pantellaria Island forces it to surrender on the 11th. Italian propaganda had falsely hailed it as an impregnable fortress and, consequently, the Allies had considered it an obstacle blocking their plans to invade Sicily and the mainland.

specially-designed "bouncing bombs." The dams generate electricity and supply water to the Ruhr region. The squadron led by Wing Commander Guy Gibson loses eight aircraft. The raid causes some disruption to industry, and boosts morale in Great Britain. German casualties are high, particularly among forced foreign workers.

MAY 16

HOME FRONT, *POLAND*
The Warsaw Ghetto uprising ends. Some 14,000 Jews have been killed, 22,000 sent to concentration camps, and 20,000 to labor camps.

MAY 22

SEA WAR, *ATLANTIC*
Admiral Karl Doenitz suspends patrols in the northern Atlantic. Some 56 submarines have been destroyed since April alone in a campaign of attrition the Germans cannot afford.

▶ Communist partisans on the move in Montenegro as an Axis force of 120,000 men launches a campaign to wipe them out. The offensive failed.

Escalating losses of both vessels and experienced crews force him to redeploy his remaining forces to less hazardous Caribbean waters and the Azores. Improved tactics, radar, code-breaking, air cover, and the increased building of escorts have combined to strengthen convoy defenses.

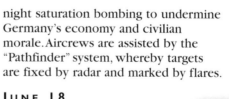

◄ *Operation Pointblank in action: the ruins of a German fighter factory after being bombed by the Allies.*

Claude Auchinleck succeeds him as commander-in-chief of India although a new East Asia Command will reduce his importance. Churchill has made these appointments as he has lost confidence in their capabilities and wishes to limit their military roles.

JUNE 20–24

AIR WAR, *GERMANY/ITALY*

The Allies launch their first "shuttle" raid. British bombers attack Friedrichshafen in Germany and then fly on to refuel in North Africa. On their return flight to Britain, they attack La Spezia naval base in Italy.

JUNE 21

PACIFIC, *SOLOMONS*

US forces begin an offensive against the New Georgia Island group. Munda airfield is the first major objective. The Solomon offensives are aided by vital reconnaissance information provided by Allied "coastwatchers" based on these little-known islands and equipped with high-powered radios. New Georgia airfields sustain air and sea bombardments while US warships mine the surrounding seas to destroy ships bringing reinforcements and supplies.

JULY 5

POLITICS, *POLAND*

General Wladyslaw Raczkiewicz, prime minister

JUNE 3

POLITICS, *FREE FRENCH*

Rival leaders General Charles de Gaulle and General Henri Giraud agree to share the presidency of the Committee of National Liberation.

JUNE 10

AIR WAR, *GERMANY*

Operation Pointblank is launched. The offensive by British and US bomber forces will last until the 1944 cross-Channel invasion. US strategy concentrates on daylight precision raids to destroy Germany's aircraft industry and its air force. British attacks focus on

► *The blazing hull of a Japanese ship hit by US aircraft off the Solomon Islands.*

night saturation bombing to undermine Germany's economy and civilian morale. Aircrews are assisted by the "Pathfinder" system, whereby targets are fixed by radar and marked by flares.

JUNE 18

POLITICS, *BRITAIN*

Field Marshal Sir Archibald Wavell becomes Viceroy of India. General Sir

JULY 5–6

▶ *Both sides lost heavily at Kursk. This Soviet tank crew fell foul of a German antitank gun and panzergrenadiers.*

of the Polish government-in-exile, is killed in an air crash. His deputy, Stanislaw Mikolajczyk, replaces him.

JULY 5–6

PACIFIC, *SOLOMONS*
The US 43rd Infantry Division leads the main landing on New Georgia. That night US and Japanese destroyers clash at the Battle of Kula Gulf. One Japanese destroyer is sunk.

JULY 6

EASTERN FRONT, *UKRAINE*
Soviet intelligence has uncovered the plans for the offensive by 900,000 German troops against Kursk. The Germans believe that a victory on the Eastern Front will bolster domestic morale and preserve the Axis coalition, while also demonstrating to the Allies that the Nazis can still achieve victory.

From March to July, they gather 900,000 troops but the Red Army succeeds in establishing numerical superiority in men (1.3 million) and equipment. Consequently, German units are exposed to aerial and land bombardment while the Red Army prepares for the attack.

The German Army Group Center's Ninth Army, south of Orel, and Field Marshal Erich von Manstein's Fourth Panzer Army, north of Kharkov, open Operation Citadel with an offensive

against the salient. The Ninth Army under Field Marshal Gunther von Kluge only penetrates six miles (9 km) and loses 250,000 men. Over 6000 German and Soviet tanks and assault guns take part in the war's greatest armored battle. Special attention is given by the Soviets to antitank guns and obstacles. The Germans deploy 200 aircraft for the operation and the Soviets 2400.

JULY 6–9

EASTERN FRONT, *UKRAINE*
Increasing numbers of German troops reinforce the Kursk offensive but the

▼ *Polish President Wladyslaw Raczkiewicz, seen here reviewing sailors, was killed in a plane crash on July 5.*

Red Army stands firm. The Soviets counter the Germans with a deep defensive network while heavily-armed antitank units deliver concentrated fire against German armor. The Soviets quickly gain air superiority and fighters provide valuable tactical support. These measures combine to prevent the German attacks penetrating the Soviet defenses.

JULY 7–13

PACIFIC, *PAPUA NEW GUINEA*
The Japanese strongpoint at Mumbo, 10 miles (16 km) inland from Salamaua, is seized by the Australians. US and Australian forces are battling to dislodge the Japanese from the high ground they have retreated to.

▼ *The Royal Navy brings troops ashore as Allied units push farther inland on Sicily.*

Allied reinforcements are to be landed in order to clear the Japanese from northeast New Guinea.

JULY 9

MEDITERRANEAN, *SICILY*
Chaotic US and British airborne landings begin the attack on Sicily. Preparatory bomber attacks have already hit air bases on Sicily, Sardinia, and on the mainland. Mussolini expects the Allied attack to be against Sardinia. The main strategic objectives are to clear the Mediterranean sea-lanes, divert Axis forces from the Eastern Front, and possibly apply pressure on Italy to accelerate its capitulation.

JULY 10

MEDITERRANEAN, *SICILY*
An invasion fleet of 2500 vessels carries General Bernard Montgomery's Eighth Army and General George Patton's Seventh Army

▲ *German armored personnel carriers and assault guns (note armored skirts) rumble forward at the Battle of Kursk.*

to southern Sicily. The Italians are surprised as they did not expect an attack during stormy weather. The Allies will eventually land 160,000 men to fight General Guzzoni's Sixth Army (230,000 Italian and 40,000 German troops). Landings are assisted by a new amphibious truck – the DUKW.

JULY 11-12

MEDITERRANEAN, *SICILY*
The German *Hermann Goering* Panzer Division almost reaches US forces on the coast near Gela and Licata but the counterattack is obstructed by US paratroopers. General Sir Harold Alexander, overall commander of the operation, expects the Eighth Army to advance up the east coast toward the key bases at

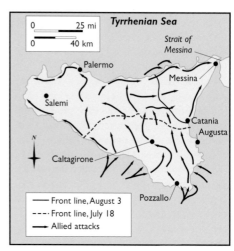

▲ *The Allied invasion of Sicily involved the largest seaborne assault mounted to date. During the initial assault seven divisions, one armored combat team, two commandos, and an assault brigade were put ashore against an enemy almost equal in numbers.*

Catania and Messina. The less experienced Seventh Army is to protect the British flank and rear.

JULY 12-13

EASTERN FRONT, *UKRAINE*
At Kursk, the Soviets launch a counteroffensive around Prokhorovka and an enormous tank battle develops. Field Marshal von Manstein's Fourth Panzer Army advances 25 miles (40 km) but loses 10,000 men and 350 tanks. Farther north, the Soviet Bryansk and West Fronts begin an offensive around Orel. Adolf Hitler calls off Operation

JULY 15–23

Citadel on the 13th. The last major German offensive on the Eastern Front has been a costly failure with the loss of over 550 tanks and 500,000 men killed, wounded, or missing. It is a major disaster for Germany, not least because the carefully-gathered strategic armored reserves have been wiped out in the fighting.

KEY PERSONALITIES

FIELD MARSHAL ERICH VON MANSTEIN

Erich von Manstein (1887–1973) was chief of staff to General Gerd von Rundstedt in 1939 before being demoted for challenging the high command's strategy for the invasion of France in 1940. He advocated a surprise thrust through the Ardennes, and when Hitler adopted this plan, his fortunes changed. Manstein led an infantry corps with distinction during the invasion of France and then took command of an armored Corps, which he led at the start of Operation Barbarossa.

By September 1941, he had risen to command the Eleventh Army on the Eastern Front. His conquest of the Crimea earned him a reputation as a top field commander and he became a field marshal in 1942. Manstein's use of armor to seize Kharkov in February 1943, when he yielded ground in the face of Soviet numerical superiority before counterattacking with his panzer corps when the enemy was suffering attrition and at the end of his supply lines, was the greatest German counteroffensive of the war.

His appreciation of the need for a flexible defensive strategy brought him into conflict with Hitler. The Führer's narrow strategic view of the Eastern Front was based on holding ground. The field marshal's plans were thus considered an abandonment of Germany's front. As a result of this conflict over strategy, Manstein was dismissed in 1944.

▲ Troops of the British Eighth Army in Catania, Sicily, in July 1943. Palermo, the capital, fell at the end of the month.

SEA WAR, PACIFIC
At the Battle of Kolombangara, off New Georgia, a Japanese squadron led by Admiral Izaki engages three US light cruisers and 10 destroyers. One US destroyer is sunk and one New Zealand and two US cruisers are damaged. The Japanese lose a cruiser.

JULY 15–23

MEDITERRANEAN, SICILY
The US Seventh Army advances westward aiming to seize the capital Palermo with an armored thrust.

JULY 17

EASTERN FRONT, UKRAINE
The Soviet Voronezh Front, just to the south of Kursk, and the Steppe Front,

to the west of Kharkov, begin pursuing the German forces, which are now retreating in some confusion.

JULY 17–18

MEDITERRANEAN, SICILY
The British Eighth Army strikes northward toward the Axis stronghold at Catania but meets determined resistance from the Hermann Goering Division on the plain beneath Mount Etna. The British therefore decide to go around Catania toward Mount Etna, while the US Seventh Army moves along the north coast toward Messina.

JULY 19

POLITICS, AXIS
Benito Mussolini and Adolf Hitler meet at Fletre in northern Italy. The Italian dictator fails to tell Hitler that his country is to cease fighting and instead endorses the proposal for Germany to

assume military control in Italy. The first major Allied air raid is made on the Italian capital, Rome, by US bombers on the same day.

JULY 23

MEDITERRANEAN, *SICILY*
The US Seventh Army enters Palermo and the west coast ports of Trapani and Marsala.

JULY 23–24

EASTERN FRONT, *UKRAINE*
The German armies have now withdrawn to the lines held at the start of Operation Citadel at Kursk.

JULY 23–30

MEDITERRANEAN, *SICILY*
The Allies drive to Messina while German forces try to save the Sicilian bridgehead and the airfields around Catania. US forces move along the north coast and Highway 120 inland.

JULY 24

POLITICS, *ITALY*
The Fascist Grand Council, the key constitutional body for debating government and party decisions, meets for the first time since 1939. Dino Grandi, former minister of justice, proposes that military authority should be given to the king and not Mussolini. His motion is approved.

JULY 24–AUGUST 2

AIR WAR, *GERMANY*
A series of massive British raids are made on Hamburg. The attacks are made over four nights and last until August 2. The dropping of foil strips to confuse German radar equipment (the "Window" system) helps the bombers. Around 50,000 people are killed and 800,000 are made homeless. The attack on the 27th–28th creates a firestorm, which blazes so intensely that the flames suck oxygen from the area nearby. This creates a "hurricane" effect that feeds the flames, which travel at great speed.

JULY 25

POLITICS, *ITALY*
The king of Italy relieves Benito Mussolini of his office. Mussolini is arrested and Marshal Pietro Badoglio forms a new government that lasts only six weeks. The government deters Germany from occupying the entire country by promising to fight on. Badoglio hopes, however, that the

Allies will land and occupy most of Italy quickly and therefore confine any fighting to the north.

JULY 26

EASTERN FRONT, *UKRAINE*
The German high command orders forces around Orel to withdraw to the previously-prepared Hagen Line, just to the east of Bryansk.

AUGUST 1

AIR WAR, *ROMANIA*
A US force of 178 bombers make a 1000-mile (1500-km) flight from Libya to attack the Ploesti oil fields, which provide essential supplies to Axis forces. The low-level attack is met by fierce antiaircraft fire and 54 aircraft are lost. Damage to the oil fields is

superficial but increases Hitler's fears over the area's susceptibility to air raids or ground attack.

AUGUST 2

EASTERN FRONT, *UKRAINE*
Adolf Hitler orders Field Marshal Erich von Manstein to hold the line firmly around Kharkov. Hitler is keen to prevent the Eastern Front being pushed farther westward by the likely Soviet summer offensive. However, German forces in the region lack the manpower, tanks, and artillery to halt the Red Army permanently.

▼ *The aftermath of the raids on the city of Hamburg. The bombing and firestorms killed an estimated 50,000 people.*

AUGUST 3

POLITICS, *ITALY*

The Italian regime puts out peace-feelers to the Allies. In reply, the Allies lay down the following conditions for an armistice: the handing over of the fleet; all Italian territories to be made available to the Allies for military operations; Allied prisoners in Italy to be freed and not be allowed to fall into German hands; and the disarming of all ground and air forces.

AUGUST 3–16

MEDITERRANEAN, *SICILY*

Italian forces withdraw from Sicily. Catania surrenders to the British on the 5th.

AUGUST 4–11

EASTERN FRONT, *UKRAINE*

Red Army units retake Orel and Belgorod by the 5th. The Voronezh and Steppe Fronts are near Kharkov.

AUGUST 5–22

PACIFIC, *SOLOMONS*

US forces capture the important Munda airfield on New Georgia Island. Japanese resistance on the island disintegrates and the defenders are not to be reinforced. A sea evacuation is made from the north of the island to neighboring Kolombangara on the 22nd.

AUGUST 6

MEDITERRANEAN, *ITALY*

German reinforcements begin arriving in Italy. Hitler orders four operations: the rescue of Mussolini from imprisonment by the new Italian government, the formation of a strong Italian defense line, the revival of fascism, and the seizure of the Italian fleet. Hitler also wishes to occupy as much of Italy as possible, using it as a bastion to keep the war as far away from Germany as possible.

AUGUST 6–7

SEA WAR, *PACIFIC*

Four Japanese destroyers carrying troops and supplies to Kolombangara in New Georgia fight a night action against six US destroyers at the Battle of Vela Gulf. Torpedo strikes sink three Japanese destroyers and claim 1210 lives. No US vessels are damaged.

AUGUST 8–17

MEDITERRANEAN, *SICILY*

US forces advancing along the coast are assisted by amphibious landings east of San Stefano. British, Canadian, and Free French Moroccan troops

▲ *The Quebec Conference, where a British plan for a cross-Channel invasion of Europe in mid-1944 was agreed.*

have fought a series of bitter actions to overcome determined German resistance to the southwest of Mount Etna. The Germans finally start withdrawing on the 11th and evacuate 100,000 Axis troops before US forces enter Messina on the 17th.

Around 10,000 Germans have been killed or captured during the campaign. The Italians have lost 132,000 men, mainly prisoners. The British and US forces have suffered 7000 fatalities and 15,000 men have been wounded. The capture of Sicily means the Allies have a springboard for the invasion of Italy.

▼ *US bombers on their way to hit the Romanian Ploesti oil fields at the beginning of August.*

AUGUST 13–24

POLITICS, *ALLIES*

British Prime Minister Winston Churchill and US President Franklin D. Roosevelt attend the First Quebec Conference in Canada. Britain reaffirms US control over the Pacific theater, where it is intensifying operations. Further Chindit operations are proposed for Burma and aid to Chiang-Kai-shek in China will continue. Vice Admiral Lord Louis Mountbatten takes charge of Southeast Asia Command.

Fighting in Italy will intensify to capitalize on Mussolini's downfall. They adopt British General Sir Frederick Morgan's plan for the cross-Channel invasion, Operation Overlord, scheduled for May 1, 1944. Floating artificial ports (Mulberry Harbors) are to be built in Britain and towed to the French beaches. The supreme commander for the invasion will be a US senior general.

AUGUST 15

PACIFIC, *ALEUTIANS*

A US and Canadian amphibious assault on Kiska Island finds that the Japanese garrison has been evacuated.

AUGUST 17–18

AIR WAR, *GERMANY*

The rocket research center at Peenemünde on the Baltic Sea is attacked by 597 British bombers. The center has been developing a remote-controlled, pulse-jet-powered "Flying Bomb" (V1) and a faster, liquid-fuel model (V2) as terror weapons to undermine the morale of enemy populations. The raid kills 732 people and delays V2 testing. The British lose 40 aircraft. A raid by 230 US bombers is made on ball-bearing works at Schweinfurt and Regensburg. Around 20 percent of the bombers are destroyed.

AUGUST 19

PACIFIC, *PAPUA NEW GUINEA*

Allied forces finally take the Japanese strongpoint of Mount Tambu. Japanese troops are now wedged between Salamaua and the Francisco River.

AUGUST 22–23

EASTERN FRONT, *UKRAINE*

Kharkov is retaken by the Red Army. The Soviets now seriously threaten the southern area of the German front in Ukraine and are well placed for advancing to the Dniepr River. The Soviets have

won victories at Kursk, Orel, and Kharkov by exhausting the enemy with fierce defensive actions followed by decisive counterattacks.

AUGUST 26

EASTERN FRONT, *UKRAINE*

Soviet forces begin their offensive to seize the eastern Ukraine and cross the Dniepr River. The river forms a key part of the German defenses established to halt Red Army advances.

AUGUST 28

POLITICS, *DENMARK*

The Danish government resigns after refusing a German demand for the repression of "saboteurs." The Danish authorities have tried to avoid collaboration with Germany. Martial law is declared on the 29th, the army is disarmed but many Danish warships are scuttled or sent to Sweden before the Germans can seize them.

SEPTEMBER 3

MEDITERRANEAN, *ITALY*

General Bernard Montgomery's Eighth Army crosses from Sicily to seize a bridgehead in Calabria. The British encounter little opposition as the Germans in southern Italy have orders to withdraw.

SEPTEMBER 4–5

PACIFIC, *PAPUA NEW GUINEA*

An Allied offensive is launched to capture the major settlement and airfield at Lae. Amphibious landings are made

▶ *Red Army artillery pounds German units outside Kharkov in the Soviet advance to the Dniepr River.*

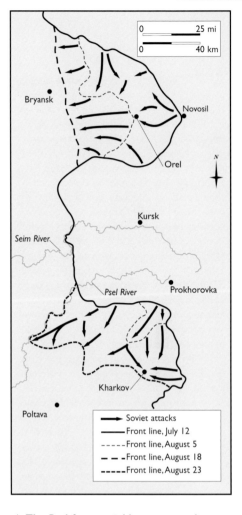

▲ *The Red Army quickly recaptured Kharkov following the collapse of Germany's Citadel attack.*

STRATEGY & TACTICS

STRATEGIC BOMBING

Strategic bombing – air offensives against an enemy's industrial centers and population – using fleets of bombers had been considered a war-winning formula by its prewar proponents. After Germany began its first major raids against Britain in 1940, however, its limitations were exposed.

Although attacks were highly destructive, they failed to paralyze the economy or undermine morale; indeed, the opposite seemed the case as the population steeled itself for the onslaught. The effect of Allied raids on Germany met with similar results, especially as they sustained heavy losses during daylight raids, in which they were easily targeted, and were forced to make less-accurate night raids. Britain's answer was to use saturation bombing to destroy homes and factories across wide areas.

US bombers began operations over Europe in 1942 and were primarily trained for daylight, high-level precision attacks. They soon found that enemy fighters and poor weather seriously undermined the effectiveness of their missions. Fighter, flak, and radar defenses combined to make bomber raids increasingly hazardous. The Allies countered this with a series of technological innovations to enhance navigation and bomb aiming. The defensive firepower of bombers and fighter escort cover was also improved. Nevertheless, aircrew losses were often heavy and Britain's Bomber Command lost 55,573 men while the US 8th Army Air Force (based in Britain) had 43,742 airmen killed.

While the Allied bombing of Germany's oil industry and transport system did play a key role toward the end of the war, the bombers were never capable of completely defeating the enemy alone as its prewar proponents had often predicted (Germany industrial output actually increased during the Allied bomber offensive).

Raids against Japan began in 1944. Although the attacks against 65 cities succeeded in undermining the faltering economy, the nation did not capitulate until the nuclear strikes in 1945. Although the earlier bombing raids did not force Japan to surrender, they did reduce whole cities to ashes and killed many thousands.

The questionable impact such raids had on the economic and psychological capacity of a population to continue fighting, and the moral concerns over civilian deaths, subsequently led many to question this method of waging war.

▶ *Free French troops catch their first glimpse of Corsica as they arrive off the island on an Allied troopship.*

around 20 miles (30 km) east of Lae on the 4th. US paratroopers land at Nadzeb on the 5th and begin securing the Markham River valley.

SEPTEMBER 8

POLITICS, *ITALY*
The surrender of Italy is officially announced by the Allies. German forces take over the north of the country and occupy coastal defenses in anticipation of a major Allied invasion. They disarm Italian ground units but the navy succeeds in sending 24 warships to Malta.

SEPTEMBER 9

MEDITERRANEAN, *ITALY*
Lieutenant General Mark Clark's US Fifth Army, plus the British X Corps, lands in the Gulf of Salerno.

SEPTEMBER 10–11

MEDITERRANEAN, *SARDINIA/CORSICA*
The Germans withdraws 25,000 men from Sardinia to Italy, via Corsica. A 7000-strong French and US force leaves Algeria to occupy Corsica at the beginning of October.

SEPTEMBER 11–15

PACIFIC, *PAPUA NEW GUINEA*
Salamaua is captured on the 11th and Lae four days later. These victories deny the Japanese a key port and airfield. The Japanese are now left occupying the Finschhafen fort. The fort has to be taken to clear the peninsula, which is adjacent to the sea approaches to New Britain – the next Allied objective.

SEPTEMBER 12

POLITICS, *ITALY*
German airborne troops led by Lieutenant Colonel Otto Skorzeny rescue Mussolini from imprisonment in Gran Sasso in the Abruzzi Mountains. Mussolini, however, will now be under Germany's control.

SEPTEMBER 12–18

MEDITERRANEAN, *ITALY*
German forces fiercely counterattack the Allies around Salerno and threaten the entire bridgehead. Only massive aerial and artillery support saves the besieged Allied units.

SEPTEMBER 15

MEDITERRANEAN, *AEGEAN SEA*
British forces land on the island of Kos in the Dodecanese. The islands, off southwest Turkey, are a potential approach to southeast Europe and a base for air operations against German communications and oil resources in Romania. A victory here might also persuade Turkey to support the Allied cause as the threat of German air raids from Rhodes would be eliminated. Kos is to be a springboard for an assault against the German stronghold on Rhodes. By the end of September,

▲ *German troops on their way to the Dodecanese following the landing of British forces on the islands.*

▼ *Jubilant German paratroopers photographed after their rescue of Mussolini from the Gran Sasso hotel.*

British forces make contact with cooperative Italian troops on most of the neighboring islands.

SEPTEMBER 17
EASTERN FRONT, *SOVIET UNION*
The Red Army capture Bryansk.

SEPTEMBER 19-23
SEA WAR, *ATLANTIC*
The German U-boat packs resume operations against Allied convoys. They are now equipped with electronic monitoring devices, improved anti-aircraft guns, and acoustic torpedoes. Twenty U-boats inflict serious losses on warships and merchant vessels in convoys ON-202 and ONS-28 from the 18th to the 23rd.

SEPTEMBER 21
SEA WAR, *FAR EAST*
Australian commandos sink two Japanese transports after canoeing into Singapore harbor.

SEPTEMBER 22
EASTERN FRONT, *CRIMEA*
The Soviet Thirteenth Army crosses

the Dniepr River south of Kiev and bridgeheads gradually emerge along it.
PACIFIC, *PAPUA NEW GUINEA*
Allied land and seaborne offensives begin against the Japanese on the Huon Peninsula.
SEA WAR, *ARCTIC*
A raid by British midget submarines to destroy the German battle squadron at Altenfiord in Norway cripples the battleship *Tirpitz*. The submarines, however, are unable to attack the battlecruiser *Scharnhorst* as it is at sea, and the pocket battleship *Lützow* could not be found. The three midget submarines involved in the attack on the *Tirpitz* are sunk.

SEPTEMBER 22-23
MEDITERRANEAN, *ITALY*
The Eighth Army's 78th Division lands at Bari. British forces then advance to seize Foggia and its valuable airfield five days later.

SEPTEMBER 23
POLITICS, *ITALY*
Benito Mussolini announces the formation of the Italian Social Republic in

SEPTEMBER 25

northwest Italy. Germany, however, is given control of some northern areas by this "republic."

SEPTEMBER 25

EASTERN FRONT, *SOVIET UNION*
The Soviets recapture Smolensk in their continuing offensive. Germany's Army Group Center is now falling back in some disarray.

OCTOBER 1–8

MEDITERRANEAN, *ITALY*
British troops enter Naples on the 1st, and the US Fifth Army advances northward. Its move north is stopped on the 8th at the Volturno River; all the bridges have been destroyed by the retreating Germans.

OCTOBER 2–11

MEDITERRANEAN, *ITALY*
British commandos land at Termoli on the 2nd and a British brigade arrives nearby on the next night. German forces counterattack but fall back as the British take control of the town by the 11th.

OCTOBER 3–4

MEDITERRANEAN, *AEGEAN SEA*
A force of 1200 German paratroopers capture Kos. Around 900 Allied and 3000 Italian troops are made prisoner. The Germans shoot 90 Italian officers for fighting against their former ally.

OCTOBER 6

MEDITERRANEAN, *AEGEAN*
A German convoy bound for Leros is attacked by two British cruisers and two destroyers. Seven German transports and one escort are sunk. British vessels are also making hazardous sailings without adequate air cover to reinforce their troops on Leros.

OCTOBER 9

EASTERN FRONT, *CAUCASUS*
The Red Army reaches the Kerch Strait. This completes the liberation of the north Caucasus.

▼ *A German sailor struggles to keep his footing on a U-boat during an operation in the Atlantic Ocean.*

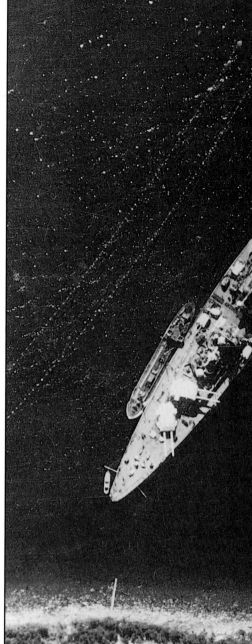

OCTOBER 10–23

EASTERN FRONT, *UKRAINE*
Strong Red Army units continue to strengthen and expand their Dniepr bridgeheads and destroy fiercely defended German positions around Zaporozhye and Melitopol.

OCTOBER 12–22

MEDITERRANEAN, *ITALY*
US forces makes slow progress across the Volturno River and through the mountain terrain in the face of increasingly bad weather. The British Eighth Army begins advancing north across the Trigno River on the 22nd. Field Marshal Albert Kesselring, the German commander-in-chief of Italy since September, has created a strong defensive system along the Garigliano and Sangro Rivers. It is known as the Gustav Line.

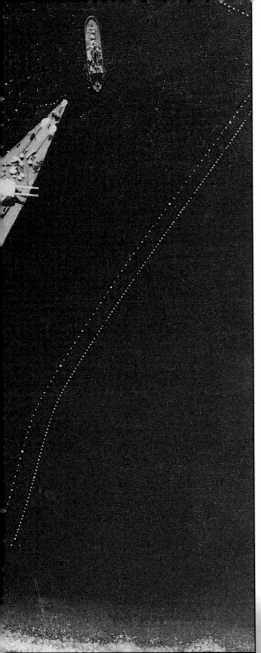

OCTOBER 13

POLITICS, *ITALY*

Marshal Pietro Badoglio's government, which has some power in southern Italy, declares war on Germany.

OCTOBER 14

AIR WAR, *GERMANY*

A second raid is made on the Schweinfurt ball-bearings complex by 291 US B-17 Flying Fortress bombers. Sixty aircraft are lost and 140 damaged for little gain. Following this operation, the US 8th Army Air Force halts unescorted daylight raids due to the high losses it has sustained. Daylight bombing raids will be given escorts of long-range fighter aircraft.

▲ *Disarmed Italian troops pictured at an internment camp in Bozzano following the German occupation of their country in late September.*

OCTOBER 19

POLITICS, *ALLIES*

Representatives from the main Allied nations attend the Second Moscow Conference in the Soviet Union. Agreements are reached over security for postwar China, the punishment of war criminals, and the establishment of advisory councils to consider the fate of Italy and Europe as a whole.

OCTOBER 21

POLITICS, *BRITAIN*

Admiral John Cunningham is appointed commander of British naval forces in the Mediterranean after Admiral Andrew Cunningham becomes the First Sea Lord.

▲ *The German battleship* **Tirpitz** *was attacked by British submarines on September 22.*

▼ *A British mortar fires on German positions during the fighting north of Naples in early October.*

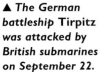

OCTOBER 25

◀ *Japanese antiaircraft troops watch for enemy warplanes following the US invasion of the Solomon Islands.*

island is of strategic importance as it offers the Allies airfield sites that can be used for operations against the Japanese base at Rabaul. The island is defended by 40,000 troops and 20,000 sailors. Most of these are concentrated in the south but US forces land farther west at Empress Augusta Bay, where there are fewer defenders.

NOVEMBER 1–2

SEA WAR, *PACIFIC*
A Japanese force of three heavy cruisers, one light cruiser, and six destroyers attempts to disrupt the Bougainville landings at Empress Augusta Bay. A lack of radar and over-complicated maneuvers enable US Task Force 39 to sink a light cruiser and a destroyer. Two heavy cruisers and a destroyer are damaged. Only one of Task Force 39's 12 vessels is damaged by the Japanese.

NOVEMBER 5–11

SEA WAR, *PACIFIC*
US Rear Admiral Frederick C. Sherman's Task Force 38, including the heavy carrier *Saratoga* and light

OCTOBER 25

FAR EAST, *BURMA*
The Burma to Siam rail link is completed by Allied POWs and indigenous forced labor. This Japanese project to build a track through dense jungle forests is achieved at tremendous human cost. A fifth of the 61,000 Allied prisoners on the project die as a result of accidents, abuse, disease, and starvation. This is the largest of Japan's many projects across Asia. The Japanese captors show complete indifference to the sufferings of their captives.

OCTOBER 27–28

PACIFIC, *SOLOMONS*
Landings are made on the Treasury Islands and Choiseul by US and New Zealand forces. These are diversionary

raids for the main Bougainville attack. It succeeds in drawing attention to the Shortland Islands and bases around Buin, southern Bougainville, rather than the US landing area farther west.

OCTOBER 30

EASTERN FRONT, *UKRAINE*
Soviet units reach the northern Crimea and have virtually cleared the Germans from the left bank of the Dniepr.

NOVEMBER 1

PACIFIC, *SOLOMONS*
US forces land on Bougainville; their final objective in the campaign. The

▶ *American troops pose for a photograph in a captured Japanese command post in the Solomons.*

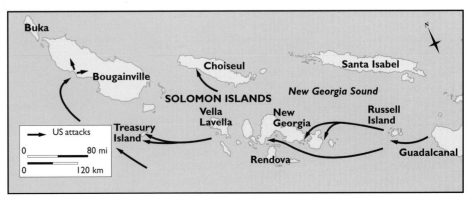

▲ *An American Hellcat takes off from the carrier USS Essex during Admiral Frederick Sherman's attack on Rabaul.*

carrier *Princeton*, attacks Rabaul. A surprise attack by 97 aircraft damages eight cruisers and destroyers commanded by Vice Admiral Takeo Kurita. A second air attack by 183 aircraft, launched from the heavy carriers *Bunker Hill* and *Essex*, plus the light carrier *Independence*, hits Rabaul on the 11th. One light cruiser and a destroyer are sunk; five other destroyers and light cruisers are damaged. The Japanese also lose more than 55 aircraft during the raid and their counterattack.

NOVEMBER 6

EASTERN FRONT, *UKRAINE*
The Soviets recapture Kiev. The Seventeenth Army is trapped in the Crimea

as Adolf Hitler orders the region not to be left. Two bridgeheads – at Kiev and southwest of Kremenchug – have been created by the Red Army for the offensive to liberate the western Ukraine.

NOVEMBER 10

MEDITERRANEAN, *AEGEAN SEA*
The island of Kos is now under German control and British destroyers shell the craft anchored in the harbor. Despite the attack, the Germans sail for Leros on the 12th. Shore batteries and infantry counterattacks attempt to halt the invaders. Strong air support

▼ *The US conquest of the Solomons was a superb example of amphibious warfare operations conducted on a vast scale.*

NOVEMBER 15

and an airborne assault help the Germans to stabilize their positions.

NOVEMBER 15

MEDITERRANEAN, *ITALY*

The Supreme Allied Commander in the Mediterranean, General Sir Harold Alexander, orders the Fifteenth Army Group, comprising the US fifth and Eighth Armies, to rest and reform after fighting against determined German delaying tactics. The war in Italy is proving to be very attritional.

SEA WAR, *ARCTIC*

Britain resumes its Arctic convoys.

NOVEMBER 16

MEDITERRANEAN, *AEGEAN SEA*

Germany completes the capture of Leros and defeats the British attempt to seize the Dodecanese. Poor planning and enemy air superiority have led to the failure of the operation. Britain sustains more than 4800 casualties, and loses 20 vessels and 115 aircraft. Germany has 12 merchant ships and 20 landing craft sunk, and suffers 4000 casualties during the short campaign.

▼ *An American soldier fires his Thompson submachine gun against a Japanese position on Cibik Ridge, Bougainville.*

NOVEMBER 18–26

PACIFIC, *SOLOMONS*

At the Battle of Piva Forks on Bougainville, the Japanese desperately try to hold a key strongpoint known as Cibik Ridge, but US troops finally capture the heavily-fortified position.

NOVEMBER 18

AIR WAR, *GERMANY*

A five-month British bomber offensive on Berlin begins. Over 6100 people are killed, 18,400 injured, and vast areas of the city are destroyed. Fifty diversionary raids are made on other cities.

NOVEMBER 20–23

PACIFIC, *GILBERTS*

US Task Force 53 lands 18,600 troops on Tarawa and Betio following several days of preparatory bombardment. Tarawa's network of bunkers, containing some 4800 Japanese defenders, manages to escape destruction.

The landings are hampered by this determined garrison and also because amphibious craft are grounded on the reef around the islands, which means the troops have to wade ashore. This makes them easy targets to hit.

Over 1000 US troops are killed before the island is captured on the 23rd. Of the garrison, only 110 Japanese soldiers survive. Nearby Makin Island is captured by the US 27th Infantry Division during the same operation.

▲ *Following the resumption of Arctic convoys, a depth-charge explodes near a U-boat closing in for an attack.*

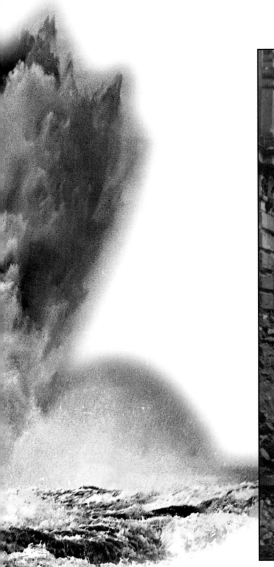

▲ Bomb damage in Berlin – a familiar sight to those who suffered the RAF's five-month campaign against the city.

◄ The Lancaster was an integral part of RAF Bomber Command's arsenal used against the German capital.

NOVEMBER 20–24

MEDITERRANEAN, *ITALY*
The Allies resume the offensive toward Rome but halt at the defenses of the Gustav Line. The British establish a small bridgehead across the Sangro River by the 24th.

NOVEMBER 22–26

POLITICS, *ALLIES*
British Prime Minister Winston Churchill, US President Franklin D. Roosevelt, and China's Chiang Kai-shek meet in Cairo, Egypt. They mainly consider postwar planning for China and Burma. A second conference, between December 4–7, draws up a schedule for the Pacific "island-hopping" campaign.

333

NOVEMBER 24

SEA WAR, *PACIFIC*

A Japanese submarine sinks the US escort carrier *Liscombe Bay* off Makin Island, claiming 644 lives.

NOVEMBER 25

SEA WAR, *PACIFIC*

At the Battle of Cape St. George, a Japanese destroyer-transport force is attacked by five US destroyers after landing troops at Buka, next to Bougainville. The Japanese lose three vessels during the last surface action in the Solomons.

NOVEMBER 28

POLITICS, *ALLIES*

British Prime Minister Winston Churchill, US President Franklin D. Roosevelt, and the Soviet leader Joseph Stalin meet in Tehran, Iran. Top priority is given to Operation Overlord, the cross-Channel invasion of German-occupied Europe, and a landing in southern France, Operation Anvil, in May 1944. The Soviets have been lobbying for the opening of the Second Front for some time.

DECEMBER 9–26

PACIFIC, SOLOMONS

US advances on Bougainville ensure that air bases can now be opened and missions launched.

DECEMBER 20

PACIFIC, *PAPUA NEW GUINEA*

The Allies achieve supremacy on the Huon Peninsula, although Japanese resistance persists.

DECEMBER 24–29

POLITICS, *ALLIES*

The commanders for the liberation of Europe are announced: General Dwight D. Eisenhower, Supreme Allied Commander; Air Chief Marshal Sir Arthur Tedder, Deputy Supreme Commander; General

Sir Henry Maitland Wilson, Supreme Allied Commander, Mediterranean; Admiral Sir Bertram Ramsay, Allied Naval Commander-in-Chief; Air Chief Marshal Sir Trafford Leigh Mallory, Allied Air Commander-in-Chief; and General Sir Bernard Montgomery, Commander-in-Chief of British Armies.

DECEMBER 25

PACIFIC, *SOLOMONS*

Allied forces land on New Britain and begin advancing to isolate the base of Rabaul from the west.

▲ *Chiang Kai-shek (seated, extreme left), Roosevelt and Churchill at the Cairo Conference in November 1943.*

▼ *A Sherman searches out the enemy during the Allied drive to Rome in November.*

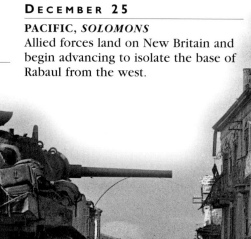

DECEMBER 26

SEA WAR, *ARCTIC*

At the Battle of the North Cape, the German battleship *Scharnhorst* is sunk during an ill-planned operation against convoys JW-55B and RA-55A, which are escorted by the British Home Fleet's battle squadron. The battleship first has its radar and fire control damaged. A running battle follows until the *Scharnhorst* begins to lose speed and is finally sunk by torpedo strikes. Only 36 of *Scharnhorst*'s 1800-strong crew survive.

▲ *Australian troops in typical jungle terrain near Lae, Papua New Guinea, during an offensive against the Japanese.*

▼ *The British battleship HMS* Duke of York, *photographed after participating in the sinking of the* Scharnhorst.

1944

In the Pacific, Japanese defeats at the Battle of the Philippine Sea and around the Mariana Islands, plus losses in Burma, signaled the growing might of the Allies. In Europe, Axis forces suffered reverses and withdrawals in Italy, France, and on the Eastern Front, as the Allies invaded northern France and the Red Army virtually wiped out Army Group Center.

JANUARY 2

POLITICS, *FREE FRENCH*
General Jean de Lattre de Tassigny is appointed commander-in-chief of Free French forces in North Africa.

PACIFIC, *PAPUA NEW GUINEA*
Troops of the US Sixth Army land at Saidor on the north coast of New Guinea as part of Operation Dexterity, cutting off Japanese rearguard forces from their main base at Madang, only 55 miles (88 km) away. The loss of Saidor, a major supply depot, means

▼ *US troops follow a Sherman tank during mopping-up operations on the northern coast of New Guinea.*

◀ *Lancasters over Germany in early January. At this time the RAF was suffering losses of up to 10 percent per month.*

that 20,000 Japanese soldiers are now sandwiched between Australian and US forces. Their only escape route is through dense jungle.

JANUARY 3

AIR WAR, *GERMANY*

In a large-scale air raid on Berlin, the RAF loses 27 Lancasters out of 383 aircraft committed, plus 168 crew members. The damage to the German capital is negligible.

JANUARY 4

ESPIONAGE, *EUROPE*

Operation Carpetbagger – regular airborne supply drops to resistance groups in the Netherlands, Belgium, France, and Italy – begins.

JANUARY 5

POLITICS, *POLAND*

The Polish government-in-exile has authorized the Polish underground movement to cooperate with the Red Army only in the event of a resumption of Polish–Soviet relations (the Soviet Union has not yet recognized the London-based Polish government-in-exile).

▶ *Algerian troops of General Alphonse Juin's French Expeditionary Corps in action at Monte Cassino, Italy, in the middle of January.*

EASTERN FRONT, *UKRAINE*

As part of the Red Army's plan to recover the western Ukraine and the Crimea, General Ivan S. Konev's 2nd Ukrainian Front launches an offensive toward Kirovgrad. Despite desperate German resistance, the town falls on the 8th.

JANUARY 9

FAR EAST, *BURMA*

As part of the Allied attempt to break into Burma, the British XV Corps takes the Burmese town of Maungdaw.

JANUARY 10

EASTERN FRONT, *UKRAINE*

General Rodion Y. Malinovsky's 3rd Ukrainian Front launches an offensive toward Apostolovo, but the attack is halted after six days in the face of fierce German resistance.

JANUARY 11

POLITICS, *ITALY*

Count Galeazzo Ciano, the former Italian foreign secretary and Mussolini's son-in-law, is executed by firing squad in Verona. His "crime" was to have voted with other fascists to oust Mussolini in July 1943. Ciano and his wife had been lured to Bavaria in August 1943 following a report that their children were in danger. Having been promised safe passage to Spain, they were handed over to Italy's puppet fascist government.

JANUARY 12–14

ITALY, *CASSINO*

At Cassino, General Alphonse Juin's colonial troops of the French Expeditionary Corps cross the Rapido River on the Fifth Army's

northern sector. Although they fail to take Monte Santa Croce, their success fills the headquarters of the Fifth Army with renewed optimism.

JANUARY 14–27

EASTERN FRONT, *LENINGRAD*

The Soviet Second Shock Army attacks from the Oranienbaum bridgehead, and the Fifty-ninth Army attacks toward Novgorod, in an attempt to break the German blockade of the city. The next day the Forty-second Army attacks from the Pulkovo Heights. On the 19th, the three armies link up near Krasnoe, and two days later German forces in the Petergof and Streina area are wiped out. Fighting continues as the Germans try to stop the Red Army onslaught, but on the 27th a salute of 324 guns announces the end of the German blockade of Leningrad. Some 830,000 civilians have died during the long siege.

JANUARY 17

ITALY, *GUSTAV LINE*

The Allied attempt to break through the Gustav Line – a frontal assault combined with a seaborne hook to the German rear at Anzio – begins. The British X Corps attacks across the Garigliano River and strikes northwest toward the Aurunci Mountains and the Liri Valley. In response, the German commander, General Heinrich von Vietinghoff, transfers two armored divisions to counter this new threat.

Rome is open. However, although by the evening Lucas has nearly 50,000 men and 3000 vehicles ashore, he orders his forces to dig in to repel any enemy counterattacks. He thus misses the opportunity to strike inland from the beachhead.

JANUARY 24

ITALY, *CASSINO/ANZIO*
At Anzio, Allied patrols venturing inland are halted by increasing German resistance. At Cassino, the US 34th Division finally establishes bridgeheads across the Rapido River to allow the armor to cross. At the other end of the Allied line, French troops make further gains.

JANUARY 26

POLITICS, *ARGENTINA*
Argentina has severed relations with Germany and Japan following the

▲ *German paratroopers on their way to attack the Allied bridgehead at Anzio, which had been contained by late January.*

JANUARY 20

ITALY, *GUSTAV LINE*
As part of the Allied attack on the Gustav Line, the US II Corps attempts to cross the Rapido River to clear a path for the US 1st Armored Division. The German defenses are strong and the Americans suffer heavy losses.

JANUARY 22

ITALY, *ANZIO*
Troops of the Allied VI Corps make an amphibious landing at Anzio, behind the German lines. Commanded by US General John Lucas, the initial attack is almost unopposed and the road to

Map legend:
- Allied attacks
- Front line, October 12, 1943
- Front line, November 15, 1943
- Front line, 15 January, 1944
- Front line, 11 May, 1944
- Front line, 5 June, 1944

Map labels: Tiber River, Avezzano, ROME, ITALY, Sangro River, Pescara, Termoli, Valmontone, Liri River, Trigno River, Socco River, Cassino, Sezza, Pontecorvo, Mignano, Anzio beachhead, Borgo Grappa, Minturino, Naples, Gulf of Gaeta

0 — 25 mi
0 — 40 km

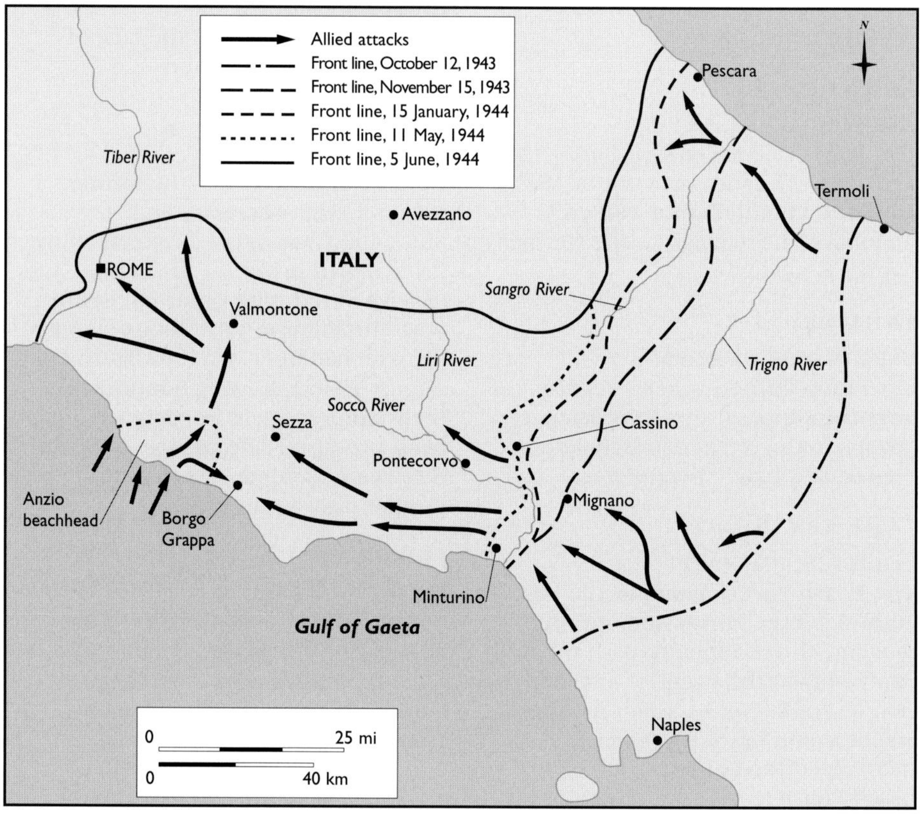

▲ *The campaign to break through the German defenses to reach Anzio was both long and costly.*

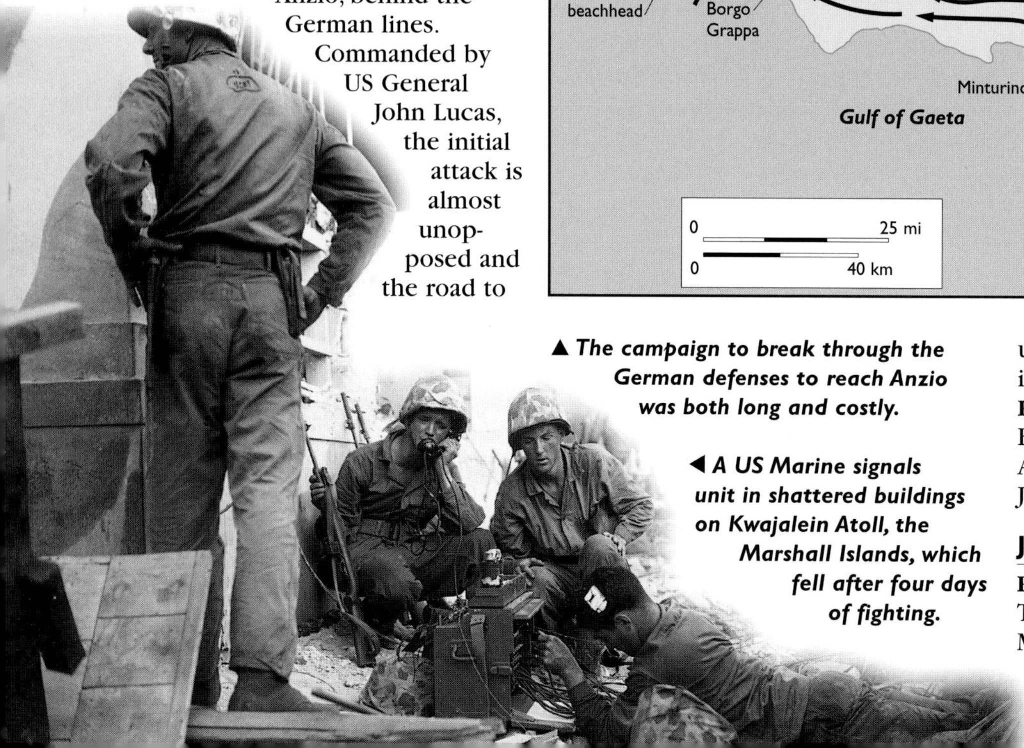

◄ *A US Marine signals unit in shattered buildings on Kwajalein Atoll, the Marshall Islands, which fell after four days of fighting.*

uncovering of a vast Axis spy network in the country.

PACIFIC, *PAPUA NEW GUINEA*
Following several days of fighting, the Australian 18th Brigade takes the key Japanese position of Kankiryo Saddle.

JANUARY 30

PACIFIC, *MARSHALLS*
The American conquest of the Marshall Islands, Operation Flintlock,

begins with an amphibious assault against Majuro Atoll. The strategy is to concentrate on key islands and their air bases. Once these have been taken, enemy garrisons on lesser islets will be starved into submission. The landing on Majuro was made on one of the atoll's islands, which was undefended.

FEBRUARY 1–4

PACIFIC, MARSHALLS
The amphibious assault against the islands of Kwajalein Atoll is launched. Some 40,000 US Marines and infantry land on the islands of Roi, Namur, and Kwajalein. Japanese resistance is fanatical. It takes the Americans two days to secure Roi and Namur at a cost of 737 killed and wounded; four days to conquer Kwajalein for the loss of 372 killed and wounded. Total Japanese losses are 11,612 men killed.

FEBRUARY 4

ITALY, CASSINO/ANZIO
Allied attacks edge closer to Monte Cassino, but then fierce German counterattacks stop the advance in its tracks. At Anzio, the Germans, located on the high ground, contain the Allied bridgehead, which now holds more than 70,000 men and 18,000 vehicles.

FEBRUARY 4–24

FAR EAST, BURMA
The Japanese launch Operation Ha-Go with their 55th Division, designed to cut off the forward troops of the Allied

▲ *General Joseph Stilwell (right), whose troops were advancing on Myitkyina in early February 1944, with Chinese allies.*

XV Corps and force the Allies back to the Indian border. Initial Japanese attacks are successful and push Allied troops back to a defensive position near Sinzweya called the "Admin Box." The Japanese ring around the position is not broken until the 25th, when the 123rd Brigade fights its way through the Ngakyedauk Pass and reaches the "Admin Box." The failure of Ha-Go is a watershed in the Burma campaign, as Japanese enveloping tactics have failed to produce the expected results.

FEBRUARY 5

FAR EAST, BURMA
The 16th Brigade of Orde Wingate's Chindits begins to move south from Ledo, India, toward Indaw in northern Burma. Its mission is threefold: to aid General Joseph Stilwell's advance on Myitkyina by drawing off enemy forces; to create a favourable situation for the Yunnan armies; and to inflict the maximum amount of damage and loss on the Japanese in northern Burma.

FEBRUARY 12

SEA WAR, FAR EAST
The Japanese submarine *I-27* sinks the British troopship *Khedive Ismail* with the loss of many lives. The submarine is then sunk by the destroyers *Petard* and *Paladin*.

KEY PERSONALITIES

MARSHAL JOSIP BROZ TITO LEADER OF YUGOSLAVIA

Tito (1892–1980) was nearly 50 years old when World War II broke out. Having seen service in the Russian Revolution and Spanish Civil War, he quickly organized resistance when the Germans invaded Yugoslavia in March 1941. By the fall of that year, he was waging a full-scale guerrilla campaign in Serbia, capturing a number of towns, including Uzice, where he set up an arms factory and printing facilities. He disagreed with the rival Chetnik resistance group and defeated them, but was then driven out of Serbia by the Germans in the first of seven major Axis offensives against the Yugoslavian partisans.

His tactics on the ground consisted of fighting as long as possible, then withdrawing into the hills with his forces, all the while maintaining tight communication and organization as he did so. In May 1943 he was attacked by forces six times greater than his own, lost a quarter of his strength and half his equipment, but still managed to keep his forces together.

In late 1942 Tito began receiving aid from the Western Allies, and the withdrawal of Italy from the war gave him Croatia and vast quantities of Italian weapons. By 1944 he had an army of 250,000 men and women, and on October 20 he took Belgrade. He became the symbol of the country's unity, and was able to establish a postwar communist government.

FEBRUARY 16–17

ITALY, *CASSINO*
The US 34th Division makes a last attempt to capture the German-held monastery. Its attack is halted, however, and the unit is replaced by the 4th Indian and New Zealand Divisions of the British Eighth Army.

FEBRUARY 16–19

ITALY, *ANZIO*
With massive artillery support, 10 German divisions attack the Anzio beachhead in an attempt to wipe it out. By the morning of the 17th, the Germans have created a wedge one mile (1.6 km) deep in the Allied line. However, that afternoon aircraft from the entire Italian front bomb and strafe the German units in an effort to save the beachhead. Allied air attacks, supported by artillery on the ground, eventually force the Germans to retire on the 19th.

FEBRUARY 18–22

PACIFIC, *MARSHALLS*
US forces complete their conquest of

▲ *American Dauntless dive-bombers returning from a strike against Japanese targets in the Marshall Islands.*

the islands with the seizure of Eniwetok Atoll. This combined army and Marine operation is a bloody affair, with 3400 Japanese defenders dying, along with 254 US Marines and 94 army personnel being killed. The Marshalls are the first Japanese prewar territories to fall to the Allies so far in the war.

FEBRUARY 26

EASTERN FRONT, *BALTIC*
The Red Army captures Porkhov and regroups on the Novorzhev and Pustoshka line. In the course of a six-week campaign the Volkhov, Leningrad, and 2nd Baltic Fronts have inflicted a shattering defeat on Germany's Army Group North. They have wiped out three German divisions, routed another 17, and captured 189 tanks and 1800 artillery pieces. In addition, units of local partisans have killed over 21,500 German troops, destroyed 300 bridges, and derailed 136 military trains during a series of wide-ranging attacks.

FEBRUARY 29

PACIFIC, *ADMIRALTIES*
As part of their strategy for isolating the Japanese base at Rabaul, American forces land on the islands, a staging

▼ *A mortar of the US 34th Division shells German-held positions around Cassino.*

KEY PERSONALITIES

GENERAL GEORGE S. PATTON

Something of an innovator in the US Army, Patton (1885–1945) had seen service in World War I and was a firm believer in the tenets of armored warfare. He was given command of the US II Corps in the Torch landings in November 1942, and was then ordered to lead the US Seventh Army in the invasion of Sicily. However, the controversial hitting of shell-shocked soldiers in a field hospital resulted in public censure.

During the campaign in France he led the US Third Army, using it to achieve quick advances to Lorraine and the German frontier. However, he strongly disagreed with Eisenhower's policy of sharing vital military supplies between US forces and Montgomery's British and Commonwealth units. Patton believed that if he had been given more supplies he could have ended the war in 1944. Instead, he fought a bitter battle of attrition on the border and intervened decisively in the Battle of the Bulge. In 1945 he conducted a masterful crossing of the Rhine, which was followed by a whirlwind advance into Czechoslovakia. Patton, the founder of the armored tradition in the US Army, was killed in an motor vehicle accident in December 1945.

post through which the Japanese can reach Rabaul. The fall of the Admiralties will secure the southwest Pacific for the Allies.

MARCH 1

FAR EAST, *BURMA*
The Chindits' 16th Brigade crosses the Chindwin River, as Chinese forces and Merrill's Marauders (a US commando force) under General Joseph Stilwell, advance toward Myitkyina.

MARCH 2

POLITICS, *ALLIES*
The Allies cut off all aid to Turkey due to its government's reluctance to help their war effort.

MARCH 5–11

FAR EAST, *BURMA*
Brigadier Mike Calvert's 77th Brigade of the Chindits begins landing by glider at two selected points code-named "Broadway" and "Piccadilly" in the Kaukkwe Valley, northern Burma. During the first lift, 61 gliders are used, although only 35 reach their target. By the 11th, the whole of Calvert's brigade has been flown in.

MARCH 7

HOME FRONT, *GERMANY*
Members of the Nazi organization for women are making house-to-house calls to recruit females between the ages of 17 and 45 to work "in the service of the community." This is to bolster Germany's depleted labor force.

▼ *Chinese infantry under the overall command of General Joseph Stilwell crossing the Chindwin River in March.*

▲ Anxious German troops wait for action as the Red Army attacks Army Group North on the Eastern Front.

MARCH 7–8

FAR EAST, *BURMA/INDIA*
Operation U-Go, the Japanese offensive to drive the Allies back into India by destroying their bases at Imphal and Kohima, begins with moves to sever the Tiddim to Imphal road. The Japanese 33rd Division has orders to cut off the 17th Indian Division at Tiddim and force the British to commit their reserves to rescue it, while the

▲ Japanese troops on the attack between Homalin and Thaungdut in their efforts to cut the Imphal to Kohima road.

▼ For German workers in 1944 it was a never-ending task of laying new railroad tracks after Allied air raids, in this case after an US 8th Army Air Force attack.

31st and 15th Divisions are to cross the Chindwin farther north and fall on Imphal and Kohima.

MARCH 8

AIR WAR, GERMANY
The US 8th Army Air Force launches a massive daylight precision raid on the Erker ball-bearing works, Berlin. A total of 590 aircraft mount the raid. There are 75 direct hits on the target, but the Americans lose 37 aircraft. This is the third US raid on Berlin under the escort of P-51 Mustang fighters. It results in the halting of ball-bearing production for some time.

MARCH 11

EASTERN FRONT, UKRAINE
General Rodion Malinovsky's 2nd Ukrainian Front reaches the Bug River, brushing aside resistance from the German Eighth Army. The Germans hope to halt the Red Army on this great water barrier.

MARCH 11–12

FAR EAST, BURMA
In the Arakan, northern Burma, the Allies recapture Buthidaung and then surround and capture the Japanese fortress at Razabil.

MARCH 15–16

FAR EAST, BURMA/INDIA
The Japanese 15th and 31st Divisions cross the Chindwin River between Homalin and Thaungdut and move forward with the intention of cutting the Imphal to Kohima road.

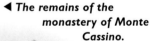

◄ *US B-25 medium bombers on their way to pound German units dug in amid the ruins of Monte Cassino.*

MARCH 18

EASTERN FRONT, *UKRAINE*

The Soviet 2nd Ukrainian Front has reached the Dniester River and seized a large bridgehead at Mogilev Podolsky. This has split the German Army Group South's front in two and has put the Red Army in a position to advance to the Romanian frontier.

MARCH 19

POLITICS, *HUNGARY*

With the Red Army rapidly approaching the Balkans, Hitler has sent troops to occupy the country. Admiral Miklós Horthy, the regent, has been ordered to appoint a pro-Nazi premier, allow the German Army to take over the transport system, and give the SS a free hand in deporting Hungarian Jews to concentration camps.

ITALY, *CASSINO*

A German counterattack against Peak 193 is unsuccessful but has loosened the Allied stranglehold. A New Zealand armored assault against the monastery is destroyed.

MARCH 20–22

ITALY, *CASSINO*

Despite further frontal attacks by New Zealand troops under General Harold Alexander, the German defenders, veterans of the 1st Parachute Division, remain in and around the monastery and repulse all efforts to dislodge

◄ *The remains of the monastery of Monte Cassino.*

MARCH 15–17

ITALY, *CASSINO*

Allied aircraft launch a massive raid against the unoccupied monastery of Monte Cassino (which is later criticized by the Vatican). The New Zealand 2nd Division then launches an assault that takes Peak 193. During the evening the 4th Indian Division attacks and captures Peak 165. All Allied attacks on the 16th are frustrated, but on the 17th a breakthrough by the New Zealanders takes Cassino railroad station. They fail, though, to complete the encirclement of the town itself.

▲ Waiting for the next Japanese attack: a British machine-gun position at Imphal in late March 1944.

▲ Major General Orde Wingate, the brilliant Chindit commander, who was killed in an air crash at Imphal.

them. On the 22nd, therefore, Alexander halts all frontal assaults.

MARCH 24

FAR EAST, *BURMA*
Major General Orde Wingate, the commander of the Chindits, is killed in a plane crash. A charismatic and controversial figure, Winston Churchill has called him a "man of genius and audacity" following the success of his long-range penetration missions in Burma.

MARCH 28

EASTERN FRONT, *UKRAINE*
As the Germans retreat in haste from the waters of the southern Bug River, Nikolayev falls to the Red Army. The 3rd Ukrainian Front is now developing an assault toward the port of Odessa.

MARCH 29

FAR EAST, *INDIA*
The Japanese 20th Division establishes itself on the Shenam Saddle near

Imphal. Japanese forces have cut the Imphal to Kohima road and begun the siege of Imphal.

MARCH 30

POLITICS, *GERMANY*
Hitler, outraged at the Soviet victories in the Ukraine, has dismissed two of his field marshals – Erich von Manstein and Paul von Kleist – for disregarding his "stand fast" orders. In addition, the Nazi leader believes that the army in the Ukraine has put up weak resistance against the Soviets.

FAR EAST, *BURMA*
The Chindits' 16th Brigade, commanded by Brigadier Bernard Fergusson, retreats following its failure to take the main Japanese supply base at Indaw.

MARCH 30–31

AIR WAR, *GERMANY*
A night raid by the RAF against Nuremberg results in little damage to the city but substantial losses are inflicted on the aircraft involved. The RAF loses 95 out of the

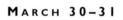

attacking force of 795 bombers, with a further 71 damaged.

APRIL 3

AIR WAR, *NORWAY*

The German battleship *Tirpitz* has been damaged in Altenfiord, Norway, by Royal Navy aircraft flown from the British carriers *Victorious* and *Furious*. *Tirpitz* has been hit 14 times, which means that it will not sail again for several months.

APRIL 4–13

FAR EAST, *INDIA*

The first stage of the Imphal battle has ended. The Japanese have failed to destroy the Allied defense line. The British IV Corps, now concentrated around Imphal, can turn its attention to the destruction of the Japanese. By April 13, the Japanese have been ejected from Nungshigum, one of the hills commanding the Imphal plain, and their 15th Division is being harried down the road to Ukhrul.

APRIL 5

EASTERN FRONT, *UKRAINE*

The Soviet 3rd Ukrainian Front captures Razdelnaya station and cuts the local German forces in two, one of which is forced to withdraw toward Odessa and the other toward Tiraspol.

APRIL 6–11

FAR EAST, *BURMA*

Japanese forces attack the Chindit fortified position at "White City," which is subsequently evacuated.

APRIL 8

EASTERN FRONT, *CRIMEA*

General Fedor I. Tolbukhin's 4th Ukrainian Front (470,000 men, 6000 field guns and mortars, 560 tanks and self-propelled guns, and 1250 combat aircraft) begins the liberation of the

▲ *General Fedor Tolbukhin, whose 4th Ukrainian Front liberated the Crimea and captured Sebastopol in April.*

peninsula. The German and Romanian forces defending the region as part of the Seventeenth Army can muster only 200,000 men, 3600 field guns and mortars, 200 tanks and self-propelled guns, and 150 aircraft.

APRIL 9

EASTERN FRONT, *UKRAINE*

The Soviet 3rd Ukrainian Front reaches the outskirts of Odessa.

APRIL 12

POLITICS, *ROMANIA*

In reply to a Romanian mission regarding the conditions for an armistice between Romania and the Soviet Union, Moscow demands that Romania break with the Germans, that its forces fight alongside the Red Army, and insists on the restoration of the Romanian and Soviet border. It also calls for reparations for damage inflicted on the Soviet Union by Romania, freedom of movement through the country for Soviet and other Allied forces, and the repatriation

◄ *A Swordfish torpedo-bomber returns to HMS* Victorious, *which took part in an attack on the German battleship* Tirpitz.

of Soviet prisoners. The Romanians reject these conditions and remain with the Axis.

APRIL 15

AIR WAR, *EUROPE*
The US 8th Army Air Force and RAF Bomber Command decide to switch bombing from German urban centers to railroads in Belgium and France to prepare for the forthcoming Allied invasion by preventing German reinforcements reaching the front.

A force of 448 Flying Fortresses and Liberators of the US 15th Army Air Force, escorted by 150 Mustang fighters, also attacks the oil fields at Ploesti and the Romanian capital, Bucharest. During the night the RAF bombs the railroad lines at Turnu Severin in Romania.

▲ *A US A-20 bomber hits an important rail junction at Busigny in northern France.*

APRIL 22

**PACIFIC,
*PAPUA NEW GUINEA***
General Douglas MacArthur, leading a 52,000-strong Allied invasion force, makes an amphibious landing in Hollandia, northern New Guinea. Hollandia will be the base for the next phase of MacArthur's Operation Cartwheel, which is

designed to drive the Japanese from northwest New Guinea.

MAY 3

POLITICS, *JAPAN*
Admiral Soemu Toyoda is appointed commander-in-chief of the Japanese Combined Fleet. He replaces Admiral Mineichi Koga, who has been killed in a plane crash on March 31.

MAY 9

EASTERN FRONT, *CRIMEA*
The Soviet 4th Ukrainian Front liberates the port of Sebastopol. It is a crushing defeat for the German defenders, who have lost 100,000 men killed and captured during the fighting.

◄ *Admiral Soemu Toyoda, the new commander-in-chief of the Japanese Combined Fleet.*

◄ *Mopping up the last pockets of Japanese resistance on the Admiralty Islands – both tedious and dangerous.*

MAY 19

HOME FRONT, *GERMANY*
Following their recapture after a mass breakout from Stalag Luft III near Sagan, Silesia, 50 Allied airmen are shot by the Gestapo. Only three of the escaped prisoners – two Norwegians and a Dutchman – reach England.

MAY 23–31

ITALY, *ANZIO*
Troops of the US VI Corps begin the breakout from the Anzio beachhead in the face of stubborn German resistance. The linkup with troops of the US II Corps occurs on the 25th, four months after the original Anzio landing. Steady gains are made by the Allies, although taking the Adolf Hitler Line, which runs from Terracina on the coast along the Foni to Pico road to Pontecorvo and across the Liri Valley through Aquino and Piedmonte to Monte Cairo, does result in heavy Allied losses. Once again the Germans have proved adept at defense.

▼ *Infantry of the British 4th Division pick their way through shattered streets during the advance to the Rapido River in Italy.*

MAY 11–18

ITALY, *CASSINO*
The Allied 15th Army Group begins its offensive to outflank the monastery. On the 12th, the French Expeditionary Corps takes Monte Faito, but the Polish 5th Division fails to capture Colle Sant'Angelo. On the 13th, the French open the way to Rome, while the US II Corps takes Santa Maria Infante, and the British 4th Division begins to enlarge its bridgehead across the Rapido River.

On the 17th, the Germans evacuate the monastery at Monte Cassino because of the deep breakthroughs by the French Expeditionary Corps and the US II Corps. The next day, the Polish 12th Podolski Regiment storms the ruins of Monte Cassino.

MAY 18

PACIFIC, *ADMIRALTIES*
The last pockets of Japanese resistance on the islands have been crushed. This effectively isolates the main Japanese bases at Rabaul and Kavieng in the southwest Pacific.

On the 25th, the US Fifth Army attacks toward Rome, but is held by the Germans, who have had time to dig in around Valmontone along the Caesar Line. It is not until the night of May 30 – when Major General Fred L. Walker's US 36th Division moves silently up Monte Artemisio and breaks the Valmontone defenses – that the final defensive line barring the entrance to Rome is cut.

MAY 25

BALKANS, *YUGOSLAVIA*

The Germans launch an air, glider, and mortar attack on the partisan headquarters at Divar, in which Marshal Tito narrowly escapes capture. The attack is believed to have been the plan of SS Major Otto Skorzeny, the officer who rescued Mussolini.

▼ *German paratroopers in Rome on the eve of their evacuation of the city in early June.*

▲ *Soldiers of the US 4th Infantry Division wade ashore under fire at Utah Beach on D-Day, the invasion of northern France.*

MAY 29

PACIFIC, *PAPUA NEW GUINEA*

The first tank battle of the Pacific campaign is fought on Biak Island, off New Guinea, between the Japanese and Americans. It is a US victory.

JUNE 1

FAR EAST, *BURMA*

Brigadier Mike Calvert, commander of the Chindits' 77th Brigade, reaches Lakum near Mogaung.

JUNE 3

FAR EAST, *INDIA*

The 64-day Battle of Kohima ends with the remnants of the Japanese 31st Division withdrawing in good order. It is the lack of supplies, rather than the attacks of the British and Indian forces, which has forced the Japanese to fall back. The fighting at Kohima has been among the most savage of the whole war.

JUNE 3–4

ITALY, *ROME*

Adolf Hitler reluctantly gives Field Marshal Albert Kesselring, the German commander-in-chief in Italy,

permission to abandon Rome. Covered by expert rearguard actions of IV Parachute Corps, the German Fourteenth Army pulls back across the Tiber River. US troops enter the city on the 5th – the first Axis capital to be captured.

JUNE 6

WESTERN FRONT, *FRANCE*
The Allies launch the greatest amphibious operation in history. The statistics for the invasion force are staggering: 50,000 men for the initial assault; over two million men to be shipped to France in all, comprising a total of 39 divisions; 139 major warships used in the assault, with a further 221 smaller combat vessels; over 1000 minesweepers and auxiliary vessels; 4000 landing craft; 805 merchant ships; 59 blockships; 300 miscellaneous small craft; and 11,000 aircraft, including fighters, bombers, transports, and gliders. In addition, the invasion force has the support of over 100,000 members of the French Resistance, who launch hit-and-run attacks on German targets.

D-Day, the Allied invasion of Normandy, code-named Operation Overlord, begins with the assault of three airborne divisions – the US 82nd and 101st on the right flank of the US forces, and the British 6th Airborne on

▲ *German prisoners are led away after their surrender on D-Day.*

◄ *British Horsa gliders litter the fields northeast of Caen on the morning of D-Day – 6 June 1944.*

▼ *After consolidating their beachhead, the Allies built up their forces for the liberation of France. Air superiority, which restricted the movement of German forces, greatly aided their efforts.*

the left flank of the British – while seaborne forces land on five beaches. Utah Beach is the target of the US 4th Infantry Division (part of the US VII Corps); Omaha Beach is the target of the US 1st Infantry Division (part of the US V Corps); Gold Beach is the landing site of the British 50th Infantry Division (part of the British XXX Corps); Juno is the target for the Canadian 3rd Infantry Division (part of the British I Corps); and the British 3rd

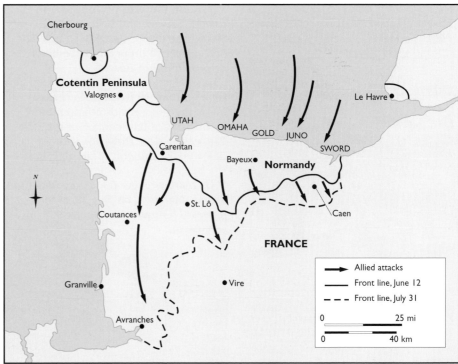

DECISIVE WEAPONS

RESISTANCE

Within those countries and regions overrun by the Germans and Japanese in Word War II, there were those among the various populations who were determined to oppose the occupiers in some way, often at great risk to themselves and their families. This resistance could be active or passive. Passive resistance involved demonstrations, industrial strikes, and slowdowns, the production of underground newspapers and leaflets, and wall slogans. Active resistance involved gathering intelligence, assisting escaped Allied prisoners of war and shot-down aircrews, sabotage, and armed action against occupation forces.

Throughout Europe and the Far East, resistance was never the preserve of any particular political grouping or social class; rather it encompassed a complete cross-section of each country's society.

The dangers of fighting back against occupiers were ever present, and resistance movements were under constant threat from enemy intelligence, collaborators, and informers, with torture and death the usual price of being caught. Ownership of a carrier pigeon, for example, warranted death by firing squad in Europe. In addition, there was often infighting between various resistance groups. In Yugoslavia, the Chetniks and Tito's forces fought each other as well as the Axis occupiers. Nevertheless, with outside help (which was often crucial in keeping the various units going), resistance groups in Europe and the Far East aided the general Allied war effort against the Axis powers.

Jubilant members of the French Resistance near Paris in August 1944, with the Germans in full retreat.

▲ *American troops march through bomb-damaged Carentan, the first French city to fall to the invaders after D-Day.*

Infantry Division (also part of the British I Corps) is tasked with seizing Sword Beach.

The initial parachute and seaborne landings have mixed results: on Utah resistance is slight and the troops are off the beach by 1200 hours; on Omaha the lack of specialized armor means the Germans can pin down the troops on the beach, with great slaughter; on Gold and Juno the specialized armor of the British and Canadians allow the troops to get off the beaches quickly, and by the afternoon they are probing inland toward Bayeux and Caen; and on Sword the troops are able to link up with airborne units that have been dropped farther inland.

This is fortunate, for it is between Juno and Sword that the Germans make their one major counterattack, comprising a battlegroup of the 21st Panzer Division. However, it is defeated. By the end of the day, at a

▼ *US Marines under fire on the island of Saipan, Marianas, on June 23, 1944. Japanese resistance was, as usual, very fierce.*

cost of 2500 dead, the Allies have a toehold in German-occupied Europe.

JUNE 9–10

EASTERN FRONT, *FINLAND*
The Soviets, in an effort to drive the Finns back to the 1940 frontier and compel them to make peace, launch a major offensive with two armies. The offensive is preceded by a sustained barrage from 5500 guns and 880 rocket-launchers. The attack shatters the Finnish front and, on the 10th, Marshal Karl von Mannerheim, Finland's military leader, orders a retreat to a stronger defensive line.

JUNE 10

WESTERN FRONT, *FRANCE*
The 2nd SS Panzer Division *Das Reich*, moving from its base at Toulouse

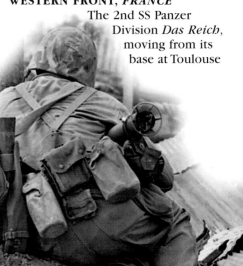

to Normandy, has been the constant target of members of the French Resistance. In retaliation, the small town of Oradour-sur-Glane is chosen as the target for a brutal reprisal, one intended to be a lesson to the people of France. The men of the village are herded into barns, the women and children into the church, and the whole town is set on fire. Those who flee are machine-gunned. In total, 642 people are killed, with only 10 able to feign death and escape.

JUNE 11

PACIFIC, *MARIANAS*
US Task Force 58 begins a heavy bombardment of Saipan, Tinian, Guam, Rota, and Pagan prior to an assault on the islands, the occupation of which will allow the US forces operating in the area to

▲ *A Japanese ship under American air attack during the Battle of the Philippine Sea, which fatally wrecked Japanese naval air strength in the Pacific.*

sever the lines of communication to Japan's units operating in the southern Pacific.

JUNE 13

WESTERN FRONT, *FRANCE*
Lieutenant Michael Wittmann, company commander of the SS 501st Heavy Tank Battalion, destroys 27 tanks and armoured vehicles of the British 4th Country of London Yeomanry in a tank battle around the village of Villers-Bocage, Normandy.
PACIFIC, *JAPAN*
The Japanese Combined Fleet is alerted to prepare for Operation A-Go, which is intended to lure the US Pacific Fleet to one of two battle areas – either the Palaus or the Western Carolines – where it can be destroyed. These areas are chosen because they are within range of the greatest possible number of Japanese island air bases, thereby counterbalancing US aircraft carrier superiority.

JUNE 15

PACIFIC, *MARIANAS*
The US Northern Attack Force arrives off Saipan. In response, the Japanese Combined Fleet is ordered to gather. On the island itself, landings are conducted on the west coast by the US 2nd and 4th Marine Divisions.
AIR WAR, *JAPAN*
The iron and steel works at Yahata on the mainland is bombed by B-29s of the US 20th Army Air Force, which is operating from bases in China.

JUNE 16

FAR EAST, *BURMA*
The 22nd Division, part of Lieutenant General Joseph Stilwell's Chinese force, has taken Kamaing, the first of his three objectives – the others being Mogaung and Myitkyina.

JUNE 18

WESTERN FRONT, *FRANCE*
US forces reach the west coast of the Cotentin Peninsula, Normandy, trapping the German garrison in Cherbourg. Hitler has ordered the garrison to fight to the death.
PACIFIC, *MARIANAS*
The warships of US Task Force 58 rendezvous west of Saipan.

JUNE 19–21

PACIFIC, *PHILIPPINE SEA*

On hearing of the US assault on Saipan, the Japanese Combined Fleet, under Admiral Jisaburo Ozawa, puts to sea immediately with five heavy and four light carriers, five battleships, 11 heavy and two light cruisers, and 28 destroyers. The US 5th Fleet, under Admiral Marc Mitscher's tactical command, numbers seven heavy and eight light carriers, eight heavy and 13 light cruisers, and 69 destroyers. Aircraft on either side total 573 Japanese (including 100 based on Guam, Rota, and Yap) and 956 American.

Ozawa's search planes locate the 5th Fleet at daybreak, 300 miles (480 km) from his advance element of four light carriers and 500 miles (800 km) from his main body. Ozawa launches an attack in four waves, while Mitscher, on discovering the enemy aircraft, sends out his interceptors.

Disaster strikes Ozawa immediately, for US submarines sink the carriers *Taiho* and *Shokaku*, and US fighters shoot down many of his aircraft. In the Battle of the Philippine Sea, nicknamed the "Great Marianas Turkey Shoot" by the Americans, the Japanese lose 346 aircraft and two carriers. US losses are 30 aircraft and slight damage to a battleship. Meanwhile, Mitscher's bombers neutralize the Japanese airfields on Guam and Rota.

On the 20th, Mitscher launches 216 aircraft, which sink another carrier and two oil tankers, and seriously damage several other vessels. While the Americans lose 20 aircraft, Ozawa loses another 65, although many US aircraft are forced to ditch into the sea.

Ozawa's costly battle deals a crippling blow to the Japanese naval air arm, not least through the loss of 460 trained combat pilots.

JUNE 20

ITALY, *UMBRIA*

The British XXX Corps opens its attack on the Albert Line, one of a series of German rearguard positions in northern Italy, south of Lake Trasimeno on either side of Chiusi. The fighting is hard; the Germans give ground grudgingly.

JUNE 22

POLITICS, *GERMANY*

Foreign Minister Joachim von Ribbentrop visits Helsinki to try to tie Finland more tightly to Germany.

FAR EAST, *INDIA*

The British 2nd Division reach the defenders of Imphal, but Japanese resistance continues.

▲ *The Red Army liberates another town in Belorussia and its soldiers are welcomed by grateful civilians.*

JUNE 22–26

FAR EAST, *BURMA*

The Chindits' 77th Brigade begins attacking Mogaung from the southeast. Following bitter fighting, it finally falls on the 26th.

JUNE 23

EASTERN FRONT, *BELORUSSIA*

The Red Army launches its Belorussian offensive. Four fronts – 1st Baltic, 1st, 2nd, and 3rd Belorussian, comprising

▼ *Allied troops in the ruins of Valognes during the drive against Cherbourg, which fell on June 29, 1944.*

1.2 million men in all – attack the German divisions of Army Group Center. The Soviets have a four-to-one superiority in tanks and aircraft.

JUNE 26

WESTERN FRONT, *FRANCE*
The British launch Operation Epsom, a drive west of Caen. Troops and tanks of the 15th, 43rd, and 11th Armored Divisions make good initial progress, but are then halted following very heavy losses.

JUNE 29

WESTERN FRONT, *FRANCE*
The port of Cherbourg finally surrenders to forces of the US VII Corps. The cost to the US has been 22,000 casualties, while 39,000 Germans are taken prisoner.

JUNE 30

TECHNOLOGY, *GERMANY*
The Germans have formed the first operational unit equipped with Messerschmitt Me 262 jet fighters.

▲ *Paratroopers belonging to the US 503rd Parachute Infantry Regiment land on Kamirir airstrip, Noemfoor, July 2, 1944.*

The unit will be deployed to France in the near future.

AIR WAR, *BRITAIN*
To date, 2000 German V1 "Flying Bombs" have been launched against England, mostly against London. In response, the British have increased the number of anti-aircraft guns, fighter aircraft, and barrage balloons.

JULY 2

ITALY, *TUSCANY*
The British XIII Corps takes the town of Foiano, northwest of Lake Trasimeno, thereby completing the breakthrough of the German Albert Line.

JULY 4

EASTERN FRONT, *BALTIC*
The Red Army offensive to clear the Baltic states begins. Three Soviet Fronts – 1st, 2nd, and 3rd Baltic – are to be used. The Baltic states are of major importance to Germany, as they are a major source of food and enable the Germans to blockade the Russian fleet and keep supply lanes to Sweden and Finland open.

JULY 7–9

PACIFIC, *MARIANAS*
The Japanese commander on Saipan, General Yoshitsugu Saito, launches a

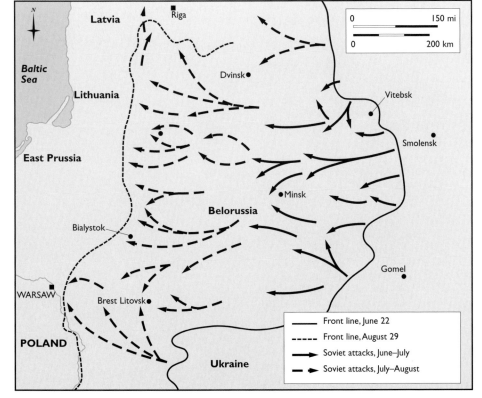

◄ *The Soviet offensive in Belorussia in mid-1944 shattered Army Group Center under a deluge of tanks and men.*

353

▲ *Admiral Miklós Horthy (center), regent of Hungary, who halted the deportation of Hungarian Jews to Auschwitz.*

mass charge against the US 27th Infantry Division at Makunsho. Despite losing hundreds of men to US gunfire, the Japanese crash through the American lines. However, they soon lose their momentum and fail. Saito commits suicide and the island is declared secure on the 9th. At least 8000 Japanese defenders and civilians have committed suicide rather than surrender.

JULY 8

POLITICS, *HUNGARY*
With the Red Army fast approaching, Hungary's leader, Admiral Miklós Horthy, orders a halt to the deportation of Hungarian Jews to Auschwitz concentration camp.

JULY 11

POLITICS, *UNITED STATES*
President Franklin D. Roosevelt announces he will run for an unprecedented fourth term in the White House.

EASTERN FRONT, *BELORUSSIA*
The Minsk area falls to the Red Army. The Germans have lost over 70,000 men killed and 35,000 taken prisoner, and their Fourth Army has ceased to exist.

▶ *Same task, different island – flushing out Japanese defenders on Tinian, one of the Mariana Islands, with a pack howitzer.*

JULY 15

EASTERN FRONT, *FINLAND*
The battle for the Karelian Isthmus ends with a defensive victory for Finland. Three Soviet armies make excellent early progress, but are unable to achieve the objectives laid down in their orders of June 21. The Soviet military leadership orders its troops in Finland to go over to the defensive on the 11th.

JULY 17

EASTERN FRONT, *UKRAINE*
Units of the Soviet First Guards Tank Army cross the Bug River into Poland.

JULY 18

FAR EAST, *BURMA*
The Japanese high command calls off Operation U-Go.

JULY 18–22

WESTERN FRONT, *FRANCE*
In the face of fanatical resistance, US troops enter St. Lô. The German 352nd Division is destroyed in the process. On the eastern sector of the front, the British and Canadians launch Operation Goodwood, a drive east of Caen to provoke heavier German concentrations in the area. The aim is to wear down German armor to such an extent that it is of no further value to them. The Allies lose over 100 Sherman tanks in the assault. By the 22nd, however, the British have cleared southern Caen.

JULY 19–21

PACIFIC, *MARIANAS*
US battleships begin the pre-invasion bombardment of Asan and Agat beaches on Guam, the most important island in the Marianas group. Two days later, troops of the 3rd Marine Division and 77th Infantry Division begin landing on the island. The Japanese fight back hard.

JULY 20

POLITICS, *GERMANY*
An attempt is made by German officers to assassinate Adolf Hitler. Count Schenk von Stauffenberg, chief-of-staff to General Friedrich Fromm, plants a bomb near Hitler in a conference room at the Nazi leader's East Prussian headquarters at Rastenburg. The bomb explodes at 1242 hours, after von Stauffenberg has left. The bomb fails to kill Hitler and the conspiracy falls apart. Josef Goebbels, Nazi minister for propaganda, acts quickly to convince the Berlin garrison that Hitler is still alive by linking them by telephone. Fromm, to allay suspicions of his involvement in the plot, has von Stauffenberg shot in the evening.

The failure of the plot results in the arrest, torture, and execution of dozens of suspects in the following months. Field Marshal Erwin Rommel is among the most notable of those senior military figures aware of the conspiracy.

JULY 21

POLITICS, *POLAND*
The Soviet-backed Polish Committee of National Liberation is formed.

JULY 23

ITALY, *TUSCANY*
After taking the vital port of Livorno on the 19th, the US 34th Division enters the town of Pisa.

JULY 25

WESTERN FRONT, *FRANCE*
Operation Cobra, the Allied breakout from Normandy, begins. Following a massive aerial bombardment, three infantry divisions of General J. Lawton Collins' US VII Corps open a breach in the German line between Marigny and St. Gilles, allowing the armor to get through. Within five days, the US spearhead reaches Avranches, turning the west flank of the German front.

JULY 25-29

PACIFIC, *MARIANAS*
A Japanese counterattack against the US 3rd Marine Division on Guam is defeated. The Japanese lose 19,500 dead, while US fatalities number 1744. On the 24th, the US 4th Marine Division lands on the island of Tinian.

JULY 27-30

EASTERN FRONT, *UKRAINE*
The Soviet 1st Ukrainian Front liberates Lvov, and goes on to establish

▲ *Hitler shows Mussolini his bomb-damaged conference room following the July assassination attempt.*

▼ *Field Marshal Erwin von Witzleben. Involved in the plot to kill Hitler, he was hanged with piano wire at Ploetzenzee.*

several bridgeheads on the Vistula River by the 30th.

JULY 30

WESTERN FRONT, *FRANCE*
Avranches falls to the US VIII Corps.

AUGUST 1

EASTERN FRONT, *POLAND*
The Warsaw uprising begins. Under the command of Lieutenant General Tadeusz Bor-Komorowski, 38,000 soldiers of the Polish Home Army battle with about the same number of German troops stationed in and around the city. Although the two sides are equal in number, the Germans are superior in weapons and can also call on tank and air support. The uprising is designed to free the city from German control and give the Polish government-in-exile in London some influence over the fate of Poland when the Red Army enters the city.
PACIFIC, *MARIANAS*
The battle for the island of Tinian ends. The entire Japanese garrison of 9000 men has been wiped out.

AUGUST 2

EASTERN FRONT, *POLAND*
The left wing of the Soviet 1st Belorussian Front establishes two bridgeheads across the Vistula River south of Warsaw.

AUGUST 3

FAR EAST, *BURMA*
The Japanese withdraw from Myitkyina following an 11-week blockade by Allied forces.

▲ US forces in Paris after its liberation. The German commander of the city chose to ignore Hitler's order to destroy it.

▶ *General Mark Clark, commander of the US Fifth Army that took Rome.*

AUGUST 4

POLITICS, *FINLAND*
Marshal Karl von Mannerheim succeeds Rysto Ryti as president of the country. Mannerheim makes it clear to the Germans that he is not bound by Ryti's promises to them.

AUGUST 8

POLITICS, *GERMANY*
Eight German officers, including Field Marshal Erwin von Witzleben, are hanged at the Ploetzenzee prison in Berlin for their part in the July Bomb Plot against Hitler. They are hanged by piano wire, their last moments recorded on film for Adolf Hitler's amusement. All the condemned go to their deaths with dignity, despite their callous treatment.

AUGUST 10

PACIFIC, *MARIANAS*
Organized Japanese resistance on Guam ends, although it is 1960 before the last Japanese soldier on the island surrenders.

AUGUST 11

WESTERN FRONT, *FRANCE*
Operation Totalize, the Canadian First Army's offensive toward Falaise, is called off after failing to meet its main objectives.

AUGUST 15

POLITICS, *SOVIET UNION*
Moscow announces that the Polish Committee of National Liberation is the official body representing the Polish nation and that de facto all negotiations with the émigré government in London are at an end.

WESTERN FRONT, *FRANCE*
Units from the US VI Corps and the French II Corps, together with paratrooper support, launch the Allied invasion of southern France, code-named Operation Anvil.

EASTERN FRONT, *UKRAINE*
The Soviet 4th Ukrainian Front, attacking to seize the passes across the Carpathian Mountains, makes some progress but fails to capture the passes themselves.

AUGUST 19

WESTERN FRONT, *FRANCE*
Allied units have closed the Falaise pocket two weeks after the Canadian First Army launched Operation Totalize to cut off the encircled German troops. Some 30,000 German soldiers escape from the pocket across the Seine River, but an estimated 50,000 are captured and another 10,000 killed. In the pocket, which has been continually strafed and bombed by Allied aircraft, are hundreds of destroyed and abandoned German vehicles. Canadian, British, and Polish forces coming from the north link up with the US First Army driving from Argentan.

AUGUST 23

POLITICS, *ROMANIA*
King Michael orders his forces to cease fighting the Allies and has his pro-Axis premier, Marshal Ion Antonescu, dismissed. He announces that the armistice terms have been accepted.

of the Eighth Army. The plan is to seize the Gemmano-Coriano Ridge complex, thereby unlocking the coastal "gate" and allowing Allied armor to break out to the plains of the Po Valley. However, German resistance is fierce.

AUGUST 27

FAR EAST, *BURMA*
The last of the Chindits are evacuated to India.

AUGUST 28

EASTERN FRONT, *POLAND*
The Polish Home Army continues to fight in Warsaw, but German air attacks and artillery fire are so heavy that the Poles have been forced into the sewers. Soviet leader Stalin has refused to help the freedom fighters, and so the Red Army awaits the outcome on the far side of the Vistula River.

AUGUST 30

EASTERN FRONT, *SLOVAKIA*
Elements of the armed forces and partisans in the Nazi puppet state stage an uprising against their German overlords as the Red Army approaches the country's eastern border.

AUGUST 31

WESTERN FRONT, *FRANCE*
The US Third Army spearheads an advance toward the Meuse River as the British XXX Corps secures all the main bridges over the Somme near Amiens.

SEPTEMBER 1–3

WESTERN FRONT, *FRANCE/BELGIUM*
The British Guards and 11th Armored Divisions, both part of the British XXX

▲ *Members of the Polish Home Army march to battle as German forces squeeze the Polish-held areas in Warsaw.*

WESTERN FRONT, *FRANCE*
The US 36th Division takes Grenoble. General Dwight D. Eisenhower, Supreme Commander of the Allied Expeditionary Force, overrules General Bernard Montgomery, commander of the 21st Army Group, regarding the latter's plea for a concentrated thrust through the Low Countries into northern Germany. Eisenhower decides that after the capture of Antwerp – a port vital to the Allies – there will be an American assault toward the Saar by General George Patton's US Third Army.

AUGUST 25

POLITICS, *ROMANIA*
The former member of the Axis power bloc declares war on Germany.
WESTERN FRONT, *FRANCE*
The commander of the German garrison of Paris, General Dietrich von Choltitz, surrenders the city to Lieutenant Henri Karcher of the French 2nd Armored Division. Choltitz, who has 5000 men, 50 artillery pieces, and a company of tanks under his command, had been ordered by Hitler to ensure that "Paris [does] not fall into the hands of the enemy except as a heap of ruins." Some 500 Resistance members and 127 other civilians are killed in the fighting for the city.

AUGUST 25–26

WESTERN FRONT, *FRANCE*
The British XII and XXX Corps cross the Seine River.
ITALY, *ADRIATIC SECTOR*
The Allied assault on the Gothic Line begins. The German defense line is 200 miles (320 km) long and runs from the valley of the Magra River, south of La Spezia on the west coast, through the Apuan Mountains and the Apennines, ending in the valley of the Foglia River, and reaching the east coast between Pesaro and Cattolica. The assault is conducted by three corps – the British V, Canadian I, and Polish –

▼ *Reconnaissance vehicles of the British Guards Armored Division in Belgium during the Allied advance on Brussels.*

SEPTEMBER 2

Corps, reach Arras and Aubigny. The Canadian II Corps, part of the Canadian First Army, liberates Dieppe.

On the 2nd, XXX Corps is instructed to slow its advance and await a projected paratroop drop. With the cancellation of the drop, the advance resumes again. The 32nd and 5th Brigades of the Guards Armored Division begin a race for Brussels, which is won by the 32nd Brigade on the 3rd. On the same day, the British XII Corps is bogged down in fighting around the town of Béthune.

SEPTEMBER 2

POLITICS, *FINLAND*
Finland accepts the preliminary conditions for a peace treaty with the Soviet Union and breaks off diplomatic relations with Germany. The Soviet Union then agrees to an armistice.

EASTERN FRONT, *BULGARIA*
The Red Army reaches the Bulgarian border.

SEPTEMBER 3

WESTERN FRONT, *FRANCE/BELGIUM*
The US First Army takes Tournai and three German corps are crushed. The British Second Army liberates Brussels.

SEPTEMBER 4

WESTERN FRONT, *BELGIUM*
The British Second Army liberates the port of Antwerp.

ITALY, *ADRIATIC SECTOR*
The British Eighth Army fails to breach the Gemmano–Coriano Ridge on the Gothic Line. The ridge is the pivot point of the German Tenth Army's second line of defense, and as such it is strongly held, particularly by anti-tank weapons. An attack by the British 2nd Armored Brigade, for example, is defeated easily, with the British losing over half their tanks.

▼ *British Eighth Army artillery shells German strongpoints on the Gothic Line in Italy. But the initial assaults failed.*

▲ *Those Allied troops who liberated Brussels experienced something akin to a Roman triumph on the streets of the city.*

SEPTEMBER 5

WESTERN FRONT, *FRANCE*
US Third Army spearheads cross the Meuse River. General Karl von Rundstedt is made Commander-in-Chief West by Hitler with orders to counterattack the Allies and split their armies apart. However, his resources for such an undertaking are scant.

EASTERN FRONT, *BULGARIA*
After declaring war on the country, Red Army units invade rapidly and reach Turnu Severin. The Soviet Union's leadership is planning to occupy the entire Balkans.

SEPTEMBER 8

POLITICS, *BULGARIA*
Bulgaria declares war on Germany.

AIR WAR, *MANCHURIA*
China-based B-29 Superfortress bombers make their first daylight raid against Japanese industrial targets at Anshan.

SEPTEMBER 8–13

WESTERN FRONT, *BELGIUM/HOLLAND*
The British 50th Division crosses the Albert Canal at Gheel. On the 10th, the British Guards Armored Division advances to De Groot.

Three days later, the British 15th Division crosses the Meuse–Escaut Canal.

SEPTEMBER 8–25

EASTERN FRONT, *SLOVAKIA*
The Soviet 1st and 4th Ukrainian Fronts begin their attacks on the Dukla Pass, the key to the Carpathian Mountain barrier separating the Red Army from eastern Slovakia. It will take the Soviets until the end of November to clear the Carpathians.

SEPTEMBER 10–14

EASTERN FRONT, *POLAND*
Despite Stalin's refusal to aid the hard-pressed Warsaw insurgents, units of Marshal Konstantin Rokossovsky's 1st Belorussian Front attack Praga, the east bank quarter of the city. Fighting is savage, and it is not until the 14th that the area is freed from German control.

SEPTEMBER 15

EASTERN FRONT, *POLAND*
Units of the Soviet-raised First Polish Army cross the Vistula River and seize bridgeheads in Warsaw.

AIR WAR, *NORWAY*
Lancasters from 9 and 617 Squadrons of the RAF attack Germany's only remaining battleship – the *Tirpitz* – in Altenfiord. However, little damage is done, chiefly due to the effectiveness of the German smokescreens.

▲ *British paratroopers in action near Arnhem. The enemy is close, as indicated by the acute angle of the mortar tube.*

▼ *Allied vehicles rumble across the bridge at Nijmegen, Holland, during the disastrous Operation Market Garden.*

SEPTEMBER 17

WESTERN FRONT, *HOLLAND*
Operation Market Garden, General Bernard Montgomery's plan for an armored and airborne thrust across Holland to outflank the German defenses, begins. The British 1st Airborne Division lands near Arnhem, the US 101st Airborne Division near Eindhoven, the US 82nd Airborne Division near Grave and Nijmegen, while the British XXX Corps advances from the Dutch border. The 82nd lands without difficulty and takes the Maas and Maas–Waal Canal bridges, but then encounters heavy resistance at Nijmegen. The 101st Division also takes its bridges, but the British paratroopers discover their way to Arnhem is blocked by German units. Only one battalion, under Lieutenant Colonel John Frost, manages to reach the bridge, where it is quickly cut off.

SEPTEMBER 19–21

WESTERN FRONT, *HOLLAND*
Forward elements of the British XXX Corps reach US paratroopers at Eindhoven, but at Arnhem all attempts to break through to the troops fail. On the 20th, the bridge at Nijmegen is captured by a combined force drawn from the US 82nd Airborne Division and the British XXX Corps. The next day, the British troops at Arnhem are

▲ A PIAT antitank weapon waits for enemy armor on the outskirts of Arnhem as the Germans close in on the British.

Canadian II Corps; its garrison of 20,000 men is taken into captivity.

SEPTEMBER 22–25

WESTERN FRONT, *HOLLAND*
Outside Arnhem, the British XXX Corps' advance is slowed by German resistance. The Polish Brigade drops south of the Neder Rijn near Driel. On the 23rd, attempts by the Poles and advance troops of XXX Corps to cross the river are driven back, and so the evacuation of the surviving paratroopers begins two days later, leaving 2500 of their dead comrades behind.

SEPTEMBER 23

AIR WAR, *GERMANY*
The RAF makes a night precision raid on the Dortmund to Ems Canal, the inland waterway that links the Ruhr with other industrial centers. A total of 141 aircraft are involved, the canal is breached, and a section drained. The RAF loses 14 bombers.

SEPTEMBER 23–30

WESTERN FRONT, *FRANCE*
The Canadian 3rd Division invests the port of Calais, which is defended by

overwhelmed. The remainder form a defensive perimeter on the northern bank of the Neder Rijn, around the village of Oosterbeek.

SEPTEMBER 21

POLITICS, *YUGOSLAVIA*
The partisan chief Marshal Tito meets the Soviet leader Joseph Stalin. They reach agreement on the "temporary entry of the Red Army into Yugoslavia."
ITALY, *ADRIATIC SECTOR*
The Eighth Army takes Rimini after a week of heavy fighting. Since the beginning of its offensive against the Gothic Line, it has lost 14,000 men killed, wounded, and

missing, plus 200 tanks. The Italian campaign has not lived up to being the "soft underbelly of Europe." A more accurate description would be "tough old gut."

SEPTEMBER 22

WESTERN FRONT, *FRANCE*
Boulogne surrenders to the

▼ Sherman tanks of the British Eighth Army on the move near Rimini during the grim battle of attrition against the Gothic Line.

▲ Beaten but defiant, these British paratroopers are led into captivity at the end of Market Garden – 2500 of their comrades were killed in the operation.

7500 men. Following heavy artillery and bomber attacks, and the use of specialized armor, Calais surrenders on the 30th.

OCTOBER 2

EASTERN FRONT, *POLAND*
After a bitter two-month battle, the last Poles in Warsaw surrender. The Germans evacuate the entire remaining population and begin the systematic destruction of anything left standing. Polish deaths number 150,000, while the German commander, SS General Erich von dem Bach-Zelewski, claims he has lost 26,000 men.

OCTOBER 3

AIR WAR, *BRITAIN*
The German bombardment of Britain with V2 long-range heavy rockets has resumed from new launch sites dotted across Holland.

▶ A British paratrooper in cover on the outskirts of Oosterbeek. The failure of XXX Corps to cross the Neder Rijn doomed the airborne operation.

OCTOBER 4

OCTOBER 4

MEDITERRANEAN, *GREECE*
Determined to prevent a communist takeover in Greece, Winston Churchill launches Operation Manna. British troops land at Patrai in the Peloponnese as German forces pull back.

OCTOBER 9

WESTERN FRONT, *BELGIUM*
Although the Allies captured Antwerp on September 4, they have not been able to use the great port because there are German units on both sides of the Scheldt estuary. Therefore, the Canadian First Army commences operations to eradicate the enemy presence in this area.

PACIFIC, *IWO JIMA*
Admiral Chester W. Nimitz, commander of all Allied forces in the Central Pacific, informs Lieutenant General Holland M. "Howling Mad" Smith, one of the leading exponents of amphibious warfare and commander of all US Marines in the Pacific, that the island of Iwo Jima will be his next target and that Smith will lead

▲ Landing craft and vehicles of the Canadian First Army engaged in clearing the Scheldt estuary near Antwerp.

▼ A German V2 rocket is readied for launch from a site in Holland. The only way to reduce the damage caused by these weapons was to bomb their launch sites and their construction factories.

the invasion with three US Marine divisions. The island is within bombing range of the Japanese mainland.

OCTOBER 10–29

EASTERN FRONT, *HUNGARY*
A massive tank battle rages around Drebrecan between two panzer divisions of Germany's Army Group Southern Ukraine, commanded by General Johannes Friessneer. The German forces have cut off three Soviet tank corps of Marshal Rodion Malinovsky's 2nd Ukrainian Front. The Soviets lose many tanks in the initial German attacks, but fresh Soviet units tip the scales against the Germans, who do not have the forces to fight attritional battles. Farther south, the German Army Group E leaves Greece.

OCTOBER 11–19

BALKANS, *YUGOSLAVIA*
The Red Army joins with the Yugoslavian First Army in the drive to Belgrade, which is abandoned by the Germans on the 19th.

OCTOBER 14

POLITICS, *GERMANY*
Field Marshal Erwin Rommel commits suicide with poison. Implicated in the July assassination plot against Hitler, he has killed himself, under pressure, to save his family from arrest. He is to be given a state funeral as part of the charade to maintain the illusion that he was an uncompromising Nazi.

▲ *A knocked-out Joseph Stalin tank at Drebrecan, the site of a massive tank battle and a German defeat.*

▼ *General Douglas MacArthur (second from left) wades ashore in the Philippines, keeping his promise "I shall return."*

OCTOBER 20

BALKANS, *YUGOSLAVIA*
The 1st Proletarian Division of Marshal Tito's Army of Liberation captures Belgrade.
PACIFIC, *PHILIPPINES*
As the US Sixth Army lands on Leyte Island, General Douglas MacArthur wades ashore and keeps a promise he made two years earlier: "I shall return." By the evening 10,000 US troops are dug in around Leyte's capital, Tacloban, and Dulag to the south.

OCTOBER 21

WESTERN FRONT, *GERMANY*
The city of Aachen surrenders to US forces following a 10-day siege.

OCTOBER 23–26

PACIFIC, *PHILIPPINES*
Following the US landings on Leyte, the Japanese put in motion their Sho Plan, in which a part of the Combined Fleet is used to decoy the US carrier force while the remainder concentrates against the landing area and attempts to destroy the amphibious armada. The resulting naval battle of Leyte Gulf has four phases: the Battle of the Sibuyan Sea, the Battle of the Surigao Strait, the Battle of Samar, and

DECISIVE WEAPONS

KAMIKAZE

Kamikaze, meaning "Divine Wind," was a suicide tactic employed by the Japanese military to destroy US military shipping by crashing explosive-filled aircraft into vessels. The cult of the kamikazes was influenced by the Bushido code of conduct based on spiritualism under the influence of Buddhism, which emphasized both bravery and conscience.

The Battle of Leyte Gulf in October 1944 saw the beginning of the Kamikaze Corps, and at the end of the war Japan had over 5000 aircraft ready for suicide missions. Kamikaze pilots endeavored to hit the deck of their target to cause maximum damage (against carriers the best point of aim was the central elevator). The overall military effect of the kamikazes was limited: during the Okinawa battles, for example, of the 1900 suicide sorties made, only 14 percent were effective.

The damaged hangar of USS Sangamon following a kamikaze attack by just one aircraft.

the Battle of Cape Engano. The result is that the Japanese Combined Fleet is finished as a fighting force, not least because its losses in trained pilots are irreplaceable. It loses 500 aircraft, four carriers, three battleships, six heavy and four light cruisers, 11 destroyers, and a submarine, while every other ship engaged is damaged. US losses are 200 aircraft, one light carrier, two escort carriers, two destroyers, and one destroyer-escort.

OCTOBER 31

EASTERN FRONT, *BALTIC*
The Soviet 1st Baltic Front isolates the remnants of Army Group North in the Courland Peninsula.

NOVEMBER 7

ESPIONAGE, *JAPAN*
The Japanese hang the spy Richard Sorge at Sugamo Prison, Tokyo. He has been working for eight years as the Tokyo correspondent for a German newspaper, and during this time has sent the Soviet Union detailed information concerning German and Japanese plans, including the attack on the Soviet Union in 1941.

NOVEMBER 8

WESTERN FRONT, *BELGIUM*
The Canadian First Army completes the clearing of the Scheldt estuary. It takes 41,000 prisoners during the operation at a cost of 12,873 men killed, wounded, and missing.

NOVEMBER 9

WESTERN FRONT, *FRANCE*
General George Patton's US Third Army (500,000 men and 500 tanks) crosses the Moselle River on a broad front toward the heart of the Reich.

▲ *The US Navy bombards the island of Iwo Jima to soften up the defenses prior to an amphibious landing.*

NOVEMBER 11–12

PACIFIC, *IWO JIMA*
The US Navy bombards the Japanese-held island for the first time.

NOVEMBER 12

AIR WAR, *NORWAY*
RAF Lancaster bombers from 9 and 617 Squadrons sink the German battleship *Tirpitz* in Altenfiord, killing 1100 of its crew when the ship capsizes.

NOVEMBER 24

AIR WAR, *JAPAN*
American B-29 Superfortress bombers mount their first raid against Tokyo from the Mariana Islands.

DECEMBER 4

FAR EAST, *BURMA*
General William Slim, commander of the British Fourteenth Army, begins the destruction of Japanese forces in Burma. The British IV and XXXIII Corps begin the offensive, heading for the Japanese airfields at Yeu and Shwebo. The Japanese Fifteenth Army, commanded by General Shihachi

Katamura, is in a weakened state following its reverses during the fighting at Kohima and Imphal.

DECEMBER 5–7

PACIFIC, *PHILIPPINES*

The final US offensive on Leyte begins with a drive by the X Corps into the northern Ormoc Valley, with simultaneous assaults by the XIV Corps in central and southwestern Leyte. On the 7th, the 77th Division lands virtually unopposed below Ormoc. Japanese forces are pressed into the Ormoc Valley, and are under intense artillery and aerial attack.

HOME FRONT, *GERMANY*

The Nazi women's leader, Gertrud Scholtz-Klink, appeals for all women over 18 to volunteer for service in the army and air force to release men for the front.

DECEMBER 8

PACIFIC, *IWO JIMA*

The US Air Force begins a 72-day bombardment of Iwo Jima, the longest and heaviest of the Pacific war, to pave the way for an amphibious assault.

DECEMBER 15

PACIFIC, *PHILIPPINES*

As part of General Douglas MacArthur's second phase of the invasion of the Philippines, the US 24th Division lands on the island of Mindoro.

FAR EAST, *BURMA*

The British 19th and 36th Divisions meet at Indaw, and set up a continuous front against the Japanese in northern Burma.

▲ *After spending most of the war in Norwegian coastal waters, the Tirpitz was finally sunk on November 12.*

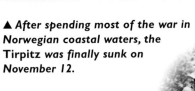

▶ *British troops of IV Corps move against the Japanese Fifteenth Army after Kohima and Imphal.*

DECEMBER 16–22

▲ *A barrage of rockets is unleashed against enemy beach defenses as the first wave of US assault units heads for Mindoro Island in the Philippines.*

DECEMBER 16–22

WESTERN FRONT, *ARDENNES*
Hitler launches Operation Watch on the Rhine, his attempt to break through the US VIII Corps on the Ardennes front, reach the Meuse River, and capture Antwerp, thereby splitting the Allies in two. The German units – 200,000 men – form Army Group B under the overall command of Field Marshal Gerd von Rundstedt. This force comprises the Sixth SS Panzer Army, Fifth Panzer Army, and Seventh Army. US forces total 80,000 men.

Surprise is total and there is dense cloud and fog, which negates Allied air superiority, but the Germans fail to take the towns of St. Vith and Bastogne immediately, which narrows their attack front. On the 17th, troops of SS Lieutenant Colonel Joachim Peiper's battlegroup murder 71 American prisoners of war at Malmédy in Belgium, leaving their bodies in a field.

By the 22nd, the Americans, having lost 8000 of 22,000 men at St. Vith, pull back from the town, but the men of the 28th Infantry, 10th, and 101st Airborne Divisions continue to hold out stubbornly in Bastogne against one infantry and two panzer divisions. On the same day the Germans mount their last attempt to reach the Meuse.

As part of their sabotage operations, the Germans are using English-speaking commandos dressed in US uniforms to spread confusion, especially at road junctions and on bridges. However, measures have been taken to defeat these infiltrators, many of whom are later shot as spies.

DECEMBER 20

MEDITERRANEAN, *GREECE*
British tanks and armored cars have lifted the siege of Kifissia RAF base by ELAS rebels (the National Liberation Army – the military wing of the country's communist party).

DECEMBER 24

AIR WAR, *BELGIUM*
The first jet bomber operation takes

south of the German "bulge" into the Ardennes. The US Third Army's 4th Armored Division relieves Bastogne as Hitler is informed by his generals that Antwerp can no longer be reached by his forces. The only hope of salvaging any sort of victory in the Ardennes is to swing the Fifth and Sixth Panzer Armies north to cross the Meuse west of Liège and come in behind Aachen. However, this presupposes the capture of Bastogne and an attack from the north to link with the panzers – both are increasingly unlikely.

DECEMBER 30

WESTERN FRONT, *ARDENNES*
At Bastogne, General George Patton, his forces swollen to six divisions, resumes his attack northeast toward Houffalize. At the same time, General Hasso von Manteuffel, commander of the German Fifth Panzer Army, launches another major attempt to cut the corridor into Bastogne and take the town. The fighting is intense, but Patton's forces stand firm and defeat the German attack.

DECEMBER 31

POLITICS, *HUNGARY*
The Provisional National Government of Hungary, set up under Soviet control in the city of Drebrecan, declares war on Germany.

▲ *Aided by secrecy and poor weather, the initial assaults of the German Ardennes offensive met with success.*

▼ *Abandoned German Panther and Panzer IV tanks in the Ardennes in late December. Shortages of fuel, stubborn defense, and Allied air attacks contributed to the failure of the offensive.*

place when twin-engined German Arado 234B bombers raid a factory and marshaling yards. The raid is led by Captain Dieter Lukesch.

DECEMBER 26

WESTERN FRONT, *ARDENNES*
The US First and Third Armies launch counterattacks against the north and

1945

In this final year of the war, Germany and Japan were defeated by a relentless tide of aircraft, tanks, ships, and men. Their cities were devastated by fleets of bombers, their armies were encircled and then annihilated, and their merchant and naval fleets were either sunk or trapped in port. There was no match for the economic might of the United States and the numerical superiority of the Soviet Union. Atomic bombs finally ended the war against Japan.

JANUARY 1

EASTERN FRONT, *CZECHOSLOVAKIA*

The Soviet 2nd and 4th Ukrainian Fronts begin an offensive against the German Army Group Center in Czechoslovakia. The German-held area contains the last foreign industrial resources under the control of the Third Reich. The Soviet fronts between them have 853,000 men, 9986 guns, 590 tanks, and 1400 combat aircraft. German forces total 550,000 men, 5000 guns, and 700 combat aircraft. Despite German fortifications and resistance, the Red Army makes good progress.

JANUARY 1–21

WESTERN FRONT, *FRANCE*

In a follow up to the attack in the Ardennes sector, General Johannes von Blaskowitz's Army Group G attacks the US Seventh Army in Alsace and Lorraine, forming the so-called Colmar Pocket. The Americans retreat, although General Dwight D. Eisenhower, commander-in-chief of Allied forces in Europe, orders Strasbourg to be held after the leader of the Free French, General Charles de Gaulle, expresses concern that the loss of the city would affect French morale. The fighting

▶ *Chinese soldiers of the Northern Combat Area Command march to the front in northern Burma.*

▲ *US troops and vehicles in Bastogne, which resisted all German assaults in December 1944 and January 1945.*

JANUARY 3–4

PACIFIC, *RYUKYUS*
The US 3rd Fleet attacks Japanese targets on Formosa, destroying 100 enemy aircraft.

JANUARY 3–16

WESTERN FRONT, *ARDENNES*
The last German attack against Bastogne is defeated. The Allied counterattack begins: on the northern flank the US First Army attacks the northern sector of the "bulge," while the southern sector is assaulted by the US Third Army. In the "bulge" itself, Hitler orders a German withdrawal to Houffalize on the 8th. However, in the face of overwhelming Allied superiority in men and hardware the Germans are forced to retreat farther east, and the US First and Third Armies link up at Houffalize on the 16th.

JANUARY 4

FAR EAST, *BURMA*
Units of General William Slim's British Fourteenth Army make an unopposed landing on the island of Akyab, securing the port and the airfield.

JANUARY 4–6

PACIFIC, *PHILIPPINES*
Prior to the landings on Luzon, the Japanese launch a series of kamikaze attacks on ships of the US 7th Fleet. Over 1000 Americans and Australians are killed in the suicide attacks, a minesweeper is sunk, and more than 30 other vessels are damaged.

JANUARY 5

AIR WAR, *BELGIUM/HOLLAND*
The Luftwaffe launches Operation Bodenplatte in support of the

▼ *The US 7th Fleet prior to the assault on Luzon. The Consolidated Catalinas are from the Air-Sea Rescue Squadron.*

is bitter. It costs the US 15,600 casualties, and the Germans, 25,000.

JANUARY 1–27

FAR EAST, *BURMA*
The Chinese units of Lieutenant General Daniel Sultan's Northern Combat Area Command and Marshal Wei Lihuang's Y Force link up in northern Burma in the face of significant resistance from the Japanese 56th Division.

JANUARY 2

TECHNOLOGY, *UNITED STATES*
An American Sikorsky helicopter is used in convoy escort duties for the first time.

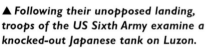
▲ *Following their unopposed landing, troops of the US Sixth Army examine a knocked-out Japanese tank on Luzon.*

Ardennes offensive with 1035 fighters and bombers attacking Allied airfields in Belgium and southern Holland. The Germans destroy 156 Allied aircraft but lose 277 of their own, losses the Luftwaffe cannot make good. It is the last major German air attack.

JANUARY 7
EASTERN FRONT, *HUNGARY*
German forces capture Esztergom, northwest of Budapest, a Nazi National Redoubt, in their attempt to relieve the garrison in the capital.

JANUARY 9
PACIFIC, *PHILIPPINES*
Preceded by a heavy bombardment, units of the US Sixth Army, command-ed by Lieutenant General Walter Krueger, make unopposed amphibious landings on Luzon.

JANUARY 10–FEBRUARY 10
EASTERN FRONT,
CZECHOSLOVAKIA
With the Red Army on their soil, Czech partisans begin to attack German units and supply lines.

JANUARY 12–17
EASTERN FRONT, *POLAND*
The Red Army begins its Vistula–Oder offensive. Soviet forces total over two million men: Marshal Georgi Zhukov's 1st Belorussian Front, Marshal Ivan Konev's 1st Ukrainian Front, and General Ivan Petrov's 4th Ukrainian Front. In addition, Marshal Konstantin Rokossovsky's 2nd Belorussian Front and General Ivan Chernyakhovsky's 3rd Belorussian Front are providing tactical and strategic cooperation. The Soviets make excellent progress, and by the 17th, Zhukov's Second Guards Tank Army has reached Sochaczew. To the north, the 1st Baltic, 2nd Belorussian, and 3rd Belorussian Fronts launch an offensive into East Prussia on the 13th.

JANUARY 14
FAR EAST, *BURMA*
The 19th Division, part of Lieutenant General William Slim's British Four-teenth Army, crosses the Irrawaddy River at Kyaukmyaung but is then violently attacked by Japanese troops holding the line of the waterway. Forced back by hordes of infantry with fixed bayonets, the division manages to hold the bridgehead in the face of the fierce onslaught.

JANUARY 15–26
WESTERN FRONT, *GERMANY*
After the containment of the German Ardennes offensive, the Allies launch a large counterattack against the Germans. In the north, Field Marshal Bernard Montgomery's British 21st Army Group presses into the Roer-mond area, while farther south General Omar Bradley's US 12th Army Group approaches the upper Roer River.

JANUARY 16
FAR EAST, *BURMA*
In the north of the country, General Daniel Sultan's Chinese New First Army occupies Namhkan. The last Japanese positions threatening the Burma Road have been eradicated.

JANUARY 18–27
EASTERN FRONT, *HUNGARY*
The German IV SS Panzer Corps launches an

▶ *One of the hundreds of Japanese soldiers killed in and around the Irrawaddy River, Burma.*

KEY PERSONALITIES

MARSHAL GEORGI ZHUKOV

Georgi Zhukov (1896–1974) was born into a peasant family and conscripted into the Imperial Russian Army in 1915. After fighting in World War I, he joined the Red Army in October 1918. He studied at the Frunze Military Academy (1928–31), and in 1938 was appointed deputy commander of the Belorussian Military District. Apparently earmarked for execution in the Stalinist purges, he escaped with his life due to an administrative error.

Zhukov's generalship skills first came to the fore in 1939, when he led the Soviet 1st Army Group to a decisive victory over the Japanese at the Khalka River (the so-called "Nomonhan Incident" over a disputed frontier in Manchuria). Following the German invasion of the Soviet Union in June 1941, Zhukov held a variety of staff positions and field commands, repulsing the enemy from Moscow in late 1941, having a hand in the great Soviet victories at Stalingrad and Kursk, and capturing Berlin in 1945. The victory at Stalingrad was particularly impressive, as the German Sixth Army had more men than Zhukov's forces. He used his units to achieve a crushing superiority over weaker Romanian armies along the front on both flanks of the Sixth Army. Once they had been smashed, he cut off the German forces in the Stalingrad area.

Zhukov was a forceful commander who possessed outstanding tactical and strategic ability – qualities that made his superiors view him as a potential threat. The fact that as a general he never lost a single battle is testament to his attributes as a military leader.

offensive to relieve Budapest. In the face of Soviet resistance, it reaches the Vali River on the 22nd, only 15 miles (24 km) southwest of the city. However, the momentum of the attack had been halted by the 25th, and two days later the Red Army counterattacks with 12 rifle divisions and strong armored support, effectively ending the German Budapest relief operation.

JANUARY 18–FEBRUARY 3

FAR EAST, *BURMA*
A vicious battle develops at Namhpakka between the Japanese 56th Division, which is

▲ *As the Red Army steamroller gathers momentum, Estonian coastguards fire a salute to welcome the Soviets.*

retreating to Lashio, and the American Mars Brigade.

JANUARY 19

EASTERN FRONT, *POLAND*
Following heavy fighting, units of the 1st Ukrainian Front liberate Cracow, the former capital of Poland. The German Third and Fourth Panzer Armies are now isolated in East Prussia, and the German front is falling apart in the face of immense pressure.

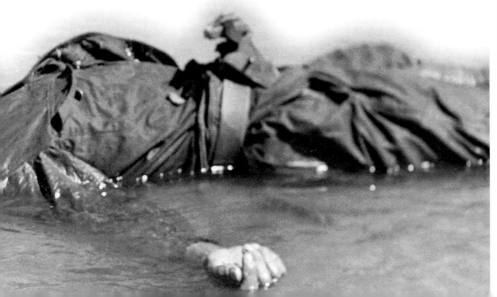

JANUARY 21

JANUARY 21

FAR EAST, *BURMA*

The island of Ramree is invaded by the British 71st Brigade. Japanese resistance is virtually non-existent, although it stiffens as Allied troops push farther inland. The island is not cleared until the middle of February, by which time General William Slim has an invaluable base for future long-range operations against Rangoon.

JANUARY 23

EASTERN FRONT, *EAST PRUSSIA*

The Soviet 2nd Belorussian Front cuts all road and rail crossings across the Vistula River, isolating German units on the east bank.

EASTERN FRONT, *POLAND*

The Soviet Second Guards Tank Army, part of the 1st Belorussian Front, storms the fortified town of Bromberg, an important strongpoint in the German Poznan Line.

JANUARY 27

EASTERN FRONT, *POLAND*

The Red Army liberates the Nazi death camp at Auschwitz. The SS has evacuated the camp nine days previously, taking 20,000 weak inmates with them. Those left number a few hundred disease-ridden inmates in the camp's hospital block.

FAR EAST, *BURMA*

Units of the Allied Y Force, pushing across the Shweli River at Wanting,

reopen the Burma Road supply route into China.

JANUARY 28

WESTERN FRONT, *ARDENNES*

The last vestiges of the German "bulge" in the Ardennes are wiped out. The total cost to the Germans in manpower for their Ardennes offensive has been 100,000 killed, wounded, and captured. The Americans have lost 81,000 killed, wounded, or captured, and the British 1400. Both sides have lost heavily in hardware – up to 800 tanks on each side. The Germans have also lost around 1000 aircraft.

▲ *German prisoners taken during the Ardennes offensive. The Wehrmacht lost over 100,000 men and 800 precious tanks.*

However, whereas the Americans can make good their losses in just a few weeks, for the Germans the military losses are irreplaceable.

JANUARY 28 – FEBRUARY 1

WESTERN FRONT, *ARDENNES*

Two corps of General Courtney Hodges' US First Army and one from General George Patton's US Third Army try to penetrate the German defenses

▼ *British troops carry a wounded comrade to a dressing station near Myitson, Burma.*

northeast of St. Vith, which lies astride the Losheim Gap. Snow and ice inhibit progress, and the Germans manage to fight back hard, thereby slowing the rate of the US advance.

▼ As fighting rages in and around Manila, the capital of the Philippines, refugees pour out of the city. This bridge was built by US engineers.

JANUARY 29

PACIFIC, *PHILIPPINES*
Major General Charles Hall's US XI Corps lands unopposed on the west coast of Luzon just to the north of the Bataan Peninsula.

JANUARY 30

EASTERN FRONT, *GERMANY*
The left wing of the 1st Ukrainian Front has reached the Oder River and some of its units have set up bridgeheads on the west bank. This ends one of the greatest strategic operations of the whole war.

The Red Army has advanced 355 miles (568 km), liberated all of Poland and a large part of Czechoslovakia, reached the Oder on a broad front, and is only 100 miles (160 km) from Berlin. In its offensive, it has inflicted losses of 500,000 dead, wounded, or captured on the Germans, and captured 1300 aircraft, 1400 tanks, and over 14,000 guns of all calibers.

JANUARY 31

PACIFIC, *PHILIPPINES*
Elements of the US 11th Airborne Division go ashore at Nasugbu Bay against light Japanese resistance. The US troops land just 50 miles (80 km) southwest of the capital Manila, which is their ultimate objective.

▲ The destruction in Manila after the city fell to the US XIV Corps. The whole of the Japanese garrison was wiped out.

JANUARY 31–FEBRUARY 21

FAR EAST, *BURMA*
The British 36th Division effects a crossing of the Shweli River at Myitson following a savage battle against the Japanese. The division's success threatens the Japanese northern approaches to the Mandalay Plain.

FEBRUARY 1

EASTERN FRONT, *EAST PRUSSIA*
The trapped German Fourth Army attempts to reach German-held Elbing but is halted by a Soviet counterattack.

FEBRUARY 3–MARCH 3

PACIFIC, *PHILIPPINES*
The US XIV Corps begins its attack against Manila, which is defended by 17,000 Japanese troops under Rear Admiral Sanji Iwabuchi. The garrison, after destroying the city (the "Rape of Manila"), is wiped out. US casualties total 1000 dead and 5500 wounded; 100,000 Filipino citizens are killed.

FEBRUARY 4–11

POLITICS, *ALLIES*
Marshal Joseph Stalin, President Franklin D. Roosevelt, and Prime

▲ *The "Big Three" at the Yalta Conference, where the postwar division of Germany and Austria was agreed.*

Minister Winston Churchill meet at the Yalta Conference in the Crimea to discuss postwar Europe. The "Big Three" decide that Germany will be divided into four zones, administered by Britain, France, the United States, and the Soviet Union. An Allied Control Commission will be set up in Berlin, and Austria will also be divided into four zones. The capital, Vienna, will be in the Soviet zone and will also have a four-power administration. The Soviet Union will declare war on Japan two months after the war in Europe has ended, while changes to Poland's borders will allow the Soviet Union to annex former Polish areas.

FEBRUARY 5

WESTERN FRONT, *FRANCE*
The German bridgehead on the west bank of the Rhine, south of Strasbourg

around the town of Colmar – the Colmar Pocket – is split by units of the French First Army attacking from the south and elements of the US Seventh Army advancing from the north. The elimination of the pocket is essential to the crossing of the Rhine.

FEBRUARY 8–24

EASTERN FRONT, *GERMANY*
Marshal Ivan Konev's 1st Ukrainian Front begins its offensive to disrupt German plans and establish an impregnable defense line along the southern Oder. By the 24th his forces have advanced 75 miles (120 km) and seized Lower Silesia, in addition to freeing 91,300 Soviet citizens and 22,500 other foreigners from German imprisonment.

FEBRUARY 9

WESTERN FRONT, *FRANCE*
Following Allied pressure against the Colmar Pocket, Field Marshal Gerd von Rundstedt, German commander-in-chief in the West, convinces Hitler to pull back the Nineteenth Army across the Rhine. The west bank of the river south of Strasbourg is now free of German troops.

FEBRUARY 10

EASTERN FRONT, *POLAND*
The Soviet 2nd Belorussian Front launches an offensive in the region of Grudziadz and Sepolno but runs into determined resistance from the German Second Army. Soviet progress is very slow.

◀ *German rockets scream through the air as the Second Army tries to halt the Soviet 2nd Belorussian Front in Poland.*

▼ *Women help clear rubble from the ruins of the Catholic cathedral in Dresden after the Allied air raids against the city.*

suburbs. The bombing triggers the worst firestorm of the war, in which at least 50,000 people are killed. The raid is controversial, as the city has negligible strategic value, is virtually undefended, and is crammed with refugees. The next morning, the city is bombed again by 400 aircraft of the US 8th Army Air Force.

FEBRUARY 14

EASTERN FRONT, *EAST PRUSSIA*
As a result of the Red Army's advance, over half of the 2.3 million population of East Prussia have fled west. Some have been taken out by boat, although most have walked or made their way by horse and wagon. Thousands have died from either cold or exhaustion, or in Soviet air and artillery attacks.

FEBRUARY 16–28

PACIFIC, *PHILIPPINES*
US forces begin to clear the Japanese from the entrance to Manila Bay, Luzon. The peninsula of Bataan falls relatively easily, though Corregidor proves a harder nut to crack. The assault begins on the 16th with a battalion of US paratroopers dropping on the southwest heights of the island. Simultaneously, an amphibious assault by a battalion of infantry takes place on the southern shore. By the evening of the 26th, almost the whole island is in US hands. It is declared secure on the 28th. The Japanese garrison refuses to surrender, and is virtually wiped out in the fighting.

FEBRUARY 11

EASTERN FRONT, *HUNGARY*
The trapped Axis garrison in Budapest attempts to break through the Soviet lines. However, of the nearly 30,000 Germans and Hungarians, fewer than 700 are able to escape.

FEBRUARY 13–14

AIR WAR, *GERMANY*
The RAF mounts a night raid on Dresden. The 805 bombers inflict massive damage on the city's old town and inner

▲ *Boeing B-17 Flying Fortress bombers of the US 8th Army Air Force unleash death and destruction on Dresden.*

▼ *American paratroopers in action on Corregidor during the operations to clear the entrance to Manila Bay.*

FEBRUARY 16

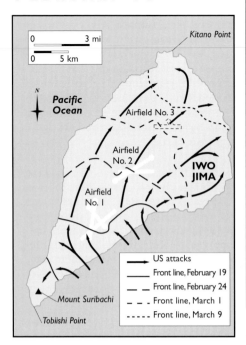

▲ The conquest of Iwo Jima was a tough battle, especially the agonizing drive to the north against a fanatical enemy.

FEBRUARY 16
PACIFIC, *IWO JIMA*
The US Navy begins a three-day concentrated bombardment of Iwo Jima. The island has to be taken for four reasons: the unescorted US bombers flying from the Marianas to Japan are suffering heavy losses, and, therefore, airfields closer to Japan are needed for fighter escorts; Iwo Jima has two air bases and is only three hours' flying time from Tokyo; Iwo

▲ US Marines head for the beaches of Iwo Jima and one of the bloodiest battles in their Pacific War. Conquering the island required the destruction of the garrison.

Jima is prewar Japanese territory, whose loss would be a severe blow to the homeland; and it is a key link in the air defenses of the Marianas.

FEBRUARY 17
PACIFIC, *IWO JIMA*
Under the command of Lieutenant General Holland M. Smith, the US 4th and 5th Marine Divisions land. Resistance is at first light, but then the attackers are hit by intense artillery and small-arms fire from the 21,000-man Japanese garrison. However, despite casualties, the Americans have 30,000 men on the island by the end of the day.

FEBRUARY 21
WESTERN FRONT, *GERMANY*
The Canadian First Army takes Goch, which ends Operation Veritable, an offensive from the Nijmegen area between the Rhine and the Maas Rivers.
FAR EAST, *BURMA*
General William Slim's British Fourteenth Army begins the reconquest of

▶ Troops of Slim's army wade across the Irrawaddy in the drive toward Mandalay.

◀ Lieutenant General Holland M. Smith, who commanded the US forces on Iwo Jima.

central Burma. Breaking out of the Irrawaddy bridgeheads, columns are directed to Mandalay, Burma's second city, and the important rail and road communications center at Meiktila.

In northern Burma, the British 36th Division breaks through Japanese positions at Myitson after a vicious three-week battle. Japanese forces are now on the retreat in the area.

FEBRUARY 23
WESTERN FRONT, *GERMANY*
The US First and Ninth Armies launch Operation Grenade, the crossing of the Roer River, and head to the Rhine. Preceded by a barrage from over 1000

that only those states that declare war before March 1 will be invited to a conference in San Francisco on the proposed postwar United Nations.

WESTERN FRONT, *GERMANY*
The US First Army begins its drive to the Rhine River, spearheaded by the VII Corps.

PACIFIC, *PHILIPPINES*
A regiment of the US 41st Division captures the island of Palawan.

MARCH 1

EASTERN FRONT, *GERMANY*
Marshal Georgi Zhukov's 1st Belorussian Front begins an offensive to destroy the German Third Panzer Army – which has 203,000 men, 700 tanks, 2500 guns, and 100 coastal artillery and fixed anti-aircraft guns – as part of the Red Army's effort to secure its flanks prior to the assault on Berlin itself.

MARCH 3

WESTERN FRONT, *FRANCE*
In snow and freezing rain, General George Patton unleashes his US Third Army over the Kyll River toward the

▼ *General George Patton's US Third Army on the move toward the Rhine River at the beginning of March.*

guns, four infantry divisions cross the river in the face of sporadic resistance. German reserves have been committed to halt Operation Veritable farther north. By the end of the day, 28 infantry battalions have crossed the river.

PACIFIC, *IWO JIMA*
US Marines raise the American flag on the summit of Mount Suribachi in the south of the island. The US Marines now have to turn north to clear the rest of the island.

FEBRUARY 25

PACIFIC, *IWO JIMA*
As the fighting on Iwo Jima becomes more intense, the US 3rd Marine Division is committed to the battle.

FEBRUARY 28

POLITICS, *SAUDI ARABIA*
Following the example of Syria on the 26th, Saudi Arabia declares war on Germany. The rush to join the Allies in part stems from the announcement

Rhine. The attack is spearheaded by the VIII and XII Corps, which make good progress.

EASTERN FRONT, *GERMANY*

In an effort to try to recapture the lost defenses on the Oder River, the German Fourth Panzer Army counterattacks from the Lauban area toward Glogau. However, strong Soviet entrenched positions stop the attack in its tracks.

▲ *A US B-29 Superfortress bomber near Tokyo, having flown from Iwo Jima.*

FAR EAST, *BURMA*

General David Cowan's 17th Indian Division and 255th Indian Tank Brigade take the communications center of Meiktila after heavy fighting.

MARCH 4

PACIFIC, *IWO JIMA*

The first US B-29 Superfortress bomber lands on the island.

MARCH 6

EASTERN FRONT, *HUNGARY*

The Germans launch Operation Spring Awakening, designed to secure the Nagykanizsa oil fields, retake Budapest, and win a prestigious victory on the Eastern Front. The Sixth SS Panzer and Second Panzer Armies make good initial progress despite very poor weather conditions.

MARCH 7

POLITICS, *YUGOSLAVIA*

Marshal Tito forms a provisional government in which he accepts representatives of the former royalist government-in-exile. This is a temporary measure, as he intends to retain full control of the government for the Communist Party, which he believes the population will accept without question as a result of partisan successes during the war.

WESTERN FRONT, *GERMANY*

Units of the US First Army capture the Ludendorff bridge over the Rhine River at Remagen. The bridge, having withstood bombs, demolition, heavy usage, and artillery shells, collapses into the river 10 days later.

MARCH 10

WESTERN FRONT, *GERMANY*

Field Marshal Bernard Montgomery's 21st Army Group completes the conquest of the area west of the Rhine River. The group has lost 22,934 casualties, although the Germans have suffered casualties totaling 90,000 men defending the area immediately west of the Ruhr.

AIR WAR, *JAPAN*

The first American fire raid on Japan, against Tokyo, burns out over 16 square miles (25.6 sq km) of the city and kills 100,000 people.

MARCH 14

WESTERN FRONT, *GERMANY*

General George Patton's US Third Army crosses the lower Moselle River to cut behind the German Siegfried Line defensive system.

MARCH 16

EASTERN FRONT, *HUNGARY*

Marshal Fedor Tolbukhin's 3rd Ukrainian Front commences the Red Army's counterattack against Operation Spring Awakening on the front between Lake Velencei and Bicske. The German IV SS Panzer Corps holds in the face of overwhelming superiority in tanks and men, but the Hungarian Third Army on the left collapses.

PACIFIC, *IWO JIMA*

The island of Iwo Jima is declared secure by the Americans following 26 days of combat. They have lost 6821 soldiers and sailors dead, while of the 21,000 Japanese garrison, only 1083 are taken prisoner. The rest have been killed or have committed suicide.

▲ Paratroopers of the British 6th Airborne Division dropping on the east bank of the Rhine on 23 March, 1945.

▼ The Rhine was a formidable barrier, but crossing it was largely a logistical rather than a military problem for the Allies.

MARCH 17–19

FAR EAST, *BURMA*
The battle for Mandalay begins. The main Japanese garrison is situated in Fort Dufferin, which is pounded incessantly by British artillery. Following an intensive aerial bombardment, the

Japanese evacuate the fort on the 19th – Mandalay is in British hands.

MARCH 18

PACIFIC, *PHILIPPINES*
In the island-hopping campaign in the theater, the US 40th Division lands on Panay, secures it, and then moves on to clear nearby Guimaras Island.

MARCH 20

EASTERN FRONT, *GERMANY*
Units of the 1st Belorussian Front storm Altdamm. There are now no German positions on the east bank of the northern Oder River.

MARCH 22–31

WESTERN FRONT, *GERMANY*
The Allied crossings of the Rhine River begin. The 5th Division of the US Third Army crosses the Rhine near Nierstein and Oppenheim and establishes bridgeheads on the east bank. By the end of the 23rd, the whole of the division is over the river. German resistance is negligible.

Field Marshal Bernard Montgomery's 21st Army Group (1.25 million men) begins crossing the river on the 23rd, when the British 51st (Highland)

▼ Prisoners taken by the Allies in their Rhine operations. Many Germans were now offering only token resistance.

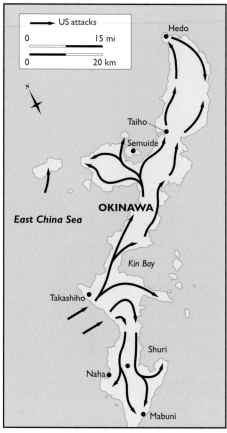

▲ *After the initial US Army and Marine thrust across Okinawa, the 6th Marine Division cleared the north of the island.*

▲ *The US II Amphibious Corps pours ashore on Okinawa. By the end of the first day, 50,000 troops had been landed.*

Division and the Canadian 3rd Division cross near Rees and Emmerich. On the 24th, the US 87th Division crosses at Boppard and the 89th at St. Goer, while farther north the British 6th and the US 17th Airborne Divisions land east of the Rhine and link up with advancing British forces.

German units, exhausted and depleted by the fierce battles west of the river, are only able to offer token resistance. By the end of the month the Algerian 3rd Division of General de Lattre de Tassigny's French First Army has crossed the river – every Allied army now has troops on the east bank of the Rhine.

MARCH 24

FAR EAST, *BURMA*
The Allied Chinese New First Army links up with the Chinese 50th Division near Hsipaw, thus bringing the campaign in northern Burma to an end.

MARCH 25–28

EASTERN FRONT, *HUNGARY*
The Soviet 2nd Ukrainian Front starts its attack across the Hron River and along the north bank of the Danube. Hungarian troops begin deserting their German allies in droves, while German commanders report a loss of confidence among their own men. By the

28th, the Red Army has reached the Austrian border in the Köszeg–Szombathely area.

MARCH 30

EASTERN FRONT, *POLAND*
Danzig is captured by the Red Army, along with 10,000 German prisoners and 45 submarines in the harbor.

APRIL 1

PACIFIC, *OKINAWA*
Operation Iceberg, the US invasion of the island, commences. Admiral Chester W. Nimitz, commander-in-chief Pacific Fleet and Pacific Ocean areas, has assigned Vice Admiral Richmond Turner as commander of the amphibious forces and Vice Admiral Marc Mitscher as commander of the fast carrier forces. The US Tenth Army is led by Lieutenant General Simon B. Buckner, and comprises 183,000 men.

The island, only 325 miles (520 km) from Japan, has two airfields on the western side and two partially-protected bays on the east coast – an excellent springboard for the proposed invasion of the Japanese mainland.

The amphibious landing by the US II Amphibious Corps and XXIV Corps is virtually unopposed. The Japanese commander, Major General Mitsuru

▶ *The conquest of islands close to Japan meant US fighters, such as these Mustangs, could escort the bombers on their missions to the Japanese homelands.*

◄ *The Japanese battleship* Yamato *under air attack. Its sinking signaled the end of the Japanese surface fleet.*

encirclement of the economically-important Ruhr region.

APRIL 4

WESTERN FRONT, *HOLLAND*
Field Marshal Bernard Montgomery's 21st Army Group begins its offensive to liberate Holland and sweep across northern Germany. As food stocks in Holland are low, this operation is important as the Dutch postwar political attitude toward the Allies will depend on the speed of liberation.

APRIL 5

POLITICS, *CZECHOSLOVAKIA*
At Kosice, the National Front government of Czechs and Slovaks announces its program and proclaims the democratic principles of the Czech Republic. Stating that the liberation of the country is the first priority, it calls on the population to undertake a broad and active struggle against the Germans.

APRIL 7

SEA WAR, *PACIFIC*
The *Yamato*, the world's largest battle-ship, is sunk at sea by US warplanes while making its way to attack US forces on Okinawa. The battleship is on a suicide mission, with just enough fuel to reach the island.

AIR WAR, *JAPAN*
Some 108 P-51s take off from Iwo Jima to escort B-29 bombers heading for Japan. They are the first US land-based fighters to reach mainland Japan.

Ushijima, has withdrawn his 80,000 men behind Shuri, where he has built a major defensive line.

APRIL 2–3

WESTERN FRONT, *GERMANY*
Units of the US First and Third Armies meet at Lippstadt to complete the

APRIL 9

PACIFIC, *OKINAWA*
The US XXIV Corps begins to attack the Shuri defenses on Okinawa. Japanese resistance is heavy and the Americans can make no headway.

APRIL 9–10

ITALY, *ARGENTA GAP*
The final campaign in Italy begins as the US Fifth and British Eighth Armies commence their fight for control of the Po Valley. The plan of Field Marshal Harold Alexander, commander-in-chief of Allied forces in Italy, is for the Eighth Army to attack westward through the Argenta Gap, while the Fifth Army strikes north, west of Bologna, thereby trapping German Army Group C between the two.

On the night of April 9, after a massive aerial bombardment and five artillery bombardments, the offensive opens with the Indian 8th and New Zealand 2nd Divisions attacking toward Lugo across the Senino River. By dawn on the 10th, Allied tanks are crossing the Senino River over three bridges, with Allied aircraft overhead providing effective support to the operation.

APRIL 10

FAR EAST, *BURMA*
General William Slim's British Four-teenth Army commences an offensive to capture Rangoon. It is a race against time to take the city before the monsoons begin in mid-May. He must

▼ *The funeral procession of US President Franklin D. Roosevelt, who died with victory in Europe a matter of days away.*

DECISIVE WEAPONS

ATOMIC BOMBS

The science behind the atomic bomb is relatively simple: a neutral neutron particle hits the nucleus of a uranium atom, which splits into two fragments: a krypton atom and a Barium atom. The reaction also releases an enormous burst of energy. One or two fresh neutrons are released, some of which find other nuclear targets and repeat the process. Each splitting or "fission" causes more – the chain reaction. A rapid chain reaction becomes a nuclear explosion. However, uranium has several isotopes, and the trick is to find a way of isolating the uranium isotope U-235, which has the highest energy factor for the development of nuclear power.

The atomic bomb dropped on Hiroshima, "Little Boy," was a "gun-type" weapon, shooting a piece of subcritical U-235 into another, cup-shaped piece to create the supercritical mass – and the nuclear explosion. The bomb used against Nagasaki – "Fat Man" – used the implosion method, with a ring of 64 detonators shooting segments of plutonium together to obtain the supercritical mass. The costs were huge: the Manhattan Project, the secret US project led by J. Robert Oppenheimer that developed the atomic bomb, cost the US government $2 billion.

also stop the Japanese forming a defensive line north of Rangoon and halting his advance.

APRIL 11

WESTERN FRONT, *GERMANY*
The US Ninth Army arrives at the Elbe River near Magdeburg. An increasing number of German towns are surrendering without a fight, while Hitler's armies fighting in western Germany are disintegrating.

APRIL 12

POLITICS, *UNITED STATES*
President Franklin D. Roosevelt dies of a cerebral haemorrhage in Warm Springs, Georgia. Vice President Harry S. Truman takes over the position of president, and one of his first decisions is to cancel a plan to launch old, pilotless aircraft packed with explosives against industrial targets in Germany following Prime Minister Winston Churchill's concern that it may provoke retaliation against London.

APRIL 13

EASTERN FRONT, *AUSTRIA*
The Red Army liberates Vienna.

APRIL 14

POLITICS, *ALLIES*
General Dwight D. Eisenhower, Supreme Commander of Allied Armies in the West, informs the Combined Chiefs-of-Staff that the Allied thrust against Berlin takes second place to the securing of the northern (Norway and Denmark) and southern (south Germany and Austria) Allied flanks. The British chiefs-of-staff are dissatisfied, but acknowledge Eisenhower's reasoning, and approve his plans on the 18th.

ITALY, *ARGENTA GAP*
The offensive by the US Fifth Army in northern Italy begins. Preceded by a bombardment by 500 ground-attack aircraft, the US 1st Armored, US 10th Mountain, and Brazilian 1st Divisions attack between Vergato and Montese, and make good progress.

APRIL 16

EASTERN FRONT, *GERMANY*
The Soviet offensive to capture Berlin commences. The Soviet plan has three parts: a breakthrough on the Oder and Neisse Rivers; the fragmentation and isolation of German units in and around Berlin; and the annihilation of said units, capture of the city, and an advance to the Elbe River.

The Red Army forces involved are the 2nd Belorussian and 1st Ukrainian Fronts, the Long Range Force, the Dniepr Flotilla, and two Polish armies – a total of 2.5 million men, 41,600 guns and mortars, 6250 tanks and self-propelled guns, and 7500 combat aircraft. German forces consist of the Third Panzer and Ninth Armies of Army Group Vistula; the Fourth Panzer and Seventeenth Armies of Army Group Center; a host of *Volkssturm* ("home guard"), security and police detachments in Berlin itself; and a reserve of eight divisions – a total of

▼ *US Private Paul Drop stands guard over thousands of German prisoners taken in the Ruhr Pocket in April 1945.*

▲ The Hohenzollern Bridge over the Rhine River near Cologne, demolished by retreating German forces in April 1945.

▲ A US truck races past the corpse of a German soldier during the Allied drive to liberate Holland.

one million men, 10,400 guns and mortars, 1500 tanks or assault guns, and 3300 combat aircraft.

ITALY, *ARGENTA GAP*
The 78th and 56th Divisions of the British Eighth Army overcome the Fossa Marina, a canal running northeast from Argenta into

Lake Comacchio, with a combination of land and amphibious assaults. The German line has been fractured, and the Allies are through the Argenta Gap.

APRIL 17

PACIFIC, *PHILIPPINES*
Elements of the US X Corps land on Mindanao.

APRIL 18

WESTERN FRONT, *GERMANY*
All German resistance in the Ruhr industrial area ceases; 370,000 prisoners fall into Allied hands.

WESTERN FRONT, *HOLLAND*
The Canadian I Corps, encountering sporadic resistance, has reached Harderwijk, thus isolating German forces in the west of the country.

APRIL 20

WESTERN FRONT, *GERMANY*
Nuremberg, the shrine of National Socialism in southern Germany, falls to the US Third Army after a five-day battle. The city had been defended by two German divisions, Luftwaffe and

▼ The taking of Berlin, Hitler's capital, was the climax of the Red Army's war.

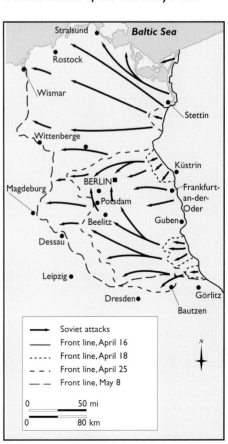

| Soviet attacks |
| Front line, April 16 |
| Front line, April 18 |
| Front line, April 25 |
| Front line, May 8 |

0 — 50 mi
0 — 80 km

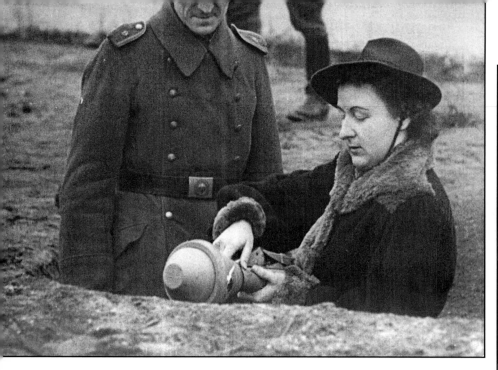

Volkssturm battalions, and ringed by anti-aircraft guns, and the German commander had vowed to Hitler that he and his men would fight to the bitter end.

EASTERN FRONT, *GERMANY*
Marshal Georgi Zhukov's 1st Belorussian Front has smashed German resistance on the Oder River and is advancing toward Berlin. The Soviet troops have had to overcome three defensive belts, each consisting of two or three layers of troops.

APRIL 22

EASTERN FRONT, *GERMANY*
The Soviet high command has ordered Marshals Georgi Zhukov and Ivan Konev to complete the encirclement of German forces in the forests southeast of Berlin by April 24 to prevent them breaking through to the city to increase the strength of its garrison. This move will also close the Red Army ring to the west of Berlin to prevent the escape of enemy units from the capital of the Third Reich. Adolf Hitler, spurning a chance to flee to Bavaria, decides to stay in the city and supervise its defense.

ITALY, *ARGENTA GAP*
The South African 6th Armored and British 6th Armored Divisions meet at Finale, north of the Reno River. The Germans are in headlong retreat from the Argenta Gap toward the Po River, leaving most of their guns, tanks, and transport behind.

▲ *The last reserves: a Berlin woman learns how to use an antitank weapon in the final days of the war.*

▶ *Soviet troops close in on "Fortress Berlin." German resistance alternated between the fanatical and token.*

APRIL 23

WESTERN FRONT, *GERMANY*
The last German defenders in the Harz Mountains are captured. Farther north, the British Second Army enters the outskirts of Hamburg.

APRIL 25–27

EASTERN FRONT, *GERMANY*
Marshal Georgi Zhukov's 1st Belorussian Front and Marshal Ivan Konev's 1st Ukrainian Front complete the encirclement of Berlin, trapping its defenders. The assault on the

▶ *As the Battle of Berlin rages, British troops mop up the last pockets of resistance in north Germany.*

city begins on the 26th, preceded by heavy air strikes and artillery bombardments, with attacks from all sides simultaneously. By the 27th, "Fortress Berlin" has been reduced to an east-to-west belt 10 miles (16 km) long by three miles (5 km) wide. German forces within the city are affected by widespread desertions and suicides.

APRIL 28

POLITICS, *HOLLAND*

The first meeting between Allied and German representatives takes place in western Holland. The Reichskommissar for the Netherlands, Artur von Seyss-Inquart, has offered the Allies the freedom to import food and coal into German-occupied western Holland to alleviate the plight of the civilian population if they will halt their forces to the east. This leads to a cessation of hostilities and saves the country from the ravages of further fighting.

POLITICS, *ITALY*

Mussolini's puppet fascist state collapses along with German resistance in the north of the country. Attempting to flee to Austria, Il Duce and his mistress Claretta Petacci are captured by partisans. On the orders of the Committee of National Liberation, Walter Audisio, a communist member of the Volunteer Freedom Corps, shoots them both. Their mutilated bodies are later hung up in the Piazzale Loreto, Milan.

EASTERN FRONT, *GERMANY*

Soviet troops begin the assault on the Reichstag by attacking across the Moltke Bridge. The Germans launch furious counterattacks, and at the strongpoints of the Ministry of the Interior (defended by SS troops) and the Kroll Opera resistance is fierce.

APRIL 29

POLITICS, *GERMANY*

Adolf Hitler, now confined to the "Führerbunker" behind the Reichs Chancellery, orders Colonel General Ritter von Greim to leave Berlin and arrest Heinrich Himmler, head of the SS, for his attempts to seek peace with the Allies. Greim had been appointed commander-in-chief of the Luftwaffe on the 23rd following Hermann Goering's attempt to negotiate with the Allies on his behalf. Hitler publishes his "Political Testament," in which he blames international Jewry for the outbreak of the war. He nominates Admiral Karl Doenitz as his successor, and marries his long-time mistress, Eva Braun.

POLITICS, *ITALY*

As a result of behind-the-scenes dealings between Karl Wolff, senior commander of the SS and police in Italy, and Allen Dulles, head of the American Office of Strategic Services (OSS) in Switzerland, Wolff and General Heinrich von Vietinghoff, German commander-in-chief in Italy, sign the instrument of unconditional surrender in northern Italy, to come into affect on May 2. The Swiss, the Allies, and many Germans and Italians in Italy have been concerned about a drawn-out campaign in Hitler's "Alpine Fortress," and the probable destruction of north Italy's industry as a result of Hitler's scorched earth policy.

▼ *Soviet rocket-launchers blast German positions in Potsdam railroad station in the final days of the Battle of Berlin.*

▲ *Hitler and his mistress Eva Braun, whom he married in Berlin just prior to their mutual suicide at the end of April.*

EASTERN FRONT, *GERMANY*

The trapped German force around Frankfurt-an-der-Oder attempts to break out of its pocket to reach Berlin. This results in three days of savage fighting in which it is annihilated. Of its original strength of 200,000 men, 60,000 are killed, and 120,000 taken prisoner. Only small groups succeed in slipping through Soviet lines.

HOME FRONT, *HOLLAND*

The RAF begins dropping food supplies to alleviate the plight of the country's starving civilians.

APRIL 30

POLITICS, *GERMANY*

Adolf Hitler and Eva Braun commit suicide in the Führerbunker in Berlin. Hitler shoots himself, while Braun takes poison. Their bodies are later cremated by the SS.

MAY 1

POLITICS, *GERMANY*
General Krebs, chief of the General Staff of the Army High Command, initiates cease-fire negotiations with the Soviets on behalf of the Nazi leadership in Berlin (Martin Bormann, Nazi Party Minister, and Josef Goebbels, Reichskommissar for Defense of the Capital). The Soviets demand unconditional surrender and the fighting in the capital and elsewhere continues.

FAR EAST, *BURMA*
In the early hours, the 2nd Gurkha Parachute Battalion makes an airborne drop to secure Elephant Point, southeast of Rangoon, to enable Allied amphibious forces to enter the Rangoon River unopposed from the sea. After a brief fight the site is secured.

MAY 2

WESTERN FRONT, *GERMANY*
The British 6th Airborne Division of the 21st Army Group moves into Wismar, just in time to prevent the Red Army entering Schleswig-Holstein.

EASTERN FRONT, *GERMANY*
Following a savage three-day battle, in which half the 5000-strong garrison has been killed, the Reichstag in Berlin falls to the Red Army and the Hammer and Sickle is raised above the shell-scarred parliament building.
  General Helmuth Weidling, commandant of Berlin, surrenders the city and its remaining troops to Marshal Georgi Zhukov. Taking the city has cost the Soviets 300,000 men killed, wounded, or missing, over 2000

▶ *The Hammer and Sickle flies over Berlin, signaling the fall of the city to the Red Army and the end of the Third Reich.*

tanks and self-propelled guns, and over 500 aircraft. The Germans have lost one million men killed, wounded, or taken prisoner.

FAR EAST, *BURMA*
The Indian 20th Division captures the town of Prome, thus severing the Japanese line of retreat from the Arakan. In the south, the Indian 26th Division makes an amphibious landing along the Rangoon River.

MAY 3

FAR EAST, *BURMA*
Following 38 months of Japanese occupation, Rangoon falls to the Allies without a fight. The city's infrastructure is in tatters, with buildings extensively damaged by bombing.

MAY 3–4

POLITICS, *GERMANY*
The whole of the northwest of the country is under British control. Admiral Karl Doenitz sends Admiral Hans von Friedeburg to Field Marshal Bernard Montgomery's headquarters at Lüneburg to discuss surrender terms. On the 4th, the German delegation signs the instrument of surrender – covering German forces in

Holland, northwest Germany, the German islands, Schleswig-Holstein, and Denmark – to come into effect at 0800 hours on May 5.

MAY 4–5

POLITICS, *DENMARK*
Some 20,000 members of the Danish Resistance movement, organized under the central leadership of the Freedom Council, come out of hiding and take over the key points in the country. Soon, they are in control of Denmark. The first Allies arrive on the 5th.

MAY 5

EASTERN FRONT, *CZECHOSLOVAKIA*
With the Red Army getting nearer, Czech nationalists begin the Prague uprising. By the end of the day, there are 2000 barricades in the city, and all the important bridges over the Vltava River have been seized. Field Marshal Ferdinand Schörner, commander of the German Army Group Center, has ordered units to the city to crush the rebellion.

MAY 7

POLITICS, *GERMANY*
General Alfred Jodl, acting on behalf of the German government, signs the act of surrender to the Allies of all German forces

◄ A grim-faced Admiral Hans von Friedeburg and Field Marshal Bernard Montgomery finalize the German surrender.

realizing that the situation is hopeless, commits ritual suicide in the early hours of the morning in a cave near Mabuni. The 82-day battle, which has seen the extensive use of Japanese kamikaze attacks, has claimed the lives of 110,000 Japanese military personnel. US Navy losses amount to 9731, of whom 4907 are killed, while the Tenth Army has suffered 7613 men killed or missing, and 31,807 wounded. There have also been over 26,000 noncombatant casualties, mostly Japanese civilians, many of whom have committed suicide.

JULY 3–11

FAR EAST, *BURMA*

The remnants of the Japanese Thirty-third Army – 6000 men – attack Allied positions at Waw from the Pegu Yomas. The aim is to threaten and, if possible, to cut the British Twelfth Army's rail and road links to Rangoon, and also draw some of its units away from the center, thus making possible the movement of the Japanese Twenty-eighth Army east between Toungoo and Nyaunglebin. However, in the face

▼ Czech nationalists fight German troops in Prague behind one of the 2000 barricades erected by the insurgents.

still in the field. Hostilities are to cease by midnight on May 8 at the latest. In Norway the German garrison of 350,000 men capitulates to the Allies. The German Army Group South surrenders to the US Third Army in Austria.

MAY 9–10

EASTERN FRONT, *CZECHOSLOVAKIA*

Prague is liberated by the Red Army with the help of the partisans. By the evening, Soviet troops have sealed off all avenues of escape west for Army Group Center. German troops, seeing the hopelessness of their situation, begin to surrender in their thousands. On the 10th, the 1st Ukrainian Front makes contact with the US Third Army on the Chemnitz–Rokycany line.

MAY 15

BALKANS, *YUGOSLAVIA*

The last German troops fighting in the country surrender.

MAY 29

PACIFIC, *OKINAWA*

The US 1st Marine Division takes Shuri after hard fighting. To date the Americans have suffered 20,000 casualties trying to take the Japanese-held island.

JUNE 1

FAR EAST, *BURMA*

Having broken and scattered all Japanese opposition in Burma, General William Slim's British Four-teenth Army is mopping up the 70,000

widely-dispersed enemy troops in the country. The Japanese Twenty-eighth Army, having been forced to retreat east to avoid starvation, has been shattered by the XXXIII Corps at the Kama bridgehead. It is now nothing more than an ill-armed rabble.

JUNE 22

PACIFIC, *OKINAWA*

All Japanese resistance on the island ends. The Japanese commander, Lieutenant General Mitsuru Ushijima,

of heavy ground and air resistance, all Japanese efforts to take Waw cease by the 11th.

JULY 12

POLITICS, *JAPAN*

War leader Shigenori Togo instructs the Japanese ambassador in Moscow to inform the authorities that the emperor wants the war to cease. To this end, Prince Konoye is to be sent as a special envoy to the Soviet Union, with authority from the emperor to discuss Soviet and Japanese relations, including the future of Japanese-occupied Manchuria. However, Togo has repeatedly stressed that the Allied demand for unconditional surrender leaves his government with no choice but to continue fighting.

Indeed, the Allies are laying plans to invade the Japanese mainland. Its is proposed that the first landings, code-named Operation Olympic, will take place in November. The second, Operation Coronet, is scheduled for March 1946. The US planners expect to suffer severe casualties. However, neither operation will take place.

JULY 16

TECHNOLOGY, *UNITED STATES*

The world's first atomic bomb is

▼ *The Soviet offensive in Manchuria was a superb example of an all-arms mobile operation on a vast scale.*

▲ *The Japanese city of Hiroshima, devastated by the first use of an atomic bomb in warfare on August 6, 1945.*

exploded at Alamogordo, New Mexico. The secret work to develop the weapon is code-named the Manhattan Project. A specialized bomber unit, the 509th Composite Group, is training to attack Japan with atomic bombs.

JULY 17–AUGUST 2

POLITICS, *ALLIES*

The Potsdam Conference takes place in Germany. The "Big Three" – US President Harry Truman, Soviet leader Marshal Joseph Stalin, and British Prime Minister Clement Attlee (who had defeated Churchill in a general election on July 5) – meet to discuss postwar policy. Japan

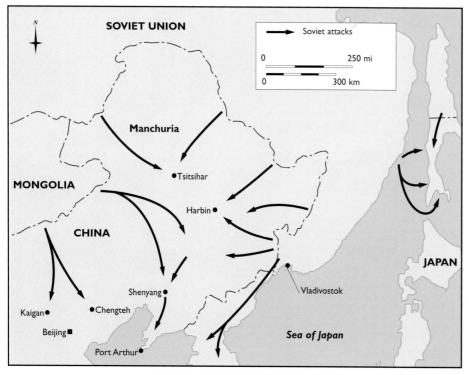

is informed that an immediate surrender would result in the continued existence of its nation, although not its empire. War criminals will be prosecuted and there will be a temporary occupation. The proclamation also makes it clear that continued resistance will lead to the "utter devastation of the Japanese homeland." This is a veiled reference to the use of atomic weapons against Japan.

JULY 19

FAR EAST, *BURMA*

The Japanese Twenty-eighth Army attempts to break out of the Pegu Yomas east across the Sittang River. Forewarned, the Indian 17th Division's guns cut down the Japanese in their hundreds, while many others drown in the river. The breakout is a shambles, and signals the end of the army.

JULY 26

PACIFIC, *PHILIPPINES*

Following an amphibious landing at Sarangani Bay on the 12th, Japanese resistance on Mindanao is overcome.

JULY 28

POLITICS, *JAPAN*

Prime Minister Kantaro Suzuki announces that both he and his cabinet will ignore the recent Allied Potsdam Proclamation.

▼ *Sailors and officials on the deck of the USS* Missouri *witness the Japanese sign surrender documents in Tokyo Bay.*

AUGUST 4

FAR EAST, *BURMA*

The last remnants of the Japanese Twenty-eighth Army are killed. The Allies have lost just 96 men killed.

AUGUST 6

AIR WAR, *JAPAN*

The B-29 Superfortress *Enola Gay* drops an atomic bomb on the Japanese city of Hiroshima, killing 70,000 and injuring the same number.

AUGUST 9

FAR EAST, *MANCHURIA*

A massive Soviet offensive by 1.5 million men begins against the Japanese Kwantung Army. The swiftest campaign in the Red Army's history has begun.

AIR WAR, *JAPAN*

A second US atomic bomb is dropped on Nagasaki, following Tokyo's non-compliance with an ultimatum that further bombs would be dropped unless there was an immediate surrender. The bomb kills 35,000 people and injures a further 60,000.

AUGUST 10

POLITICS, *JAPAN*

Following a conference, during which the emperor voices his support for an immediate acceptance of the Potsdam Proclamation, Japan announces its willingness to surrender unconditionally.

AUGUST 15

POLITICS, *JAPAN*

Emperor Hirohito broadcasts to the Japanese people for the first tine calling on them to respond loyally to his command to surrender.

AUGUST 23

FAR EAST, *MANCHURIA*

The campaign in Manchuria ends in total Soviet victory. The Japanese have lost over 80,000 dead and 594,000 taken prisoner. Soviet losses are 8000 men killed and 22,000 wounded.

SEPTEMBER 2

POLITICS, *ALLIES*

Aboard the battleship *Missouri* in Tokyo Bay, Foreign Minister Mamoru Shigemitsu and General Yoshijiro Umezo sign the Instrument of Surrender. General Douglas MacArthur, Supreme Commander for the Allied Powers, signs on behalf of all the nations at war with Japan. World War II is finally over.

KEY MOMENTS

COUNTING THE COST

World War II was probably the most destructive conflict in the history of mankind. Of the major belligerents, the Soviet Union suffered the most casualties, with an estimated 7.5 million military dead. The Nazis' racial policies and general disregard for the population of the Soviet Union resulted in an estimated 15 million Russian civilian deaths. Germany, having plunged the world into conflict, paid a huge price, its armed forces suffering 2.8 million fatalities and a further 7.2 million wounded. On the home front, a total of 500,000 Germans lost their lives. Japan suffered 1.5 million military dead in the war, and 300,000 civilians died during the US bombing campaign of the Japanese homeland. Italy had 77,000 military deaths and upward of 40,000 civilian fatalities.

The Western Allied nations lost far fewer men than the Soviet Union: the United States 292,000; Great Britain 397,762; and France 210,600. US civilian deaths were negligible, while Great Britain suffered 65,000 civilian deaths; France 108,000.

In total, the military dead during the war is estimated to be 15 million, and civilian deaths are estimated at 34 million, including some six million Jews murdered in the various Nazi extermination camps.

AFTERMATH

The end of World War II ushered in the Nuclear Age, and the political and military strategy of all nations was influenced by the confrontation between the two major nuclear powers: the United States and the Soviet Union. Both countries had achieved superpower status simultaneously, having done so amid the ruins left by World War II.

They were afraid of each other, and they represented incompatible systems: capitalism and communism. The most important strategic fact of life for each was the existence and power of the other. The friction that resulted from this confrontation was called the Cold War, and was to have a profound affect on the postwar world.

THE COLD WAR

In the postwar period, the most important confrontation was the Cold War between the superpowers.

Following the inconclusive Potsdam Conference, Stalin decided to consolidate communist control over Eastern Europe, which was occupied by one million Red Army troops. The process was gradual, and the 1945 and 1946 elections in the

region were relatively free. However, by 1947 Soviet-dominated governments had been set up in Hungary, Poland, Bulgaria, and Romania (and in Czechoslovakia in February 1948) – only Yugoslavia retained some independence. Moreover, so-called "national communist" leaders, such as Wladyslaw Gomulka in Poland, were removed, thus assuring full Soviet control.

▼ Berlin in ruins after the war. Germany's infrastructure was all but destroyed during the fighting.

◀ *A torn and twisted railroad bridge – just one example of Europe's wrecked communications network.*

since 1911 a strong regime controlled all Chinese territory, and had plans (already tested in some areas) for the regeneration of the economy and the transformation of the country. With the establishment of an industrial infrastructure, a growing petroleum sector, and a nuclear capability, China quickly became a major power in Asia.

In February 1950 China signed a Treaty of Friendship with the Soviet Union, thus creating a supposed "monolithic" structure of world communism. One tangible result of this was massive Chinese-involvement in the Korean War (1950–53), which was countered by US and other Western military forces on the Korean Peninsula. Fortunately for the West, the ideological differences and conflicting ambitions of the Soviet Union and China rapidly created major splits in their alliance.

When civil war and an attempted communist coup in Greece took place in December 1947, and the Soviet Union attempted to freeze out the Western sectors of Berlin and incorporate the whole city into the German Democratic Republic in April 1948, the United States reacted with vigor, and began a policy to "contain" the Soviet Union by a series of alliances and bases, such as the North Atlantic Treaty Organization (NATO) and the South-East Asia Treaty Organization (SEATO). By 1959, the United States had over 1400 foreign bases. Fortunately, overt hostilities between the two super-powers never took place.

The victory of Mao Zhe-dong in the Chinese Civil War in 1949 created the People's Republic of China. When the communists came to power they inherited a bankrupt economy: hyper-inflation had destroyed the currency, the banking system, and urban business. Industrial plant was in ruins, and much of the rail system was inoperative. However, for the first time

▶ *The "Big Three" nations fell out after the end of the war.*

KEY MOMENTS

THE UNITED NATIONS

The term "United Nations" was originally used during World War II to denote those countries that were allied against the Axis powers of Germany, Italy, and Japan. The earliest attempt to permanently establish the United Nations was a conference at Dumbarton Oaks, Washington D.C., where representatives of the "Big Four" (the United States, Great Britain, the Soviet Union, and China) met from August 21 to October 7, 1944, to draft preliminary proposals.

These proposals for the postwar world were discussed in more detail at the Yalta Conference in February 1945, and the decisions reached at that venue formed the basis of negotiations at the United Nations Conference held in San Francisco two months later. The resultant Charter of the United Nations was signed by 50 states in June and came into force on October 24, 1945.

The basic aims of the United Nations are the maintenance of international peace and security, the development of friendly relations between states based on the principle of equal rights and self-determination, and the encouragement of international cooperation to solve international social, economic, cultural, and humanitarian problems.

position to revitalize the world economy. The manifestation of this revitalization was the Marshall Plan (April 1948–December 1951), designed to rehabilitate the economies of 17 European nations in order to create stable conditions in which democratic institutions could survive. The aims suited US foreign policy, as it was feared that poverty, unemployment, and dislocation would reinforce the popular appeal of communism.

Aid was initially offered to almost all European nations, including those under the military occupation of the Soviet Union. However, the plan was rejected by Stalin in January 1949 and the Soviet Union and its dependencies established the Council of Mutual Economic Assistance (Comecon) in response. This left the following countries to participate in the plan: Austria, Belgium, Denmark, France, Great

▶ *French tanks and an armored personnel carrier in Indochina in 1948.*

▼ *Unloading food supplies during the 1948 Berlin blockade – an example of Soviet brinkmanship during the Cold War.*

The Cold War's main front, however, was not in Asia but in Europe, with the dividing line running through the center of the continent, and through the center of Berlin. Europe itself was politically disorganised and economically shattered. In European Russia and much of Eastern Europe, where the tides of war had ebbed and flowed, a vast wilderness had been created that was barren of everything save people. Agricultural production was in dire straits, compounded by the breakdown of the communications network, and output of coal, steel, and iron was reduced drastically compared to prewar levels. The sheer enormity of the physical damage would have prevented a rapid return to peacetime conditions anyway, but the partition of Europe into US and Soviet spheres of influence further aggravated the problem.

THE MARSHALL PLAN
Only the United States, with its surplus of production and materials, was in a

for in mid-1945 Germany had no running railroads, no postal service and in many areas no gas, electricity, or water. But US aid (also given to Japan) stimulated production and revitalized the economy. One of the benefits was a social democratic Federal Republic of Germany, which joined its former enemy France to create a bloc which promoted peace and development in Central Europe.

DECOLONIZATION

The reverberations of the changes in Europe were felt in Africa and the Middle East, where nationalism developed rapidly after World War II. In Africa, the experience of African soldiers in overseas theaters, the examples of nationalist movements in India and Indonesia, plus the influx of Allied personnel into African countries, from whom native Africans learned new skills and new attitudes, made the end of colonialism inevitable. There was a new generation of nationalist leaders, such as Jomo Kenyatta, founder of the Kenya African Union.

By the end of 1960 all the former colonies of French West and French Equatorial Africa were politically independent, and Britain and Belgium had read the signs of the times and had granted their colonies independence. Only Portugal and the white settlers in Algeria, Rhodesia, and South Africa held out, although the tide of change would eventually sweep them away. A new age had dawned out of the ashes and horrors of World War II.

Britain, Greece, Iceland, Ireland, Italy, Luxembourg, the Netherlands, Norway, Portugal, Sweden, Switzerland, Turkey, and western Germany. The US distributed some $13 billion worth of economic aid, which helped to restore industrial and agricultural production, establish financial stability, and expand trade. The European states set up the Committee of European Economic Cooperation to coordinate participation, which was later replaced by the permanent Organization for European Economic Cooperation (OEEC).

The Marshall Plan was very successful, with some states experiencing a rise in their gross national products of between 15 and 25 percent in this period. In addition, the plan contributed greatly to the rapid renewal of the Western European industries.

▶ *A "hot war" during the Cold War. British troops fire at Chinese forces during the Korean War with a Bofors Gun.*

The Marshall Plan also facilitated the integration of western Germany into Europe's political and economic infrastructure, paving the way for the Federal Republic of Germany (created in 1949) to play an active role in the European Coal and Steel Community and NATO. This was indeed remarkable,

APPENDICES

The appendices to this book recount, in brief, the careers of the leading figures, both military and political, who played a major role in the period 1914–45. Individuals who are included as features in the main body of the work are excluded here to avoid repetition.

WORLD WAR I PERSONALITIES

ALBERT I
BELGIAN RULER,
1875–1934
Albert took command of his country's small armed forces at the outbreak of World War I, but was quickly forced to retreat to Antwerp by the overwhelmingly superior German invaders. From the base at Antwerp, he launched limited counterattacks on the German right wing as it swung through Belgium for France. By the end of 1914, however, the bulk of the forces under Albert's command had retreated from Antwerp and were occupying a small strip of Belgian territory along the coast of the English Channel.

Albert, who hoped for some time after 1914 to reach a compromise peace with Germany, was at odds with the British and French as the war continued, and his small forces stood back from any major offensives until the last year of the war. In later 1918, however, Albert, now in charge of the large Flanders Army Group, led his command in the final general offensives against the crumbling German defenses on the Western Front.

ALLENBY, EDMUND
BRITISH GENERAL,
1861–1936
Allenby was the commander of the British Expeditionary Force's cavalry during 1914, but was criticized for his handling of his forces. Nevertheless, he was promoted to lead the British Third Army in 1915, and went on to play a key role in the costly Third Battle of Ypres in 1917.

Allenby's great chance came later in the year when he was transferred to Egypt, where the British offensives against the Turks had stalled. He broke through the enemy defenses in Palestine at the Battle of Beersheba in late October and had captured Jerusalem by December. Allenby's ultimate objective was Damascus, the capital of Turkish-held Syria and a key railroad center, but he was unable to begin his offensive until September 1918 due to troop shortages – many of his units had been hurriedly sent to the Western Front to combat a series of major German attacks.

When his attack did begin, it was wholly successful – the Battle of Megiddo shattered the Turkish forces blocking the road to Syria. Damascus fell on October 1. Allenby, who had conducted the campaign with resolution and flexibility, was showered with public praise and official awards.

BEATTY, DAVID
BRITISH ADMIRAL,
1872–1936
Renowned for his dash and urgency, Beatty had a meteoric rise, becoming an admiral in 1910. At the outbreak of World War I, he was commander of the British fleet's battlecruiser squadron. His battlecruisers enabled the British to inflict losses on German naval forces at the Battle of the Heligoland Bight in August 1914 and he played a prominent role in the Battle of the Dogger Bank during the following January.

Beatty took part in the Battle of Jutland in 1916, where he lost three of his warships to highly-accurate German fire and was criticized, somewhat unfairly, for the handling of his vessels. His reputation was still sufficiently high for him to be promoted to command the whole of the British Home Fleet in December 1916. In this position, he oversaw the repair of the warships damaged at Jutland and also rectified many of the fleet's shortcomings, most notably with regard to the protection of their magazines and the clear, unambiguous use of communications during battle. Beatty's last act of the war was to accept the surrender of the German High Seas Fleet at Scapa Flow in 1918.

BELOW, OTTO VON

GERMAN GENERAL,
1857–1944
Below was one of the most peripatetic German commanders of World War I. He served on the Eastern Front, taking part in the Battle of Gumbinnen and the First Battle of the Masurian Lakes in 1914. In 1915, he commanded the German Eighth Army at the successful Second Battle of the Masurian Lakes.

Below moved to the Balkans, where he was instrumental in preventing an enemy breakout from Salonika. He next transferred to Italy, where he commanded a mixed German and Austro-Hungarian force of 12 divisions during the brilliantly-executed Battle of Caporetto in October–November 1917. In the final year of the war, Below served on the Western Front, leading the German Seventeenth Army until the armistice in November.

BETHMANN HOLLWEG, THEOBOLD VON

GERMAN POLITICIAN,
1856–1921
Chancellor of Germany from 1909 until 1917, Bethmann Hollweg became increasingly involved in international diplomacy, chiefly to weaken the alliances arrayed against Germany before World War I. His efforts, mainly directed toward keeping Britain out of the war, did not come to fruition, however. When World War I began his view was pessimistic regarding its probable outcome and he believed a compromise peace would have to be agreed the longer the fighting continued.

Nevertheless, Bethmann Hollweg did have some noteworthy diplomatic coups during the war, particularly encouraging Turkey and Bulgaria to fight alongside Germany. However, he believed that Germany's commitment to unrestricted submarine warfare was a risky strategy, one likely to bring the United States into the war. This view brought him into direct conflict with Germany's military-dominated leadership and hastened his departure from government in July 1917.

BRUSILOV, ALEXEY

RUSSIAN GENERAL,
1853–1926
Considered to be one of the best generals of World War I, Brusilov stands unique in that he masterminded his country's only successful offensive of the entire conflict. Indeed, the offensive, fought in 1916, bears his name.

At the outbreak of war, Brusilov led the Eighth Army into the Austro-Hungarian province of Galicia with some success, but was repulsed in the spring of 1915, when German forces were sent eastward to prop up the Austro-Hungarian armies in the area.

In 1916, Brusilov was promoted to command four armies and he embarked on a huge offensive against Austria-Hungary that came close to knocking the tottering empire out of the war. However, the offensive ended in stalemate and tore the heart out of the Russian Army, leaving an aftermath of bitterness among the ordinary soldiers that would have profound repercussions the following year.

In 1917, as Russia fell into revolutionary turmoil, Brusilov, now commander-in-chief, coordinated its last offensive in World War I. It failed for understandable reasons, chiefly the poor morale of the ordinary Russian soldiers, and Brusilov resigned. He joined the revolutionary Red Army in 1920.

BULLARD, ROBERT LEE

US GENERAL,
1861–1947
Bullard, a veteran of the Spanish–American War of 1898, was made commander of the US Second Army when it was created in October 1918. He led the army during the final offensives against the Germans on the Western Front, chiefly in the vicinity of the Moselle and Meuse Rivers.

Bullard had already established a reputation as a tenacious "fighting" commander as he had led American troops with distinction during the Battle of Cantigny the previous May and during the Second Battle of the Marne a few months later.

BÜLOW, KARL VON

GERMAN GENERAL,
1846–1921
Bülow's standing was irreparably damaged by Germany's defeat during the First Battle of the Marne in 1914. As commander of the Second Army, he had begun well, capturing the key Belgian fortress of Liège, but failed to maintain the necessary pace of the advance through northeast France. Losing touch with other friendly forces, he opened a gap in the sweeping German attack through France that was exploited by the British and French at the Battle of the Marne.

After the Marne, Bülow was briefly given overall command of the German First and Second Armies and later took charge of the Second Army alone, a position he held until March 1915, when he was replaced due to ill-health. Bülow recovered from his illness, but never gained another army command, mainly because of his poor performance during the fighting along the Marne River.

BYNG, JULIAN

BRITISH GENERAL,
1862–1935
A distinguished commander of Canadian troops in World War I, Byng came from a British family steeped in military tradition – not all of it fortunate. One of his ancestors, a British admiral, was executed by his own country in dubious circumstances during the middle of the eighteenth century, an event that prompted French satirist Voltaire to comment that the admiral had been executed

"pour encourager les autres" ("to encourage the others").

Julian Byng was more fortunate, however. After service on the Western Front in 1914–15, he gained prominence for conducting the carefully-crafted withdrawal from the disastrous campaign against the Turkish-held Gallipoli Peninsula. Back on the Western Front, Byng was one of the prime-movers behind the attack on Cambrai in 1917, and he also kept his forces together during the great German offensives of 1918. Held in great esteem by the Canadians, he was made their governor-general after the war, a post he filled between 1921–26.

CADORNA, LUIGI

ITALIAN GENERAL, 1850–1928

Cadorna was made the head of the Italian Army in 1914, just a year before the country entered World War I. The forces he commanded were poorly trained and badly equipped, and his first job was to improve standards – unfortunately the onset of war prevented his reforms from being completed.

Cadorna's main effort during the war was directed against the Austro-Hungarian forces stretched along the line of the Isonzo River, a position he attacked on more than 10 occasions with little success. The morale of the ordinary Italian soldiers plummeted.

The Battle of Caporetto in 1917, which saw the Italians forced to retreat in almost total disorder, sealed Cadorna's fate. He was replaced by General Armando Diaz and spent a brief period as a member of the newly-created Supreme War Council, which coordinated efforts against the Central Powers, before he retired.

CASTELNAU, NOËL DE

FRENCH GENERAL, 1851–1944

As a close confident of Joffre, Castelnau was instrumental in drawing up France's Plan XVII, the country's strategy to attack Germany in the event of war. In 1914, he carried out part of this plan by advancing into Alsace-Lorraine but was soon forced to retreat. However, he played in a key role in preventing the Germans from exploiting their success in Alsace-Lorraine, which allowed Joffre to marshal his forces for the key Battle of the Marne.

In mid-1915 Castelnau was promoted to command a group of armies in the center of the Western Front and he led these in a major but unsuccessful offensive in Champagne. At the close of the year, he was made Joffre's chief-of-staff and in 1916 coordinated the defense of Verdun.

However Castelnau's role in the defense of the key frontier fortress could not save his career. Joffre was replaced at the end of the year and Castelnau, so closely identified with him, was also removed. Nevertheless, he returned to service in 1918, leading the final offensives into Lorraine.

CLEMENCEAU, GEORGES

FRENCH POLITICIAN, 1841–1929

Clemenceau became French prime minister in the latter part of 1917 and was a forceful critic of the malaise of inactivity that gripped his country's political establishments. Clemenceau immediately ruled out a negotiated peace with Germany and set about galvanizing France's war effort. Defeatist politicians were removed from power, he was able to exert his authority over recalcitrant members of the military, and he also established a more meaningful relationship with his senior commanders.

Clemenceau was also instrumental in establishing the joint Supreme War Council, which coordinated efforts against the Central Powers. However, he was foiled in his attempts during the peace deliberations to gain even more for France from the defeated Central Powers, but his wartime leadership was crucial to the final victory.

CONRAD VON HÖTZENDORF, FRANZ

AUSTRIAN GENERAL, 1852–1925

Although he often devised grandiose military strategies as the Austro-Hungarian chief of the General Staff, Hötzendorf lack firmness and was hampered by the generally poor quality of the polyglot forces under his command. Austro-Hungarian forces suffered a number of humiliations on the Eastern Front, in Italy, and the Balkans, and often had to rely on German forces to bail them out. Hötzendorf's position was weakened and his overall authority gradually undermined.

In September 1916, his position was further destabilized with the establishment of a wholly German-dominated joint command, and in March 1917 Hötzendorf was sacked. He subsequently served as a senior commander in Italy but was dismissed in July 1918 following the failure of a major Austro-Hungarian offensive the previous month.

DIAZ, ARMANDO

ITALIAN GENERAL, 1861–1928

Diaz replaced General Luigi Cadorna as chief of the Italian General Staff in November 1917. His immediate role involved stabilizing the front line following the German-led Battle of Caporetto, which came close to knocking Italy out of the war. This achieved, he set about restoring the morale of the Italian Army and building up its strength.

Despite entreaties from his allies, Diaz refrained from launching any offensives until fully prepared. Before this, he was able to blunt an Austro-Hungarian offensive, the Battle of the Piave River, in June 1918 and then launch his own onslaught. Aided by French and British troops, he initiated the Battle of Vittorio Veneto in late October and within a few weeks the Austro-Hungarian forces in Italy had been shattered.

ENVER PASHA

TURKISH GENERAL, 1881–1922

An ardent nationalist, Enver was his country's minister of war at the beginning of 1914 and, being decidedly pro-German, was partly responsible for Turkey's entry into the war. With war declared, Enver directed Turkey's strategy toward the Caucasus, where he planned to gain territory and the region's oil at the expense of Russia, Turkey's historical rival.

Enver took charge of the subsequent operations but his military skills were limited. Between 1914 and 1916, his forces suffered a series of defeats, yet he continued to attack into the Caucasus, particularly after the Russian Revolution in 1917. His attacks were accompanied by sustained and large-scale massacres of Christian Armenians by Turkish forces. In late 1918, the Turkish government collapsed and Enver was forced into exile.

FALKENHAYN, ERICH VON
GERMAN GENERAL, *1861–1922*
Falkenhayn began World War I as Germany's minister of war and was made chief-of-staff in September 1914 after the dismissal of General Helmuth von Moltke for the failure of the Schlieffen Plan. Falkenhayn combined both posts for the next six months and wielded enormous power. However, he was a prudent and cautious commander, one unwilling to launch large-scale offensives unless he thought they were absolutely necessary.

His downfall came in 1916 when he launched the onslaught against the French-held fortress of Verdun, which produced huge German casualties for little gain and cost him his position. Falkenhayn next served as a field commander in Romania and the Middle East. He was decisively beaten at the Battle of Beersheba in November 1917 and was replaced by General Otto Liman von Sanders. Falkenhayn ended the war as the commander of a small garrison in Lithuania.

FAYOLLE, MARIE
FRENCH GENERAL, *1852–1928*
Fayolle was actually retired at the outbreak of World War I, but immediately returned to active service. By 1916, he was commander of the French Sixth Army, which supported the ill-fated British offensive along the Somme sector. Fayolle was transferred to the First Army in 1917 but was soon made overall commander of the French forces on the Western Front known as the Center Army Group.

Fayolle proved to be diligent and efficient in this position and was next sent to Italy to help stabilize the front following the Battle of Caporetto. Returning to France in March 1918, he led some 40 French divisions that helped to defeat the German offensives of the spring and summer. Fayolle also took part in the subsequent successful counterattacks.

FISHER, JOHN
BRITISH ADMIRAL, *1841–1920*
Fisher, although his service in World War I was limited, was a key naval figure. His foresight and commitment to modernizing Britain's navy ensured that the country's naval forces were pre-eminent at the outbreak of war. Fisher was responsible for the creation of the *Dreadnought* battleship, the most powerful warship afloat when it was launched in 1906, and also made the crucial decision to concentrate the bulk of the Royal Navy in home waters from where it could confront Germany's naval forces.

Fisher was made First Sea Lord in October 1914 but soon began to clash with Winston Churchill, the First Lord of the Admiralty. Fisher resented Churchill's meddling in purely naval matters and was highly resistant to his plans for operations against the Gallipoli Peninsula and the Dardanelles. Indeed, Fisher resigned in May 1915, unwilling to commit more resources to the dangerous operation in the eastern Mediterranean.

FRANCHET D'ESPEREY, LOUIS
FRENCH GENERAL, *1856–1942*
An experienced officer of France's colonial campaigns, Franchet d'Esperey came to prominence during Germany's invasion of 1914. He was made commander of the Fifth Army, which he led with success during the Battle of the Marne. Between 1915–17, he rose in seniority, ending the period as commander of several armies. However, his reputation was temporarily damaged during the German offensives on the Western Front during the spring of 1918.

He was moved to take charge of the forces operating in Salonika. Here, he redeemed his reputation by launching an offensive on 15 September that effectively knocked Bulgaria out of the war.

FRANZ JOSEPH
AUSTRO-HUNGARIAN RULER, *1830–1916*
Franz Joseph was emperor of Austria-Hungary for nearly 70 years and his reign was punctuated by a series of crises that threatened to tear the empire apart. Although several of his leading military and political advisers welcomed the outbreak of World War I, the aged emperor was altogether more lukewarm in his enthusiasm.

By 1916, following a succession of military humiliations, it was clear to many, including Franz Joseph, that there was little chance of winning the war. On his deathbed he confided that "I took over the throne in the most difficult conditions and I am leaving under even worse ones." His pessimism was to prove correct – within two years the empire had broken apart.

GOUGH, HUBERT
BRITISH GENERAL, *1870–1963*
Gough served on the Western Front for most of World War I, but his career was not particularly distinguished. In 1916, he led the Fifth Army during the catastrophic Battle of the Somme, making some gains but at a terrible cost in lives. Rumors began to circulate of his shortcomings and ordinary soldiers began to believe he was profligate with their lives.

In July 1917, he spearheaded the equally-contentious Third Battle of Ypres, which resulted in severe losses for little gain. The lack of progress was partly blamed on Gough's weak command. In March 1918, the German offensive almost smashed the Fifth Army. Gough bore the brunt of the widespread criticism and was replaced.

397

GROENER, WILHELM

GERMAN GENERAL, 1867–1939

Groener was in charge of the German General Staff's key railroad department at the outbreak of war and retained the position until 1916, when he briefly became involved in food supply. Groener did, however, have two stints as an active field commander before becoming the chief-of-staff of the army group based around Kiev in March 1918.

The following October, Groener replaced General Erich Ludendorff as the deputy chief of the General Staff. Staring defeat in the face, Groener had to inform Kaiser Wilhelm II that the country was gripped by revolutionary fever and that an armistice had to be agreed. Groener also agreed that the new German government would have the support of the army. At the war's end, Groener was responsible for the demobilization of the German field armies.

HAMILTON, IAN

BRITISH GENERAL, 1853–1947

Hamilton had played a distinguished role in Britain's colonial campaigns before World War I, but was seemingly entering the twilight of his career in 1914. However, following a stint in charge of home defense, he was ordered to take overall command of an attack on Turkey through the Dardanelles in 1915. He concluded that naval forces alone would in no way be sufficient to force a route through the Turkish defenses and proposed an all-out amphibious assault on the Gallipoli Peninsula.

However, Hamilton's plans were far too ambitious for the resources at his disposal and, as the initial amphibious assault on Gallipoli descended into attritional trench warfare, he became seemingly detached from the running of the campaign. He instigated further landings on the west coast of the peninsula to break the deadlock, but these also met with little success and casualties were high. Having lost the confidence of his political masters, Hamilton was sacked on October 14, 1915.

HIPPER, FRANZ VON

GERMAN ADMIRAL, 1863–1932

For much of World War I, Hipper led the reconnaissance forces of the High Seas Fleet. He earned a first-rate reputation as a daring and resourceful officer, and led elements of his command on a number of sorties that saw them bombard ports and towns along England's east coast in 1914–15. His battlecruisers also took part in large-scale actions against the British, chiefly at the Dogger Bank in 1915 and at Jutland in 1916.

At Jutland, Hipper helped to save the German fleet from disaster and was awarded the Pour le Mérite, Germany's highest ward. In August 1918, he was promoted to replace Admiral Reinhard Scheer, becoming the last commander of the High Seas Fleet. However, his policies (chiefly a plan to lead the fleet in a "death ride" against the British) led to an outbreak of mutiny that effectively destroyed the German fleet as a cohesive fighting force.

JELLICOE, JOHN

BRITISH ADMIRAL, 1859–1935

Jellicoe was the commander of the British Home Fleet from 1914 to 1916. He expected, mistakenly as events proved, to take on the German High Seas Fleet soon after the outbreak of the war, but he had to wait until the final year of his command to do so. Although Jellicoe was able to force the High Seas Fleet to withdraw at the Battle of Jutland, there was disquiet over the number of British warships sunk and the failure to inflict crippling losses on the German fleet.

In December 1916, Jellicoe was promoted to the administrative post of First Sea Lord, where he was increasingly preoccupied by the threat posed by Germany's submarines. To counter them, he was an advocate of the convoy system, which was introduced in May 1917 and proved highly successful. However, Jellicoe had a poor working relationship with Prime Minister David Lloyd George and he was dismissed in December 1917. His replacement as First Sea Lord was Sir Eric Geddes.

KITCHENER, HORATIO

BRITISH GENERAL, 1850–1916

Horatio Herbert Kitchener was Britain's war minister from 1914 until his death in June 1916. A much-decorated veteran of Britain's colonial wars, he was one of few senior figures who did not believe that the war would be short-lived. As the war dragged on, he was responsible for the massive expansion of the British Army. It was perhaps his greatest contribution to his country's war effort.

In other areas, he was much less successful. Kitchener had a difficult working relationship with several of his senior colleagues and was criticized for the shortage of artillery shells that dogged the British forces in France during 1915. He also surrendered his role as the government's chief military adviser to General Sir William Robinson. Kitchener was killed in 1916 when the warship taking him to Russia for discussions was sunk by a mine in the North Sea. He was the most senior figure of any side to be killed during the war.

KLUCK, ALEXANDER VON

GERMAN GENERAL, 1846–1934

Kluck, a long-serving officer and veteran of the Franco-Prussian War of 1870-71, was commander of the First Army during the opening battles on the Western Front in 1914. A key part of the Schlieffen Plan, his forces on the German right flank were supposed to maneuver through Belgium and France and then swing to the west of Paris. Kluck moved rapidly, but actually advanced to the east of the capital and was in danger of being attacked in the flank.

He moved to deal with the danger, but opened a gap between his own troops and the German Second Army, which was exploited by the French and British during the critical Battle of the Marne. The German forces were forced to retreat, effectively destroying the Schlieffen Plan and Germany's hopes of a swift victory. Kluck was badly wounded by shrapnel in 1915 and retired from further active service.

LETTOW-VORBECK, PAUL VON

GERMAN GENERAL, 1870–1946

Lettow-Vorbeck was made the overall commander of the small forces available in German East Africa in 1914 and fought an outstanding guerrilla campaign until the end of the war. His chief strategy was to move quickly and launch hit-and-run raids. Among his main targets were enemy railroads, bridges, and radio stations. So effective was his strategy that he tied up scores of thousands of troops.

In November 1917, the bulk of Lettow-Vorbeck's German troops were captured, but he fought on from his base in Portuguese East Africa. Lacking any support from Germany, he improvised and lived off the land. Lettow-Vorbeck advanced into British Northern Rhodesia in September 1918 and was finally convinced to surrender on November 23, nearly two weeks after the end of World War I.

LIGGETT, HUNTER

US GENERAL, 1857–1935

At the beginning of 1918, Liggett was in command of the US Army's I Corps, which he led with considerable success in the attack on the German-held St. Mihiel salient, south of Verdun, in September. During the following October, Liggett was promoted to take charge of the US First Army, which he commanded during the advance along the Meuse–Argonne sector of the Western Front.

Liggett remained in charge of the First Army until it was disbanded on April 20, 1919, and then took over the Third Army, which was the chief US occupation force in Germany, during the following May and June. He later returned to the United States to occupy administrative posts before retiring in 1921.

LIMAN VON SANDERS, OTTO

GERMAN GENERAL, 1855–1929

Liman von Sanders spent the whole of World War I in Turkish service, after having arrived there in 1913 as a military adviser. As the Turkish military was weak, he was soon appointed as the army's inspector-general and set about a program of wholesale reorganization. At the outbreak of the war, Liman von Sanders commanded the First Army, but did not take part in any action until 1915 when, in charge of the Fifth Army, he opposed the amphibious attack on the Gallipoli Peninsula.

By 1918, Liman von Sanders was active in Palestine, where he commanded the group of Turkish armies blocking the British advance toward Syria from Egypt. Starved of men and equipment, he was unable to halt the British onslaught and had been pushed back to the borders of Turkey by the signing of the armistice.

LLOYD GEORGE, DAVID

BRITISH POLITICIAN, 1863–1945

A radical politician renowned for his oratory, Lloyd George replaced Herbert Asquith as prime minister in December 1916. Previously, Lloyd George had been a member of Asquith's cabinet, serving as minister for munitions from 1915. In June 1916, he was promoted to the position of minister of war and clashed with senior military figures over British war strategy.

As prime minister, he totally reorganized Britain's war effort, making it more efficient and effective, and was a leading advocate of implementing the convoy system against the threat posed by German submarines in 1917. He was also instrumental in establishing the Supreme War Council, which coordinated the strategies of those opposed to the Central Powers. Lloyd George was also a leading figure in the creation of the Treaty of Versailles and objected to the harsh terms that some of his colleagues wished to impose on a defeated Germany.

LUDENDORFF, ERICH

GERMAN GENERAL, 1865–1937

Ludendorff began World War I as deputy chief-of-staff of the Second Army, where he became renowned for his drive, thoughtfulness – and ambition. He gained public recognition for his role in the capture of the Belgian fortress of Liège. Ludendorff next transferred to the Eastern Front, where he played a prominent role in the great German victories at the Battle of Tannenberg and the First Battle of the Masurian Lakes. It was during this period that he forged a close working relationship with General Paul von Hindenburg.

In August 1916, Ludendorff was made Hindenburg's deputy and both men effectively ran Germany's war effort for the remainder of the war. They also dominated the country's political life. Following the defeat of Russia in 1917, which freed many units for service elsewhere, Ludendorff gambled all on a decisive breakthrough on the Western Front. The sustained offensive, launched in spring 1918, was ultimately unsuccessful and probably hastened Germany's defeat. Ludendorff, the architect of the failure, was sacked on October 26 and fled to Sweden.

MACKENSEN, AUGUST VON

GERMAN GENERAL, 1849–1944

Mackensen was one of the finest German commanders of the war and fought throughout on the Eastern Front and in the Balkans. For his string of victories, he was promoted to field marshal. Mackensen's first actions in 1914 came as commander of the Ninth Army, which attacked successfully at the First Battle of the Masurian Lakes in September and then captured Lòdz in December.

In 1915, Mackensen led the Eleventh Army to decisive victory during the offensive against the Russian forces in the vicinity of the towns of Gorlice and Tarnow in Galicia, and then led German, Austro-Hungarian, and Bulgarian troops in the successful invasion of Serbia.

In 1916, Mackensen played a key role during the invasion of Romania, capturing Bucharest, the capital, in December. Mackensen stayed in command of the various forces in Romania until the close of the war.

MANGIN, CHARLES

FRENCH GENERAL, *1866–1925*

After winning praise from his superiors (but not from his troops who considered him profligate with their lives) for his recapture of Fort Douaumont during the French counterattack at Verdun in late 1916, Mangin was promoted to command the Sixth Army, which was destined to play a leading role in the offensive planned by General Robert Nivelle in 1917. Nivelle's attack was a complete failure and Mangin, although an ardent supporter of Nivelle, was sacked by the latter.

Mangin was rehabilitated in the last year of the war, being given command of the Tenth Army and leading it in several attacks on the Western Front, most notably the Second Battle of the Marne in July.

MAX OF BADEN, PRINCE

GERMAN POLITICIAN, *1867–1929*

Max von Baden was made Germany's last chancellor in October 1918, shortly after the German government had recognized the necessity of seeking an armistice. To this end, he had two main aims designed to preserve Germany's existing political structures. First, he successfully engineered the dismissal of General Erich Ludendorff, who was obstructing any peace moves. Second, he attempted to secure the removal of Kaiser Wilhelm II. Both were essential prerequisites to achieving a negotiated peace settlement with Germany's enemies.

However, Max von Baden failed to secure Wilhelm's abdication personally, although the kaiser did finally abdicate. Max von Baden was able to announce the kaiser's abdication and the creation of a regency on November 9, but this did little to halt political unrest and the clamor for more democratic government in Germany. The existing cabinet collapsed and Max von Baden paid the price – he was removed from office to be replaced by a more democratic government. A new chancellor was announced – the leader of the Social Democrats, Friedrich Ebert.

MOLTKE, HELMUTH VON

GERMAN GENERAL, *1848–1916*

Von Moltke, a member of a distinguished military family, was made chief of the General Staff in January 1906, replacing Count Alfred von Schlieffen who had devised the strategy that Germany had chosen to win World War I outright in 1914. However, Moltke was of a lesser caliber than his predecessor. He fatally weakened the Schlieffen Plan and, distant from the action in 1914, failed to react decisively to events that were changing hour by hour.

During the crucial Battle of the Marne, he sent one of his officers to investigate the strategic situation and on his intelligence ended the attacks, a decision that effectively destroyed German plans to win a swift outright victory on the Western Front. Von Moltke was marked as the culprit behind the offensive's demise and was replaced by General Erich von Falkenhayn on September 14.

NICHOLAS II

RUSSIAN RULER, *1868–1918*

Although Nicholas II was initially less than wholehearted about Russia's entry into World War I, his subsequent position as the commander of its armed forces, a role he performed badly, did much to hasten his own fall and initiate the Russian Revolution of 1917. Nicholas was dogmatic, headstrong, and wholly opposed to liberal political reform. He became his country's overall commander in September 1915, despite having no military experience. Although inexperienced, he listened little to his military chiefs.

As the Russian position on the Eastern Front became increasingly untenable in 1916–17, the country was thrown into political turmoil. The czar, abandoned by many of his senior commanders and advisers, was forced to abdicate in early 1917 and arrested by the new Provisional Government. He and his family were subsequently held at Ekaterinburg, Siberia, by the Bolshevik revolutionaries and were executed in July 1918.

NIVELLE, ROBERT

FRENCH GENERAL, *1856–1924*

Nivelle had a meteoric rise in France's military hierarchy during the war. A regimental commander in 1914, he was in charge of the Second Army by 1916. Nivelle became a national figure during the Battle of Verdun, where his tactics allowed the French to regain much of the territory they had lost to the Germans. Nivelle was subsequently made the commander of the French Army on the back of his successful defense of Verdun.

Nivelle's downfall began when he suggested that he had a strategy to end the war at a single stroke. He planned a massive offensive along the Aisne River, which he claimed would punch a huge hole through the German defenses and inflict unsustainable casualties on the enemy. In the event, his boasts were ill-judged. Beginning in mid-April 1917, Nivelle's attack was an unmitigated disaster and led to widespread mutiny. Within a month of its opening, Nivelle was sacked. He was sent to North Africa, his reputation destroyed.

ORLANDO, VITTORIO

ITALIAN POLITICIAN, *1860–1952*

Following Italy's disastrous defeat at the Battle of Caporetto in 1917, Italy's incumbent prime minister, Paolo Boselli, was replaced by Orlando. Orlando was considerably more energetic than Boselli. He was able to win increased support from his allies to shore up the front and removed the country's chief-of-staff, General Luigi Cadorna, replacing him with General Armando Diaz. Orlando also paid attention to the morale of Italy's war-weary citizens.

Diaz had many strengths but he was also cautious and refused to launch any attacks against the Austro-Hungarians until goaded into action by Orlando. Diaz's offensive in 1918, known as the Battle of Vittorio Veneto, was successful. Orlando was one of the leaders involved in drafting the World War I peace treaties, but his demands for large Italian territorial gains were rebuffed by his peers.

PLUMER, HERBERT

**BRITISH GENERAL,
1857–1932**

Considered to be one of his country's best generals of the war, Plumer became a corps commander in December 1914 and took charge of the Second Army the following April. For the next two years, he was in charge of part of the "quiet" Ypres sector of the Western Front.

In 1917, he was ordered to launch a major offensive against a piece of German-held high ground that dominated the salient. The ensuing Battle of Messines was meticulously planned and brilliantly executed. Plumer took over the whole of the sector and became embroiled in the Third Battle of Ypres. A disaster for the British, its only redeeming feature were the gains made by Plumer's old command, the Second Army.

Following a brief secondment to Italy, Plumer returned to Ypres in 1918, where he held the salient in the face of large-scale German attacks. In the final months of the conflict, he took part in the wholesale advance along the Western Front. After the end of the war, Plumer was made the commander of occupied territory in Germany and was ennobled.

POINCARÉ, RAYMOND

**FRENCH POLITICIAN,
1860–1934**

Poincaré was the president of the French Third Republic throughout the war and took a full and active part in directing his country's military effort, despite the supposedly quasi-ceremonial position he occupied. In the early years of the war, he often determined the politicians to serve in the war cabinet and influenced planning.

In 1917, France was thrown into disarray due to the failure of General Robert Nivelle's Aisne offensive and the subsequent mutinies. By November, Poincaré asked Georges Clemenceau to form a new government. However, Clemenceau was a more forceful personality than his predecessors and he resented Poincaré's interference. The two men hardly got along and the simmering tensions between them surfaced during discussion over the peace to be imposed on the defeated Central Powers, chiefly Germany. Poincaré demanded much more from the defeated but lost out to Clemenceau. The president finally left office in 1920.

PUTNIK, RADOMIR

**SERBIAN GENERAL,
1847–1917**

Putnik had experienced senior command before World War War I, leading Serbia's Army during the 1912–13 conflict in the Balkans. When Serbia was invaded by Austria-Hungary in 1914, Putnik responded with characteristic vigor, pushing back two attacks in quick succession.

In 1915, however, Serbia was invaded in considerable strength by Austro-Hungarian, German, and Bulgarian forces. The much smaller Serbian Army was forced to retreat but Putnik displayed outstanding generalship by avoiding any significant losses, thereby ensuring that his forces were still available to combat the Central Powers. Putnik and his troops were eventually evacuated from Albania to Corfu, but the general's health was wrecked and he took no further part in the war. He died in Nice, France, in May 1917.

RAWLINSON, HENRY

**BRITISH GENERAL,
1864–1925**

Rawlinson was made commander of the new Fourth Army in late 1915 but his first major offensive, along the Somme in 1916, was a disaster, although the blame was far from his alone. In 1917, he played a role in the later stages of the equally sanguine Third Battle of Ypres. After Ypres, Rawlinson temporarily took charge of the Second Army.

However, Rawlinson totally redeemed his bruised reputation on August 8, 1918, when, at the head of the Fourth Army again, he inflicted heavy losses on the German forces around Amiens. In the final weeks of the war, his forces advanced some 60 miles (96 km), winning several battles.

RENNENKAMPF, PAVEL

**RUSSIAN GENERAL,
1853–1918**

In August 1914, Rennenkampf led the Russian First Army and was involved in the invasion of East Prussia in conjunction with the Second Army. The German response was swift and devastating. While holding off Rennenkampf with light forces, they destroyed the Second Army at the Battle of Tannenberg. The Germans next attacked Rennenkampf at the First Battle of the Masurian Lakes in September, forcing him to retreat with severe casualties.

Rennenkampf, much criticized for his performance in 1914, was sacked toward the end of the year and never again held high field command. He was a victim of the Russian Civil War, shot by the Bolsheviks for declining an offer to serve them as a general.

ROBERTSON, WILLIAM

**BRITISH GENERAL,
1860–1933**

Robertson, although from a humbler background than most of his country's generals, enjoyed high office for most of World War I. He served as chief of the Imperial General Staff, the military's war planning body, from 1915 until February 1918. In 1914, Robertson had displayed excellent administrative skills by keeping the British Expeditionary Force in France supplied in the field as it retreated in the face of the German advance.

As chief of the Imperial General Staff, he invariably sided with Field Marshal Sir Douglas Haig, who continued to pursue an attritional strategy on the Western Front, despite the grave reservations of Prime Minister David Lloyd George. Lloyd George grew increasingly skeptical of Robertson's abilities and replaced him with General Sir Henry Wilson.

RUPPRECHT, CROWN PRINCE

**BAVARIAN GENERAL,
1869–1955**

Rupprecht commanded the Bavarian Sixth Army during the 1914 invasion of France and

Belgium as Bavaria remained nominally independent of German military control. Attacking through the Vosges region, he was repulsed at Nancy. Later in 1914, he took charge of a new Sixth Army, which eventually held the line in Flanders. Rupprecht was to remain in this sector of the front until the end of the war. His successes in defeating a number of British attacks led him to be promoted to command an army group, which was named after him.

Rupprecht was an astute and farsighted general, one who often expressed doubt over Germany's war strategy. Nevertheless, despite recognizing that Germany was likely to lose the conflict at a far earlier stage than many of his colleagues believed, he fought doggedly to the end of the war.

SARRAIL, MAURICE

FRENCH GENERAL,
1856–1929
Sarrail, unusually, was a senior officer in the French Army with radical political views and he displayed his independence during the fighting around Verdun in September 1914, where his refusal to retreat from the frontier fortress, despite orders to do so, had an adverse impact on the German Schlieffen Plan. In 1915, however, Sarrail was sacked, probably because of his unpopularity with the high command.

Nevertheless, Sarrail had political "friends in high places" and was appointed to command forces in Salonika, where he arrived in October 1915. Sarrail was in charge of a multinational force beset by national rivalries, and he quickly lost any support he had, being considered a "political" general. In late 1917, he was replaced by General Marie Guillaumat.

SCHEER, RHEINHARD

GERMAN ADMIRAL,
1863–1928
Scheer, who had begun the war as the commander of the High Seas Fleet's 2nd Battle Squadron, became the German fleet's overall commander following the retirement through poor health of

Admiral Hugo von Pohl in January 1916. Scheer was a more imaginative and aggressive leader than his predecessor; he sought a decisive engagement with the British navy and backed the greater deployment of U-boats.

However, the Battle of Jutland, Scheer's hoped-for decisive victory over the British, ended in a strategic defeat, one which left Germany reliant on its submarines to starve Britain into submission. By 1918, with Germany's defeat increasingly likely, Scheer was given an administrative position, but one that could not influence the outcome of the conflict.

SIMS, WILLIAM

US ADMIRAL,
1858–1936
Sims, an innovator who greatly improved the combat-readiness of the US Navy before World War I, was also a forthright and often controversial figure, but one who played a key role in coordinating Anglo-US naval policy. Sims rightly recognized the threat posed by Germany's submarines and argued successfully for the commitment of more US warships to the Atlantic sea-lanes to protect convoys.

A keen supporter of Britain, he was made Commander US Forces Operating in European Waters in June 1917, a post he held throughout the war. In this position, he made an invaluable contribution to the defeat of Germany, and was promoted to admiral in December 1918.

SMUTS, JAN CHRISTIAAN

SOUTH AFRICAN GENERAL,
1870–1950
Smuts, a leading figure in postwar South African politics, was the dominant figure in his country's military leadership between 1914 and 1918. In 1915, he was a firm supporter of South Africa's successful intervention in German Southwest Africa, and was given charge of the British and Commonwealth forces operating in East Africa against Germany's General Paul von Lettow-Vorbeck.

The hunt for the elusive Lettow-Vorbeck proved protracted, ending

in 1918, but Smuts was recalled from East Africa the year before. Smuts went to Britain to serve as South Africa's representative on the Imperial War Cabinet but was soon given a position within the British War Cabinet. Smuts, who had the confidence of Prime Minister David Lloyd George, undertook several roles, not least investigating the need for an independent air force. At the end of the war, Smuts was one of South Africa's delegates at the Paris Peace Conference.

TIRPITZ, ALFRED VON

GERMAN ADMIRAL,
1849–1930
Tirpitz, as Germany's secretary of state for the navy (1897–1916), was responsible for the rapid expansion of his country's fleet before the outbreak of the war. Despite his naval pedigree, his request to be promoted to the position of the navy's commander-in-chief in 1914 was rejected and he was increasingly excluded from discussions of naval strategy.

Tirpitz wished to seek a decisive engagement with the British fleet but some of his superiors were more concerned with avoiding such a battle. He also supported the use of unrestricted submarine warfare, a policy which his compatriots rejected until 1917. Tirpitz, frustrated by his isolation, surrendered his position in 1916.

TROTSKY, LEON

COMMUNIST REVOLUTIONARY,
1877–1940
Trotsky was appointed the Bolsheviks' commissar of foreign affairs after the revolutionaries took power in Russia during November 1917. One of his first major acts was to sign an armistice with Germany during the following December; the Bolsheviks urgently wanted to end Russia's involvement in World War I. The subsequent peace treaty, signed at Brest-Litovsk on March 3, 1918, was a humiliation which saw Russia surrender vast tracts of territory.

During the Russian Civil War (1919–21), Trotsky, although with no military experience, was made commissar for war and created the Red Army, which swept away all opposition to the Bolshevik regime. However, Trotsky was a victim of political infighting within the Bolshevik leadership. Exiled in 1935, he was finally assassinated in Mexico by an agent working for his erstwhile colleagues.

WILHELM II
GERMAN RULER, 1859–1941

Wilhelm was made Germany's emperor and the king of Prussia in 1888, and became increasingly associated with the expansion of his country's armed forces. His main aim was to make Germany the equal of the world's leading powers, based on industrial might, military power, and colonial expansion. Wilhelm, however, was far from being a strong character and his reading of international affairs was often flawed, particularly with regard to Britain.

Wilhelm did little to prevent the outbreak of World War I, and presented an image of a strong war leader for public consumption. Reality, however, was somewhat different. In effect, Germany was increasingly run by senior generals as the conflict progressed and Wilhelm became little more than a figurehead. In November 1918, he was forced to abdicate and fled to the neighboring Netherlands, where he remained, despite calls from the victors to have him tried as a war criminal, until his death.

WILSON, WOODROW
US POLITICIAN, 1856–1924

Wilson, a Democrat and the 28th president of the United States, adopted a policy of strict neutrality on the outbreak of World War I, but increasingly offered indirect support to those opposed to the Central Powers. He became, as did his fellow Americans, increasingly outraged by Germany's submarine campaign, which was punctuated by the deaths of US civilians and the loss of US vessels.

However, Wilson was initially unwilling to become embroiled in a European war and his foreign policy, at least in 1915–16, was geared to brokering a peace settlement. In 1916, he was mandated

for a second term, partly on a ticket of keeping the United States out of the war.

The situation was transformed in 1917, chiefly because of German actions, not least the initiation of an unrestricted submarine campaign and the publication of the Zimmermann telegram in which Germany attempted to win Mexico as an ally. Wilson moved toward involvement and, on April 6, the United States declared war on Germany.

Wilson was also responsible for the 14 Points, which provided the basis on which the treaties ending World War I were made. However, he had to give ground to his allies, who successfully demanded that harsh terms be imposed on the defeated Central Powers.

Wilson was also unable to secure the backing of his own political establishment for the peace settlements. Returning to the United States to promote his cause, he suffered a stroke in late 1919. Wilson was awarded the Nobel prize for peace in December 1920 and remained in office until March 1921, when he was replaced by Republican Warren G. Harding.

WORLD WAR II PERSONALITIES

ALEXANDER, HAROLD
BRITISH GENERAL, 1891–1969

Alexander was one of Britain's most popular and successful generals of the war. However, his first campaigns, those in France in 1940 and in Burma the following year, ended in defeat. Nevertheless, Alexander was made Britain's commander-in-chief in August 1942 and oversaw the defeat of Rommel at the Second Battle of El Alamein in November 1942. In the final stages of the North African war, he led the 18th Army Group.

For the invasions of Sicily and the Italian mainland, he was named Supreme Allied Commander in the Mediterranean, where he served until taking the German surrender in northern Italy on April 29, 1945.

ANTONESCU, ION
ROMANIAN POLITICIAN, 1882–1946

Antonescu, the leader of the fascist "Iron Guard" movement, was the dictator of his country from September 1940 until August 1944. On his accession to power, he immediately offered his support to both Germany and Italy – a position that was ratified when Antonescu formerly joined the Axis alliance in September 1940.

Antonescu sent Romanian divisions to fight on the Eastern Front, but they were shattered during the Soviet counterattack around Stalingrad. From this point on, Antonescu attempted to leave the Axis, but Romania's oil-producing facilities were too vital to the cause for this to be a realistic proposition. By 1944, with the Red Army approaching Romania, Antonescu was arrested following a fractious meeting with King Michael. He was later executed for war crimes.

ARNOLD, HENRY
US GENERAL, 1886–1950

A leading air force figure throughout the war, Arnold did much before 1941 to ready the US air arm for war: he increased aircraft production and bolstered its manpower. During the conflict, Arnold was a member of both the US Joint Chiefs-of-Staff and the Allied Combined Chiefs-of-Staff. In the later role, he was a key figure in devising the strategic air offensive against Germany with his British counterparts, despite initial disagreements over tactics.

In 1944, Arnold, a popular commander, was made a full general in the US Army and later became the newly-independent US Air Force's first five-star general.

AUCHINLECK, CLAUDE
BRITISH GENERAL, 1884–1981

Auchinleck was a career soldier who had served with distinction in prewar India. At the outbreak of war, he was serving in Britain but was briefly made commander-in-chief in India in 1941. However, Auchinleck was promoted to

Commander-in-Chief, Middle East, in June the same year.

Auchinleck had several tussles with Rommel's Afrika Korps over the following 12 months, but was finally successful in blocking the Axis advance on Egypt and the Suez Canal at the First Battle of El Alamein in July 1942. Despite this success, Auchinleck was replaced by Montgomery, primarily because the former had failed to prevent Tobruk from falling into Axis hands before Second Alamein. Auchinleck was sent to India, where he remained the commander-in-chief of the Indian Army throughout the war.

BADOGLIO, PIETRO
ITALIAN GENERAL, 1871–1956

Badoglio, a career officer, saw service in World War I and throughout the interwar years. He took part in the Italian occupation of Ethiopia in 1935–36 and was made the country's viceroy after the swift Italian victory.

At the outbreak of World War II, Badoglio was appoint Italy's chief-of-staff, a position he had also occupied directly after World War I. His second tenure of the post was short-lived, however, as he resigned following Italy's disastrous invasion of Greece in December 1941. He returned to the spotlight in 1943, when he was the chief figure behind the overthrow of Mussolini. His final act of the war was to sign his country's armistice with the Allied powers.

BEDELL SMITH, WALTER
US GENERAL, 1895–1961

Bedell Smith did not see active service during World War II, but he was a major figure in the sometimes fraught relationship between the United States and Britain. In 1941, he was made secretary of the US Joint Chiefs-of-Staff and secretary of the Anglo-American Combined Chiefs-of-Staff.

Bedell Smith crossed the Atlantic in 1942, when he became the chief-of-staff of General Dwight D. Eisenhower. As the war drew to a close, he created the foundations on which the Italian armistice was

signed in 1943, and also oversaw the surrender of German forces in Western Europe during 1945.

BOCK, FEDOR VON
GERMAN GENERAL, 1885–1945

Bock was one of three German army group commanders at the outbreak of war. He led Army Group North during the successful attack on Poland in September 1939 and repeated the feat with Army Group B during the invasion of the Low Countries and France the following year.

Bock led Army Group Center during the invasion of the Soviet Union in the summer of 1941, reaching the outskirts of Moscow by the end of the year. This was the pinnacle of his career. Suffering from illness and with his forces spread thinly, he was unable to block the Red Army's winter counterattack, much to Hitler's displeasure. Bock was sacked but reinstated in early 1942, when he took charge of Army Group South. Later in 1942, while his army group was attacking in the Caucasus, he disputed strategy with Hitler and was sacked.

BRADLEY, OMAR
US GENERAL, 1893–1981

Bradley spent World War I in his home country, where he specialized in training recruits. He gained a reputation as a fair officer, one who was acutely concerned for the well-being of the men under his command. It was a trait that made him one of the most popular senior officers of World War II.

Bradley first saw major action in World War II during the latter stages of the North African campaign in 1943. He subsequently took part in the invasion of Sicily and played a major role in the D-Day landings in 1944. During the breakout from Normandy, Bradley led the US 12th Army Group, which also bore the brunt of the German Ardennes offensive. In the final months of the war, his forces drove through Germany and in April linked up with Soviet units on the Elbe River.

CHIANG KAI-SHEK
CHINESE LEADER, 1887–1975

Chiang was leader of the country's Nationalists, who had been battling the Japanese invaders since 1937. However, his efforts were undermined by a lack of supplies, the unreliability of his own forces, and a difficult relationship with China's communists. In early 1942, matters improved somewhat because of the entry of the United States into the war, although Chiang remained suspicious of US General Joseph Stilwell, who was his chief-of-staff and commanded two field armies.

More than anything, Chiang requested aircraft, a wish that was granted but one that prompted a major Japanese attack in 1943. Chiang's forces were far too limited to launch an all-out counterattack, chiefly because he was often more concerned with fighting the Chinese communists. Despite his limitations, Chiang was recognized as China's legitimate leader by the Allies, but he could not prevent the country from sliding back into civil war after 1945.

CHUIKOV, VASILI
SOVIET GENERAL, 1900–82

Although he was foul-mouthed and prone to fits of violence, Chuikov is recognized as the outstanding architect of the Red Army's defense of Stalingrad, a battle that was a key point in World War II. By the time of his appointment to the Sixty-second Army at Stalingrad, he had taken part in the occupation of Poland and the attack on Finland.

During the siege of Stalingrad, Chuikov ordered his men to defend every inch of ground and fight at very close quarters, tactics which prevented the attackers from deploying their armor and aircraft effectively. Chuikov remained in command of the Sixty-second Army for the remainder of the war, taking part in the final battle for Berlin.

CLARK, MARK
US GENERAL, 1896–1984

Clark's first role in the war was as General Dwight D. Eisenhower's deputy during Operation Torch, the Allied landing in North Africa during November 1942. Shortly before the operation, Clark traveled secretly to North Africa to negotiate with Vichy French leaders to ensure that their forces did not oppose Torch.

Clark later led the US Fifth Army during the capture of Sicily and spearheaded the subsequent landings at Salerno on the Italian mainland. Clark's command took part in the fighting around Monte Cassino and played a role in the botched Anzio landings. After months of bitter fighting, his forces captured Rome, which he finally entered in triumph during early June 1944.

Clark spent the remainder of the war fighting in Italy, being promoted to commander of the 15th Army Group in December 1944 and accepting the surrender of some 230,000 German troops in the theater in April 1945. He was then placed in charge of the US forces occupying Austria.

CUNNINGHAM, ANDREW

BRITISH ADMIRAL, *1883–1963*

As the acting commander-in-chief of the Mediterranean Fleet in 1939, Cunningham had the responsibility of neutralizing Italy's naval forces. In this task, he was supremely successful. The air attack on Taranto put three Italian warships out of commission in November 1940 and the subsequent Battle of Cape Matapan inflicted further woes on the Italians. However, Cunningham's forces lost heavily during the struggle for Crete, chiefly due to repeated attacks by land-based German aircraft.

After this setback, Cunningham became briefly involved in Allied naval planning and was then made General Dwight D. Eisenhower's naval deputy for the Torch amphibious landings in North Africa in November 1942 and the Allied invasion of Sicily. In October 1943, Cunningham returned to England, where he was made First Sea Lord. In this key planning role, he advised Prime Minister Winston Churchill on naval matters and related strategy for the remainder of the war.

DARLAN, JEAN FRANÇOIS

VICHY FRENCH ADMIRAL, *1881–1942*

At the outbreak of the war, Darlan commanded France's navy and after his country's defeat he served as Vichy France's minister of the navy, whose vessels were sent to ports in North Africa for safety. However, many of the ships were sunk or damaged by the British in July 1940.

In the spring of 1942, Darlan was made the overall commander of Vichy French forces in North Africa, but he agreed not to oppose any Allied landings following negotiations with US General Mark Clark shortly before Operation Torch in November 1942. As part of the deal, Darlan was to be recognized as head of the French government by the United States, despite Britain supporting the exiled General Charles de Gaulle. What might have become a source of friction between the two Allies evaporated after Darlan was assassinated by one of his own countrymen in late December.

DE GAULLE, CHARLES

FREE FRENCH LEADER, *1890–1970*

De Gaulle served on the Western Front during World War I and gained a reputation as a forward-thinking theorist on armored warfare during the interwar years. During the German invasion of France in 1940, de Gaulle led French tanks against the invaders with limited success, but his superiors were sufficiently impressed to promote him to the cabinet.

After France's capitulation, de Gaulle became the effective head of those French citizens who opposed the German occupation of their country and the creation of the puppet Vichy French regime. His first aim was to secure France's overseas colonies, which were held by Vichy French forces. The results were mixed, but de Gaulle was increasingly seen by both the Allies and most French nationals as France's legitimate leader.

On June 13, 1944, de Gaulle returned to France and on August 25 entered recently-liberated Paris, where he received a thunderous reception. However, although de Gaulle was made president of the Committee of National Liberation, he was excluded from the Allied conferences at Yalta and Potsdam, and he greatly resented France's "second-power" status within the Allied camp.

DOENITZ, KARL

GERMAN ADMIRAL, *1891–1980*

Doenitz, who had served on submarines during World War I, was placed in charge of Germany's secret U-boat expansion plan during the interwar years, and when the arm's existence was made known in 1935, he was announced as its commander. In this role, he planned U-boat strategy and tactics during the war, not least the use of "wolf packs."

Although the fortunes of the U-boats fluctuated during the war, they generally had the upper hand until mid-1943, when the Allies gained the ascendancy in the Battle of the Atlantic. By this stage, Doenitz was commander-in-chief of all Germany's warships, having replaced Admiral Erich Raeder in the previous January. During the final part of the war, Hitler made Doenitz his successor and head of state, a position he assumed on April 30, 1945.

GOERING, HERMANN

GERMAN LEADER, *1893–1946*

Goering was a highly-successful fighter ace in World War I and credited with 22 air victories. An early supporter of the Nazi cause, he joined the party in 1922 and Hitler made him his successor in 1939. Six years earlier, he had been given responsibility for, among other roles, expanding the Luftwaffe.

Although the Luftwaffe played a vital role in the early German victories of World War II, subsequent events, chiefly the Battle of Britain in summer 1940 and the attempted air supply of Stalingrad in 1942–43, highlighted the force's shortcomings. Goering lost Hitler's confidence and was marginalized until the closing stages of the war, when he mistakenly reminded Hitler that he was the Führer's chosen heir. The message further soured the relationship between them. Hitler ordered Goering's arrest, but he was captured by the Allies before the order could be carried out.

HALSEY, WILLIAM

US ADMIRAL,
1882–1959
Halsey, known for his energy and short temper, was a leading advocate of naval aviation and played a decisive role in the naval operations that accompanied the war in the Pacific. He had charge of the carrier *Hornet* during the Doolittle attack on mainland Japan in April 1942, but was too ill to take part in the Battle of Midway in June.

On returning to active service, Halsey fought in the Solomons until 1943, when he transferred to command the 3rd Fleet in the Central Pacific, winning a victory at the Battle of Leyte Gulf in October 1944, despite the near disaster which befell one of his groups of surface warships that was intercepted by the Japanese.

HIROHITO

JAPANESE RULER,
1901–89
Hirohito, a shy and somewhat weak emperor, was little more than a figurehead, although he did try to curb the militarists in his cabinet. However, all government proclamations were issued in his name.

As the war turned against Japan, he attempted to seek a peace settlement with the Allies, but this came to nothing. On August 14, 1945, following the use of atomic weapons, Japan was forced to surrender, and the announcement of the decision to the Japanese people was made by Hirohito. The emperor kept his throne after the war, but had to renounce his divinity in 1946.

JODL, ALFRED

GERMAN GENERAL
1890–1946
In 1938, Jodl was made head of the operations section of the body that planned and coordinated the country's armed forces, and a year later was promoted to the position of chief-of-staff to Field Marshal Wilhelm Keitel, the head of the coordinating body. Jodl, a more dominant figure than Keitel, effectively ran all of the operations of the armed forces, save those on the Eastern Front.

Jodl thus became a close confident of Hitler and was chiefly responsible for turning the Führer's plans into practical propositions. Jodl stayed loyal to the cause until the end of the war; his last act was to sign the surrender of the German Army at Reims in 1945.

KEITEL, WILHELM

GERMAN GENERAL,
1882–1946
Keitel was made head of the unified German command structure in 1938, not because of his brilliance but because of his subservience to Hitler. Indeed, Keitel was nicknamed by his fellow generals "Lakaitel" (*Lakai* meaning "lackey"). Keitel was willing to offer Hitler his opinions, but only if they were requested.

Keitel was closely involved in the various repressions instigated by the Nazis, but his last act for his leader was to sign the final ratification of Germany's surrender in Berlin on May 8, 1945.

KESSELRING, ALBRECHT

GERMAN GENERAL
1885–1960
Kesselring is widely regarded as one of the best commanders of ground forces in World War II, although he had joined the fledgling Luftwaffe in 1933. In the first stages of the war, he commanded large groups of aircraft that operated over Poland, France and the Low Countries, and Britain.

In 1941, Kesselring was sent to the Mediterranean theater and directed air operations in support of the North African campaign. By 1943, Kesselring was directing the opposition to the Allied landings on Sicily and the Italian mainland. His key strategy was to withdraw slowly, holding a series of strong defensive lines until the last minute, thereby inflicting heavy casualties on the Allies.

In 1945, Kesselring was moved at the instigation of Hitler, becoming the commander-in-chief of the German forces in Western Europe. However, the war was effectively lost and Kesselring could do little to prevent the Allied victory.

KING, ERNEST

US ADMIRAL,
1878–1956
King was a dominant figure in US strategic planning throughout World War II. Following US entry into the conflict, he was made commander-in-chief of the country's naval forces and became the head of naval operations in March 1942. He also held several other posts, including memberships of the US Joint Chiefs-of-Staff and the Combined Chiefs-of-Staff, the body which directed overall Allied strategy.

King was not always popular with the British as he believed that the war could be won in the Pacific by the US Navy if it were given greater resources at the expense of the war in Europe – a strategy totally at odds with the British and many of his US colleagues, who placed greater emphasis on concluding the war against Germany first.

MARSHALL, GEORGE

US GENERAL,
1880–1959
Marshall spent much of time before his country's entry into the war successfully reorganizing the army's structure and increasing its strength. Shortly before hostilities began, he was made its chief-of-staff and carried out further structural reforms. After Pearl Harbor, he became the effective, although reserved, chairman of the Joint Chiefs-of-Staff, where he backed the strategy to defeat Germany first rather than deal with the Japanese in the Pacific.

Marshall attend the major Allied conferences of the war, either in the company of the president or as his personal representative. After the war, he became the US secretary of state and devised the wholly successful plan to rebuild Europe's shattered economies that bears his name.

MITSCHER, MARC

US ADMIRAL,
1887–1947

An advocate of and expert in aircraft carrier operations, Mitscher was the commander of carrier forces in the Far East throughout the conflict. In this role, he took part in the Battle of Midway in June 1942 and had charge of all the air units committed to operations over Guadalcanal from April 1943.

As the noose tightened around Japan, Mitscher was given charge of Task Force 58 in the Central Pacific. His record was excellent, the task force accounting for close to 800 enemy ships and 4400 aircraft destroyed between January and October 1944.

His units took part in some of the Pacific war's most decisive naval engagements, including the Battle of the Philippine Sea, and also supported numerous amphibious operations, not least the assaults on Iwo Jima and Okinawa.

OZAWA, JISABURO

JAPANESE ADMIRAL,
1896–1966

Ozawa was undoubtedly one of Japan's finest naval strategists and a keen supporter of carrier operations. He was the commander of the Japanese Mobile Fleet from November 1942 until 1945, but did not take charge of his country's carrier forces until after they had been decimated by the US Navy. Ozawa committed what was left of the navy to the Battle of the Philippine Sea in June 1944. The battle was a disaster for Japan.

Ozawa also took part in the Battle of Leyte Gulf the following October, where his force acted as a decoy to lure the US Navy into a trap. The ruse almost worked but the Japanese had to retreat with severe losses. Ozawa was made commander-in-chief of the Japanese Combined Fleet in 1945, but there was little left to lead.

RUNDSTEDT, GERD VON

GERMAN GENERAL,
1875–1953

Rundstedt came out of retirement on the eve of World War II to lead Germany's Army Group A in the invasion of Poland in September 1939 and the offensive against France and the Low Countries in May the following year. During the invasion of the Soviet Union, Rundstedt led Army Group South into the Caucasus, but was sacked by Hitler in November 1941 after he asked to withdraw.

Rundstedt returned to active service in 1942, when he was made the commander-in-chief of Western Europe with responsibility for building up Germany's defenses there against any Allied invasion. However, his strategy proved ineffective on D-Day and he was sacked on July 1, 1944.

Again, he was reinstated and was the architect of the Ardennes offensive in the winter of 1944, although he had little hope of the attack succeeding. Its failure led him to be sacked in March 1945.

SLIM, WILLIAM

BRITISH GENERAL,
1891–1970

The outbreak of World War II found Slim in East Africa, where he led a successful offensive against the Italians in which he was wounded. After recovering, he was active in Syria and Iran in 1941. In 1942, however, he was transferred to Burma, where he performed outstandingly, holding together his battered command as it retreated some 900 miles (1440 km) in the face of the Japanese onslaught.

In late 1943, Slim was placed in charge of the British Fourteenth Army, which initially made little progress in recapturing parts of Burma. However, it performed excellently to defeat the Japanese offensive directed toward Imphal and Kohima in 1944.

Slim went over to the offensive himself, driving southward into central Burma. He captured Mandalay in March 1945 and took Rangoon in the south by May, inflicting the greatest defeat of the war on Japanese land forces.

SPAATZ, CARL

US GENERAL,
1891–1974

Spaatz was the senior officer in charge of US air forces primarily in Europe but also in the Pacific. In July 1942, Spaatz reached Britain, where he was commander of the US Eighth Army Air Force, which was based in eastern England. US bombers were committed to the offensive against Germany, carrying out daylight precision raids.

Spaatz next spent some time in charge of air units in North Africa and Sicily, but returned to Britain in January 1944, when he became closely involved in planning the air operations in support of the D-Day landings. As the war with Germany drew to a close, Spaatz left Europe in March 1945 and took command of the strategic bombing offensive against Japan during the following July. Two of his bombers dropped the atomic bombs on Hiroshima and Nagasaki.

SPRUANCE, RAYMOND

US ADMIRAL,
1886–1969

Probably the US Navy's most successful commander of the war, Spruance was initially in charge of a cruiser squadron but was placed at the head of Task Force 16 during the defense of Midway in June 1942. His actions in the battle ensured a major victory, a role that was recognized by his promotion to the position of Admiral Nimitz's chief-of-staff.

In mid-1943, Spruance again took active command. His first major engagement was in support of the amphibious assault on Tarawa in November; similar supporting operations followed into 1944.

Spruance's greatest battle was that in the Philippine Sea in June 1944, which effectively smashed what remained of Japan's naval aviation arm. In the final stages of the war, he assisted in the attack on Iwo Jima and launched air raids on the Japanese mainland.

STILWELL, JOSEPH

US GENERAL,
1883–1946

The commander of US and Chinese forces in Burma, Stilwell was also a seemingly ideal figure to be the chief-of-staff to Chinese Nationalist leader Chiang Kai-shek as he had considerable experience in the Far

East. During World War II, he began his career as the commander of US forces in China, Burma, and India, but also had the role of improving the efficiency of the Chinese Army. He was leading two Chinese armies in Burma when he was made Chiang's chief-of-staff in 1942.

Following a major reorganization of the Allied command structure in August 1943, Stilwell was promoted to the Deputy Supreme Allied Commander under Britain's Lord Louis Mountbatten. In late 1943, Stilwell took charge of forces operating against Myitkyina in Burma, but it took until the following August for the town to fall.

However, Stilwell's career in China was coming to an end, chiefly due to the intrigues of Chiang. He left the theater in October, but had one last role to perform. Following the death of a commander on Okinawa, he took charge of the US Tenth Army.

STUDENT, KURT

GERMAN GENERAL
1890–1978
Student, who saw service as a pilot during World War I, joined the fledgling Luftwaffe in 1934 and was chosen to develop its paratrooper arm and the gliders and transport aircraft it would need.

Paratroopers were used with great success in the early stages of the war, but they suffered a major setback during the costly invasion of Crete in 1941, which signaled the end of large-scale parachute operations. Despite the losses on Crete, the strength of Germany's paratrooper force continued to grow and its units were employed in conventional ground roles. Student was on hand to oppose the Arnhem operation in 1944, by which stage he was commander of Army Group G in Holland. He held this post until the end of the war.

TEDDER, ARTHUR

BRITISH AIR MARSHAL,
1890–1967
Tedder came to prominence as the leader of the British air units committed to the fighting in North Africa, a campaign in which he correctly stressed the importance

of gaining total air superiority. He was particularly keen on close cooperation between air and ground units. Promotion came in January 1943, when Tedder was made deputy army and air force commander to US General Dwight D. Eisenhower. In this role, Tedder oversaw the land and air operations during the invasions of Sicily and the Italian mainland.

In 1944, he played a key coordinating role in the Anglo–American air offensives that supported the D-Day preparations. Once the Allies were ashore, Tedder took charge of the Tactical Air Force, which backed Allied ground attacks. In May 1945, he signed the surrender documents of the German forces in Western Europe.

TOGO, SHIGENORI

JAPANESE POLITICIAN,
1882–1950
Togo was Japan's war minister on two occasions: at the outbreak of World War II and in its final months. Unlike a number of his colleagues, he was alarmed at his country's military ambitions and was an advocate of avoiding war with the United States. Unable to prevent the schemes of the militarists, he resigned once the fighting had begun.

Togo was recalled to political service in April 1945, when he was made foreign minister on the understanding that the Japanese leadership would actively seek peace. However, any undertakings given to reassure Togo were false as the militarists continued to fight on, rejecting any "humiliating" peace discussions. Togo resigned in August, shortly after the peace he had wanted so much earlier had been signed.

TOJO, HIDEKI

JAPANESE POLITICIAN,
1884–1948
Tojo, a confirmed militarist and expansionist, was Japan's prime minister and actively sought war in the Pacific. He effectively directed his country's war effort until 1944. Tojo was a military man and enjoyed the unquestioning support of his brother officers. In

1938, as Japan slid toward war in the Pacific, he was, unusually, allowed to hold both senior military office and also be a member of the cabinet. In October 1941, he was appointed prime minister.

As war became inevitable, Tojo accrued even more power, becoming not only prime minister, but also minister of war and the chief of the army staff. As the tide of war turned against Japan, his dominant position was called into question and he surrendered some of his powers. However, these concessions were not enough and Tojo resigned on July 18, 1944. Held responsible for innumerable war crimes, he was executed by the Allies.

WAVELL, ARCHIBALD

BRITISH GENERAL,
1883–1950
Wavell was made commander-in-chief of the Middle East and North Africa in July 1939 and gained great fame for smashing a huge Italian invasion force in Egypt in 1940-41. He next turned his attention to East Africa and again decisively defeated the Italians. However, the arrival of Rommel saw Wavell's forces pushed back into Egypt. Wavell was transferred and made commander-in-chief in India and then the overall leader of the American, British, Dutch, and Australian forces defending the Dutch East Indies. Wavell could not prevent the region from being overrun, however, and he moved to Burma, where his offensive against the Japanese in December 1942 failed. In June 1943, he was given the position of viceroy of India. Wavell was a general often given difficult tasks by his superiors, and did well with the resources at his disposal, but he was never really trusted by Prime Minister Winston Churchill, who had little faith in him – despite his outstanding performance in North Africa.

YAMAMOTO, ISOROKU

JAPANESE ADMIRAL,
1884–1943
Yamamoto, Japan's minister of the navy from 1938 and the overall commander of the 1st Fleet from

1939, was the leading figure behind the expansion of the country's navy. He also believed that Japan could not win a long war with the United States and planned Pearl Harbor, which was developed to knock the United States out of the war with a single blow.

The attack failed and Yamamoto again sought a decisive battle, but Midway in June 1942 was a disaster for the Japanese. It was a massive blow to Yamamoto's confidence and, although his warships later won several battles around the Solomons, Japanese losses were increasingly heavy. While the Americans could replace their losses in men and equipment quickly, the Japanese could not. As Yamamoto believed, Japan could not win a protracted war against the industrial might of the enemy.

On April 18, 1943, Yamamoto set off on an inspection tour of the western Solomons, but his aircraft was intercepted and shot down by American fighters. His death deprived the Japanese of their finest naval strategist.

YAMASHITA, TOMOYUKI

JAPANESE GENERAL, 1885–1946
Yamashita was an outstanding commander, one whose victories in Malaya and at Singapore are considered some of the greatest defeats in British military history. Despite the scale of Yamashita's triumphs in 1941–42, he was next sent to Manchuria to train troops and was not given another active command until 1944, when he was ordered to defend the Philippines from attack.

The US operations against the islands began shortly after Yamashita had arrived, and he had little opportunity to prepare his defenses. He was gradually pushed out of the various islands and finally surrendered on September 2, 1945. Yamashita was executed by the Allies after the war for atrocities committed in Manila, although many have suggested that he was not in direct charge of the troops at the time the killings took place.

BIBLIOGRAPHY

WORLD WAR I

Brown, M. *The Imperial War Museum Book of the First World War.* London, 1991.

Bruce, A. *Illustrated Companion to the First World War.* London, 1989.

Evans, R., and Strandmann, H. von. *The Coming of the First World War.* London, 1960.

Garrett, R. *The Final Betrayal: The Armistice 1918 and Afterwards.* London, 1989.

Griffiths, W.R. *The Great War.* Wayne, New Jersey, 1986.

Haythornthwaite, P.J. *Gallipoli, 1915: Frontal Assault on Turkey.* London, 1991.

Haythornthwaite, P.J. *The World War One Source Book.* London, 1992.

Herwig, H.H., and Heyman, N.M. *Biographical Dictionary of World War I.* Westport, Connecticut, 1982.

Hough, R. *The Great War at Sea, 1914–18.* Oxford, 1983.

Kennedy, David M. *Over Here: The First World War and American Society.* Oxford, 1980.

Kennet, Lee. *The First Air War: 1914–18.* New York, 1991.

Liddle, P. *The Airman's War, 1914–1918.* Poole, 1987.

Livesey, A. *Great Battles of World War I.* London, 1989.

Middlebrook, M. *The First Day of the Somme.* London, 1971.

Nicolle, D. *Lawrence and the Arab Revolt.* London, 1989.

Simpkins, P. *Air Fighting 1914–18: The Struggle for Air Supremacy over the Western Front.* London, 1978.

Stone, N. *The Eastern Front, 1914–17.* London, 1975.

Taylor, A.J.P. *War by Timetable: How the First World War Began.* London, 1969.

Terraine, J. *The Smoke and the Fire: Myths and Anti-Myths of War.* London, 1980.

Toland, John. *No Man's Land: 1918 – The Last Year of the Great War.* New York, 1980.

Tuchman B. *The Guns of August.* New York, 1962.

Warner, P. *Passchendaele: The Story Behind the Tragic Victory of 1917.* London, 1987.

INTERWAR YEARS AND WORLD WAR II

Allen, Louis. *Burma: The Longest War, 1941–45.* London, 1986.

Beevor, Antony. *The Spanish Civil War.* New York, 1983.

Beevor, Antony. *Stalingrad.* London, 1999.

Breuer, William B. *Retaking the Philippines: America's Return to Corregidor and Bataan, October 1944 – March 1945.* New York, 1986.

Campbell, John. *The Experience of World War II.* Oxford, 1989.

Clark, Alan. *Barbarossa: The Russo-German Conflict, 1941–1945.* London, 1965.

Fess, Joachim. *Hitler.* London, 1974.

Gilbert, Martin. *The Holocaust: The Jewish Tragedy.* London, 1986.

Griess, Thomas E. (editor). *The Second World War: Asia and the Pacific.* Wayne, New Jersey, 1984.

Keegan, John. *Six Armies in Normandy: From D-Day to the Liberation of Paris.* London, 1982.

Keegan, John. *Who's Who in World War II.* London, 1994.

Kennett, Lee. *The American Soldier in World War II.* New York, 1987.

Rhodes, Richard. *The Making of the Atomic Bomb.* New York, 1988.

Salisbury, Harrison E. *The 900 Days: The Siege of Leningrad.* London, 1986.

Slowe, Peter, and Woods, Richard. *Battlefield Berlin: Siege, Surrender, and Occupation, 1945.* London, 1988.

Spector, Ronald H. *Eagle Against the Sun: The American War With Japan.* New York, 1984.

Strawson, John. *The Italian Campaign.* New York, 1988.

Thomas, Nigel, and Abbott, Peter. *Partisan Warfare, 1940–45.* London, 1985.

Toland, John. *Battle: The Story of the Bulge.* University of Nebraska, 1999.

Weinburg, Gerhard L. *Germany, Hitler, and World War.* Cambridge, 1996.

Entries in **bold** refer to major battles or offensives; page numbers in *italics* refer to picture captions.

A

A-Go, Operation 351
Aachen 363
ABDA 276, 277, 285
Abe, N. 220
Admiralties 340–41, 347
Adolf Hitler Line 347
Adriatic 69, 83, 92, *96*, 97, 104, 112, 134, 168, 183
Aegean (WWI) 158
Aegean (WWII) 246–47
  see also Mediterranean (WWII)
Africa (interwar)
  Eritrea 202
  Ethiopia 198, 201, 202, 212
  Italian E. Africa 202
  Italian Somaliland 201, 202
Africa (post-WWII), decolonization 393
Africa (WWI) 8
  Cameroons 21, 84
  East 17, 43–44, 85, 152–53, 155
  N. Rhodesia 186
  sea war 72, *73*
  South 53
  Southwest 56–57, 59, 67, 72
  Togoland 27
Africa (WWII)
  Algeria 301
  British Somaliland 234
  Egypt 236–37, 241, 251, 299, 300, 301
  Eritrea 202, 243, 246, 248
  Ethiopia 248, 250, 255, 265
  Italian E. Africa 243
  Italian Somaliland 243, 244
  Libya 229, 242–50, 253–54, 259, 264, 268, 277, 279–80, 281, 293, 296–97, 301, 308
  Madagascar 291, 301
  Morocco 301
  sea war 237–38
  South 215, 229

Tunisia 302, 303, 307, 310, 312, 313, 314–15, 316, 317
Afrika Korps 244, 251, *268, 280, 296*
aircraft
  helicopters 369
  WWI 62, 74, *75*, 87, 94, 132, 134–35, 136, *138, 140*
  WWII *217, 234, 235, 284, 285, 303, 310, 314, 333, 337, 340, 343, 375, 378, 380*
airships (WWI) 21, 36, 51, 70–71, 81, 87, 96, 106–07, 143, 152–53
Aisne 35
Aisne–Marne 133
Aisne River *37*, 166–67, *169*
Alamein 247, 299
Alamein 300, 301
Albania (interwar) 197, 208
Albania (WWI) 86, 88, 92
Albania (WWII) 245
Albert 103
Albert I, *king of Belgium* 20, 34, 39, 178, 180, 394
Albert Line 352, 353
Aleppo 179
Aleutians 317, 325
Alexander, *king of Greece* 191
Alexander, H. 228, 285–86, 298, 314, 317, 321, 332, 343–44, 381, 403
Alexandria 203, 232, 240
Alfonso XIII, *king of Spain* 198
Algeria *see* Africa (WWII)
Allenby, E. 136, *137*, 145–47, 148–50, 152, 157, 176, 179, 394
Allies (WWII), politics 214, 220, 221, 244, 256, 274–75, 276, 278, 284, 285, 296, 298, 308, 317, 325, 329, 333, 334, 341, 373–74, 388–89
Alsace-Lorraine 17, 18, 184, 190, 368
Amba Alagi 250

Amboina 277
Amiens 173–75
Amritsar, atrocity at 190
Ancre 116, 117
Anders, W. 259
Anglo-German Naval Agreement 208
Anti-Comintern Pact 203, 209, 213
Antonescu, I. 240, 356, 403
Antwerp (WWI) 34, 38
Antwerp (WWII) 357, 358, 362, 367
Anvil, Operation 334, 356
ANZACs 64, 65, 68, 76, 77, 106, 112, 120, *145*, 175
Anzio see Italy (WWII)
appeasement 212
Arabia *see* Middle East (WWI)
Arcadia Conference 274–75, 276
Archery, Operation 275
Arctic, sea war 260, 279, 314, 327, 332, 335
Ardennes (WWI) 21–22
Ardennes (WWII) 366, 367, 369, 372–73
Area Bombing Directive 282
Argentina, politics 338
Ark Royal 216, 237, 252, 263–64
Armenia *see* Middle East (WWI)
armistice 182–85, 187
Arnhem 359–60
Arnim, J. von 312
Arnold, H. 403
Arras 128–29
artillery (WWI) 15, *22*, 30, *48, 59, 83, 102, 108, 114, 155, 169, 175*
  howitzers 20, *41, 53, 78, 84, 88, 130, 179*
  mortars 78, *97*
  Paris guns 161
artillery (WWII)
  howitzers *225*
  mine-throwers *254*
  mortars 295, *329*
  rocket-launchers 264
Artois I 37
Artois II 66, 71
Artois III 79
Asturias 201
Ataturk *see* Kemal, Mustafa
Atlantic Charter 259–60, 276
Atlantic (WWI) *46*, 47–48, 65, 66, 92, 114, 118, 121, 126–27
Atlantic (WWII) 215, 216, 219, 231, 237, 239, 243, 244, 252, 260, 263, 265, 271, 278, 281, 282, 288, 299–300, 306–07, 312,

313, 316–17, 318, 327
Attlee, C. 388–89
Aubers Ridge 66, *67*
Auchinleck, C. 255, 297, 298, 319, 403–04
Augsburg 288
Aung San 277–78
Auschwitz 260, 354, 372
Australia (WWI) 35, *38*, 39
  see also ANZACs
Australia (WWII)
  air war 284
  politics 214, 229, 237, 285, 286–87, 293
Austria 184
Austria (interwar)
  German take-over 203, *204*, 205
  politics 191, 201
Austria (WWII) 382
Austria-Hungary 13
  Home Front 57
  politics 10, 12, 13, 17, 50, 52–53, 57, 84, 117, 125, 159, 183, 184
Avranches 355
Axis powers 203, 213, 240, 244, 246
  politics 238, 270–71, 322–23
Azana, M. 202

B

Badajoz 203
Badoglio, P. *240*, 241, 323, 329, 404
Baedeker Raids 289
Baghdad 66, 69, 125
Baku *158*, 159, 176, 185–86
Balfour, A. *146*, 147
Balfour Declaration 147
Balkans (interwar) 200
  Albania 208
Balkans (WWI) 81, 138
  Albania 86, 88, 92
  Corfu 93
  Greece 96, 108, 111, 112, 132–33, 176
  Macedonia 114
  Montenegro 80, 85–86, 105
  Romania 111, 113, 114, *115*, 117–18, 119
  Salonika 79, 80, 83, 93, 96, 101, 106, 111, 119
  Serbia 13, *18*, 19, 33, 44, 47, 80, 81–83, 105, 117, 119
Balkans (WWII)
  Greece *238*, 239, 240, 244, 248, 249, 250
  Romania 238
  Yugoslavia 247–48, 318, 348, 363, 387
Ball, A. 132
Baltic (WWI), sea war 116
Baltic (WWII) *see* Eastern Front (WWII)

Barbarossa, Operation 241, 254, 259
Bardia 242
Barents Sea 305, 307
Barker, W. 182
Basra 60
Bastogne 367, 369
Bataan 280, 287
Bath *289*
Battleaxe, Operation 253
Beatty, D. 51, 98, 118, 186, 394–95
Beda Fomm 244
Bedell Smith, W. 404
Beersheba 146, 147
Beijing 204
Beirut 179
Belgium (interwar) 204
Belgium (WWI)
  espionage 74–75
  see also Western Front (WWI)
Belgium (WWII)
  air war 366–70
  see also Western Front (WWII)
Belgrade (WWI) 13, 44, *45*, 80
Belgrade (WWII) 363
Belorussia *see* Eastern Front (WWII)
Below, O. von 114, 143, 151, 160, 395
Benes, E. *257*
Benghazi 280
Berlin 309, 332, *333*, 337, 342, 391
Berlin 382, 384, 385, 386, *390*
Berlin blockade *392*
Bessarabia 231
Bethmann Hollweg, T. von 395
Beveridge, W. 303
Bilbao 204
Bir Hacheim 293, 296
Biscay, Bay of 287
Bishop, B. 135
Bismarck 252
Bismarck Sea 312–13
Bizerta 317
Black Sea 84
Blackshirts 195
Blamey, T. 286–87
Blaskowitz, J. von 368
Blitz, the 236, 251
Blitzkrieg 217, 227
  on France *228*
  on Norway/Denmark *222*
Bloody Ridge 300
Blücher and Yorck, Operations 166
Blum, L. 284
Bock, F. von 224, 228, 254, 278, 297, 404
Bodenplatte, Operation 369–70
Boehn, M. von *170*, 171, 179

Boelcke, O. 115
Bohemia 207
Bojna, B. von 169
Bolero, Operation 283
Bolimov 53
bombs/bombing
    atomic 382, *388*, 389
    bouncing 318
    flying 325, 353
    strategic 326
Bor-Komorowski, T. 355
Bormann, M. 251, 386
Borneo 272, 277, 279
Bosnia, politics 12
Botha, L. 56, 59, 67
Bou Aoukaz, Djebel 316, 317
Bougainville 330, 334
Boulogne 226, 360
Bradley, O. 370, 404
Brauchitsch, W. von 214, 274
Braun, E. 385
Brazil (WWI) 144
Brazil (WWII) 299
Bremén 315
Brest-Litovsk 77, 254
Brest-Litovsk, Treaty of 23, 159–60
Brevity, Operation 251
Brihuega 203
Britain 232, 235, 238
British Expeditionary Force (WWI) 15
British Expeditionary Force (WWII) 216
Bromberg 372
Brooke, A. 285
Brooke, R. 63
Brownshirts 199, 201
Brusilov, A. 93–94, 101, 102, 137, 395
Brusilov Offensive *100*, 101, 102, 105, 107
Brussels (WWI) 21
Brussels (WWII) 358
Bryansk 261, 327
Bryansk front 260
Bucharest (WWI) *117*, 118, 119
Bucharest (WWII) 346
Bucharest Treaty 166
Buckner, S.B. 380
Budapest 371, 375, 378
Budënny, S. 256
Bulgaria (WWI) 13, 73, 78, 80, 81, 111, 179
Bulgaria (WWII), politics 244, 358
Bulge *see* **Ardennes (WWII)**
Bullard, R.L. 180, 395
Bülow, K. von 20, 29, 395
Bundy, O. 167
Burma *see* Far East
Burma Corps 286, 289
Burma Road 206, 233, 289, 370, 372
Byng, J. 153, 154, 160, 162, 175, 395–96

C

Caballero, F. Largo *see* Largo Caballero, F.
Cadorna, L. 74, 144, 147, 150, 396
Caen 354
Cairo Conference 333, *334*
Calais 226, 361
Calinescu, A. 217
Calvert, M. 341, 348
Cambrai 153–57
Canada (WWI), politics 82
Canada (WWII), politics 216, 219, 229, 237, 292
Canton 206
Cape Matapan *246*, 247
Cape St. George 334
Caporetto 143–44, 145, 147–48, 150–52
Carpetbagger, Operation 337
Cartwheel, Operation 311, 346
Casablanca Conference 308
Casado, S. 207
Casement, R. 94
Cassino *see* Italy (WWII)
Castelnau, N. de 396
casualties
    WWI 49, 187
    WWII 389
Catalonia 201, 205, 207
Catania 321, 323, 324
Caucasus (WWI) *see* Middle East (WWI)
Caucasus (WWII) *see* Eastern Front (WWII)
Cavell, E. 74–75
Celebes 277
Ceylon 286, 287
Chamberlain, N.
    interwar 206, 212
    WWII 214, 223–24
Champagne–Marne *see* **Marne II**
Champagne I 49
Champagne II 79, 80
Channel Dash 282
Channel Is. 231
Château-Thierry 172
Chemin des Dames 132, 166
Cherbourg 351, *352*, 353
Chernyakhovsky, I. 370
Chiang Kai-shek 196, 197, 198, 204, 276, *277*, 325, 333, *334*, 404
China (interwar) 197, 204–05, 206
    politics 196, 197, 198, 205
China (WWI) 44, *45*, 97
China (WWII) 267, 276, *277*, 307
Chindits *310*, 311, 325, 339, 341, 344, 345, 352, 357
Chindwin River *341*, 342
Choltitz, D. von 357

Christmas truce 49
Chuikov, V. 404
Churchill, W. 225
    and WWI 51, *68*, 69, 76
    and WWII 214, 224, 233, 237–38, 245, 255, 259–60, 274–75, 296, 298, 308, 311, 317, 319, 325, 333, 334, 344, 362, 374, 382
Ciano, G. 206, 337
Citadel, Operation 314, 320, 321–22, 323
Clark, M. 307, 326, *356*, 404–05
Clemenceau, G. *188*, 189, 396
Cobra, Operation 355
Cold War 390–92, *393*
Colmar Pocket 368
Cologne 293
colonies 393
Comecon 392
concentration camps 253, *279*, 318, 343, 354
Conrad von Hötzendorf, F. 13, 26, 78, 84–85, 169, 396
Constantine I, *king of Greece* 191, 193
Constantinople 182, 185, *194*, 195
convoys, ship 299, *311*, *332*
Coppens, W. 165
Coral Sea 290, 291, 292, 313
Corfu 86, 93
Corfu, Pact of 138
Coronel 41–42
Coronet, Operation 388
Corregidor Is. 276, 287, 291
Corsica 207, 326
Coventry 240
Crace, J. 292
Cracow 371
Crete 237, 239, 250–52
Crimea *see* Eastern Front (WWII)
Croatia 248, 249
Cruewell, L. 259
Crusader, Operation 264, 279
Ctesiphon 82
Cunningham, A. 243, 247, 248, 264, 329, 405
Cunningham, J. 329
Curzon Line 191
Cyrenaica 242, 254, 264
Czech Legion 170, 172, *173*, 186
Czechoslovakia (interwar) 189
    politics 192, 201, 205–06, 207, 211, 212
Czechoslovakia (WWI) 185
Czechoslovakia (WWII)
    Home Front 293, 295–96

politics 257, 381
see also Eastern Front (WWII)

D

D-Day *348*, 349–51
Dakar 237, 238
Daladier, E. 206, 212, 216, 221, 284
Damascus 179
dams, raid on 317–18
D'Annunzio, G. 152, 191
Danzig 207, *212*, 213
Dardanelles 50–51, 62, 64, 185
Dardanelles 56, 59
Darlan, J.F. 259, 301, 305, 405
Dawes Plan 196
de Gaulle, C. 90, 226, 230, *236*, 237, 319, 368, 405
de Robeck, J. 59
Debeney, E. 178
decolonization 393
defense-in-depth 110, 112, 124
Deniken, A. 191
Denmark
    politics 325, 386
    see also Western Front (WWII)
Dentz, H. 253, 256
depth charges 84, 92
Desert Mounted Corps *145*, 149, 177
Devers, J. 317
Dexterity, Operation 336–37
Diaz, A. 170, 180–81, 396
Dieppe 298
Dniepr River 255, 260, 311, 325, 327, 328, 330
Dobell, C. 127, 131
Doenitz, K. 307, 318, 386, 405
Dogger Bank 51–52
Dollfuss, E. 201
Doolittle, J. 288
Doorman, K. 285
Dorpat, Treaty of 193
Dortmund 318, 360
Dowding, H. 234
Dreadnought 9–10
Dresden *314*, *374*, 375
Drina River 33
Dujaila Redoubt 91
Dulles, A. 385
Dunkirk evacuation 227, 228
Dunsterville, L.C. *158*, 159, 176
Dutch East Indies 238–39
    see also Far East
Dyer, R. 189–90
Dyle Plan Line 224, 225
Dynamo, Operation 227, 228

E

Easter Rising 94–95
Eastern Front (interwar)
    Latvia 188
    Poland 191–2
    Russia 192
Eastern Front (WWI) *55*, 61
    E. Prussia 20, 21, 22–23, 26–27, 34–35, 55
    Galicia 26, 27, 30, 35, 37–39, 45–46, *53*, 54, 56, *57*, 59, 65, 70, 71
    Poland 72–73
    Russia 53–54, 77, 78, 91–92, 93–94, 101, 105, 107, 137–38, 140–41, 157, 176, 185–86
Eastern Front (WWII)
    Austria 382
    Baltic 258, 260, 340, 353, 364
    Belorussia 255, 352–53, 354
    Bulgaria 358
    Caucasus 297, 306, 307, 309, 310, 328
    Crimea 292, 297, 327, 345, 346
    Czechoslovakia 368, 370, 386, 387
    E. Prussia 372, 373, 375
    Finland 218, 219, 220, 221, 350, 354
    Germany 373, 374, 377, 378, 379, 382–86
    Hungary 363, 370–71, 375, 378, 380
    Poland 214, 215–16, 217, 309, 316, 355, 357, 359, 361, 370, 371, 372, 374, 380
    Slovakia 357, 359
    Soviet Union 254–55, 257–58, 261, 262–63, 264, *266*, 276, 277, 280, 299, 327, 328
    Ukraine 255, 259, 260, 261, 263, 279, 295, 297–98, 302, 303–04, 310, 311, 313–14, 320, 322–25, 328, 330, 331, 337, 342–45, 354–56
    see also **Leningrad; Stalingrad**
Eastern Solomons 299
Eben Emael 224
Ebert, F. 189
Eden, A. 214
Egypt (interwar) 203
Egypt (WWI) *see* Middle East (WWI)
Egypt (WWII) *see* Africa (WWII)
Eisenhower, D.D. 283, 297, 301, 334, 357, 368, 382
El Alamein *see* Alamein
English Channel 52, 87,

126, 131–32
Eniwetok 340
Enver Pasha *15*, 16, *48*, 49, 50, 101, 396–97
Epsom, Operation 353
Eritrea *see* Africa (interwar; WWII)
Estonia (WWI), politics 159
Estonia (WWII), politics 218, 233
Ethiopia
  politics 250
  see also Africa (interwar, WWII)
Europe (interwar), politics 195–96
Europe (WWII), air war 346
extermination camps 279, 309, 372, 389

F

Faisal, *regent of Iraq* 247
Falaise 356
Falkenhayn, E. von *34*, 35, 37, 39, 41, 61, 78, 87, 104, 110, *111*, 113, 117–18, 152, 397
Falklands *46*, 47–48
Far East (WWII)
  Borneo 272
  Burma 277–78, 282–83, 285–86, 287–88, 289, 290, 292–93, 311, 330, 337, 339, 341–42, 344, 345, 348, 351, 352, 354, 355, 357, 364–65, 369–73, 376, 378, 379, 380, 381–82, 386–89
  Dutch East Indies 277, 286, *287*
  Hong Kong 270
  India 293, 341–42, 344, 348, 352
  Indochina 237
  Malaya 270, *271*, 277, 286
  Manchuria 389
  sea war 270, 280–81, 284, 285, 287, 327, 339
  Singapore 281, 282, 327
  Thailand 270
Fayolle, M. 397
Festubert 67–68, 69
Final Solution 240, 253, *258*, 259, 260, 261, 279, 299
Finland (interwar), politics 193
Finland (WWI), politics 158, 159, 162, 165–66, 187, 254
Finland (WWII)
  politics 218–19, 356, 358
  see also Eastern Front (WWII)
Fisher, J. 397

Five-Power Naval Conference 201
Five-Power Naval Limitation Treaty 194
Flers–Courcelette 112
Fletcher, F. 291, 299
Flintlock, Operation 338–39
Foch, F. 32, 119, 161–62, 163, 164, 173, 178, 184
Fonck, P.R. 130
Formosa 369
Four-Power Act 194
14 Points 158, 159, 179, 187, 190
France 227
France (interwar) 195–96, 210
  politics 201, 207
France (WWI)
  air war 30, 57, 74, 87
  espionage 138
  Plan XVII 18
  politics 10, 14, 18, 72, 81, 83, 88, 96, 113, 116–17, 119, 120–21, 157, 161–62, 164, 173, 184, 187
  technology 89, 132
  see also Western Front (WWI)
France (WWII)
  air war 298, 310
  politics 214, 216, 221, 230
  sea war 303
  see also Free French; Vichy France; Western Front (WWII)
Franchet d'Esperey, L. 119, 176, 397
Franco, F. 202–03, 204, 207, 208
Franz Ferdinand, *archduke* 11, 12
Franz Joseph, *emperor of Austria-Hungary* 397
Free French *236*, 237, 319, 336
Freikorps 189
French, J. 24, 39, 58, 59, 65–66, 67, 69, 72, 81, 83, 121
Freyberg, B. 252
Friedeburg, H. von 386, *387*
Friedrichshafen 319
Friendship, Treaty of 391
Friessneer, J. 363
Fromm, F. 355
Frontiers *see* **Ardennes; Lorraine; Mons**

G

Galicia *see* Eastern Front (WWI)
Galliéni, J. 31
Gallipoli 57, 59
Gallipoli 64, 65, 66, 68,

70, 75–76, *77*, 80–81, 82, 83, 86
Gamelin, M. 226
Gandhi, M. 189
gas, poison 196
  WWI 53, 62–64, 79
  WWII 260, 279
Gaulle, C. de *see* de Gaulle, C.
Gaza I 127
Gaza II 131
Gaza III 145–47
Gazala Line 293
Geneva Protocol 196
George II, *king of Greece* 249
Georgette, Operation 163
Germany (interwar) 195–96
  politics 189, 191, 196–209
  see also Weimar Republic
Germany (WWI) 10, 11
  air war 21, 36, 42, 55–56, 62, 69
  Home Front 55, 109, 117
  politics 13, 14, 15, 55–56, 61, 69–70, 74, 77, 78, 83, 87, 90, 91, 95, 102, 104–05, 106, 110–11, 113–14, 115, 119, 123–24, 138, 156, 159–60, 179, 181–82, 184–87
  strategies 17, 25, 33–34, 61, 110, 112
  see also airships
Germany (WWII)
  air war 215, 226, 235, 282, 285, 287, 288, 293–94, 296, 309, 313, 315, 317–18, 319, 323, 325, 329, 332, 337, 342, 344–45, 360, 375
  Final Solution 260, 279
  Home Front 311, 313, 341, 347, 365
  politics 217, 220–21, 232–38, 241, 250, 254, 259, 274, 278, 282, 299, 300, 307, 312, 344, 352, 355, 356, 363, 385, 386–87
  technology 353
  see also Eastern Front (WWII); Western Front (WWII)
Germany First strategy 275
Ghormley, R. 286, 300
Gibraltar 238, 250
Gibson, G. 318
Gilbert Is. 281, 332
Gneisenau 229, 244, 282
Gneisenau, Operation 168, *169*
Gnila Lipa 27
Goebbels, J. 355, 386
Goering, H. 164, *209*, 232, *233*, 234, 405–06

Gomulka, W. 390
Gondola, Operation 310
Goodwood, Operation 354
Gorlice–Tarnow 61, *64*, 65, 70
Gort, Lord 216, 228
Gothic Line 357, 358, 360
Gough, H. 397
Graf Spee 219
Graziani, R. 236–37
Great Britain (interwar), politics 208
Great Britain (WWI) 10, 15
  air war 51, 70–71, 81, 87, 96, 118, 134–35, 136, 143
  espionage 44, 123
  Home Front 19, 39, 59, 70, 72
  politics 13, 14, 15, 19, 49, 50–51, 52, 57, 69, 73, 80–81, 88, 89, 96, 118, 120, 121, 125, 133, 136, 140, 147, 303
  recruits 16, 18, 90, 97
  strategy 61
  technology 76, *77*, *86*, 87
Great Britain (WWII)
  air war 232, 234–35, 236, 240, 250, 251, 288–89, 353, 361
  espionage 233, 317
  Home Front *236*, 237, *251*
  planned invasion of 232–33, 282
  politics 214, 223–34, 233, 235–36, 238, 251, 255, 259–60, 265, 284, 285, 286, 287, 293, 298, 303, 319, 329
  technology 240
Great Depression 198, 199
Greece (interwar)
  politics 191, 200
  war with Turkey 193–95
Greece (WWI)
  politics 62, 79, 103, 117, 136
  see also Balkans (WWI)
Greece (WWII) 237, 244
  see also Balkans (WWII); Mediterranean (WWII)
Greenland, sea war 249
Groener, W. 181, 182, 398
Guadalcanal 298, *299*, 300–01, 302–03, 307, 309
Guam 351, 352, 354, 355, 356
Guam Is. 269
Guderian, H. 216–17, 226, 257–58, *259*, 261, 312
Guernica 203
Guise 29
Gumbinnen 21
Gustav Line 328, 333, 337–38
Guynemer, G. *140*, 141

H

Ha-Go, Operation 339
Haakon VII, *king of Norway* 221–2, 228
Hagen Line 323
Haig, D. 40, 79, 83, 111, 112, 121, 129–30, 135, 139, 142, 145, 156, 161, 164, 184
Haile Selassie 202, 250
Halberd, Operation 261
Halder, F. 234, 300
Halfaya 251, 279
Halsey, W. 300, 406
Hamburg 323, 384
Hamilton, I. 398
Hanna 86
Harding, W. 195
Harris, A. 284
Harwood, Admiral 293
Heligoland Bight 28
Hess, R. 251
Heydrich, R. *258*, 259, 279, 293, 295
Hindenburg, P. von
  interwar 196, 197, 199, 200, 201, 211
  WWI 21, 23, 35, 38–39, 46, 53, 55, 61, 110–11, 112
Hindenburg Line 110, 112, 124, 154, 175, 178, 179
Hipper, F. von 51, 99, 182, 398
Hirohito, *emperor of Japan* 389, 406
Hiroshima 382, *388*, 389
Hitler, A. 218
  interwar 196, 198, 199–200, 201, 204, 205–06, 207, 209, 210–11, *213*, 218
  WWI 19–20
  WWII 217, 218, 220, 233, 237, 241, 246, 250, 254, 267, 274, 278, 282, 297, 298, 304, 305, 313, 322–23, 324, 344, 351, 355, 356, 384, 385
Hodges, C. 372
Holland
  air war 369–70
  Home Front 385
  politics 385
  see also Western Front (WWII)
Hong Kong 270, *271*
Hoover, H. 199
Horthy, M. 191, 343, 354
Hungary (interwar), politics 189, 191, 206–08, 255
Hungary (WWI), politics 184, 185
Hungary (WWII)
  politics 240, 343, 354, 367
  see also Eastern Front (WWII)
Huon Gulf 307

Hutier, O. von 140, *141*, 160, 161, 168

I

Iceberg, Operation 380–81
Iceland, sea war 256
Immelmann, M. 102
Imphal 344, 345
India (interwar), politics 189–90
India (WWII)
    politics 287
    see also Far East
Indian Ocean 36
Indochina *see* Far East
Inönü I 193
Inönü II 193
Inter-Allied Military Control Commission 197
Iran *see* Middle East (WWII)
Iraq
    politics 247, 253
    see also Middle East (WWII)
Ireland
    Civil War 189
    Easter Rising 94–95
    politics 194
Iron Guard 238
Ironclad, Operation 291
Isonzo I–XI 71–72, 74, 81, 82, 90–91, 107, 108, 112, 114, 115, 133–34, 140
Isonzo XII *see* **Caporetto**
Italy (interwar) 208
    politics 191, 195, 197, 200–01, 203, 204, 207, 208–09, *211*, 212
Italy (WWI)
    politics 14, 65, 68, 76, 81, 97, 110
    see also Western Front (WWI)
Italy (WWII) 231
    Adriatic sector 357, 358, 360
    air war 300, 318, 319
    Anzio 337, 338, 339, 340, 347–48
    Argenta Gap 381, 382, 383
    Cassino 337, 338, 339, 340, 343–44, 347
    Gustav Line 337–38
    politics 229, 238, 240, 241, 323, 324, 326, 327–28, 329, 337, 385
    Tuscany 353, 355
    Umbria 352
    see also Mediterranean (WWII)
Iwabuchi, S. 373
Iwo Jima *see* Pacific

J

Jadar River 19
Japan (interwar) 198, 201, 203, 204–05, 206, 209, 212–13
Japan (WWI) 19, 24, 44, 157
Japan (WWII)
    air war 288, 351, 364, 378, 381, 389
    espionage 364
    politics 220, 238–39, 241, 249, 261–62, 315, 316, 346, 388, 389
    resources 233, *258*, 259
    see also Pacific
Java 277
Jellicoe, J. 98, 99, 109, 118, 398
Jerusalem *127*, 136, *137*, 152, 157
Jews
    interwar 206–07, 211
    WWII 295–96, 343, 354
    see also Final Solution; Warsaw Ghetto
Jodl, A. 386–87, 406
Joffre, J. 18, 23, 25–26, 27, 30, 35, 37, 72, 83, 89, 115, 116–17, 119, 120–21
Juin, A. 337
July Bomb Plot 355, 356
Jutland 98–100, 104–05

K

Kalewa 292
kamikaze 364, 369, 387
Kapp Putsch 189
Karcher, H. 357
Károlyi, M. 189
Kasserine Pass 310
Katamura, S. 364–65
Katyn Forest *314*, 315
Keitel, W. 406
Kellogg–Briand Pact 198
Kemal, Mustafa 64, 65, 76, 107, 190, 192, 194–95, 196
Keren 246
Kerensky Offensive 137–38
Kesselring, A. 328, 348, 406
Kharkov *313*, 314, 325
Kiev (interwar) 189, 191
Kiev (WWII) 255, 260, 261, 331
Kimmel, H. 272
King, E. 243, 274, 286, 291, 406
Kirovgrad 337
Kitchener, H.H. 18, 24, 57, 72, 80, 82, 102, 398
Kleist, P. von 299, 344
Kluck, A. von 20, 24, 29–30, 398
Kluge, G. von 320
Knox, F. 231
Koga, M. 316, 346
Kohima 342, 348
Kokoda Trail 307
Kolchak, A. 186, 191

Kolombangara 322
Kolubra 47
Kommandorsky Is. 314
Konev, I.S. 337, 370, 374, 384
Konoye, F. 262
Köprüköy 86
Korea (interwar) 212
Korean War 391
Koritza 240
Krasnik 26
Krasnov, P. 191
Kristallnacht 206–07
Krithia 64, 66, 70, *76*
Krueger, W. 370
Kuala Lumpur 277
Küchler, G. von 278
Kun, Béla 189, 191
Kursk 310, 314
Kursk 320, 321–22, 323
Kut-el-Amara 77–78, 79, 85, 86–87, 91–95, 124
Kut II 124

L

La Spezia 319
labor camps 318
Lae 325–6
Lake Naroch 91, 93
Lanrezac, Charles 24
Largo Caballero, F. 203, 204
Lattre de Tassigny, J. de 336
Latvia (interwar) 188
Latvia (WWII), politics 218, 233
Lausanne, Treaty of 196
Laval, P. 288
Lawrence, T.E. 114, 176
Leahy, W. 297
Lebanon 179
Leeb, W.R. von 224, 254, 278
Leigh Mallory, T. 334
Lemberg 54
Lend-Lease 245, 263
Lenin, V.I. 126, 128, 141, 150, *192*, 196
Leningrad 254, 258, 259, 260, 280, 290, 337
Leopold III, *king of Belgium* 226–27
Lettow-Vorbeck, P. von 85, 153, 155, 186, 399
Leyte 363, 365
Leyte Gulf 363–64
Libya *see* Africa (WWII)
Liebknecht, K. 95
Liège 17, 18, 20
Liggett, H. 179–80, 399
Liman von Sanders, O. *28*, 59, 64, 176, 399
List, W. 216, 299
Lithuania (interwar) 207
Lithuania (WWI), politics 170, 183
Lithuania (WWII), politics 218, 233
Little Entente 192

Little Entente powers 201
Litvinov, M. 198, 208
Lloyd George, D. 399
    and post-WWI peace *188*, 189
    and WWI 105, 118, 120, 133, 148
Locarno Conference 196–97
Locarno Pact 202
Lofoten Is. 245, 275
Lombok Strait 284
London (WWI) 134, 136
London (WWII), air raids *234*, 235, 236, 251
London Naval Conference/Treaty 199, 201
Long March 198
Loos 24, 79, *80*, 81
Lorraine 19
Los Angeles 285
Lübeck 287
Lucas, J. 338
Ludendorff, E. 21, 22, 23, 35, 61, 110, 112, 160, 161, 163, 164, 166, 167, 168, 169, 170, 171, 172, 175, 181–82, 399
Lufbery, R. 166
Luke, F. 173
Lukesch, D. 367
Lusitania 66, 82
Luxembourg 14
    see also Western Front (WWI)
Luxemburg, R. 95
Luzon 269, 274, 370
Lys River *163*, 164

M

MacArthur, D. 156, 269, 276, 286, 287, 307, 309, 311–12, 346, 363, 365, 389
Macassar Strait 280
McCudden, J. 142, 170
Macedonia 111, 114, 133
machine guns 15, *63*
    aircraft 62, 74
Mackensen, A. von *52*, 53, 61, 71, 80, 111, 114, 117, *118*, 119, 399
Madagascar 291, 301
Madrid 203, 208
Maginot Line 197, 224, 227, *228*, 229
Magruntein 122
Maitland Wilson, H. 334
Makin Is. 332
Malaya *see* Far East
Malinovsky, R.Y. 337, 342, 363
Malta 231, 258, 298
Manchukuo *see* Manchuria
Manchuria (interwar) 198, 212, 213
Manchuria (WWII) 358, 389
Mandalay 286, 289, 290, 376, 379

Mangin, C. 400
Manhatten Project 388
Manila 274, *275*, 276, 373
Manna, Operation 362
Mannerheim, K. von *186*, 187, 218, *219*, 254, 350, 356
Mannerheim Line 218, 219, 220
Mannock, E. 173
Manstein, E. von 221, 303–04, 311, 313, 320–23, 344
Manteuffel, H. von 367
Mao Zhe-dong 197, 198, 391
March on Rome 195, *211*
Mareth Line 310, 312, 313, 314
Marianas *see* Pacific
Marita, Operation 246
Market Garden, Operation 359, *361*
Marne I *28*, *29*, 30–34
Marne II 170–71, 172, 173
Mars, Operation 162
Marshall, G. 406
Marshall Is. 281, 338–39
Marshall Plan 392–93
Marwitz, G. von der 160, 161
Massicault 317
Masurian Lakes I 23, 34–35
Masurian Lakes II 55
Mata Hari 95, 138
Maude, F. 119, 124, 125, 132, 142, 153
Max of Baden, *prince* 400
Medenine 313
Mediterranean (WWI), sea war 15–16, 17–19, 56, 59, 62, 82, 109, 117, 185
Mediterranean (WWII)
    Aegean Sea 326–27, 328, 331–32
    air war 238
    Corsica 326
    Greece 362, 366
    Italy 324, 325, 326, 327, 328, 332, 333
    Sardinia 234, 326
    sea war 229, 232, 234, 235, 237, 240, 250–51, 258, 261, 263–64, 271, 272–73, 286, 293, 298, 302–03, 306, 310
    see also Crete; Sicily
Medjez-el-Bab 303, 316
Megiddo 176–77, 179
Memel 207
Menzies, R. 237
Mercury, Operation 250
Merrill's Marauders 341
Mesopotamia *see* Middle East (WWI)
Messina 321, 322, 323, 324
Messines 135–36, 141
Metaxas Line 248

Meuse–Argonne 133, 177–80, 182–83
Mexico (WWI) 91, 116, 122–23, 125
Mexico (WWII) 293
Michael, *king of Romania* 356
Michael, Operation 160–61, 162–63
Middle East (WWI)
Arabia 84, 96–97, 114, 115
Armenia 49, 60, 62, 86, 88, 94, 101, 106, 107, 113, 160
Caucasus 46–47, 49–50, 78
Egypt 49, 55, 56, 92, 106, 107, 112, 120, 122
Lebanon 179
Mesopotamia 40, 47, 60, 66, 69, 74, 77–78, 79, 82, 83, 85, 86–87, 92–95, 105, 119, 125, 132, 142, 153, 159, 181, 183
Palestine 51, 122, 127, 131, 145–50, 152, 176–79
Syria 179
Turkey 39, 64, 65, 66, 68, 70, 75–76, 80, 81, 82, 83, 86
Middle East (WWII)
Iran 260
Iraq 250
Syria 253, 256–57
Midway 279
Midway 292, 293, 294–95, 313
Mikolajczyk, S. 320
Mindoro Is. *366*
Mitscher, M. 352, 380, 407
Molotov, V. 208, 209
Molotov Cocktails 219
Moltke, H. von 13, 17, 25, 33, 35, 400
Monastir 112, 117, 119
Mongolia 196
Mons 15, 24–25
Montdidier 162
Montenegro (WWI)
politics 17, 186
see also Balkans (WWI)
Montenegro (WWII) 318
Montgomery, B. 298, 300, 301, 314, 316, 321, 334, 357, 370, 378, 379, 381, 386, *387*
Moravia 207
Morgan, F. 325
Morocco *see* Africa (WWII)
Moscow 234, 254, 258, 259, 261, *262*, 263, 264, 267
Moscow, Treaty of 221
Moscow Conference, Second 329
Mosul 183
Mount Sorrel 101

Mountbatten, L. 325
Mudania, Convention of 195
Mukden 198
Munich 196, 311
Munich Agreement 206, 207, 212
Munich Putsch (coup) 196, 211
Murray, A. 122, 127, 131, 136
Mussolini, B. 239
interwar 195, 202, 206, *211*, 212
WWI 90, 152
WWII 229, 231, 245, 321, 322–23, 324, 326, 327–28, *355*, 385
mutinies 131, 132, 134, 159, 182
Mutual Aid Agreement 284
Mutual Assistance Pact 256
Myitson 376

N

Nagasaki 382, 389
Nagumo, C. 265, 294
Namur 23
Nanking 205
Naples 328, *329*
Narvik II 222, 223
Nations, League of 190, 196, 200, 201, 202, 204, 208, 212, 213, 218–19
NATO 391
Navarre, H. 102
Neame, P. 248
Negrín, J. 204, 207
Nelson, D. 279
Netherlands 13, 95
Neutrality Act 218
Neuve-Chapelle 24, 57–58
New Britain 279, 311, 326, 334
New Caledonia 286
New Georgia Is. 319, 324
New Ireland 279
New Zealand (WWI) 39, 102
see also ANZACs
New Zealand (WWII), politics 214, 229
Nicaragua, interwar 197
Nicholas, *grand duke* 12, 77, 78
Nicholas II, *czar* 13, 77, 93, 125, 126, 171–72, 400
Night of the Long Knives 201
Nijmegen 359
Nimitz, C. 291, 294, 311–12, 313, 362, 380
Nine-Power Pact 194
Nivelle *130*, 131, 132, 141
Nivelle, R. 27, 117, 119, 128, 130–31, 134, 400
North Cape 335
North Sea (WWI) 28, 36, 40, 43, *50*, 51–52, 83, 95,

98–100, 101–02, 108–09, 142–43, 186
North Sea (WWII) 218, 220, 221, 229, 275, 282, *283*, 285
Norway (WWII) 220, 275
air war 345, 359, 364
politics 238, 281
sea war 222
see also Western Front (WWII)
nuclear technology 303
Nuremberg 344, 383–84
Nuremberg rallies *210*
Nuremberg War Crimes Trials 279

O

O'Connor, R. 237, 241, 243, 248
Odessa 189, 259, 345
Okinawa *see* Pacific
Olympic, Operation 388
Olympic Games *211*
Oradour-sur-Glane 351
Orlando, V.E. *188*, 189, 400
Orlau-Frankenau 27
Oslo *222*
Ostend 164, 165
Ourcq 31
Overlord, Operation 325, 349–51
Ozawa, J. 352, 407

P

Pacific
Admiralties 340–41, 347
air war 265–66
Aleutians 317, 325
Gilberts 332
Guadalcanal 307, 309
Iwo Jima 362–63, 364, 365, 376–79
Japan 351
Marianas *350*, 351, 353–54, 355, 356
Marshalls 338–39, 340
New Caledonia 286
Okinawa 380–81, 387
Papua New Guinea 291, 306, 307, 309, 320–21, 325–26, 327, *335*, 336–37, 338, 346, 348
Philippine Sea *351*, 352
Philippines 269, 274, *275*, 276, 280, 282, 286, 287, 291, 363–64, 365, 369, 370, 373, 375, 377, 379, 383, 389
Ryukyus 369
sea war 41–42, 264–65, 279, 281, 285, 290–91, 292, 298, 299, 300, 303, 307, 312–13, 314, 322, 324, 330–31, 334, 381
Solomons 279, 290, 298, 300, 302, 303, 311–12,

319, 320, 324, 330, 332, 334
Pact of Steel 208, *209*
Pagan 351
Palestine *see* Middle East (WWI)
Pantellaria 261, 318
Papagos, A. 239, 249
Papen, F. von 100, 198, 199
Papua New Guinea *see* Pacific
Paris
WWI 30, 87, 161
WWII 229–30, *356*, 357
Paris Peace Conference 190
Pasha, N.-ud-D. 78, 79, 82
Passchendaele 142, 144
Patch, A. 303
Pathfinder system 319
Patton, G. 321, 341, 357, 364, 367, 372–73, 377–78, 378
Paulus, F. von 237, 304, 310
Pearl Harbor 264–65, 266–67
Pedestal, Operation 298
Peenemünde 325
Peiper, J. 366
Percival, A. 282
Pershing, J. 91, 123, 133, 136, 176, 180
Pétacci, C. 385
Pétain, H.-P.
WWI 27, 66, 89, 93, 95, 134, 161
WWII 230, 288, *305*
Peter II, *king of Yugoslavia* 246
Petrograd 125
Petrov, I. 370
Philippine Sea *see* Pacific
Philippines
politics 282
see also Pacific
Piave River 169–70
Picardy 36–37
Pilsudski, J. 184–85, 191–92, 197
Piraeus 248
Piva Forks 332
Plan XVII 18
Plan Yellow 217
Plate River 219
Ploesti oil fields 238, 323, 346
Plumer, H. 401
Plymouth 250
Poincaré, R. 110, 401
Pointblank, Operation 319
Poland (interwar)
invasion by Germany 209, 213, 214
politics 191, 193, 197, 200, 208, 213
see also Eastern Front (interwar)
Poland (WWI) 26, 27, 30, 116, 184–85

see also Eastern Front (WWI)
Poland (WWII)
Final Solution 240, 260, 299
Home Front 315, 318
politics 217, 259, 319–20, 337, 355
see also Eastern Front (WWII)
Polish Corridor 190, 207, 213
Port Moresby 290–91, 307, 309, 315
Portugal 89, 90, 107
Potsdam Conference 388–89
Pound, D. 285, 297
Pozières Ridge 106
Poznan Line 372
Prague 386, 387
Pridham-Wippell, H. 246
Prussia, E. *see* Eastern Front (WWI; WWII)
Przemysl 54, 59, 70
Pu-Yi, *emperor of China* 198
Punta Stilo 232
Putnik, R. *18*, 19, 44, 47, 401

Q

Quebec Conference, First *324*, 325
Quezon, M. 282
Quisling, V. 238, 281
Qurna I 47
Qurna II 69

R

Rabaul 279
Rabaul 331, 341–42
Race to the Sea *34*, *36*, 37
Raczkiewicz, W. 319–20
radar 238, 240, 265
Raeder, E. 307
Ramadi 142
Ramree Is. 372
Ramsay, B. 334
Rangoon 286, 381–82, 386, 387
Rapallo, Treaty of 191
Rashid Ali 247
Rasputin *120*, 121
Rava Ruska 30
Rawlinson, H. 178, 401
Red, Operation 228
Regensburg 325
Reichenau, W. von 215, 257, 278
Reichstag 199–200, 386
Remagen 378
Rennenkampf, P. 401
resistance 350
Reynaud, P. 221, 230, 284
Rhine River 379–80
Ribbentrop, J. von 206, 209, 352

Richthofen, M. von 112, 139, 164
Rickenbacker, E. 162
Riga 140
Riga, Treaty of 193
Ritchie, N. 264, 296, 298
Robertson, W. 401
Röhm, E. 201
Rokossovsky, K. 359, 370
Romani 112
Romania (interwar), politics 189, 192, 208
Romania (WWI)
  politics 14–15, 108, 109, 118, 157, 166
  see also Balkans (WWI)
Romania (WWII)
  air war 323
  politics 217, 240, 345–46, 356, 357
  see also Balkans (WWII)
Rome 323, *334*, 348
Rome–Berlin Axis 203
Rome–Berlin–Tokyo Axis 213
Rommel, E. 145, 244, 245–46, 247, 248, 249, 259, 264, 268, 277, 279–80, 293, 296–97, 300, 301, 307, 308, 310, 313, 355, 363
Roosevelt, F.D. 275
  death *381*, 382
  interwar 199, 207
  WWII 227, 229, 230–31, 239, 241, 242, 245, 252, 259–60, *266*, 274–75, 284, 296, 308, 317, 325, 333, 334, 354, 373–74
Rostov 263, 297–98
Rota 351, 352
Rotterdam 224
Ruhr 195, 210, 294, 313, 318, 360
Rundstedt, G. von 224, 226, 229, 254, 255, 263, 358, 366, 374, 407
Rupprecht, *crown prince* 401–02
Russia (Civil War) 126, 172, 188, 189, 191, *192*, 193, 195
Russia (interwar), politics 193
  see also Eastern Front (interwar)
Russia (WWI) 10, 13
  peace treaty 159–60
  politics 13, 77, 78, 81, 88, 89, 114, 121, 125–26, 128, 135, 138, 139, 141, 150, 156, 170, 171–72, 185, 186
  see also Eastern Front (WWI)

S

Saarland 202

St. Germain, Treaty of 191
St.-Gond 32
St. Mihiel 59–60
St. Mihiel 133, 175–76
St. Nazaire 287
Saipan *350*, 351
Saito, Y. 353–54
Sakkaria 193
Salerno 326
Salonika (WWI) *see* Balkans (WWI)
Salonika (WWII) 248
Sannaiyat 92–93
Santa Cruz 300
Sardinia 234, 326
Sarikamish 49–50
Sarrail, M. 402
Saudi Arabia, politics 377
Savo Island 298
Scapa Flow 191, 218
Scharnhorst 229, 244, 282
Scheer, R. *86*, 87, 104, 402
Scheldt Line 225–26
Schlieffen Plan 17, 25, 33–34
Schweinfurt 325, 329
Sealion, Operation 232–33, 236, 237, 238, 282
Sebastopol 295, *296*, 297
Seeckt, H. von *190*
Serbia 10, 11, 12–13, 17, 74, 78, 80, 81, 187
  see also Balkans (WWI)
Sèvres, Treaty of 192, 196
Seyss-Inquart, A. von 385
Shanghai 197, 204
Sharqat 181
Sheikh Saad 85
Sherman, F.C. 330–31
Shigemitsu, M. 389
ships
  interwar 191, 199, 201
  WWI 11–12, 15
  WWII 235–36, 242, 278, 299, *311*
Sicily 308, 317, *320*–24
Sidi Barrani 241
Siegfried Line 110, 378
Simovic, D. 246, 277
Sims, W. 402
Singapore *see* Far East
Sinn Fein 189
Sirte 286
Sittang River 282–83
Skoropadski, P. 185
Skorzeny, O. 326, 348
Sledgehammer, Operation 283
Slim, W. 286, 288, 364, 369, 370, 372, 376, 381–82, 387, 407
Slovakia 189
Smith, H.M. 362–63, 376
Smolensk 254, 257, 328
Smuts, J.C. 215, 402
Solomon Is.
  air war 315
  see also Pacific
Somaliland *see* Africa (interwar; WWII)

Somerville, J. 286
Somme I 27, 83, 88, 103–04, 105–06, 111, 112, 113, 116, 117, 121
Somme II *see* Michael, Operation
Sorge, R. 364
South Africa *see* Africa, South (WWI; WWII)
Soviet Union (interwar)
  dispute with Japan 205
  politics 195, 196, 198, 199, 201, 208, 209, 213, 237, 255
Soviet Union (WWII)
  Home Front 290
  politics 218, 224, 233, 244, 249, 256, 289, 356
  see also Eastern Front (WWII)
Spaatz, C. 281, 407
Spain (interwar)
  Civil War 202–03, 204, 205, 207–08, *213*
  politics 198, 199, 201, 202, 203, 204, 207
Spartacus League 95
Special Operations Executive 233
Spee, M. von 41–42, 47
Spring Awakening, Operation 378
Spruance, R. 407
SS (*Schutzstaffel*) 299
Stalin, J. 126, 196, 209, 213, 256
  post-WWII 392
  WWII 218, 255, 256, 261, 262–63, 276, 289, 298, 310, 334, 357, 360, 373–74, 388–89
Stalin Line 255
Stalingrad 297, 298
Stalingrad 299, 302, *303*, 304, 307, *309*, 310
Stark, H. 286
Stauffenberg, S. von 355
Stilwell, J. 286, 290, 339, 341, 351, 407–08
Stimpson, H. 231
Strasbourg 368, 374
Student, K. 408
submarines (WWI) 23, 36, *52*, 55, 62, 66, 76, 78, 82, 84, 90, 92, 109, 114, 118, 121, 123–24, 126
  and convoys 132
submarines (WWII) 237, 238, 279, 281, 282, 288, *289*, 307, 327, *328*
Substance, Operation 258
Sudetenland 205–06, 212
Suez Canal 49, 51, 55, 106, 107, 203, 250, 301
Sultan, D. 369, 370
Sun Yat-sen 196
Supreme War Council 220
Sykes–Picot Agreement 96
Syria *see* Middle East (WWI; WWII)

T

Takagi, T. 291
tanks
  WWI 76, *86*, 87, 89, 112, 132, 154, *157*, *166*
  WWII 264, *334*, *336*, *360*, *363*, *367*
Tannenberg 23, *26*, 27
Taranto 240
Tarawa 332
Tassafaronga 303
Tedder, A. 334, 408
Tehran Conference 334
Thailand 270, 280, 281
Third International 201
Tientsin 204
Tiger, Operation 250
Timoshenko, S. 220, 224, 256, 279
Tinian 351, *354*, 355
Tirana, Treaty of (I) 197
Tirana, Treaty of (II) 197
Tirpitz 327, *329*, 359, 364, *365*
Tirpitz, A. von 88, 402
Tito (Josip Broz) 256, 318, 339, 348, 360, 378
Tobruk I 242–43
Tobruk II 249, 250, 253, 259, 264, *267*, 268
Tobruk III 296
Togo, S. 388, 408
Tojo, H. 261–62, 408
Tokyo 378
Tolbukhin, F.I. 345, 378
Torch, Operation 296
Totalize, Operation 356
Townshend, C. 69, 74, 77–78, 79, 82, 86, 94, 95
Toyoda, S. 346
Transylvania 109, 113, 189
Trentino *96*, 97, 102, 182
Trianon, Treaty of 192
Trident Conference 317
Tripartite Pact 238, 240, 246
Trondheim 222–23
Trotsky, L. 126, 141, 150, *192*, 402–03
Truman, H.S. 245, 382, 388–89
Tsingtao 44, *45*
Tunisia (interwar) 207
Tunisia (WWII)
  air war 316
  see also Africa (WWII)
Turkey (interwar) 190, 193–95
  politics 192, 196, 200
Turkey (WWI)
  politics 14, 15, 40, 44, 56, 60, 179, 182, 185
  see also Middle East (WWI)
20-Year Friendship Pact 198
Two Morins 32
Typhoon, Operation 261, 263

U

U-Go, Operation 341–42, 354
Ukraine
  Final Solution 261
  see also Eastern Front (WWII)
United Nations 276, 377, 392
United States (interwar)
  economics 198
  politics 195, 197, 199, 200, 207, 227, 281
United States (post-WWII), Marshall Plan 392–93
United States (WWI) *148*
  Home Front 72
  politics 15, 72, 82, 86, 91, 97, 98, 113, 123, 124, 126, 127–28, 133, 134, 156, 187
United States (WWII)
  espionage 293
  Home Front 284, 285
  joins the war 270–71
  politics 215, 218, 229, 230–31, 233, 235–36, 239, 241, 242, 243, 245, 247, 252, 259–60, 263, 272, 274, 279, 281, 283, 286, 297, 300, 303, 317, 354
Ushijima, M. 380–81, 387

V

V1 and V2 325, 353, 361, *362*
Valdai Hills 277
Vandegrift, A. 303
Vardar River 176
Verdun 23, 87–90, *92*, 93, 95, 102, 104, 112, 115, 117, 120
Veritable, Operation 376, 377
Versailles, Treaty of 190–91, 196, 197, 201, 202, 210, 211–12
Vichy France 230, 237
  Final Solution 253
  politics 239, 259, 284, 288, 305
  see also Western Front (WWII)
Vienna 374, 382
Vietinghoff, H. von 337, 385
Villa, Pancho 91, 123
Vimy Ridge 66, 70, 79
Vimy Ridge 129
Visconti-Prasca, S. 239, 240
Vistula–Oder 370
Vitry-le-François 32
Vittorio Veneto *180*, 181, 182
Vladivostok 157, 170
Voroshilov, K. 224, 256
Voss, Werner 142

W

Wainright, J. 287, 291
Wake Is. 269, 285
Wannsee Conference 279
Warsaw (WWI) 69, 73
Warsaw (WWII) 215–16, 357, 359, 361
Warsaw Ghetto *240*, 279, 299, *300*, *308*, 309, *315*, 316, 318
Washington Conference, Second 296
Washington Treaty 201
Wavell, A. 241, 242, 253, 254, 276, 285, 319, 408
Weimar Republic 189, 211
Western Front (WWI) *16*, 61
    air war 57–58, 87, 92, 102, 112, 115, 129, 130, 132, 135, 138–39, 141, 142, 162, 164, 165, 166, 170, 173, 176, 182
    Belgium 17, 18, 20–25, 34, 39–40, 41, 48–49, 62–64, 65–66, 68, 101, 135–36, 138, 139–40, 141–42, 144, 163–65
    France 18, 19, 27, 29–33, 36–37, 39–40, 48–49, 58, 59–60, 66, 67–68, 69, 71, 79, 80, 81, 115, 128–31, 132, 136, 148, 155–56, 160–61, 162–64, 166–80
    Italy 71–72, 74, 81, 82, 90–91, 97–98, 102, 107, 108, 112, 114, 115, 133–34, 140, 143–44, 145, 147–48, 150–51, 169–70, 180–81, 182
    see also Hindenburg Line; **Somme I**; **Verdun**
Western Front (WWII)
    Belgium 220, 224, 225–27, 357–59, 362, 364
    Denmark 221
    France 216, 225, 226, 227, 228–30, 231, 285, 298, 349–51, 353–61, 364, 368–69, 374, 377–78
    Germany 215, 363, 370, 376–84, 386
    Holland 224, 358–60, 381, 383
    Luxembourg 224
    Norway 221–23, 227–28, 245, 312
    Vichy France 301
    see also **Ardennes**
(WWII)
Weygand, M. 226, 229
Wilhelm II, *kaiser* 8, 10, 11, 23, 28–29, 61, 69, 184, 403
Wilson, W. 91, 97, 98, 113, 123, 124, 126, 127–28, 187, 403
    and post-WWI peace 187, *188*, 189
    see also 14 Points
Wingate, O. *310*, 311, 339, 344
Wolf Packs 237, 271, 313

Y

Yalta Conference 374, 392
Yamamoto, I. 316, 408–09
Yamashita, T. 270, 277, 409
Young Turks 179
Ypres I 40, 41, *48*, 49
Ypres II 24, 62–64, 65–66, 68
Ypres III 121, 136, 138, 139–40, 141–42, *143*, 144–45
Yugoslavia (interwar) 192
Yugoslavia (WWII), politics 246, 248, 249, 256, 277, 360, 378
    see also **Balkans (WWII)**

Z

Zamosc-Komarów 27
Zeebrugge 164–65
Zhukov, G. 205, 244, 263, 276–77, 310, 370, 371, 377, 384, 386
Zimmermann, A. 125

ACKNOWLEDGMENTS

David King Collection, pages: 190–91, 192(top), 192–93(top and bottom).
Hulton Getty, pages: 189(top), 190(top), 194(bottom), 195(top), 196(bottom), 196–97, 198(bottom).
Robert Hunt Library, pages: 2–3, 8, 9(top and bottom), 10, 11, 12(both), 14(top right and bottom), 15(bottom), 16–17, 20(bottom), 23, 24(top left and right), 25, 26(top), 28–29, 30(top), 33(top and center), 35(top), 40–41(top), 42(bottom), 44–45(bottom), 48–49(bottom), 51(bottom), 52(bottom), 54(top), 57(top), 60–61(bottom), 64(top left), 66(top), 67(top), 68–69(top), 70(top), 71(center left), 76–77(top), 84, 85(center), 86(bottom), 88(both), 90 (bottom), 92(bottom), 95(center and bottom), 96(bottom), 100–01(center), 102–03(bottom), 120(bottom), 121(bottom), 123(top and bottom), 124(top), 126(top and bottom left), 128 (top), 130–31, 133(top), 137(top), 138((top and bottom), 142–43(top and bottom), 148 (bottom), 150(top), 155(bottom), 156–57(top), 172–73(top), 186–87(bottom), 188, 189 (bottom), 195(bottom), 197(bottom), 199, 202(bottom), 202–203(top), 204(bottom), 204 (both), 205, 206(both), 207(bottom), 208–09(bottom), 209(top), 211(top and bottom), 212 (bottom), 212–13(top), 213(bottom), 215(both), 216(top and bottom), 217(bottom left and right), 218–19(top), 219(top center and bottom), 220, 221(all three), 222(bottom), 222–23 (top), 223(top), 224(bottom left), 225(bottom), 226–27(all four), 228(top), 229(bottom), 230 (both), 232(bottom), 233(all three), 234(top right), 235(both), 236(bottom left and right), 237(both), 238(bottom), 239(all three), 240(top left and right), 242–43(top and bottom), 244(bottom), 245(bottom right), 246(bottom), 247(bottom right), 248(bottom), 248–49(top), 249(bottom right), 250(top), 251(all three), 252(bottom), 254(both), 256(top left and bottom), 258–59(all four), 260–61(top), 261(bottom), 262(top and bottom), 262–63(center), 264–65 (top), 266(top), 266–67(top and bottom), 269(bottom), 270–71(all three), 272–73(top and bottom), 274–75(all four), 276, 277(top and bottom left), 278(top), 279(top), 280(top and bottom), 280–81, 282(both), 285(both), 286(bottom), 286–87(top), 287(bottom), 288 (bottom), 289(both), 290(both), 294–95(bottom), 296(top), 296–97(bottom), 298, 303, 304–05(bottom), 308(bottom), 311(bottom), 312(center right and bottom), 313(bottom), 314–15 (bottom), 315(bottom), 316(both), 318(bottom), 322(both), 324(both), 326 (top), 327(top), 330(top), 332–33(top), 333(top), 339(both), 342(top), 345(top), 346(bottom) 346–47(top), 348(top and bottom), 351(top), 352(top), 354(top), 357(top), 359(both), 360(top), 363(bottom), 366–67(top and bottom), 370(top), 370–71(top), 371(top), 374(top and bottom), 375(top), 374–75(bottom), 376(bottom left and right), 377(bottom), 378–79(bottom), 381(bottom), 382(bottom), 384(top), 384–85(top), 385(top and bottom), 386, 387(bottom), 388(top), 388–89(bottom), 389(bottom).390, 391(bottom), 392(bottom), 392–93(top).
Robert Hunt Library/Australian War Memorial, pages: 38(top), 146(bottom), 149(bottom), 281(top), 295(top).
Robert Hunt Library/Bapty, pages: 13(top), 48–49(top), 72(top), 152–53(top).
Robert Hunt Library/Bayerische Hauptstaatsarchiv, Munich, pages: 24–25(bottom), 41 (bottom), 103(top), 108(both), 130(bottom), 160(top).
Robert Hunt Library/Bibliotheque Nationale, Paris, pages: 22(top), 62(bottom), 75(bottom).
Robert Hunt Library/Bundesarchiv, pages: 9(center), 13(bottom), 53(top), 73(top), 85(top and bottom right), 141(bottom), 151(top), 155(top), 158–59(top), 161(bottom), 186(top), 186–87(top), 200(bottom), 208(top), 214, 216–17(top), 224(top), 228(top), 230(top), 232(top), 245(bottom left), 248(top), 255(top), 257(bottom), 263(bottom), 278(bottom), 302(bottom), 302–03(top), 309(bottom), 313(center), 317(top), 321(top), 323, 338(top), 355(bottom).
Robert Hunt Library/CAR, Warsaw, page: 185(top).
Robert Hunt Library/Central News, page: 21(bottom).
Robert Hunt Library/ECPA, pages: 89(bottom), 90(top), 120–21(top), 132–33(bottom), 140–41(bottom), 166–67(bottom), 168(bottom), 169(both), 173(top), 223(bottom), 225(top), 230(bottom).
Robert Hunt Library/Faruk Kenc, page: 50(bottom).
Robert Hunt Library/Heeresgeschichtliches Museum, Vienna, pages: 104–05(top).
Robert Hunt Library/Imperial War Museum, London, pages: 1, 4–5, 14 (top left), 16(top), 24–25(center), 27, 28(top and bottom), 29(top), 31(bottom), 32–33(bottom), 34(top), 34–35(top), 36(top), 36–37(bottom), 37(top and center), 38–39(bottom), 39(top), 40(top), 41(top), 42(top), 42–43(top), 43(top), 45(bottom), 46–47(bottom), 47(bottom), 48(top), 49(bottom), 50–51(bottom), 52(top), 53(top), 54(top), 54–55(bottom), 56

(top), 57(bottom), 58–59(all five), 60–61(top), 62(top), 63(top), 64(top right), 64–65(bottom), 65(top), 66–67(bottom), 68(bottom), 69(bottom), 70–71(top), 73(bottom), 74–75(top), 76 (center), 76–77(bottom), 77(top), 78–79(all four), 80(top), 81(top), 82–83(all four), 86–87 (top), 87(center), 91(both), 92–3(top), 93(top), 94(top), 95(top), 96(top), 96–97(center), 97 (bottom), 98–99(all three), 100(bottom), 101(top), 102(top), 103(top), 104(top), 104–05 (bottom), 105(top and center), 106(both), 107(bottom), 109(all three), 110–11(all three), 112 (top), 114(bottom), 114–15(all four), 116–17(all three), 118–19(all three), 120–21(bottom), 122(bottom), 122–23(top), 124(bottom), 125(both), 126(bottom right), 127(top), 128 (bottom) 128–29(top), 129(both), 130(top), 131(top), 132(top), 133(bottom), 134–35(all four), 136(bottom), 139(both), 140(top), 141(top), 142(top), 143(bottom), 144–45(all four), 146(top and center), 147(both), 150–51(top), 152(bottom), 153(top and bottom), 154 (both), 157(top and bottom), 158(bottom), 159(bottom), 160(both), 163(bottom left), 164–65 (all four), 168(center), 170(bottom), 172(top), 172–73(top), 174(top), 176–77(all four), 178(top and bottom), 180(left), 180–81(top), 181(bottom), 182(top), 183(top), 184(bottom), 184–85(bottom), 194(top), 201, 210–11(center), 218, 234(top left), 236(top), 238(top), 240 (bottom), 241(both), 246(top), 249(bottom left), 250(center), 252(bottom and center right), 253(both), 255(bottom), 256–257(bottom), 264(bottom), 264–265(bottom), 267(top), 268 (top), 273(top right), 284(bottom), 288(top), 291(bottom), 292(both), 292–93(top), 293 (top), 294(bottom), 299(bottom), 301(bottom), 309(top), 310(both), 317(bottom), 318(top), 319(top), 320(bottom), 320–21(bottom), 325, 326–27(bottom), 328–29(top), 329(both), 332 (bottom), 333(bottom), 334–35(all four), 336–37(top), 337(bottom), 341(bottom right), 342 (bottom), 342–43(top), 343(bottom), 344(top left and right), 346(bottom), 347(bottom), 348–49 (bottom), 349(top), 350(bottom), 355(top), 356(bottom), 357(bottom), 358(both), 360 (bottom), 361(both), 362(both), 365(both), 366(top left), 368, 370–71(bottom), 372(bottom), 379(bottom right), 381(top), 383(bottom), 384(bottom), 387(bottom), 393(bottom).
Robert Hunt Library/Kriegsarchiv, Vienna, pages: 22(bottom), 26–27, 38(center), 46 (bottom), 51(bottom), 56–57(bottom), 63(bottom), 69(top), 71(bottom), 72(left), 80–81 (bottom), 85(top left bottom), 93(bottom), 97(top), 149(top), 181(top).
Robert Hunt Library/Military Museum, Belgrade, pages: 44–45(bottom).
Robert Hunt Library/Musée de la Guerre, Vincennes, pages: 34(bottom), 89(top).
Robert Hunt Library/Museo del Risorgimento, Milan, pages: 74(top), 107(top).
Robert Hunt Library/Museo Storilo Navale, Venice, page 168(bottom).
Robert Hunt Library/National Library of Ireland, page: 94(bottom).
Robert Hunt Library/National Maritime Museum, London, page: 260(bottom).
Robert Hunt Library/Naval Ministry, Rome, page: 86(bottom).
Robert Hunt Library/Roger Viollet, pages: 16(bottom), 18–19, 19, 20(top), 21(top).
Robert Hunt Library/SADO, Brussels, pages: 277(bottom right), 284(top), 287(top), 292 (center), 305(top), 307(bottom), 313(top), 328(bottom).
Robert Hunt Library/SIPHO, Brussels, pages: 234(bottom), 255(center left), 268(bottom), 283(bottom), 307(top), 311(bottom), 312(top), 314(bottom), 320(top), 341(top).
Robert Hunt Library/US Air Force, pages: 314–15(top), 378, 380–81(bottom).
Robert Hunt Library/US Army, pages: 279(bottom), 283(top), 336(bottom), 341(bottom left), 350(top), 352(bottom), 353(top), 356(bottom), 369(both), 372(bottom), 372–73(bottom), 373 (top), 375(bottom), 379(top), 382–83(bottom and top), 391(top).
Robert Hunt Library/US Information Agency, pages: 191, 200(top), 340(top).
Robert Hunt Library/US Library of Congress, page: 113(top).
Robert Hunt Library/US Marine Corps, pages: 306, 330–31(bottom), 331(top), 338(bottom), 350–51(bottom), 354(bottom), 376–77(top).
Robert Hunt Library/US National Archives, pages: 74(bottom), 112(bottom), 136–37(top), 137(bottom), 148(top), 156(bottom), 162(bottom), 162–63(top), 163(bottom right), 166(top), 166–67(center), 167(top), 170(top), 171(both), 174(bottom), 174–75(top), 175(top), 179 (top), 182–83(bottom), 198–99(top), 207(top), 210(bottom), 224(bottom), 291(top), 294(top).
Robert Hunt Library/US Naval Academy, pages: 178–79(bottom).
Robert Hunt Library/US Navy, pages: 242(top), 297(bottom), 299(top), 301(top), 340(bottom), 344–45(bottom), 364(both), 380(top).
Robert Hunt Library/US Office of War Information, pages: 304–05(top).
Robert Hunt Library/Vereenigde Fotobureaux, Amsterdam, pages: 22–23.
Robert Hunt Library/VHU, Prague, pages: 30–31, 54(bottom), 70–71(bottom), 100(top).
Robert Hunt Library/YIVO Institute for Jewish Research, pages: 300(top), 308(top).